FACILITY AND EVENT
MANAGEMENT
APPLICATION IN SPORT

Kendall Hunt
publishing company

JEFFREY C. PETERSEN | LAWRENCE W. JUDGE | JOHN J. MILLER
Baylor University *Ball State University* *Troy University*

Cover image © T-Mobile Arena.

www.kendallhunt.com
Send all inquiries to:
4050 Westmark Drive
Dubuque, IA 52004-1840

Published in the United States of America

Brief Contents

Table of Contents

Jeffrey C. Petersen

For both the fan and the athlete, nothing can match the energy and excitement of a contest in a packed stadium or arena. However, these fans and athletes seldom, if ever, realize the tremendous level of planning and work in the successful development and operation of the facility and event. Indeed, sport occupies an immense and growing element of the local, regional, national, and even global interest and attention. At a national level in the United States, the National Football League's 2014 Super Bowl attracted a record television audience of 112.2 million American viewers (Ellingson, 2014b), and the 2014 Winter Olympic Games in Sochi included NBC broadcasts rights fee of $775 million as a part of a $4.38 billion deal for the 2014–2020 games (Crupi, 2011) capturing an American audience averaging 21.4 million between the opening and closing ceremonies (Ellingson, 2014a).

On a global stage, the 2014 FIFA World Cup set records for television viewers from Argentina, Brazil, Croatia, France, Germany, Italy, Japan, the Netherlands, the United Kingdom, and the United States ranging from 11 to 48 million in audiences for opening round games on various broadcast networks contracted with FIFA (Parker, 2014). In addition to the spectator interest in sport, the facility and infrastructure investments of these three examples are equally stunning. The 2014 Super Bowl was hosted in a single venue, Met Life Stadium, that opened in 2010, at a total cost of $1.7 billion (Meyers, 2010). The 2014 Winter Olympics Games in Sochi were noted as the most costly in history with facility spending at $51 billion, almost 25% more than the prior cost leader, the Beijing Games of 2008 (Panja, 2014). While the 2014 FIFA World Cup host in Brazil tallied $3.5 billion in costs for six new and six refurbished soccer venues with total event costs topping $11 billion (Koba, 2014). When considering the entirety of the global sport market, PricewaterhouseCoopers has estimated that total sport industry revenues in 2015 reached $145.34 billion USD representing a 35% level of growth since 2006 (PwC, n.d.). Given the tremendous global interest and financial resources associated with sport, it is not surprising that there is a continuing need to develop leaders and managers to effectively and efficiently operate sporting events and venues from the highest international levels down to the local and grassroots levels.

Formally training and developing leaders in the sport management in general and sport facility and event management specifically can be traced to a number of university-based programs. Since the development of the first sport management academic program at Ohio University as a graduate program in 1966, this academic discipline has experienced substantial growth (NASPE/NASSM, 1993). By the late 1970s, sport management academic offerings included 20 graduate and three undergraduate programs (Parkhouse, 1978) The number of undergraduate schools with sport management programs grew to 274 by the mid 2000s (Jones, Brooks, & Mak, 2008). Most recently, review of the North American Society for Sport Management (NASSM) website revealed that there are currently 450 colleges and universities offering academic degrees in the field of sport management in the United States. This includes 385 programs offering bachelor's degrees, 221 offering master's degrees, and 33 doctoral degree programs. While this growth is extensive, it only represents roughly 16% of the four-year colleges and universities within the nation. Although, the greatest number of programs are found within United States, there are significant markets within other regions including Canada, Europe, Asia, and Australia/New Zealand.

Curricular content within the academic discipline of sport management varied widely until the establishment of curricular standards by academic leaders in the field. The first major adoption of content curriculum was developed by a joint commission of the National Association for Sport and Physical Education (NASPE) and the North American Society for Sport Management (NASSM) in 1992, and these NASPE/NASSM curriculum standards for program approval included 10 content areas: behavioral dimensions in sport, management and organizational skills in sports, ethics in sport management, marketing in sport, communication in sport, finance in sport, economics in sport, legal aspects of sport, governance in sport, and field experience in sport management (NASPE/NASSM, 1993). Later revisions to the NASPE/NASSM curriculum occurred in 1999, and these revisions included adoption of a specific competency regarding facility management (Sport Management Program Review Council, 2000). The development of the Commission of Sport Management Accreditation (COSMA) in 2008 through NASSM created a new system of Common Professional Components (CPC) for academic programs that included "sport operations management/event & venue management" as a portion of its bachelor's degree programs (COSMA, 2010). The inclusion of specific instruction via CPC adoption in COSMA related to facility and event management further establishes the importance of these topics within the academic curricula.

Due to the growth in the sport industry combined with the formal recognition of the facility and event management as a valued component of the sport management discipline, this text has been created as a resource for use in the training and development of facility and event managers in sport. This textbook resource is designed to fit within the broader education of individuals at both the undergraduate and graduate levels within sport management programs. This text seeks to provide a balanced approach between the theoretical and research based approaches of academia and the pragmatic best practices of professionals in the field. This new text will provide coverage of content that is common to both facility management and event management while also highlighting the unique aspects of both areas within the context of sport. As the recent research in the areas of facility and event management in sport is limited but growing, this text seeks to include all contemporary research in these fields while also maintaining a strong connection to sport industry practitioners and their best practices.

The text is designed with a total of 18 chapters that are organized into three primary units: Foundations, Facility Operations, and Event Planning and Implications. The Foundations unit includes five chapters covering: 1) History of Sport Facilities and Events, 2) Types of Facilities and Events in Sport, 3) Basic Management Theories, 4) Strategic Planning and Budgeting, and 5) Managing Human Capital. The Facility Operations unit spans seven chapters including: 6) Facility Construction/Planning Process and Building Life Cycle, 7) Facility Maintenance, 8) Changeover Management and Temporary Venues, 9) Sport Facility Safety and Security, 10) Customer Service, 11) Alcohol Management, and 12) Media Support. The third and final units deals with Event Planning and Implications and includes six chapters: 13) Booking and Scheduling, 14) Bidding Processes, 15) Tour and League Events, 17) Facility and Event Impact and Legacy, and 18) Sport and Recreation Facilities as Leverageable Assets. While the text is generally designed to flow and build upon the prior content, each chapter's content retains the ability to stand in its own right, thereby allowing for instructor freedom in reorganizing the content order or in eliminating content or adding additional personal content to a course of study.

To increase the effectiveness of this text resource for both the teaching faculty and the students, multiple features are included at the start and conclusion of each chapter. Each chapter begins with a statement of objectives. These objectives identify key knowledge, skills and competencies for the students that are addressed in behavioral terms to frame the chapter content and assist in student learning by guiding their reading. A second key feature to begin each chapter is a section of key terms and key acronyms associated with the content. Acronyms and terms within the field of facility and event management in sport become a vital part of the language of the professional, and students must master this "language" in order to serve as a competent professional. The listing of key terms is provided at the start of each chapter, and key terms are bolded within the reading with call outs including short working definitions found within the margins of the text. Additionally, a full glossary of key terms and list of acronyms with definitions are provided at the end of the textbook.

In order to connect students to many career paths and varied professional roles in the field, each chapter includes a Practitioner Spotlight. This feature is designed to enhance career development and foster knowledge of specialized job opportunities within facility and event management in sport. Each Practitioner Spotlight includes a photo of the professional, a photo of their venue or event, detailed job duties, and the career path taken to secure their position.

Each chapter concludes with a series of discussion questions and a mini case study. The discussion questions can be used for individual student reflection and review, or they may be used to facilitate a dialogue within the class for small group or whole class discussion. The mini case studies provide a short scenario that will allow for students to work individually or within groups to create a solution to a more open-ended case that is connected to the content covered within the chapter.

Where appropriate in the text, some chapters include pull outs for Technology and Innovation Spotlights or Management in Action sections. The Technology and Innovation Spotlight defines and describes a new product, practice, or technique that significantly impacts that area of facility and event management taken from the perspective of professional practitioners in the field. The Management in Action section seeks to create a practical application of a key chapter concept or process by an industry practitioner embedded within a specific venue or event.

Students and instructors alike will benefit from the special features provided within each chapter. Additionally, a full complement of ancillary materials for instructors are available including presentation slide decks and test bank questions for each of the 18 chapters.

REFERENCES

COSMA (2010). Accreditation Principles & Self Study Preparation. Retrieved from http://www.cosmaweb.org/accreditation-manuals.html

Crupi, A. (2011) NBC Bids $4.38 Billion for Olympic Gold No Ebersol, no problem: Lazarus delegation nabs rights through 2020. *Adweek*. Retrieved from http://www.adweek.com/news/television/update-nbc-bids-438-billion-olympicgold-132319

Ellingson, A. (2014a). TV ratings: Sochi Olympics down 12 percent from Vancouver. *L.A. Biz*. Retrieved from http://www.bizjournals.com/losangeles/news/2014/02/26/ratings-sochi-olympicsdown-12-percent-from-2010.html

Ellingson, A. (2014b). TV ratings: Super Bowl propels Fox to top spots. *L.A. Biz*. Retrieved from http://www.bizjournals.com/losangeles/news/2014/02/05/tvratings-super-bowl-propels-fox-to-top-spots.html

Jones, D. F., Brooks, D. D., & Mak, J. Y. (2008). Examining sport management programs in the United States, *Sports Management Review, 11*(1), 77–91.

Koba, M. (2014). World Cup by the numbers: Most expensive ever! *CNBC*. Retrieved from http://www.cnbc.com/id/101750395#

Meyers, G. (2010). Welcome to the Meadowlands: Exclusive tour of Giants, Jets brand new $1.7 billion stadium. *New York Daily News*. Retrieved from http://www.nydailynews.com/sports/football/meadowlands-exclusive-tour-giantsjets-brand-new-1-7-billion-stadium-article-1.175650

NASPE-NASSM Joint Task Force on Sport Management Curriculum and Accreditation. (1993). Standards for curriculum and voluntary accreditation of sport management education programs. *Journal of Sport Management, 7*, 159–170.

Panja, T. (2014). Sochi Olympics $51 billion price tag deters host cities. http://www.bloomberg.com/news/2014-10-30/sochi-olympics-51-billion-pricetag-deters-host-cities.html

Parker, R. (2014). FIFA: 2014 World Cup TV ratings break records around the world. *LA Times*. Retrieved from http://www.latimes.com/entertainment/tv/showtracker/lana-nn-fifa-2014-world-cup-tv-ratings-20140620-story.html

Parkhouse, B. L. (1978). Professional preparation in athletic administration and sport management. *Journal of Physical Education and Recreation, 49*(5), 22–27.

PwC. (n.d.). Global sports market—total revenue from 2006 to 2015 (in billion U.S. dollars)*. In Statista—The Statistics Portal. Retrieved from https://www.statista.com/statistics/194122/sporting-event-gate-revenue-worldwide-by-region-since-2004/

Sport Management Program Review Council. (2000). Sport Management Program Standards and Review Protocol. Oxon Hill, MD: AAHPERD Publications.

Primary Authors

Dr. Jeffrey C. Petersen | Baylor University

Dr. Petersen is an Associate Professor of Sport Management, director of the Graduate Program in Sport Management, and the coordinator of graduate programs for Baylor's School of Education. Prior to his time at Baylor, Petersen served as coordinator of the Sport Administration undergraduate program at Ball State University, the division chair and Sport Management program director at Loras College, and has experience as a teacher, coach, athletic director, and New Mexico Activities Association district chair at the high school level.

Dr. Petersen's research and scholarship has received recognition from the Sport Marketing Association naming him Best Paper Award winner in 2012 and a best paper finalist in 2011. His research has also been recognized by the American Alliance of Health, Physical Education, Recreation and Dance with the designation of Research Fellow. He has published more than 65 peer-reviewed journals and has made over 125 presentations at state, national, and international conferences. Petersen's primary research areas include sport facility design and management, sport management curriculum and pedagogy, the Youth Olympic Games, and interscholastic sport sponsorship. He currently serves on the editorial board of the *Journal of Facility Planning, Design and Management* and has published work in leading journals such as the *International Journal of Sport Management, Journal of Strength and Conditioning Research, Journal of Physical Education, Recreation & Dance, Journal of Venue and Event Management and Sport Marketing Quarterly*. Petersen's academic training includes a PhD from the University of New Mexico with an emphasis in Sports Administration, an MA from New Mexico Highlands University in Human Performance and Sport, and a BS from Taylor University in Biology and Secondary Education.

Dr. Lawrence W. Judge | Ball State University

Dr. Judge is a professor and the Associate Chair of the School of Kinesiology at Ball State University in Muncie, Indiana. From 2009 to 2016 Dr. Judge has been involved in 220 peer-reviewed presentations with participation in leading state, national and international conferences. His research has led to a strong scholarly contribution in written forms including authorship of 121 peer-reviewed manuscripts from 2009–2015. This includes 65 first-author publications in prestigious journals such the *International Review for the Sociology of Sport, Journal of Strength & Conditioning Research*, the *Journal of Physical Education, Recreation and Dance*, and the *International Journal of Sports Science & Coaching*. Dr. Judge has also been active in the area of textbook publishing, contributing 12 textbook chapters and has co-authored three books. Dr. Judge co-authored the textbook, *Sport Governance and Policy Development: An ethical approach to managing sport in the 21st century*, and authored the books *The Complete Track and Field Coaches' Guide to Conditioning for the Throwing Events* and *The Shot Put Handbook*. He was recently honored by the Society of Health and Physical Activity (SHAPE) as a research fellow and was named a registered strength and conditioning coach emeritus by the National Strength and Conditioning Association (NSCA).

At the national level within the coaching education field, Dr. Judge has served as the President for the National Council for the Accreditation of Coaching Education and as the National Chairman of the United States Track and Field Coaching Education. Dr. Judge has lectured in 37 different countries and serves as a level II and level III instructor in the IAAF coaching education program, an instructor/trainer in the International Paralympic Committee Coaching Education program and also lectures in the Professional Figure Skaters Association nationwide coach's education program.

Dr. John J. Miller | Troy University

Dr. Miller serves as a full professor of Sport Management at Troy University in Troy, AL. Prior to his time at Troy, Miller served in a number of roles in the university and college levels as a professor and department curriculum and assessment coordinator at Texas Tech University and as an assistant professor at Western New Mexico University, Saint Mary's (MN) University, and Willamette University. Dr. Miller is a Research Fellow in the Research Consortium as well as the Sport and Recreation Law Association. He is also a Fellow in the North American Society of Health, Physical Education, Recreation, Sport and Dance Professionals.

Dr. Miller has published more than 70 refereed articles in peer-reviewed journals and has made over 219 presentations at regional, national, and international conferences. Miller is the co-author of the book, *A Practical Guide to Sport Management Internships* and has authored over 35 chapters in various publications. He received the Distinguished Scholar Award from the School and Community Safety Society of America in 2005. Miller's primary areas of research include legal issues in sport and recreation risk management, sport marketing and promotion affecting consumer behavior in sports, issues dealing with sport management pedagogy, and issues in student leadership.

CONTRIBUTING AUTHORS

J. Patrick Marsh | Baylor University

Patrick Marsh is a doctoral candidate at Baylor University in the Department of Health, Human Performance, and Recreation with a concentration in Sport Management. Prior to Baylor, Marsh received his bachelor's and master's degrees in Sport Administration at the University of North Carolina. Marsh also served as an assistant facility director at both Carmichael Arena and the Dean E. Smith Center during his time at the University of North Carolina. In his various roles at UNC, Marsh hosted hundreds of collegiate athletic events including the annual UNC—Duke basketball game, NCAA women's basketball, baseball, softball, lacrosse, soccer, and field hockey championship events, and ACC wrestling, swimming and diving, track and field, and women's lacrosse championship events. In addition to the athletic events, Marsh also hosted numerous concerts, graduation ceremonies, and a visit from President Barak Obama.

Marsh's research and scholarship has focused on athletic facility and event management, the student-athlete experience, and sport management education. Marsh has published in the *Journal of Amateur Sport* and the *Journal of Physical Education, Recreation, and Dance*. Marsh has presented at the North American Society of Sport Management, the College Sport Research Institute, Sport and Entertainment Venues Tomorrow, the Applied Sport Management Association, the National Strength and Conditioning Association, and Texas Association for Health, Physical Education, Recreation, and Dance conferences.

Ricardo Gonzales | University of New Mexico

Mr. Gonzales currently serves as a principal with RGA in Santa Fe, New Mexico. Prior to this, he was the director of project planning and development at the University of Wisconsin—Eau Claire, the executive director of physical resources at Savannah College of Art and Design, the design and construction bureau manager for the state of New Mexico, and the project planning and development group leader at the University of California—Los Alamos National Laboratory. Gonzales received a master's degree in urban and regional planning, as well as an MBA from the University of Colorado Denver.

Mr. Gonzales authored textbook chapters in both the 12th and 13th editions of *Facility Planning and Design for Health, Physical Activity, Recreation, and Sport.* He has been both a presenter and a panelist at the AAHPERD National Convention.

Dr. Marshall Magnusen | Baylor University

Dr. Magnusen is an associate professor of Sport Management and serves as a faculty advisor to the Baylor Sport Management Association. He is an Associate Editor for the *Sport Management Education Journal* and serves as an editorial board member for the *Journal of Applied Sport Management, Journal of Amateur Sport,* and the *Journal of Global Sport Management.* Magnusen also served as a co-editor for a 2016 special issue of the *Journal of Applied Sport Management* entitled, "The Political Arena: Power and Political Behavior in Sport Organizations".

Dr. Magnusen has published over 35 peer-reviewed articles and several book chapters. In addition, he has made over 40 presentations at both national and international conferences. Magnusen is an Oral History Research Fellow at Baylor University, receiving research grants in 2012 and 2015. His primary research areas include recruiting and personnel selection, leadership and social effectiveness in sport, organizational politics and political behavior in sport organizations, and the allure of sport to participants, spectators, employees, and stakeholders.

Seth Dorsey | Texas A&M University

Mr. Dorsey is the assistant athletic financial manager at Texas A&M University. Prior to his time at Texas A&M, Dorsey served as the assistant manager of business and ticket operations at Princeton University, and he has also served as the director of operations for Baylor Baseball. He has a master's in sport management and degrees in economics and finance from Baylor University.

Dr. Deanna Kolar | Purdue University

Dr. Kolar is a clinical assistant professor and academic director of the MSHRM program at Purdue University. Prior to her arrival at Purdue, Kolar taught International Legal Management and Leadership at IAE Aix-en-Provence Graduate School of Management in France and International Management at ISC Paris School of Management. Kolar has additional professional experience with both the Hyundai Corporation and Borders Group Incorporated.

Dr. Kolar's primary areas of research within human resource management include stigmatizing professions, employee autonomy, and employee embeddedness.

Dr. Lynsey A. Madison | Troy University

Dr. Madison is an assistant professor of Hospitality, Sport, and Tourism Management. Prior to her time at Troy, Madison served in teaching assistant positions at Auburn University and the University of Alabama. She served as assistant events coordinator at the University of Alabama's Culverhouse College of Commerce and in nutrition services at DCH Regional Medical Center in Tuscaloosa. Madison has completed a number of projects in the Tuscaloosa and Auburn areas including College of Health and Human Services Homecoming, Alabama Hall of Fame Induction Ceremony, and Hospitality Gala "An International Affair" as the marketing team leader.

Dr. Madison's areas of research include the various aspects of event planning and event management. Within hospitality management she teaches courses in human resource management in hospitality, hotel management, and revenue management.

Dr. Shannon Powers | Ball State University

Dr. Powers works as an assistant professor of physical fitness and wellness and health/physical education teacher education at Ball State University. She has had extensive experience with student experiential learning and working with the community. Dr. Powers has researched and published work regarding intercollegiate athletic departments and worked at intercollegiate football bowl games. Her research focus is focused on the consumer's experience with organized sport, exercise, and health programs.

Powers earned her Ph.D. in Higher Education Leadership from Colorado State University, and has master's degrees from both Columbia University and California State University along with a BA in communications from Loyola Marymount University.

Kelsey L. Jones | Ball State University

After earning a BS in hospitality and food management from Ball State University, Kelsey Jones worked in upper-level management within the catering and food industry. Jones later returned to Ball State for a MA in public relations and is currently employed in that field. Ms. Jones specializes in customer service, community engagement, event planning, and social media management.

Acknowledgements

Dr. Jeffrey C. Petersen | Baylor University

The time, energy, and resources required to bring this text from a concept to a reality is indeed a tremendous team effort, and I am deeply indebted to a wide array of individuals whose investment and insight have contributed to the creation of top-quality product. If I had known what I was in for from the very beginning I might have run in the opposite direction, but these people transformed the seemingly impossible and insurmountable tasks into ones that were actually possible.

First to my co-authors Larry and John, our team approach on this text helped keep this project manageable, and your personal skill sets and knowledge added much to the scope of this book. The work of additional contributing authors also added depth to key areas such as HRM, strategic planning, recruiting, finance and budgeting. My doctoral student, Patrick Marsh, brought a wealth of industry experience and broke new ground with the coverage of changeover and temporary facilities. This development and multiple rounds of revisions were greatly aided by the work of my graduate assistants Amy Gaston, Tess Moore, Jimmie Simpson, and Jordan Strickland over the past two years. I also must acknowledge the 18 industry practitioners who shared their expertise and insights in the Spotlight features within the text. These spotlights link the content to the industry and provide career path insights that are so vital for students.

The key staff members from Kendall Hunt Publishing who provided the necessary support and patience in the long journey of bringing this book to press are also deserving of my thanks. First, Perry Carty shared my visions for an innovative new text in this segment of the sport management discipline and invested in this endeavor. Lynne Rogers patiently worked through the long process of chapter content development and review including the seemingly unending process of seeking necessary permissions. Anne Luty and her team at Composure Graphics copyedited and artfully laid out the text content into a beautiful final product. All of this technical support made my first foray into leading a group of authors a memorable one.

My students over the years in classes like PHE 611 Development and Utilization of Accountability and Facilities in Athletics at Loras College, SPTAD 676 Administration of Athletic Programs, SPTAD 190 Introduction to Sport Administration, and ACE 692 Organization and Administration for Coaches at Ball State University along with HP 4393 Facilities and Equipment, HP 5327 Financial Management in Sport, SPM 5372 Legal Issues in Sport, SPM 5373 Sport Management and SPM 5376 Facility and Event Management at Baylor University have provided me with insights regarding important content and effective teaching methods. These experiences teaching over the years have given me the necessary inspiration to undertake the development of a new textbook in the area of facility and event management. I am quite sure that I have learned as much from my students as they have learned from me.

The foundation of faith and family cannot be overlooked in the completion of this textbook project. In all things, I do continue to acknowledge the presence and inspiration of God, for without Him we can do nothing. When the tasks at hand threatened to overwhelm me, I recalled Isaiah 40:31, "…they that wait upon the Lord shall renew their strength; they shall mount up on wings as eagles; they shall run and not be weary" and Philippians 4:13, "I can do all things through Christ who strengthens me." The completion of this book was also inspired by those in my family that have been committed to teaching, learning and writing including my grandfather Harold Lindbloom. His signed copy of the *Our State: Colorado* book project that he led in the 1960s with Old West Publishing adorns a place of honor in my office to this day. My parents Jerry Petersen, Betsy LeGray and John LeGray, along with my in-laws Fred and Sandra Pomeroy whose careers in education helped lead and influence my own. My wife, Sherry, and our kids, Jeremy, Joel and Jadie, who endured much of my time being taken by this project including our traditional summer vacation of 2016, I celebrate with you all the completion of this project and your inspiration and help along the way that was indeed beyond measure, and I dedicate this work to you.

Dr. Lawrence W. Judge | Ball State University

I want to take this opportunity thank my mother, Joan and my father, Ira, for everything that you have both done for me. I could not have asked for better parents or role models. I also want to thank and acknowledge my brother Mike. Mike Judge (Throw1deep) has quietly emerged as one of the country's best coaches and is really making a difference in the grass roots development of the hammer throw in the United States. The real "Coach Judge," my father Dr. Ira Judge, would be very proud. And finally, I would like to dedicate this work to all of my current and former students and athletes. The bond that we all share shall never be broken.

I would also like to acknowledge Dr. Jeffrey Petersen for the faith he showed in me as I transitioned from 18 years of collegiate coaching to full time academia. Dr. Petersen took a chance and hired me as a contract faculty member at Ball State University in 2006. He and I quickly became friends and began working on many projects together. Our collaborations and friendship have continued over the years, and I am grateful for the opportunity to contribute to this textbook.

I also want to acknowledge the contributions of my chapter co-authors, Dr. Deanna Kohler (Managing Human Capital/Strategic Planning and Budgeting), Dr. John Miller and Ricardo Gonzalez (Strategic Planning and Budgeting), Dr. Shannon Powers and Ms. Kelsey Jones (Customer Service), Dr. Jeffrey Petersen (Mega-Events and Sport Festivals/Tour and League Events) and Mr. Patrick Marsh (Media Support) for their expertise and insights. Without their work, these chapters would have been far less comprehensive and valuable. I would also like to acknowledge my graduate assistants Kara Holtzclaw and Brianna Leitzelar and student assistant Dagny Zupin for all of their support with this project. I would also like to thank the individuals (Mr. Frank Caraway, Ms. Dawn Ellerbe and Ms. Dana Schoen-wetter) who volunteered to be part of the practitioner spotlight. Their valuable contributions will allow students to understand the facility and event management profession in much more depth.

It is a near impossible task to thank each individual who has helped me and travelled with me along my journey. However, I would like to say to the many individuals I have learned from and the many folks who I have shared these experiences with, thank you for all you have given and enjoyed with me. Finally, I would like to give a special thanks to my mentor Dr. Thomas Sawyer for all of his guidance, friendship and support over the years. He is responsible for igniting my interest in the topic of facility planning, design and management. This book is a compilation of the ideas that I have drawn from my experiences, academic coursework from experts like Dr. Sawyer, or from studying his/their articles in the literature. I take credit only for the errors.

Dr. John J. Miller | Troy University

I would like to acknowledge the contributions of my chapter co-authors, Dr. Lynsey Madison (Alcohol Management) and Mr. Ricardo Gonzales (Facility Construction / Planning Process and Building Life Cycle), and Mr. Patrick Marsh (Facility Maintenance) for their expertise and insights. Without their work, the chapter information would have been substantially less. I would also like to thank the individuals who volunteered to be part of the practitioner spotlight. Their contributions will allow students to understand the facility and event management profession more in-depth. Finally, I would like to thank my wife, Laura, for taking the time to proof read my writings. I can put the words down, but she helps put them into the proper order.

History of Sport Facilities and Events

Jeffrey C. Petersen

OBJECTIVES

After studying this chapter, the student should be able to:

- Identify and describe key facilities types and events for sport in ancient Greece and Rome.
- Trace the development of key sport facilities and events and apply these examples to larger trends in facilities and events in sport.
- Apply the concepts of diffusion of innovation and place attachment to the development of sport facilities.
- Understand the development of the profession of facility and event management.
- Describe various professional organizations that serve and lead this profession.

KEY TERMS

Amphitheater	Gymnasion	Pankration
Certification	Hippodrome	Place Attachment
Circus	Palaistra	Stadium
Diffusion of Innovation		

KEY ACRONYMS

AFL	American Football League	**MLB**	Major League Baseball
ALSD	Association of Luxury Suite Directors	**NASC**	National Association of Sport Commissions
FIFA	Federation Internationale de Football Association	**NBA**	National Basketball Association
IAVM	International Association of Venue Managers	**NCS4**	National Center for Spectator Sports Safety & Security
IFEA	International Festival and Events Association	**NFL**	National Football League
IFMA	International Facility Management Association	**SMA**	Stadium Managers Association

Introduction

A historical perspective of sport facilities and events provides a framework for the interpretation of the contemporary and current trends of sport. This perspective can not only provide knowledge of the past but also can provide insights for the development of innovative venues and events for the future. The basic human interest in play and sport through many cultures has been elevated into elaborate systems of facilities and events that, at times, can encompass great significance from both social and economic perspectives. Both historically and today, the particular sporting events and venues deemed of great importance may vary by geographical area and climatic conditions, as well as cultural or national traditions.

While historical, anthropological, and archaeological evidence exists for the long traditions of sport and at times sport facilities across many nations, areas, and cultures, significantly more information is available regarding the development of sport and sport facilities in the ancient Greece and the Roman Empire. Therefore, the majority of this examination of ancient history sporting facilities will focus upon Greece and Rome, but this should not discount the unique development of sport, sport facilities, and sport events in other areas of the world such as North and South America, Mesoamerica, Africa, Asia, and Oceana. For example, the game of lacrosse can be traced back as far as 1100 AD as a large team game with a ball and sticks with a hooped net played by the native tribes in the Northeast regions of North America (Fisher, 2002). In Mesoamerica, an ancient ballgame connected to pre-Columbian peoples dates back to court/facility remains from 1400 BC. This game is thought to be connected to a more modern game form called *ulama* in which a heavy rubber ball is kept in play using the hips to strike the ball (Hill, Blake, & Clark, 1998). In ancient China, Wu Shu (martial arts) can be traced to forms using the body and forms using weapons back through the Xian Qin Period (770–221 BC), and ball games more similar to western sports like Cu Ju (similar to soccer) can be traced back more than 2000 years (Xikuan, 1991). Variations of dart throwing (somewhat analogous to a javelin throw for distance) have been noted in several Oceanic cultures including the

Remains of a Mayan stadium type structure in Chichen Itza, Mexico with stone hoops located high upon the walls near the midpoint of the structure.

Details of the stone hoop element of the ancient Mesoamerican ball game in the ruins at Quintana Roo, Mexico.

Maori of New Zealand, the Samoans of the South Pacific, and the Tikopians of the Hebrides chain of islands (Craig, 2002). The ancient Hawaiians held Makahiki, an annual festival of games that included competitions in surfing, spear throwing, wrestling, and holua, a competition of dry-land sledding perhaps somewhat similar to bobsledding (Craig, 2002). These ancient ties to sport, sport facilities, and sport events serve as important examples to compare and contrast with the current state of sport.

Sport Events and Facilities in Ancient Greece

The development of sport events and facilities was an important and integral part of the culture within ancient Greece. Ancient Greek athletic games connected to funeral games honoring past warriors can be traced back to Homer's epic poetry of the *Iliad* and the *Odyssey* of the late eighth or early seventh century BC (Young, 2004). The ancient Olympic Games were held on a quadrennial basis for more than a millennium from approximately 776 BC to 400 AD. The scope of events grew over time. While much attention is properly directed toward the ancient Olympic Games, there was a broader interest with the development of common facilities related to sport for physical, intellectual, and spiritual development. Indeed, sport in ancient Greece was connected to religious worship and festivals, and common places for training and development as well as for competition were developed in many cities including common structures like the gymnasion, the palaistra, the hippodrome, and the stadium. Throughout the Pan-Hellenic world, hundreds of city-states and religious sanctuaries conducted games and built public athletic facilities (Kyle, 2014). It is important to understand what these common facilities were and what roles they played in the athletic culture of this era.

The Greek *gymnasion* was a multi-use type of facility used for recreation, exercise, athletic practice, and physical education that also occasionally hosted organized competitions for young males, and has a literal translation as a "place for nude exercise" (Scott, 2014). This form of exercise was the cultural norm for this society. The gymnasion was often built on the outskirts of the city where space and topography might aid in the facility development suitable for varied training activities. The gymnasion would include both the park-like natural setting and spaces used for training along with the structures built for athletic and other purposes as a part of the facility. The basic form of the gymnasion complex included straight running tracks (dromoio) in both open air (paradromis) and roofed (xystos) varieties along with a *palaistra*, a rectangular shaped building with an open courtyard (Scott, 2014). The individual sports connected with modern track and field (running, javelin, and discus) were practiced in the track areas. Combat sports like wrestling, boxing, and pankration were conducted in the palaistra. While nearly all of these sports continue in our modern era, the pankration does require definition. *Pankration* was a combat sport combining aspects of boxing and wrestling including strikes to the face and body and grappling forms with falls, chokes, foot and arm locks, plus kicks. Virtually all contact except biting and gouging of the eyes was allowed. (Georgiou, 2008). The pankration can be viewed as

Gymnasion a multi-use public venue for recreation, athletic practice, and physical education in ancient Greece.

Palaistra a structure with an open courtyard for training and combat sports in ancient Greece built in combination with gymnasion and track or as a stand-alone structure.

Pankration a combative submission sport combining the skills of wrestling and boxing.

similar to modern mixed martial arts (MMA) contests as a submission sport. The gymnasion would also often contain rooms for baths and dressing as well as spaces for education. While the gymnasion was a larger and more complex public facility, there is evidence that private palaistra facilities may have been located throughout many cities providing space for physical training (Scott, 2014). These ancient Greek training facilities had significance in blending sport, civic education, and military training within this society and culture.

Stadium a spectator venue associated with a running track (stade) in ancient Greece typically with sloped surroundings on three sides.

While the gymnasion may have been primarily a place of training, it was often combined with sites of competition and performance in Greece. The two primary facilities used for competition included the stadium and the hippodrome. The classic Greek *stadium* was somewhat rectangular in shape and was at least one stadion or stade in length (approximately 600 feet) to conform to the primary sprint race distance, and it included turning posts for the longer races, along with a stone starting line (balbis) and a starting mechanism (hysplex) that worked on a catapulting principle (Miller, 2014). Other features that developed within the Greek stadium were related to spectator seating and the athlete entrance area. Many Greek stadiums were constructed near a hill or in a valley, thus allowing audiences seated upon the surrounding slopes to watch the running competitions. If one end of the stadium was rounded and sloped for seating it could also be used in a multi-purpose format as a theater (Tekin & Ekici, 2005). Seating in the early stadiums was primarily directly on the grassy slopes, and some permanent stone seating was developed for judges and officials as seen in the stadium at Olympia and at Nemea (Miller, 2014). Stadiums developed in later time periods within ancient Greece did begin to incorporate more permanent stone seating for spectators as visible in the stadium remains located in Messene.

Remains of a palaistra, or fighting arena, at ancient Olympia in Greece.

Ruins of the Gymnasion at Pergamum (Turkey) on a hillside location.

The stadium entrance tunnel was another element that became a featured aspect of the stadium in ancient Greece. This structure likely created a separation of athletes from the spectators and created a dramatic entrance for the events. This stone barrel vaulted structure was discovered at the stadium at Nemea and is also noted at Olympia where it was called the *krypte esodos* or hidden entrance (Scott, 2014). In the stadium ruins of Nemea, the tunnel entrance for the stadium was also connected to dressing area or perhaps better stated as an undressing room as athletes in ancient Greece competed in the nude, a practice that is traced to ancient Sparta (Christesen, 2014). This combination of stadium, tunnel, and changing room/ locker room facilities mirrors features found in stadiums of the modern era, and this likely created a more dramatic entrance of the athletes into the stadium for competition.

The Greek *hippodrome* was the venue used for the racing of horses and chariots. The nature of this sport required large and relatively flat areas that remained fairly undeveloped from an architectural and structural perspective. Ancient literary sources have specifically identified hippodromes in Athens, Delphi, Olympia, and Alexandria, but few remains have been fully documented leading some to speculate that these tracks might have often been located on river flood plains where annual floods would discourage building, but may have provided generally flat sand and gravel surfaces to act as a track (Scott, 2014). The Greek hippodromes differed from the later Roman tracks in that they did not include a central dividing barrier in the middle of the track to prevent head-on collisions, but provided only turning posts at each end of the hippodrome to designate the course (Kyle, 2014). While the importance and interest in horse and chariot racing in ancient Greece is evident, fewer physical remains of the hippodromes have been found than of other facilities associated with sport from this time period.

Hippodrome a venue for horse and chariot races developed in ancient Greece.

Stadium and Gymnasion ruins in Messene showing spaces for both competition and training.

Ancient Olympia

The facilities at ancient Olympia represent a combination of structures that have cultural, religious, and athletic significance. Olympia was located in the western Peloponnese peninsula of Greece and the sanctuary site included the Temple of Zeus, the Temple of Hera, and the Pelopion as an altar for animal sacrifices during the Games. The site was backed on one side by Mount Kronos and on another by the Kladeos River. From an athletic facility perspective, Olympia featured the stadium for the running events utilizing the sloping land for seating, a gymnasion, a palaistra, baths, and likely a hippodrome adjacent to the stadium for the horse and chariot races. Not every contest was held in the stadium at Olympia; it appears that the combat contests of boxing, wrestling, and pankration were held in open areas of the sanctuary (Scott, 2014). The initial Olympic Games in 776 BC included only one athletic event, the stadion or sprint, and the winner of that event

The athlete entrance into the stadium in Olympia including an arched entrance tunnel.

A view of the stadium remains in Olympia. Note the stone seating area for officials and judges on the right side of the sloped seating area.

was honored with the Games being given his name. As this festival of worship, sacrifices, and sport grew, events were slowly added to the athletic elements of the festival as noted in Table 1.1. These ancient contests, held every four years, spanned nearly 1200 years and would form the basis for many aspects of the later modern Olympic Games.

Interestingly, the ancient Olympics were located in a somewhat remote location, and the site of these most venerated games did not move from one city to another. The Olympics were a highly prestigious event, and there is evidence of important dignitaries requiring special accommodations such as the guesthouses constructed in Olympia during the fourth century (Scott, 2014). However, the Olympic Games were not the only large athletic contests or festivals held in ancient Greece. Many cities or city-states hosted major festivals including sporting contests noted in Delphi and Athens.

Table 1.1 *Summary of Event Development in the Ancient Olympic Games*

Year	Olympiad	Competition Added
776 BC	1	Stade race or sprint
724 BC	14	Diaulos or two stade race
720 BC	15	Dolichos or long race
708 BC	18	Pentathlon and wrestling
688 BC	23	Boxing
680 BC	25	Four-horse chariot races
648 BC	33	Pankration and horse racing
632 BC	37	Wrestling and running for boys
628 BC	38	Pentathlon for boys
616 BC	41	Boxing for boys
520 BC	65	Race in armor
444 BC	84	Trotting race on mares
408 BC	93	Two-horse chariot race
384 BC	99	Four-horse chariot races with foals
256 BC	131	Horse race on a foal
200 BC	145	Pankration for boys

Adapted from Kotynski (2006)

Rome

The Roman culture and political empire supplanted the Greeks with the development and expansion of the Roman Empire, and it formed the next level of development of sport and facilities in the ancient world. From the iconic structures of the Flavian Amphitheater, also known as the Roman Colosseum, and the Circus Maximus, both in Rome, to public facilities built for shows and spectacles throughout their empire, the Romans fostered community and identity in their amphitheaters, circuses, and stadia that served as sites for spectacle and sport.

Amphitheaters

The amphitheater is likely the single most distinctive form of Roman architecture and was the primary venue of sport and spectacle in the Roman world. The general design of the **amphitheater** is an oval arena completely surrounded by seating that was tiered in elevation to create better lines of sight for the spectators. While events such as beast hunts, aquatic displays and mock battles were hosted within amphitheaters, the facilities were most commonly used for and associated with gladiatorial contests or munera (Dodge, 2014a). While early munera can be traced back to the third century BC, the development of permanent structures to house these contests lagged while temporary wooden structures may have provided models and influences to the permanent structures designs that followed.

Amphitheater an oval shaped arena completely surrounded by seating developed by the ancient Romans.

One of the earliest permanent amphitheaters is found south of Rome in the city of Pompeii and dates from the first century BC. This sizeable structure (135 × 105 meters) included many features of the typical amphitheater design; however, there was no vaulted substructure below the arena floor common in later designs, and the support of the seating was made with the dirt removed to create the sunken arena rather than by stone and concrete (Dodge, 2014a). This early venue did have indications that the spectator seating area was capable of being shaded from the sun by the use of awnings.

Remains of the Amphitheater in Pompeii, Italy, featuring the classic oval design and arched entryways.

The Flavian Amphitheater in Rome, also known as the Colosseum, is the most well known and influential structure as it modeled features repeated throughout the empire and seen, in some extent even today in the design of spectator facilities. The Colosseum was

Interior ruins of the Flavian Amphitheater in Rome, Italy, noting the infrastructure located below the surface level of the venue.

© Lloyd/Shutterstock.com

Exterior remains of the Flavian Amphitheater in Rome from street level.

initially constructed from AD 75–80 and included an arena floor space measuring approximately 80 × 50 meters with exterior dimensions of 188 × 156 meters. It rose nearly 50 meters above the ground level (Dodge, 2014a). This massive structure became an icon of design and was the largest of the amphitheaters in the Roman world. From a design perspective, the Colosseum included a number of features specifically related to the spectators. With an estimated capacity of 45,000 to 50,000 people, the Colosseum provided 76 public access points for ease of movement, but many of the seating areas were physically separated by social rank and gender, including a five-meter vertical drop between the upper two tiers and the lower level seating (Dodge, 2014a). From an operational and performance perspective, the Colosseum and many other similar structures included substructures with access via trap doors for the movement of animals or participants in the events. The Colosseum and other amphitheaters served primarily as a venue for gladiatorial contests and combat reenactments, but amphitheaters were also utilized for other entertainment forms such as animal displays, acrobatics, and dancing. Perhaps some unique Colosseum events were the naumachia or naval battles conducted within the amphitheater, with records of Emperor Domitian holding such a battle in 85 AD (Coleman, 1993). Such events demonstrated the tremendous versatility of this venue.

Amphitheaters were constructed throughout the Roman Empire, and the remains of more than 150 of these structures are scattered across Europe, Great Britain, North Africa, and the Middle East (Chase, 2002). While the amphitheater was the most iconic of the Roman sport facilities, it was not the largest in scope and capacity.

Circuses and Circus Maximus

Circus a venue for horse and chariot races used within ancient Rome.

While the development of Greek hippodromes or horse tracks has been previously mentioned, the development of the *circus* (the Latin term for horse track) reached new levels in the Roman world. The circus was the largest venue type used for sport and entertainment as it would need to accommodate up to 12 chariots in a single race (Dodge, 2014b). The length of the arena floors varied in size from some of the smallest courses being 250 to 300 meters in length to the largest at approximately 580 meters in length (Humphrey, 1986). Some of the common features for these racing venues included the spina or euripus that was a structure composed of a central barrier or wall with turning posts at each end that divided the track. Walls also separated the seating areas from the base of the track, and these walls were known as the podium. Many of the circus seating areas were designed with the long sides curving slightly outward from the midpoint of each of the long sides in order to improve visibility and sight lines for the spectators. The addition of statues and obelisks along the central spina also became common within the circuses. While there is evidence of circuses located in cities throughout the Roman world, they are much less commonly found than amphitheaters and theaters, and the presence of a circus seemed to mark a city as a center of power (Dodge, 2014b).

Circus Maximus, located in Rome, was the largest and most well-chronicled facility of its type in the Roman world. This facility may have sprung from humble beginnings of grassy slopes along a valley between the Palatine and Aventine Hills, but over time it was transformed into a grand facility for sport and spectacle. Modern estimates for the spectator capacity of Circus Maximus vary from 150,000 to 350,000, and the highest estimates appear to be quite credible for the Trajanic period of 99–117 AD (Dodge, 2014b). As a mass spectator facility for sport, this facility was without match in the ancient world and it rivals the largest facilities for sport even today.

Ruins of Circus Maximus in Rome with the race course in the foreground.

The massive size of the Circus Maximus is evident with remains of the seating structures visible on the left side.

Panathenaic Stadium— A Bridge from Past to Present

While nearly all the facilities used for sport in the ancient world are either completely lost or lie in ruins, one restored facility remains in use today, acting as a bridge from the facilities of the past to the modern facilities used today. The Panathenaic Stadium can be traced back to wooden structures as far back as 556 BC and served as host to the athletic elements of the Panathenaic Games, the largest festival held in the city of Athens that included religious ceremonies, cultural events, and athletic competitions with prizes (Young, 2004). This stadium was reconstructed in stone from 330 to 329 BC. with major renovations made in 140 to 139 BC by Herodes Atticus bringing the facility to a capacity of 50,000 spectator seats made of cut marble (Sanada, 2010). The Panathenaic Games continued for a span of over 800 years into the third century AD (Allen, 1999).

The restored Panathenaic Stadium in Athens, Greece, boasting 50,000 marble seats date back to the 6th century BC.

The Panathenaic Stadium currently still serves as the finish line for the Athens Classic Marathon shown here and was the finish line for the 2004 Olympic Marathon.

A restoration of this stadium was initiated in 1869, and the Greek Olympia Games, a precursor to the modern revival of the Olympic Games, were held there in both 1870 and 1875 (Sanada, 2010). In preparation for the inaugural modern Olympic Games in 1896, the Greek Crown Prince Constantine appealed to George Averoff of Alexandria, Egypt for financial support to continue stadium renovation. This additional work on the Panathenaic Stadium restored most of the stadium back to its ancient form and glory with the first few rows of seats restored to their marble surface. British archaeologist, Charles Waldstein (1856–1927), praised the restoration efforts to maintain the historic accuracy based upon documentary records stating, "This Stadium, especially when filled with such a vast population, brings us face to face with the grandeur and power of the ancient community of Athens" (Waldstein, 1896, p. 490).

The 1896 Olympics were not the only use of this restored stadium. In 1906, an Intermediate or Intercalated Olympic Games was hosted in the Panathenaic Stadium, and at that time all the remaining stadium seats were restored to marble (Sanada, 2010). Almost 100 years later, the 2004 Olympic Games in Athens featured contests held in this stadium including archery and the finish line of the marathon. In addition to Olympic uses, the Panathenaic Stadium serves as the finish line for the Athens Classic Marathon held annually, as well as for concerts and other cultural events. This historic site and venue indeed boasts an incredible tradition and history of use bridging a span of over 2,500 years.

Historic Fenway Park located in the Back Bay area of Boston, MA.

Historic Facilities in America

The history of sporting venues in the United States is considerably shorter than what has been noted for the Greco-Roman world. However, the level reverence for selected older sport facilities still in use within the United States has created an iconic presence for two venues in professional baseball and one in professional football that are worthy of special consideration. Although sport historians and even fans of a particular team can identify with numerous past stadiums and/or ballparks, Fenway Park in Boston and Wrigley Field in Chicago for baseball and Soldier Field in Chicago for football provide a link to the more distant past and the emergence of sport as a leading element in the national culture.

The oldest remaining venue for professional team sports in the United States is Fenway Park the home field of the Boston Red Sox since 1912. Its original construction was on an asymmetrical lot that has helped to create some of the unique features of this field. Most notable would be the towering left field wall known as the "Green Monster." The proximity of Lansdowne Street compacted the field space, creating a 310' to 315' shallow left field that is compensated for with a 37-foot tall wall. This wall has included a manually updated scoreboard since 1934, and in 2003 a total of 269 new seats were added to the park atop the "Green Monster" (2003 Renovations, 2016). In recent years a sell-out streak for home games has added to the mystique of the venue. From May 15, 2003, to April 10, 2013, a total of 820 Red Sox home games were sold out, totaling more than 30 million spectators breaking the former United States' major professional sports team record of the NBA's Portland Trailblazers selling out 814 home games in a row from 1977 to 1995 (Levinson, 2013). Fenway has not only hosted the Red Sox but numerous other team and events that have expanded this facility's impact on the region. From a team perspective, Fenway was the home venue for: the Boston Braves of the MLB National League (1914–1915), the Boston Redskins of the NFL (1933–1936), the Boston Shamrocks of the American Football League (AFL) (1936–1937), the Boston Bears of the AFL (1940), the Boston Yanks of the NFL (1944–1948), the Boston Patriots of the AFL (1963–1968), and the Boston Beacons of the North American Soccer League (1968) (Foulds, 2005).

From an events perspective Fenway has hosted major music concerts, the NHL Winter Classic outdoor game, the college football College Shamrock Series game of 2015 featuring Notre Dame and Boston, and even the Polartec Big Air at Fenway snowboard and ski competition as a part of the International Ski Federation's world tour of 2016. Although one of the smallest parks in the MLB by spectator capacity (37,949), Fenway remains a landmark and icon of professional baseball and of sport, and the park was added to the National Register of Historic Places in 2012. The historic roots of Fenway Park, however, have not precluded significant investments in

Wrigley Field on the north side of Chicago, IL opened in 1914.

facility renovations and upgrades. During a span from 2002–2011, the Red Sox ownership spent approximately $285 million in refurbishments and upgrades including new Green Monster seats, a manual scoreboard, a new playing field, improved concourses, new and renovated suites and club levels, new seats, new restrooms and concession stands, along with roof and waterproofing repairs (Strauss, 2011).

Halfway across the country, another new professional baseball venue opened on the north side of Chicago constructed as a single deck grandstand of steel and concrete. Originally opened as Weeghman Park in 1914 as the home of the Chicago Federals of the Federal Baseball League, the field had a capacity of 14,000 (Osacky, 2014). After an ownership and name change to Wrigley the venue was renovated with the addition of an upper deck in 1927 expanding capacity to just over 38,000. The famous ivy along the outfield walls was planted in 1937 (Riess, 1999). In addition to serving as the home venue of the MLB's Chicago Cubs since 1916, Wrigley Field has served as the home venue for numerous professional football teams including the Chicago Tigers, Hammond Pros, Chicago Cardinals, and the Chicago Bears. Beyond football and baseball, other notable uses have included professional soccer, the NHL's 2009 Winter Classic hockey game, and a limited number of concerts since the mid 2000s. Wrigley Field had been a hold-out for the tradition of day baseball and did not install field lights and play its first night game until 1988 (Vettel, 1988). While much of the mystique of Wrigley is connected to its historic roots, this venue has undergone recent renovation while maintaining most of its original charm. The Cubs new ownership, led by Tom Ricketts, began a four-phase $575 million privately-funded renovation project in 2014 that included outfield bleacher expansion, a new clubhouse, a broadcast center, upgraded concessions and parking, and new club and suite premium seating options (1060 Project, 2014). Both Wrigley and Fenway have maintained a strong connection with their primary structure and design along with the loyalty of their fans while undergoing significant renovation investments to maintain their viability.

While the majority of venues for the National Football League are relatively new, several stadiums still in use with more historic ties are still in use. This would include the Los Angeles Memorial Coliseum opened in 1923, home of the Rams (1946–1979 and 2016–2019) and the Raiders (1982–1994), Lambeau Field in Green Bay, WI opened in 1957 serving as the home of the Packers. However, most unique would be Soldier Field in Chicago that opened in 1926 and serves as the home of the Bears (1971–2001 and 2003–present) (Ford, 2009). Soldier Field was developed initially in an effort to attract the Olympic Games to the city and was connected to master planning efforts for the city tied to the progressive City Beautiful movement that drew architectural inspiration from ancient Greece and Rome (Ford, 2009). The use of arched openings, classic columns, and the red tiles roof details on the iconic

The iconic status of both Fenway Park and Wrigley Field is noted in the 2001 national commemoration of these venues in United States postage stamps.

colonnades all connect the original design of this stadium to antiquity. This stadium was grand in size and scope, with a seating capacity of 100,000 plus ample standing room for larger crowds, and it established a collegiate football attendance record in the 1927 Notre Dame and USC contest with more than 123,000 spectators (Historical Timeline, n.d.). Outside of football, the original Soldier Field hosted sporting events such as midget and NASCAR stock car racing, boxing (most notably the Tunney-Dempsey rematch of 1927), FIFA World Cup (1994), and Women's World Cup (1999) as well as non-sport events, like concerts, religious events like the Eucharistic Congress (1926) or the Billy Graham Crusade (1962), and political events like the Chicago Freedom Movement with Dr. Martin Luther King Jr. (1964 and 1966) or the Franklin D. Roosevelt campaign appearance (1944) with over 150,000 attending (Ford, 2009). The move of the NFL's Bears to Soldier Field began the start of numerous facility transformations including the enclosure of the formerly open north end of the stadium with seating (1974), the addition of artificial turf (1979), the creation of a press box and 60 sky boxes (1982), and the change back to natural grass plus an additional 56 more skyboxes (1988) (Historical Timeline, n.d.). However, the most substantial renovation occurred in 2002–2003 when an entirely new stadium structure was constructed within the confines of the original bowl and colonnades of Soldier Field. A modern design, stainless steel, and glass finished stadium with a capacity of 61,500 was constructed at a cost of $690 million, and sought to retain the classic design elements of the original stadium by building within the outer shell of the original (Kamin, 2014).

Since reopening after the major renovation, Soldier Field has accommodated a greater number of major musical concerts and several iterations of outdoor hockey at both the professional and collegiate levels in addition to its more typical football offerings. The hockey events began in 2013 with the Hockey City Classic pitting Notre Dame against Miami (OH) and Wisconsin against Minnesota, followed in 2014 with the NHL stadium series with the Blackhawks facing the Penguins, and the 2015 Hockey City Classic featuring games of Miami (OH) versus Western Michigan and Michigan versus Michigan State (Banks, 2012; Belson & Klein, 2013; Sipple, 2015). Much of the expanded events in the stadium can be attributed to the upgraded infrastructure, the improved sightlines, and the closer proximity of the stands to the field.

The review of these three historical American sport venues shows different methods of maintaining a connection to the past while attaining modern features and functionality. Wrigley and Fenway have worked to maintain much of their original appearance and

© Richard Cavalleri/Shutterstock.com

Historic Soldier Field in Chicago, IL, with the new construction located within the superstructure of the original venue.

features in many aspects and that has garnered them historical landmark or National Register of Historic Places status even after the recent renovations. However, Soldier Field was originally granted National Historic Landmark status in 1987 only to have that status revoked in 2006 due to the extensive nature of the stadium renovations that occurred despite claims that 90% of the original architectural design was preserved (Ahmed-Ullah, 2006).

Development of Sport Facilities in the United States

While the consideration of key historical sport venues still in use creates a modern tie to the historical development of sport facilities in the United States, larger trends must be considered that fostered the investment in and construction of stadiums, arenas, ballparks and other facilities for sport. Several sport historians have attempted to describe the development of sport facilities as ideal types over the past nearly 170 years through the concepts of innovation diffusion and historical ideal-type. This process began with Bale's (1984, 2001) four-stage application to the modern English soccer stadium, expanded to Seifried's (2010) six-stage evolution of professional baseball and football stadiums in the United States and now has been applied as a five-stage model for the development of the ideal collegiate football stadium (Tutka, 2016). This theoretical concept of *diffusion of innovation* seeks to identify how, why, and at what rate new ideas and technology spread (Rogers, 1962). While historical ideal-type can be traced to the original concepts of the early sociologist Max Weber, it allows for a combination of quantitative, qualitative, legal, and historical data to create a staged yet more open-ended explanation of stadium development (Tutka & Seifried, 2015).

Diffusion of Innovation a theory describing the communication and spread of an innovation over time in a social system.

A further examination of Tutka's (2016) five-stage model in combination with Siefried's (2010) six stage model of stadium development can create a framework for interpreting major stadium development in the United States at both the professional and collegiate levels. The development of professional baseball preceded college and professional football and began the stadium development movement in America (see Table 1.2). For Seifried's (2010) model, stages one and two primarily appeared before the beginning of the 20th century and included facilities constructed as temporary structures generally small and inexpensive. Stages three and four materialize as the first permanent professional baseball and football facilities are constructed and many of the first generation baseball facilities are renovated. For example, the classic Tiger Stadium was expanded twice in this time frame (1923 and 1938) along with Ebbets Field in 1926 and 1931 (Smith, 2000). Seifried's stage five aligns with the rise of the multi-purpose facility which attempted to accommodate both professional football and baseball equally, and during this stage professional football overcame baseball in general popularity. Finally, stage six represents a break away from the multi-purpose facility back to a more specialized single-purpose structure with a growing emphasis on spectator amenities including luxury and club areas. While professional baseball and football facilities were limited in some ways by their location, the economic goals of league and franchise leadership drove much of the professional sport facility development and change in America. Thus, professional sport facilities transformed from simple temporary structures into more opulent permanent structures to accommodate larger crowds along with special amenities, which created highly effective selling machines for these professional leagues.

Interestingly, the sport of football rose to popularity and fame at the collegiate level far ahead of the popularity and interest in the professional leagues. The investment in the creation of permanent and dedicated facilities for college football was far ahead of professional football in the size and scope of facilities. The work of Tutka (2016) to chronicle the development of Division I NCAA football facilities dovetails with much of the stage development within professional football and baseball (see Table 1.3). While the professional model has two stages, prior to the turn of the 20th century the collegiate football model had only one in that early time period, and then both models have four stages from 1903 to the present, with minor differences in the transition dates for the stages based on the differences in the facilities

Table 1.2   Professional Baseball and Football Development Stages

Stage	Time Frame	Primary Innovations	Facility Examples
1	1850–1884	Enclosure, Ticketed Admission, Temporary Facilities	Union Grounds (NYC), Avenue Grounds (Cincinnati), South End Grounds (Boston), Polo Grounds (NYC)
2	1885–1902	Wood Construction, Grandstands, Pavilions, Manual Scoreboards,	West Side Park (Chicago), Polo Grounds II & III (NYC)
3	1903–1919	Concrete and Steel Construction, Baseball Specific Venues	Forbes Field (Pittsburgh), Shibe Park (Philadelphia), Ebbets Field (NYC), Comiskey Park & Wrigley Field (Chicago), Crosley Field (Cincinnati)
4	1920–1952	Renovations (adding seating, restrooms & concessions), Electric Scoreboards, Lights, Multiple Decks	Yankee Stadium (NYC), Memorial Stadium (Baltimore), Cleveland Stadium, Los Angeles Memorial Coliseum
5	1953–1991	Multi-purpose, Artificial Turf, Domes	Astrodome (Houston), Three Rivers (Pittsburgh), Riverfront (Cincinnati), Qualcomm (San Diego), Metrodome (Minneapolis), Silverdome (Pontiac)
6	1992–present	Luxury Boxes, Club Seating, Retractable Roofs, Retro Design Features	Oriole Park at Camden Yards (Baltimore), Miller Park (Milwaukee), Cowboy/AT&T Stadium (Arlington)

Adapted from Seifried (2010)

Table 1.3 *Division I FBS College Stadium Development Stages*

Stage	Time Frame	Primary Innovations	Facility Examples
1	1869–1902	Wooden Bleachers, Enclosures (Fences, Walls)	College Field (Rutgers), Yale Field, Camp Randall Field (Wisconsin), Regents Field (Michigan), Beaver Field (Penn State)
2	1903–1929	Reinforced Concrete & Steel Construction, Press Areas, Parking	Harvard Stadium, Yale Bowl, Rose Bowl (Pasadena), Michigan Stadium
3	1930–1945	Press Boxes, Radio Broadcasts, Lights, Restrooms, Concessions, Electronic Scoreboards	Notre Dame Stadium, Amon G. Carter Stadium (TCU), Rutgers Stadium, Memorial Stadium (Clemson)
4	1946–1984	Television Broadcasts, Large Scoreboards, Artificial Turf, President's Boxes	Doak Campbell Stadium(FSU), Aloha Stadium, Rice Stadium (Utah), Carrier Dome (Syracuse)
5	1985–2014	Luxury Suites, Video Boards, Disability Seating, Complete Reconstructions	Papa John's Cardinal Stadium (Louisville), TFC Bank Stadium (Minnesota), McLane Stadium (Baylor)

Adapted from Tutka (2016)

studied. Unifying points would be the advent of concrete and steel construction methods connected most notably with Harvard Stadium for college football and Shibe Park for professional baseball. Additionally, both models rely on key innovations to move forward such innovations as media technologies in scoreboards, radio and television, along with spectator amenities ranging from the provision of restrooms and concessions to luxury boxes and club seating. Many of these innovations contribute to the use of these current modern stadia as event venues for other sport and non-sport events (Parrish, Lee, & Kim, 2014).The facility design features noted for baseball and football venues could and should also be considered for arena design and development where similar innovations have impacted their design and construction. The history of facility development for spectator sport in the United States can and should lend insight into the future development of these facilities types.

History of Key Sport Events

This chapter has already highlighted several aspects of the ancient athletic facilities in Greece and more specifically the facilities and event of the ancient Olympic Games. However, the modern Olympic Games are arguably the largest and most complex of sport events in the world. The creation of the modern Olympic Games is typically credited to the efforts of Pierre de Coubertin, and were officially approved by the delegates of International Congress of Paris for the Study and the Propagation of the Principles of Amateurism in 1894 and resulted in the inaugural 1896 games being held in Athens, Greece (Spears & Swanson, 1983). Since that modern inception, the Olympic Games have grown significantly in size and scope. While the first modern Olympics included 241 athletes (men only) from 14 nations, the 2012 London Olympics boasted 10,568 athletes (5,892 men, 4,675 women) from 204 countries (IOC, 2013). In 1924, the Olympic family of events expanded with the Winter Games hosted in Chamonix, France including 258 athletes (247 men, 11 women) from 16 countries that grew to 2,781 athletes (1,660 men, 1,211women) from 88 nations in the 2014 Sochi Games (IOC, 2014).

The rise of the Olympic Games' popularity can be tied to television coverage of the events for a global audience. For example, the 2012 London Olympics, drew an unprecedented level of broadcast coverage by NBC Universal in the United States providing 5,335 hours of coverage across multiple platforms and networks such as NBC, NBC Sports Network, MSNBC, CNBC, Bravo, Telemundo, NBCOlympics.com, a pair of dedicated channels specifically covering basketball and soccer competitions on some cable systems, and a 3D platform (Deitsch, 2012). Olympic Games broadcasts draw highly significant levels of viewership. For example, the Nielsen Company has reported global audiences over the span of recent Summer Games at 3.2 billion for Atlanta in 1996, 3.6 billion for Sydney in 2000, 3.9 billion for Athens in 2004, and 4.7 billion for Beijing in 2008 (Hui, 2008). This total from 2008 equates to roughly 70% of the entire global population at that time.

The popularity of the Olympic movement spawned numerous multi-sport festivals based upon unique characteristics such as geographic region (e.g. Pan-American Games and Asian Games both established in 1951), language/culture (e.g. Commonwealth Games established 1930 and Pan-Arab Games established 1963), participant occupation (e.g. World University Games established 1959 and World Police and Fire Games established 1985), and disability (e.g. Paralympic Games established 1960 and Special Olympics World Games established 1968) (Bell, 2003). Beyond the replication of multi-sport festivals similar to the Olympic Games, new sporting events not included in Olympic competition also began to develop with specific target audiences, most notably the X Games. As a unique creation of the ESPN television network, the X Games and Winter X Games, begun in 1995 and 1997 respectively, were established to appeal to a younger audience and connected to sports seen as more individualist and extreme (Pickert, 2009). The International Olympic Committee followed this trend of seeking to engage a younger audience with the development of the Youth Olympic Games starting summer games in 2010 and winter games in 2012 both following the typical Olympic four-year cycle (Petersen, Deitz, Leitzelar, Bellar, & Judge, 2015). While these types of large, multi-sport festival-style events are typically international in nature and classified as mega-events, there are a number of single sport competitions that rival the Olympics and other sport festivals in interest and popularity on global and national levels. The World Cup and the Super Bowl will next be considered as highly influential single-sport events.

World Cup

The history of the World Cup is broad enough to be the topic of an entire book in its own right, which it indeed has been many times. However, a brief history of this event brings perspective to the rapidly changing and developing environment of single sport events that have grown to mega-event status.

To a degree the World Cup is connected to the Olympic Games as the official addition of football (soccer) to the London Olympics in 1908 further spurred interest in international tournaments. The founding of the Federation Internationale de Football Association (FIFA) in 1904 included the exclusive right to organize a global football competition, and in 1924 FIFA agreed to assume responsibility for the organization of the Olympic football tournament (Street, Frawley, & Cobourn, 2014). This Olympic involvement ultimately prompted FIFA as the international governing body of the sport to create their own tournament better representing competitive equity by allowing both professionals and amateurs the ability to play beginning in 1930. As the early Olympic Games limited participation to athletes of an amateur status, the newly formed World Cup would allow participation of all of the world's top players. Table 1.4 summarizes the World Cup from a host nation, tournament size, venues utilized and championship game details perspective.

An examination of the data in this table provides a number of key insights related to the growth and success of this event. First, it should be noted that the World Cup remains strategically timed to fall directly between the four year cycle of the Summer Olympic Games, and this serves to heighten global interest in this event. Second, the World Cup has been hosted in five of the six populated continents of the world with only Australia not yet serving as a host. The World Cup has grown in size and scope from its inception in 1930 from a single city event of 13 teams to its status for the 2018 event in Russia with 32 teams playing in 12 venues spread throughout 11 cities. This growth in the number of teams invited to participate in the event included the move from 16 to 24 teams for the 1982 Cup in Spain, and the expansion from 24 to 32 teams in 1998 for the World Cup in France. This data also reveals that the number of venues utilized for the event has grown, and FIFA has created nine areas of technical requirements for World Cup stadiums including specifications for the field of play, other competition areas, public area, operational areas, VIP areas, media tribune, media centers, broadcast areas, and hospitality areas (Street et al., 2014). The World Cup also continues to grow from a financial perspective with the revenues associated with the 2011–2014 cycle (including the World Cup in Brazil) totaling $5.718 billion dollars and representing nearly a 47% increase in earnings from the prior 2007–2010 reporting period of $3.890 billion (FIFA, 2015). Much of this revenue is associated with the global television rights connected with the World Cup. Solberg and Gratton (2014) reported that 56.4% of the FIFA revenues in 2003–2006 came from

Table 1.4 FIFA World Cup Venues Summary

Year	Country	Teams	Cities	Stadiums	Finals City	Finals Venue	Attendance
1930	Uruguay	13	1	3	Montevideo	Centenario	80,000
1934	Italy	16	8	8	Rome	Nazionale PNF	50,000
1938	France	15	9	10	Paris	Olympique	45,000
1950	Brazil	16	6	6	Rio de Janeiro	Maracana	174,000
1954	Switzerland	16	6	6	Berne	Wankdorf	60,000
1958	Sweden	16	12	12	Stockholm	Rasunda	51,800
1962	Chile	16	4	4	Santiago	Nacional	69,000
1966	England	16	7	8	London	Wembley	93,000
1970	Mexico	16	5	5	Mexico City	Azteca	107,412
1974	West Germany	16	9	9	Munich	Olympiastadion	75,200
1978	Argentina	16	5	6	Buenos Aires	River Plate	71,483
1982	Spain	24	14	17	Madrid	Santiago Bernabeu	90,000
1986	Mexico	24	9	12	Mexico City	Azteca	114,600
1990	Italy	24	12	12	Rome	Olympico	73,603
1994	United States	24	9	9	Pasadena	Rose Bowl	94,194
1998	France	32	10	10	Saint-Denis	Stade de France	80,000
2002	Korea/Japan	32	20	20	Yokohama	International Stadium	69,029
2006	Germany	32	12	12	Berlin	Olympiastadion	69,000
2010	South Africa	32	9	10	Johannesburg	Soccer City	84,490
2014	Brazil	32	12	12	Rio De Janeiro	Maracana	74,738
2018	Russia	32	11	12	Moscow	Luzhniki	TBD

Adapted from FIFA World Cup Finals (2007) and FIFA Tournaments (2016)

television rights of the 2006 World Cup in Germany, while 61.9% of FIFA revenues in 2007–2010 came from the television rights of the 2010 World Cup in South Africa.

While the World Cup remains the mainstay of revenue for FIFA, this organization has sought some diversification and growth with the operation and support of nine other global soccer events for men and boys. These events include 1) the FIFA U-20 World Cup (begun in 1977 as the World Youth Championship held one year prior to the World Cup; 2) the FIFA U-17 World

Maracana Stadium in Rio de Janeiro, Brazil, was the venue for the 2014 World Cup Final.

Cup (begun in 1985 as the U-16 World Championship) held every two years; 3) the FIFA Futsal World Cup (began as the Futsal World Championship in 1989) now held every four years on the same year as the Summer Olympics; 4) the FIFA Beach Soccer World Cup (began in 2005) held annually from 2005–2009 and now held every two years on odd years; 5) the FIFA Club World Cup (began in 2000) held annually since 2005 as an 8v8 format competition; 6) the FIFA Confederations Cup (begun in 1992 as the Intercontinental Champions Cup) now held every four years on the year preceding the World Cup; 7) Blue Stars/ FIFA Youth Cup (begun in 1939 and operated by FIFA since 1991) held every year; 8) the Men's Olympic Football Tournament (begun in 1908 and organized by FIFA since 1924) held during summer Olympic Games years, and 9) the Youth Olympic Football Tournament for boys (begun in 2010) held every four years (FIFA, 2016).

The World Cup inspired tournament play has also expanded and developed with global events for women and girls. The Women's World Cup was launched in 1991 with China hosting 12 nations, and this tournament, held every four years, expanded to 24 teams for the 2015 event hosted by Canada (FIFA, 2016). FIFA also sponsors four other global tournaments specifically for females including 1) the FIFA U-20 Women's World Cup (begun in 2002) held every two years; 2) the FIFA U-17 Women's World Cup (begun in 2008) held every two years; 3) Women's Olympic Football Tournament (begun in 1996) held during the summer Olympic Games every four years, and; 4) the Youth Olympic Football Tournament for girls (begun in 2010) held every four years (FIFA, 2016).

The growth and development of the World Cup, along with its ancillary tournaments and events, serves as a model of success in many ways for other sports and sport organizations. The tremendous financial gains associated with the event have in many ways helped to invest in the global game through the expansion of other soccer-based tournaments and global initiatives for this sport's continued development at both professionals and grass-roots levels.

Super Bowl

Although only a singular game-based event compared to the multigame format of the World Cup and multisport format of the Olympics, the Super Bowl is the most significant single sport and sport media event in the United States. The Super Bowl is much younger than the World Cup and the Olympics with the first game held in 1967. The game began as part of the efforts to formally unite two rival professional football leagues—the older and established National Football League and the younger upstart American

Football League. The merger of these two leagues was agreed upon in 1966 and went fully into effect in 1970, but the agreement included a common draft and a championship game to begin during the interim (Tinley, 2012). Lamar Hunt, then owner of the Kansas City Chiefs, is credited coining the name "Super Bowl" to replace the game title of AFL-NFL World Championship Game, and Hunt is also credited with suggesting the use of Roman numerals in the game designation to denote greater prestige (Tinley, 2012). Table 1.5 summarizes the first 50 years of the Super Bowl.

Levi's Stadium in Santa Clara, CA, host venue for the Super Bowl 50.

A review of the Super Bowl venues reveals that the stadiums used for this event were all previously existing professional or college football facilities, as opposed to the Olympics and World Cup that often include new construction or significant venue renovations. However, many NFL teams with new stadiums are often in a strong position to vie for a successful bid to host the big game. The Super Bowl has been hosted at a neutral site as opposed to the rest of the NFL playoffs that are held at the home venues of the higher-seeded team. However, since the bidding process is typically completed three to five years in advance of the playoffs, the possibility of a home stadium Super Bowl for a team remains possible although it has not occurred to date. It should be noted that the possibilities of a home crowd advantage would be highly reduced since the NFL controls the sales distribution of Super Bowl tickets rather than the host team or host venue. The Super Bowl is typically viewed as a destination event, and the vast majority of the host stadiums have been in warm climates for this mid-winter event like Florida, Louisiana, California, Arizona, Georgia, and Texas.

From a media perspective, the Super Bowl is tremendously popular as a televised sports event. The Super Bowl occupies the top four spots of most-watched broadcasts in the United States, and in 2015 set the top mark at 114.4 million viewers (Baron, 2015). While the popularity of the professional football in America is a driving force for this level of viewership, the creation of an extended 30 minute halftime with top musical performers has added to the allure of the Super Bowl as an entertainment spectacle. While the early years of the Super Bowl included halftime shows often featuring collegiate marching bands, the 1993 halftime performance by pop music superstar, Michael Jackson, transformed halftime into an event that attracted top musical performers as featured acts. The Jackson performance in Super Bowl XXVII drew a total audience during the halftime show of 133.4 million viewers (Knapfel, 2016).

Table 1.5 *Super Bowl Venues and Following*

Year	City/Market	Venue	Attendance	Network	US TV Audience
1967	Los Angeles	Memorial Coliseum	61,946	NBC & CBS	51,180,000
1968	Miami	Orange Bowl	75,546	CBS	39,120,000
1969	Miami	Orange Bowl	75,389	NBC	41,660,000
1970	New Orleans	Tulane Stadium	80,562	CBS	44,270,000
1971	Miami	Orange Bowl	79,204	NBC	46,040,000
1972	New Orleans	Tulane Stadium	81,023	CBS	56,640,000
1973	Los Angeles	Memorial Coliseum	90,182	NBC	53,320,000
1974	Houston	Rice Stadium	71,882	CBS	51,700,000
1975	New Orleans	Tulane Stadium	80,997	NBC	56,050,000
1976	Miami	Orange Bowl	80,187	CBS	57,710,000
1977	Pasadena/ Los Angeles	Rose Bowl	103,438	NBC	62,050,000
1978	New Orleans	Superdome	75,583	CBS	78,940,000
1979	Miami	Orange Bowl	79,484	NBC	74,740,000
1980	Pasadena/ Los Angeles	Rose Bowl	103,985	CBS	76,240,000
1981	New Orleans	Louisiana Superdome	76,135	NBC	68,290,000
1982	Pontiac/Detroit	Silverdome	81,270	CBS	85,240,000
1983	Pasadena/ Los Angeles	Rose Bowl	103,667	NBC	81,770,000
1984	Tampa	Tampa Stadium	72,920	CBS	77,620,000
1985	Palo Alto/ San Francisco	Stanford Stadium	84,059	ABC	85,530,000
1986	New Orleans	Louisiana Superdome	73,818	NBC	92,570,000
1987	Pasadena/ Los Angeles	Rose Bowl	101,063	CBS	87,190,000
1988	San Diego	Jack Murphy Stadium	73,302	ABC	80,140,000
1989	Miami	Joe Robbie Stadium	75,129	NBC	81,590,000
1990	New Orleans	Louisiana Superdome	72,919	CBS	73,852,000
1991	Tampa	Tampa Stadium	73,813	ABC	79,510,000
1992	Minneapolis	Metrodome	63,130	CBS	79,590,000
1993	Pasadena/ Los Angeles	Rose Bowl	98,374	NBC	90,990,000
1994	Atlanta	Georgia Dome	72,817	NBC	90,000,000
1995	Miami	Joe Robbie Stadium	74,107	ABC	83,420,000
1996	Phoenix	Sun Devil Stadium	76,347	NBC	94,080,000

1997	New Orleans	Louisiana Superdome	72,301	FOX	87,870,000
1998	San Diego	Qualcomm Stadium	68,912	NBC	90,000,000
1999	Miami	Pro Player Stadium	74,803	FOX	83,720,000
2000	Atlanta	Georgia Dome	72,625	ABC	88,465,000
2001	Tampa	Raymond James Stadium	71,921	CBS	84,335,000
2002	New Orleans	Louisiana Superdome	72,922	FOX	86,801,000
2003	San Diego	Qualcomm Stadium	67,603	ABC	88,637,000
2004	Houston	Reliant Stadium	71,525	CBS	89,795,000
2005	Jacksonville	Alltel Stadium	78,125	FOX	86,072,000
2006	Detroit	Ford Field	68,206	ABC	90,745,000
2007	Miami	Dolphin Stadium	74,512	CBS	93,184,000
2008	Glendale/ Phoenix	University of Phoenix Stadium	71,101	FOX	97,448,000
2009	Tampa	Raymond James Stadium	70,774	NBC	98,732,000
2010	Miami	Sun Life Stadium	74,059	CBS	106,476,000
2011	Arlington/ Dallas	Cowboys Stadium	103,219	FOX	111,041,000
2012	Indianapolis	Lucas Oil Stadium	68,658	NBC	111,346,000
2013	New Orleans	Mercedes-Benz Superdome	71,024	CBS	108,414,000
2014	East Rutherford/ New York	Metlife Stadium	82,529	FOX	111,488,000
2015	Glendale/ Phoenix	University of Phoenix Stadium	70,288	NBC	114,400,000
2016	Santa Clara/San Francisco	Levi's Stadium	71,088	CBS	111,900,000

Adapted from data from Alder (2012), Nielsen (2014), and the NFL (2016)

Place Attachment

There continues to be a high level of interest and engagement in sport both nationally and globally, and the phenomenon that seems to be recurring throughout history is for large groups of people to gather together to share in witnessing sport events. The positive experiences and fond memories that each individual may have of time spent participating in or watching sporting events in a particular site may develop into a strong connection to a particular location or venue. Behavioral and environmental scientists investigating these phenomena have developed place attachment as a theoretical construct to explain this relationship.

Place Attachment
a concept from environmental psychology describing the emotional connection between a person and a place that is founded on a three component model of person, process and place.

At the most basic level, *place attachment* can be defined as the emotional bond between a person and a place, and this concept draws from a foundation in environmental psychology (Florek, 2011). This place attachment bond is not a simple cause and effect relationship, but it is dependent upon the relationships between behavior and experiences that can apply to both individuals and groups (Rollero & De Piccoli, 2010). Place attachment is also related to the meaning of thoughts, feelings, memories, and interpretations connected to the landscape or place. In order to better understand place attachment, a conceptual framework, known as the Tripartite Model, has defined three place attachment variables (person, process and place) or the three Ps (Scannell & Gifford, 2010).

The person element of the Tripartite Model defines the "who" of the attachment. This person can be an individual or a group. For the individual the place derives meaning from personal experiences or perhaps life milestones or significant growth. For the group or community setting, places connect meaning typically to religious, historical or other cultural events, and these behaviors can lead to place attachment for both the groups as a whole and for the individuals (Scannell & Gifford, 2010). The process element of the model addresses the "how" of the place attachment. This process is connected to affective, cognitive, and behavioral elements. The affective or emotional elements are most typically positive in their associations. Sometimes even referred to as *topophilia*, or love of place, Cronin (1998) noted that sport stadia could form such emotional connections by being viewed in five ways including sacred places, scenic spaces, home, tourist places, or as a place of local patriotism. The cognitive or mental elements are related to the knowledge and memories of the place and the related meanings that individuals or groups will connect with the place. The third part of the process element is behavioral, and this behavioral aspect is the physical manifestation of the person-place bonds. This can be seen either in proximity-maintaining behaviors (staying close to the place) or in efforts to recreate aspects of the place when it is not accessible. The final element of the Tripartite Model, place, addresses the "what" of the attachment and can be any geographical location natural or human-created.

While the application of place attachment theory has been very limited in directly relating to sport venues or events, it has been connected with concepts of space planning for buildings or monuments (Manzo & Perkins, 2006) and has been heavily used within recreational settings (Kyle, Graefe, & Manning, 2005). There has also been some connection of place attachment to more recreational or participatory sport settings such as marathon running (Kaplanidou, Jordan, Funk, & Rindinger, 2012), but there has been virtually no direct connection of major spectator sport venues to this theoretical perspective. Given the tremendous individual and group passion for sport in so many nations around the globe, it is likely that this theory will expand its application within spectator sport and sporting venues in the near future.

History of Facility/Event Management as a Profession

The long history of facilities and events in sport was, of course, dependent upon people for organization and management. However, a more formal recognition of these unique job roles as a profession made little traction until the 1980s. During that decade, a number of professional association were formed for practitioners; publications and trade journals for facility management first appeared; manufacturers and consultants began to market directly to facility managers and a new segment of buyers with clout, and colleges and universities began to develop degree programs directed within facility management (Rondeau, Brown, & Lapides, 1995). More specifically, university-based degree programs can be traced back to Cornell University claiming the first specific degree in Facility Planning and Management established in 1980.

The further professionalization of facility and event management is connected to the direct identification of key job responsibilities or duties. For example, the International Facility Management Association (IFMA) sanctioned a "Global Job Task Analysis" in 2009. Through this process, eleven core competencies were identified in facility management including:

- communication,
- emergency preparedness and business continuity,
- environmental stewardship and sustainability,
- finance and business,
- human factors,
- leadership and strategy,
- operations and maintenance,
- project management,
- quality,
- real estate and property management, and
- technology (Roper & Payant, 2014).

The development of facility and event management as professions has also led to some levels governmental attempts to organize and or train facility managers from the US federal government level. Most recently the Facility Management Institute (FMI) was established within the General Services Administration (GSA) as an online or "cloud based" institute to provide training resources to fulfill the mandates of the Federal Buildings Personnel Training Act that was passed by Congress in 2010 as Public Law 111-308. Although not specific to sporting venues or events, this federal law and training program did further the professional recognition of these roles.

Professional Organizations

As with any growing profession, the development of professional or trade organizations signifies the value and importance of these job roles along with the financial and human resources associated with them. These professional organizations in general provide educational and professional development opportunities for their members often along with tangible goods and services such as hosting conferences, conventions, and seminars, conducting research, providing professional *certifications*, and publishing trade publications and resources.

Certification the validation of specific professional training related to a professional practice or professional organization.

These professional organizations range in geographic scope from the international to the national, regional, state, and sometimes local levels. These organizations can also represent either broad or more limited scopes based upon the types of facilities or events covered within their organizational mission. For example, both the International Facility Management Association (IFMA) and the International Association of Venue Managers (IAVM) are international in scope, but the IFMA has a broad facility focus while the IAVM is more narrowly focused on large public assembly facilities. A professional organization like the Florida Facility Managers Association (FFMA) would have a more narrow geographic scope while still maintaining a broader scope of venue type, whereas the Wisconsin Ice Arena Management Association (WIAMA) would be rather narrow in its facility type and geographic scope yet both organizations still serve an important professional role. It will be well beyond the scope of this text to describe all of the applicable professional organizations in facility and event management and more specifically sport facility and event management. However, seven organizations will be highlighted that demonstrate the variety of associations available to foster the continued development of the profession. For the student, many of these organizations offer significantly reduced rates for membership or conference attendance, and engagement with these associations can create tremendous professional development and networking opportunities that can aid in launching a career. For both young and established professionals, connection with professional organizations provides a vital link to continuing education and networking that will help foster a vibrant career path.

International Facility Management Association (IFMA)

The IFMA is the broadest professional organization overviewed in this chapter, and its scope encompasses all facilities, not being limited to sport or public assembly settings. While the IFMA is relatively young, being founded in 1980, it has a membership of over 24,000 spread throughout 105 nations. This organization hosts two major conferences on an annual basis *World Workplace* and *Facility Fusion* and publishes *FMJ magazine* six times per year in both a print and online format. In addition to the magazine, members have access to a bi-weekly newsletter (*The WIRE*) and are sent four different regionally-focused weekly news briefs (*IFMA Insider*). This organization also publishes research reports, how-to guides, and white papers that are discounted to members and sold also to non-members. The IFMA has three different credential programs that combine focused online learning modules to enhance professional development and recognition. These credentials include the base-level Facility Management Professional (FMP), the Sustainability Facility Professional (SFP) and the Certified Facility Manager (CFM) that requires both educational and work experience requirements along with the CFM examination.

International Association of Venue Managers (IAVM)

One of the oldest, largest, and most influential professional organizations within the field of facility and event management is the International Association of Venue Managers (IAVM). Unlike the IFMA, the IAVM has a specific focus on facilities used for public assembly and sport. This organization can be traced back to a founding in 1924 with a meeting of seven professionals held in Cleveland, Ohio where the Association of Auditorium Managers was formed. Ten years later, in 1934, the organization was expanded and renamed the International Association of Auditorium Managers, and in 1996 the organization was retitled the International Association of Assembly Managers to more broadly encompass all the public assembly facilities (PAFs) that encompassed the organization (Williams, 2010). The current title for the organization was adopted in 2010 where the term *Assembly* was replaced with the term *Venue*, and this change placed a greater emphasis on the facility itself over the gathering of people and also made the organization more marketable and understandable to the general public.

The IAVM is structured in eight geographic regions with the strongest presence within the United States and Canada. Each of the regions 1–7 includes at least five states with the Canadian provinces, Africa, Mexico, Central and South America strategically spread throughout the regions, while Australia, New Zealand and countries of the Asia Pacific Rim form the final region (Regions and Chapters, n.d.). The IAVM hosts an annual broad-based conference, *VenueConnect*, plus three more focused industry sector conferences including the Arena Management Conference (AMC), the International Convention Center Conference (ICCC), and the Performing Arts Managers Conference (PAMC).

As of 2015 the IAVM boasted a professional worldwide membership of more than 5,000. This organization also offers numerous certification and education programs. The Certified Venue Professional (CVP) is viewed as the entry-level certificate for practicing professionals. The CVP program began in 2015 for middle to senior level managers to demonstrate competence and assist in professional development. The CVP process adheres to a set of competency standards and requires three to five years minimum industry experience, IAVM involvement, commitment to an IAVM code of ethics, recommendations from three professional references, along with passing a written examination. A second and more advanced certification, the Certified Facilities Executive (CFE), has been developed for top level venue managers

© Eugenio Marongiu/Shutterstock.com

Professional meetings, conferences, conventions, and trade shows are all important elements associated with professional organizations in facility and event management.

with job titles such as General Manager, CEO, President, Executive Director, or Senior Manager. This program requires at least seven to ten years of industry experience, a college degree(s), IAVM involvement in conferences, professional programs and continuing education, leadership training, publishing, speaking, mentoring and service. The CFE program was first initiated in 1976, and includes 1) an application with documentation of work, education and service background plus an ethical code commitment; 2) a written essay; 3) a written examination; and 4) an oral interview conducted by a panel of the Certification Board that assesses the candidate ability to articulate their professional experience, management philosophy, professional contributions, and overall management within public assembly facilities, including arenas, stadiums, convention centers, or performing arts venues.

From an educational perspective, IAVM offers training in guest experience and crowd management via their GuestX conference. The organization also offers the Trained Crowd Manager educational program that aligns with the assembly occupancy requirement from the 1994 Life Safety Code from the National Fire Protection Association. Special one-day training sessions occur on Severe Weather Preparedness, and a more intensive two-year program conducted with two intensive one-week sessions is offered as the Academy for Venue Safety and Security. Additionally, the IAVM offers members access to numerous webinar sessions and the association also provides *FM Facility Manager Magazine*, a quarterly online and print publication, along with maintaining an industry blog *Front Row News*.

Stadium Managers Association (SMA)

The SMA has a more narrow focus than the IAVM with a specific focus on stadiums as a subset of PAFs with unique considerations for optimal management of the stadium environment. The SMA can be traced back to an initial meeting in 1974 called the Stadium Seminar that was organized by Robert Sigholtz from RFK Stadium in Washington, D.C. These annual seminars continued through 1991 when the SMA was officially incorporated as a trade association (History of SMA, n.d.). The annual convention or seminar as it is titled by the SMA is a week-long event. One unique aspect of this organization is that student members can apply for the Seminar Student Intern Program that provides hotel accommodations, registration, and meals for the event while the student assists in organizational and operational elements of the seminar. From an organizational mission perspective, the SMA remains committed to issues and solutions that enhance the safety, profitability, and service of their stadiums and their three-prong mission for their members is to network, educate, and involve.

College Event and Facility Management Association (CEFMA)

Somewhat a niche organization, the Collegiate Event and Facility Management Association was developed within the larger parent organization, the National Association of Collegiate Directors of Athletics (NACDA). This facility and event-focused organization was founded in 2007 as the National Association of Collegiate Event Managers, but was reorganized, expanded and renamed CEFMA in 2008. The primary mission of this professional association is to provide educational programs, share best practices, enhance professional development and provide networking opportunities within all levels of collegiate event and facility management (CEFMA, n.d.). An annual convention in June has been held since 2009, and educational efforts have expanded into CEFMA webinars and a smaller regional conference held in December. CEFMA is student-friendly and provides reduced rates for student membership and conference or convention attendance. This association has also grown to nearly 700 individual members, which is impressive given that the total number of NCAA member schools is just over 1100.

Association of Luxury Suite Directors (ALSD)

A relatively new, and tightly focused, professional association is the Association of Luxury Suite Directors. Founded in 1990, the ALSD meets the professional needs of those who sell and service premium level seating. As both the number of venues with premium seating and total number of luxury seats available has increased, so has the membership and interest in this portion of venue management. Members hail from the NFL, NBA, MLB, NHL, MLS, minor leagues, racing venues, universities, theater and concert venues along with food and beverage vendors. ALSD hosts an annual conference and tradeshow and publishes *SEAT* magazine, a quarterly print and online trade magazine. Educational programming at the conference typically includes concurrent trainings such as the Sport Sales Boot Camp (What is ALSD, n.d.).

National Center for Spectator Sports Safety & Security (NCS4)

While the first four professional organizations progressed from broad to narrow venue types or even venue components, the National Center for Spectator Sports Safety & Security emphasizes an operational aspect within the sport venue realm. The NCS4 is an example of a professional organization in sport facility management with a focus upon security and safety as the priority through training and professional development, academic programs, and research. The NCS4 has much more direct academic connection since it is housed at the University of Southern Mississippi and was founded in 2006 partly as preventative response to the 9/11 terrorist attacks. The academic programs connected to the NCS4 include a master's degree in sport management with an emphasis in sport event security management, master's in business administration (MBA) with an emphasis in sport security management, and a 12 credit hour graduate certificate in sport security management, all offered through the University of Southern Mississippi; the program faculty have a vast array of research writings and presentations related to sport-based security (NCS4, n.d.).

The NCS4 has hosted a national conference since 2010, and also hosts separate summit meeting sessions such as the Marathon Summit, Intercollegiate Summit, and the Interscholastic Summit. Additionally, the NCS4 in collaboration with the Department of Homeland Security (DHS) and Federal Emergency Management Administration (FEMA) provides training workshop in four areas: Sport Event Risk Management, Sports and Special Events Incident Management, Sports and Special Events Enhanced Incident Management, and Sport Event Evacuation Training Exercise. A specialized, one-day training for the interscholastic athletics and after-school activities setting has also been developed. In addition to providing training, the NCS4 has established a certification program, the Certified Sport Security Professional (CSSP), to indicate knowledge, skills and abilities with current techniques and effective strategies in handling safety and security risks within sport venues. The CSSP credential requires candidates to meet educational and experience benchmarks as well as complete a written examination.

National Association of Sport Commissions (NASC)

In addition to professional organizations related primarily to venues, there are also organizations tied to events. The development of sport commissions in the United States can be traced back to 1979 when the City of Indianapolis formed the Indiana Sports Corporation in order to strategically attract and support sporting events in the Indianapolis metropolitan region. As more cities and regions began to implement similar models, the need for a professional organization to meet the unique needs of these professionals developed. The National Association of Sport Commissions (NASC) was formed in 1992 with 15 inaugural member organizations and has grown to over 700 member organizations in 2014 (FAQs, n.d.). Formed as the first trade association within the sport tourism industry, the NASC works to provide a communication outlet among sport commissions, destination marketing organizations, and event rights holders along with key suppliers within the sport tourism industry. This professional development organization has a goal to provide its membership with quality education, relevant industry research and professional networking opportunities. The NASC is currently headquartered in Cincinnati, Ohio and hosts an annual meeting, the NSCA Sports Event Symposium on a rotating basis of host cities and venues.

The International Festivals and Events Association (IFEA)

The IFEA can trace its origins to 1956 when the first meeting of the Festival Managers Association was held in the Park Sheraton Hotel in New York City. This professional association seeks to provide the answers, guidance, information, resources, contacts, programming, benefits, and support that are needed for success in the event and festival management field. The International Festivals and Events Association has a number of products and services for its members in the educational and professional development and networking realms including their annual convention and trade expo, numerous webinars for office-based training, and their Event Management School for new and mid-career professionals. The IFEA also publishes a trade magazine *IE—The Business of International Events* originally launched in 1994 as *Festivals* (About IFEA, n.d.).

The organization oversees the Certified Festival & Event Executive (CFEE) program that was founded in 1983 and reorganized in 2003 with the goal of enhancing the professional stature among one's peers and recognizing those who worked to exceed expectations to be the best in their profession. This comprehensive certification program includes completion of a core and elective curriculum, five years minimum of professional experience, IFEA involvement including conference attendance, speaking presentations, and a publication in the IE magazine.

Expectations of spectacle in sport continue to drive interest and attendance in sport events such as this fireworks display as a part of a New York Mets game at Citi Field.

Conclusion

The development of the current profession of facility and event management in sport is inexplicably tied to the historical development of sport and the sport venues that house these activities and events. While this chapter introduces several classic facilities from both ancient times along with the more recent past, it remains somewhat cursory in relation to the depth of information available regarding other similar facilities not specifically covered within this chapter.

CHAPTER DISCUSSION QUESTIONS

1. Compare and contrast the sport facility types and their features found in ancient Greece with those in ancient Rome.

2. Explain how historical sport facilities still in use today effectively bridge the past and present.

3. How does innovation drive facility development and change historically and what are some primary eras and innovations within sport facilities in America?

4. Compare and contrast the Olympic Games, the World Cup, and the Super Bowl as mega-events in sport.

5. Define place attachment and describe how it applies to sport events and sport venues.

6. How has the profession of facility and event management in sport become professionalized, and what role do professional and trade organizations help develop this profession?

SUGGESTED ACTIVITIES

1. Select a sport and trace the development of this activity and the most noted facilities for this sport at the local, national, and global levels (as applicable) via an illustrated timeline.

2. Select a sport team/franchise at a professional or collegiate level and trace the facility history including all primary competition venues along with relevant details (location, initial cost, renovations etc.) from the team/franchises inception to the present day.

3. Identify a local sporting event such as a specific race, tournament, etc. and document the development of this event with consideration of where this event may be in its lifecycle.

4. Explore the website of one of the professional organizations (IAFM, IAVM, NCS4, NACS, SMA, or others) and hypothetically plan your attendance at a conference or training program including a consideration of costs and benefits for you.

MINI CASE STUDY

Assume that you are working in the role of as Director of Facilities for Kokernot Field in in the small rural town of Alpine, Texas. This field serves as the home baseball venue for Sul Ross State University and for the Alpine Cowboys, an independent league professional baseball franchise. There is currently a debate regarding whether this historic, but old, facility should be renovated or replaced. The facility was originally opened in 1947 at a cost of $1.25M and currently has a capacity of 1,400 spectators (Dawidoff, 1989). You are leading the facility planning committee that will determine the recommendation between renovation/restoration and new construction. A review of Dawidoff's article from *Sports Illustrated*, The Best Little Ballpark in Texas or Anywhere Else, will provide further background for this mini case study.

1. Describe how the concept of place attachment might influence which direction would be taken by the facility planning committee?

2. What general constraints might be encountered with renovations to an historic stadium, arena or ballpark, and what specific constraints might you encounter with Kokernot Field?

3. If a new facility is proposed as the solution, should any tribute or homage be paid to the original facility? If so how, and if not, why not?

4. What professional organizations related to facility and event management might provide resources or insight to your committee?

PRACTITIONER SPOTLIGHT

Photo courtesy of Robert Drumm.

NAME: Robert Drumm

ORGANIZATION: SMG—Superdome and the Smoothie King Center

CURRENT JOB TITLE: Manager of Event Services, October 2015–Present

EDUCATIONAL PREPARATION: BA in Marketing, Louisiana State University MSEd in Sport Management, Baylor University

CAREER PATH: Initially, I worked part-time with the Superdome in events after completing my graduate internship experience there. My first full-time position was within SMG in Bossier, Louisiana at the LA Century Link Center as the Event Coordinator. I held this position from April of 2011 through November of 2012 when I returned to the Superdome to assume the role of Event Coordinator in New Orleans. Since that move, I experienced two promotions. The first was to take on the role as Assistant Manager of Event Services beginning in July of 2014. The second promotion was to my current duties as the Manager of Event Services that began in October of 2015.

AS AN OLDER AND HISTORIC VENUE WHAT CONSTRAINTS DO YOU FACE WITHIN THE MERCEDES-BENZ SUPERDOME IN HOSTING YOUR REGULAR EVENTS (I.E. NFL GAMES) AND SPECIAL EVENTS LIKE BOWL GAMES, FINAL FOURS, SUPER BOWLS ETC.?

The biggest constraint for us is technology. The Superdome was opened in 1975 and has to be updated when we want to add new technology to keep us competitive from a venue perspective. We are also constrained in terms of land around the facility. There is no room to grow or expand seeing as we are landlocked in downtown New Orleans. Finally, our concourses aren't wide enough. The newer venues have larger concourses which help with food and beverage sales distribution, along with general traffic flow in the venue. Our concourses simply weren't large enough so our 2011 renovation project expanded them on the 100 level and added to new club-level "bunker" lounges.

HOW HAVE FACILITY RECENT RENOVATIONS AND UPGRADES IMPACTED HOW YOU OPERATE EVENTS IN THE SUPERDOME?

The Mercedes-Benz Superdome and Smoothie King Center in New Orleans, LA.

The most recent and impactful facility upgrades that we have done was the installation of stadium Wi-Fi and new HD LED video boards in the end zones that are 330' × 35'. These were critical seeing as both are headed toward the norm within facilities of our type. They added a layer to the fan experience, which is obviously a huge plus when you talking about getting fans into the venue and creating an atmosphere that they can enjoy. Another major factor that has helped us out from a revenue standpoint is was an upgrade to the suites on the 300 and 400 level. We upgraded a total of 153 suites which has greatly impacted the premium seating revenues within the venue.

The facility also had significant renovations and upgrades with the post-Katrina repairs and three-phase renovation project.

HOW HAS THE HISTORY AND TRADITION OF THIS FACILITY IMPACTED WHAT TYPES OF EVENTS ARE HOSTED AS WELL AS IMPACTED POSSIBLE AND ACTUAL CHANGES MADE IN THE FACILITY?

The Superdome is rather old but that also creates a great sense of history and tradition for the facility. We have had Pope John Paul II, the Rolling Stones, seven Super Bowls (XII, XV, XX, XIV, XXXI, XXXVI, and XLVII), five NCAA Men's Final Fours (1982, 1987, 1993, 2003, and 2012), Muhammad Ali's third and final World Heavyweight Championship victory in 1978, and many other historic events hosted in the Superdome. I don't know if any of these events changed the facility per se, but it has definitely added to the historic perspective of the venue. When you think Superdome, historic events come to mind, and that is a major selling point for our venue.

WHAT IS THE MOST REWARDING ASPECT OF YOUR JOB?

The most enjoyable part of this position to me is seeing every detail and plan come together on "game day." There are a lot of moving pieces such as security, food and beverage operations, ticketing, production, and many more which require a significant amount of planning and coordination. It's extremely gratifying when all of these facets come together seamlessly to make a great event that the fans can enjoy.

WHAT IS THE MOST CHALLENGING ASPECT OF YOUR JOB?

The most challenging part of this role is the sheer volume and variation of events that we have over the course of a year. It becomes rather difficult managing all of these different events and keeping everyone on the same page while working on them. Another difficulty is communicating the needed information to everyone effectively. People have different communication styles and you have to properly navigate that to make sure that each of our entities has the information they need to help run the event effectively.

WHAT DO YOU SEE AS THE MOST IMPORTANT SKILL(S) TO DEVELOP?

The most important skill in my opinion is to be organized and to be an effective multitasker. A lot of what we do is time sensitive, and being organized is a huge part of being successful in this role. If you don't have your "ducks in a row" it may be difficult to get your tasks done effectively, and this can impact the entire organization.

WHAT PARTING WORDS OF WISDOM DO YOU HAVE FOR STUDENTS AND YOUNG PROFESSIONALS IN THE FIELD?

Get out there and volunteer as much as you can. Get as much experience as you can whenever you can because any experience in the field is valuable. People in this business seldom turn down volunteers. Make sure to use your volunteer work to network with people, and don't be afraid to ask if you can help them.

Reprinted by permission of Robert Drumm.

REFERENCES

1060 Project. (2014). Cubs host 1060 Project groundbreaking ceremony at Wrigley Field. Retrieved from http://chicago.cubs.mlb.com/chc/restore-wrigley/media-center/releases/cubs-host-1060-project-groundbreaking-ceremony-at-wrigley-field-101114/

2003 Renovations. (2016). Fenway Park Living Museum Fund. Retrieved from http://boston.redsox.mlb.com/bos/fenway-park-living-museum/timeline/index.jsp?year=2003

About IFEA. (n.d.). International Festival and Events Association. Retrieved from http://www.ifea.com/p/about

Ahmed-Ullah, N. S. (2006, April 22). Soldier Field loses landmark status. *Chicago Tribune.* Retrieved from http://articles.chicagotribune.com/2006-04-22/news/0604220145_1_historic-landmark-designation-soldier-field-blair-kamin

Alder, J. (2012). Super Bowl attendance. Retrieved from http://football.about.com/od/histo2/a/SBattendance.htm

Allen, S. H. (1999). Finding the walls of Troy: Frank Calvert and Heinrich Schliemann at Hisarlik. Berkeley, CA: University of California Press.

Bale, J. (1984). International sport history as innovation diffusion. *Canadian Journal of History of Sport, 15,* 38–63.

Bale, J. (2001). *Sport, space, and the city.* Caldwell, NJ: Blackborn.

Banks, P. M. (2012, July 11). College hockey doubleheader coming to Soldier Field: Hockey City Classic. *Chicago Sports Guru.* Retrieved from https://web.archive.org/web/20120725035223/http://www.chicagonow.com/chicago-sports-guru/2012/07/college-hockey-doubleheader-coming-to-soldier-field-hockey-city-classic/

Baron, S. (2015, February 2) Super Bowl XLIX most-watched show in U.S. television history with 114.4 million viewers. *TV by the Numbers.* Retrieved from http://tvbythenumbers.zap2it.com/2015/02/02/super-bowl-xlix-is-most-watched-show-in-u-s-television-history/358523/

Bell, D. (2003). *Encyclopedia of international games.* Jefferson, NC: McFarland & Company.

Belson, K., & Klein, J. Z. (2013, May 1). NHL Stadium Series announces date in Chicago. *New York Times.* Retrieved from http://www.nytimes.com/2013/05/02/sports/hockey/nhl-stadium-series-announces-date-in-chicago.html?_r=1

CEFMA. (n.d.). About Us. Retrieved from http://www.nacda.com/cefma/aboutus.html

Chase, R. G. (2002). *Ancient Hellenistic and Roman amphitheatres, stadiums, and theatres: The way they look now.* Portsmouth: NH, P. E. Randall Publishing.

Christesen, P. (2014). Sport and democratization in ancient Greece with an excursus on athletic nudity. In P. Christesen & D. G. Kyle (Eds.), *A companion to sport and spectacle in Greek and Roman antiquity.* (pp. 211–235). West Sussex, UK: John Wiley & Sons.

Coleman, K. M. (1993). Launching into history: Aquatic displays in the early empire. *Journal of Roman Studies, 83,* 48–74.

Craig, S. (2002). *Sports and games of the ancients.* Westport, CT: Greenwood Press.

Cronin, M. (1998). Enshrined in blood: The naming of Gaelic Athletic Association Grounds and Clubs. *Sports Historian, 18*(1), 90–104.

Dawidoff, M. (1989, July 31). The best little ballpark in Texas or anywhere else. *Sports Illustrated.* Retrieved from https://www.si.com/vault/1989/07/31/120250/the-best-little-ballpark-in-texas-or-anywhere-else-travel-with-us-to-beautiful-kokernot-field-a-gem-of-a-place-where-time-has-stopped-and-small-town-baseball-has-been-elevated-into-a-work-of-fine-art

Deitsch, R. (2012, July 26). The Olympic television guide. *Sports Illustrated.* Retrieved from https://web.archive.org/web/20120731005714/http://sportsillustrated.cnn.com:80/2012/olympics/2012/writers/richard_deitsch/07/16/olympics-NBC-TV-preview/

Dodge, H. (2014a). Amphitheaters in the Roman World. In P. Christesen & D. G. Kyle (Eds.), *A companion to sport and spectacle in Greek and Roman antiquity.* (pp. 545–560). West Sussex, UK: John Wiley & Sons.

Dodge, H. (2014b). Venues for spectacle and sport in the Roman world. In P. Christesen & D. G. Kyle (Eds.), *A companion to sport and spectacle in Greek and Roman antiquity.* (pp. 561–577). West Sussex, UK: John Wiley & Sons.

FAQs. (n.d.). National Association of Sport Commissions. Retrieved from https://www.sportscommissions.org/Membership/FAQs#NASC-FAQs

FIFA. (2016). FIFA Tournaments. Retrieved from http://www.fifa.com/fifa-tournaments/

FIFA. (2015). Financial report 2014. Retrieved from http://www.fifa.com/mm/document/affederation/administration/02/56/80/39/fr2014weben_neutral.pdf

FIFA. (2007). FIFA World Cup finals: All-time recap. Retrieved from http://www.fifa.com/mm/document/fifafacts/mcwc/ip-301_09a_wc-finals_alltime_8864.pdf

Fisher, D. M. (2002). *Lacrosse a history of the game.* Baltimore, MD: Johns Hopkins University Press.

Ford, L. T. A. (2009). *Soldier Field: A stadium and its city.* Chicago, IL: University of Chicago Press.

Foulds, A.E. (2005). *Boston's ballparks & arenas.* Lebanon, NH: University Press of New England.

Georgiou, A. V. (2008). Pankration: A historical look at the original mixed-martial arts competition. *Black Belt, 48,* 92–97.

Florek, M. (2011). No place like home: Perspectives on place attachment and impacts on city management. *Journal of Town & City Management, 1*(4), 346–354.

Graham, P. J., & Ward, R. (2004). *Public assembly facility management: principles and practices.* Coppell, TX: IAAM Inc.

Hill, W. D., Blake, M., & Clark, J. E. (1998). Ball court design dates back 3,400 years. *Nature, 392,* 878–879.

Historical Timeline. (n.d.). Soldier Field history. Retrieved from http://www.chicagobears.com/tradition/soldier-field-history/historical-timeline.html

History of SMA. (n.d.). Stadium Managers Association. Retrieved from http://www.stadiummanagers.org/index.php/history-of-sma-53/history

Hui, A. (2008). The final tally—4.7 billion tunes into Beijing 2008—more than two in three people worldwide. *Nielsen.* Retrieved from http://www.nielsen.com/content/dam/corporate/us/en/newswire/uploads/2008/09/press_release3.pdf

Humphrey, J. H. (1986). *Roman Circuses: Arenas for chariot racing.* Berkley, CA: University of California Press.

International Olympic Committee. (2013). Factsheet: The games of the Olympiad, update October 2013. Retrieved from: http://www.olympic.org/Documents/Reference_documents_Factsheets/The_Olympic_Summer_Games.pdf

International Olympic Committee. (2014). Factsheet: The Olympic Winter Games, update September 2014. Retrieved from: http://www.olympic.org/Documents/Reference_documents_Factsheets/The_Olympic_Winter_Games.pdf

Kamin, B. (2014, March 9). Soldier Field expansion raises questions about feasibility. *Chicago Tribune.* Retrieved from http://articles.chicagotribune.com/2014-03-09/news/ct-met-kamin-soldierfield-20140309_1_new-seating-bowl-soldier-field-chicago-bears

Kaplanidou, K., Jordan, J. S., Funk, D., & Rindinger, L. L. (2012). Recurring sport events and destination image perceptions: Impact on active sport tourist behavioral intentions and place attachment. *Journal of Sport Management, 26*(3), 237–248.

Knapfel, J. (2016, January 22). How an Elvis impersonator helped change Super Bowl history. *VIPtickets.com.* Retrieved from https://www.viptickets.com/blog/how-an-elvis-impersonator-helped-change-super-bowl-history/

Kotynski, E. J. (2006). The athletics of the ancient Olympics: A summary and research tool. Retrieved from http://www.oocities.org/ejkotynski/Olympics.pdf

Kyle, G., Graefe, A., & Manning, R. (2005). Testing the dimensionality of place attachment in recreational settings. *Environment and Behavior, 37*(2), 153–177.

Kyle, D. G. (1987). Athens—The Athletic. *Canadian Journal of History of Sport, 18*(2), 15–25.

Kyle, D. G. (2014). Greek athletic competitions. In P. Christesen & D. G. Kyle (Eds.), *A companion to sport and spectacle in Greek and Roman antiquity.* (pp. 21–35). West Sussex, UK: John Wiley & Sons.

Levinson, M. (2013, April 11). Red Sox sellout streak ends at 820 games with loss. *Bloomberg.* Retrieved from http://www.bloomberg.com/news/articles/2013-04-10/red-sox-s-fenway-sellout-streak-ends-at-794-regular-season-games

Manzo, L. C., & Perkins, D. D. (2006). Finding common ground: The importance of place attachment to community participation and planning. *Journal of Planning Literature, 20*(4), 335–350.

Miller, S. G. (2014). The Greek stadium as a reflection of a changing society. In P. Christesen & D. G. Kyle (Eds.), *A companion to sport and spectacle in Greek and Roman antiquity.* (pp. 287–294). West Sussex, UK: John Wiley & Sons.

NCS4. (n.d.). National Center for Spectator Sport Safety and Security. Retrieved from https://issuu.com/ncs4/docs/ncs4_brochure/1?e=8954340/8732659

NFL. (2016). Super Bowl History. Retrieved from http://www.nfl.com/superbowl/history

Nielson. (2014). Super bowl XLVII Draws 111.5 million viewers, 25.3 million tweets. Retrieved from http://www.nielsen.com/us/en/insights/news/2014/super-bowl-xlviii-draws-111-5-million-viewers-25-3-million-tweets.html

Osacky, M. (2014, March 21). 11 things you didn't know about Wrigley Field. *Parade Magazine.* Retrieved from http://parade.com/271495/michaelosacky/11-things-you-didnt-know-about-wrigley-field/

Parrish, C., Lee, S., & Kim, J. (2014). Marketing stadiums as event venues. *Journal of Applied Sport Management, 6*(3), 20–40.

Petersen, J. C., Deitz, S., Leitzelar, B., Bellar, D., & Judge, L. W. (2015). Youth Olympic Games awareness: An analysis of parents of elite youth sport athletes. *Global Sport Business Journal, 3*(3), 29–42.

Pickert, K. (2009, January 22). A brief history of the X Games. *Time.* Retrieved from http://content.time.com/time/nation/article/0,8599,1873166,00.html

Regions and Chapters. (n.d.). International Association of Venue Managers. Retrieved from http://www.iavm.org/regions/chapter-meetings-overview

Riess, S. A. (1999). *Touching base: Professional baseball and American culture in the progressive era.* Champaign, IL: University of Illinois Press.

Rogers, E. M. (1962). *Diffusion of innovations.* New York, NY: Free Press of Glencoe.

Rollero, C., De Piccoli, N. (2010). Place attachment, identification and environment perception: An empirical study. *Journal of Environmental Psychology, 30*(2), 198–205.

Rondeau, E. P., Brown, R. K., & Lapides, P. D. (1995). *Facility management.* New York, NY: John Wiley & Sons.

Roper K. O., & Payant, R. P. (2014). *The facility management handbook* (4th edition). New York, NY: American Management Association.

Sanada, H. (2010). Concept of the Intermediate Olympic Games of 1906: Continuity with the past Olympics. *International Journal of Sport & Health Science, 8,* 7–14.

Scannell, L., & Gifford, R. (2010). Defining place attachment: a tripartite organizing framework. *Journal of Environmental Psychology, 30,* 1–10.

Scott, M. (2014). The social life of Greek athletic facilities. In P. Christesen & D. G. Kyle (Eds.), *A companion to sport and spectacle in Greek and Roman antiquity.* (pp. 295–308). West Sussex, UK: John Wiley & Sons.

Seifried, C. S. (2005). *An analysis of the American outdoor sport facility: Developing an ideal type on the evolution of professional baseball and football structures.* (Doctoral dissertation, The Ohio State University). Retrieved from http://rave.ohiolink.edu/etdc/view?acc_num=osu1116446330

Seifried, C. S. (2010). The evolution of professional baseball and football structures in the United States, 1850 to the present: Toward an ideal type. *Sport History Review, 41,* 50–80.

Sipple, G. (2015, February 8). Hockey City Classic in Chicago full of problems. *Detroit Free Press.* Retrieved from http://www.freep.com/story/sports/college/2015/02/08/michigan-msu-hockey-city-classic/23083555/

Solberg, H. A., & Graton, C. (2014). Broadcasting the World Cup. In S. Frawly & D. Adiar (Eds.), *Managing the football World Cup* (pp. 47–62). New York, NY: Palgrave Macmillan.

Smith, R. (2000). *The ballpark book: A journey through the fields of baseball magic.* St. Louis, MO: The Sporting News.

Spears, B., & Swanson, R. A. (1983). *History of sport and physical activity in the United States* (2nd ed.). Dubuque, IA: William Brown Publishers.

Strauss, B. (2011, December 15). Fenway and Wrigley find two sides to landmark status. *New York Times.* Retrieved from http://bats.blogs.nytimes.com/2011/12/15/fenway-and-wrigley-find-two-sides-to-landmark-status/?_r=0

Street, L. Frawley, S., & Cobourn, S. (2014). World Cup stadium development and sustainability. In S. Frawly & D. Adiar (Eds.), *Managing the football World Cup* (pp. 104–132). New York, NY: Palgrave Macmillan.

Tekin, A., & Ekici, S. (2005). Antique sports places in Anatolia. *Journal of Sport and Tourism, 10*(3), 175–186.

Tinley, J. (2012, January 31). Super Bowl – Why do we call it that? *Midwest Sport Fans.* Retrieved from http://www.midwestsportsfans.com/2012/01/super-bowl-why-do-we-call-it-that-why-roman-numerals/

Tutka, P. M. (2016). *An ideal-type through innovation diffusion: Recording the construction history of football stadiums in the National Collegiate Athletic Association Division I football bowl subdivision.* (Doctoral dissertation, Louisiana State University). Retrieved from http://etd.lsu.edu/docs/available/etd-03252016-202739/

Tutka, P. & Seifried, C. (2015). The historical ideal-type as a heuristic device for academic storytelling by sport scholars. *Quest, 67,* 17–29.

Vettel, P. (1988). The Cubs get lights at Wrigley Field. *Chicago Tribune.* Retrieved from http://www.chicagotribune.com/news/nationworld/politics/chi-chicagodays-wrigleylights-story-story.html

Waldstein, C. (1896, May 16). The Olympic Games at Athens. *Harper's Weekly,* 490.

What is ALSD? (n.d.). Association of Luxury Suite Directors. Retrieved from https://www.alsd.com/content/what-alsd

Williams, K. (2010). International Association of Assembly Managers changes name to International Association of Venue Managers. *PRWeb.* Retrieved from http://www.prweb.com/releases/IAVM/name_change/prweb4744694.htm

Xikuan, Z. (1991). China: Sports activities of the ancient and modern times. *Canadian Journal of History of Sport, 22*(2), 68–82.

Young, D. C. (2004). *A brief history of the Olympic Games.* Malden, MA: Blackwell Publishing.

2

Types of Facilities and Events in Sport

Jeffrey C. Petersen

OBJECTIVES

After studying this chapter, the student should be able to:

- Identify and define primary facility types including stadium, arena, fieldhouse, indoor practice facility, gymnasium, natatorium, recreation center, and sportsplex.
- Compare and contrast facility types based upon characteristics such as spectator capacity, field/surface type, and sport function.
- Differentiate between stand-alone events, league events, and tour events.
- Identify and explain management implications for the various types of sport facility types and event types.

KEY TERMS

Arena

Fieldhouse

Gymnasium

Indoor Practice Facility

Natatorium

Recreation Center

Sport League

Sport Tour

Sportsplex

Stadium

KEY ACRONYMS

ATP	Association of Tennis Professionals
COTA	Circuit of the Americas
F1	Formula 1
FINA	Fédération Internationale de Natation
LPGA	Ladies' Professional Golf Association
NFHS	National Federation of State High School Associations
PAF	Public Assembly Facility
PGA	Professional Golf Association
WTA	Women's Tennis Association
YMCA	Young Men's Christian Association

Introduction

In order to better understand the myriad of types and variations in both sport facilities and sport events, this chapter has been developed to provide a definitional framework. From the prior coverage of facility and event history, this chapter will create a contemporary system of classification. However, the continued development of new facilities, events, and technologies can result in changes and even exceptions to the proposed working definitions. This chapter is structured to provide an overview and typology of sport facilities and sport events.

Sport Facilities

A large number of distinct types of built environments or facilities provide the setting or place for sport to occur. These facilities can be indoor or outdoor, and they are typically designed and operated from three distinct perspectives: the participants, the owner/operators, and the spectators (Sheard, 2000). The first would be facilities designed primarily with the needs of the athlete/participant as the top consideration. Sport facilities like recreation centers and sportplexes, focused upon youth and adult sport and participation, would align with this first perspective. The second perspective relates to the owners/operators who expect to make a return on investment by producing operating income from the events. A third perspective for sport facility design and operation would focus primarily upon the spectators and their experience at a sporting event. A large category of structures with a heavy emphasis on the spectator would be Public Assembly Facilities (PAFs). By definition PAFs are a classification of structures where people congregate in large numbers to attend events. PAFs include sport facilities like stadiums and arenas along with typically non-sport facilities like convention centers and theaters. While stadiums and arenas represent the primary PAFs related specifically to sport, this chapter will also consider a number of other facility types related to sport and recreation.

However, the effort to create clear and distinct definitions related to facility types can be challenging due to the broad use of many different terms for similar facilities. For example, the sport of baseball has used up to 14 different names within their titles to describe their venues (see Table 2.1). While the use of park, stadium, or field may be more common within baseball, it does not preclude the common usage of many other descriptive names. So while this chapter may seek to provide a strong sense of definition for many facility types, the varied and at times creative interpretation and use of terms in this profession remains challenging.

Stadium an outdoor or domed facility that provides a large space typically with turf to host sport and other non-sport events.

Stadiums

At the most basic level, a *stadium* is an outdoor or domed facility that provides a large space to host sport and other non-sport events. Stadiums typically include a large turf surface that can accommodate larger team sports

Table 2.1 *Baseball Venue Name Variations*

Name	Example Title	Location	Years Played
Park	Fenway Park	Boston, MA	1912–present
Stadium	Tiger Stadium	Detroit, MI	1912–1999
Field	Wrigley Field	Chicago, IL	1914–present
Grounds	Polo Grounds (I, II, & III)	New York, NY	1880–1911
Dome	Astrodome	Houston, TX	1965–1999
Diamond	Sunken Diamond	Stanford, CA	1931–present
Bowl	Baker Bowl	Philadelphia, PA	1895–1938
Cricket Grounds	St. George Cricket Grounds	New York, NY	1886–1889
Lot	Belair Lot	Baltimore, MD	1884
Palace	Palace of the Fans	Cincinnati, OH	1902–1911
Coliseum	Oakland Coliseum	Oakland, CA	1966–present
Commons	Case Commons	Cleveland, OH	1866–1870
Oval	Dyckman Oval	New York, NY	1923–1938
Dell	Sulphur Dell	Nashville, TN	1870–1963

Adapted from Lowery (1986)

such as football, soccer, baseball, rugby, cricket, lacrosse, track and field, and others. Because of the large size of the playing areas for these sports, early stadiums were completely outdoor structures. Over time, developments in construction technology allowed for the creation of shaded structures for spectators, followed by the development of fully enclosed or domed stadiums.

The dome stadium era began in 1965 with the opening of the Astrodome (originally the Harris County Domed Stadium) in Houston, Texas that was coined the "eighth wonder of the modern world." Domed stadiums provided protection from inclement weather and virtually eliminated the need for postponed or delayed contests. These structures also provided a climate-controlled environment that could provide heating or cooling to both the seating areas and playing field. The creation of enclosed stadiums also created a need for artificial playing surfaces as the growth and maintenance of natural turf within an indoor stadium was nearly impossible. As artificial turf technology advanced and developed, it began to be used in both indoor and outdoor stadium applications.

BC Place in Vancouver, British Columbia was originally constructed as an air supported fabric dome stadium (as shown here), and after the 2010 Olympic Games it was renovated and converted to a retractable roof stadium.

Eilat Ice Mall in Israel an example of a wooden dome construction spanning an athletic, shopping and entertainment venue.

Rogers Centre, home of the Toronto Blue Jays of the MLB, was the first retractable roof stadium.

As the interest in fully enclosed stadiums increased, so did additional technologies and techniques for dome construction. This has included roof structures such as air-supported fabric structures like the Carrier Dome (Syracuse University) and the Tokyo Dome; cable-supported fabric like the Georgia Dome (Atlanta); and wooden geodesic domes like the Walkup Skydome (Northern Arizona University) and the Superior Dome (Northern Michigan University) (Seidler & Miller, 2013). As convenient as the domed stadiums are in avoiding inclement weather, the traditional aesthetic of exposure to the outdoors and the use of natural turf is still appealing to many when the weather conditions are acceptable. This appeal has led to the next advancement in stadium design technology.

The most recent advance in the development and construction of stadiums is retractable roofs, as these structures allow the use of an indoor or outdoor environment within the same facility depending upon weather conditions. Retractable roof stadiums and arenas can be traced back to the 1960s when the Civic Arena opened in Pittsburgh, Pennsylvania. This arena was originally constructed as a home for the city's civic opera, but it was also used as the home venue for the NHL's Pittsburg Penguins (Eberson, 2010).

While this initial application of retractable roofs was of a smaller scale, the technology was soon applied to larger structures for football and baseball beginning in the late 1980s and beyond including Rogers Centre (Blue Jays, MLB) 1989, Chase Field (Diamondbacks, MLB) 1998, Safeco Field (Marlins, MLB) 1999, Minute Maid Park (Astros, MLB) 2000, Miller Park (Brewers, MLB) 2001, NRG Stadium (Texans, NFL) 2002, University of Phoenix Stadium (Cardinals, NFL) 2006, Lucas Oil Stadium (Colts, NFL) 2008, AT&T Stadium (Cowboys, NFL) 2009, Marlins Park (Marlins, MLB) 2012, and Mercedes-Benz Stadium (Falcons, NFL) 2017. It should be noted that retractable roof stadiums are not just a North American phenomenon.

There are at least 12 other retractable roof stadiums with a capacity of over 50,000 currently located in Europe, Asia, and Australia.

The seating capacity of stadiums can vary greatly depending upon the sport played and the market demand for tickets. Currently, the largest sport stadium for spectator capacity is located in North Korea. The Rungrado May Day Stadium has an official capacity of 150,000 yet does not serve as a "home venue" for any particular professional league or team. Table 2.2 lists the ten largest stadiums by spectator capacity in the world. An examination of this list reveals an interesting trend in that collegiate football in the United States occupies eight of the nine largest stadiums globally. This fact may relate to the unique nature of college football compared to many other spectator sports. However, stadiums as a facility type are not limited to those that are massive in scope. For example, the state of Texas includes 1,305 stadiums used for

Table 2.2 *World's Ten Largest Stadiums*

Stadium Name	Seating Capacity	Year Opened	Location	Primary Activity
Rungrado May Day Stadium	150,000	1989	Pyongyang, North Korea	Soccer (national)
Michigan Stadium	107,601	1927	Ann Arbor, MI, USA	American Football (college)
Beaver Stadium	107,282	1960	State College, PA, USA	American Football (college)
Ohio Stadium	104,944	1922	Columbus, OH, USA	American Football (college)
Kyle Field	102,512	1927	College Station, TX, USA	American Football (college)
Neyland Stadium	102,455	1921	Knoxville, TN, USA	American Football (college)
Tiger Stadium	102,321	1924	Baton Rouge, LA, USA	American Football (college)
Bryant-Denny Stadium	101,821	1928	Tuscaloosa, AL, USA	American Football (college)
Darrell K Royal— Texas Memorial Stadium	100,119	1924	Austin, TX, USA	American Football (college)
Melbourne Cricket Ground	100,024	1853	Melbourne, Victoria, Australia	Cricket & Australian Football

Adapted from worldstadiums.com

The Rungrado May Day Stadium on the Banks of the Taedong River in Pyongyang, North Korea is presently the largest stadium in the world with a seating capacity of 150,000.

home high school football games. While nine of these Texas high school stadiums have a capacity exceeding 16,500 spectators, the majority of the schools' stadia (39.3%) have a seating capacity between 1,001 and 5,000 (McSpadden, 2015).

Stadiums vary in their size, shape, and structure based upon the primary sport hosted within the facility. Sports like baseball and cricket with expansive variations in field size can impact the size and design of the stadium. Stadiums designed for athletics (track and field) typically have a large enough infield area for a football field or soccer pitch. However, current trends toward sport-specific stadiums have led many multi-purpose stadiums with running tracks to remove the track in favor of creating more spectator seating and seating closer to the field of play. While many stadiums will include seating that completely surrounds the playing area, many smaller-scale stadiums may provide seating on only one or two sides of the field space.

Racing Venues

In addition to stadiums there are two other very large outdoor sport venues to consider—racetracks for motor racing or for horse racing. Much of early spectator sport was focused upon the racing of humans and of horses; this later expanded to numerous types of motorized vehicles. Specialized venues for horse races and chariot races were present in ancient Greece as hippodromes and in ancient Rome as circuses. As motorized vehicles were developed, interest in racing grew to include various forms of motor sport races

such as Formula One (F1), IndyCar, NASCAR, MotoGP (motorcycles), and many others. These races could be seen as the next step in progression from the chariot races of antiquity.

Given the larger size and scope of the race tracks for both horse racing and motor sports in comparison to stadiums, it is not surprising that racing venues have the largest capacities of all sporting venues. Large singular and signature events at these tracks are typically associated with these venues, and the massive capacity for spectators often includes a mix of permanent fixed seating, temporary seating, and premium/luxury seating options. Several

Daytona International Speedway is the largest capacity NASCAR venue and the second largest motor sport venue in the United States.

Table 2.3 *Top Ten Motor Sport Venues by Capacity*

Rank	Venue	Capacity	Country	Signature Event
1	Indianapolis Motor Speedway	257,325	USA	Indianapolis 500 (IndyCar)
2	Circuit de la Sarthe	234,800	France	24 Hours of Le Mans
3	Shanghai International Circuit	200,000	China	Chinese Grand Prix (F1)
4	Daytona International Speedway	168,000	USA	Daytona 500 (NASCAR)
5	Charlotte Motor Speedway	167,000	USA	Coca-Cola 600 (NASCAR)
6	Bristol Motor Speedway	160,000	USA	Food City 500 (NASCAR)
7	Istanbul Park	155,000	Turkey	Turkish Grand Prix (F1)
8	Texas Motor Speedway	154,861	USA	AAA Texas 500 (NASCAR)
9	Nürburgring	150,000	Germany	German Grand Prix (F1)
10	Silverstone Circuit	150,000	UK	British Grand Prix (F1)

Adapted from worldstadiums.com

motor sports rank among some of the most popular global sports including Formula 1 or F1 (#6), Moto GP (#19), NASCAR (#20), and IndyCar (#33) (Brown, 2016). Table 2.3 identifies the largest auto racing venues globally with three venues at or above a 200,000 spectator capacity.

More recently developed motor sport venues have also sought to combine the track and spectator components into a broader event facility. This trend is exhibited in the Circuit of The Americas (COTA) Grand Prix facility, which opened in 2012 outside Austin, TX,. This 3.41 mile long track is first and foremost the host of the annual Formula 1 United States Grand Prix which drew 117,429 spectators in its debut (Spurgeon, 2012). COTA also serves as a racing venue for a MotoGP (motorcycle) event, the Red Bull Grand Prix of the Americas, and a Lone Star LeMans event. However, the events at COTA have expanded beyond racing to many other events including the ESPN Summer X Games that utilized various portions of the track, grandstands, and hospitality areas (McKelvey, 2015). COTA also incorporates an outdoor amphitheater concert venue with a

© Tricia Daniel/Shutterstock.com

A portion of the race track at the Circuit of The Americas near Austin, TX.

fixed seating capacity for 5,240 and a total capacity of 14,000. The creation of a broader entertainment complex beyond strictly motorsport make the COTA facilities more heavily utilized and thereby draw more total attendees which creates a greater economic impact for the region.

Motor sport venues have a number of important design considerations related to safety for the racers on the track and the spectators in the stands. Walls, fences, and other barriers between the track and the fans require expert engineering and design in order to minimize the risks of injuries to racing participants and racing fans. These barriers need to function from a safety perspective while making minimal disruption to the sightlines or views of the race track.

While the global popularity of horse racing may have dropped to some degree as motor sports have developed, a significant number of massive venues remain around the globe—most notably in Japan and in the United States. Horse racing still remains a major global sport ranking 23rd in total following according to an international assessment of sports news websites (Brown, 2016). Many horse tracks feature annual signature events that provide tremendous prize money or purses and attract tremendous crowds such as the Kentucky Derby where a record crowd of 170,513 gathered at Churchill Downs in Louisville in 2015 (Galofaro, 2015). A summary of the largest horse racing tracks globally is provided in Table 2.4. Eight venues with a capacity of 100,000 or more are featured.

Table 2.4 *Top Ten Horse Racing Venues by Capacity*

Rank	Venue	Capacity	Country	Signature Event
1	Tokyo Racecourse	223,000	Japan	Japan Cup, Japanese Derby
2	Nakayama Racecourse	165,676	Japan	Arima Kinen, Satsuki Sho
3	Churchill Downs	165,000	USA	Kentucky Derby
4	Hanshin Racecourse	139,877	Japan	Takarazuka Kinen
5	Flemington Racecourse	130,000	Australia	Melbourne Cup
6	Epsom Downs	120,000	UK	Epson Derby
7	Kyoto Racecourse	120,000	Japan	Kikuka Sho
8	Hippodromo de San Isidro	100,000	Argentina	GP Clarlos Pellegrini
9	Pimlico Race Course	98,983	USA	Preakness Stakes
10	Belmont Park	90,000	USA	Belmont Stakes

Adapted from worldstadiums.com

Current designs and renovations to venues for both motor sports and horse racing have mirrored other sports with an increased emphasis on luxury seating options and suite development in order to meet the needs of high income individuals and corporate interests in providing hospitality to current and potential business clients. Most racing venues host a regular schedule of races and events, but these racing venues are also structured around a single signature event that draws significantly more fan and media interest than their other events.

Churchill Downs in Louisville, KY, home of the Kentucky Derby, is the largest spectator capacity horse racing venue in the United States.

Arenas

An *arena* is a structure that is completely enclosed to provide playing space on a central area, court, or floor surrounded by spectator seating with a high ceiling clearance. The primary sports utilizing arenas for competition include basketball, volleyball, team handball, badminton, gymnastics, tennis, figure skating, and hockey. Due to their relatively smaller spectator capacity, arenas often serve as multipurpose venues hosting concerts and other non-sport events, and many arenas can serve two primary sport tenants. Arenas typically have a limited amount of court space and are not usually heavily used as a practice facility for teams.

Arena completely enclosed sport venue providing playing space on a central area, court, or floor with a high ceiling clearance surrounded by spectator seating.

The sport of basketball greatly influenced the development of the modern arena. Basketball was created in 1891 by Dr. James Naismith at the YMCA training school in Springfield, Massachusetts (Rains, 2009). In the early years, this game was played in gymnasiums that were used for multiple purposes like gymnastics and physical education and training. These early gyms were not constructed with spectators in mind, but as the interest in the game of basketball grew at the college level new facilities with greater spectator capacity were constructed or retrofitted into existing structures.

The era of the Great Depression in the 1930s created a number of publicly funded municipal auditoriums that were used for basketball as well as other functions, and this era included facilities such as the New Orleans Municipal Auditorium (1930), Convention Hall in Philadelphia (1931), the Kiel Auditorium in St. Louis (1934), the Cleveland Public Auditorium (1937), and Buffalo Memorial Auditorium (1940) (Scott, 2016). These municipal, multi-purpose venues provided a large capacity for college basketball events and also helped foster the formation of professional basketball leagues. During this same era, on-campus basketball arenas like Alabama's Foster Auditorium (1939), Duke University's Cameron Indoor Stadium (1939), and Michigan State's Jenison Fieldhouse (1940) were being constructed. Some have capacities hovering around 10,000 (Scott, 2016).

Other sports also influenced arena development, most notably ice hockey. While the sport of ice hockey can be traced back to the early 1800s as an outdoor sport, the first indoor contest was held in 1875 in the Victoria Skating Rink in Montreal, Canada (McLaren, 2012). The development of refrigeration technology allowed for the creation of indoor rinks that corresponded to the growth of hockey as a spectator sport. The formation of the National Hockey League (NHL) in 1917 was also tied to key facilities to host the games, and the most famous of the early era of the NHL were the facilities associated with the "original six" which included the first Madison Square Garden in New York City (1926–1968) home of the Rangers, the Boston Garden (1928–1995) home of the Bruins, the Montreal Forum (1926–1996) home of the Canadiens, Maple Leaf Gardens in Toronto (1931–1999) home of the Maple Leafs, Chicago Stadium (1929–1994) home of the Blackhawks, and the Olympia in Detroit (1927–1979) home of the Red Wings (McLaren, 2012). Interestingly, the four venues located in the United States also served as home venues for professional basketball franchises at some point in their histories.

Table 2.5 *World's 12 Largest Arenas*

Arena Name	Seating Capacity	Location	Primary Sport Activity
Philippine Arena	55,000	Santa Maria, Philippines	Basketball
Saitama Super Arena	36,500	Saitama, Japan	Basketball
Olympic Stadium	35,000	Moscow, Russia	Basketball, Tennis
Gwangmyeong Velodrome	30,000	Gwangmyeong, South Korea	Cycling
Mineirinho Arena	25,000	Belo Horizonte, Brazil	Volleyball
Baku Crystal Hall	25,000	Baku, Azerbaijan	Volleyball
Kombank Arena	25,000	Belgrade, Serbia	Basketball
Araneta Coliseum	25,000	Quezon City, Philippines	Basketball
Palau Sant Jordi	24,000	Barcelona, Spain	Basketball
Arthur Ashe Stadium	23,771	New York, NY, USA	Tennis
Rupp Arena	23,500	Lexington, KY, USA	Basketball
Greensboro Coliseum	23,500	Greensboro, NC, USA	Basketball

Adapted from worldstadiums.com

This shared-use function between hockey and basketball has become a fairly common feature of many large arenas.

The modern arena has a number of design features that have become commonplace. This would include an emphasis on loading docks and access for changeover between sport and concert/event uses. Similar to stadiums, the modern arena design places an emphasis on premium seating including suites, and club level options along with access to amenities like concessions and restrooms. In general, arenas are constructed on a smaller scale than stadiums. However, a number of arenas have been constructed with very large spectator capacity. A summary of the largest arenas by capacity is provided in Table 2.5.

The Field House

Perhaps one of the most confusing terms used within the sport facility genre would be the field house, which is also commonly referred to as a single word—*fieldhouse*. In fact, of the 65 facilities in the United States, with names in this category 36 used the two-word title, field house, compared to 29 using the one word title of fieldhouse. From the early to mid-1900s the term fieldhouse was commonly used for a competitive indoor athletic venue for basketball, volleyball, and even at times hockey. However, many of the original fieldhouse facilities have since been replaced with new competitive venues, and the remaining structure has been converted to use for other sports or activities.

Fieldhouse a large multipurpose indoor facility that typically incorporates an indoor track plus additional court facilities.

The state of Kansas provides two examples of the varied term use mentioned above. First, Ahern Field House, on the campus of Kansas State University, was opened as the primary basketball venue in 1950, and this structure known as "The Barn" was used for basketball through 1988. When a new basketball arena at Kansas State opened, Ahern Field House was modified for use for indoor track and volleyball. At the University of Kansas, Allen Fieldhouse was opened in 1955 as the largest basketball venue in the state with an original capacity of 17,000. Allen Fieldhouse, affectionately called "the Phog," remains the home venue of the Jayhawks with a current capacity of 16,300 (Scott, 2016). Two universities in Indiana further illustrate this point. Gladstein Fieldhouse (originally called New Fieldhouse) on the campus of Indiana University originally opened in 1960 and served as the home of Indiana Basketball through 1971. This fieldhouse was then converted to an indoor track and field facility. Similarly, Lambert Fieldhouse (originally named Purdue Fieldhouse) opened in 1937 as a basketball facility for Purdue University but was converted to indoor track and field use in 1967.

In many cases the term fieldhouse now encompasses a large multipurpose indoor facility that incorporates a track plus additional court use. This may be in part due to the number of historic fieldhouse facilities that have been converted to track uses. Additionally, a few modern competitive basketball or hockey venues have adopted the use of fieldhouse within their title

Historic Hinkle Fieldhouse on the campus of Butler University in Indianapolis opened in 1928.

in recent years. The terms *arena* or *events center* have become a much more common moniker for these types of large spectator venues. The lone exception to this would be Bankers Life Fieldhouse (home of the Indiana Pacers (NBA) and Fever (WNBA), and this is likely due to the strong historical connections in the city of Indianapolis to the historic Hinkle Fieldhouse on the campus of Butler University that is known as "Indiana's Basketball Cathedral." In fact, when Hinkle Fieldhouse opened in 1928, it was the largest basketball arena in the United States until 1950 (Branch, 2010). This fieldhouse was immortalized in the classic basketball film *Hoosiers*. These examples all illustrate the confusing status of many terms used to describe athletic venues.

Indoor Practice Facilities

Indoor Practice Facility large indoor practice facilities with artificial turf that provide large spaces for practice in inclement weather conditions.

While fieldhouse may be a term that is somewhat dated and declining in common use, the use of large *indoor practice facilities* with artificial turf has been growing primarily with specific sport applications for football in the United States. For example from 2009–2015 a total of 10 universities in the Atlantic Coast Conference constructed new turfed indoor practice facilities, and across the nation 37 NCAA Division I and II schools constructed indoor practice facilities with an average cost of $14.1 million in that same time span (Attwood, 2014). These collegiate facilities are often constructed with secondary uses to provide indoor practice space for other sport teams.

These indoor practice facilities are most ideally located in close proximity to the outdoor fields and to the supporting locker room and strength training areas. Important considerations for the operation of these facilities include air quality and movement through the use of varied combinations of heating, air conditioning, and ventilation fans; observation decks for coaching and filming; sound systems to simulate game conditions; and lighting via natural sources (windows/skylights) and via direct or indirect lighting fixtures.

An innovation for indoor practice facilities at the professional football level has been to seek partnerships with other organizations such as school districts to share the facility use and cost. The new headquarters and training facilities for the NFL's Dallas Cowboys, The Star, included an indoor practice facility with seating for 12,000 spectators that serves as a competition venue for the Frisco Independent School District (Prisbell, 2016). The indoor practice facility portion of The Star totaled $260 million with $30 million covered by the school district and $60 million provided by the city of Frisco. The Dallas Cowboys funded the balance of the costs.

Gyms and Gymnasiums

A *gymnasium* would be currently defined as an indoor facility including a high ceiling for sport competition, practice, and physical education. It would differ from an arena in the fact that the arena places a greater emphasis on spectator seating, while the gym places greater emphasis on the activity area or playing floor and may or may not include formalized seating areas. While the concept of the open-air gymnasium dates back to the ancient Greeks, the modern era gyms began in Europe and the United States in the 1850s. Prior to the Civil War, gymnasiums were constructed in Cincinnati, Boston (Tremont Gymnasium), and Chicago (Metropolitan Gymnasium) with the Chicago facility boasting a 108' × 80' floor surrounded by 20' walls and 40' high dome over its center (Spears & Swanson, 1995).

Gymnasium an indoor facility with high ceilings for sport competition, practice and/or physical education.

Much of the early gymnasium construction was also connected to the Turner movement started in Germany, and this movement included fitness training via gymnastics. YMCAs in America soon followed with a formal resolution committing the organization to physical education. Thus, the first gymnasiums were constructed in YMCA facilities in New York and San Francisco in 1869 (Spears & Swanson, 1995). Much of the expansion of gymnasium activities beyond gymnastics training and physical exercise can be connected to the development of popular games and team sports at the YMCA including basketball and volleyball.

Colleges and universities began to incorporate physical education and fitness in the 1860s led by institutions like Harvard University and Dr. Dudley Sargent when they constructed Hemenway Gymnasium in 1878, along with Amherst College and Dr. Edward Hitchcock who built Pratt Gymnasium in 1884 (Spears & Swanson, 1995). The further development of physical education and sport at the scholastic level led to the widespread inclusion of the gymnasium as a standard part of school construction from the elementary through the high school levels.

Currently, gymnasiums typically fill a multi-functional purpose and often employ telescoping or temporary bleacher seating during competitive events. These seating options can allow for maximal floor space to be available for other non-competition activities such as sport practices or physical education classes. The gymnasium must provide a high ceiling in order to accommodate games such as basketball and volleyball that require at least 22 feet of clearance. Because of their generally large size, school gymnasiums are sometimes configured for use as an auditorium or assembly space, and at times as dining space. A gymnasium facility is also a common component within recreation centers, health and fitness clubs, and even many churches.

Natatoriums and Aquatic Facilities

The development of swimming pools constructed for recreation, therapy, and ceremony can be traced back to more than 5,000 years ago. Archaeological remains of a vessel known as The Great Bath located in the ancient Pakistani settlement of Mohenjodaro includes a complex array of benches and steps surrounded by a terraced deck area. This pool was constructed with tightly fitted bricks finished with gypsum plaster along with a waterproofing tar membrane that surrounded the outside of the structure (Herman, 2013). The ancient Romans were noted builders of pools and baths, and the ruins and remains of Roman baths can be found throughout much of their former empire in Europe. These aquatic structures included the creation of the first recorded heated pool by Emperor Gaius Marcenus in the first century B.C. and the construction of a 900,000 square foot pool facility in Rome in 305 A.D. (Herman, 2013).

The creation of the modern pool can also be traced to the development of floating baths in the mid to late 1700s. Floating baths, located along rivers, included barges with bathhouses for changing and permeable wooden basins or slats that allowed for continual water flow. Such baths were noted in Paris, Frankfurt, and Vienna in the 1760s (Van Leeuwen, 1998). A transition from floating baths to floating pools began in Paris with the opening of a massive structure (106 meters by 30 meters) on the Seine River that became known as the Royal Swimming School in 1796 (van Leeuwen, 1998). The development of swimming schools and floating pools were also connected to military training. As the military strength of the French grew in the early 1800s, floating pools and swimming training were developed in rival nations like Austria and Germany.

The transition from floating pools to the fully contained indoor pool occurred in 1842 in Vienna where the Dianabad added a 36 meter by 12 meter pool to its bathing facilities that were first established in 1804. In London, passage of the Mansion House Act in 1844 helped to establish wash, bath, and swimming facilities in large numbers. This began with the opening of the Paddington Bath House in 1847 and would expand to a total of 13 similar facilities throughout London by 1854 (van Leeuwen, 1998).

In the United States, the first public pool or bath opened in 1868 in Boston on Cabot Street in the Roxbury area, and this facility included separate pools for males and females each 20 feet by 24 feet (Wiltse, 2007). With the technology of that time period lacking water filtration and chemical disinfectants, the pools were maintained by emptying and refilling with fresh water. This initial municipal pool facility was closed in 1876, but many others pool facilities soon followed. In 1887, a community-owned indoor swimming pool that remained in operation until 1958 opened in Brookline, Massachusetts, just outside Boston (Gabrielsen, 1987). The first pool in a collegiate setting opened at the University of Pennsylvania in 1896 and was housed within the lower level of the student union building. This 10 feet by 30 feet pool hosted the first intercollegiate competition in 1897 when swimmers from Penn competed with swimmers from Columbia (ISHOF, 2016).

Natatorium a building containing a swimming pool or an indoor competitive swimming and diving facility.

While swimming pools can be constructed for a wide variety of uses in both private and public settings and in both recreational and competitive contexts, the natatorium will be the primary focus of this text. A *natatorium* is most basically defined as a building containing a swimming pool, but it typically refers to a competitive swimming facility that should contain a number of features for effective operation. Natatoria are complex and expensive facilities, and they are often the most expensive type of sport facility when considering cost per square foot. These high costs are connected to the actual basin or pool construction along with the extensive plumbing required for water treatments including filtration, disinfection, and heating. Natatoria also require specialized systems for maintaining required air temperature and humidity through heating, ventilation, and air conditioning (HVAC) systems. In addition to the pool itself and the associated mechanical systems, a competitive natatorium would require spectator seating areas, athlete seating areas, locker rooms, and public restrooms. Sport governing bodies from the international level via the Fédération Internationale de Natation (FINA), or the national levels through USA Swimming, the NCAA or the National Federation of State High School Associations (NFHS) establish specifications for the swimming and diving areas of the pool for competition.

Competitive venues for international swimming include a 50-meter pool for long course competitions, and a 25-meter pool for short course competitions, while the standard for interscholastic and intercollegiate competition in the United States is a 25-yard pool. Competitive diving requires diving boards and platforms of required heights as well as a diving well that is constructed to the appropriate depth and specifications. A total of five platform heights are to be provided (1 m, 3 m, 5 m, 7.5 m and 10 m) along with springboards at 1 m and 3 m heights (FINA, 2015).

As the aquatic sports have been foundational in the Olympic sport movement, it is not surprising that swimming was included in the inaugural 1896 Athens Games with water polo added in 1900 and diving in 1904. The natatoria of the Olympic Games have often been seen as iconic structures highlighting the latest in design and technical performance such as the Beijing National Aquatic Center or Water Cube from the 2008 Games. The London Aquatics Centre, host of the 2012 Olympic

The "Water Cube" as the iconic natatorium of the 2008 Olympic Games in Beijing.

The London Aquatics Center includes the full complement of diving platforms and springboards required to host diving competitions.

Interior of the London Aquatics Center the site of the 2012 Olympic swimming and diving competitions after the temporary wing seating removal along the window area of both sides.

swimming, diving, and synchronized swimming competitions, included a 50-meter competition pool, a 50-meter warm-up pool and a 25-meter diving well. This facility was designed with a spectator capacity of 17,500 for the Games, but was converted to a post-Olympic configuration seating 2,500 ("History," n.d.).

Most large natatoria in the United States are constructed and operated by colleges, universities, and public school districts. The natatorium in the United States with the largest spectator capacity is the Indiana University Natatorium located on the campus of the Indiana University-Purdue University in downtown Indianapolis. This aquatic facility was first opened in 1982, in preparation for the 1987 Pan American Games. Its original cost was $21 million and includes an eight lane 50-meter competition pool and diving well, plus a six lane 50-meter instructional pool with an adjustable depth floor (from 0 to 4'–6") on one end (Campus Recreation, 2016). This facility has hosted hundreds of championship competitions at the state, NCAA, USA Swimming, and USA Diving levels, and in 2015–2016, $20 million in renovations took

Table 2.6   Top Competitive Swimming Facilities in the United States

Venue Name	Institution	City	Year Opened	Spectator Capacity
Herb McAuley Aquatic Center	Georgia Tech	Atlanta, GA	1996	1,950
Lee and Joe Jamail Texas Swimming Center	University of Texas	Austin, TX	1977	2,600
Indiana University Natatorium	IUPUI	Indianapolis, IN	1982	4,700
McCorkle Aquatic Pavilion	Ohio State University	Columbus, OH	2005	1,400
Freeman Aquatic Center	University of Minnesota	Minneapolis, MN	1990	1,346
Avery Aquatic Center*	Stanford University	Palo Alto, CA	2001	2,530
Kiphuth Exhibition Pool	Yale University	New Haven, CT	1932	2,187
Gabrielsen Natatorium	University of Georgia	Athens, GA	1996	2,000
Denunzio Pool	Princeton University	Princeton, NJ	1990	1,700
Trumbull Aquatic Center	Denison University	Granville, OH	2012	750

*outdoor facility

Adapted from collegeranker.com

place including an interior redesign, a new roof, heating and cooling system, pool deck, pool filtration, lighting, skylights, bulkheads, starting blocks, and modernized locker rooms ("IU Natatorium," 2015). Table 2.6 provides a summary of the top competitive swimming and diving facilities in the country.

The relatively modest spectator capacity for these aquatic facilities has created a market for temporary competition pools to be constructed within large arenas to host major events such as the U.S. Nationals and Olympic Trials (2004, 2008, 2012, 2016) or FINA World Championship events (2007, 2011, 2013, 2015), and even some Olympic Games (2016) (Guo, 2016). Such temporary venues create a solution to the need for large spectator capacity for a singular event, but recently there has been some concern raised with variances in pool conditions and race results in these pools. A trio of researchers have recently determined a possible impact in elite swimming race results due to lane bias occurring more in temporary pools (70% of lanes) than in permanent pools (35% of lanes) due to the possibilities of water currents developing within the pool (Cornett, Brammer, & Stager, 2015).

Recreation Centers

Recreation centers would be classified as facilities designed for the pursuit of fitness, wellness, and sport, and are multipurpose based upon the needs of the users. Recreation centers are primarily indoor facilities, and they occur in non-profit settings like community centers, YMCAs, and college campuses, as well as for-profit health and fitness clubs. On college and university campuses, the pursuit of recreational sport and fitness activities has been a part of the student experience for more than a century. However, prior to the 1970s few institutions had dedicated facilities for recreation. Two exceptions were the Intramural Sports Building at the University of Michigan, opened in 1928 as the first dedicated general student use facility and the Intramural Activities Building at the University of Washington opened in 1968. These are often seen as the forerunners of the modern campus recreation center (Turman & Hewitt, 2009). While the early years of campus recreation had programs housed as a third-tier priority in physical education and athletic departments, campus recreation facilities have become a standard campus amenity and expectation for students.

Recreation Center a multipurpose facility designed for the pursuit of fitness, wellness, and sport based upon the needs of the users.

In some ways the development of private athletic clubs in the era following the Civil War began the development of sport facilities for the training of the socially and economically elite. The New York Athletic Club (NYAC), founded in 1866, opened its first permanent clubhouse in 1885. It was five stories tall and cost $150,000 (Willis & Wettan, 1976). Other athletic club facilities followed suit

© Rob Wilson/Shutterstock.com

The $19.5M student wellness and recreation center at the University of North Florida includes three levels and 82,000 square feet of space.

and opened throughout New York City (e.g. the Staten Island Athletic Club, the Manhattan Athletic Club, and the Berkeley Athletic Club) and across the nation. By 1883 more than 150 athletic clubs had been formed (Rader, 1977). The minimal facility expectations for these clubs included a gymnasium, a swimming pool, club rooms, and dining rooms. Many clubs provided features like bowling alleys, rifle ranges, billiard parlors, and Russian and Turkish baths (Willis & Wettan, 1976). These athletic clubs not only built facilities but also organized athletic competitions. The NYAC sponsored a number of the first amateur national championships in sports such as track and field (1876), swimming (1877), boxing (1878) and wrestling (1878). The Amateur Athletic Union (AAU) was created from several of these early clubs (Rader, 1977). Many of these historic athletic clubs still exist today, but their membership levels and influence pale in comparison to the growing fitness center movement that is accessible to greater segments of the population.

In addition to campus and community recreation centers and private athletic clubs, a more recent development in the fitness industry would be the development of for-profit fitness centers both as stand-alone small businesses and as franchised brands. Many would trace the beginnings of the modern fitness centers to Vic Tanny in the 1940s. Tanny is credited with moving gyms out of the cellar by creating multi-purpose facilities with plenty of chrome, carpeting, and walls painted in aesthetically pleasing colors. Tanny also began to franchise his fitness centers, which expanded to 84 facilities throughout the nation by the 1960s (Buck, 1999). While Vic Tanny's fitness centers worked for mass appeal, others sought to focus specifically on the niche market of body builders. Joe Gold established the original Gold's Gym in 1964. Located in Santa Monica Beach, California, it set the standard for serious weightlifting and bodybuilding (Buck, 1999). Throughout the 1960s and 1970s, interest in fitness centers continued to grow. In 1978 there were just over 3000 private fitness clubs in America. That number expanded to nearly 20,000 by 2002, and total fitness center membership increased from 1.7 million in 1972 to 42.7 million in 2006 (Stern, 2008). In 2016 the top fitness centers with annual revenues over $1 billion included LA Fitness, 24 Hour Fitness, Life Time Fitness, ClubCorp and Equinox. Other trends of growth include hospital-based fitness centers that are making a strong impact on the fitness center industry (Kufahl, 2016).

Whether a community recreation center, a for-profit fitness center, a campus recreation center, or a private fitness club, this group of facilities typically includes a number of common elements. Areas for cardiovascular training and conditioning (cardio) often includes an area with numerous machines such as treadmills, elliptical trainers, stationary bikes (upright, spin, and recumbent) and stair machines/steppers. Cardio training areas also often include a jogging/walking track that in many instances is suspended above the open court areas. Rooms or areas for strength training include weight lifting equipment such as free weights (bars, plates, and dumb bells) along with benches and racks, as well as machine weights. The machine weights can include selectorized machines that are self-contained machines with a variable weight stack and pin and with a design to target specific muscles and movements within a controlled range of motion. Plate loaded machines provide a similarly specified and controlled range of motion, but utilize the standard weight plates with the machine to provide the source of resistance.

A gym with a multi-purpose court or courts (basketball, volleyball, badminton, pickleball etc.) is another common feature in the recreation center. Additional specialized indoor courts can also be included. Examples include fully enclosed courts for racquetball, squash, handball, or wallyball. Some recreation and fitness center may opt to provide indoor tennis courts, as well.

Aquatic features are another common element of recreation and fitness centers. The inclusion of a swimming pool is quite common. Several different types of pools might even be provided such as a lap swimming pool, a therapy pool (smaller with warmer water temperature), a leisure pool (with slides and other play features), or a hot tub/whirlpool.

Ancillary or support spaces typically included would be locker rooms, rest rooms, and lounges. At times the locker rooms could include other amenities such as saunas or steam rooms (Turkish baths) as well as areas for massage or other spa-type treatments. Areas for product sales such as snack bars or juice bars for food and beverages sales or pro shops for the sale of apparel and sporting goods might also be features found in Recreation Centers.

Many campus recreation centers have included wellness offices and services within their facilities by incorporating the campus health center or counseling center within the facility. Many of the newer hospital-based fitness centers may also incorporate physical therapy or cardiac rehabilitation services within their centers. It is also not uncommon to find rock climbing walls or free standing climbing structures with belays and smaller bouldering walls for free climbing within campus recreation centers.

The Sportsplex

The *sportsplex* or sport complex would be broadly defined as an indoor, outdoor, or combination of both facility with multiple fields and/or multiple courts used for competitive or recreational sport. The sportsplex may be designed or operated with a single sport focus such as softball or soccer, or it can be operated on a multi-sport basis such as volleyball, basketball, soccer, football, lacrosse etc. The sportsplex is typically large in size and scope due to the large amount of space needed for multiple fields and/or courts.

Leisure pools with water features such as slides, zero depth entry, large capacity hot tubs, and other amenities have become more common in community and college campus recreational centers.

© Vereshchagin Dmitry/Shutterstock.com

Sportsplex a large multiple field and/or multiple court complex used for competitive or recreational sport.

Seminole County Sports Complex in Sanford, FL during final construction phase noting the artificial turf on the nine baseball fields.

Photo courtesy of Medallion.

© BrazilPhoto/Shutterstock.com

The ESPN Wide World of Sports Complex is one of the premier sportsplex destinations.

© Alison Hancock/Shutterstock.com

This multipurpose football goal post and soccer goal can facilitate rapids changeover for multiple sport use on this synthetic turf field in a sportsplex setting.

© John Panella/Shutterstock.com

A Pop Warner youth football Super Bowl game held at the ESPN Wide World of Sports Complex in Lake Buena Vista, Florida.

The large size of most sportsplex facilities led much of the early development to be connected with public agencies like municipal parks and recreation departments or with established not-for-profit sport organizations like Little League Baseball. These entities relied upon taxpayer funding or sponsorship and donation funding to support the facility construction and operation. As the size, scope, and interest in youth and adult recreational sport has grown, the development of private for-profit sportplex facilities has grown as well. One of the most recognized for-profit sportsplex would be the ESPN Wide World of Sports Complex in Orlando, Florida that originally opened in 1997 as the Disney Wide World of Sports. This complex covers more than 200 acres with nine primary venues that can host multiple amateur and professional sporting events including a 9,500 seat baseball stadium, a 5,000 seat arena, a multi-court arena (six basketball courts or 12 volleyball courts), a multi-purpose fields area (15 total fields with one expandable to 3,000 seats), a baseball quadraplex, a six field softball diamondplex, a 10-court tennis complex (Centre Court capacity of 8,500), a cross-country running course, and a nine-lane track and field complex with seating for 500 ("The Complex," n.d.). These facilities at the ESPN Wide World of Sport Complex host professional sports like the Atlanta Braves (MLB) spring training and collegiate basketball and cross-country events, but the majority of events hosted are geared toward youth sport in baseball, softball, basketball, cheerleading, lacrosse, soccer, and volleyball. The growing interest in organized large participation events in team sports continues to foster the development of both moderate-scale and large-scale sportplexes. Table 2.7 identifies some of the nation's top sportsplex facilities for hosting basketball tournaments.

Table 2.7 *The Top Six Amateur Basketball Tournament Facilities*

Venue Name	Location	Venue Features
ESPN Wide World of Sports	Orlando, FL	12 courts in 2 facilities
A-Game Sportsplex	Franklin, TN	10 courts in 2 facilities
Boo Williams Sportsplex	Hampton, VA	8 courts in 1 facility
Jackson Sports Academy	McClellan, CA	15 full courts
The Big House Sports Complex	Tavares, FL	9 maple courts
Rocky Top Sports World	Gatlinburg, TN	6 hardwood courts

Adapted from Walton (2014)

While the outdoor field or indoor court facilities are the primary driver for a sportsplex operation, other key facility needs include parking, restrooms, spectator and team seating, and concession sales. More recently some facilities have incorporated full-service restaurants, lodging, strength training areas, full fitness facilities and sport specific training areas like batting cages. Multi-use courts and fields within sportsplexes can benefit from equipment that can be easily transitioned from one sport to another such as goal post and soccer goal combinations, or floor-sleeved standards for volleyball, tennis, or badminton courts. Professional organizations such as the Sportsplex Operators and Developers Association (SODA), founded in 1981, have helped to meet the need for assistance in planning, operations, and risk management within this unique facility type.

Sport Events

While the facilities are foundational to conduct sporting events for both the sport participants and the spectators, the competitions or events themselves are what drives the sport industry at the local, regional, national, and international levels. There are several ways that sport events may be organized from the most simple, single, stand-alone event, to the most complex international, global sport festivals like the Olympic Games. Sport events may be organized into leagues with recurring events or contests at "home" venues, or it may be organized as a tour of individual competitors traveling from venue to venue to compete. The development of operational definitions of sport event types can assist in organizing and understanding the sport event and aid the sport manager in its effective and efficient operation.

Stand-Alone Events

Sport Tour a group of tournaments established around a single sport or single ownership/leadership that travels from city to city around a nation, region, or even the world and brings high caliber athletes and events to various fan bases.

To a degree, nearly every *sport tour* or league can be traced back to early singular contests or events that began to generate greater interest in the given sport. This often developed into either a tour or league structure. For example, intercollegiate athletics in several sports can be traced to initial singular events. The earliest intercollegiate contest was held in 1852 in crew (rowing) between Harvard and Yale (Dealy, 1990). The first baseball game was a contest between Amherst College and Williams College in 1859, and the sport of football followed with the first contest held in 1869 with Rutgers and Princeton (Davenport, 1985). These sports with beginnings in singular contest have developed into league events under the direction of intercollegiate conferences and the NCAA.

However, some singular events have remained as important within the landscape of organized sport without transitioning to a league or tour status. The system of post-season bowl games in collegiate football could be seen as stand-alone singular events. Each of these games operates as an independent organization that seeks to provide a single game in a neutral site to generate revenue while providing a service to the participating teams and fans. These early bowl games began with the Rose Bowl in Pasadena California (1902), the Orange Bowl in Miami, Florida (1933), the Sugar Bowl in New Orleans, Louisiana (1935), the Sun Bowl in El Paso, Texas (1936), and the Cotton Bowl in Dallas, Texas (1937). These bowl games have expanded to more than 40 events annually (Klein, 2013).

Spectators line this portion of the Boston Marathon course in Newton, MA.

The Boston Marathon is a stand-alone annual event that is the oldest continually contested footrace in the United States and the oldest annual marathon in the world. First held in 1897 from the inspiration of the inaugural Olympic Games marathon, the Boston Athletic Association (BAA) has hosted this race that has grown from 15 entrants in the first year to a record of 38,708 entrants during the 100th anniversary event in 1996 (Douglas, 2014). The Boston Marathon draws an estimated 500,000 to one million spectators along the 26.2 mile course. The impact of this event in 2014 with 35,660 runners was reported at $175.8 million including $103.7 million in spending by athletes and guests, $27.5 million raised for local charities by participants, $20 million spent by race spectators, $4 million spent in sponsorships and media coverage, and $10.6 million spent by the BAA in event operations (DeLuca, 2014).

Stand-alone sporting events as a single game or contest could also be expanded into a tournament allowing multiple games to be played within a single event. Tournaments can be structured in a number of ways in order to vary the total number of games played or the method by which the winner is determined. Byl (1998) has identified a number of different tournament types including single elimination, double elimination, multi-level, round-robin, and round-robin split (double, triple, or quadruple), also referred to as pool play.

Single elimination is the most simple tournament structure where losers are eliminated and the winners move to the next round until only a single contestant or team remains as the champion. This tournament form requires the least amount of contests and therefore requires the least amount of time and facility space resources. The elimination creates more limited opportunities for participation as one-half of the field is eliminated from play with each round.

One alternative to single elimination is to utilize a double elimination format. A double elimination tournament uses a winners' bracket and a losers' bracket, and a participant is not eliminated from the tournament until two losses have occurred. This format guarantees a minimum of two contests for all participants, and it also allows one to overcome a single poor performance with an opportunity to feed back into the winners' bracket. However, the double elimination format has a much greater number of rounds, and those performing well in the tournament play a greater number of games.

The multi-level tournament structure is identical to the single elimination format on the winners' side of the bracket, but each time a team loses it continues to play down one level in a consolation round. This format allows each team to play the same total number of games and it tends to move teams toward contests with opponents of similar ability/performance levels. This format is more time efficient than the double elimination format in terms of total tournament rounds.

The round-robin format calls for all individuals or teams to play each entry an equal number of times. This format does not require seeding or ranking of teams in advance as the total results determine the final standings. This type of format can be effective as a single day tournament when the total participant numbers are few and the games progress quickly. Round-robin play has been adapted for larger team or participant numbers into split groups or pool play (double split for two groups or pools, triple split for three groups or pools, and quadruple split for four groups or pools). Each of the participants in each pool plays all others within their pool, and the results of this pool-play are used to seed championship tournament play or consolation play with a traditional tournament bracket. These tournament formats provide a high amount of game play opportunities, and also reduce the importance of pre-event seeding or ranking on the final outcome of the tournament. Sample tournament brackets for each of these tournament types are provided in Appendix A at the end of the chapter. A comparison of the total number of games played and rounds required for completion of each tournament bracket type is summarized in Table 2.8. This is based upon the assumption of having four venues or four courts/fields available for tournament. The goals and objectives for the tournament can influence the choice of bracket structure selected.

Table 2.8 *Tournament Characteristics Based upon Bracket Structure*

Bracket Type	Total Teams	Total Games	Total Rounds
Single Elimination	8	7	3
Double Elimination	8	14–15	6–7
Multi-Level (3 Game Guarantee)	8	12	3
Double Split Group Pool Play	8	19	6
Quadruple Split Group Pool Play	16	38	10

League Events

Professional sport leagues and their basic structure are typically traced back to the 1870s and the development of organized baseball in the United States (Crosset & Hums, 2009). The league by its nature is highly dependent on the existence and use of a home venue. Within leagues, a group of teams compete either at their home venue or the home venue of another league member. These recurring events result in about half of the games or matches being completed in the home venue. League play generates recurring revenue for the home contests of league members and fosters the development of place attachment for the fans of each team. There are several examples of leagues in different sports that operate wholly within the league model such as Major League Baseball, the National Hockey League, and the National Basketball Association. In each of these examples, all contests for the regular season and the post-season playoffs are conducted in the "home" venues of the competing league members. Much of intercollegiate sport within conferences in the United States operates as a form of league play where the hosting of home contests and the generation of revenue from those games is important to the individual schools and the conferences/leagues.

The value of league play in relation to total annual revenues is massive. Globally, the top three professional sport leagues in terms of revenues are the National Football League (NFL), Major League Baseball (MLB), and the National Basketball Association (NBA). For example, the NBA recorded $5.2 billion in total revenues for the 2014–2015 season from their 30 franchise teams ("Forbes Releases," 2016). Major League Baseball has experienced record growth from 2003 to 2015 with annual revenues for 2015 of approximately $9.5 billion (Brown, 2015). The NFL posted the highest of all leagues in total revenue with just over $13 billion from the 2015–2016 season (Belzer, 2016). These values are driven by media rights, sponsorships, and licensing/merchandising as well as via ticket and suite/premium seating sales.

Sport leagues serve to gather and organize players/talent to play for given teams or franchises. The recurring games of the regular season provide a stream of interest and revenue that is capitalized upon via some type of

Sport League an organization of team sports dependent upon the use of a home venue. Within leagues, a group of teams competes either at their home venue or at the home venue of another league member throughout a set season of competition.

season ending tournament or play-off. League play was revolutionized by William Hulbert, an early manager for the National League of Professional Baseball Players in the 1870s. Hulbert drove spectator interest in the regular season games by creating a pennant race where the sport would be viewed as a series of games rather than single events. This created value for parity amongst the teams where even the best teams would be expected to lose a substantial portion of their games (Leifer, 1995). These tactics along with the print media coverage of baseball helped establish interest and attendance in the regular season games of the league.

Tour Events

While leagues are a common structure for team events, many individual sports are organized through a tour structure. A group of tournaments established around a single sport or single ownership/leadership becomes a tour. The tour travels from city to city around a nation, region, or even the world and serves to bring high caliber athletes and events to various fan bases.

Some of the largest and most successful tour events include the sports of golf and tennis. The creation of the professional golf tournament and tour would be credited to Fred Corcoran who began work with the Professional Golf Association (PGA) in 1937 and in 1949 worked to organize the women's tour known as the Ladies' Professional Golf Association (LPGA). Other examples of sports that operate on a tour basis would be many auto racing organizations such as Formula 1, NASCAR, and IndyCar, as well as track and field in the Diamond League.

The revenues associated with tour play at the highest levels are great. In 2013, the total revenues for the PGA were $1.075 billion with $364.8 million coming from television rights and an additional $290 million from sponsors, and the total LPGA revenues were $102.8 million with $14.6 million coming from television rights and $5.8 million from sponsors (Saffer, 2016). In professional tennis, the Association of Tennis Professionals (ATP) for men's tennis reported total tour revenues for media and sponsorship at $107.1 million, and the Women's Tennis Association (WTA) reported total tour revenues for media and sponsorship at $69.7 million for 2014 (Kaplan, 2015). These revenues did not include individual tournament revenues including both the Grand Slam events and other affiliated tournaments. Tennis Grand Slam event revenues are summarized in Table 2.9 and these major stops in the tour add tremendous financial resources to the sport.

The tour play format has a number of venue management implications. First the governing bodies or organizations leading tour-based sports typically determine host sites via a competitive bid process. The bid process can create competition between potential host sites regarding the venue features and characteristics as well as with the supporting infrastructure. This can lead to high levels of facility investment, yet at the same time many tour events will make only one stop or host one primary event in the venue, and this can create a venue that is under-utilized for the balance of a competitive season.

Table 2.9 *Grand Slam Tennis Tournament Revenues (ATP & WTA combined)*

Tournament	Location	Year	Total Revenue in millions (USD)	Total Profit in millions (USD)
Australian Open	Melbourne, Australia	2015	$174.6	$8.2
French Open	Paris, France	2015	$204.7	N/A
Wimbledon	London, England	2014	$240.5	$79.5
U.S. Open	Flushing Meadows, New York	2013	$253.0	N/A

Adapted from Carter (2016)

Sport Festivals

The largest and most complex of the tour events would be sport festivals or multi-sport events. These large-scale events are more complex due to the logistical and facility needs to conduct multiple and varied events. The Olympic Games would be an example of a sport festival on the grandest of scale. These sport festivals typically move from city to city for hosting the event whether on a four-year basis like the Olympics, on a bi-annual basis like the Special Olympics World Games, or on an annual basis like the X-Games. The topic of sport festivals and mega events will be further explored in Chapter 15 of the text, and a more detailed examination of tour and league events in sport will be provided in Chapter 16.

As with the prior discussion of facility definitions and types, there is some level of cross over at times between the classification of sports and events as stand-alone, league, or tour. For example, the NFL operates in a league fashion for its regular season and its post-season playoffs with the exception of the Super Bowl. This final game operates more as a tour event with bids obtained for hosting this culminating event by various cities and venues. Similarly, men's basketball at the NCAA Division I level functions as a league through the regular season within conference and non-conference games. However, the NCAA Tournament or March Madness operates as a tour event with the various rounds of the single elimination tournament moving from city to city. These locations are based upon the bids accepted by the NCAA for venues to serve

© A. RICARDO/Shutterstock.com

The Maracana Stadium and Sport Complex in Rio de Janeiro as a part of the 2016 Olympic Games a major global sports festival event.

as hosts for the various portions of the tournament including, the first four, the opening rounds, regionals, and the final four that spans a time period of roughly three weeks.

Conclusion

A common understanding of the basic structure of sport facilities and events can create a foundational knowledge for the sport facility and sport event manager. While the basic definitions of facility and event types can create a common basis of communication, this chapter has demonstrated a number of instances of exceptions or crossover between the various types of sport facilities and sport events. However, the continued development of new variations in facilities and events within sport should not diminish the importance of the primary need for venues to host and carry out successful sport events. The information provided in this chapter has provided an overview and typology of sport facilities and sport events that can assist in an ongoing dialogue within this profession.

CHAPTER DISCUSSION QUESTIONS

1. Define the term stadium and identify examples of stadia that are open-air, domed or completely enclosed, and those with a retractable roof.

2. Define the term *arena*, and explain how an arena is different from a stadium.

3. Summarize the development from early indoor swimming pools to modern natatoria.

4. Compare and contrast the following terms and facilities: Arena, Gymnasium, Fieldhouse, Indoor Practice Facility, and Recreation/Fitness Center.

5. Explain the basic differences between league and tour organizational structures for sport, and how these two forms of organization impact venue operations.

6. Create a referenced list of the largest venues for a particular sport either globally or within a single nation.

MINI CASE STUDY

You are currently serving as the Director of Parks and Recreation for a large suburban community. This community has a great interest and following for the sport of basketball, and there is the desire to create a new facility that could include both basketball practices and competitive games from the youth level through the senior adult level. You have been granted an ample budget to propose a new indoor facility to accommodate this interest in basketball that could also be expanded to other sports or activities.

1. What type of facility would you propose? What design elements of an arena, gymnasium, fieldhouse, indoor practice facility or recreation/fitness center would be incorporated into the facility that you would propose?

2. What other sports or activities would you add to your facility and programming offerings beyond basketball, and why?

3. If you determined that a swimming pool should be a part of this facility, then what components of a natatorium would you plan to include and what size of pool(s) would you include?

4. For the basketball programming portion of this new facility, what type of game and tournament scheduling would you recommend for the youth levels and for the adult levels? Would these scheduling and tournament types vary for these levels or be the same throughout the basketball program? Explain your rationale.

PRACTITIONER SPOTLIGHT

NAME: Nikki Epley

ORGANIZATION: College Football Playoff

CURRENT JOB TITLE: Director of Stadium and Game Operations, 2013–Present

EDUCATIONAL PREPARATION: BA in Sport Business, Wichita State University, 1994; M.Ed. in Sport Administration, Wichita State University, 1997

Photo courtesy of Nikki Epley.

MEMBERSHIP IN PROFESSIONAL ORGANIZATIONS:

- Collegiate Event and Facility Management Association (CEFMA)
- Stadium Managers Association (SMA)
- National Association of Collegiate Women Athletic Administrators (NACWAA)

CAREER PATH: As an undergrad, I played softball and also worked as an intern in the athletic department at Wichita State University. As a part of the master's program at WSU, I completed a graduate internship in the Wake Forest University athletic department where I worked for Michael Kelly, the current COO for the College Football Playoff, for the first time. I have now worked for Michael in four different roles. After Wake Forest, I interned with the Missouri Valley Conference for a year before taking my first full time job in the University of New Mexico's athletic department. After UNM, I worked in the athletic department of Colorado State University and in the alumni association at Wichita State before rejoining Michael Kelly as the Director of Special Events for Super Bowl XXXIX in Jacksonville. After the Super Bowl in Jacksonville, I joined Michael in South Florida to work as the Director of Operations and Events for Super Bowl XLI. Both Super Bowls had end dates. After the second Super Bowl, I took a job working with

A rooftop view of University of Phoenix Stadium before the 2016 CFP Championship Game.

Photo courtesy of Nikki Epley.

the NCAA Men's Basketball Championship for a couple of years before moving back into alumni relations at the University of Kansas. While at KU, I started working with the Super Bowl as a consultant and have done so for the past six games. In 2013, I rejoined Michael in my current role at the College Football Playoff.

WHAT ARE YOUR JOB RESPONSIBILITIES WITH THE COLLEGE FOOTBALL PLAYOFF?

My role is primarily to oversee everything that occurs on the stadium campus for the CFP National Championship Game. This includes everything that happens in the areas outside of the stadium such as accreditation, parking, security screening, ESPN functions, and the Championship Tailgate. I work with multiple vendors that I call stadium operations planning partners, which help facilitate everything that must take place in and around game day. We have a parking vendor, a security consultant, a game producer, a pageantry director, a credentialing company, a signage team, a décor company, radio provider, IT liaison, frequency coordinator, timeout coordinator, game officials, PA announcer, a field crew, instant replay technicians, etc., We also use a sports architecture firm, Populous, to help us design drawings of how the facility will function for the event. We have meetings at the host facility every month for three days to bring all of the planning partners together. We work through credentialing, parking, logistics for the teams, pageantry elements such as the bands, the cheerleaders, the national anthem, and the trophy presentation. We also work with public safety to discuss security and we go through "what happens if…" scenarios. We lay out and design all of the décor for the facility. When I am back in the office, I have meetings and calls with our planning partners and I create operations manuals for various areas.

WHAT IS THE MOST CHALLENGING ASPECT OF YOUR JOB?

It is new and different every year. We aren't in the same city doing the same game every year. We start with a blank slate each time and everything is different. It's a challenge to have to build everything from scratch every year. It's what I love, but it's also extremely challenging. The reward is I can go from not knowing anything about a particular stadium to being an expert on everything about it in a year.

WHAT IS THE MOST REWARDING ASPECT OF YOUR JOB?

I love starting from a blank slate. It is so rewarding for me when we get to game week and it's such a family environment at the stadium as we see all of our work and everything that we have done over the past year come together. It's so great to see the student-athletes raise the trophy and to see the confetti drop. We are all down on the field feeling really great about what we have done. Then right after a game ends we start all over again with a blank slate for the next year.

AS THE CFP USES EXISTING FOOTBALL VENUES, WHAT ARE THE WAYS THAT YOUR ORGANIZATION WORKS AND COORDINATES WITH THE EXISTING STAFF OF THE VENUE FOR THE CHAMPIONSHIP GAMES?

We work primarily with the management group of each stadium and they are essential to what we do. I talk with the stadium's general manager, director of operations, and/or various event managers almost daily. They know the facility in and out and they work directly with the city, county, and local vendors and ensure that we are able to communicate with the appropriate people to get what we need. They become one of us and are a significant part of our team and a part of putting on the game. The host NFL team within the venue also plays a large role. They typically will provide IT and audiovisual support and other necessary stadium support as the host tenant. The stadium management group also provides all of the guest services (ticket taking, concessions, general operation of the venue for game day, etc.).

AS YOU HAVE EXPERIENCE WITH BOTH THE SUPER BOWL AND THE CFP CHAMPIONSHIP GAME, WHAT ARE SOME KEY SIMILARITIES AND DIFFERENCES OF THESE EVENTS FROM AN OPERATIONS PERSPECTIVE?

One of the biggest differences lies within the fan bases and clientele for each event. The Super Bowl is very corporate and everything is very high priced. Attendance of the game is more about being at the Super Bowl than the teams. With the College Football Playoff, fans are there because they are fans of the team. The Super Bowl is also an international event and college football is not. So while the CFP National Championship is certainly a huge media event, it isn't quite to the scale of a Super Bowl from an international perspective. I think that the CFP National Championship is quickly bringing college football to the level of a Super Bowl and the Final Four in terms of being a mega-event that draws people to a city for several days of events. I think we have done a great job of creating events around the game that allow fans to come and enjoy themselves for an entire weekend and not just for one game day

WHAT IS A UNIQUE ASPECT OF YOUR CAREER?

I came from a school that didn't play football. Growing up, college basketball was always my passion, and it wasn't until I went to Wake Forest, New Mexico, and Colorado State that I was able to start working with football game operations and be exposed to college football. I developed a passion for college football and then I had the opportunities with the Super Bowl. I have found that so much of what goes on operationally is transferable from college to professional sports and from one sport to another. I have been able to learn so much from each of my experiences that I can apply to what I do now. It has been an interesting path to working for the College Football Playoff from a school without a football program.

WHAT ARE YOU PARTING WORDS OF WISDOM FOR STUDENTS AND YOUNG PROFESSIONALS IN THE SPORTS WORLD?

Do as much as you can. Even if it's volunteering with an event, get involved in anything and everything. You can always learn from any event. Even now, I volunteer with the Big XII Gymnastics Championship and other events when I can. You can learn so much from just being on site and observing what is happening. Work to critique different processes and different management styles. Make as many connections as you can and learn from as many people and experiences as possible. Keep well read on sports issues. Read journals, manuals, and game bids. People in the industry love to have students and young professionals come and talk to them and seek advice or volunteer opportunities. Make these connections, keep in touch with them, and learn from them.

Reprinted by permission of Nikki Epley.

REFERENCES

Attwood, E. (2014). Designing the modern college football practice facility. *Athletic Business.* Retrieved from http://www.athleticbusiness.com/gym-fieldhouse/designing-the-modern-college-football-practice-facility.html

Belzer, J. (2016, February 29). Thanks to Roger Goodell, NFL revenues projected to surpass $13 billion in 2016. *Forbes.* Retrieved from http://www.forbes.com/sites/jasonbelzer/2016/02/29/thanks-to-roger-goodell-nfl-revenues-projected-to-surpass-13-billion-in-2016/#69e8e1033278

Branch, J. (2010, March 16) It's the bricks that make Butler basketball special. *New York Times*. Retrieved from http://www.nytimes.com/2010/03/17/sports/ncaabasketball/17butler.html?ref=sports&_r=0

Brown, M. (2015, December 4). MLB sees record revenues for 2015. *Forbes*. Retrieved from http://www.forbes.com/sites/maurybrown/2015/12/04/mlb-sees-record-revenues-for-2015-up-500-million-and-approaching-9–5-billion/#66fbb2ea2307

Brown, M. (2014). Biggest global sports: A statistics-based analysis of the world's most popular sports. Retrieved from http://www.biggestglobalsports.com/

Buck, J. (1999). The evolution of health clubs. *Club Industry*, http://clubindustry.com/forprofits/fitness_evolution_health_clubs

Byl, J. (1998). *Organizing successful tournaments* (2nd ed.). Champaign, IL: Human Kinetics.

Campus Recreation (2016). Facilities Pools. Retrieved from http://studentaffairs.iupui.edu/health-wellness/campus-rec/facilities/pools.shtml

Carter, A. (2016, January 20). Grand Slam 2016: Tennis' four majors by the numbers, *Forbes*. Retrieved from http://www.forbes.com/sites/alikocarter/2016/01/20/grand-slam-2016-tennis-four-majors-by-the-numbers/#43b2e11820de

Cornett, A., Brammer, C., & Stager, J. (2015). Current controversy: Analysis of the 2013 FINA world swimming championships. *Medicine & Science in Sports & Exercise*, 47(3), 649–654.

Crosset, T. W., & Hums, M. A. (2009). History of sport management. In *Principles and Practice of Sport Management* (3rd ed.) L. Masteralexis, C. Barr, & M. Hums (Eds). Sudbury, MA: Jones and Bartlett Publishers.

Davenport, J. (1985). From crew to commercialism- the paradox of sport in higher education. In D. Chu, J. O. Segrave, & B. J. Becker (Eds.), Sport and higher education (pp. 5–16). Champaign, IL: Human Kinetics.

Dealy, F. X. (1990). *Win at any cost*. New York, NY: Carol Publishing Group.

DeLuca, N. (2014, March 14). Race officials predicting highest Boston Marathon spending impact ever. *City News*. Retrieved from http://bostinno.streetwise.co/2014/04/14/how-much-money-will-the-2014-boston-marathon-generate/

Douglas, S. (2014, April 10). A brief history of the Boston Marathon. *Runner's World*. Retrieved from http://www.runnersworld.com/boston-marathon/a-brief-history-of-the-boston-marathon

Eberson, S. (2010, May 30) Arena timeline: Highlights of 50 years of entertainment. *Pittsburgh Post-Gazette*. Retrieved from http://www.post-gazette.com/neighborhoods-city/2010/05/30/Arena-timeline-Highlights-of-50-years-of-entertainment/stories/201005300240

FINA. (2015). FINA facility rules 2015–2017. Retrieved from https://www.fina.org/sites/default/files/finafacilities_rules.pdf

Forbes releases 18th annual NBA team valuations (2016, January 20). *Forbes*. Retrieved from http://www.forbes.com/sites/forbespr/2016/01/20/forbes-releases-18th-annual-nba-team-valuations/#686a7d56e3e5

Gabrielsen, M. A. (1987). *Swimming pools: A guide to their planning, design, and operation* (4th ed.). Champaign, IL: Human Kinetics.

Galofaro, C. (2015, May 3). The latest: Keep black cats away from Baffert. *Associated Press*. Retrieved from http://bigstory.ap.org/article/7c6d91b3926346b9b8989426a666044e/latest-fans-stream-churchill-downs-derby-day

Guo, J. (2016, September 1). These charts clearly show how some Olympic swimmers may have gotten an unfair advantage. *Washington Post*. Retrieved from https://www.washingtonpost.com/news/wonk/wp/2016/09/01/these-charts-clearly-show-how-some-olympic-swimmers-may-have-gotten-an-unfair-advantage/

Herman, E. (2013). Pools: A history of innovation. *Aqua Magazine*. Retrieved from http://aqua-magazine.com/pools/pools-a-history-of-innovation-part-i.html

History. (n.d.). London Aquatics Centre. Retrieved from http://www.londonaquaticscentre.org/about/history

International Swimming Hall of Fame. (2016). Swimming in America—one hundred years ago. Retrieved from http://www.ishof.org/assets/1916-one-hundred-years-ago-in-swimming.pdf

IU Natatorium Renovation (2015). Retrieved from http://iunat.iupui.edu/renovation/index.html

Kaplan, D. (2015, November 23). ATP outstrips WTA in revenue growth. *Street & Smith's SportsBusiness Journal*. Retrieved from http://www.sportsbusinessdaily.com/Journal/Issues/2015/11/23/Leagues-and-Governing-Bodies/ATP-revenue.aspx

Klein, C. (2013, January 1). A brief history of college bowl games. *History*. Retrieved from http://www.history.com/news/a-brief-history-of-college-bowl-games

Kufahl, P. (2016, August 8). Club Industry's top 100 health clubs of 2016. *Club Industry*. Retrieved from http://clubindustry.com/profits/club-industrys-top-100-health-clubs-2016

Leifer, E. M. (1995). Making the majors: the transformation of team sports in America. Cambridge, MA: Harvard University Press.

Lowery, P. J. (1986). *Green cathedrals*. Cooperstown, NY: Society for American Baseball Research.

McKelvey, S. (2015). Industry insider: Geoff Moore. *Sport Marketing Quarterly, 24*, 75–77.

McLaren, I. (2012). The ice rink: A brief history. *The Hockey Writers*. Retrieved from http://thehockeywriters.com/the-ice-rink-a-brief-history/

McSpadden, R. (2015). Texas football stadium database. Retrieved from http://texasbob.com/stadium/tbt_stadium_fcts.html

Prisbell, E. (2016, July 18). Inside The Star: The Cowboys new $1.5B headquarters. *USA Today*. Retrieved from http://www.usatoday.com/story/sports/nfl/cowboys/2016/07/18/the-star-frisco-dallas-practice-facility/86763256/

Rader, B. G. (1977). The quest for subcommunities and the rise of American sport. *American Quarterly, 29*(4), 355–369.

Rains, R. (2009). *James Naismith: The man who invented basketball*. Philadelphia, PA: Temple University Press.

Saffer, M. (2016, April 8). Dollars but no sense: Golf's long history of shortchanging women. *ESPNW*. Retrieved from http://www.espn.com/espnw/sports/article/15160220/big-gap-earnings-men-women-professional-golfers

Scott, J. (2016). Arenas through history—part 1: Early years. Retrieved from http://www.bigblue-history.net/bb/arenas.html

Seidler, T., & Miller, J. (2013). Design trends in stadiums and arenas, 1975–2012. In T. Sawyer (Ed.), *Facility design and management for health, fitness, physical activity, recreation and sports* (13th ed.). (pp. 393–405). Champaign, IL: Sagamore.

Sheard, R. (2000). *Sports Architecture*. London, GB: Taylor & Francis.

Spears, B., & Swanson, R. A. (1995). *History of Sport and Physical Activity in the United States* (4th ed.). Dubuque, IA: William Brown Publishers.

Spurgeon, B. (2012, November 18). Formula One makes successful return to US. New York Times. Retrieved from http://www.nytimes.com/2012/11/19/sports/autoracing/grand-prix-successful-in-return-to-united-states.html?_r=0

Stern, M. (2008, January). The Fitness Movement and the Fitness Center Industry, 1960–2000. In *Business History Conference. Business and Economic History On-line: Papers Presented at the BHC Annual Meeting* (Vol. 6, p. 1). Business History Conference.

The Complex. (n.d.). Retrieved from https://www.espnwwos.com/complex/

Turman, J. C., & Hewitt, C. N. (2009). The planning process through the eyes of the campus master planner and the recreational sports director. In M. Callender (Ed.), *Campus recreational sports facilities: Planning, designing and construction guidelines* (pp. 3–34). Champaign, IL: Human Kinetics.

van Leeuwen, T. A. P. (1998). *The springboard in the pond: An intimate history of the swimming pool*. Boston, MA: MIT Press.

Walton, P. (2014). Six best basketball venues. *Connect Sports*. Retrieved from http://www.con-nectsports.com/feature/6-best-basketball-venues/

Willis, J., & Wettan, R. (1976). Social stratification in New York City athletic clubs, 1865–1915. *Journal of Sport History, 3*(1), 45–63.

Wiltze, J. (2007). *Contested waters: A social history of swimming pools in America*. Chapel Hill NC: University of North Carolina Press.

Sample Tournament Brackets for Various Tournament Structures

SINGLE ELIMINATION | 8 TEAMS

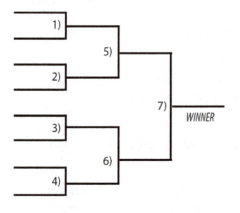

DOUBLE ELIMINATION | 8 TEAMS

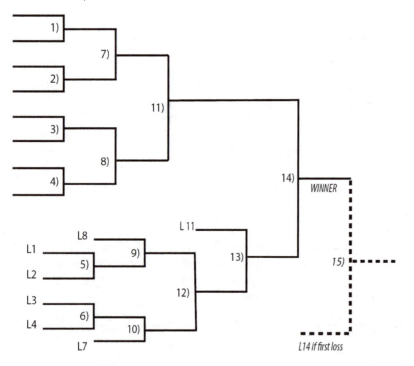

THREE GAME GUARANTEE | 8 TEAMS

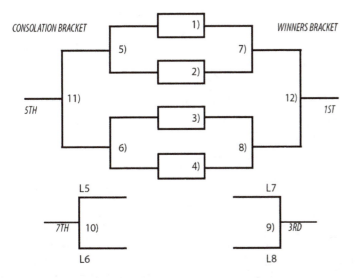

POOL PLAY | 8 TEAMS

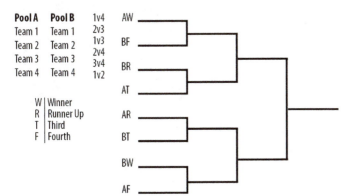

POOL PLAY | 16 TEAMS

Pool A	Pool B	Pool C	Pool D	1v4		
Team 1	Team 1	Team 1	Team 1	2v3	W	Winner
Team 2	Team 2	Team 2	Team 2	1v3	R	Runner Up
Team 3	Team 3	Team 3	Team 3	2v4	T	Third
Team 4	Team 4	Team 4	Team 4	3v4	F	Fourth
				1v2		

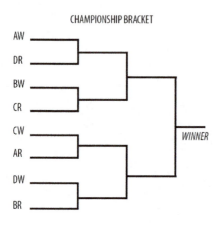

CHAMPIONSHIP BRACKET

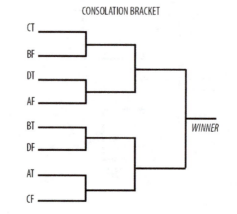

CONSOLATION BRACKET

3

Basic Management Theories and Perspectives

J. Patrick Marsh and *Jeffrey C. Petersen*

OBJECTIVES

After reading this chapter, the student should be able to:

- Define sport facility and event management and its common tasks within the context of the 3 P model of place, process, and people.
- Identify the primary management leaders and apply their theories within the process aspect of the 3 P model.
- Identify the primary management leaders and apply their theories within the people aspect of the 3 P model.

KEY TERMS

Allocation of Resources

Division of Labor

Emotional Intelligence

Expectancy Theory

Hawthorne Effect

Management by Objectives

Maslow's Hierarchy of Needs

Motivator-Hygiene Theory

Say's Law

Scientific Management

Theories X and Y

3 P Model

KEY ACRONYMS

CBA	Collective Bargaining Agreement
CSR	Corporate Social Responsibility
MBO	Management by Objectives

PSL	Personal Seat License
TQM	Total Quality Management

Introduction

The successful operation and management of facilities and events within sport settings can be modeled through the inter-relationships among three primary factors: place, process and people. This is commonly referred to as the *3 P model*. While facility management may at times have a greater emphasis on the "place" element relating to the physical or built environment than to the event management element that emphasizes the "process," both facility and event management will most often reside in that central nexus where all three factors intersect (see Figure 3.1). This model can be traced back to the 1970s and the work of an early non-profit educational and research organization called the Facility Management Institute (Rondeau, Brown & Lapides, 1995). More recently these conceptual elements of the 3 P's were reinforced in the 2007 adoption of the European Standard (EN15221-1) for facility management. This standard noted that the scope of Facility Management included both "Space and Infrastructure" (i.e. planning, design, construction, maintenance, furnishings and cleaning) and "People and Organization" (i.e. catering, information/communication technology, human resource management, accounting, marketing, and hospitality). Although the terms may be slightly altered from the 3 P model, the place, process and people are fully evident in this more recently developed standard.

3 P Model the inter-relationships among three primary factors (place, process, and people) for the management of facilities and events in sport.

When examining facility and event management as the nexus of the place, process, and people model, it is easy to identify the place elements. Facility and event managers generally manage a specific facility or group of facilities and the events that occur within them. Every facility is different, and it is important for managers to know every detail of their facility so that they can apply managerial concepts involving processes and people in the best way possible. With a strong understanding of the place, facility and event managers can look to management history and theory for applications of both process and people oriented managerial principles. Much of early management theory and practice focused on *process* elements such as efficiency and expansion. The field of management would later shift its focus toward *people* elements, primarily motivation and engagement, thus completing the 3 P model.

Courtesy Jeffrey Petersen.

Figure 3.1 The 3 P Model of Facility and Event Management—the central nexus of these factors is a common mode of operation for the manager.

Athletic facility and event management is a branch of the larger field of sport management. Sport management is a specialized field of management that applies the study and practice of managerial concepts to the sport industry (Chelladurai, 2005). To best understand the study and practice of athletic facility and event management, one must begin with an understanding of general management principles and the historical process that generated these concepts.

The term *management* has been defined by scholars and practitioners in a multitude of different ways. While different sources have different definitions of management, the same concepts and ideas appear in the vast majority of these definitions. A simple definition for management is the process of organizing and utilizing people and limited resources to achieve specific goals and objectives. This definition of management emphasizes both the *process* and *people* elements of the 3 P model, and when combined with a specific *place*, a sport facility, the model for facility management is complete.

While clear definitions are an important part of the academic process, management is often better understood through the exploration of its functions. In the early 20th century, French management theorist, Henri Fayol (1917), described five functions of management: planning, organizing, command, coordination, and control. These five functions have been adapted and redefined by scholars throughout the management field. Bridges and Roquemore's (2004) adaptation of Fayol's work identifies four main functions of management in the sport setting: planning, organizing, implementing, and controlling. When performing these four functions, a person is engaging in the basic process of management.

Planning, as a managerial function, involves the setting of goals and objectives and the development of detailed methods to achieve these goals and objectives in an efficient manner. Planning can be thought of as designing the bridge between where we are and where we want to be (Robbins, 1976). Good planning minimizes the problems of getting from point A to point B and maximizes the efficiency of the process. The planning process covers a large spectrum of time. Facility and event managers will plan for short-term activities, lasting only a few hours, such as the set-up of an event. They will also create plans for longer time periods such as a yearly facility schedule or a five-year capital improvement plan. Regardless of the objective or the time frame, well thought out and detailed planning is the foundation of a successful operation, and the failure to plan properly is the leading cause of organizational failure.

Organizing is the process through which a manager coordinates the efforts of employees to achieve the goals outlined in the planning process. Organizing the efforts of employees is a two-part process. The first aspect of organizing employees is the identification of specific jobs designed in the planning process and identifying specific employees who are best suited to perform each job. A manager must put each employee in a position to succeed. The second part of organizing employees is to establish the relationships among each job task and facilitate the effective and efficient coordination between these job tasks and the employees that are performing them. By placing each employee in a position and creating a system to coordinate and facilitate cooperation among the employees, a manager puts the entire organization in a position to work towards a common goal.

Implementation is the process of putting the plans and processes into action. Planning and organization are the foundations for the implementation function. Without implementation, the planning and organization functions are wasted. Implementation involves the manager working directly with employees towards the goals and objectives defined in the planning process. Implementation, as a managerial function, is very people-centric. Communication and motivation are at the core of the implementation process. Managers who are successful as implementers are those who are able to work with a variety of different people and personalities in order to create unity and efficiency within the entire organization.

The control function of a manager is to keep the performance of employees on schedule and according to the plan. In theory, if the planning, organizing, and implementation functions were done perfectly, the control function would not be necessary. This is rarely if ever the case, so the regulation and control of processes within an organization are a necessity. The control process has three essential steps: establishing a standard, appraising conformance to the standard, and correcting non-conformance to the standard (Bridges & Roquemore, 2004). The level of control required of a manager is dependent upon several factors including the precision required in completing the task, the ability and skill of the employee(s), and the time and resources required to correct mistakes. Control programs should be implemented with relatively high levels of control and then scaled back on control levels as the direct control becomes less necessary.

Understanding facility and event management within the context of sport also requires consideration of the primary functions of the people working in this field. Roper and Payant (2014) identified a number of commonly performed job functions for facility managers that expanded beyond the general organizational management elements of planning, organizing staffing, directing, controlling, and evaluating. A total of 14 functional areas were identified as follows: facility planning and forecasting; lease administration; space planning, allocation and management; architectural/engineering planning and design; workplace planning, allocation and management; budgeting, accounting and economic justification; real estate acquisition and disposal; sustainability; construction project management; operations maintenance and repair; technology management; facility emergency management; security and life-safety management; and general administrative services (Roper & Payant, 2014, pp. 5–8). The International Facility Management Association (IFMA) has worked to establish a group of 11 competencies for facility managers, and their professional training and programming aligns with this competency classification. The 11 competencies identified were:

1. Communication
2. Emergency Preparedness
3. Environmental Stewardship and Sustainability
4. Finance and Business
5. Human Factors
6. Leadership and Strategy

7. Operations and Maintenance
8. Project Management
9. Quality
10. Real Estate and Property Management
11. Technology (IFMA, 2005).

Similar to these 11 competencies, Curtland (2012) sought to identify key facility management tasks across five broad areas: operations and maintenance; planning and budgeting; sustainability and energy management; life-safety and security; and communication and technology.

While the study and practice of basic managerial principles has been around since the earliest of times (Chelladurai, 2005), very little of what we would recognize as managerial practice was seen prior to the industrial revolution (McGrath, 2014). Prior to the Industrial Revolution, only a few kinds of organizations such as churches, military, and large trading companies employed any recognizable management principles. The Industrial Revolution changed everything as it relates to the field of management. Rather than owners of an enterprise performing all of the coordinating tasks, the emergence of large-scale production created a necessity for owners to delegate many of these responsibilities (McGrath, 2014). This new classification of employees known as managers served as the initial practitioners in the emerging field of management.

Throughout the 19th century, early managerial concepts were applied by business leaders to create industrial corporations of tremendous stature. The improvements in the efficiency in steel production, petroleum refinement, textile production, and transportation created many of the wealthiest people in American history such as Rockefeller (oil), Carnegie (steel), Ford (autos), and Vanderbilt (railroads). While managerial principles were behind the rapid growth of industry, the ownership of capital was still the primary basis for economic well-being (McGrath, 2014). While knowledge of managerial principles steadily accumulated throughout the 19th century, it wasn't until the late 19th century that business management was introduced into the American higher education system.

The introduction of business management into higher education sparked a new era in the field of management. Management study and practice would begin emphasizing expertise and scientific inquiry. Management study began to incorporate statistical analyses and mathematical principles in the optimization of business practices. Managerial research was becoming common, and the research was giving way to evidence-based practice. As managerial research progressed, a new concept began to emerge. Managerial experts were beginning to shift from the idea of management being about command and control towards emphasizing motivation and engagement (McGrath, 2014).

Currently, management is experiencing another shift in thinking as scholars, practitioners, and the public at large reconsider the purpose of many organizations. Many of the organizations developed during the Industrial Revolution, with capitalistic expansion ideals, are being viewed as fostering inequality by promoting profiteering at the expense of employees and consumers. Managers are being asked to manage with a greater sense of empathy than ever before and to emphasize the greater good over corporate profit (McGrath, 2014). Within facility and event management in sport this is evidenced with a growing emphasis on sustainability and green practices as well as with corporate social responsibility (CSR) initiatives. The intersection of these two factors can be seen the drive toward green or sustainable stadium design (Kellison & Hong, 2015). The development of new stadiums and arenas that can be seen as eco-friendly may impact both perceptions of the fans of the sport organization as well as possible pro-environmental social change among the spectators (Kellison, Trendafilova, & McCullough, 2015).

As the study and practice of management has evolved, so has the study and practice of sport management and facility and event management. The field of sport management and the sub-discipline of facility and event management in sport can both trace their roots back to the administration of physical education programs in primary, secondary, and post-secondary institutions. Courses in the organization and administration of physical education programs can be traced back to the late 19th century, and a primary focus of these early courses was the organization and maintenance of facilities (Chelladurai, 2005).

Sport management as an academic field of study began to emerge in the 1960s with the formation of programs at Ohio University, the University of Michigan, the University of Illinois, and the University of Western Ontario (Chelladurai, 2005). Today, over 500 colleges and universities throughout the United States offer a program in sport management, and nearly 100 international institutions offer programs as well ("Academic Programs", 2016). Over a period from 1990 to 2005 the rate of program growth has exceeded 100% (Chelladurai, 2005). The growth of academic sport management programs has been a product of the remarkable growth in the global sport industry along with tremendous student interest.

One of the most visible areas of growth within the sport industry has been in facilities. The sport industry has seen a construction boom over the past two decades. From 1997 to 2017, 20 new NFL stadiums, 17 new NBA arenas, and 16 new MLB ballparks have been constructed. Sport organizations are seeking new ways to attract fans to events and compete with the technological advances in television viewing. New facilities with innovative features and an ever-expanding schedule of events have created a demand for knowledgeable and competent facility and event managers to operate these facilities. Throughout this chapter, general managerial principles will be discussed from their origins to their application to facility and event management in the sport setting. These principles will be organized around the broad categories of *process* and *people* as they are each applied to the *place* context within facility and event management.

Process

Adam Smith

Adam Smith was a prominent moral philosopher in the 18ᵗʰ century. He is best known for his 1776 book, *An Inquiry into the Nature and Causes of the Wealth of Nations*, which is commonly shortened to *The Wealth of Nations*. This text is widely considered to be one of the foundational works of modern economics and is one of the most influential works in business history. In *The Wealth of Nations*, Smith presents several ideas that are fundamental to modern economic practices. Smith's work was so influential and wide reaching that many prominent scholars have differing views on Smith's most important contributions to the study of business. From a managerial point of view, the two most important concepts presented by Smith are the allocation of resources and the division of labor.

Noble Prize winning, American economist, George Stigler (1976) believes that Smith's most "overwhelmingly important triumph" and "the crown jewel of *The Wealth of Nations*," is the concept of pursuing self-interest under conditions of competition. This is the foundation of the theory of *allocation of resources*. This theory holds that under competition, the owner of resources (capital, human, natural) will seek to use the resources in the most profitable way. This concept is central to the formation of a capitalistic economy, and examples can be found throughout any capitalistic system.

Allocation of Resources this theory holds that under competition, the owner of resources (capital, human, natural) will seek to use the resources in the most profitable way.

One example of the theory of allocation of resources from the sport industry comes from the National Football League (NFL). The NFL uses a revenue sharing system that is negotiated with the NFL Players Association (NFLPA) as part of a collective bargaining agreement (CBA). The CBA (2011) outlines what revenues are shared among the teams and with the players and what revenues are not subject to revenue sharing. Revenue generated from media contracts, merchandising, concessions, parking, local sponsorships, and general ticket sales are shared between the teams and with the players. However, one prominent source of revenue not shared is personal seat license (PSL) and premium seating charges. This has led to a construction boom within the NFL. NFL teams and the communities that host them are choosing to allocate resources towards new stadiums or stadium renovations in efforts to increase premium seating options and opportunities to sell PSLs. This is all a plan to maximize revenue that is not subject to revenue sharing and increase profits for owners. The pursuit of facility resources to increase team profits demonstrates this form of competition amongst the NFL franchises. Those NFL ownership groups with the greatest level of success in developing these facility resources will see the greatest return in these areas of revenue that are not shared amongst the league.

Another of Adam Smith's observations with important managerial implications involves the division of labor. The *division of labor* is the separation of tasks within a system. This allows for specialization, which increases efficiency, productivity, and the quality of the labor and of the product produced.

Division of Labor the separation of tasks within a system.

Smith based his writing on the division of labor on his observations of pin manufacturing and the building of ships. The ability of laborers to specialize in the use of specific equipment and the performance of specific tasks allows them to become experts within their division. This expertise gives way to innovation in the way of developing new equipment and processes to enhance the ability of the laborer to perform the task.

While the division of labor is most commonly associated with manufacturing and assembly lines, the concept is important to human resource management in many industries. The division of labor is quite common within the sport industry. Sport organizations have employees who specialize in a variety of different areas including facility and event management. Within facility and event management there is even further division of labor. Administrators, marketing specialists, maintenance engineers, turf specialists, change-over specialists, and housekeepers all have specific areas of responsibility and expertise. The ability of these specialized laborers to perform their duties efficiently and in concert with one another creates a process that is advantageous to the organization.

For example, venue entry requires several different employees to work together to create an efficient entry system for patrons. The process begins with the ticketing staff having efficient sales and will call processes to allow patrons to purchase and obtain their tickets. The patrons then go through a security screening process that will involve an employee checking their bag and another employee operating a metal detector. The patron's ticket is then scanned by another employee, and finally the patron receives a promotional item from a marketing representative. The ability of the patron to enter the facility efficiently is dependent upon each of these five employees performing their responsibilities efficiently and in coordination with the other employees. As a manager, it is important to observe the entire process closely and to identify any bottlenecks so that the overall process can be improved.

© Rob van Esch/Shutterstock.com

Statue memorializing economist Adam Smith in Edinburgh, Scotland.

JB Say

Say's Law a product is no sooner created, than it, from that instant, affords a market for other products to the full extent of its own value.

Say's law or the law of markets is an early 19th-century economic theory developed by French economist, Jean-Baptiste Say. Say's law states: "A product is no sooner created, than it, from that instant, affords a market for other products to the full extent of its own value" (Say, 1880, p. 134). This is often restated and simplified with phrases such as "supply creates its own demand" or "if you build it, they will come." While the debate over supply creating demand or demand creating supply continues among modern economists, applications of Say's law can be found throughout the business world.

Applications of Say's law are particularly prominent in the area of facility and event management. The construction of new athletic facilities in efforts to attract patrons is common practice in the sport business. Sport franchises are continually constructing, expanding, renovating, or otherwise improving their stadiums and arenas to add more amenities for fans. These in-stadium experiences are developed in an effort to compete with the increasing pull for in-home viewing via high definition television (HD TV) as well as to increase revenue through premium seating options.

An etching of J. B. Say from a medallion circa 1870s.

While luxury suites and club level seating are staples of modern facilities, sport franchises have been creative in their creation of premium seating options. In 2011, the Arizona Diamondbacks installed a pool in Chase Field, just beyond the wall in right-center field. The pool and surrounding area were available for rent as a suite for 35 guests for $5,000–$7,000 per game. Many NBA teams have created a unique premium experience by positioning courtside seats between the team benches and the scorer's table. This literally puts the patron in the middle of the action and allows them to experience the game from a unique vantage point. In addition to premium seating options, sport organizations are also creating enhancements to the in-stadium viewing experience through upgraded concessions and other stadium amenities. Craft beer selections and local specialty dining options are becoming popular stadium enhancements. Sport facilities are also investing in technology upgrades such as larger video boards and improved WiFi connectivity. All of these amenities are provided in hopes of creating and maintaining a strong demand for live sport attendance. These examples can be viewed as a practical application of Say's law in the realm of spectator sport venues.

Frederick Taylor

Frederick Taylor was an American engineer and early managerial consultant. During the late 19th and early 20th centuries, Taylor was a pioneer in industrial efficiency. In 1911, Taylor published his defining work, *The Principles of Scientific Management*, laying out his managerial theory. Taylor's theory of *scientific management* was one of the first attempts to apply scientific and engineering principles to management. Taylor outlined four principles for scientific management. The first is that managers should develop a science for each task. This means that each task should be studied and perfected rather than broadly applying concepts to different tasks. The second principle is that managers should scientifically select, train, and develop workers for specific tasks. This is meant to place workers in the best possible position for productivity. The third principle is for managers to cooperate with their employees to ensure that all tasks are being done with the scientific approach that has been developed. The final principle is that there should be an equal division of work and responsibility between

Scientific Management the application of scientific and engineering principles to management.

management and the workforce. This means that managers should take on the work and responsibilities within the organization for which they are better suited than their employees.

Applications of Taylor's theory of scientific management are abundant in facility and event management. One area of facility and event management in which the principles of scientific management are particularly applicable is in change-over management. In change-over management, a variety of different tasks must be completed as efficiently as possible to prepare a facility for the next event. Applying the principles of scientific management to this process, managers should study each task independently to determine the most efficient way to complete the task. The manager would then select the employee or employees best suited to perform each task and train them on the optimal performance methods. Managers should include themselves in the division of labor and perform the tasks for which they are most suited. By participating in the change-over process with their employees, managers are able to ensure that the optimal methods for each task are being employed and that the change-over is completed as efficiently as possible.

Peter Drucker

Management by Objectives a managerial concept by which managers manage their employees by setting specific, short-term goals for employees, and the organization then works towards those goals.

Peter Drucker was an Austrian born, American management consultant and theorist. Drucker is best known for his development of the concept of *management by objectives.* Management by objectives is a managerial process that Drucker described in his 1954 book *The Practice of Management.* The basic concept of management by objectives is for managers to manage their employees by setting specific, short-term goals for employees and for the organization and then to work towards achieving those goals. Management by objectives is intended to produce a clear understanding of each employee's role and responsibilities as well as a clear understanding of how their role contributes to the achievement of the organization's goals. This understanding and clear delineation of responsibilities gives employees a sense of importance in their work and a sense of accomplishment upon the completion of a task.

Management by objectives has been implemented and praised for its effectiveness by numerous large companies and has clear applications to facility and event managers. Management of a large, multi-purpose facility is a complex process involving numerous employees and job tasks. Utilizing the management by objectives concept, a facility manager can outline the responsibilities of the maintenance workers, custodians, concessions workers, gate staff, sales team, marketing team, ushers, and hospitality staff. This outline of responsibilities provides the entire staff with a picture of how their roles fit together in the successful operation of the facility. This, in turn, provides the staff with clarity and a sense of purpose in their work. It also provides the entire staff with a sense of unity and promotes cooperation.

Another example of how management by objectives can be applied to facility and event management is in assisting patrons with disabilities. Perhaps a child is using a wheelchair that is smaller than a normal wheelchair and has difficulty seeing over the railing. When a patron asks an usher for assistance, it is important for the usher to know how they are supposed to handle the situation from a customer service point of view as well as how others within the organization can help. In this case, a maintenance engineer can assist. The maintenance engineer can install a ramped box to lift the chair a few inches to allow the child to see over the rail.

Disability seating areas can sometimes require slight modifications to meet the needs of the patron. Effective communication between the maintenance staff and ushers is essential to efficiently make the required modifications.

While it is important for the maintenance engineer to know how to install the ramped box, it is also important for them to understand the customer service objectives of the usher so that the entire process is efficient and helpful to the patron. Communication between the usher and maintenance engineer is key to understanding the objectives and capabilities of each person and how to work together for the optimal result.

W. Edwards Deming

A final landmark contributor to the process aspect of management would be William Edwards Deming and his approaches to management that are associated with the development of the total quality management (TQM). Deming was educated as an engineer, mathematician, and physicist and was known for his use of statistical analysis for the solution of problems related to manufacturing and sales. He is credited with being instrumental in the rebuilding of the Japanese manufacturing industry and economy after the devastation of World War II. In his 1950 speech, Deming challenged Japanese managers to address four key issues: 1) improve service through better product design, 2) create higher levels of uniform product quality, 3) improve product testing in research centers and the workplace, and 4) generate greater sales through global markets (Chung, n.d). Deming called for statistical product quality administration that would lower manufacturing costs, economize raw materials, improve production levels and uniform product quality, and allow producers and consumers to gain agreement on product quality. The embracing of these concepts by many of the businesses in Japan led to a position of dominance in technology and automobile manufacturing in the 1970s and 1980s.

In 1982 Deming's concepts and ideas were published in his book *Quality, Productivity and Competitive Position* that was re-titled and released again in 1986 as *Out of the Crisis*. The following are his 14 points for transformation management that became the foundation of the total quality management movement:

1. Create constancy of purpose toward improvement of product and service, with the aim to become competitive and to stay in business, and to provide jobs.

2. Adopt the new philosophy. We are in a new economic age. Western management must awaken to the challenge, must learn their responsibilities, and take on leadership for change.

3. Cease dependence on inspection to achieve quality. Eliminate the need for inspection on a mass basis by building quality into the product in the first place.

4. End the practice of awarding business on the basis of price tag. Instead, minimize total cost. Move toward a single supplier for any one item, on a long-term relationship of loyalty and trust.

5. Improve constantly and forever the system of production and service, to improve quality and productivity, and thus constantly decrease costs.

6. Institute training on the job.

7. Institute leadership. The aim of supervision should be to help people and machines and gadgets to do a better job. Supervision of management is in need of overhaul, as well as supervision of production workers.

8. Drive out fear, so that everyone may work effectively for the company.

9. Break down barriers between departments. People in research, design, sales, and production must work as a team, to foresee problems of production and in use that may be encountered with the product or service.

10. Eliminate slogans, exhortations, and targets for the work force asking for zero defects and new levels of productivity. Such exhortations only create adversarial relationships, as the bulk of the causes of low quality and low productivity belong to the system and thus lie beyond the power of the workforce. Eliminate work standards (quotas) on the factory floor. Substitute leadership. Eliminate management by objective. Eliminate management by numbers, numerical goals. Substitute leadership.

11. Remove barriers that rob the hourly worker of the right to pride of workmanship. The responsibility of supervisors must be changed from sheer numbers to quality.

12. Remove barriers that rob people in management and in engineering of their right to pride of workmanship.

13. Institute a vigorous program of education and self-improvement.

14. Put everybody in the company to work to accomplish the transformation. The transformation is everybody's job (Deming, 1985, pp. 23–24).

The application of Deming's TQM concepts to sport facility and event management could take many forms. For example, improvements in product design have been a hallmark of new venue construction in the efforts to provide a better spectator experience through the features of the venue itself.

The improvement of customer experience at sport venues and events is also addressed through efforts in employee training and employee empowerment where the front line event workers take pride in their work and its contribution toward the overall event experience.

The progression of managerial concepts related to process within the 3 P model has included the pioneering work of Adam Smith, J.B. Say, Frederick Taylor, Peter Drucker, and W. E. Deming. The consideration of managerial concepts for facility and event management will now shift to the *people* component of the 3 P model with an examination of the contributions of seven other leaders in managerial thought and theory.

People

Robert Owen

Robert Owen was an early 19th-century Welsh businessman and social reformer. Owen is considered to be one of the founders of utopian socialism, a precursor to modern socialism, which focused on the creation of idealistic societies. During his lifetime, Owen attempted to create utopian communities in both the United Kingdom and the United States such as New Lanark, Scotland and New Harmony, Indiana; however, both projects failed to reach their ultimate goals. Despite the failures of Owen's utopian experiments, many of his ideas remain influential in the business world.

Owen moved from Wales to his new bride's home of New Lanark, Scotland in 1799. He began working for his father-in-law, the proprietor of a large cotton mill, where he eventually would become a part-owner and manager. The mill's workers were mostly from the lowest social class and included nearly 500 children from Scottish poorhouses. People from respectable social classes refused to work the long hours of difficult labor in the mill. Owen became increasingly tired of the pressure and restrictions of the mill's investors who wanted the mill to be run with purely commercial and capitalistic ideals. Owen arranged to have these investors bought out by more progressive investors who would allow Owen to operate the mill as he saw fit ("Robert Owen Time Line," 2008).

One of the first practices that Owen changed was the elimination of the truck system. Truck systems were common among 18th- and 19th-century British employers. In a truck system, employers would pay employees in tokens or vouchers that were only able to be used to purchase goods from a truck store that was owned by the employer. The truck store would often mark up the prices in the store as the employees had no alternative option for purchasing goods. Owen began paying his employees in common currency and opened a general store in which he sold quality goods at competitive prices. Owen also took an active role in supporting the children of the mill by reducing their hours and investing in their education (Carradice, 2011). The improvements in the treatment of employees led to increased morale and commercial success.

Perhaps the most recognizable of Owen's ideas is the eight-hour work day. Prior to the Industrial Revolution in Britain, it was common for factory workers, including children, to work up to 16 hours per day for six days a week. Owen instituted a ten-hour day at the mill and began to champion an eight-hour day as a political activist. Owen used the slogan: "eight hours labour, eight hours recreation, eight hours rest" (Peaucelle & Guthrie, 2016, p. 91). While the eight-hour workday would not become standard until after Owen's death, it remains a significant aspect of his legacy.

While employment practices and working conditions have changed drastically since Owen's time, his ideas are still applicable to facility and event managers today. Facility and event management can often require long hours and physically demanding labor. It is important for leaders within an organization to recognize and reward the work done by their staff. This comes in the form of both standard rewards such as appropriate pay, including overtime, and supplemental rewards such as special access to events or other perks. One of the most important factors in running a successful facility is having a staff that feels respected and appreciated. Being innovative and proactive in supporting employees is Robert Owen's legacy and something that today's managers should continue to emulate.

Elton Mayo

Elton Mayo is an Australian born psychologist best known for his research at the Hawthorne Works factory in Illinois. Mayo was commissioned by the Hawthorne Works, a factory producing electrical equipment, to examine ways to increase productivity by their employees. While Mayo conducted several experiments at the Hawthorne Works, the most famous and influential study involved changes in the lighting levels at the factory. In this study, Mayo would alter the intensity of the light in which employees worked. The study found that employees were more productive after changes in the lighting were made, but productivity slumped upon the conclusion of the study. Similar studies involving cleaning work stations, moving work stations, and clearing obstacles from the floor all produced similar short-term increases in productivity.

Hawthorne Effect the concept of the increased attention of being a subject in a study creating a temporary increase in productivity.

Mayo originally interpreted these results to mean that increased attention to workers needs would create improvements in productivity. Later interpretations of Mayo's research suggested that the increased attention of being a subject in a study creates a temporary increase in productivity. This concept has become known as "the *Hawthorne effect*." While applications of "the Hawthorne effect" are much more prevalent in conducting research, concepts from Mayo's research can be applied to everyday managerial situations. Mayo's research shows that employees can be motivated by attention. Being present, and interacting with employees is a great motivational technique. Facility and event management often requires workers to perform menial tasks such as cleaning the facility or setting out chairs for an event. By assisting in these tasks from time to time, and interacting with the staff, managers can show the attention to their employees that can lead to increases in motivation and productivity.

Abraham Maslow

Abraham Maslow is an American psychologist, best known for his theory of psychological health, also known as *Maslow's hierarchy of needs*. Maslow first proposed his hierarchy of needs in his 1943 paper, "A Theory of Human Motivation" and fully developed the concept in his 1954 book, *Motivation and Personality*. In describing the hierarchy of human motivations, Maslow used a pyramid structure beginning with physiological needs and moving up through safety and security, love and belonging, self-esteem, and culminating in self-actualization.

Maslow's hierarchy begins with physiological needs. These needs are physical requirements for human survival. If they are not met, a person cannot survive. Humans must have air to breathe, food and water for sustenance, clothing, and shelter from the elements, and sexual instinct to maintain adequate birth rates. Without these things, humans will not survive; thus, these needs must be met first.

The next stage of human motivation, according to Maslow, is safety and security. Safety needs begin with physical safety such as safety from war, violence, abuse, or natural disasters. Humans then meet their need for health and well-being and economic and financial wellness. Having economic and job security provides the financial ability to sustain one's self and family. Safety needs are most important to children, as they generally have a greater need to feel safe, whereas, economic and financial security needs are generally more important to adults as they feel the need to provide for their families.

Maslow's next stage of motivation is love and belonging. Humans need to feel a sense of belonging within their social circle. Social circles can be large groups or clubs, small family units, or didactic relationships. While the need for love and belonging is above the need for safety in Maslow's hierarchy, it is important to note that there are many instances in which the need for belonging can be strong enough to override the need for safety. This can be seen in people who remain in abusive relationships or participate in dangerous activities in an effort to gain acceptance.

Maslow's fourth level of human motivation is esteem. Humans have a need to feel respected and esteem is typically the product of the respect and acceptance of others and themselves. The need for the respect of others is what Maslow called the "lower" version of esteem. The "higher" version of esteem comes from self-respect and self-esteem.

The pinnacle of Maslow's hierarchy of needs is self-actualization. Self-actualization is the need to achieve one's full potential. Humans have a desire to accomplish everything that they can accomplish and become the best version of themselves possible. This can manifest itself in a variety of different ways. An athlete may desire to be the best athlete that they can be. Others may desire to reach the pinnacle of their profession or become the best parent or spouse possible.

Maslow's Hierarchy of Needs a pyramid structure for human motivation beginning with physiological needs and moving up through safety and security, love and belonging, self-esteem, and culminating in self-actualization.

Maslow's hierarchy of needs

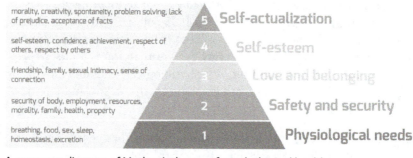

morality, creativity, spontaneity, problem solving, lack of prejudice, acceptance of facts — **5 Self-actualization**

self-esteem, confidence, achievement, respect of others, respect by others — **4 Self-esteem**

friendship, family, sexual intimacy, sense of connection — **3 Love and belonging**

security of body, employment, resources, morality, family, health, property — **2 Safety and security**

breathing, food, sex, sleep, homeostasis, excretion — **1 Physiological needs**

© Pyty/Shutterstock.com

A summary diagram of Maslow's theory of psychological health.

Maslow's hierarchy of needs can be applied to a variety of different situations. Bill Sutton (2016) proposed an application of Maslow's hierarchy to sport management when he proposed a model for building fan relationships. In his model, Sutton postulated that sport organizations must first meet physical needs of fans such as enjoyment and affordability. The organization must then build trust and a piece of mind within fans. Fans then need to feel a sense of belonging to the organization. This can come in the form of membership programs and fan loyalty groups. Fans then need to feel recognized. This can be accomplished through benefits based upon longevity such as priority access to long time patrons. Finally, fans can achieve self-fulfillment or the complete love and adoration of the team. When a fan reaches this stage of belonging, other benefits lose their significance and only the success of the team matters. The fan is at this point fully invested in the team.

Douglas McGregor

Theories X and Y two competing theories on the motivation of workers. Theory X assumes that workers are intrinsically lazy, and Theory Y assumes that workers are intrinsically motivated.

In his book, *The Human Side of Enterprise* (1960), former MIT management professor and motivation theorist, Douglas McGregor, outlined his *Theory X and Theory Y* of motivation. Theory X and Theory Y are two opposing models of workforce motivation that can be applied by managers. The two contrasting models provide managers with contrasting styles of management and supervision. According to McGregor, while Theory X and Theory Y are contrasting and opposing styles of management, they are not opposite ends of the same continuum. The two theories should instead be viewed as two separate continua that can be applied in combination when appropriate.

Theory X is predicated on a negative or pessimistic view of the worker. It assumes that the employee has little ambition, is less intelligent and lazy, and is working merely for a paycheck. Managers employing a Theory X approach emphasize close supervision of their employees and a strong reward and penalty system. According to McGregor, a Theory X managerial approach often produces strong consistency of work and a systematic work flow. Theory X is often viewed as an appropriate managerial approach in manual labor or assembly line settings.

Theory Y is predicated on the assumption that workers are intrinsically motivated. Theory Y holds that employees are a valuable asset for the organization and will take responsibility for the quality of their work and have a sense of pride in the quality of their organization's product. Managers employing a Theory Y managerial style tend to allow their employees to work with more freedom and less supervision. Theory Y managers also tend to place a greater emphasis on relating to employees rather than directing them. Theory Y is often viewed as an appropriate managerial approach for administrative and professional environments.

The wide range of job tasks and work environments found within facility and event management will likely necessitate managers to employ both Theory X and Theory Y styles of management in some form. The manual labor, assembly style tasks associated with change-over management, food and beverage service, and security screening may lend themselves to a Theory X style of management. Other tasks such as marketing or hospitality operations may function better under Theory Y style management. It is important for facility and event managers to choose their managerial style carefully given the type of tasks being performed and the employees performing them.

Frederick Herzberg

American psychologist, Frederick Herzberg, was a prominent management scholar best known as the developer of the *motivator-hygiene theory*. Herzberg's motivator-hygiene theory creates two categories of factors that lead to job satisfaction: motivators and hygiene factors. Motivators are factors that give positive satisfaction, and hygiene factors are factors that do not give positive satisfaction, but the absence of these factors creates dissatisfaction. Herzberg's theory postulates that job satisfaction and job dissatisfaction act independently of one another (Chelladurai, 1999).

Motivator-Hygine Theory a two-factor model for factors that create job satisfaction and job dissatisfaction.

Motivators are factors that create job satisfaction. These factors create satisfaction as a result of the intrinsic conditions of the job itself. The challenge of the work, doing something that is meaningful, and having a sense of importance are all motivators. These motivators are what drive an individual to higher performance and achievement. Hygiene factors do not necessarily drive individuals to achieve, but the absence of these factors leads to dissatisfaction. Hygiene factors include pay, benefits, and work conditions. The presence of these factors is viewed as maintenance for the employee by keeping them happy, but not motivational to perform better (Chelladurai, 1999).

There are four possible combinations of the two factors each with a different work environment. The ideal combination is high motivation and high hygiene. This combination creates an environment in which employees are highly motivated and have very few complaints. Low motivation combined with high hygiene creates an environment in which employees are generally happy, but not very motivated. These job situations are typically viewed as "just collecting a paycheck." High motivation combined with low hygiene results in an environment where the employees are motivated by exciting and/

or challenging work, but the work conditions are subpar and the employees have a lot of complaints. Low motivation combined with low hygiene generates the worst work environment. In these environments, employees have little desire for achievement and many complaints about their work conditions.

Motivator-hygiene theory is extremely applicable to sport management and facility and event management. Working in athletics is generally associated with a high level of motivating factors. There is often a strong sense of attachment to the organization that a person works for and a desire to help that organization achieve its goals. Employees in sport settings also have a strong connection to the athletes they are supporting with their work and are motivated by their personal connections with the athletes. While there are generally a number of motivators in athletics, the quality of several hygiene factors is often lacking. Pay in the sport management field is often subpar, the hours can be long and demanding, and working on special events during holidays is common. As a manager, it is important to work towards improving these hygiene factors as much as possible. Managers can work to improve compensation. While huge pay increases are likely not an option, small increases in salary or instituting a performance bonus structure can significantly improve morale. Managers can also work to mitigate some of the work-life balance issues with flex time, rotating holiday schedules for, and/or designating family times at the facility or on road trips. Managers and organizations that create positive hygiene factors will have the most success in creating a positive work environment and retaining their employees.

Victor Vroom

Expectancy Theory this theory postulates that an individual will select a specific behavior over other behaviors based upon the expected result of the selected behavior.

Victor Vroom is a former Yale management professor and leading scholar on motivation. Vroom is best known for his development of the *expectancy theory* of motivation. Vroom's expectancy theory postulates that an individual will select a specific behavior over other behaviors based upon the expected result of the selected behavior. In other words, the motivation for behavior is the desirability of the outcome.

Expectancy theory has three components: expectancy, instrumentality, and valence. Expectancy is the belief that effort results in performance. In order for an individual to believe that effort results in the desired performance, individuals must have confidence in their abilities at least to the extent that the desired performance is within their ability. Setting unrealistic performance goals produces low expectancy. Instrumentality is the belief that the desired performance will result in a reward. The reward may come in a variety of different forms such as monetary rewards, recognition, or a sense of accomplishment. Commission based work is an example of instrumentality. The more one sells, the greater the reward. Valence is the value that an individual places on the reward. Positive valence is defined as the individual's preference for obtaining the reward as opposed to not obtaining it (Chelladurai, 1999).

The application of expectancy theory urges organizations to tie rewards to performance. Organizations should reward the performance of its employees to the extent that the reward is deserved. Better performance levels should result in greater levels of reward. In order to effectively reward the performance of employees, a manager must identify what the employees value as a reward or valence. Do the employees value monetary rewards, recognition, advancement and promotion, or something else? Once the valences of different reward structures have been identified, managers can tie the rewards to performance. For example, if the employees of an organization value recognition for their work, an "Employee of the Month" program based on performance might be a very motivating program. If the employees value monetary rewards, a performance bonus system could be very beneficial. The important thing is for the reward to be desired by the employees, and it is equally important that the reward be tied to attainable performance goals.

Daniel Goleman

The most recent area of emphasis in management research and practice has centered on the emotions of employees and how work is intertwined with emotion. A great deal of the current thinking on emotions and their ties to management is based on Daniel Goleman's 1995 work *Emotional Intelligence.* *Emotional intelligence* is a theoretical construct under the larger umbrella of social effectiveness, the ability to read, understand, and control social interactions (Ferris, 2002). Goleman's work on emotional intelligence focuses on the ability of individuals to recognize the emotions of others and themselves and to use this recognition to guide their thinking and behavior in the pursuit of one's goals.

Emotional Intelligence the ability of individuals to recognize the emotions of others and themselves and to use this recognition to guide their thinking and behavior in the pursuit of one's goals.

In a 1998 work, *Working with Emotional Intelligence,* Goleman outlined five main constructs for emotional intelligence. The first construct is self-awareness. This is the ability to recognize your own emotions, motivations, and values and to recognize how your emotions impact others. The second construct is self-regulation. Self-regulation is the ability for an individual to control their impulses and disruptive emotions. This gives the individual an ability to adapt to changes in their environment. The third construct is social skill or the ability to manage one's relationships. The ability to manage relationships provides the individual with a means of guiding others in a desired direction. The fourth construct is empathy. Being empathetic means taking other people's feelings into consideration when making decisions. The final construct is motivation. Goleman defines motivation as being driven to achieve for the sake of achievement. In order to motivate others, one must be motivated themselves.

Emotional intelligence is still a relatively poorly understood idea. Emotional intelligence is difficult to quantify and measure making it difficult to study and predict. While the word intelligence is in the name of the construct, there has not been any evidence to support emotional intelligence being associated with cognitive ability. The lack of understanding of emotional intelligence within the academic community has not diminished the popularity of the theory. Scholars are still actively attempting to gain a better understanding, and practitioners are still attempting to apply the ideas behind emotional intelligence. Better recognition and understanding of emotions, both our own and of those around us, certainly has beneficial implications for managers. Humans are emotional beings and the ability to guide different emotions into motivation is extremely valuable.

There are many applications of the concept of emotional intelligence to the management processes for sport facilities and events. Emotional intelligence demonstrates an integrated approach to management combining the rational and emotional nature of our human existence. Embracing emotional intelligence requires recognition that these two natures cannot be fully separated in the work setting. For example, an event manager who is reaching the end of a 12-hour event work day should be cognizant of her own emotional state and also empathetic to her event staff. Through self-regulation, this manager would ideally control the impulse to respond with anger or impatience regarding the remaining tasks to complete the event tear-down process. She would seek to engage, encourage, and motivate the staff toward the successful completion of the event. Maintaining such an emotional connection with herself and her staff allows this manager to apply the rational and task-oriented elements of the job at hand while maintaining the positive personal connection and motivation with the event staff. This type of integration demonstrates the application of the constructs of emotional intelligence to such a work setting, and it shows how these constructs lead to a more positive and productive work environment through the influence and leadership of this event manager.

Conclusion

Management can be defined as the process of organizing and utilizing people and limited resources to achieve specific goals and objectives. By combining the *process* and *people* elements of this definition with a facility, or *place*, the 3 P model of facility management takes form. Throughout this book, different facility and event management topics will be discussed. When thinking about these topics, it is important to remember the basic managerial principles discussed in this chapter and how they may be specifically applied to each topic. Begin to think as a facility and event manager. Think of how to best plan, organize, implement, and control situations in specific facilities.

Think of how processes can be modified to become more efficient. Think of how to train and motivate employees to work towards specific common goals. Most importantly, think of how you can begin developing your own management style. This chapter discussed a variety of different theories on how to manage. As a manager, you must analyze the different approaches and how you can best apply them to create an efficient and successful organization.

CHAPTER DISCUSSION QUESTIONS

1. Explain the basis for the 3 P model of management and why it specifically relates to facility and event management in the sport setting.

2. Identify and describe the four elements or tasks of management outlined in the definition of Bridges and Roquemore (2004).

3. Place in rank order your perception of the value and importance of the contributions of Smith, Say, Taylor, Drucker, and Deming to the *process* aspect of facility and event management.

4. Determine and defend a ranking of the top three contributions to the *people* aspect of facility and event management from the works of Owen, Mayo, Maslow, McGregor, Hertzberg, Vroom, and Goleman.

MINI CASE STUDY

The city of Fargo, North Dakota is building a new arena, The Dairy Queen Center, to host their new NHL team, the Fargo Blizzard. The previous arena in Fargo was plagued by an inefficient entry process, creating long lines outside in the North Dakota winter. Sarah Waters was hired as the facility manager and is tasked with establishing efficient operations within the facility. With puck drop for the next season opening only six months away, Sarah must create a plan for game day operations and hire a staff for the facility. Having been made well aware of past inefficiencies, Sarah knows that a smooth entry process must be a priority.

Approaching management as the nexus of place, process, and people and applying management theories and principles from this chapter discuss how Sarah should perform the four main functions of management.

1. Planning

2. Organizing

3. Implementing

4. Controlling

PRACTITIONER SPOTLIGHT

NAME: Debb Stevens, CAA

ORGANIZATION: Caston Junior/Senior High School

CURRENT JOB TITLE: Athletic Director K–12

- Year started in this role: 1991
- Also serves on the Executive Board of the Indiana High School Athletic Association (IHSAA) as well as acting as the chair of the IHSAA Executive Committee.

Photo courtesy of Debb Stevens.

EDUCATIONAL PREPARATION:

- **Undergrad degree**: BS in PE/Health K-12 from Indiana State University
- **Graduate degree:** MS in PE/Health with a Coaching Track from Indiana State University
- **Special Certification(s) associated with your job:** Certified Athletic Administrator (CAA) from the National Interscholastic Athletic Administrators Association (NIAAA)

CAREER PATH:

- **Entry level job:** My work in sport started with teaching elementary physical education (K–6) plus coaching varsity basketball, volleyball, and track & field at the Bloomfield school district in Southern Indiana.

WHAT IS THE MOST REWARDING ASPECT OF THIS JOB?

Watching students succeed and display pride in their school and their home community.

WHAT IS THE MOST CHALLENGING ASPECT OF THIS JOB?

At the interscholastic level it is challenging to deal with parents when they are unhappy about some aspect of their child's experience within their sport. This is definitely a people aspect of management, but in this area the parent's emotions can sometimes create a challenge.

AS THE ATHLETIC DIRECTOR IN A RURAL SCHOOL DISTRICT, DESCRIBE THE SIZE AND SCOPE OF YOUR ATHLETIC PROGRAM IN TERMS OF SPORTS, PARTICIPANTS AND FACILITIES.

Our school district is in class 1A, the smallest classification of high schools in the state of Indiana. However, Caston High School sponsors nine sports for boys and nine sports for girls including baseball, basketball, cross country, football, golf, soccer, track & field, volleyball, and wrestling. With a total high school enrollment of about 250 students, at least 80% are participating in sport. From a facilities perspective, we have a football/soccer stadium, a competition gym, an eight-lane all-weather track, a baseball field and a softball field all on the school campus. We really have great facilities and outstanding programs in place.

WHAT ARE YOUR MOST CHALLENGING EVENTS TO HOST AND MANAGE?

Spring sports proved to be the greatest time challenge with three major programs operating at the same time creating a high number of events for baseball, softball and track & field during the same time frame. Our school has also served as the host for Sectionals, Regionals and Semi-State competitions in volleyball, and these were really big events for our school to host. These major events were stressful, but I looked at them as a lot of fun too.

WHAT MANAGEMENT THEORY OR CONCEPTS DO YOU RELY UPON WITHIN YOUR JOB ROLE AS AN AD?

I have primarily created my own style from key ideas from others around me. It is vital to "pick the brains" of other leaders. That means there is a lot of communication with other athletic directors and coaches about what works for them and then adapting it to my situation. I see my role as being there to help our coaches with anything they needed to be successful.

The facilities of Caston Junior/Senior High School.

Photo courtesy of Debb Stevens.

HOW DO YOU COORDINATE YOUR EVENT STAFF, SECURITY, AND OTHER PERSONNEL WITHIN A SMALLER SCALE OF INTERSCHOLASTIC SPORT?

The smaller scale does not take away from the attention to detail when running events. We coordinate Emergency Medical Service (EMS) coverage through the local hospital, and event security is established with the Sheriff's Reserve from Fulton County. Most other event workers come from the school faculty and staff. There are typically few key personnel that have proven to be reliable that work in critical positions such as staffing ticketing at the gate, working the clock or book, or providing general event supervision.

OF ALL THE EVENTS AND/OR POLICY DECISIONS YOU HAVE BEEN A PART OF, WHICH HAVE BEEN THE MOST REWARDING AND WHY?

Two projects that stand out would be the development of the Wall of Fame and the Coaches Handbook. The Wall of Fame would be considered a very "people-focused" project that rewarded and recognized students for being Academic All-State, or a Conference or Loganland MVP with a picture added to the designated Wall of Fame. The creation of the Coaches Handbook was more of a "process-focused" project. The school never had a handbook for coaches, so this provided each coach with the policies and procedures that help them accomplish each part of their job responsibilities throughout the year from pre-season to post-season.

WHAT ADVICE WOULD YOU OFFER TO THOSE SEEKING A SIMILAR CAREER?

To do this job right you have to be ready to put in a lot of time!

WHAT DO YOU BELIEVE ARE THE MOST IMPORTANT SKILL(S) TO DEVELOP?

For this type of role the most important skills are organization, communication, and public relations. Much of your success relates to being a people person and having the organizational skills to use your time wisely.

WHAT PARTING WORDS OF WISDOM DO YOU HAVE FOR STUDENTS AND YOUNG PROFESSIONALS IN THE FIELD?

If you don't want to put in 12 hour days, 6 days a week, then this is not the job for you. The kids and fans are depending on you to handle all of the operational aspects of the job in order for the games, matches, and meets to run smoothly. Remember that your name is essentially "signed" on everything you do.

Reprinted by permission of Debb Stevens.

REFERENCES

Academic programs. (2016). North American Society of Sport Management. Retrieved from https://www.nassm.com/Programs/AcademicPrograms

Bridges, F. J., & Roquemore, L. L. (2004). *Management for athletic/sport administration: Theory and practice* (4th ed.). Decatur, GA: Educational Services for Management.

Carradice, P. (2011). Robert Owen, socialist and visionary. *BBC Wales.* Retrieved from http://www.bbc.co.uk/blogs/wales/entries/b39285e4-19eb-347e-9af3-06b2391b525f

Chelladurai, P., (1999). *Human resource management in sport and recreation.* Champaign, IL: Human Kinetics.

Chelladurai, P. (2005). *Managing organizations for sport and physical activity: A systems perspective* (2nd ed.). Scottsdale, AZ: Holcomb Hathaway.

Chung, H. (n.d.). Deming's 1950 lecture to Japanese Management. Retrieved from http://hclectures.blogspot.com/1970/08/demings-1950-lecture-to-japanese.html

Collective bargaining agreement. (2014, August 4). National Football League—National Football League Players Association. Retrieved from https://nfllabor.files.wordpress.com/2010/01/collective-bargaining-agreement-2011-2020.pdf

Curtland, C. (2012, November 5). What does a facility manager manage? *Buildings.* Retrieved from http://www.buildings.com/news/industry-news/articleid/14904/title/what-does-a-facility-manager-manage-.aspx

Deming, W. E. (1982). *Quality, productivity, and competitive position.* Cambridge, MA: Massachusetts Institute of Technology, Center for Advanced Engineering Study.

Deming, W. E. (1986). *Out of the crisis.* Cambridge, MA: Massachusetts Institute of Technology, Center for Advanced Engineering Study.

Drucker, P. (1954). *The practice of management.* New York, NY: Harper.

Fayol, H. (1917). *Administration industrielle et générale; prévoyance, organisation, commandement, coordination, controle.* Paris: Dunod et E. Pinat.

Ferris, G. R., Perrewe, P. L., & Douglas, C. (2002). Social effectiveness in organizations: Construct validity and research directions. *Journal of Leadership and Organizational Studies, 9*(1), 49–63.

Goleman, D. (1995). *Emotional intelligence.* New York, NY: Bantam Books.

Goleman, D. (1998). *Working with emotional intelligence.* New York, NY: Bantam Books.

IFMA. (2005). *Current trends and future outlook for facility management.* Houston, TX: IFMA.

Kellison, T. B., & Hong, S. (2015). The adoption and diffusion of pro-environmental stadium design. *European Sport Management Quarterly, 15,* 249–269.

Kellison, T. B., Trendafilova, S., & McCullough B. P. (2015). Considering the social impact of sustainable stadium design. *International Journal of Event Management Research, 10*(1), 63–83.

Maslow, A. H. (1943). A theory of human motivation. *Psychological Review, 50*(4), 370–396.

Maslow, A. H. (1954). *Motivation and personality.* New York, NY: Harper.

McGrath, R. G. (2014). Management's three eras: A brief history. *Harvard Business Review.* Retrieved from https://hbr.org/2014/07/managements-three-eras-a-brief-history

McGregor, D. (1960). *The human side of enterprise.* New York, NY: McGraw Hill.

Peaucelle, J. L., & Guthrie, C. (2016). *Henri Fayol, the manager.* New York, NY: Taylor & Francis.

Robbins, S. P. (1976). *The administrative process: Integrating theory and practice.* Englewood Cliffs, NJ: Prentice Hall.

Robert Owen Time Line. (2008). Retrieved from http://robert-owen-museum.org.uk/time_line

Rondeau, E. P., Brown, R. K., & Lapides, P. D. (1995). *Facility Management.* New York, NY: John Wiley & Sons.

Roper, K. O., & Payant, R. P. (2014). *The facility management handbook.* New York, NY: AMACOM.

Say, J. B. (1880). *A treatise on political economy or the production, distribution, & consumption of wealth.* New York, NY: Augustus M. Kelley.

Smith, A. (1776). *An inquiry into the nature and causes of the wealth of nations.* London: W. Strahan.

Stigler, G. J. (1976). The successes and failures of Professor Smith. *Journal of Political Economy, 84*(6), 1199–1213.

Sutton, W. A. (2016). How teams can use Maslow's hierarchy to build fan relationship. *Street & Smith's Sport Business Journal, 18*(37), 15.

Taylor, F. (1911). *The Principles of Scientific Management.* New York, NY: Harper & Brothers.

4

Strategic Planning and Budgeting

Lawrence W. Judge, John J. Miller,
Deanna Kolar, and Ricardo Gonzalez

OBJECTIVES

After studying this chapter, the student should be able to:

- Understand the importance of the strategic planning process.
- Generate effective solutions to problems of organizational performance.
- Understand the significance of element in developing a comprehensive master plan.
- Analyze the different techniques to determine facility needs in planning stages.
- Independently assess and/or predict business performance based on the detailed analysis of a specific problem, case, or company.
- Examine the reasons why organizational philosophy, facility accessibility issues, sustainability issues, and external forces affect the planning of a facility.
- Correctly apply concepts of strategic facility management.
- Evaluate organizational strategies, structures, and strategy implementation.
- Grasp the importance of the budgeting as well as the types of budgets a facility manager may consider.

KEY TERMS

Budgeting	Integrated Planning	Sustainability
Comprehensive Master Plan	Strategy	Values
	Strategic Facility Planning	Vision or Vision Statement

KEY ACRONYMS

ADA	Americans with Disabilities Act	**SCAN**	strategic creative analysis
ADAAG	Americans with Disabilities Act Accessibility Guidelines	**SFP**	strategic facilities plan
		SLP	systematic layout planning
FC	fixed costs	**SMART goals**	strategic, measurable, attainable, realistic and timely goals
GHG	green house gas		
IP	integrated planning	**VC**	variable costs
PPBES	planning programming budgeting evaluation system	**VIK**	value in kind
		ZBB	zero based budget

Introduction

Creating a successful program, event, or facility with impact in the community is a continuous process. By working with current and potential users/customers, facility managers can help to shape program offerings, hours of operations, and create a useful strategic plan for a facility and its community. *Strategy* is defined simply as the plan and process of defining the organization's goals and objectives (Bora & Chungyalpa, 2015). During the planning process, it is necessary to choose a course of action to realize these goals and objectives within the environment both inside and outside the organization. Strategic planning is vital for ensuring an organization still will be a leader in its field 20 years in the future, and it can propel an organization to the forefront in its field. Strategic planning for sport facilities and events encompasses both the long term and short term forms of strategy:

> strategies can be defined at a very high level, i.e. the strategic level encompassing the business vision and mission and long-term goals, or it can be defined at a more granular level where it more or less specifies performance targets, plans, and schedules for operation. (Bora & Chungyalpa, 2015, p. 73)

The strategic plan is a tool leadership can use as a guide to the future. Preparing this plan can assist in judging an organization's health at that moment. The primary purpose of planning is to offset future uncertainties by reducing the risk surrounding the organization's operations. Strategic planning and budgeting are both planning processes at their core, and it is vital for organizational success that the resource allocation (i.e. budget) aligns with the overall strategic goals and objectives of the organization. These two processes must be integrally linked in order to foster success. A budgeting system is a combination of information flow and processes that shape short planning and goals of an organization. This chapter emphasizes strategic planning and implementation across a broad spectrum of sport business contexts. It focuses on the managerial, multi-business, multi-industry, multicultural, and multinational complexities of achieving and sustaining a competitive advantage. This chapter integrates content from foundational courses such as economics, human resource management, marketing, supply chain/operations management, accounting, and finance with the development of analytical, communication, and teamwork skills. The overarching goal of the chapter is to have students demonstrate their capacity to develop and execute organizational strategies in actual or simulated sport business situations.

The information presented in this chapter will help students to sharpen critical thinking skills and independent problem-solving techniques relevant to the analysis of sport business problems and the generation of feasible strategic solutions through both strategic planning and budgeting processes. This applies specifically to sport facility and event management in that sporting arenas and organizations can struggle to accurately factor all the "peripheral" factors into their budget and strategic planning. This is precisely where strategic planning becomes important. The actual "contest on the field" is considered to

Strategy a method or plan chosen to bring about a desired future state such as goal achievement or problem solution.

be the "core service product" for sporting arenas (Hassan & Trenberth, 2012). In contrast, the arena, team website, team merchandise, entertainment before, during, and after games, sponsor roles, and community involvement are considered "peripherals" (Hassan & Trenberth, 2012). These peripherals are the "wider view of a sports service product" (Hassan & Trenberth, 2012, p. 219). These peripheral aspects are perhaps some of the most important aspects to consider when preparing a strategic plan for a sports facility or event management. A strategic plan and budget are important for a successful sport facility because it takes into account all aspects of a team and event, instead of just those that might be obvious to the general public.

Core v peripheral

Private and public organizations capital planning and funding processes can vary so much that it is not possible to address the numerous ways that this can take place in such distinctly different environments. Understanding the environment and what it takes to make a concept a reality is essential to the success of any project. The essential steps in any institutional environments can vary greatly. On the surface who, what, where, when, why, and how projects proceed from concept to reality may appear to have no similarities from one organization to the next, but there are likely to be more similarities than there are differences.

Role of Strategy in the Business Plan

While strategy can vary greatly from business to business and from sport to sport there are common checkpoints that warrant widespread use. A number of key benefits and rationales have been identified related to the application of strategic planning within general business settings, and these elements are also applicable to settings in sport facilities and sport events. Four elements with nearly universal application include:

- It provides direction—The strategy of an organization provides future direction to the firm.
- It focuses effort—Strategy promotes coordination of activities. It ensures that people in the organization are working towards uniform objectives and goals as a cohesive team.
- It defines the organization—Through strategy employees and other stakeholders can come to understand the organization. Strategy encompasses an organization's, vision, mission, and values—defining traits of any organization.
- It provides consistency—Strategy provides a plan of action. It reduces ambiguity and provides order. It ensures consistent action over uncertain environment (Bora & Chungyalpa, 2015; Mintzberg, Ahlstrand, & Lampel, 2009).

The strategic planning process for facilities includes several elements that may be used in combination or association with one another including comprehensive master planning (CMP), strategic facility planning (SFP), and integrated planning (IP).

Comprehensive Master Plan

Strategic Facility Planning a connection of an organization's strategic planning to a mid- or long-term facility plan.

Comprehensive Master Plan a long-range and general plan to guide land and building development based upon committee assessment of data.

Confusion for many facility managers concerns the difference between a *strategic facility plan* (SFP) and a *comprehensive master plan* (CMP). For example, is the CMP part of a master plan or something else such as downtown or campus renovation? The confusion exists between a CMP and SFP since they may both answer the same question: What building, buildings, and space are needed to support our strategic goals? The strategic facility plan guides a master plan by adding long-range strategic analyses of project drivers and restrainers.

The CMP is a living document that represents the values that this institution is looking to protect in the long term. As a work "in progress," it provides the campus with a common baseline of information and begins to correlate the programmatic efforts with infrastructure and facility needs. This approach is crucial both to the revitalization of existing facilities and towards bringing new initiatives to reality. The CMP must accommodate these evolving programs in the development of timely, flexible, and quality facilities to meet the needs of these programs and to position the institution for the dynamic future.

The CMP is the institutional plan that will guide future physical development. The CMP will be the tool to identify the physical needs and program initiatives and will integrate those needs within the comprehensive planning process. The plan will identify both programmatic and operational needs, assess the site's physical capabilities to respond, recommend planning solutions, and identify projects and funding sources or budgets needed to implement the development required. The CMP should contain four primary elements:

1. Descriptions of the principles, assumptions, and strategies affecting planning and the environment in which planning and development evolve,
2. Needs analysis and determination of the physical objectives to be met by development,
3. Plans that illustrate the proposed development improvements, and
4. Implementation strategies, priorities, and phasing of future developments for realizing the plan's objectives.

The CMP identifies an outline for the physical environments that incorporate the buildings. Master planning creates the site-specific combination of programmed elements, natural conditions and constructed infrastructure and systems at the functional, aesthetic and temporal levels. The development of a CMP starts with alternative organizational configurations, often referred to as scenarios. These scenarios or alternatives represent differing priorities and criteria, as well as present choices for organizational and site/facility models. The nature of the plan will influence, and be influenced by, the context of the project location beyond the property lines. Alignment with community needs and expectations is a critical factor of this phase.

Components of a CMP include regulatory analysis; infrastructure and transportation plans; amenities and support plans; corporate image; security strategies; phasing plans; cost projections; and environmental design. Expert planners need to ensure the outcome is achievable, yet flexible enough to preserve future options. Master plans can include varying levels of detail but usually include some or all of these space-use analyses:

1. Zoning, regulation, covenant assessments
2. Space standards/benchmarks descriptions
3. Program of space use
4. Workflow analyses
5. Engineering assessment and plan
6. Block, fit or stacking plans
7. Concept site plan or campus plan
8. Architectural image concepts
9. Long-term maintenance plan
10. Construction estimates
11. Phasing or sequencing plan (the sequence of projects)

The CMP is often summarized with color-coded site drawings or timelines of projects which, in some cases, is referred to as the master plan. The three types of facility plans and some of their major components are shown in Table 4.1 to help distinguish between them. Items in each row are not comparative, but each cell stands on its own.

Table 4.1 *Summary of SFP and CMP Elements*

Strategic Facility Plan	Comprehensive Master Plan
Existing condition analysis	Site-specific physical plan for buildings
Organizational needs statement (linking FM to strategy)	Infrastructure and systems within the site
Gap analysis	Aesthetics of buildings and grounds
Recommendations for new spaces/buildings	Phasing plans for building
Facility cost projections/life cycle cost analysis	Construction estimates
Capacity analysis and use recommendations	Engineering assessments

Strategic Facility Plan

Many facility managers may be unfamiliar with the best way to accomplish this type of planning or are not sure where to begin the process. When beginning to develop a strategic facility plan (SFP), it is important to determine the scope of the project to ascertain key objectives, milestones, and data gathering activities. Strategic facility planning process adheres to the concept that that every decision has a direct impact on the organization's comprehensive master plan.

To be successful in achieving the needs, an SFP must be employed. An International Facility Management Association white paper (Roper, Kim, & Lee, 2009) defines the strategic facility plan:

> A strategic facility plan (SFP) is defined as a two-to-five year facilities plan encompassing an entire portfolio of owned and/or leased space that sets strategic facility goals based on the organization's strategic (business) objectives. The strategic facilities goals, in turn, determine short-term tactical plans, including prioritization of, and funding for, annual facility related projects. (p. 3)

Roper, Kim, and Lee (2009) further indicate that four steps must be considered for the effective implementation of a strategic facility plan. The first step is an understanding of the organization's mission, vision, values, and goals. The mission statement provides focus, defines the institution, clarifies the *values* are important, and establishes an overall philosophy. By understanding the organizational mission four key measurements can be addressed: financial performance of the facility, the customer knowledge, internal business processes, and learning and growth. The second step is an examination of the range of potential organization's facility needs. This step requires a thorough examination of current facility assets to plan and react to changing facility needs. When the organization's business plan has been created with an in-depth comprehension of the assets and capabilities, it is possible to identify future strategic business goals for the facility. The third step assesses the ability to meet the long-term needs of the organization. Once a clear definition of the state of the organization's assets is understood a consideration as to how to balance present facility needs with long-term needs and issues is necessary. These items may include workforce demographics, organizational structure and culture, and market position. The fourth step to consider is the ability to incorporate potential future changes and updates. The cyclical nature of continuous preparation for the fluctuating future requires changing of plans to meet the needs of the facility. These changes and updates must be managed on a regular basis to ensure they are achievable.

Planning is a process for instilling quality while working to arrive at a desired physical end state. Planning implementation is often long term in nature; in some cases, many years will pass before any significant change can be observed. Developing the strategic facility plan is a process that may involve discussion with a number of different stakeholder groups and should take place over a period of time. An organization's planning efforts must be

Values principles or standards related to significance or importance for person or organization.

both flexible and agile so it is able to exercise leadership, and to respond with scientific, engineering, and technical solutions to a wide range of emerging challenges. By creating quality processes, quality outcomes will be the result. The widespread use of integrated planning concepts will always add value.

Integrated Planning

To provide a comprehensive strategic facility plan or a comprehensive master plan, various business goals must be integrated into the facility plan analyses. Planning by its unique nature requires that most decisions be made by consensus and not within a vacuum. Developing the facility plan is a process that may involve discussion with a number of different stakeholder groups and should take place over a period of time. *Integrated planning* (IP) establishes the mission and *vision* framework, the "big picture," and not just for one project but holistically for an entire institution, community, or organization. In public environments, this shows commitment on the part of the institution and indicates it is willing to have a stake in the investment. Community members who are skilled facilitators should be identified and included to assist with coordinating the process between the planning committee and the community at-large.

The IP process requires direct alignment of all of the organizational facility plans. Without the direct alignment, different organizations are marching to the beat of different drums. The intent is to get everyone moving in the same direction, at the same time, and to speak with one voice. This is achieved because the process is intended to be open, inclusive, transparent, collaborative, future driven, and respectful. To accomplish these items, here are a few key questions to ask:

- Have we undergone an IP effort that closely aligns the institution's mission and vision to the institutional, academic, financial, physical, and capital plans?
  - If yes, when was it last updated to reflect changes and pressures in the external and internal environments?
- When you look at the plan and compare when it was published against your current physical state, does it appear that the plan has been followed?
  - If not, have you done at least some portion of the IP and is there a plan to integrate the rest?
- When you speak with your peers and colleagues how do they feel about the current plan?
- What changes would your peers and colleagues recommend?

The value of community and stakeholder engagement should not be underestimated when planning for facilities or programs. It can provide important insights into community values and views, ensure the plans and facility/program location is in tune with local sentiments and provides important information about the likely use of the facility. It can also act as a community capacity building initiative in its own right. Such community involvement

Integrated Planning planning process linking the organization's values, vision, mission and priorities and all departments/areas with the event or facility plan.

Vision or Vision Statement a statement of an organization's desired achievements or accomplishments in the mid-term or long-term future.

will generally strengthen community ownership and the validity of the findings. Broad community consultation may identify opportunities to share resources, extend an existing service, enter into a partnership or co-locate complementary services.

Facility Planning Committee

Ideally, an integrated committee should have a diverse range of expertise in facility project management, building design, recreation planning, business/financial management, facility management, maintenance management, security, parking and transportation, and community development. Key constituents and stakeholders who comprise the planning committee should include community administrators/leaders, facility maintenance and management, occupants and end users. It is important to note that such facility planning committees are recommending bodies only and not decision making.

While it is important to have adequate representation from key constituents, the facility planning committee must be able to function and not collapse under its own weight. According to Waite (2005) at least one "opponent" of the project should be on the committee as well. The role of critic and devil's advocate provides a check to the often unbridled enthusiasm of project proponents.

Although the roles, responsibilities, and the power of a facility planning committee can vary greatly within various organizations, it is ultimately the responsibility of this committee to review planning recommendations and provide input, comments, and recommendations to the appropriate leaders. Activities under the purview of the committee could include the need to:

- Represent key institutional interests and needs
- Review, advise, and endorse priorities, plans, and funding
- Resolve conflicts between internal organizations on planning issues when necessary

When effectively done, integrated planning (IP) can provide the decision makers a way to provide the intended services to its stakeholders. Where appropriate, a cooperative approach can achieve maximum effectiveness and efficiency. Integrated planning ensures participation of all stakeholders and affected parties.

Responsibilities of the Strategic Planning Committee

The strategic planning committee should decide what investigative methods will be used in undertaking the strategic plan study. A number of different methods are used to identify and gather relevant information. Some commonly recommended methods are literature search, community surveys, site visits to existing facilities in other localities, discussions with experienced facility managers and governing bodies, researched information regarding technical data or usage patterns, direct interviews with key groups and individuals, or community workshops with key groups and individuals.

When the results from a combination of the aforementioned methods are interpreted and used by the committee, it is imperative that they are analyzed properly. Such examination may be accomplished by using analytical techniques such as surveys and interviews, scenario planning, systematic layout planning (SLP), SMART processes, strengths, weaknesses, opportunities and threats analysis (SWOT), strategic creative analysis (SCAN), or benchmarking.

Surveys and Interviews

Surveys and interviews are great instruments for obtaining information that would otherwise be unobtainable. There is an art and a science behind the development and analysis of these instruments. At times, people can feel that they are questioned too much about their opinions on matters, so it is important to construct instruments that are brief, concise, constructive, have a well-defined purpose, and target persons only within the population area. It is unlikely that any survey instrument will be able to capture data from the entire desired population, but statistically it may provide important insights. A number of types of surveys would prove useful to the planning committee. This section of the chapter will consider integrating environmental surveys with current customer surveys.

Environmental Survey: Conduct an Environmental Survey of the Building

An environmental survey is an excellent starting point when determining and allocating future resources for buildings and planning programs. This important tool can be used to help review the current uses of the facility, current offerings, and trends. In addition, the environmental survey reviews exterior forces that impact the facility and its customers. The internal capabilities of the facility are important; however, the external factors of a facility are just as essential to creating a detailed strategic plan (Mintzberg, 1994). External forces could include competing programs, economic issues, emerging trends in technology, or other issues that impact the building and its customers. The content received from an environmental survey is also closely related to differentiation tactics that will be discussed later on in the chapter. The exterior environmental survey for a building provides management with a current view of their business's landscape. These exterior environmental factors are a guideline showing management what is resonating with the public, as well as what the current standards are within the industry, based on the offerings of competitors. While the external environmental factors are important to a business or sports facility, the internal results of the environmental survey provide an up-to-date blueprint of the company's current standing. When coupled with the findings of the external environment survey, the internal survey allows management to compose a strategic plan by setting benchmarks and specific goals for their facility.

Current and Potential Customers: Who are they and how do they use the resources?

Start with a study of the customers who currently use the building and its resources. Customers can vary based on the entity conducting research, and the exact focus of their research. Fitness facility customers, stadium spectators, and teams/players can all be considered customers. Scan current sources of information to discover what statistics are kept concerning attendance at past programs, usage numbers by day or time, and any demographic records that are recorded for study. If the population and demographic information are not available at the current time, a sampling of statistical data or direct observation over a specific time period may be used to provide a starting point for determining the habits of current users. The review of current usage should help in creating priorities for programming, links to open hours and usage, and assist in developing a priority list for services.

Review resources concerning the demographics of the entire community served by the facility; resources for demographics could include federal census records for the area, school demographics, or other databases that provide general information about the community. Compare the current users' demographics with the demographics of the general population and record any trends that are discovered. The research may demonstrate that the current users reflect the community demographics in gender, age, and geographic location from the building. The research may also highlight portions of the community demographics that are not using the building and provide target populations for the strategic plan and future customer growth. Diversifying customers, as well as finding the correct clientele to target for the facility, is an essential part of a strategy as it pertains to strategic planning (Thompson & Strickland, 2001).

The survey process can also be modified to reach future customers who do not use the facility and are not familiar with the current offerings or ideas for future programs. Using the results from the review of current users, develop a survey to determine the impact on those who do not currently use the facility. Create a list of ideas generated from the user surveys and have non-users prioritize or indicate which ideas generate interest. Using the data about non-users created during the Environmental Survey process, management now has the ability to effectively reach non-users. The data obtained from the environmental survey process provides a strategic plan and guideline for reaching the non-users of a program. A currently unreached geographic area is a good target for future customers; provide informational booths and conduct information interviews to find out the priorities

Input from current and potential sport consumers can form an important aspect of strategic plan development.

of the non-user. If the demographics indicate older individuals are frequently non-users, reach out to local senior centers and social groups that provide senior services to access the opinions of this non-user demographic.

Scenario Planning

Scenario planning allows the decision makers to identify a variety of future issues such as expansion of the facility and parking as well as the changes in the consumer interests. The objective is to create solutions which perform the best under all scenarios. According to Owen and Daskin (1998), "…scenario planning approaches move away from reactive analyses of solution sensitivity toward models which formalize the complexity and uncertainty inherent in real-world problem instances" (p. 424). In some situations, scenario planning may substitute as a way of forecasting potential trends and changes of the consumers (Mobasheri, Orren, & Sioshansi, 1989). Additionally, scenario planning may be employed to prepare for and solve specific operational problems (Mulvey, 1996).

Systematic Layout Planning (SLP)

As developed by Muther (1973), systematic layout planning (SLP) is an organized way to conduct layout planning. It consists of a framework of phases, a pattern of procedures, and a set of conventions for identifying, rating, and visualizing the elements and areas involved in planning a layout. Based on the understanding of the roles and relationships between activities, a flow analysis and an activity relationship analysis are performed. From the analyses performed, a relationship diagram is developed.

The relationship positions the activities spatially. Proximities are typically used to reflect the relationship between pairs of activities. Although the relationship diagram is normally two dimensional, there have been instances in which three-dimensional diagrams have been developed when multistory buildings, mezzanines, and/or overhead space were being considered. The next two steps involve the determination of the amount of space to be assigned to each activity. Departmental services and area requirement sheets would be completed for each planning department. Once the space assignments have been made, space templates are developed for each department or program, and the space is hung on the relationship diagram to obtain the venue's overall space relationships. Based on modifying considerations and practical limitations, a number of layout alternatives, such as the shapes of the activity and office areas, are developed and evaluated. The preferred alternative is then identified and recommended. The SLP procedure can be used sequentially to develop first a block layout and then a detailed layout for each planning department. In the latter applications, relationships between activity areas, offices, storage locations, as well as entrances and exits from the department are used to determine the relative location of activities within each department.

SMART Process

The SMART process refers to developing goals that are specific, measurable, attainable, realistic, and timely. According to Donahue (1998), goals can be attained through the following steps:

1. **Specific**—What is the unique goal to be evaluated? Who should be involved? What is trying to be accomplished? What is the purpose and benefit of this goal?

2. **Measurable**—Benchmarking or other types of measurement tools to determine whether or not the goal is attained. How will we know when we have accomplished this goal?

3. **Attainable**—Actions required to attain goal(s). Goals can seem unattainable given current organizational or resource limitations, but the gap to achieve the goal can be reduced by developing skills, abilities, financial capacity, and attitudes. This is also known as "stretch goals" whereby incremental improvements or change allows an institution to extend itself beyond current capabilities.

4. **Realistic**—What can realistically be achieved given the available resources? The institution must be willing and able to do what is necessary to achieve each goal.

5. **Timely**—Assign a time frame to achieve the specific goal. Without a time frame there is no sense of urgency.

The framing of goals statements within the overall strategic plans improved the likelihood of success in goal achievement.

Strengths, Weaknesses, Opportunities, and Threat (SWOT) Analysis

Strengths, weaknesses, opportunities, and threat (SWOT) analysis is another planning tool used to strategically evaluate the strengths, weaknesses, opportunities and threats in a project or in a business venture. SWOT uses business objectives and identifies both internal and external factors that are either favorable or unfavorable to achieving that objective. The four areas considered are:

1. Strengths: attributes within the organization helpful to achieving the objective and describing how they can be leveraged

2. Weaknesses: attributes within the organization harmful to achieving the objective and how they can be minimized or neutralized

3. Opportunities: external conditions helpful to achieving the objective

4. Threats: external conditions harmful to achieving the objective

Strategic Creative Analysis (SCAN)

This is a process designed for strategic planning, decision making, and analyzing case studies (Winer, 1993). This method should be used in conjunction to the SWOT analysis by developing objectives that correspond with the results of the SWOT. The relative importance of each SWOT objective should be rank ordered so that the highest ranked objectives are analyzed. Analysis questions are based on the SWOT findings. For example:

1. How can we use this strength?
2. How can we overcome this weakness?
3. How do we exploit this opportunity?
4. How do we defend against this threat?

The end goal is to determine whether objectives are attainable, develop strategies for success, develop action plans, evaluate progress, and monitor the implementation.

Benchmarking and Review of Current Offerings

Benchmarking utilizes much of the organizational understanding gained in the first step of SFP to compare practices and metrics to recognized leaders. Networking with peer organizations, competitors, and especially for facility organizations, visiting award-winning facilities provide insight to bring back and adapt to your operations. Adaptation is the key—recognizing a good process or practice and using it in a familiar way within the organization is the basis of successful benchmarking. In order for SFP to serve as the right mechanism to analyze and improve current facility operations, a proactive approach to benchmarking practices and services of those organizations recognized as industry leaders is needed. Benchmarking may be undertaken as part of a broader process reengineering initiative, or it might be conducted as a freestanding exercise. It may be used when visiting existing facilities in other localities to discuss potential issues or barriers other facility managers experienced. In summary, benchmarking is the practice of being humble enough to admit that others may be better at something and being wise enough to learn how to match, and even surpass, them at it.

Within educational and recreational settings, the determination of current programs and the impact on the community will assist in the creation of a strategic plan and help determine the future building program. A review should assess the current programs, the hours of operation, and popularity of the different offerings provided by the institution. After a review of the current offerings, research other institutions for comparison. Other institutions may be selected using standards of shared geography, similar budget size, or the general population served by either number or type. Review the offerings and services of the comparison organizations and create a picture of how the organization stands in relation to its cohort. An important part of reviewing the current offerings is looking at ways to differentiate the facility

Great American Ballpark along the Ohio River in Cincinnati.

from current programs. The differentiation tactics used should be sustainable. Differentiation in business process and knowledge are very hard to duplicate and will give a facility a uniqueness that is sustainable (Bora & Chungyalpa, 2015). One way of differentiation that has become popular in MLB lately, for example, has been ensuring the family and kid friendliness of stadiums. The outreach programs and areas designed specifically for children have become an important part of benchmarking with other stadiums. At the Great American Ballpark in Cincinnati Ohio, the Reds have set the mark for family friendly quite high for their fellow MLB teams. The Reds stadium includes interactive kids' games, a playground, a family Picnic Deck, scheduled "Family Days" at the park, as well as several firework nights throughout the season. All these events and amenities show a significant step by the Great American Ballpark to position themselves as a family destination. While the Reds seem to be leading the way in this aspect, other MLB teams such as the Milwaukee Brewers, Detroit Tigers and Texas Rangers are trying to duplicate this differentiation.

Emerging Trends and Issues

After the completion of the analytic steps within the SFP process, the strategic facility planning committee should consider examining the following items as overarching issues and emerging trends that can impact the process: 1) organizational philosophy, 2) facility accessibility, 3) facility sustainability, and 4) external forces.

Organizational Philosophy

Organizations are collections of people that are more organic than mechanistic. They are a complex inter-relationship of emotions, politics, judgments, ambitions, intent, power, opportunity, and of course, processes. Of all these things, processes are the most tangible. They can be seen, measured, and mapped with relative ease. This can cause some individuals to tend toward a singular focus on process, on structured problems, but this ignores the also important unstructured and more organic problems facing organizations.

Creating organizations where people want to work towards their own individual visions, while contributing towards the common good of the organization is paramount, and also relates to the concept of integrated planning (IP) discussed earlier in the chapter. Creating effective organizations requires an environment where change is welcome because changes occur every day. This environment must also tap the true potential and creativity of every individual. Changing processes alone will not solve problems of values, beliefs, vision, flexibility, as well as management philosophy and style.

It is crucial that the organizational philosophy and values are determined at the outset of the strategic facility planning process. The strategic facility plan identifies the type, quantity, and location of spaces required to fully support the organization's business initiatives and should be framed within the organization's philosophy. The strategic facilities plan includes three primary components: an understanding of the organization's culture and core values and an analysis of how existing and new facilities must manifest that culture and core values within the physical space or support their change, an in-depth analysis of existing facilities—including location, capability, utilization and condition, and an achievable and affordable (approved) plan that translates the goals of the business plan into an appropriate facility response.

The organizational philosophy should define the social, financial and environmental outcomes that could be expected from the facility. It should clarify your position regarding the following policy issues:

- Financial costs—user contributions to capital, maintenance, and operation
- Equity/access—community access to the facility
- Multi/single use—usage and programming

Organizational philosophy and processes will clearly impact how the SFP is achieved. For example, profit, non-profit, and government organizations will have both parallels and contrasts regarding management preferences. These relationships will be encountered across three main kinds of organizations: service business, manufacturing business, and governmental/ academic institutions.

In a service business, there is a consistent focus on people and facility design. Service business differs from manufacturing business in that whereas the manufacturer emphasizes the characteristics buyers will value, service designers tend to focus on the experiences customers desire (Frei, 2008). Most of these businesses have centralized information-gathering and interpretation methods, as well as established processes to utilize the data.

Manufacturing businesses tend to adhere to more measurable and standardized outputs in terms of their specifications. Woon (2000) reported that the service organizations generally revealed a decreased implementation of Total Quality Management (TQM) when compared to manufacturing organizations in terms of information and analysis, process management, and quality performance. However, Huq and Stolen (1998) revealed no significant difference between manufacturing and service in terms of mission statement, customer focus, management commitment, empowerment, and communications.

Academic institutions that are funded by the government are susceptible to changes in economic budgets, desired levels of service and public opinion. All institutions can have various needs to meet its academic, athletic, recreation, foodservice, and support facility (parking, security, etc.) needs. Few institutions have the financial wherewithal to address all needs simultaneously. These organizations utilize both centralized and decentralized information-gathering, which makes long-range planning the norm for organizations in this category. Publically funded sport organizations, such as municipal or county parks and recreation departments and programs fall into similar funding susceptibilities.

Since differences in organizational type, culture, and processes strongly influence how the strategic facility plan is accomplished, the recommended strategic facility plan will need to be adjusted in accordance with the different type, culture, and process specific to the organization. Depending on which category the organization is best aligned, the proposed SFP will need to be adjusted. The process of establishing the SFP begins with categorizing the types of organization. When the organization is categorized, it becomes easier to gather more relevant information and utilize SFP techniques that have been discussed previously, such as scenario planning modeling, SLP and SWOT analyses, to effectively analyze the accumulated data.

Facility Accessibility Issues

Another area that needs extensive attention in developing an SFP deals with accessibility issues or universal design. According to the U.S. Census Bureau Report, American with Disabilities 2010, about 56.7 million people—19% of the population—had a disability in 2010. Although members of the general population obtain most of their physical activity in outdoor settings such as neighborhood streets, shopping malls, parks, and walking/ jogging paths, access to walking may be limited for those with mobility disabilities or those who have difficulty walking due to arthritis or extreme obesity. Other examples may include the inability to walk due to paralysis or vision impairments that make these inaccessible environments (Humpel, Owen, & Leslie, 2002). Yet, among the reasons that people with disabilities often do not visit places of public accommodation for physical activity or sport include architectural and transportation barriers or safety concerns (Grady & Finnegan, 2012; Pate, Bemiller, & Hardin, 2010).

Policy and legislation aimed at improving accessibility are also not without their limitations (Rimmer, Riley, Wang, & Rauworth, 2004). Considerations must be made to address the Americans with Disabilities Act (ADA) of 1990. According to the ADA (2010), accessibility can be defined as having a site, facility, work environment, service, or program that is easy to approach, enter, operate, participate in, and/or use safely and with dignity by a person with a disability. It is important to note that ADA is an antidiscrimination law that sets forth minimal standards for equal access. To comply with the ADA (2010), any facility or part of a facility constructed by, on behalf of, or for the use of a public entity shall be designed and constructed in such manner that the facility or part of the facility is readily accessible and usable by individuals with disabilities, if the construction was commenced after January 26, 1992.

Within ADA of 1990, the two most applicable aspects when developing a facility concept design are Title II and Title III. Title II of the ADA prohibits disability discrimination by government entities by providing that "no qualified individual with a disability shall, by reason of such disability, be excluded from participation in or be denied the benefits of the services, programs, or activities of a public entity, or be subjected to discrimination by any such entity" (42 U.S.C. § 12132). Sport facilities must ensure that individuals with disabilities have physical access to facilities and an equal opportunity to participate in and benefit from all programs and activities offered to students, faculty, staff, and guests of the university. The term "public entity" includes any state or local government and their departments, agencies, special purpose districts, or other instrumentalities (42 U.S.C. § 12131(1)). A public entity that has authority over streets, roads, or walkways must include in its transition plan a schedule for providing curb cuts, "giving priority to walkways serving entities covered by the Act, including State and local government offices and facilities, transportation, places of public accommodation, and employers, followed by walkways serving other areas" (28 C.F.R. §35.150(d)(2).

Title III of the Americans with Disabilities Act of 1990 (1991) prohibits discrimination on the basis of disability by places of public accommodations. According to the ADA Accessibility Guidelines (ADAAG, 2000), within Title III, it is asserted that "[a] public accommodation shall afford goods, services, facilities, privileges, advantages and accommodations to an individual with a disability in the most integrated setting appropriate to the needs of the individual...." (28 C.F.R. § 36.203(a)). The ADAAG (2000) defines a facility as "all or any portion of buildings, structures, sites, complexes, equipment, rolling stock or other conveyances, roads, walks, [and] passageways, parking lots..." (28 C.F.R §35.104). As a result, the priority of public accommodation must provide access from public sidewalks and parking lots, including providing accessible parking spaces (28 C.F.R. § 36.304(c)(1)). Accordingly, the ADAAG states:

> This priority on "getting through the door" recognizes that providing actual physical access to a facility from public sidewalks, public transportation, or parking is generally preferable to any alternative arrangements in terms of both business efficiency and the dignity of individuals with disabilities. (28 C.F.R. pt. 36, App. B.)

Regarding individuals with disabilities' access to goods, services, and employment opportunities on an equal basis with the general public, reserved parking, and specialized treatment are necessary items. The significance of accessible and ample parking for a driver with a disability is a vital prerequisite for the place of public accommodation. The protections afforded by the ADA may also come back into play and trigger additional legal obligations, such as obligations found in premises liability, to ensure a safe environment for tailgating for people with disabilities and people without disabilities. The owner/operator or supervisor of the "event" has an affirmative duty, per the ADA, to ensure that services are provided to individuals with disabilities in a non-discriminatory manner and must not be denied the full and equal enjoyment of the goods, services, and facilities (42 U.S.C. § 12182).

Petersen and Piletic (2006) stated that there are three main structural barriers within fitness, physical activity, recreation, and sport facilities: access to the facility, including parking and entry; access to activity spaces, including gyms, cardio areas, weight rooms, group exercise and dance areas, and pools; and access to support facilities, including locker rooms and rest rooms. Yet, Cardinal and Spaziani (2003) found that none of the 50 facilities surveyed in western Oregon were in 100% compliance with ADA guidelines. Whereas exterior entrances or doors (90%) and telephone accessibility (88%) were the areas with the highest compliance, accessibility to and around exercise equipment (8%) and the customer-service desk (37%) were lowest in compliance.

In another facilities study, Rimmer, Riley, Wang, and Rauworth (2005) reported that combinations of accessible and inaccessible features existed. Most of the facilities in the study had accessibility features consistent with the ADA Accessibility Guidelines pertaining to elevators, bathrooms, entrance doors, water fountains, and parking areas. However, many others did not have adequate access routes and curb cuts; power-assisted or pushbutton-operated doors; visual and audible signals in elevators; hand-held shower-head units; and obstacle-free paths to lockers (Rimmer et al., 2005).

According to the U.S. Department of Justice, the revised regulations for Titles II (public entities and public transportation) and III (public accommodations and commercial facilities) of the ADA of 1990 are most applicable to sport and recreation settings. These revised regulations resulted in enforceable accessibility standards called the 2010 ADA Standards for Accessible Design. Key 2010 ADA interior requirements that can apply to sport, athletic, and recreational facilities and are important for a practitioner to know of are as follows:

- Standard 102 Dimensions for Adults and Children—This standard recognizes that facilities must meet the physical needs of people of varying size.
- Standard 103 Equivalent Facilitation—Even though the 2010 ADA can be quite specific as to certain standards, it does allow some deviation "to encourage flexibility and innovation while still ensuring access, by allowing alternatives that result in substantially equivalent or greater accessibility and usability."
- Standard 104 Conventions—This standard states that certain construction tolerances are absolute dimensions that must be met, such as the mounting heights of grab bars in toilet facilities.
- Standards 201 Application and 202 Existing Buildings and Facilities—All areas of newly designed, newly constructed buildings, facilities and altered portions of existing buildings, and facilities shall comply with these requirements.

- Standard 203 General Exceptions—Spaces with limited means of access, such as ladders or very narrow passageways, and that are visited only by service personnel for maintenance, repair, or occasional monitoring of equipment may be exempt from accessibility requirements. This does not mean that all mechanical, electrical, IT, or plumbing areas are not required to comply.

- Standards 204 and 307 Protruding Objects—Prohibits protruding objects in the circulation paths.

- Standard 206 and Chapter 4 Accessible Routes—Provides specifications for accessible routes to and within built environments.

- Standard 207 Accessible Means of Egress—Requires the same number of accessible means of egress to be provided as the number of exits required by applicable life safety (building and fire) codes.

- Standards 208 and 502 Parking Spaces—This standard establishes the requirement for dedicated disabled parking spaces based on the number of building occupants and the size of the lot.

- Standards 210 and 504 Stairways—This standard requires that stairs to be accessible only when they provide access to floor levels not otherwise connected by an accessible route (e.g., where the accessible route is provided by an elevator, lift, or ramp). The standard further requires that all newly constructed stairs that are part of a means of egress to comply with the requirements for accessible stairs, which include requirements for accessible treads, risers, and handrails.

- Toilets, bathing areas, drinking fountains, lavatories, washing and drying machines, dressing, fitting, locker rooms, and storage such as those found in locker rooms must comply with ADA Standards 211, 212, 213, 214, 222, 225 respectfully. ADA requirements require that there must be at least one toilet and shower facility per gender that meets these requirements. The required number can increase based on the total number of occupants for a given facility. The primary difference between accessibility standards for lavatories and for vanities is the need for forward approach clearance with knee space. Accessibility standards include requirements for faucets, mirror height, and pipe protection.

- 216 Signage—This standard address signs that include seat and row designations in assembly areas; occupant names, building addresses; company names and logos; signs in parking facilities (except those identifying accessible parking spaces and means of egress); and exterior signs identifying permanent rooms and spaces that are not located at the door to the space they serve.

ADA compliance should be a significant consideration in strategic planning for facilities and events.

Many guidelines within the ADA are primarily intended for newly constructed facilities. The ADA focuses heavily on access to the built environment and does not address other types of barriers such as equipment and programs. As such, accessibility guidelines are general principles or strategies for creating a barrier-free environment, which might or might not apply to the specific needs of the individual with a disability (Rimmer et al., 2005). Thus, every effort to accommodate individuals with disabilities must be made in the strategic facility plan not only for ethical but also legal reasons.

Facility Sustainability Issues

Sustainable design practices have been applied in American buildings for millennia, as evidenced in the exquisite structures of the Hopi Indians over a thousand years ago. However, the term sustainable or green architecture as a modern, integrated design philosophy appears to be very recent. The first references to "green architecture" and "green building label" reportedly appeared in the British publication *The Independent* in London in early 1990, followed by the first American use of the term "green architecture" in mid-1990.

The American Institute of Architect's Committee on the Environment started in 1989. In 1991, the first green building program in the United States was established. The Green Building committee of the American Society for Testing and Materials (ASTM) also formed in 1991 (Kats, 2003). Thus, the modern green building movement appears to be little over 25 years old. In the last 25 years, countless numbers of "sustainable" buildings have been constructed. However, sport, athletic, and recreational facilities have been behind the curve as it relates to adopting sustainable design practices. Facilities of this type comprise a very small percentage of LEED certified facilities. Known sustainable sport facilities that have been completed to date include the following: Montclair State University; Grinnell (IA) College; Detroit Lions training center; University of South Carolina baseball stadium, Minnesota Twins Target Field, and Orlando Magic Amway Center, to name a few.

Sustainability Defined

No common definition of sustainability exists. Green design, socially responsible design, high-performance buildings, ecologically efficient, environmentally friendly, healthy buildings, eco-design, natural resource efficient, whole building design, and other terms are widely used synonymously. However, according to the *Green Building Encyclopedia* (2007), *sustainability* is the condition of being able to meet the needs of present generations without compromising those needs for future generations. This sustainability is achieved through a balance among extraction and renewal and environmental inputs and outputs as to cause no overall net environmental burden or deficit. To be truly sustainable, a human community must not decrease biodiversity, must not consume resources faster than they are renewed, must recycle and reuse virtually all materials, and must rely primarily on resources of its own region.

Sustainability the use of materials or methods that do not use resources that cannot be replaced and that do not harm the environment.

Sustainability Issues

Sustainability is an important social and economic issue. The need to become more sensitive to global warming, rising energy prices, increased contamination, the increase in environmental related diseases and ailments, material shortages, overflowing landfills, and other related issues has caused significant concern not just in the scientific community but with the general public as well. The main objectives of sustainable design are to reduce or completely avoid depletion of critical resources like energy, water, and raw materials, and prevent environmental degradation caused by facilities and infrastructure throughout their life cycle (Whole Building Design Guide, 2015).

The need to become more sensitive to global warming, rising energy prices, increased contamination, the increase in environmental related diseases and ailments, material shortages, overflowing landfills, and other related issues has caused significant concern not just in the scientific community but with the general public as well. Increased news coverage, Academy Award winning documentaries, Nobel Peace prizes along with increased awareness has brought this issue to the forefront of human concern (Gonzales & Petersen, 2013). Thus, an evaluation of sustainable design opportunities and strategies appropriate for project program, site, and budget must be strongly considered in the strategic planning phase of a building.

Building the case for sustainability should start with the group that has the most knowledge of the long-term costs and methodologies of managing physical assets. The integration of facility sustainability will be developed from the strategic facility planning committee's understanding of the organization's overall strategy. Some of the sustainable design guidelines that should be addressed include:

1. Energy Use
   a. Consider local climate and site influences on building energy use. Utilize "free" energy sources where feasible, such as solar energy, daylight, exterior temperature variations, and winds.
2. Water Use
   a. Opportunities for achieving water-use reductions should be identified in the course of routine maintenance improvements and renovation projects.
3. Building Materials
   a. Recycled Content Materials: Use materials with post-consumer or post-industrial recycled content where feasible.
   b. Renewable Materials: Consider use of products that are comprised of raw materials that are in abundant supply or come from renewable sources.
   c. Local Materials: Use products produced regionally where possible.
   d. Construction Waste Management: Contractors are to develop a plan for sorting, storing, and recycling of waste materials on projects.

4. Indoor Environmental Quality

    a. Consider environmental needs of people in terms of daylight, ventilation, exterior views and thermal/acoustic/visual comfort for interior spaces. A direct line of sight to exterior view via windows or doors from 90% of all regularly occupied spaces is a long term goal.

    b. Optimize the amount of fresh air provided to building spaces.

5. Site Work

    a. Consider the impact of project on the surrounding ecosystem. Investigate methods to minimize impacts on natural habitats and watersheds.

    b. Limit off site storm water runoff and employ methods to increase on-site infiltration.

    c. Provide site facilities to encourage pedestrian, bicycle and bus transport, where feasible.

    d. Minimize site lighting levels and off-site light spillover/glare, while providing for adequate levels for security and way finding.

    e. Utilize drought resistant plant materials and low flow irrigation techniques, where feasible. Consider use of native plant species (Hodges, 2005).

Reasons for Sustainability

People and organizations can have many different reasons why they adopt or promote sustainable design methods. According to Gonzales and Petersen (2013) some reasons why such sustainable practices should be considered include but are not limited to the following:

- Demonstrating altruistic objectives—displaying a commitment to environmental stewardship and social responsibility through a notable transformation of the built environment.

- Reducing energy consumption—decreasing the amount of energy used while creating a similar work outcome. This practice may result in an increase of financial capital, environmental value, national security, and human comfort. Both individuals and organizations as consumers of energy may seek to conserve energy in order to reduce energy costs and promote economic, political and environmental sustainability as well as to increase efficiency and maximize profit.

- Reducing non-biodegradable waste—discouraging use of disposable products and designing products that use less material to achieve the desired purpose. The construction challenge is producing high quality projects with minimal waste generation.

- Conserving water—seeking to limit the withdrawal of fresh water from an ecosystem to at or below its natural replacement rate.

- Reducing greenhouse gas (GHG) emissions—major sources of GHG include heating and cooling, electricity production, and transportation. Carbon dioxide, methane, nitrous oxide and three groups of fluorinated gasses (sulfur hexafluoride, HFCs, and PFCs) are the major greenhouse gasses that contribute to global warming.

- Protecting the rights of future generations—commitment to development that meets current needs without compromising the ability of future generations to meet their needs. This definition implicitly recognizes the rights of future generations to achieve a sustainable level of development and the right to be able to utilize natural resources.

- Improving air quality—eliminating sick building syndrome, improving occupant health and psyche, reducing lost work time, and improving productivity.

- Reducing toxic chemical production—moving away from use and reliance on chemicals that can harm human health or disrupt the ecosystem or environment.

- Moving America away from oil dependency—developing alternative fuel sources that benefit the environment, economy, and national security interests.

- Saving the wild lands—defending the wild places of the world including forests, prairies, deserts, wetlands, and wilderness areas.

- Reviving the oceans—protecting the largest portion of the planet from pollution, over fishing, and habitat destruction.

- Receiving financial incentives—some local communities, state agencies, and federal agencies may provide some form of financial incentives for constructing sustainable facilities. The restoration of an historic structure with sustainable features may also qualify for financial incentives.

Sustainability and green building approaches to facilities will profit an organization via increased financial returns, improved standing in the community, enhanced productivity and a decrease of detrimental effects on the environment (Hodges, 2005). However, not many of sustainable buildings have been in operation long enough to determine whether or not the financial benefits have or will be fully realized.

Sustainability is not a concept that should be applied on an as needed basis. It is an overall philosophy that should guide an institution on a daily basis. Not just for new buildings, it can be applied to existing buildings, land use, and all day-to-day operations. The integration of facility sustainability will be developed from the facility planning committee's understanding of the organization's overall strategy.

To ensure that sustainability is at the forefront of all sports and recreation events and facilities provisions regarding the design, construction, use of natural resources, and sustainable transport should assure respect for the environment. A primary incentive for following sustainable and green building practices is the reduction in energy consumption. The likelihood of rising energy costs and the reduction of long-term operating costs could be a very attractive alternative to relatively low first costs required for construction. The rise in environmental awareness and interest continues to keep sustainability a priority in the planning process.

External Forces

For a full understanding of all the external forces that impact a building and its customers, a planner must consider external forces in the planning process. Economic trends, changes in the law and social issues all may impact the planning process. Using local news, talking with local government officials, and speaking with local business groups may provide a better understanding of community obstacles or issues that require consideration and a plan to overcome them. For example, spending time and effort to create a fantastic sports program will be hindered if the Department of Transportation is planning on construction all summer and the customers are not able to access the facility easily. When it comes to reviewing external trends and issues relative to a new facility, it is important to consider the environmental dynamism. Environmental dynamism is defined as the degree of effervescence and change expected in the environment (Reklitis, Konstantopoulos, & Trivellas, 2007). The expected change could refer to any economic, governmental, or social issues that would affect the facility. When the dynamism of an external environment is considered to be high, management may need to be prepared with strategic alternatives. Environments that are highly munificent provide the best external environment for a facility or organization, as it provides the most supportive environment for sustainable growth (Reklitis et al., 2007).

An external governing body or structure of a sport facility or sport event can greatly influence the potential success of a strategic planning process. This governing body could be from elected local government officials like a city or county council, from appointed government officials like a city manager, or from sport governing bodies like national or international sport federations. Different facilities and events would have different tiers of governing bodies whose input should be sought. Regardless of the type of governing body encountered, creating an opportunity for the appropriate governing body to review the current strategic plans can provide assistance in avoiding roadblocks to a successful implementation. Regardless of the type of governing body encountered "proper and well-defined structure provides a solid foundation for

FIFA headquarters in Zurich, Switzerland, is an example of governing structure that would influence events such as the World Cup and facilities such as stadia within the realm of international football (soccer).

any successful sport entity" (Lam, 2014, p. 25). Whatever governance structure is set in place, this structure must be made clear to all those involved in governance and planning decisions in order to avoid noncompliance with rules and regulations, and spare their organizations from corruption scandals like those that have plagued FIFA as of late.

Developing and Communicating the Strategic Plan

The facility or event manager, along with the planning committee, will assume the responsibility for the development of the strategic plan. After reviewing all the pertinent data from the surveys and interviews, scenario planning, systematic layout planning (SLP), strengths, weaknesses, opportunities and threats analysis (SWOT), strategic creative analysis (SCAN), benchmarking and external issues, planners create ideas for consideration that will ultimately lead to the shaping of goals and objectives. Whether the charge of the committee is to create a comprehensive master plan (CMP), a strategic facility plan (SFP), or another planning document, it is important to maintain the integrated planning (IP) process. This IP process will keep the committee and its plans grounded in the organizational values, vision, and mission. Once the key elements of the strategic plan are determined, these elements must be crafted into a draft document that can be presented to all the stakeholders of the organization both internal and external.

The strategic plan should be viewed as a living document that will require regular efforts to update and review. A strategic plan that is not consulted or reviewed after initial development creates minimal organizational impact. The ideas and structure of the plan should be presented with accessible language that fosters ease of access, and it should include steps encouraging plan review and amendment. For example, a local community sport facility conducts annual focus groups as a form of communication to allow both external and internal stakeholders to become informed of and provide ongoing input to the strategic plan.

The role of both staff and volunteers in the successful communication and implementation of strategic planning should not be underestimated. The staff and volunteers are on the front line of the services for facilities and events and work with the strengths and weaknesses of the physical structures. A series of meetings and discussions with all levels of staff and volunteers are beneficial for a review of the results of the strategic planning. The plan and strategy of a facility or event should be communicated to employees frequently to keep them up to date on the goals and image of the organization (Sotoducho-Pelc, 2013). As staff and volunteers often have the most access to customers, it is important that they portray an image that aligns with the strategy chosen by top management. Make sure that staff and volunteers are conscious of their contribution to the realization of the company strategy. The process of developing the ideas and creating the steps in the strategic plan are best created through individual input methods and over a series of meetings in small and large groups. Using a longer process and variety in methods of input allow individuals to participate without social or organizational structure limiting participation. The development and implementation of the strategic plan works best with input from all levels of staff and volunteers. The different perspectives allow for development of successful ideas and identification of issues that might hinder successful implementation. The "buy-in" of staff to an organization and its mission results in not only a more well-run facility or event but translates into a more pleasant experience for spectators and customers as well. This pleasant experience for spectators and a well-operated facility typically translates into higher revenue. Thus, the importance of these internal communication strategies cannot be underestimated. Staff and volunteers should be made aware of strategic plans and facility/company goals. As Pichot, Tribou, and O'Reilly (2008) conclude: "External perception is mainly based on information communicated by employees" (p. 420). A facility's employees are their ambassadors to consumers.

Budgeting

Budgeting a plan of operations based on estimates of income and expenses over a given time period.

The allocation of financial resources should ideally be tied to the organizational mission, values, and philosophy for any sport facility or event. *Budgeting* is the process to accomplish such an allocation of funds, and it is best accomplished in alignment with the strategic plans.

Most basically, a budget is a document that lists the planned costs and revenues for a facility or event. However, sporting organizations also use budgets to estimate costs of their facilities over a certain period of time. Budgeting is defined as the "internal approval, external adoption, and allocation of funds required in the operation of an organization" (Wooldridge, Garvin, & Miller, 2001, p. 87). Along with budgeting, accounting is an essential component of strategic planning. Accounting records all business spending and income, and these records are vital sources of information used by management to make financial decisions regarding a facility. Accounting, therefore, provides the means for budgetary control (Wooldridge et al., 2001).

The budget is a manager's best means of monitoring operations to determine whether the flow of money is positive or negative. The purpose of budgets is to allot the appropriate funds to the appropriate categories, with the ultimate goal of balancing the cash in with the cash out (Gage, 2012). Budgeting performs four basic functions that are essential for an organization to attain its strategic objectives (Sandu, 2011). These functions include planning, coordinating and communicating, monitoring progress, and evaluating performance. Planning, budgeting, and forecasting are the most important management functions. Within the context of these functions, planning is considered a strategic prediction of organizational performance at a summary level. Plans are defined by upper-level managers who react to shifting market conditions and opportunities. The planning process should be conducted frequently and completed quickly.

Table 4.2 *Planning, Budgeting, and Forecasting Characteristics*

	Frequency	**Speed**	**Detail Level**	**Personnel Involved**
Planning	Often	Quick	Summary	Senior Management
Budgeting	Annual	Slow	Very detailed	All areas
Forecasting	Monthly	Quick	Summary, minimal detail	Finance

Adapted from Ivanova, & Rachev (2004)

Budgeting is a form of planning that is disseminated to specific areas of responsibility across the organization. Budgeting is a relatively slow process often taking weeks or months, has significantly more individuals, and is performed in greater detail than planning. Forecasting occurs when a revision of the budget is needed. The revisions should mirror any fluctuating market conditions, strategic plan modifications, error corrections, or adjusted assumptions in the initial accepted budget (Sandu, 2011). Usually, organizations forecast on a monthly basis by employing a small number of personnel to partake in the process. Ultimately, the primary purpose of these functions is to allow upper-level management personnel to view and respond to a variety of business scenarios (Sandu, 2011).

Budget Preparation

Because of the importance of budgets as instruments for planning and controlling organizational finances, the action of budgeting impacts organizations of every type and size. Proper budgeting practices can assist an organization to use limited financial and human resources so as best to take advantage of existing business opportunities.

Smart budgeting integrates good business judgment with appropriate review and examination of historical trends and data that is relevant to the business. This review and analysis helps an organization to make decisions regarding the amount of money to be invested, the type and number of employees to hire, as well as the marketing strategies that may be needed. During the budgeting process, the organization often develops long-term and short-term plans to execute its strategies as well as to conduct continuing assessments of its performance. While the process of budgeting can be laborious and pricey for many businesses, it can also deliver various benefits including an increased understanding and appreciation of costs, a coordination of efforts to achieve organizational goals and objectives, an enhanced communication at all management levels, and a basis for conducting performance evaluations.

To be successful, budgets should be prepared in accordance with the following:

1. Realistic and Quantifiable—Due to limited resources, an organization should ration the resources it possesses by setting goals and objectives which can be reasonably attained. Realism often creates loyalty and commitment among employees which may motivate them to perform to their highest capability (Mowday, Porter, & Steers, 2013). An organization should assess each foreseeable activity and identify which ones will provide the most suitable resource allocation. An organization may achieve this identification by studying the empirical observations of prior costs and benefits of the activities (Malone et al., 1999).

2. Historical—The budget should expose a sharp comprehension of prior results as well as a powerful sense of anticipated potential financial changes. Although previous results are not absolute predictors, they can be utilized to indicate significant events and standards.

3. Period Specific—The budget period must be a rational piece of time. Although plans and projects often vary in length and scope, usually organizations prepare each budget on a yearly basis. However, a shorter budget period will necessitate increased detail and control mechanisms. The length of the budget period influences the time restrictions for commencing possible budget modifications.

4. Standardized—Managers should use standardized forms, formulas, and research techniques to most effectively expedite the budgeting process. Due to computer-aided accounting, the examination and report of computer-aided accounting allows the managers to study "real time" results while providing them the flexibility to try out the latest products.

5. Inclusive—Well-organized companies decentralize budgeting process to include the smallest level of responsibility. All areas managers such as aquatics director, wellness and fitness directors, or concession directors become responsible for the development of their own budgets as well as learn how their activities are interrelated with the other areas of the facility and organization. While each area manager creates a budget and establishes its goals, they also should meet with other area managers to exchange ideas and objectives, to learn innovative concepts, and to decrease any redundancies of activities. Being inclusive in the budgeting process provides a better understanding of the entire process and accountability of most, if not all, of the areas.

6. Successful Evaluation—Decentralization does not omit a comprehensive and systematic review of budget proposals at the higher levels of management. A budget review at higher levels of management provides a sense of checks and balances that substantiates an appropriate fit within the final master budget and alignment with the overall strategic plan of the organization.

7. Officially Accepted and Circulated—When the upper levels of management have compiled the master budget and formally accepted it as the operating plan for the organization, the master budget must be distributed it in a timely manner to the responsible area managers.

In the end, an efficient organization utilizes a well-conceived budget program as a valuable tool for predicting feasible results for a particular period of time (typically one year). By controlling and implementing an effective budget plan, an organization may be in a position to successfully plan and coordinate a variety of offerings.

Budget Planning Factors

As sport organizations enter the budgeting process, a number of factors must be considered including fixed and variable costs, various expense categories, and revenue types related to sport.

Fixed Costs versus Variable Costs

When designing a budget, individuals must take into account both fixed costs and variable costs. Fixed costs do not change based on output that is produced (Mankiw, 2015). Examples of fixed costs are employee salaries, building rent, etc. Variable costs are those costs that fluctuate with the output of the company (Mankiw, 2015). In the case of sporting facilities, output can be measured by event attendance and money spent. Examples of variable costs for a sport facility could include increased security costs and event concessions corresponding with increased attendance levels.

Typical Expense Categories

Although not an all-encompassing list of expense categories, these are typically the expenses involved in running a successful event (Supovitz, 2005): facilities (rent, capital replacement fees, facility usage fees, or ticket sales commissions); facility labor; player/game expenses; event operations; marketing and promotion; sponsor fulfillment; guest management and hospitality; event presentation (halftime shows, video feed, playbacks/highlights, lighting, etc.); capital investment and amortization; and contingency expenses. Depending on the nature of the event or facility the number of specific categories and subcategories for expenses can be quite extensive. Appendix 4.1 at the conclusion of the chapter provides an extensive sample of possible expense categories that could be encountered in sport facility or sport event applications.

Usually revenues and expenses are intertwined. Excess revenue over expenses can usually be used to cover other expenses of the organization—for example, programs that do not generate revenue and administrative expenses. Some different types of expenses the manager or board will need to anticipate during the budget year include a) direct costs related to a specific program or project; b) capital expenditures; and c) indirect or overhead costs such as postage, telephone, internet service, or copier usage.

Event Revenue

There are several ways in which an event can pay for their costs, termed *revenue streams*. One primary avenue for revenue is ticket sales. Many facilities keep a percentage of the total ticket sales as part of the contract for using the facility. In other cases, a special event may rent or lease a facility and those charges become another revenue source. Special events can also generate revenue to the sale of media rights to broadcast an event via television, radio, or streaming media.

© Lester Balajadia/Shutterstock.com

Fans awaiting ticket sales for an MLB game in Toronto. Ticket sales remain a strong revenue stream for sport facilities and events.

Another common revenue stream for both facilities and events comes from sponsorship and advertising. This depends on the available resources in the area of the event and if the goals of the event match with the goals of potential sponsors or advertisers. From grassroots handshake deals involving a few hundred dollars to the multimillion-dollar contracts negotiated with the Olympic Games and professional major league sports, the guiding principle is generally the same—"the event must deliver certain benefits for a sponsor: sales opportunities both on-site and at its regular retail locations, exposure at the event and in the media, and goodwill, among others" (Supovitz, 2005, p 65).

Some sponsors will offer goods or value in kind (VIK) instead of cash. If this is accepted, the cash value of the goods must be entered into the budget. Some events receive revenue from selling merchandise; however, this varies on the size and scope of the event. Some established events receive a large amount of revenue because of the recurring nature of the events. Annual mega events such as the Indianapolis 500, Super Bowl, and the Masters are practically guaranteed large amounts of revenue based on their firm establishment with fans and the annual reoccurrence that creates hype surrounding the event. However, smaller or newer events may not want to rely on revenue from merchandise. Most sporting events offer concessions and the revenue comes from the money left after paying for the expenses of concessions. Less typical sources of revenue include tournament fees, grants and donations, and other miscellaneous sources of revenue. These types of revenue are possible but are specialized ways of finding revenue based on the nature of the event.

Classification and Types of Budgets

The formation of a complete organizational budget, referred to as the master budget, combines all of the organizational activities into a complete plan. The following information illustrates the different types of budgets a facility manager must be familiar. The budgeting process is often predicated on information gleaned from prior budgets. However, a budget can also be created without specific information from a similar, preceding budget.

Master Budget

A master budget is not, as its name would imply, one single document. Rather, it is a compilation of various budgets that are interconnected and encapsulates an organization's business pursuits for the upcoming year. Responsible parties often refer to the master budget to guide the creation and implementation of their own department budgets. On a frequently repeated basis, area managers should compare master budget with their own budgets. To realize the greatest outcomes, budgets must be perfected to fit the specific business needs of the organization. The master budget integrates operational and financial budgets and is created with an iterative process during which information flows back and forth from each element of the master budget. The two primary components of the master budget are the operating budget and the financial budget.

Figure 4.1 Relationship of typical budget components in the master budget.

Adapted from Sandu (2011)

Operating Budget

The operating budget is an accumulation of the projected results of the operating decisions made by a company regarding the available business opportunities. The operating budget consists of budgets from such various departments or areas such as research and development, production, marketing, distribution, and customer service while providing the budgeted income statement (Sandu, 2011). The primary emphasis of an operating budget is to warrant that sufficient funds will be available to continue the operation of a business as well as to disseminate the funds in the most cost-efficient way.

A business operating budget will often include monthly line items for continuing expenses. These continuing expenses usually involve employee salaries and wages, health insurance, and other provided employee benefits. Additionally, the operating budget will analyze production costs as well as any essential expense that allows the organization to earn profits. In the final analysis, the operating budget provides a projected (pro forma) income statement which illustrates the positive revenue flow the organization expects for the upcoming year. This net income reveals the extent to which the organization is able to react to the market in supplying the right product at an appealing cost and provides a profit to the organization. As with any type of budget, an operating budget may be modified or revised on occasion. Such modifications or revisions may be the result of monthly revenue changes or estimated fluctuations in consumer demand.

Financial Budget

The financial budget includes the capital expenditure budget, the budgeted balance sheet, and the cash and cash flow budget. It identifies the future projections for cash and balance sheet item such as assets and liabilities. There are several benefits related to a well-thought out financial budget. The first benefit addresses the budgetary process of establishing short-term and long-term goals for the organization. Second, if the data used to produce the budget is accurate, the financial budget may function as a month-to-month operational blueprint for operations. Additionally, the document offers the manager the opportunity to contemplate the long-term benefits of staying within the budget. When this occurs, the financial budget becomes a powerful instrument for evaluating how well the organization meets its short-term and long-term financial goals.

Assuming that the budget is thoroughly thought out and is able to set parameters for each area of the operation, there generally is minimal demand to modify in budget line items. Under the best of circumstances, a financial budget offers a relatively secure roadmap to the future that permits an organization to satisfactorily focus on every operational aspect, rather than concentrating solely on financial matters. It is important to note that a financial budget will include a capital expenditure budget as well as a cash budget.

Budget Development Methods

Budgeting is a quantitative expression of a plan for a defined period of time and is an important component of financial success. It is an action plan; it helps a business allocate resources, evaluate performance, and formulate plans. Companies may use several types of managerial budgets concurrently. While there are different types of budgets, all budgets serve the same function for a business. The budgets differ in the way they categorize expenses, the amount of explanation provided for expenses, the timeline, and the starting point of the budgets. Some budgets will begin at zero with each new year, while others will begin with the data and funding level from the previous year as a starting point. The following seven types of budget development methods are commonly used by venue and event managers.

Line Item Budget

This is a budget where items are grouped into categories. These categories encompass specific items and objects, but don't fully consider their function relative to the overall organizational environment (Wooldridge et al., 2001). For example, in Appendix 4.1 the budget category of Sponsor Fulfillment Costs includes a number of items within it including agency commissions, sales expenses, banners and signage, complimentary tickets, hospitality, and sponsor gifts. Each of these categories and items is assigned a specific individual code, and planned costs and revenues are assigned in all areas. It is a fairly simple and commonly used method, and it is often based on the previous year's budget, only making edits to the budget based on changes or elevated costs in the listed departments, programs, or specific items. However, it is not specifically connected to organizational goals and objectives.

Performance Budget

This budget takes a closer look at the each item's full function and takes the object's performance into budgetary consideration (Wooldridge et al., 2001). The performance budget is often seen as an extension of the line item budget with an additional assessment step related to performance impact upon the organization.

Program Budget

This is a budget where items are grouped by program need. Each category is a program (e.g., swim program, basketball program), and items needed for that program are noted beneath that program of operation. The cost of each item is also listed so event planners can compare the costs of each program. Program budgeting is a broader form of budgeting that looks at big picture activities instead of specific objects to be purchased. Program budgeting defines what funds will be spent on and why it is imperative to spend them (Wooldridge et al., 2001). This would be used in an event that includes several programs or across large areas that require expenses.

Zero Based Budgeting (ZBB)

This type of budgeting is more complex than the previous methods mentioned. Financial planners using this type of budgeting to create a new budget from scratch, or "zero," each year. Each program develops a "decision package" that must include information of the program goals and objectives, how the program will be executed, costs of the program, output criteria, and alternate plans for reaching goals (Wooldridge et al., 2001). From this point, event planners rank the decision packages and programs based on their goals and financial allocations in the budget are made accordingly. As such this budgeting system requires specific justifications for each area of expense that would be considered in the "decision package."

Planning-Programming-Budgeting-Evaluation System (PPBES)

This type of budgeting focuses on the outcome of the programs. It includes planning of goals, programming how to reach those goals, budgeting for the costs of the program, and evaluating the outcomes of the program. By including evaluation to this type of budgeting, administrators can assess the individual programs within a larger organization and determine where to fully fund, partially fund, or not fund.

Capital Expenditure Budget

Capital budgeting is one of the most important decisions that face the financial managers (Ryan & Ryan, 2002). A capital expenditure budget represents the organizational plan for financing its operation and capital investment activities. The capital expenditure budget applies to the purchases of the physical plant (buildings), property, or equipment with a useful life of more than one year. It is often used to undertake new projects or investments by the organization. This type of outlay is also made by companies to maintain or increase the scope of their operations (Johnston, 2015). These expenditures can include everything from repairing a roof or purchasing a new major piece of equipment. The budget for these purchases must come from cash on hand to qualify as capital budget expenditures.

The escalation of capital expenditures can begin an escalation of the operational budget, primarily because these assets must be maintained. Conversely, the operational budget can reduce the capital budget. Should daily expenses grow to be cumbersome, the organization may end up paying bills in cash instead of setting it aside for capital expenditures. The rationale for maintaining low operational costs is to have some remaining income for the purchase of additional assets (Johnston, 2015).

Cash Budget

Cash, also referred to as liquidity, is the amount of assets that an organization has available to spend immediately. A cash budget calculates the budgeted cash inflows and outflows both during a specific period as well as the budgeted cash balance at the end of the period. By crafting a cash budget an organization generates a compilation of the projected revenues, operating expenditures, and the sale and purchase of assets.

A full replacement of strength and cardio equipment in a fitness center would be an example of a capital expense.

The cash budget assists managers in identifying if any excessive cash or cash shortage will be incurred during a specific time. A cash budget can help to avoid having a shortage of cash during periods of numerous expenses. However, it is significant to note that cash budgeting is a continuous process that must be verified for consistency and exactness by evaluating the actual budgeted sums with the expected amounts. Such knowledge helps the managers to budget accordingly.

Budget Preparation

It would be an enormous task to have one or two individuals to develop and implement an organizational budget. As such, it is strongly recommended that the annual facility budget be conducted by a budget committee. The task of the budget committee is to develop the budget for the next year (or future years, in the case of a multi-year budget). There are several ways in which to prepare a budget. Appenzeller and Lewis (2000), suggest the following ten steps in constructing a budget:

1. Examining the organization's present mission, objectives and goals in relationship to the previous year's budget,

2. Collecting the necessary information relative to the needs, strengths, and resources of the organization,

3. Soliciting input from others with expertise in the collection and evaluation of information needed,

4. Reviewing the data collected and analyzing it in terms of what was done previously, what is required presently, and what the future may hold immediately,

5. Preparing the budget document in accordance with the stipulations and requirements established by the organization, or governing body,

6. Checking to ensure the document is accurate, feasible and realistic,

7. Submitting a "rough draft" for critical analysis by an expert or colleague, prior to making the formal presentation to the board or administration,

8. Preparing prior to the presentation for anticipated outcomes,

9. Implementing the approved budget (once changes have been made as needed) with the knowledge that flexibility may be necessary as time progresses and events transpire, and

10. Auditing the budget following the conclusion of the budget year to assist the sport manager in gaining proficiency and competence as a fiscal manager (pp. 81–82).

Conclusion

When developing a new sport facility, it is important to have a strategic plan and budget in which to follow. Developers must first develop the goals of the project through various survey techniques. They may want to consider an environmental survey to assess the current customers of similar facilities, evaluate the current and similar services available, and assess any outside forces that may impact the success of the facility. Once these aspects are considered, planners can then develop a plan which they openly discuss with employees, community members, and government officials in order to gain support and make any changes which would increase the success of the facility. The final plan should be disseminated to the community.

An important aspect of strategic planning is budgeting. Once the goals/vision of the facility are in place, it is important to make a financial plan in order to cover the expenses of the facility and the events or program one plans to host in the facility. Several important aspects of budgeting are listed including expense documents, revenue streams, as well as different types of budgets. Planners must choose the methods that make the most sense for their needs and match the goals of their facility.

Research has indicated that a majority of organizations are satisfied with their planning and budgeting processes (Hagel, 2014). Budgeting and planning processes often are recognized as barriers to effective strategic employment. However, organizations need to employ both the strategic planning and budgeting processes to gain and or maintain a competitive advantage. Strategic planning, in particular in facility planning, must be aligned with the budgets to be truly value based. While appropriate consideration to the details of either of these processes will most likely result in the organization being a successful, miscalculations or lack of attention could result in potential failure.

KEY LEARNING POINTS

1. One must survey various aspects of the community before developing a strategic plan.

2. Once a strategic plan is developed, it must be disseminated to the community and adjusted to fit the input from these stakeholders.

3. Expenses and revenue streams must be determined, and a budget must be made in order to ensure the success of the plan.

CHAPTER DISCUSSION QUESTIONS

1. Assume that you are the manager of a sports medicine clinic with a budget of 1.3 million dollars and four organizational units that report to you. You are a consultative, democratic manager. Develop a process for the preparation of the budget based upon your management style.

2. Explain how a mission statement helps a company with its strategic planning.

3. Describe how a sport organization analyzes its internal environment.

4. Describe the external environment a sport organization may face and how it is analyzed.

5. Explain why some strategic planning strategies work for some companies, but not others.

6. Describe the different types of budgets, and what situation works best for each budget.

7. Select a specific sport event or facility and for that selection review Appendix 4.1 to determine applicable and non-applicable line-item budget categories.

MINI CASE STUDY

Under the direction of a newly hired facility manager, the Pippe Falls Area Multi-plex (PFAM), began a strategic planning process in September, 2017. This school and community facility includes outdoor fields for football, soccer, lacrosse, baseball and softball, and indoor facilities including a 50m competition pool, courts for basketball and volleyball, a fitness center for strength and cardio training and locker rooms. One reason strategic planning is important in an educational setting is to assist the organization in establishing and monitoring its goals. Without attainable goals in place, the organization does not know what it is supposed to do or how to achieve future successes. At a time when many school districts are facing budget cutbacks, many people were surprised when the Pippe Falls Area Multi-plex announced that it would be conducting a major strategic planning process. However, with a new superintendent, a fresh approach was needed to ensure that the PFAM was meeting the needs of the students, staff, and community members that it serves. The realization of the intricacies involved in the process seemed overwhelming to some and it was evident that a clear plan was needed to make the process a success. Now, two years into the planning process, the strategic planning process has stalled, and Pippe Falls Area Multi-plex is still in the midst of transition and uncertainty.

Use the following questions to recommend potential solutions:

1. What are some potential reasons for the Pippe Falls Area Multi-plex (PFAM) to complete a strategic planning initiative?

2. Determine a potential timeline and outcomes that the facility has for the strategic planning process.

3. Identify resources to assist the PFAM in completing the strategic planning process.

4. Provide suggested methods for coping with potential cultural change during strategic planning to ease employee resistance.

PRACTITIONER SPOTLIGHT

NAME: Dan Smith

ORGANIZATION: Troy Parks and Recreation, Troy, Alabama

CURRENT JOB TITLE: Director of Parks and Recreation

YEAR STARTED IN ROLE: I began working in Parks and Recreation in 1990 as the Adult Activities Coordinator.

EDUCATIONAL PREPARATION: Graduate of Troy State University in 1981 with a BS in Art with emphasis in graphic design and some studies in Journalism.

Photo courtesy of Dan Smith.

CAREER PATH:

- Entry level job

My first real job, one year after graduation, was as a newspaper photographer, which evolved into sports writing and sports photography, and I became the Sports Editor one year after joining The Troy Messenger newspaper. I was there from 1982 until 1990, and also served as Managing Editor of the newspaper as well as an Alabama contributor to USA Today Sports.

- Job path both inside and outside sport (as applicable) leading to this current role.

My eight years as a newspaper photographer, writer and sports editor placed me in daily workings and interactions with Troy State University athletics, local high school athletics, and also day-to-day news and events of Troy Parks and Recreation. My style of writing was always that of positive promotion and not considering negative angles. I say this because this strengthened my professional relationships and friendships with administrative personnel at all levels.

In 1990 I took a job with Troy State University as the Operations Coordinator, but only six months later I was approached by the Director of Parks and Recreation of the City of Troy about a new ballpark under construction, the Troy Sportsplex, and he wanted me to apply for that position. After much deliberation and consideration, I did apply for that job and was hired in April of 1990. I served as Adult Activities Coordinator from 1990 to 1995 and was appointed as Director in 1995.

WHAT IS THE MOST REWARDING ASPECT OF THIS JOB?

Without question, it is receiving positive feedback from customers regarding facilities, programs, special events, and the growth and direction of our department.

WHAT IS THE MOST CHALLENGING ASPECT OF THIS JOB?

Dealing with budgets, dealing with parents who do not have the fundamental recreation philosophies for all children at heart, and dealing with controversy created by parents and coaches, and dealing with customers in our Recreation Center that are involved in stealing, fighting and profanity among other things. Time management is also difficult during peak busy seasons.

WHAT IS A UNIQUE ASPECT OR TASK OF YOUR JOB THAT MANY WOULD BE SURPRISED TO HEAR ABOUT?

We believe in helping every department in the City of Troy with any request. Whether it be Police, Fire, Public Works, Library, City Hall, Travel and Tourism, whomever, it is our belief that we do not say no, but rather, the attitude that if they are asking for something it is because they need assistance, and sooner or later, we are asking help of them as well for support of our special events. The spirit of cooperation and teamwork must be there or there will be negative results eventually.

WHY IS FACILITY STRATEGIC PLANNING AND BUDGETING SO IMPORTANT TO A SUCCESSFUL FACILITY?

A parks and recreation organization should strive to maintain facilities to the highest of quality standards, but realistically the age and heavy public use of a major facility from year to year can present issues, repair needs and significant capital outlay challenges that can make keeping up with these demands difficult.

Facility maintenance improvements should be expected and written into the annual operating budget, but one must also prepare for the unexpected with a segment of the facility maintenance budget applied to unforeseen needs for replacement or repairs.

WHAT METHODS DO YOU USE TO STRATEGICALLY PLAN FOR THE FUTURE?

Charting the history of recurring budget needs for the upkeep of a facility are vital, going back as far as five years. This spreadsheet will show patterns and trends in revenue increases or decreases, and the same goes for expenses. However, one must also be aware of improvements to facilities that were not available a decade ago, especially with technology. Improvements to swimming pools such as variable frequency drives can save electricity over the course of a year, as well as automation to lighting, irrigation, air conditioning and heating.

Doing your research before your budget meetings to present a thorough case to your Mayor or appropriate decision makers will show you are prepared. You still may not get what you ask for, but if you have done your homework and can state your case for need, then you will know you gave it your best shot.

A budget should be looked upon, not as a suggestion, but respected as exact parameters for a department to provide the funding for the maintenance needs of a large facility. Record keeping by spreadsheet and software reports, for example, can show where the money is going year after year for repeat expenses, but in planning for the future, one must begin preparation months in advance. Providing the detailed documentation of repairs and maintenance history to your Mayor, City Council, Recreation Board or Department Head will strengthen your case in selling the point as to why you need a new air conditioning system for your gymnasium or renovation of an outdoor pool.

Photo courtesy of Dan Smith.

The Troy Recreation Center (left) and Sports-plex (right) in Troy, Alabama.

WHAT ARE THE TWO MOST IMPORTANT ITEMS YOU CONSIDER WHEN PLANNING AND BUDGETING FOR YOUR FACILITY?

Without question the most demanding needs are considered first. What cannot wait? What is needed immediately? There are always wants and needs. There are things we want and there are things we need. What does your facility need immediately?

The second is preparation. Don't wait until three days before a budget meeting to start pulling numbers together. If it is important to you to get the end results of capital outlay or major repairs, then make this a consistent responsibility of yours to always be monitoring where the money goes, and where you need it most for the future.

WHAT ADVICE WOULD YOU OFFER TO THOSE SEEKING A SIMILAR CAREER?

Without a doubt, a college graduate must be prepared to find a job straight out of college in any profession, in order to make a paycheck and pay bills, and that job is going to show your next employer that you are in the work force, a good employee, but looking for a career in your field of study.

Also be willing to relocate to any city, anywhere. Today while many employers are required by law to advertise for 10 days, that job announcement may only be online on that city's website for only one day, so bookmark those websites and check them daily.

It is also very important to have an impressive resume. Extracurricular activities, volunteer hours, service projects and part-time jobs while in college show a future employer that you are motivated, driven and responsible.

Once you are fortunate enough to be hired in a profession in which you are seeking as a career path, then be prepared and expect to start at the ground and work your way up. Do not expect your dream salary that first year, and maybe not even after 10 years. The greatest qualities in an employee are hard work, honesty, loyalty conscientiousness, and a positive attitude. You will make mistakes, but learning from those mistakes and accepting responsibility is important.

WHAT DO YOU BELIEVE ARE THE MOST IMPORTANT SKILLS TO DEVELOP?

The ability to multi-task, working on many projects in the same hour, day, and week is vital. One must be a good communicator. Let your bosses and fellow employees know what is on your work schedule, and do not be afraid to ask questions. It is often more impressive when someone asks questions than someone that appears uninterested in their job assignments. Public relations and customer service skills are also imperative. Become a list maker and work hard to be organized. When times are demanding, it is important to make a daily to-do list and prioritize those items that require action first. Also, return every phone call and email when possible. This is just common courtesy. Acquiring and strengthening personal qualities of character, dependability, organizational skills, honesty, integrity, and loyalty not only will make life more fulfilling, it will also create more positive relationships with your coworkers, bosses, mayor and City Council members.

WHAT PARTING WORDS OF WISDOM DO YOU HAVE FOR STUDENTS AND YOUNG PROFESSIONALS IN THE FIELD?

In the career of parks and recreation, do not expect to get rich, to work 40 hours a week, or to make everyone happy, but if you love your job, which is easy to do in this profession, you will find it to be very, very rewarding. There are many, many people that tell me they would never want to have my job, and there are just as many people that tell me we have the best job in the world. I agree with the latter. I do not want to be tied down to a desk eight hours a day, and in our job no two days are ever the same. Currently, for example, we are working on opening a new municipal lake, we are making additions to a playground, and have received a grant for an extension to our walking trail, in addition to our normal day-to-day activities and programs. Our customers in our recreation center come from every demographic and profession, and a great reward is getting to know these people.

Be a good listener, be a "doer" and not one that immediately says, "That can't be done."

Never, ever say, "That's not my job." In any profession, you will accomplish more by working WITH people than expecting others to work for you and/or to do their assignments while you carry less of the load.

Regardless of your dream job, you can and will get there, but you must commit yourself in school to give your best effort, do an internship if possible, and understand that there is more to preparing yourself for the real world other than making A's and B's. You must become mature and well-rounded, and that will come with experience and more experience.

Reprinted by permission of Dan Smith.

REFERENCES

Appenzeller, H., & Lewis, G. (2000). *Successful sport management.* Durham, NC: Carolina Academic Press.

Bora, B., & Chungyalpa, W. (2015) Towards conceptualizing business strategies. *International Journal of Multidisciplinary Approach and Studies, 2*(1), 73–83.

Cardinal, B. J., & Spaziani, M. D. (2002). ADA compliance and the accessibility of physical activity facilities in western Oregon. *American Journal of Health Promotion, 17,* 197–201.

Frei, F. X. (2008). The four things a service business must get right. *Harvard Business Review, 86*(4), 70–80.

Gage, A. (2012). Budget success means changing past practices. Retrieved from http://www.facilitiesnet.com/maintenanceoperations/article/Budget-Success-Means- Changing-Past-Practices--13621?source=previous

Gonzales, R., & Petersen, J. (2013). Sustainable design, construction and building operation. In T. H. Sawyer (Ed.), *Facility design and management for health, fitness, physical activity, recreation and sports* (13th ed.). (pp. 29–38). Champaign, IL: Sagamore.

Hagel, J. (2014). How to better connect planning, forecasting, and budgeting. *Journal of Accountancy, 217*(4), 20–21.

Hassan, D., & Trenberth, L. (2012). *Managing Sport Business: An Introduction.* New York, NY: Routledge.

Hodges, C. (2005). A facility manager's approach to sustainability. *Journal of Facilities Management, 3*(4), 312–324.

Humpel, N., Owen, N., & Leslie, E. (2002). Environmental factors associated with adults' participation in physical activity: A review. *American Journal of Preventive Medicine, 22,* 188–199.

Huq, Z., & Stolen, J. D. (1990). Total quality management contrasts in manufacturing and service industries. *International Journal of Quality & Reliability Management, 15*(2), 138–161.

Ivanova, A., & Rachev, B. (2004). *Multidimensional models—Constructing data cube.* Paper presentation at the International Conference on Computer Systems and Technologies. Rousse, Bulgaria.

Johnston, K. (2015). Differences and similarities of capital and operational budgeting. *Chron.com.* Retrieved from http://smallbusiness.chron.com/differences-similarities- capital-operational-budgeting-33149.html

Kats, G. (2003). *The costs and financial benefits of green buildings.* Report to California's Sustainable Building Task Force, Retrieved from http://www.usgbc.org/Docs/Archive/General/Docs1992.pdf

Lam, E. (2014). The roles of governance in sports organization. *Journal of Power, Politics & Governance, 2*(2), 19–31.

Mintzberg, H. (1994). *Rise and fall of strategic planning.* New York, NY: Simon and Schuster.

Mintzberg, H., Ahlstrand, B., & Lampel, J. (2009). *Strategy safari* (2nd ed.).New York, NY: Prentice Hall.

Malone, T. W., Crowston, K., Lee, J., Pentland, B., Dellarocas, C., Wyner, G., ... & Klein, M. (1999). Tools for inventing organizations: Toward a handbook of organizational processes. *Management Science, 45*(3), 425–443.

Mobasheri, F., Orren, L. H., & Sioshansi, F. P. (1989). Scenario planning at southern California Edison. *Interfaces, 19*(5), 31–44.

Mowday, R. T., Porter, L. W., & Steers, R. M. (2013). *Employee—organization linkages: The psychology of commitment, absenteeism, and turnover.* New York: Academic Press.

Mulvey, J. M. (1996). Generating scenarios for the Towers Perrin investment system. *Interfaces, 26*(2), 1–15.

Muther, R. (1973). Systematic layout planning (2nd ed.). Boston, MA: Cahners Books.

Owen, S. H., & Daskin, M. S. (1998). Strategic facility location: A review. *European Journal of Operational Research, 111*(3), 423–447.

Petersen, J. C., & Piletic, C. K. (2006). Facility accessibility: Opening the doors to all. *Journal of Physical Education, Recreation & Dance, 77*(5), 38–44.

Pichot, L., Tribou, G., & O'Reilly, N. (2008). Sports sponsorship, internal communications, and human resource management: An exploratory assessment of potential future research. *International Journal of Sport Communication, 1*, 413–423.

Reklitis, P., Konstantopoulos, N., & Trivellas, P. (2007). Organizational strategy and business environment effects based on a computation method. *American Institute of Physics, 2*, 1094–1097.

Rimmer, J. H., Riley, B. B., Wang, E., & Rauworth, A. E. (2005). Accessibility of health clubs for people with mobility and visual disabilities. *American Journal of Public Health, 95*, 2022–2028.

Rimmer, J. H., Riley, B. B, Wang, E., & Rauworth, A. (2004). Development and validation of AIM-FREE: Accessibility Instruments Measuring Fitness and Recreation Environments. *Disability Rehabilitation, 26*, 1087–1095.

Roper, K. O., Kim, J. H, & Lee, S. H. (2009). *Strategic facility planning: A white paper.* Houston, TX: International Facility Management Association.

Ryan, P. A., & Ryan, G. P. (2002). Capital budgeting practices of the Fortune 1000: How have things changed. *Journal of Business and Management, 8*(4), 355–364.

Sandu, D. I. (2009). Multidimensional model for the master budget. *Journal of Applied Quantitative Methods, 4*(4), 408–421.

Sotoducho-Pelc, L. (2013). Methods for communicating strategy in companies. *International Journal of Contemporary Management, 12*(4), 45–60.

Supovitz, F. (2005). *The sports events management and marketing playbook.* Hoboken, NJ: John Wiley & Sons, Inc.

Thompson, A. A., & Strickland, A. J. (2001). *Strategic management* (12th ed.). New York, NY: McGraw Hill/Irwin.

Waite, P. S. (2005). *The Non-Architect's Guide to Major Capital Projects: Planning, Designing and Delivering New Buildings.* Ann Arbor, MI: Society for College and University.

Whole Building Design Guide. (2015). Building for environmental and economic sustainability (BEES). *Wbdg.com.* Retrieved from http://www.wbdg.org/tools/bees.php

Winer, L. (1993). *The strategic creative analysis (SCAN) process.* New York: Center for Applied Research. Lubin School of Business, Pace University.

Wooldridge, S., Garvin, M., & Miller, J. (2001). Effects of accounting and budgeting on capital allocation for infrastructure projects. *Journal of Management in Engineering. 17*(2), 86–94.

Woon, K. C. (2000). TQM implementation: Comparing Singapore's service and manufacturing leaders. *Managing Service Quality, 10*(5), 318–331.

Appendix 4.1 Event Expense Budget Worksheet (adapted from Supovitz, 2005)

Acct. No	Expenses	Budget	Forecast	Actual	Variance	Comment
1000	*Player Cost*					
1001	*Player Appearance Fees*					
1002	*Player Prize Money*					
1003	*Player Gifts*					
1004	*Player Travel, Air*					
1005	*Player Travel Ground Trans*					
1006	*Player Travel, Hotel*					
1007	*Player per Diem*					
1008	*Player Scheduled Meals*					
1009	*Player Guest Expenses*					
1010	*Uniforms and Equipment*					
1011	*Insurance*					
1012	*Officials*					
1013	*Officials, Travel Expenses*					
1014	*Trainers*					
1015	*Trainer Expenses*					
1016	*Medical Staff*					
1017	*Ambulance*					
1018	*Player/Athlete Transportation/Parking*					
1050	*Ticketing Expenses*					
1051	*Capital Replacement Fees*					
1052	*Sales and Amusement Tax*					
1053	*Box Office/Ticket Processing Labor*					
1054	*Remote Ticket Fees*					
1055	*Credit Card Commissions*					
1056	*Ticket Printing*					
1057	*Group Sales Commissions*					
1058	*Mailings, Creative*					
1059	*Mailings, Printing*					
1060	*Mailings, Postage*					
1100	*Facility Expenses*					
1101	*Facility Rental*					

1102	Facility Labor					
1103	Carpenters					
1104	Electricians					
1105	Laborers					
1106	Riggers					
1107	Cleaners					
1108	Field/Ice Mountain Crew					
1109	Ushers					
1110	Ticket Takers					
1111	Security					
1112	House Supervisors					
1113	Medical/First Aid					
1114	Scoreboards					
1115	Video and Matrix Crew					
1116	Stagehands					
1117	Spotlights					
1118	Changeover Crew					
1119	Miscellaneous Facility Labor					
1120	Bleachers/Additional Seating					
1121	Playing Surface Prep Expenses					
1123	Rope and Stanchion					
1124	Barricades					
1125	Fencing					
1130	Utility Costs					
1131	Generators					
1132	Power Distribution					
1133	Water					
1134	Waste Receptacles and Dumpsters					
1135	Portable Toilet Facilities					
1140	Arena Décor and Signage					
1141	Tenting					
1142	Flooring and Carpeting					
1143	Pipe and Drape					
1200	**Guest Services**					
1201	Invitation Design and Printing					

1202	Invitation Postage					
1203	Guest Management Expenses					
1204	Guest Transportation					
1205	Guest Gifts					
1206	Guest Hospitality					
1207	Complimentary Tickets					
1208	Information Guides					
1209	Directional Signage and Info Desks					
1210	Hotel Lobby Décor					
1211	Hotel Staff Gratuities					
1212	Hotel Attrition Contingency					
1300	**Event Operations**					
1301	Temporary Staff and Interns					
1302	Volunteer Staff Expenses					
1303	Staff Travel Expenses					
1304	Staff Meals or Per Diem					
1305	Staff Wardrobe/Uniforms					
1306	Site Surveys/Planning Trips					
1307	Pre-Event Planning and Tie-Down Mtgs.					
1308	Event Location Office Rent					
1309	Event Location Office Furnishings					
1310	Computer and Printer Rental					
1311	Copiers and Fax Machines					
1312	Televisions and VCRs					
1313	Phone Lines					
1314	T-1 Lines					
1315	Phone Equipment					
1316	Phone Service and LD Charges					
1317	Event Location Office Supplies					
1318	Radios					
1319	Cellular Phone Rental and Service					

1320	Accreditation					
1321	Postage and Overnight Services					
1322	Storage					
1323	Shipping and Trucking					
1324	Liability Insurance					
1325	Event Cancellation Insurance					
1326	Legal Services					
1330	Police					
1331	Sanitation					
1332	Fire					
1333	Other City Services					
1334	Permits					
1335	Miscellaneous Op. Costs					
1500	**Marketing/Promotion**					
1501	Logo Development					
1502	Advertising Agency and Creative					
1503	Advertising Agency Expenses					
1504	Advertising, Print					
1505	Advertising, Radio					
1506	Advertising, Outdoor					
1507	Poster and Handbills					
1508	Public Relation Agency					
1509	Public Relations Agency Expenses					
1510	Telephone Information/ 800 Service					
1511	Street Banners, Design and Printing					
1512	Street Banners, Installation					
1513	Airport Greeting Signage					
1514	Promotional Items (caps, pins, t-shirts)					
1515	Miscellaneous Marketing					
1600	**Media Expenses**					
1601	Press Conferences					

1602	Media Pre-/Postgame Meals					
1603	Media Center F&B					
1604	Media Tabletops, Phones, etc.					
1605	Photocopier/Fax					
1606	Media Office Expenses					
1607	Media Guide					
1608	Photography					
1609	Media, Miscellaneous					
1610	Media Gift					
1700	**Sponsor Fulfillment Costs**					
1701	Agency Commissions					
1702	Sales Expenses					
1703	Banners and Signage					
1704	Complimentary Tickets					
1705	Hospitality					
1706	Sponsor Gifts					
1707	Other Fulfillment Expenses					
1800	**Broadcasting**					
1801	Broadcast Expenses					
1802	Airtime Purchase					
2000	**Production Costs**					
2001	Stage Risers and Platforms					
2002	Set Design					
2003	Set Construction/Rentals					
2004	Set Refurbishment					
2005	Lighting					
2006	Audio					
2007	Props and Flags					
2008	Draping					
2009	ClearCom					
2010	Video Production					
2011	Video Projection					
2012	Production Management Fees					
2013	Production Management Expenses					
2014	Production Labor, Installation					

2015	*Production Labor, Rehearsal and Event*					
2016	*Production Labor, Dismantle*					
2020	*Equipment Rental*					
2025	*Talent Fees*					
2026	*Talent Expenses*					
2030	*Costumes and Wardrobe*					
2031	*Floral*					
3000	**Associated Events and Programs**					
3001	*School/Educational Outreach*					
3100	*Welcome Party*					
3200	*Closing Party*					
3300	*VIP Hospitality*					
3400	*Spouse Program*					
4000	**Other Expenses and Adjustments**					
4100	*Amortization of Prior Year Assets*					
4200	*Deferral of Capital Assets—5yr*					
4300	*Deferral of Capital Assets—3yr*					
4400	*Contingency*					
	Total Expenses					

5 Managing Human Capital

Deanna Kolar and *Lawrence W. Judge*

OBJECTIVES

In this chapter students will look at the fundamental functions of human resource management. Students will examine human resources in the context of facility and event management as a relationship between personnel management and an organizations' emerging role of internal administration and strategic policy development.

After studying this chapter, the student should be able to:

- Identify and discuss the key elements and main tasks associated with human resource management.
- Explain the relationship of key HR elements to people in the facility.
- Consider and explain how the law, societal expectations, and the desires/needs of individual employees impact the management of human resources.
- Explain the importance of the cultural context for managing people.

KEY TERMS

Compensation	Employee Development	Recruitment
Employee Benefits	Performance Management	Selection

KEY ACRONYMS

ACA	Affordable Care Act	**FMLA**	Family and Medical Leave Act
ADA	Americans with Disabilities Act	**FUTA**	Federal Unemployment Tax Act
BFOQ	bonafide occupational qualification	**HRM**	Human Resource Management
EAP	employee action plan	**KSAs**	knowledge, skills and abilities
EEOC	Equal Employment Opportunity Commission	**OSHA**	Occupational Safety and Health Administration
FLSA	Fair Labor Standards Act		

Introduction

Human capital describes the knowledge, skills, and capabilities of individuals that have economic value to an organization (Snell, Morris, & Bohlander, 2016). The process of human resource management (HRM) identifies and cultivates the human capital in order to facilitate the organization's planned objectives. This involves a variety of activities including acquiring, training, appraising, and compensating employees as well as attending to labor relations and health, safety, and fairness concerns (Dessler, 2013). The human resource function serves as a vital link between an organization's management and its employees.

Human resource management is a key component of facility and event management. A facility that is well maintained and managed is one of the best tools in an organization's arsenal. An organization's facility and event manager must become involved in many tasks including leadership, facility/event admission access control, property and event security, emergency operations, facility maintenance, and operational policies and procedures (Sawyer & Judge, 2012). These functions cannot be effectively accomplished without a solid human resource management system in place.

This chapter will consider the management of human capital within a facility management context. Four sections will be utilized to provide an overview of the HRM process: the staffing process, employee performance and development, employee well-being, and compensation and benefits. Throughout this chapter, the legal perspective and standards from the United States will be utilized, but the practitioner and student should be aware that various laws at the state level can also impact human resource practices, policies, and procedures adopted at the organizational level.

I. The Staffing Process—Job Analysis, Recruitment, and Selection

Human resource strategy should integrate with the organization's overall strategic plan. Forward thinking managers recognize the strategic potential of their human capital. An organization should analyze its competitive environment and then acquire and retain key people so a firm's strategy can be successfully implemented to beat the competition.

With those objectives in place, an organization should be continually adding value through its staffing process. The three primary phases of organizational staffing are: 1) identifying and clarifying the staffing need, 2) attracting the right applicants, and 3) selecting the best candidate. Before beginning the hiring process, it is critical to be aware of the legal regulations that govern this aspect of human resource management.

Legal Regulations

Anyone involved with the staffing function in an organization should be aware of the applicable state and federal regulations. Labor laws are enacted to protect the rights, health, and financial remuneration of workers. In the United States, both potential and existing employees receive protections based on the regulatory framework in place. The following section provides an overview of the major Federal employment laws. Within every jurisdiction, managers should also be mindful of state and local laws that may provide additional protections within the employment environment.

Civil Rights Act of 1964—Title VII

The Civil Rights Act of 1964, commonly referred to as "Title VII," grants significant protection from discriminatory practices in the workplace. Title VII has also served as a vehicle to promote fairness and equality in the workplace. Specifically, Title VII makes it illegal for an employer

> 1) to fail or refuse to hire or to discharge any individual, or otherwise to discriminate against any individual with respect to compensation, terms, conditions, or privileges of employment, because of such individual's race, color, religion, sex or national origin; or 2) to limit, segregate, or classify employees or applicants for employment in any way which would deprive or tend to deprive any individual of employment opportunities or otherwise adversely affect status as an employee, because of such individual's race, color, religion, sex or national origin. (Civil Rights Act of 1964)

The Act applies to organizations with 15 or more employees working 20 or more weeks a year that are involved in interstate commerce, as well as state and local governments, employment agencies and labor organizations (Civil Rights Act of 1964). Generally, Federal regulation supersedes state and local labor laws. However, when federal and state laws conflict, the U.S. Department of Labor instructs employers and employees to follow the law that provides the highest level of protection to employees and the strictest standard for employers.

Title VII language also helps to interpret types of discrimination as well as to delineate possible defenses available to employers when faced with discrimination claims. Title VII identified three types of discrimination: disparate treatment, disparate impact, and pattern or practice discrimination.

Sexual Harassment

In the federal context, sexual harassment is considered to be a form of sex discrimination under Title VII of the Civil Rights Act of 1964. According to the Equal Employment Opportunity Commission (EEOC) unwelcome sexual advances, requests for sexual favors, and other verbal or physical conduct of a sexual nature constitutes sexual harassment when submission to or rejection of this conduct explicitly or implicitly affects an individual's employment, unreasonably interferes with an individual's work performance or creates an intimidating, hostile or offensive work environment.

Harassment does not have to be of a sexual nature, however, and can include offensive remarks about a person's sex. For example, it is illegal to harass a woman by making offensive comments about women in general. Both victim and the harasser can be either a woman or a man, and the victim and harasser can be the same sex. The harasser can be the victim's supervisor, a supervisor in another area, a co-worker, or someone who is not an employee of the employer, such as a client or customer.

There are two different general forms of sexual harassment claims. The first would be *quid pro quo* and the second would involve the creation of a hostile work environment. *Quid pro quo* sexual harassment occurs when a supervisor or one in an authority position requests sex, or a sexual relationship, in exchange for not firing or otherwise punishing the employee, or in exchange for favors, such as promotions or raises. A hostile work environment sexual harassment claim can be filed when a work environment is demeaning or when sexual photographs, jokes, comments, or threats have taken place. The inappropriate behavior or conduct must be so pervasive as to, as the name implies, create an intimidating and offensive work environment.

Although the law doesn't completely prohibit jokes, offhand comments, or isolated incidents that are not viewed as very serious, harassment is illegal when its frequency or severity creates a hostile or offensive work environment or when it results in an adverse employment decision (such as the victim being fired or demoted).

Types of Discrimination

Disparate treatment (also sometimes called adverse treatment) occurs when individuals who are similarly situated are intentionally treated differently, and that treatment is based on an individual's membership in a protected class. A person's legally protected class status can include race, color, religion, nationality, sex, disability, etc. The key distinguishing feature of disparate treatment is the intentional nature of the behavior. Examples of practices that may be subject to a disparate impact challenge include written tests, height and weight requirements, educational requirements, and subjective procedures, such as interviews. For example, The EEOC (Equal Employment Opportunity Commission) filed a lawsuit against Bass Pro Outdoor World in 2011. The EEOC accused Bass Pro of racially discriminatory hiring practices since at least 2005. The suit claimed that qualified African-American and Hispanics were denied jobs nationwide based on their race. The EEOC alleged that Bass Pro managers, specifically those in the Texas and Louisiana areas, had made racially derogatory comments insinuating that the hiring of

African-Americans and Hispanics "did not fit the corporate profile" (EEOC, 2015). Because the prospective employees were repeatedly denied jobs based on their race, the treatment is considered intentional, classifying it as disparate treatment, rather than disparate impact.

In another case highlighting disparate treatment, an African-American woman was passed up for a job after she appeared for an interview with her hair in ethnic braids. After an initial interview, the woman in question was given word that the company, Alliant Techsystem, wanted to hire her. The HR department contacted her for a finalizing interview, which she attended wearing her hair in ethnic braids. The next day, her offer was promptly revoked, and Alliant's HR informed her that they were no longer interested in hiring her. Several months later, Aliant hired a white male to fill the position. Once again, the nature of the treatment was proved intentional (EEOC, 2015).

Disparate impact (also sometimes called adverse impact) occurs when a facially neutral employment practice disproportionately excludes the members of a protected group. Although it is generally considered to be unintentional, the lack of intent does not diminish the discriminatory nature of the conduct (Lussier & Hendon, 2016). Disparate impact claims commonly relate to failure to hire and failure to promote allegations. In these claims, the employer's policy for hiring or promoting puts a protected class at a disadvantage. Other examples of disparate impact claims may relate to pay increases, pregnancy, transfers, training programs, leadership programs, and firing policies. *Ricci v. DeStefano* (2009) is an example of a disparate impact case dealing with race. In *Ricci v. DeStefano* the focus was on the possible effects felt by African-American employees due to an employer's written promotion exams (Wu, 2012). In this case, the lawsuit is classified under disparate impact because the alleged treatment is not intentional. Cases can also be centered on gender-based disparate impact. The only gender-based disparate impact case to be judged by the Supreme Court is *Dothard v. Rawlinson* (1977). In this suit, a woman was denied a job as a correctional counselor because she did not meet a 120-pound weight requirement. During the suit, the plaintiff provided evidence showing that the 120-pound weight limit prohibited over 40% of females from applying for the job, while only 1% of males would be excluded based on the weight requirement. In *Dothard v. Rawlinson*, the claim was classified as disparate impact rather than treatment because of the unintentional nature. The woman was not intentionally discriminated against because of her gender; however, requirements for the job gave an unfair advantage to male applicants.

Other example are timed mile runs and wall climbs. These types of tests or assessments can be part of employer testing and hiring processes. These types of tests can keep women from entering a field dominated by males, as they are physiologically disadvantaged to compete with their male counterparts. Cases such as these are difficult to judge and are often taken on a case-by-case basis, depending on the employer and job. There is no doubt that the nature of these tests is having a disparate impact on women; the question is how necessary these tests are to their corresponding job, and whether they are being used by employers for disparate treatment.

Pattern-or-Practice discrimination refers to behavior occurring over a significant period of time, which is intended to deny the rights outlined in Title VII. In general, individuals do not bring pattern-or-practice discrimination lawsuits against an organization. Instead, a class of plaintiffs will be involved and the attorney general files the lawsuit. For example, many private golf clubs in Ireland, the United Kingdom, and the United States provide membership to men only. In 2009 Ireland's Supreme Court ruled that the Portmarnock Golf Club could continue to uphold its male-only membership rule, without violating anti-discriminatory laws. Male-only golf clubs have been around for generations. Thus this gender discriminatory pattern has been firmly established. The Portmarnock's gender policy was able to bypass the anti-discriminatory laws by adhering to the Equal Status Act, "which allows exclusion of certain members only if the club promotes activity tailored for a specific group" (Song, 2007, p. 181). Ireland's Supreme Court reasoned that although women were not allowed to become members of the men-only golf clubs, this pattern of discrimination was legal because the Portmarnock Golf Club was operating to fill the needs of men exclusively. This specific example was able to evade the pattern-or practice discrimination verdict, as gender discrimination by male-only golf clubs in Ireland, the United Kingdom, and the United States stem from a multi-generational precedent.

Employer Defenses to Discrimination Claims

Title VII also describes several ways an organization can defend its actions when facing a discrimination claim: bona fide occupational qualification (BFOQ), business necessity, and job relatedness.

Bona fide occupational qualifications generally only apply to occupations where the BFOQ is considered necessary to do a particular job. The qualification cannot merely be a preferred quality; it must be one that is inherently necessary for the job to be performed. An example of a bona fide occupational qualification includes mandatory retirement ages for bus drivers and airline pilots, for safety reasons. Advertising and acting roles may lawfully advertise for models of a specific gender. In 1991, *EEOC v. Sedita* was a loss for corporations and sports facilities looking to justify their hiring with BFOQs. A health club was forced to argue in court that their policy of hiring only females for manager, assistant manager, and instructor positions was a BFOQ due to their clientele. Because the health club was for female patrons only, the club owners argued that having staff members who were females as well was a BFOQ (Miller, 1997). The health club lost the lawsuit after the court sided with the plaintiff, finding the female only staff to be a preference, instead of a BFOQ.

Fitness testing such as a timed run or another physical task in some instances can be used to assess a BFOQ.

A business necessity is a legitimate business purpose that justifies an employment decision as effective and needed to optimally achieve the organization's goals and ensure that operations run safely and efficiently (Cascio & Aguinis, 2010). The premise behind job-relatedness is that even though the requirement may cause a disparate impact, it is essential to performing the job in question. If the knowledge, skills, and abilities needed to perform the job's essential task and duties have not been identified, the employer has no way of linking the listed requirements to actual job performance (Robinson & Franklin, 2015). Sports facility management needs to make sure they are up to date and aware of all hiring policies to minimize lawsuits against the facility. Any sort of discriminatory hiring can affect the public's view of the facility and team.

Pregnancy Discrimination Act of 1978

The Pregnancy Discrimination Act of 1978 is a United States Federal statute that amended Title VII of the Civil Rights Act of 1964 to "prohibit sex discrimination on the basis of pregnancy" (42 U.S.C. § 2000(e) et seq.). The act covers discrimination "on the basis of pregnancy, childbirth, or related medical conditions." This law is applicable to all employers with 15 or more employees. Pregnancy discrimination involves treating female job applicants or employees unfavorably because of pregnancy, childbirth, or a medical condition related to pregnancy or childbirth.

Age Discrimination in Employment Act of 1967

The Age Discrimination in Employment Act of 1967 (ADEA) protects individuals who are 40 years of age or older from employment discrimination based on age. The ADEA's protections apply to both employees and job applicants. Under the ADEA, it is unlawful to discriminate against a person because of his/her age with respect to any term, condition or privilege of employment, including hiring, firing, promotion, layoff, compensation, benefits, job assignments, and training.

It is also unlawful to retaliate against an individual for opposing employment practices that discriminate based on age or for filing an age discrimination charge, testifying or participating in any way in an investigation, proceeding or litigation under the ADEA. The ADEA applies to employers with 20 or more employees, including state and local governments. It also applies to employment agencies and labor organizations, as well as to the federal government.

Americans with Disabilities Act of 1990

The Americans with Disabilities Act (ADA) prohibits discrimination on the basis of disability in employment, state and local government, public accommodations, commercial facilities, transportation, and telecommunications. A person is considered disabled if he or she either actually has, or is thought to have, a physical or mental impairment that substantially limits one or more "major life activities." The ADA requires employers with 15 or more employees to provide qualified individuals with disabilities an equal opportunity to benefit from the full range of employment-related opportunities available to others. Title I of this law prohibits discrimination in recruitment, hiring, promotions, training, pay, social activities, and other privileges of employment. It restricts questions that can be asked about an applicant's disability before a job offer is made, and it requires that employers make reasonable accommodation to the known physical or mental limitations of otherwise qualified individuals with disabilities, unless it results in undue hardship.

Under the ADA, employees are protected from disability discrimination in the workplace. However, employers don't have to hire an employee who can't do the job, regardless of whether or not the employee has a disability. Essential job functions are used to determine which employees are protected by the ADA and which are not.

An employee who is otherwise qualified (for example, because the employee has the degrees, license, and experience required for the position) is protected from disability discrimination if he or she can perform the essential job functions. As long as the employee can perform the essential functions of the job, with or without reasonable accommodation, the employee is protected from discrimination by the ADA.

Providing reasonable accommodations for employees with disabilities is a primary provision of the ADA.

This is why the labeling of job functions as "essential" or "nonessential" is so important. As the name suggests, essential job functions are the fundamental, not marginal, duties of a job. If a function is truly essential, and an applicant or employee cannot perform it even with a reasonable accommodation, then that person is not qualified for the job as a legal matter. If a function is not truly essential, the employer cannot exclude a person with a disability from consideration just because that person is unable to perform the function.

Job Analysis

A staffing plan is a system that works to monitor and control the costs of human capital while creating an infrastructure to support effective decision-making in an organization. An analysis of the relevant workload and outcome measures can aid organizations in assessing current and future staffing needs.

Before hiring parameters can be set, an organization needs to be conscious of its current worker population and the tasks performed by each employee. The overarching goal of job analysis is to gain insight into an organization's personnel demands and to determine the right person to fill that staffing need. It is important to note that job analysis underpins the majority of the other human resource functions (e.g., HR planning, staffing, training, performance management, safety and health, compensation and legal compliance).

Job analysis is the comprehensive process of assessing worker roles and aids in the creation of job description and person specification. Managers consider knowledge, skills and abilities (KSAs) to distinguish the "qualified candidates" from the "unqualified candidates." Individual KSAs are demonstrated through qualifying experience, education, or training.

Knowledge is a person's comprehension of an organized body of information, usually factual or procedural in nature. *Skill* is indicated by a person's proficiency at mental, manual, or verbal manipulation of data or things. A person's *ability* is the actual power or capacity to perform an activity or task.

Job Descriptions

Job analysis produces information used for writing job descriptions which, at the most basic level, explains what the job entails. A job description should also provide the organization with a description of how a particular position fits into the overall structure of the organization. A job description reveals the job's goals, responsibilities, and duties. These are key determinant factors in preparing job (person) specifications (i.e., the level of experience, education, skill, required for the job).

A job description should include a job title, outline to whom that person will report, describe the position's major and minor duties and lastly, define how the job relates to other positions in the company. Which positions are subordinate and which are of equal responsibility and authority are questions that should be addressed. Well-researched and carefully crafted job descriptions not only provide guidance in the staffing process, but they continue to provide clarity for employees and their managers once a candidate has been selected for a position.

A job (person) specification outlines what kind of person to hire for the job. The job specification describes the personal requirements expected from the employee. This might include educational requirements, desired experience, and specialized skills or knowledge required. The job specification will also lay out salary range and benefits. Lastly, a job (person) specification will list any physical or other special requirements associated with the job, as well as any occupational hazards.

Attracting Potential Applicants

Before a position can be filled, a facility must first search for and obtain candidates to interview for possible hire. Before the interviewing and hiring process can begin, the facility must be sure that the number and quality of potential candidates are sufficient to ensure an appropriate hire. Based on the job and person specification, the organization needs to consider how expansive the job search needs to be to find the right candidate. Informal personal contacts, formal personal contacts (career fairs, open days, leaflet drops, notice boards), advertising (newspapers, specialty publications, Internet), and external assistance (job centers, career services, employment agencies) are examples of methods to find the right candidates for a specific job. In the sporting world, many new job searches are started by word of mouth *recruitment*. Current employees of the sporting organization bring the news to fellow colleagues within the trade. This word-of-mouth technique has caused some to criticize the "political hiring in sport" (Covell & Walker, 2013, p. 315). These same critics point to the pattern of "'old-boy' network...in sports that dictates the hiring of friends, associates and/or colleagues" (Covell & Walker, 2013, p. 315). Whether it is wrong or simply part of the process to finding a good candidate, word of mouth is heavily used to attract potential candidates in the sporting world. Another method is to utilize media dedicated specifically to the sports industry. Sporting magazines and websites can provide a valuable platform in order to attract worthy employees.

Recruitment the process by which an organization enlists new workers and members.

Selecting an Appropriate Candidate

Once an acceptable pool of candidates has been achieved through recruiting efforts, hiring managers begin the task of predicting which candidates will provide the best contribution to the organization. Based on the essential and desired qualities for the position, the applicants need to be sorted. Those lacking the essential characteristics will be eliminated from the process. From those candidates who meet the basic qualifications, employers then go about the process of determining which candidate best fits the job description and can help meet the overall goals of the organization.

Selection the process of choosing someone (or something) deemed to be the most acceptable candidate.

Within the *selection* process, employers must exercise due diligence to verify the background of the potential employees. Creating a procedure to check applicant experience can help avoid hiring employees who are a poor fit for the job or detrimental to the organization. Once employee backgrounds are verified for experience, it may also be beneficial to complete a criminal background check. Some organizations may complete such a check at the screening stage while others may complete a criminal background check just prior to hiring. With the completion of background checks, the organization can then begin the interview process. Time and expense both play critical roles in deciding how the interviewing process should progress. Some organizations will opt for a phone or Internet-based contact as the mode for initial contacts. This allows for additional filtering of applicants before in-person meetings are sought.

Interviews—Style and Content

During the selection process, hiring managers have several interviewing options for extracting the relevant information about potential employees. Using a structured interview approach, interviewers ask all candidates the same list of prepared questions. This form of questioning is generally regarded as containing the least amount of interviewer bias. This style also eliminates the opportunity for follow up questions based on applicant responses. Many interviews are conducted using a semi-structured approach that begins with a list of planned questions but also permits for unplanned questions to follow up on areas of interest.

An unstructured interview begins with no pre-planned questions or even general sequence of topics. While this approach allows for the most interviewer latitude to gather information about the candidate, it is also the most susceptible to discrimination claims because of the greater potential for interviewer bias.

The interview is still an integral part of the employee selection process.

Illegal inquiries

As addressed earlier in the chapter, job applicants enjoy legal protection from discrimination. Because employers are not allowed to discriminate when hiring, certain questions may not be asked by the interviewer during the recruitment and selection process. A summary of subject matter and the types of questions that are generally problematic is provided in Table 5.1.

Once candidate interviews are complete, the hiring committee should discuss individual perceptions of the interviews, compare candidates' qualifications, assess person-organization fit via coworkers' impressions, and consider diversity. Once an agreement is reached, the best candidate should be offered the position. If the candidate refuses, or accepts but soon leaves, offer the job to the next-best candidate.

Worker Classifications

When staffing a sports facility, a manager may interact with individuals who possess different working relationships with the organization. In particular, the status of "employee" carries with it statutory requirements regarding pay, benefits, and working time. Independent contractors, interns, and volunteers do not benefit from those protections. It is critical that an employer appreciates the distinctions of the different classifications of the people performing work at the facility.

The Fair Labor Standards Act (FLSA) defines "employ" as including to "suffer or permit to work" which focuses on work that the employer directs or allows to take place. A key differentiator is economic dependence. Applying the FLSA's definition, workers who are economically dependent on the business of the employer, regardless of skill level, are considered to be employees, and most workers are employees (U.S. Department of Labor, 2014). Most employees in the United States are "employees at will." Those considered to be employed "at will" are able to be discharged by the employer for good cause, bad cause, or no cause at all, while at the same time these "at will"

Table 5.1 *Summary of Permissible and Impermissible Questions in the Job Selection Process*

Subject Area	Permissible Questions	Potentially Illegal Questions
Name	May ask current legal name as well as whether the applicant has ever worked under a different name.	Asking applicant about her maiden name or whether the applicant has changed his or her name.
Address	Current address and time at that address.	Whether an applicant rents or owns their home (unless it is a BFOQ).
Age	Whether a person is of the legal age to perform the work in questions (e.g. 21 years of age to serve alcohol).	Asking an applicant's age, birthdate or how long the he or she plans to work before retiring.
Sex	Can ask gender if it is a BFOQ.	May not ask about sexual preference.
Marital/ Family Status	May inquire whether an applicant can work the hours required for the position.	Asking about spouse and/or children.
National Origin	Whether a candidate may legally work in the country with or without sponsorship.	Specific inquiries about applicant's national origin, citizenship or race.
Language	Whether a candidate speaks a specific language if it is a BFOQ.	Where the candidate learned the language or the language spoken when not working.
Religion	May ask about religion only if it is a BFOQ.	Any inquiry about religious beliefs and affiliations are illegal if not a BFOQ.
Disabilities	Whether a candidate is able to perform the essential functions of the job.	Whether a candidate has a disability and specific information relating to the disability.
Military Record	Asking about military experience as it relates to the job.	Dates and conditions of military discharge.
Criminal Record	Whether the candidate has been convicted of a crime. If yes, an employer may ask details of the conviction if it relates to the job.	Whether a candidate has ever been arrested for a crime.

employees are free to quit, strike, or otherwise cease their work. While a few select workers may possess an employment contract, most employees may be released for no cause at all, and volunteers are provided even less protection than paid employees (U.S. Department of Labor, 2011).

Exempt versus Non-Exempt Employees

Paid employees of an organization can fall into two broad classifications: non-exempt or exempt. A non-exempt employee is also referred to as an hourly employee while the exempt employee is generally classified as a salaried employee. Employees must meet three requirements to qualify as exempt including a salary basis test, a salary level test, and a duties test. In order to meet the salary basis test, an exempt employee must be paid a fixed salary that has been predetermined and is not subject to reduction based on work quality or quantity. The salary level test requires a fixed minimum amount of annual salary to qualify as exempt. The duties test calls for exempt employees work to primarily involve executive, administrative, or professional duties. A professional employee is a person hired in his or her professional capacity. Typically the employee's primary duty must be the performance of work requiring advanced knowledge, defined as work that is predominantly intellectual in character and includes work requiring the consistent exercise of discretion and judgment. This group of employees are grouped together under the classification of executive, administrative, and professional and can be classified as exempt from mandatory overtime pay for duties performed above 40 hours per week.

Since 2004, the Department of Labor has established a minimal salary level that an employee can be considered exempt at $23,600 annually. However, in 2016 President Obama signed a memorandum specifying that the Department of Labor increase the annual income an employee is required to make to remain an exempt employee by more than $20,000. Effective December 1, 2016, employees must make $47,476 annually in order to be considered an exempt employee (Davidson, 2016). This new rule also includes an automatic update of salary levels every three years. This new ruling regarding exempt employees has implications for senior management related to budgeting and worker scheduling, and it has implications for entry-level management employees regarding possible eligibility for overtime pay if their initial base salary falls below the federal minimum standard.

Part-Time and Hourly Employees—Non-Exempt

A part-time worker is a form of employment that carries fewer hours per week than a full-time job. They are required to be paid minimum wage as well as overtime, if more than 40 hours is worked over the course of one week. An hourly worker or hourly employee is an employee paid an hourly wage for their services, as opposed to a fixed salary. Hourly workers may often be found in service occupations. Overtime pay constitutes time-and-a-half hourly wage, for each hour worked over the 40-hour limit. Some employers may pay double time for holidays, but it is not mandatory unless it is specified in the employees' contract.

When a non-exempt employee is not compensated for overtime work, or for work done after clocking out, they are being treated as an exempt employee. When this occurs, claims may be filed with the department of labor. Employees working for an hourly wage are almost exclusively non-exempt employees (U.S. Department of Labor, 2008). They work in shifts but remain on call while off duty and during annual leave. The shifts are often rotational. Workers are considered to be part-time if they commonly work fewer than 30 hours per week. Large sporting events and facilities require lots of workers to ensure the event runs smoothly from set-up to clean up, and to keep the arena clean and pleasant for spectators. In order to perform all of these duties, facilities hire many non-exempt employees by paying hourly wages. When hiring workers, a facility needs to take into account how many hours will be required to keep the event running smoothly, and how many workers are needed. By hiring enough workers, the facility is able to meet the service needs of the event and avoid expensive overtime pay or tasks performed after a shift officially ends. Non-exempt workers are suited to fit these tasks, as long as labor laws are followed, and the facility is not under-staffed.

Independent contractors are workers with economic independence who are in business for themselves. Independent contractors, by definition, are self-employed and are not direct employees. Independent contractors are not covered by employment, labor, and related tax laws.

Volunteers form a vital part of the work force for many sport events and sport organizations.

Volunteers

Volunteers are often utilized during large events at sports facilities. The use of volunteers within sport venues is a vital aspect of organizational success specifically for facility and event management in sport. The idiosyncratic nature of volunteer recruitment for events, fast track training, as well as "perk" compensation makes this a unique topic of discussion. The Fair Labor Standards Act defines "volunteer" as an individual who performs hours of service for a public agency for civic, charitable, or humanitarian reasons without promise, expectation or receipt of compensation for services rendered. Volunteer services must be offered freely and without pressure or coercion, direct or implied, from the employer. Volunteering is considered a "leisure experience"; it is something the volunteer actively chooses to do out of enjoyment, without any sort of coercion or personal gain (Engelberg, Zakus, Skinner, & Campbell, 2012, p. 192). Because volunteering is defined as a leisure activity, the act must remain enjoyable in order for the facility to keep its volunteers. Facilities, therefore, should provide opportunities for their volunteers to learn new tasks and be able to perform them with mastery. The volunteer must realize that their work is worthwhile and needed, or the activity no longer becomes one of chosen leisure, causing them to leave the facility. If facilities wish to have volunteers return for future sporting events, they should be sure volunteers are satisfied after each event (Bang & Ross, 2009). Among sport volunteers in particular, it was found that commitment to the organization ties the volunteers to the facility, and assures them of their relevance (thus this sense of relevance ensures continued leisure experience). Many facilities offer perk compensations for their volunteers. These kinds of perk compensations keep the volunteers feeling tied to the facility, and committed to their work and the team (Engelberg et al., 2012). Some possible perks to offer facility volunteers could include free or discounted tickets for themselves or family members, free concessions, free parking, or free uniforms or other apparel (Fried, 2015).

There are some limitations to the use of volunteers from a legal perspective. For example, an individual may not be a volunteer if otherwise employed by the same public agency or organization to perform the same type of services as those the individual performs as an employee according to the provisions of the Fair Labor Standards Act (U.S. Department of Labor, 2011).

II. Managing Employee Performance and Development

Performance management is the process of identifying, measuring, managing, and developing the performance of human resources (Turk, 2016). Performance appraisal is the ongoing process of evaluating employee performance. All employees should be evaluated. An effective performance management plan aids with workplace communication, employee motivation, and helps to maintain a fair and informed system when making employment-related decisions. Employee feedback and goal setting are an important part of the performance management process, as well, and can help an employee to improve specific areas of their work before the next official performance management meeting (Turk, 2016). Performance management data can also help when allocating promotions and raises, can assist in *employee development*, and help to decide when a worker should receive discipline or be terminated. Different businesses and venues handle performance management in different ways. Some management teams find it helpful to outline the organization's broad goals, thus ensuring that goals between management and employees become a shared end product. Today's performance management strategies tend to involve a more relaxed agenda, where constructive feedback is offered between management and employees to foster developmental growth (Turk, 2016).

Performance Management a communication process where employer and employee collaborate to attain the organization's specific goals.

Employee Development an employer supporting an employee by providing access to training programs that introduce new skills to the employee and organization.

The task of assessing performance is a difficult and extremely complex undertaking. Central to any sport organization is ensuring that the mission and vision of the organization remain consistent. This means that everyone from the director to the volunteers should all be well versed in the policy and practices of the organization (Turk, 2016). Organizations that conduct evaluations and perform routine observations of support staff have greater success in achieving these ends. For this reason, significant planning and supervisory time should be devoted to the appraisal process (Sawyer & Judge, 2012). Supervision and evaluation can sometimes have a negative connotation, so it's important that sport organizations are clear that the primary goal in utilizing both of these tools is to support the development and success of the employee. Appraisal measures should be valid, reliable, acceptable, feasible, specific, and sensitive (Lussier & Hendon, 2016). Malaysia's public stadiums are an example of how poor appraisal measures can affect the longevity and maintenance of a facility. Malaysian stadiums and sporting facilities are built using government assets; in an effort to promote healthy lifestyles, a facility is erected in every district and state. Despite the government money used to erect these facilities, the stadiums and arenas are being poorly maintained by the event staff, thus making the arenas appear unsafe and causing them to be underutilized by the public. One could argue that the disarray of the Malaysian sporting facilities could point to poor performance management of employees and volunteers. By not providing the employees with direction as to the mission and vision of the sporting facility, maintenance is not being kept in the desired manner. When communication between management and employees is poor, a sport facility cannot function as it should (Harun, Salamudin, & Hushin, 2013).

Discipline

A key component of performance management deals with unwanted workplace conduct or poor productivity. The major objective of coaching, counseling, and discipline is to change behavior to maximize the organizational benefit.

It is very difficult to terminate an employee for job performance deficiencies. By implementing a progressive discipline process, sport organization can provide employees and volunteers with an opportunity to correct challenges found on the assessment tool and become a productive part of organizational culture. Progressive discipline is meant to be corrective rather than punitive, with the overall aim to rehabilitate the behavior of the employee. Except in the most serious of situations, termination of employment is, and always should be, the last alternative. This final step should be taken only after the employee is provided with several chances to improve behavior. The employer provides the employee with opportunities to learn from the results of the evaluation, and progressive discipline approaches the situation in stages. These steps can include: 1) an initial informal coaching talk 2) an oral warning, 3) a written warning, 4) suspension of the employee, and 5) ultimately termination if the other steps fail to correct the behavior (Fried, 2015). Any termination progressing through such steps becomes more defensible if challenged and/or taken to court. While progressive discipline policies are not a requirement of federal or state law, courts may challenge an organization that terminates an employee without following their own policies of progressive discipline steps. However, any progressive discipline policy should include language allowing for progressive discipline to be skipped for egregious actions by an employee.

Training and Development

Employee training is essential for a facility's success. Providing regular, planned, and systematically implemented in-service education programs for the staff can only benefit the organization and staff members (Sawyer & Judge, 2012). Despite the importance of training, a trainer can encounter resistance from both employees and managers.

To ascertain what types of training are needed, an organization should conduct a needs assessment. This type of assessment is a systematic analysis of the specific training activities an organization requires to achieve its objectives (Rue et al., 2011). The needs analysis phase involves establishing employee development priorities and objectives, defining specific training requirements, and establishing evaluation criteria.

Methods of Training

Specific types of sports facility workers require specialty competencies (e.g., security, athletic trainers, lifeguards). Employee training can be accomplished in many forms. Common training methods include on the job training, classroom training, E-Learning, and simulations. Each of these forms of training has strengths and weaknesses.

For example, on the job training can be customized and is interactive with the ability to give the learner instant feedback. The knowledge can also be transferred immediately to the job. However, on the job training has the potential to

Employee training through various modes and methods is essential for organizational success.

disrupt the work environment and trainers may not be capable of imparting their knowledge or may transfer their own bad habits. This can be avoided by providing trainers with a standardized training plan.

Classroom training can provide standardized knowledge to a large number of people at the same time, which is cost effective. Trainers tend to be skilled at teaching and can create an interactive environment. However, groups of students may have different learning styles, and the teaching pace might not fit everyone in the class.

E-Learning provides flexible, non-disruptive training to workers, but not all subject matter can be trained in this manner. Assessment can also be difficult due to logistics and employee dishonesty. Additionally, lack of interaction with trainers and the solitary nature of this style of training can lessen motivation. Simulation-training allows students to practice challenging situations in a realistic setting. Trainers are also able to assess student progress visually and through simulator data collection. However, simulation costs may be expensive to create and maintain.

In addition to choosing the training method, organizations should carefully consider who will deliver the training, the program content, and how the training will be scheduled. At the conclusion of training, managers should assess whether the appropriate knowledge was transferred. Facility managers may consider whether to try other methods or use different trainers. Lastly, they should evaluate whether the benefits outweigh the costs and inconvenience.

III. Employee Well-Being

Worker Well-Being is a broad category that includes some elements of risk management. Risk management is the process of planning, organizing, and controlling activities that contain an element of risk of injury to the worker. Risk Management involves identifying, assessing, and analyzing potential workplace hazards. As with any workplace, facility managers need to clearly state the workplace safety policy. Accidents and "near miss" incidents should be investigated and trends analyzed to determine root causes and aid in accident prevention.

Occupational Safety and Health Act of 1970 (OSHA)

The Occupational Safety and Health Administration (OSHA), a division within the Department of Labor, is charged with overseeing the practical application of the Occupational Safety and Health Act of 1970. This federal legislation seeks to "ensure safe and healthful working conditions for working men and women by setting and enforcing standards and by providing training, outreach, education and assistance" (Occupational Health and Safety Administration, n.d). OSHA creates and communicates federal safety and health standards to employers. It also conducts health inspections (made without any advance notice) in response to worker complaints, targeted inspections, and suspected dangerous working conditions.

To avoid OSHA penalties, facility managers should keep the building and equipment well maintained by conducting regular inspections with detailed checklists. Organizations can also protect their workers by establishing and communicating emergency plans and by integrating comprehensive safety training as part of its risk management program.

Workplace Violence

The risk of workplace violence raises several concerns for employers, including the potential for liability. Workplace violence lawsuits have resulted in millions of dollars in settlements and judgments. Beyond monetary costs, employers must contend with lower employee morale and negative publicity.

Given the threat of workplace violence between workers and from third parties, facility managers should create a well-defined, written policy. As with other workplace safety objectives, employees need to be trained on the policy as well as how to deal with potentially violent scenarios. Swift disciplinary action must be taken against employees who behave violently at work and incidents should be tracked to determine if patterns arise.

Negligent Hiring

To avoid violent or inappropriate conduct in the workplace, sport facility managers need to perform adequate background research during the hiring process (e.g., contacting references, criminal background checks). A facility could face a civil lawsuit for "negligent hiring" if one worker harms another. This type of liability is more likely if a sufficient background investigation might have easily uncovered a violent reputation or record. The important thing is to exercise due diligence by asking questions about prior misconduct. Even if a facility manager does not obtain usable information from references or if the applicant lies, the fact that the employer asked the questions helps decrease liability.

Employee Wellness Programs/Employee Assistance Programs (EAP)

Employee wellness programs attend to employees' physical and mental well-being through education and training programs. Weight and lifestyle management, health risk assessment services, access to fitness equipment and fitness classes are examples of the offerings in wellness programs. Healthy, fit employees handle stress better, are more productive, and are usually more engaged which can lead to higher productivity and overall, happier employees.

Employee Assistance Programs (EAP) provide access to counseling and other services to help employees resolve personal issues that may affect their work. EAPs may consist of in-person assessments; short-term counseling; career coaching and referrals to community resources and providers.

IV. Employee Compensation and Benefit Packages

Employee *compensation* consists of three primary components: direct compensation, indirect compensation, and nonfinancial compensation (Snell et al., 2016). The sum of these various types of compensation is called the worker's "total compensation." Direct compensation includes all compensation (base salary and/or incentive pay) that is paid directly to an employee. Indirect compensation is composed of rewards that are not paid directly to an employee and is calculated in addition to base salary and incentive pay (e.g., employer-paid portions of health and dental insurance, retirement benefits, relocation expenses, and paid time off).

Compensation the salary or pay an employee receives for performing a job.

Nonfinancial compensation differs from direct and indirect pay because it lacks monetary value and is not part of an employee's pay. Examples of this type of compensation include achievement awards, team leadership opportunities, personal days, prizes, paid training, workspace upgrades, and parking or transit passes.

Organizations develop and implement salary structures to provide a framework for administering their employee compensation programs. Most companies determine their employee pay levels by evaluating market pay levels for the majority of their jobs. Facility managers should "benchmark" similar jobs at comparable organizations.

Fair Labor Standards Act of 1938 (minimum wage and overtime pay)

The FLSA requires that most employees in the United States be paid at least the federal minimum wage for all hours worked and overtime pay at time and one-half the regular rate of pay for all hours worked over 40 hours in a workweek.

As of July 2009, the federal government mandates a nationwide minimum wage level of $7.25 per hour (U.S. Department of Labor, 2011). Youth under 20 years of age may be paid a minimum wage of no less than $4.25 an hour during the first 90 consecutive calendar days of employment with an employer. Employers may not displace any employee to hire someone at the youth minimum wage. Some states and municipalities have set minimum wage levels higher than the federal level so managers should be aware of the minimum wage required by local law.

Additionally, 14 and 15 year olds may work *outside school hours* no more than three hours on a school day, 18 hours in a school week, eight hours on a non-school day, and 40 hours in a non-school week. Further, 14 and 15 year olds may not work hours before 7 a.m. or after 7 p.m. on any day, except from June 1st through Labor Day, when nighttime work hours are extended to 9 p.m. Additionally, 16 and 17 year olds cannot be employed in jobs deemed to be hazardous, but their work hours are unrestricted (U.S. Department of Labor, 2013).

Employee Benefits

Employee Benefits
non-monetary compensation awarded to employees by employers. Benefits can include health benefits, special perks or vacation time.

Benefits are indirect compensation offered to employees in addition to salary. Benefits that encourage healthier behavior are a cost effective way to keep up employee morale, improve employee retention, and decrease absenteeism. Certain *employee benefits* are mandated by federal and state law while others are optional based on the desires of the firm. Common benefits include medical, disability, and life insurance; retirement benefits; paid time off, dental care, free parking and public transportation vouchers. A summary of common employee benefits including those that are required by law and those provided on a voluntary basis by some organizations are provided in Table 5.2.

Table 5.2 *Summary of Employee Benefits*

Statutory Benefits	Voluntary Benefits
Workers' Compensation	Group Health Insurance
Unemployment Insurance	Paid time off
Family and Medical Leave Act (FMLA)	Health and Dental Insurance
Consolidated Omnibus Budget Reconciliation	Transportation vouchers
(COBRA)	Gym memberships
Employee Retirement Income Security (ERISA)	Free or low-cost meals during working hours

Unemployment Insurance

The Federal Unemployment Tax Act (FUTA), along with state unemployment systems, provides for payments of unemployment compensation to workers who have lost their jobs. Despite federal guidelines, each individual state determines the eligibility, amount, and duration of benefits. Keeping the number of unemployment insurance claims filed by former employees to a minimum can produce significant payroll tax savings (Federal Unemployment Tax Act, 2011).

In order to qualify for this benefit program, an employee must have worked during a specified period, usually in the past 12 to 18 months, and earned a minimum amount of wages as set by each state. There must also be a determination that the former employee became unemployed through no fault of his or her own and meet other eligibility requirements determined under state law.

Family and Medical Leave Act of 1993 (FMLA)

The Family and Medical Leave Act allows 12 work weeks of unpaid leave in any 12-month period for eligible employees when they or immediate family members are faced with medical issues. To qualify, the employer must have at least 50 employees and the employee must have worked at least 1,250 hours for the employer in the 12 months before the leave (Family and Medical Leave Act of 1993, 2006).

Examples of eligible leaves include the birth and care of the employee's child within one year of birth, placement with the employee of a child for adoption or foster care within one year of the placement, care of an immediate family member (spouse, child, parent) who has a serious health condition, and for the employee's own serious health condition that makes the employee unable to perform the essential functions of his or her job (Department of Labor, 2012).

The Patient Protection and Affordable Care Act

The Affordable Care Act (ACA) guarantees that health care is available to any legal US resident who cannot otherwise obtain "good" healthcare through their employer. This federal act gives employers with over 50 employees the choice between providing insurance that meets the standards of the act or paying a penalty. This penalty helps to offset the cost of employees who aren't covered through their employer to purchase insurance through the public health insurance exchanges instead of using emergency services. Employers with fewer than 25 employees may qualify for tax credits, tax breaks, and other assistance for insuring employees. The Affordable Care Act ensures employees understand the true cost and value of the benefits they receive from the firm as well as provides information through multiple communication channels more often than just once a year during open enrollment.

Conclusion

This chapter has provided an introduction to human resource management and has made the point that the work and structure of the human resource function will only continue to grow more complex. Human resource departments were added to organizations in recent years. The behavioral sciences played a strong role in helping to understand the needs of workers and how the needs of the organization and its workers could be better aligned. Various new theories were spawned and many were based on the behavioral sciences. This is all the more reason to invest time in clarifying roles, interdependencies, and interfaces. By achieving a greater level of such clarity around its own work, HR departments will be well positioned to enable the businesses they support to operate quickly and flexibly under changing conditions. In the process, HR can maintain its seat at the strategic table as facilities move forward to face the global challenges of the coming decades.

KEY LEARNING POINTS

The key learning points in this chapter were as follows: explain the role humans play in modern organizations, implement a basic job description analysis, implement a basic job specification analysis, identify the different employee selection methods and their characteristics, match job specifications with appropriate selection methods, identify different performance appraisal approaches and techniques and their characteristics, design appropriate employee selection instruments, and design appropriate performance appraisal instruments.Mini Case Study

MINI CASE STUDY

A newly redesigned recruiting and interviewing system of a fast growing multi-sport facility shortened the open position "Time to Fill" benchmark by almost 40%. Methodology required the recruiter to quickly sort the top 15 to 20 resumes received within the first five days of the placement of an advertisement for a position. The recruiter would email a worksheet/exercise to be completed and returned by the applicants, which often resulted in a response rate of about 80% from seriously interested candidates. A 20-minute phone interview would then be scheduled with the candidates to (A) review all the potential "deal-breakers" such as salary, benefits, hours of work, etc. and (B) ask five structured interview questions about prior employment. The top five to eight candidates would be scheduled for a 30 to 40 minute soft-skill phone interview with the recruiter to assess their soft skills in relation to the top 10 soft skills that we identified for each position. Finally, the top three to five candidates would be invited for in-person interviews at the school, with the recruiter getting permission to check certain references of the top candidates before they arrived for the interview. We also worked with the managers to create structured interview questions for each position so that all applicants would be measured by the same benchmarks. Finally, we trained the managers to score the responses to interview questions as a method for weighing the quality of candidate responses.

Analyze the above scenario discuss the strengths and weaknesses of the HR hiring practices.

1. What is one method or action the recruiter could have done differently to obtain the best candidate?

2. Name one method the recruiter used that would be beneficial in searching for the right candidate.

3. Are there any major limitations to the methodology that HR used?

CHAPTER DISCUSSION QUESTIONS

1. What should managers consider in order to distinguish the "qualified candidates" from the "unqualified candidates"?

2. Discuss two examples of bona fide occupational qualifications (BFOQ) that might relate to work within facility and event management in sport.

3. When writing job descriptions, an employer should focus on which component to facilitate compliance with the Americans with Disabilities Act (ADA) of 1990?

4. The Occupational Safety and Health Act of 1970 grants which right to employees?

5. In your opinion, what is the most effective on the job training? Discuss strengths and weaknesses of each method of training.

PRACTITIONER SPOTLIGHT

NAME: Jordin Westbrook

ORGANIZATION: SMG McLane Stadium

CURRENT JOB TITLE: Operations and Events Manager

- Year started in this role: officially January 2016, but took over responsibilities in July 2015 after a staffing change.

EDUCATIONAL PREPARATION:

- **Undergrad degree:** BA in Communications with minor in Entrepreneurship at Baylor University
- **Graduate degree:** Masters in Sport Management, Baylor University
- **Special Certifications associated with your job:** OSHA Safety Training 30-Hour Compliance Course

Photo courtesy of Jordin Westbrook.

CAREER PATH:

- **Internship(s), entry level job:** I choose to do my internship here (at SMG) since I was already here for my graduate assistantship. I was in charge of all staffing of the new stadium. This presented challenges both for our staff and workers as it was new for everyone. We had a lot of customer service complaints that first year just because we were all still learning.

WHAT IS THE MOST REWARDING ASPECT OF THIS JOB?

I get to work at a university that I love. I work in a building that is unlike any other that SMG manages. Usually, we would be in charge of every aspect like, concessions, HVAC, and housekeeping, but here we have seven different companies that we outsource to for those services. The best thing we do is Baylor football. We do it six days a year, and they are the best six days that we do. The stadium is full, and the atmosphere is awesome. There's just nothing that compares to it.

WHAT IS THE MOST CHALLENGING ASPECT OF THIS JOB?

I would say handling the seven companies I work with on a daily basis. Finding ways to make everyone happy or to find compromises that work out in the best possible way. I put out a lot of fires and deal with a lot of various conflicts. Everyone always wants something. You're on call 24/7 in this role. You have to be willing to get calls and emails at all hours of the day and night. I serve as the main contact for the Baylor Police Department if something happens at the stadium. There is just always something that needs to be tended to.

HOW IS YOUR ROLE CONNECTED TO THE RECRUITMENT AND TRAINING OF EVENT STAFF?

I was responsible for hiring all game day staff for the opening of this stadium. Our number for that was somewhere north of 225, and we had to find them from scratch. We still facilitate all of the hiring of game day personnel here at the stadium, and each of those workers serves as an employee for SMG. These workers are also then eligible to work other Baylor athletic events in other venues on the campus.

HOW DOES YOUR STAFFING PLANS AND PATTERNS CHANGE BASED UPON THE TYPE OF EVENT HOSTED?

The Baylor Athletic Department is responsible for staffing game day. All other events at the stadium I handle. So for movie nights, if it's for a small group like a sorority or fraternity, we usually have two on duty. If it's for a bigger group, like a student activities' or a community event, we'll have six to eight because we will have field security and bag checker duties required. Our biggest challenge is when the event allows for anyone with a Baylor ID to enter. That's potentially 15,000 students and we need to be ready for that level of attendance. At Pee-Wee football

McLane Stadium the home of Baylor University Football in Waco, TX is managed by SMG.

games it calls for about 20 event staff members. For those events we have to look at entry for teams, for fans, how people get on the field and ticket takers. Basically, no two events are the same.

HOW ARE PART-TIME AND FULL-TIME ROLES AND RESPONSIBILITIES BALANCED WITHIN YOUR ORGANIZATION?

SMG does not employ part time staff on a daily basis. They are solely event staff not in a full time role. Everyone who works full time is here every day and works on the day to day operations of the stadium.

WHAT ARE SOME OF THE DUTIES OF YOUR POSITION IN RELATION TO HUMAN RESOURCE MANAGEMENT OF EVENT STAFF?

Our HR designee is not here for all events so that becomes my responsibility. I handle any issues that arise on those occasions including discipline, correction, and praise with our staff.

WHAT IS A UNIQUE ASPECT OR TASK OF YOUR JOB THAT MANY WOULD BE SURPRISED TO HEAR ABOUT?

As the building manager you are responsible for the safety and security in this place. You are responsible for any person that walks through the door. It's a lot of pressure to assume in that role. For example, if someone walks in off the interstate and there is an incident, I'm responsible for that. Therefore, you're watching cameras, checking doors, seeing how people might get in without going through proper channels. I'm in charge of all access points. It's not just an event planning position. You coordinate with the client, but you are in charge of so much more.

WHAT DO YOU BELIEVE ARE THE MOST IMPORTANT SKILL(S) TO DEVELOP?

Three key skills would be communication, relationship building and flexibility. If you're not, this is not the right position for you. Professional conversations and cold calls on clients are a must. You have to be able to show empathy to the patron so there's the customer service side. You have to be able to talk to your staff and brief them effectively. You have to be able to separate yourself as the boss in those situations. You must be adaptable and even keeled. Learn to mask your stress when necessary, and get the task at hand done.

WHAT PARTING WORDS OF WISDOM DO YOU HAVE FOR STUDENTS AND YOUNG PROFESSIONALS IN THE FIELD?

Give this profession a chance. You're always in a position to have a good day. You just have to set yourself up to have that happen. Prepare as best as you can. Even if that means staying up until 2 a.m. the night before, you have to show up the next day ready to do the job. Don't leave important task for the day of the event. The more advanced planning you have, the more you will be set up for success. Don't let your lack of planning constitute an emergency on someone else's part. Be a "yes" person…within reason, and make the things happen that need to for a successful event.

Reprinted by permission of Jordin Westbrook.

REFERENCES

Bang, H., & Ross, S. D. (2009). Volunteer motivation and satisfaction. *Journal of Venue and Event Management, 1,* 61–77.

Cascio, W. F., & Aguinis, H. (2010). *Applied psychology in human resource management,* Upper Saddle River, NJ: Prentice Hall.

Civil Rights Act of 1964 § 7, 42 U.S.C. § 2000e et seq. (1964).

Covell, D., & Walker, S. (2013). *Managing sport organizations: Responsibility for performance* (3rd ed.). New York, NY: Routledge.

Davidson, P. (2016, May 18). Millions more Americans to be eligible for overtime pay. *USA Today.* Retrieved from http://www.usatoday.com/story/money/2016/05/17/overtime-pay-eligible-employees-workers/84504890/

Dessler, G. (2013). *Human resource management* (13th ed.). Upper Saddle River, NJ: Pearson/Prentice-Hall.

Dothard v. Rawlinson, 433 U.S. 321 (1977).

EEOC v. Sedita, 755 F. Supp. 808 (1991).

Engelberg, T., Zakus, D., Skinner, J., Campbell, A. (2012). Defining and measuring dimensionality and targets of the commitment of sport volunteers. *Journal of Sport Management, 26,* 192–205.

Family and Medical Leave Act of 1993, 29 U.S.C. §§ 2601–2654 (2006).

Federal Unemployment Tax Act, 26 U.S.C. §§ 3301–3311 (2011).

Fried, G. (2015). *Managing sport facilities* (3rd ed.). Champaign, IL: Human Kinetics.

Harun, M., Salamudin, N., Hushin, H. (2013). Appraisal of the sport facilities maintenance management practices of Malaysian stadium corporations. *Asian Social Science, 9*(12), 93–98.

Lussier, R. N. & Hendon, J. R. (2016). *Human resource management: Functions, applications, skill development.* (2nd ed.). Thousand Oaks: Sage.

Miller, L. (1997). *Sport business management.* Gaithersburg, MD: Aspen Publishers.

Occupational Safety & Health Administration, 29 C.F.R. §24 (n.d.).

Ricci v. DeStefano, 557 U.S. (2009).

Robinson, R. K. & Franklin, G. (2015). *Employment regulation in the workplace: Basic compliance for managers.* Routledge: New York.

Rue, L., Ibrahim, N., & Byars, L. (2011). *Human resource management.* New York: McGraw Hill.

Sawyer, T. H., & Judge, L. W. (2012). *The management of fitness, physical activity, recreation, and sport.* Sagamore Publishing: Champaign, IL.

Significant EEOC Race/Color Cases (2015). *EEOC.* Retrieved from https://www1.eeoc.gov//eeoc/initiatives/e-race/caselist.cfm?renderforprint=1#hiring

Snell, S. A., Morris, S. S., & Bohlander, G. (2016). *Managing human resources* (17th ed.). Boston, MA: Cengage.

Song, E. (2007). No women (and dogs) allowed: A comparative analysis of discriminating private golf clubs in the United States, Ireland and England. *Washington University Global Studies Law Review, 6,* 181–203.

Turk, K. (2016). Performance management of academic staff and its effectiveness to teaching and research-based on the example of Estonian universities. *TRAMES: A Journal of the Humanities & Social Sciences, 20* (70/65), 17–36.

U.S. Department of Labor. (2014). *Am I an Employee?: Employment relationship under the Fair Labor Standards Act.* Retrieved from http://www.dol.gov/whd/regs/compliance/whdfs13.htm

U.S. Department of Labor. (2013). *Child labor provisions for nonagricultural occupations under the Fair Labor Standards Act.* Retrieved from. https://www.dol.gov/whd/regs/compliance/childlabor101_text.htm

U.S. Department of Labor (2011). *The Fair Labor Standards Act of 1938 as Amended.* Retrieved from https://www.dol.gov/whd/regs/statutes/FairLaborStandAct.pdf

U.S. Department of Labor. (2008) *Exemption for executive, administrative, professional, computer & outside sales employees under the Fair Labor Standards Act.* Retrieved from https://www.dol.gov/whd/overtime/fs17a_overview.htm

Wage and Hour Division (2008). *U.S. Department of Labor.* Retrieved from www.dol.gov/whd/overtime/fs17a_overview.pdf

Wu, Y. (2012). Scaling the wall and running the mile: The role of physical-selection procedures in the disparate impact narrative. *University of Pennsylvania Law Review, 160,* 1195–1237.

Facility Construction/ Planning Process and Building Life Cycle

6

John J. Miller and *Ricardo Gonzales*

OBJECTIVES

After studying this chapter, the student should be able to:

- Understand the importance of facility design principles.
- Determine the level of architect inclusion in planning and designing a facility.
- Comprehend the life cycle cost analysis process.
- Understand the application of life cycle assessments.
- Analyze the facility space needs, including ancillary spaces.
- Become familiar with facility construction processes.

KEY TERMS

Ancillary Space

Architect

Architect Supplemental Instruction

Bidding

Change Order Requests

Concourse

Construction Process

Cradle-to-Cradle

Cradle-to-Grave

Deconstruction

Egress

Facility Construction Document

Facility Design Development Phase

Facility Pre-Planning Phase

Facility Programming Phase

Facility Schematic Design Phase

Feasibility Study

Ingress

Life Cycle Assessment

Life Cycle Cost

Line of Sight

Notice of Delay

Request of Information

Substantial Completion

Vertical Circulation

Vomitory

KEY ACRONYMS

AIA	American Institute of Architects	**LCCA**	Life Cycle Cost Analysis
ASI	Architect Supplemental Instruction	**NPV**	Net Present Value
CMP	Comprehensive Management Plan	**RFI**	Requests for Information
COR	Change Order Requests	**RFP**	Request for Proposal
HID	High Intensity Discharge	**RPS**	Request for Professional Services
LCA	Life Cycle Assessment		

Introduction

Facility design and construction focus on maximizing the functional life of the sport and recreational spaces. Evidence suggests that the construction of appropriate and sufficient sports facilities has considerable influence on participation in sport. The presence of appropriate sports and recreational facilities, access to those facilities, and the conditions under which a facility operates can either encourage or discourage participation or attendance. A number of geographical, environmental, and population demographic factors are important in determining the impact a sporting facility has on the community.

Facility construction is a complex business, whose projects are increasingly more technically sophisticated as well as subjected to shorter execution schedules and costs due to market demands. When best practice construction principles are applied, sports facilities can service the greatest breadth of spectator and participant base. During the construction phase, projects are affected by uncertainty resulting from urgent requirements, non-consistent construction sequences, project scope changes, and poor quality, among other factors (Gonzalez, Alarcon, & Mundaca, 2007). In some cases, the major sports or recreational opportunities are clear while other variables such as financing plan, site location, and construction costs require work to turn a concept into a meaningful plan.

Within professional sport in the United States, team owners have pushed the communities for larger, grander, and more exclusive venues in response to similar actions from other teams. It is a very high priced arms race that has been fought for decades with no end in sight. In 2016, the NFL owners agreed to allow the St. Louis Rams to move to the lucrative Los Angeles market, vacating Edward Jones Stadium that was built in 1995. However, under the terms of the lease, the Edward Jones Dome stadium had to be ranked in the top tier of all NFL stadiums through the 2015 season. Yet, *Time Magazine* ranked Edward Jones stadium as the seventh worst major sports stadium in the United States (Carbone, 2012). As a result, the Rams were free to break the lease and relocate without penalty due to the terms of the lease (deMause, 2016). The Edward Jones Dome cost about $435 million at the time of its original construction. This fact begs the question as to how civic leaders and design teams missed the mark so badly.

In stadiums and arenas, the demand for luxury boxes, premium seating, plush dining accommodations, and other amenities has led to extremely high construction costs. Such teams are always looking for an edge that will boost team visibility demand, and ultimately increase revenue. Presently, no consensus exists on what type of services and amenities these types of facilities should include. Each new facility is typically designed and constructed to meet the need of the respective end user(s). This is consistent with the inherent differences between arenas. These differences also make it difficult to equitably compare one facility with another. Many different factors can impact the cost of space. These can include but are not limited to required utilities, sound control, security systems, wall and floor finishes, lighting, casework, and seating, just to name a few of the more common cost contributing factors.

An ugly conception may very likely be an ugly project from beginning to end. It takes great skill to take poorly conceived concepts and turn them around to end up as well executed projects. Thus, the facility design concept phase translates the facility construction needs.

Facility Concept Design

The concept design gives a public face to the organization. Components of the detailed concept design include detailed programming of user space and equipment needs; conceptual site, architectural and engineering design; detailed systems design; materials selection; and construction documentation. It is essential to develop a conceptual design for each potential solution, at least in schematic form as early as possible in the process.

Design Principles

According to the American Institute of Architects (AIA), there is significant interest in reducing the impact that facility design has on the environment. As the architectural and construction industries increasingly emphasize sustainability, more comprehensive methods are being developed to evaluate and reduce environmental impacts. Tools like energy modeling assist in predicting and, through good design, reducing the operational energy in buildings.

Design principles support the institution's mission by working to address the quality of the environment in order to attract and

© fotogestoeber/Shutterstock.com

Building design principles must consider sustainability as it intersects with the available resources, environment, and profitability.

© Dimitar Sotirov/Shutterstock.com

Planning and design development is typically led by an architectural firm.

retain quality faculty, students, and staff personnel as well as to instill sustainability. The facility should be functional and attractive, so that its fits within the natural landscape. The institution's architectural design should reflect its stature. The design principles constitute an important tool to achieve these goals. Additionally, the design principles link institutional goals with detailed architectural and engineering design standards.

Ultimately, the principles provide a bridge between the comprehensive management plan (CMP) and various construction design codes and manuals. The goals of the design principles are to 1) create an attractive physical environment and a sense of place, 2) reduce operational costs, 3) understand that design complexity and spaces that create a "wow" factor come at a price, 4) promote higher levels of pride and create branding opportunities, 5) promote functional and visual consistency and compatibility, and 6) provide guidance to facility designers. The design principles for future development at an institution include a set of principles and detailed guidance with respect to land development, landscape architecture, and building architecture as well as space and furniture standardization.

The design principles provide a transition from the conceptual nature of planning to the detailed specifics of architectural and engineering design and define administrative processes for reviewing and approving design. They provide a framework for making decisions without precluding innovative solutions to design problems. Elements that provide a basis for evaluating proposed design solutions and recognize the existing diversity in architecture as well as their relationship to one another and the surrounding environment should be roughly agreed upon. This information will be useful when an architect is chosen.

Architect Involvement

Architect a person who designs buildings as well as often supervises the construction.

In 1943 Winston Churchill said "we shape our buildings, and afterwards our buildings shape us" (Churchill, 2003, p. 358). That being the case, architecture is too important to be left to *architects* alone. That is why it is essential that a facility administrator and selected committee members must be involved in the process. The administrator and committee have important information, valuable insights, and worthwhile priorities that must be brought to bear on the process of shaping architecture. Even though the facility administrator may not be an architect, that person can exercise leadership in the capital project process because leadership is, at its root, influence.

Architect selection is a critical part of the process. Architects are generalists by training. Through the architectural registration process, all architects are legally allowed to lead the design efforts for projects ranging from complex engineering structures to backyard decks. Architects can provide various professional services including urban planning, master planning, environmental design, landscape architecture, interior design, environmental planning, facility planning, cost estimating, and other key services. Not all architects are qualified to provide professional services for every type of project imaginable. This is not the time to select a neighbor, relative, or good friend unless they have demonstrated that they have the skills (design, facilitation, team building, and management of various specialized consultants), past performance history on similar projects, and the resources (skilled staff and time) to successfully complete the task.

Reviewing the qualifications of these key design professionals is critical to ensure that an institution hires the best team possible for their unique project. Checking their references and making sure that they have done work regularly and recently that most closely resembles the scope and magnitude that of your project cannot be stressed enough. The selection process is not just for an architect, but for the entire design team. In the planning of a facility it is important to recognize the close relationship between the architect and building committee. Broadly speaking, design is a process of creating the description of a new facility, usually represented by detailed plans and specifications. Innovative design concepts are highly valued not for their own sake but for their contributions to reducing costs and the improvement of aesthetics, comfort, or convenience as embodied in a well-designed facility. The most important aspect of design innovation is the necessity of communication within the partnership of the architect and the building committee.

Generally speaking, architects may perform a minor percentage of the overall design work. Specialized consultants such structural, electrical, mechanical, plumbing, site development engineers as well as space programmers, environmental and interior designers, must be consistently utilized. Architects are typically the leaders, coordinators, and record keepers for the design team; thus it is critical that all members of the design team work well together and hopefully have worked together on past successful projects.

As the leader of the design team, architects will typically select the specialized consultants for the project. The planning committee should not hesitate to review the past performance histories of these potential consultants and should have the final say on whether certain consultants should join the project. For example, an institution may feel very comfortable with a particular architectural firm, but may also have had bad previous experiences with certain engineers on a past project while those firms worked under a different architect's direction. The design process would typically include a number of key steps as follows:

- Development of selection criteria
- Development of a Request for Proposal (RFP), also known as a Request for Professional Services (RPS)
- Advertise the RFP
- Receive letters of interest and proposals
- Reviewing credentials
- Short listing of teams
- Design competition if required
- Design team selection pending state, regent, board of governors, administration, owners, or lenders approval.
- Design contract negotiation
- Contract approval
- Notice to proceed

Most often, architects will make certain that the design of the facility will meet or exceed all applicable building and fire codes. They also will design facilities that are pleasing to the eye both internally and externally. However, beyond these basic items, the architect and chair of the design committee must consider the needs and liabilities that are unique to sports and/or recreation programs such as the heating, ventilation, and air conditioning (HVAC) systems.

Heating, Ventilation, and Air Conditioning (HVAC) Systems

The HVAC system (heating, ventilation, and air conditioning) is a critical but often overlooked component in the design of a facility. While many patrons primarily relate HVAC to temperature control, doing so overshadows its ability to provide ventilation throughout the facility (Broadhag, 2009b). Sport and recreation facilities provide a unique and perplexing environment for HVAC systems as the presences of large groups of people, either attending a contest or working out, causing heat to be released causing the temperature of the area to rise. As the room temperature increases, patrons or spectators will begin to perspire, resulting in an increase of humidity. Finally, a large number of people will elevate the amount of carbon dioxide (CO_2) in the area. All of these factors must be accounted for in the design of a sport or recreation facility. It is important to note that a monitoring system should be implemented to make

© withGod/Shutterstock.com

Specialized consultants are often needed for structural, mechanical, electrical, HVAC, and other complex systems in stadium and arena settings.

sure CO_2 levels stay within acceptable ranges. Basic guidelines for the HVAC system include acceptable temperature ranges of 68 degrees to 78 degrees (depending upon space usage), humidity of 60% or less, and air circulation of 8% to 12% (Broadhag, 2009b).

Lighting

It has been estimated that 25% of all energy used is consumed through lighting. Of that, three-fourths is used in commercial and industrial settings. In the commercial facility, natural light and lighting fixtures combine to light the space with levels typically measured in foot-candles. A foot-candle may be defined as the illumination produced by a source of one candle at a distance of one foot and equal to one lumen incident per square foot. Illumination levels for sport settings both indoor and outdoor are often specified by sport governing bodies in consideration of both safety and for media coverage. For example, in 2013 the National Collegiate Athletic Association (NCAA) developed best practices guidelines for events ranging from a low of 30 foot-candles for track (running) to 125 foot-candles for most televised national championship events. Lighting fixtures are designed for various functions—ambient light, task light, or accent light. These fixtures can be grouped into three major categories: the basic light fixture, linear fluorescent, and high intensity discharge (HID). Each fixture has its own specific function.

Previously, energy efficiency was associated with replacing the basic incandescent light bulb with the compact fluorescent light bulb (CFL) (Broadhag, 2009a). However, linear fluorescent and HID were curbed because they could not be controlled via dimming, or often took up to 10 minutes or more. In the design and construction of a sport or recreation facility, energy-efficient bulbs must be considered to save electricity. For example, the standard CFL bulb can save anywhere from 50% to 80% energy cost from the normal light bulb with no loss in light quality. The primary reason for such savings is due to the fact that the ratio of a CFL to a traditional incandescent light bulb is 3:1 in comparable energy usage (Broadhag, 2009a). This means that a 60-watt light bulb can be replaced with a 20-watt CFL. Also, the CFL fluorescent may last eight to ten times longer than the incandescent (Broadhag, 2009a). Lastly, these new energy-efficient bulbs create much less heat, which keeps the temperature down in the gym. As a result, the use of energy-efficient bulbs in the life cycle planning and analysis as they save money in utility charges as well as natural resources by using fewer bulbs over time, thus creating less harmful byproducts in conversion to energy.

Life Cycle Planning

Life cycle planning (LCP) is a significant part of managing sport and recreation facilities. One of the primary benefits of developing a life cycle plan is the opportunity it offers to plan financially for each future stage. Life cycle planning is a process that establishes the fully-anticipated cost of a structure, product, or component over its expected useful life (Snodgrass, 2013). It is very important to recognize the significance of integrated building systems design in the overall efficiency of the design. The most effective approach to LCP is to appropriately integrate it into the design process. According to the Manitoba Culture, Heritage Recreation and Citizenship (1995) the life cycle of a facility generally follows a pattern of five predictable stages. The first stage includes the initial pre-construction planning of a location, site plans, and design alternatives. Stage two focuses on equipment and building component selection, and ongoing facility inspections and maintenance. Stage three considers the potential renovations, repairs and/or replacements of equipment. Stage four concentrates on the changing desires of the community as well as the potential deterioration of the facility over time. Finally, stage five recognizes the "end" of the facility that is often predicated on the maintenance and attention the facility received during the first four stages.

The building design evolves from general concepts to detailed analysis. An LCP needs to follow the same approach paralleling the focus to the current level of detail study. In general, LCP aids in the selection of all building systems that influence energy use: thermal envelope, passive solar features, fenestration, HVAC, domestic hot water, building automation, and lighting (GSA, 2003). Additionally, the LCP process can also be applied to facility characteristics or involve costs related to occupant productivity, system maintenance, environmental impact and any other issue that affect costs over time (GSA, 2003).

Life Cycle Cost Analysis

The procurement and advancement of a new facility is often a costly, time-sensitive project. Suitable locations must be recognized, correct facility capacity requirements must be established for present and anticipated future use, and the appropriate sums of capital must be earmarked prior to the purchase and construction of a facility. While the objectives in identifying a sports facility location may often be highly dependent on the organization's relationship with the university or city, the high costs connected with this process make almost any location project a long-term investment. Because sport facilities are generally expected to remain in a location for an extended time, elements that should be considered are any anticipated shifts of population as well as the possibility of expanding and adapting the sport facility to meet potential consumer market changes.

The financial impact is an additional consideration for all facility design plans. Because funding is often limited, designers and facilities managers have usually concentrated on decreasing the initial cost of the facility. However, employing this exercise has created structures with needlessly high operation and maintenance costs. To best address potential financial issues and minimize additional expenses, a life cycle cost analysis (LCCA) should be conducted.

Over the life of a facility it has been estimated that the operation and maintenance cost more than initial construction (Ive, 2006) Since this cost estimation applies to new construction as well as major replacement and improvement projects, the inclusion of operation and maintenance costs is extremely practical. Additionally, for items that last longer than a couple of years, the cost analysis process is a more accurate way of assessing costs than merely using the purchase price. As such, the operation and maintenance costs should be added to the purchase price.

Basic Life Cycle Cost Analysis Calculation

The LCCA formula works for all projects, large or small. It is much easier to calculate the *life cycle cost* of a window air conditioner than of a large laboratory building (Snodgrass, 2013). Two factors make it difficult to use the formula for large projects (Snodgrass, 2013):

1. A lot of information has to be assembled and manipulated.
2. All costs must be adjusted for inflation.

The term "present value" in the formula describes costs that have been adjusted for inflation, or "discounted." The emphasis on present value is important when considering expensive structures or components that function for many decades because inflation can influence affordability. It's usually not worth calculating present value when analyzing the life cycle costs of small or short-lived structures, products, or components. The Office of Management and Budget (OMB) Circular A-94 (2015) requires that life cycle cost analysis be calculated in terms of "net present value." Net present value (NPV) is the difference between the discounted present value of benefits and the discounted present value of costs (Office of Management and Budget Circular, 2015). NPV is computed by assigning monetary values to benefits and costs, discounting future benefits and costs using an appropriate discount rate, and subtracting the discounted costs from the discounted benefits. Discounting benefits and costs transforms gains and losses occurring in different time periods to a common unit of measurement. Programs with a positive net present value increase social resources and are generally preferred. Programs with negative net present value should generally be avoided (Office of Management and Budget Circular, 2015).

Life Cycle Cost process that considers the total expenditures of project options to choose the design that best guarantees the facility will offer the lowest overall cost of ownership in relationship with quality and function.

Basic Formula for Calculating Life Cycle Cost

The formula for calculating life cycle cost is (Snodgrass, 2013):

LCC = I + Repl – Res + E + W + OM&R + O

Where:

LCC = Total life cycle cost in present value (PV) dollars of given alternative

I = Initial cost

Replacement (Repl) = PV capital replacement costs

Residual (Res) = PV residual value (resale value, salvage value) less disposal costs

Energy (E) = Total energy cost (PV)

Water (W) = Total water costs (PV)

Operating (O) Maintenance (M) & Repair (R) = Total operating, maintenance, and repair costs (PV)

Other (O) = Total other costs, if any—contract administration costs, financing costs, employee salaries and benefits, and so forth (PV)

Life Cycle Cost Analysis Works for Small Decisions

Life cycle cost comparisons for building components or equipment can be accomplished relatively easily if there are no significant financing costs or differences in procurement costs among the options (Snodgrass, 2013). For a simple lifecycle cost analysis, the following items are added together: a) the initial cost of each system; b) replacement costs expected life (most often in years) of each system; c) anticipated average yearly maintenance, operation, and repair costs of each system; d) any salvage or other residual value you will get out of the system; e) time period for the analysis and figure the cost for each system over that time period; and f) yearly average operating, maintenance, and repair costs (including fuel and utility costs) (Snodgrass, 2013).

Simple Formula for Calculating Life Cycle Cost

The formula used to determine life cycle cost has been defined as (Snodgrass, 2013):

$$LCC = I + Repl - Res + L (OM\&R)$$

Where:

I = Initial cost

Repl = Replacement cost for any system that isn't expected to last the full time period. The replacement cost may need to be proportioned. For example, if the selected time period is 30 years, but the system will only last 20 years, you will need to include a replacement cost that is one-third of the full replacement cost. This is because two-thirds of the expected life of the replacement system will occur after the end of the time period you've chosen. Don't proportion the cost if the time period you select is the life of the structure, because once the structure's gone, you cannot get years of service from the system.

Res = Any remaining value you can recover at the end of the time period. If you can't sell it or trade it, there's none.

L = The time period you have chosen for the analysis.

OM&R = The yearly average operating, maintenance, and repair costs (including fuel and utility costs).

Life Cycle Cost Analysis Works for Big Decisions

An LCCA that evaluates large systems or whole buildings usually considers so much information that assembling and tracking all of it becomes a major undertaking. Adding to the complexity, LCCA normally is used to compare the cost of several alternative designs of buildings and building systems. The guidelines and discount rates in OMB (2015) Circular A-94 must be used for determining present value for life cycle cost analysis on projects.

Life Cycle Assessments

Life cycle assessment (LCA) is emerging as one of the most functional assessment tools. The LCA process is governed under ISO 14000, the series of international standards addressing environmental management. According to the International Organization for Standardization (ISO) 14040 (2006), LCA is a "compilation and evaluation of the inputs, outputs and the potential environmental impacts of a product system throughout its life cycle" (p. 2). LCA is a tool that allows architects and other building professionals to understand the energy use and other environmental impacts associated with all life cycle phases of the building: procurement, construction, operation, and decommissioning. The LCA can further be used to:

Life Cycle Assessment a technique to measure the environmental effects related to all the periods of a product's life from cradle to grave.

1. Evaluate the environmental costs associated with a product, process, structure, or activity.
2. Identify energy and materials used and wastes released to the environment.
3. Take into account the whole-of-life implications of acquiring, operating, maintaining and disposing of a building asset.
4. Make decisions at both strategic and operational levels.
5. Provide confidence regarding the optimum timing for equipment replacements and upgrades (ISO 14040, 2006).

While a life cycle cost analysis is a financial tool, a life cycle assessment evaluates the environmental costs associated with a product, process, structure, or activity by identifying energy and materials used and wastes released to the environment (Snodgrass, 2013). In this context, the term "life cycle" means the assessment considers everything that goes into or is produced as a result

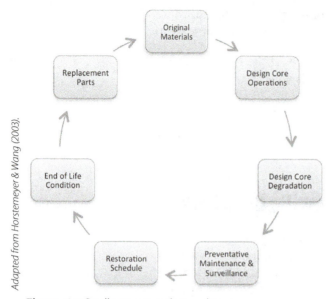

Figure 6.1 Cradle-to-grave design diagram.

of the product or service. This starts with production of raw materials and includes manufacturing, distribution, use, disposal, transportation, and the energy used by the product, process, structure, or activity. This is sometimes referred to as a "cradle-to-grave" assessment (see Figure 6.1).

LCA as a *cradle-to-grave* approach evaluates the environmental impacts that occur throughout the complete life cycle of a product, process, or activity (Hermann, Kroeze, & Jawjit, 2007). The cradle-to-grave approach is an analysis of the impact of a product from the beginning of its source gathering processes, through the end of its useful life, to disposal of all waste products. The sum of the cradle-to-grave environmental costs is the life cycle environmental cost of the product.

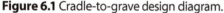

Cradle-to-Grave refers to a process in which an organization being accountable for the removal of goods it has manufactured without putting the components back into service.

Cradle-to-Cradle process in which all material inputs and outputs are viewed as technical (recycled or reused items with no loss of quality) or biological nutrient (items that can be composted or consumed).

Cradle-to-Cradle

Some products can be partly or completely reused or remanufactured into new products after they have served their original purpose. In these cases, the cycle is often referred to as "*cradle-to-cradle*" (McDonough & Braungart, 2010). A phrase invented by Walter R. Stahel in the 1970s, cradle-to-cradle is a process that seeks to create production techniques that are not just efficient but are essentially waste free (Dictionary of Sustainable Management, 2016). An example of a cradle-to-cradle product is an aluminum beverage can. Aluminum production is extremely energy intensive, but aluminum is fully recyclable no matter how many times it has already been recycled. Manufacturing new cans from recycled cans cuts energy use by 95%, making aluminum cans a cradle-to-cradle product. Unfortunately, only about half of the aluminum cans produced in the United States are recycled, so there's still some "grave" in aluminum can production.

With the tremendous long-term cost and impact of facility decisions, the financial analysis is an extremely critical component. A number of financial tools are available to evaluate scenarios, options, or alternatives; however, two components are critical to provide the complete business case for any Strategic Facilities Planning (SFP). First, the SFP must demonstrate that the facility supports the organization's core mission and strategy, and the financial analysis must demonstrate that the recommendations will yield the highest return at the lowest risk. To understand the financial analysis, the facility plan must address life cycle planning.

Life Cycle Assessment Stages

The life cycle assessment may be used in the pre-design, schematic design, and design development stage. Each of these stages will be explained in the following information.

Pre-Design Stage

During this stage, LCA can help define the environmental goals of a project. LCA could be used to make decisions regarding the building footprint among several options. The basic decisions for choosing a structural system can also be based on LCA. Trade-offs between impacts from the manufacturing phase and operational phase can be evaluated to select assembly types.

Schematic Design Stage

Choices regarding selection of building products and assemblies can be made with the help of LCA. Energy conservation measures can be assessed for their environmental burdens and an informed decision can be facilitated by the use of LCA.

Design Development Stage

In the design development stage, LCA can help evaluate the life-long impacts of proposed lighting and HVAC systems. The most crucial stages in a system's life can be identified in terms of environmental impact, and appropriate modifications to the system design can be proposed. Material finishes can also be compared with the help of LCA results, and the right choices can be made.

Facility Space Considerations

All facilities are different as are their space requirements. The needs for sports arenas and stadiums, health clubs, physical and sport instruction, gymnasiums, etc. will all be unique. As a result, facilities should be designed to be as flexible as possible to allow as many uses as possible to ensure economic viability. When the life cycle cost analysis and assessments of the overall structure have been completed, it is imperative that individual spaces for programs be considered. At minimum this should consist of a statement of intent, target audience, equipment requirements, space requirements, staffing needs, frequency, and an outline of the program structure. The analysis of space should include not only the primary activity areas but also the support or ancillary spaces needed within a facility for optimal operation.

Primary Activity Spaces

The primary purpose of any facility constructed for health, fitness, physical activity, recreation, or sport is for users to engage in the activity or the event itself. All facility users may generally be classified into four basic user groups: members (or users of the fitness/recreation center), team members (or event participants), spectators, and service providers (McDonald, 2011). The overall experience of each group needs to be top-quality in order for the project to flourish. As a result the understanding of the needs and desires of each population must be achieved (McDonald, 2011). Thus, the need and construction of appropriate primary activity spaces begin with good planning. While being careful not to duplicate services provided by others in the area, once the market is closely identified including needs and wants of the patron population, the primary activity spaces can start to be constructed.

Multipurpose Sports Fields

Multipurpose sports fields have become a popular choice in recent years. There are obvious exceptions to multipurpose use fields such baseball, which has highly specialized field requirements. However, outdoor sports such as soccer, lacrosse, and Ultimate Frisbee provide multipurpose opportunities. It is important to ensure that the patrons of multipurpose playing fields are provided the opportunity to participate in the sports of their choice safely. Whether the facility will be new construction or renovation of existing outdoor primary activity spaces, some questions that need to be addressed include:

1. How will the soil characteristics of the area?
2. How will urbanization surrounding the area affect the activity space?
3. What are the geographic location issues that may impact the design and construction?

Soil Testing

Soil testing is crucial to ensure that the field is on solid ground. A soil analysis, which needs to take place before design and construction, starts with digging. The soil analysis will indicate the condition of the topsoil and subsoil. Evaluating a field's soils can make a significant difference in the long term. For example, heavy soils will hold a good deal of water, which makes the area vulnerable to compaction, thereby creating a possible standing water and drainage problems. These issues will impact the use of the field in the short- as well as long-term use. Amending the soils of a natural grass field can make the field more resilient and less likely to compact, which also makes it easier to maintain—all big pluses for a long lifespan (Nardone, 2014).

Environmental Considerations

Another important consideration when designing and constructing an activity field is the environment immediately around the site. Questions that should be addressed are:

1. What features are near the field that will have an impact on what you can build, and where?
2. What type of lighting can be installed for night games?

3. What are the local traffic patterns?

4. Are there any wetlands or bodies of water around the field that could negatively affect participation due to flooding or underground water saturation?

5. What are the wind patterns and could they have a negative impact on the competition?

6. Would the position of the sun at certain times of the day have an adverse impact on the games?

Geographic Location

The geographic location must also be considered when designing and constructing sports fields. For example, in areas subject to freezing, keep a close eye on metal post caps that might be loosened and removed, which may allow moisture to accumulate and eventually freeze inside the posts, leading to fracture. Special attention should be paid to review any old outdoor equipment for signs of deterioration where it meets the ground as well as all of the post tops. Inspections don't always need to be complicated and time-consuming. For example, a weekly scan for corrosion and wear on points of connection, such as field goal or soccer posts, are effective. The Consumer Product and Safety Commission (CPSC) checklist for routine inspection and maintenance includes these items:

1. Broken equipment such as loose bolts, missing end caps, cracks, etc.

2. Broken glass and other trash

3. Cracks in plastics

4. Loose anchoring

5. Hazardous or dangerous debris

6. Insect damage

7. Problems with surfacing

8. Displaced loose-fill surfacing

9. Holes, flakes, and/or buckling of unitary surfacing

10. User modifications (such as ropes tied to parts or equipment rearranged)

11. Vandalism

12. Worn, loose, damaged, or missing parts

13. Wood splitting

14. Rusted or corroded metals

15. Rot

It is important to ensure that the playing fields patrons with the opportunity to participate in the sports of their choice safely and properly. In the end, the facility is liable for checking on the safety of the outdoor spaces. However, it is key to note that all participants should report any kind of potential issues that may compromise the safety of the area. If participants see something, they should say something.

Multipurpose Indoor Sport Spaces

The popularity of multipurpose indoor facilities has increased as estimates place the number of privately operated multipurpose indoor sports facilities in the United States at more than 300 (Popke, 2006). A multipurpose facility offers a range of services such as sport and recreational activities in one location. Sport and recreation facilities may consider using indoor multi-purpose spaces for several reasons such as:

1. Trends in lifestyle and activity participation
2. Consumer expectations
3. Programming advantages
4. Environmental and economic factors.

Indoor multi-purpose facilities, in particular, are helpful to growing physical activities as well as to accommodate individual, unstructured activities. Such multi-purpose facilities help to provide opportunities to cross-program individual facility components and to offer one-stop recreation programming for families and other groups, with varying individual interests. From an operational standpoint, centralizing facilities under one roof decreases the level of energy consumption associated with a number of decentralized indoor locations. Energy costs are thereby reduced, as are other costs including staffing, office equipment, among others.

However, multipurpose facilities go well beyond simply taking down the volleyball nets and putting up tennis nets in the same area does not necessarily constitute making a facility a multipurpose space. Nor does having several different sports being conducted simultaneously make the facility multipurpose. To truly determine if the facility can be considered multipurpose, the following questions must be asked:

1. Does the area have the ability to provide sufficient barriers so others do not interfere with the play? In some facilities, the basketball and volleyball courts are located so close together that an errant ball enters another court. Situations such as this do not only interfere with play but may cause injury to one or more of the participants.

2. Does the space offer sufficient flexibility to conduct various categories of types of events while maintaining facilitate flow, security, and visibility? One mistake that sometimes occurs in a facility is the inability to supervise several different events at the same time due to the lack of visibility. For example, a desk supervisor should be able to view the actions on the basketball courts, volleyball courts, and weight/cardiovascular rooms without obstruction. The lack of visibility increases the likelihood of theft, fights, and other actions that would be harmful to the client.

3. Are the acoustic issues satisfactory for the participants as well as the spectators? It used to be that large video displays and high-quality sound systems were luxury items, but now they are design standards.

Having specific venues adjacent to each other requires that particular attention be paid to acoustics and sightlines. For example, some weight and cardio rooms have heavy metal music playing loudly to enhance the experience. While this may be fine for those in the area, it would take away from a yoga session if the music from the weight room infiltrated the nearby yoga room.

Multipurpose Unique Offerings

In many cases, indoor basketball courts can host volleyball contests by having appropriate lines. Outside of the facility, football fields can be modified to host soccer contests. Facility specifications of the more traditional facility specifications may be viewed in Table 6.1.

While these specifications are useful, an effective facility manager must be aware of the more unique activities that may be provided in a sport facility. Several new opportunities for such activities that have recently emerged include pickleball, underwater hockey, kayak polo, Wallyball, and Quidditch (from the Harry Potter books and movies).

Spectator Seating Issues

Spectator seating issues begin when the bleachers or individual seats are purchased by the facility. When buying the selected type of seating, it is important to determine the local code requirements. Such code requirements may include guardrails, openings between seating components, types of non-skid surfaces, and accessibility. Similar to many building codes, individual communities may have unique circumstances that mandate specific standards be met for compliance. Such circumstances may be due to a previous incident or an extraordinary environmental reason (i.e. snow, rain, heat, etc.). Once the spectator seating is deemed to be fully compliant with relevant codes, it is the responsibility of the facility director to ensure the codes are followed. This may best be accomplished by performing regular inspections (prior to and after every event) to verify that the seats are safe.

Spectator Amenities

More than 50 years ago sports facility design and construction processes did not take into account different types of seating, amenities, and services. Generally, seating bowls had simple, linear, mostly symmetrical layouts. The seats themselves were constructed of wood and metal, often in a limited a 16-to-18 inch wide seating space on a continuous bench without a seat back.

Nowadays, sports facilities offer preferred seat locations. These seat locations are close to the action but still provide excellent viewing points and lines of sight. Since these seats are the highest priced in the facility, many facility operators cite the 80-20 rule—80% of the revenue comes from 20% of the attendees.

Table 6.1 *Traditional Multipurpose Activity Specifications*

Activity	Specifications
Badminton	A standard badminton court measures 20' × 44' and can be used for both singles and doubles play. The diagram includes specifications for long service, short service, center and side lines.
Baseball	A standard baseball diamond measures 90' from base to base and 60'6" from pitcher's plate to home. Diagrams include specifications for base lines, batter's box, catcher's box, foul line, pitcher's plate, home plate, coach's box, on-deck circle, and grass lines. The PDF includes variations for youth league, pony league and senior league fields.
Basketball	Optimum dimensions of a basketball court are 94' × 50' (professional/college) or 84' × 50' (high school). Diagrams include specifications for sidelines, three-point line, free-throw lane, center circle, coaching box and scorers' table.
Field Hockey	Optimum dimensions for field hockey are 100 yards × 60 yards with the grass cut to a height of ¾"–1½". The diagram includes sidelines, striking circle and penalty stroke line.
Football	A standard football field measures 360' × 160' (including end zones). Diagrams of professional, college and high school feature pylon specifications, goal post detail, recommended yard-line numbering and end zone detail.
Ice Hockey	Recommended ice hockey dimensions vary in the range of 85'–100' × 185'–200'. Diagrams include specifications for face-off configuration, crease and goal frame.
Soccer	Soccer field dimensions may vary in the range of 50–100 yards × 100–130 yards. The PDF includes specifications for both outdoor and indoor soccer fields.
Softball	The distance between bases on a softball field varies from 60' (fast pitch) to 65' (slow pitch). The PDF includes in-field diagram, home plate details, official distance table and wheelchair softball specifications.
Swimming	Included here are the facility standards of FINA and USA Swimming; APSP construction dimensions for class B and C pools; and NCAA recommended dimensions for collegiate competition (long-course swimming, short-course swimming and diving facilities).
Tennis	A standard tennis court measures 36' × 78' (including doubles alleys).
Track & Field	Dimensions for track and field events based on requirements set forth by the NFHS. Diagrams serve merely as examples; rules allow variation in geometry and layout. The PDF includes specifications for 400 meter track, 400 meter events (with staggers and hurdle settings), track/playing field configuration, shot put pad, suggested discus/hammer cage, javelin runway, pole vault landing area, long jump/triple jump pit plan and high jump detail.

Volleyball	A standard volleyball court measures 29'6" × 59' (9m × 18m). The PDF includes diagrams for both indoor and outdoor volleyball courts.
Water Polo	A standard water polo course measures 25m x 20m with a recommended water depth of 2m. The PDF includes diagrams of both floating goal and wall-mounted goal variations.

Adapted from Facility Specification Guide (2016). athleticbusiness.com/images/pdf/316-SpecGuide_web_high.pdf

The 20% attendees are sitting in the premium seats, buying premium food and beverages, and, arguably, paying premium prices (Lamberth, 2005).

The luxury/private suite concept has become a staple of many new sport facilities. Generally, a standard suite holds up to 16 people with fixed seats in a living room environment. Suites often include drink rails, bar stools, a buffet, and a kitchenette area. A combination of television monitors, dedicated phone lines, computers with Internet access, and wireless hot spots are now standard features (Lamberth, 2005). Restrooms should be placed in a separate location from the suite environment to improve cleanliness, odor control, and cost savings in construction and maintenance (Lamberth, 2005).

New expansive nightclub style lounges, fine dining, loge seating, bunker suites or lounges, and field or courtside suites are trending in the field of spectator seating design. According to Lamberth (2005), nightclub style bars offer fashionable, lounge style environments for fans who wish to be close to the action. Full-service sit-down restaurants, build-your-own buffets, and stand-alone dessert carts offering premium menu selections are being provided in sports facilities. The loge seat concept takes the suite out of the suite and into the open bowl. Loge seating includes comfortable office style chairs, a dining counter top for in-seat food service, dedicated television and Internet access, and occasionally a small refrigerator. Bunker suites and lounges do not offer any views of the action. However, bunker suites provide a large environment that provides all of the finishes, amenities, and services of a suite or lounge. Finally, Lamberth indicates that courtside and field suites, like the ones at CenturyLink Field in Seattle, are suites placed right down in the front row, bringing the fans even closer to the action.

Line of Sight

A key spectator seating issue is the line of sight. In particular, the spectator's line of sight is an important element in the design of viewing venues. Quality lines of sight, unobstructed views, comfortable seating or premium seating were not paramount design elements in the past. However, they are significant considerations for today's sports facility designs. During the design, architects and engineers, as well as the planning committee must carefully consider how the spectator seats are arranged without compromising on the quality of every spectator's view. The line of sight is a straight line along

Line of Sight the ability of a spectator to see a predetermined point of focus (such as the nearest touchline or outside lane of a running track) over the top of the head of the spectators sitting immediately in front.

which an observer observes an object. *Line of sight* refers to the ability of a spectator to see a predetermined focal point of the area of activity over the top of the head of the spectators immediately in front or to the side. It is an imaginary line that stretches between observer's eye and the object that he is looking at. If the object being observed is above the horizontal, then the angle between the line of sight and the horizontal is called angle of elevation. If the object is below the horizontal, then the angle between the line of sight and the horizontal is called the angle of depression.

Ensuring adequate sightlines is, therefore, an important part of providing safe seated accommodation. While the lines of sight may be augmented by the presence of an extremely large video screen, balancing an uninterrupted view of the field from each seat without sacrificing structure, cost, and safety considerations is critical. Ineffective views can result in spectators jumping up for a better view during exciting play. This action may result in irritation to others and lead to fights in the stand. In large crowds, this can be a serious safety threat. The better the sightline, the more likely it is that spectators will remain seated during the event. Finally, when a physical barrier or fence exists, the architects, engineers, as well as the planning committee must consider the lines of sight. When any type of physical barrier is required, it must not present a risk or danger to spectators or players (FIFA Stadium Safety, n.d.).

The lines of sight in the horizontal plane should be contemplated for the front row spectators as they may need to look sideways as the action of the sport is played. At the end of the front row, spectators could have their view blocked by the heads of spectator sitting next to them or across the aisle. During exciting plays, spectators tend to jump out of their seats to gain a better view. A straight view for all front row spectators is often assured by the use of curved stands (Guide to Safety at Sports, 1997).

Concourse a circulation area providing direct access to and from spectator accommodation, via stairways, ramps, vomitories, or level passageways, and serving as a milling area for spectators for the purposes of refreshment and entertainment. It may also provide direct access to toilet facilities.

The presence of individuals with disabilities is another consideration regarding lines of sight at sports contests. According to the U.S. Department of Justice (n.d.) wheelchair seating locations must provide lines of sight comparable to those provided to other spectators. In stadiums where spectators can be expected to stand during the event (i.e., football, baseball, basketball games), all or a majority of the wheelchair seating locations must provide a line of sight over standing spectators. A comparable line of sight, as illustrated in the figure below, allows a person using a wheelchair to view the playing action between the heads and over the shoulders of the persons standing in the row immediately in front and over the heads of the persons standing two rows in front (U.S. Department of Justice, n.d.).

Stadium or Arena Concourse Areas

An element that must be addressed in the design of a sport or recreation facility is a concourse area. A *concourse* is defined as a circulation area that offers direct access to and from viewing accommodation that may be connected by vomitories, passageways, stairs, or ramps (Guide to Safety at Sports

Grounds, 2008). The concourse area allows spectators to visit, obtain refreshments, use restrooms, and be part of the entry and exit routes.

It is not uncommon for new sports facilities to have three or more concourse levels. As a result, more vertical circulation should strongly be considered in a sport facility design and construction. *Vertical circulation* is the movement of people and/or products between floors of multi-level facilities (Civil Engineering, 2016). Allotting stairs, escalators, and elevators for which public, private, and service use is independently assigned is essential to avoiding the congestion and frustration of moving so many people throughout the venue. For example, allowing food service to transport the goods in the same elevator will most likely clog up the use of the elevator. Working closely with a vertical transportation consultant to manage these issues may even reduce the original estimated requirements (Lamberth, 2005).

Vertical Circulation the movement of people and/or products between floors of multi-level facilities.

Progressively, concourses also form a significant access route to facilities provided for the comfort and enjoyment of spectators. As referred to in Chapter 1, access routes are also referred to as vomitoria in the early Roman venues. The *Guide to Safety at Sports Grounds* (2008) defines a *vomitory* as "an access route built into the gradient of a stand which directly links spectator accommodation to concourses, and/or routes for ingress, egress and emergency evacuation" (p. 75). As a result, it is crucial that neither the design nor management of concourses negatively impact the safety of spectators. This is a particular concern at existing grounds where concourses, initially designed solely for general circulation, have been fitted with additional facilities, which considerably add to the concourses' usage during peak times. Circulation routes and areas must be clear particularly when there may be a large number of spectators moving through it at any given time. Additionally, all circulation routes must be free of trip hazards and have slip-resistant floor surfaces (Guide to Safety at Sports Grounds, 2008).

Vomitory an access route built into the gradient of a stand, which directly links spectator accommodation to concourses, and/or routes for ingress, egress or emergency evacuation.

Being in a crowded situation can create a sense of easiness among spectators. Everywhere possible, new facilities should be planned so that there are uninterrupted circulation routes that are associated with both ingress and egress routes. Moreover, facility management should assure that sufficient access and egress is afforded to emergency vehicles to the facility. Wherever possible such routes should be separate from those used by spectators or, alternatively, provide for the parking of emergency vehicles so that spectator routes are not obstructed. Finally, the police, fire, and ambulance authorities should be consulted about the suitability of access routes in generating an agreed plan of action, including access for emergency vehicles, for all foreseeable incidents.

Beyond ingress, egress, and life safety issues, circulation within sports facilities must flow, promoting ease of access, even when at capacity. To allow for sufficient flow, concourses are becoming wider. Allowing an additional 15–20% of the required code width can make a huge difference. Also, adding lobby and entry space allows for a larger queue area that supports effective security screening (Guide to Safety at Sports Grounds, 2008).

To ensure that concourses are designed and construction to provide for smooth circulation during peak hours as well as to provide patron safety and security the following items must be deliberated:

1. The positioning of travel routes—for general ingress, egress or access to toilets or catering outlets—should be determined, and should not create cross flows; that is, people moving along the concourse should not be impeded by large numbers crossing their path.

2. To avoid congestion and discomfort, there should be an adequate number of toilets and concession areas provided. These should be spaced sufficiently apart in concourses to avoid queues for each becoming disorderly, thereby creating additional potential congestion.

3. The positioning of concessions and restroom entrances should be such that the lines do not impede the circulation of people along the concourse nor the entry of spectators into the concourse direct from turnstiles.

4. The positioning of concessions and restroom entrances immediately next to the foot of vomitories or stairways leading from spectator accommodation. This is to avoid congestion in the vomitories owing to the potential build-up of queues.

5. The location of television monitors, or any other forms of display that might encourage large numbers of people to stand around (Guide to Safety at Sports Grounds, 2008).

Additionally, the design and management of ingress and egress routes should take into consideration the following:

1. Entrances to each part of the ground should, wherever practicable, be designed and located so as to allow for the even distribution of spectators.

2. Walls, fences, and gates should not provide the opportunity for hand or footholds which might assist climbing. They should be regularly inspected.

3. The installation of closed circuit television should be considered in order to assist in the monitoring of crowd densities outside the ground and throughout the ingress/egress routes.

4. The design of the turnstile and its housing should allow for the operator to see and communicate clearly with entrants.

5. Turnstiles are not suitable for use by wheelchair users, visually impaired spectators, and people with assistance dogs. The most practical design solution is to provide level access via a gate or door, with an appropriate vision panel, which is staffed by a steward. Arrangements must be in place to ensure that all those entering by such routes are counted among the spectators attending the event.

6. Entrances should be located so that the flow of people to the spectator accommodation can be evenly distributed. Where this distribution is uneven, it gives rise to congestion at an entrance. Consideration should be given to changing the turnstile or entry point arrangements.

7. Entry routes should not be obstructed. Amenities such as refreshment kiosks or toilets should be located away from the immediate area of the turnstiles and entry routes.

8. *Ingress* and *egress* routes are often common to each other and in such cases, the considerations that apply to exit routes also apply to entry routes (Guide to Safety at Sports Grounds, 2008).

Ingress a place or means of access or entrance to a facility.

Egress action of going out of or exiting a facility.

Modern sports facilities have dramatically changed in the United States over the past 25 years. The sophisticated fan of today not only wants but often expects to be entertained with non-game elements; the game itself has become only a part of the entire experience. Therefore, current features and systems for patron comfort and safety are should be considered in every step of facility design and construction.

Ancillary Spaces

Support spaces are often overlooked or simply not given the attention provided to other, more visible areas. Yet, when a storage area or team locker room doesn't work, it will take a toll on the efficiencies of programs and the satisfaction of everyone involved. However, the actual use of the activity space is typically dependent upon additional support spaces such as locker rooms, administrative offices, storage spaces, restrooms, and others. In fact, the effective use of any activity space can be greatly impacted by the design, quality, and condition of such *ancillary spaces*.

Ancillary Space spaces that are used to house or contain operating, maintenance, or support equipment and functions.

Despite the fact that a building may have a designated primary usage, it is important to note that any health, sport, recreation, fitness, and physical activity building will require ancillary spaces in order to function appropriately. Ancillary spaces are essential as they provide the necessary support to the primary activities or operation of the organization. Yet, ancillary spaces of all types are often overlooked, or simply not given the attention provided to other more visible areas. When a storage area or team locker room doesn't work, it will take a toll on the efficiencies of programs and the satisfaction of everyone involved. Ancillary spaces such as equipment storage rooms and staff offices are often overlooked because they are considered back-of-house areas. Yet, they are absolutely critical to how the front end of the program functions. As such areas of support need to be addressed in the planning phase.

During the *programming phase*, architects and organizational committee members will need to have discussions around the following topics. Start by answering a basic set of questions for every space:

Facility Programming Phase involves collecting information from the anticipated facility occupants and user groups through focus group and/or individual interviews.

1. How will the space be used by different groups?
2. How does it need to function for each group?
3. What's the best arrangement?
4. How much space is needed?

The more detailed the answers, the better the facility will be in the long run. Committee members who are working in the facility must be prepared to present a detailed picture of the needs and applications of every space in the athletic facility.

Quality ancillary spaces have been linked to retention of professional athletes (Bynum, 2005), recruitment and retention of collegiate athletes (Dahnert & Pack, 2007), and as a general factor in attracting and retaining college students to campus recreation facilities (Miller, 2011). The design of these support areas is vital to the overall success of the physical activity, recreation, or sport facility. Ancillary spaces may include, but are not limited to the following areas: locker rooms, equipment and storage rooms, office space, laundry rooms, showers, and restrooms.

Locker Room Considerations

The classic example of a locker room has progressed from a plain, no-frills area to store clothes and personal effects while working out into nearly a spalike environment for relaxing after a challenging workout. Increased consideration is being provided for the features of a locker room as the end users continue to insist on nicer facilities. Nowadays, it not unusual for a locker room to have large flat screen TVs, saunas, or computer access capabilities. In most physical activity based facilities the locker room will be the largest and most complex of the ancillary spaces. The locker room is much more than just a room full of lockers. The locker room fulfills a number of functions related to dressing, storage, personal grooming, social interaction, instruction, safety, and privacy. The most basic of components for all locker rooms include lockers, toilets, showers, and grooming stations. Key design factors include the location of the locker room in relation to the activity spaces as well as the arrangement of the locker room components. Whenever a pool or other aquatic venue is a part of the activity spaces, the locker room should be on the same floor level to prevent patrons from slipping while climbing up or descending downs stairs (Petersen & Gonzales, 2013).

Non-custom, small, vented, metal lockers as a part of a low-end locker room finish.

Locker rooms typically fall into three design categories based upon cost, finishes, and features: low, medium, and high-end. The low-end locker room typically will include sealed concrete floors, standard metal lockers, basic lighting, non-finished ceilings, and gang showers. The mid-level locker room might upgrade to customized metal lockers, integrated bench systems, showers with tile floors and walls, and finished ceilings. The high-end locker room tends to feature custom wooden lockers, completely tiled floors and walls, carpeted areas, individual showers, solid-surface countertops (stone,

Corian, etc.), and extra amenities like saunas, steam rooms or whirlpools, lounge spaces, and televisions (Fickes, 1999). Regardless of the design category and cost, all locker rooms have common basic components that all need to be carefully planned for an effective locker room design.

According to McGowan and Kruse (2004), locker room entrance and exit doors should have vision barriers. Heavy-duty moisture resistant doors at locker room entrances and exits should be of sufficient size to handle the traffic flow and form natural vision barriers. Entrance and exit doors for the locker room area should be equipped with corrosion resistant hardware.

The best facilities employ an approach that looks at more than just surfaces. For locker rooms that offer both fitness and aquatic pool facilities, it is advisable to divide wet versus dry areas in the locker room. Using hard, nonporous surfaces and even antimicrobial-treated laminates are best wherever possible, but there is more to think about. The mix of wet and dry area concerns makes flooring selection of great importance for the locker room. One key factor in flooring selection is slip resistance. A wet area of the locker room must provide enough traction to reduce or eliminate slips and falls. However, there is a balance to be maintained in creating high traction floors. As a floor surface is made more textured for anti-slip purposes, this rougher surface becomes more difficult to keep clean and can be more uncomfortable on bare feet. Primary floor choices in the locker room include lower cost options like coated concrete and flow-through interlocking tiles, mid-priced options like ceramic tile and poured epoxy, and higher end options like high-grade carpet, porcelain, slate, or marble tile (Popke, 2006).

Air flow is another key component to keeping your facility in top shape. For optimal performance, damp, humid air from showers and locker rooms must be directed away with a fresh-air exchange system with negative air pressure. Lockers and shelving that promote air flow and drying will help curb the growth of mold or mildew. Mobile storage and fixtures that can be cleaned under and around are another important consideration when designing your space. Creating a space that is easy to clean, has the right air flow, and is built using hard surfaces will greatly reduce your chances of having costly sanitation issues or virus outbreaks.

The determination of the total number of lockers to be provided in the locker room is vital to the planning and design process. A peak load of facility users should be determined or projected in order to provide adequate numbers of lockers for all users. Where total space is limited, this may require a mix of locker sizes and configurations in order to meet user demand. However, locker sizes must still be able to

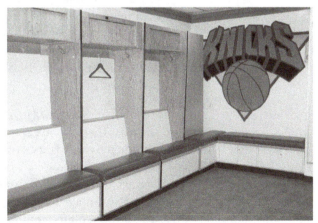

A portion of a locker room with higher end finishes in an NBA venue.

fully accommodate the storage needs of clothing and equipment for the users. Ideally, the number of lockers should exceed the current peak use in order to accommodate for program growth without the need for immediate facility renovation (Petersen & Gonzales, 2013).

Final selection of lockers should take into consideration a number of factors including cost, appearance requirements, durability and abuse resistance, corrosion resistance, locking systems, size and configuration options, and installation requirements. Lockers should be selected early in the design process to help ensure that that they are not overlooked and underfunded at the end of the design and building process. Additionally, the specifications for each locker model installation are important in the planning process. Locker selection and locker room design should also take into account that at least 5% of each type of locker must be accessible to persons with disabilities and include easy to operate handles or latches that do not require pinching or grasping to operate as well as a maximum 54" side reach height (ADA Accessibility Guidelines, 2002).

Storage and Equipment Room Considerations

The equipment room is often the part of a sports facility that receives the least amount of allocated space. To ensure that traffic flow will be easily maintained, double doors in high-traffic areas where equipment will be moving through would be a wise selection. High-density storage is usually far preferred to traditional storage, which requires more space and is more difficult to organize. Additional considerations are the removal of traditional wire cages and stationary shelves, which are not usually flexible enough to function adequately.

A typical equipment room is a square box with some lumber-made shelves bolted to the wall. Often, the equipment ends up on the floor because the staff is in a hurry or the placement of equipment is not identified. This blocks access to the shelving so more stuff gets dumped on the floor. These rooms are quickly rendered inefficient, unsanitary, and costly. They rob facility staff of time spent searching for the appropriate equipment. It wastes space and expensive gear degrades quickly because it's not properly cared for. The related sanitation issues increase liability, which also increases program costs. When it comes to reflecting pride in the program these rooms can be an embarrassment.

To adequately address storage issues, a consideration is to have small separate storage areas. These storage spaces would be located near the individual team or program activity spaces. An advantage to this system is that individual coaches or program leaders would control their own access to equipment. This arrangement may allow for equipment to be stored closer to its point of use. The disadvantage to this system is that control of access to the multiple areas can be difficult to monitor.

In many instances, facilities do not have enough storage space or have outgrown their existing storage space. Utilization of "just-in-time" purchasing and delivery is one option to reduce the amount of storage space required. For example, rather than ordering and receiving your facility cleaning supplies in bulk for the year, the items could be purchased in bulk but delivered on a monthly or bi-monthly schedule. This would reduce the amount of storage space that would need to be dedicated to these types of supplies. This form of purchasing, however, does not work well with large equipment or non-consumable items (Petersen & Gonzales, 2013).

Regardless of whether the storage space is arranged in a large centralized space or in smaller "point-of use" areas, the total amount of space available must be adequate for the proper storage equipment and supplies. Proper storage would include keeping equipment secure and protecting it from inappropriate use or theft. Proper storage is also necessary to reduce liability for the facility operators and owners. In fact, the American College of Sports Medicine (ACSM) Guidelines for Health/Fitness Facility Design and Construction call for separate spaces from activity areas for operational storage (Tharrett, McInnis, & Peterson, 2007). In addition, proper storage should include adequate temperature and humidity controls for equipment that could be adversely impacted by environmental extremes. The use of overhead roll-up doors or oversized double doors also can help maximize use and access of storage space.

Storage space must be suited for the intended purpose. The storage requirements for boxed files are quite a bit different than the requirements of large two person kayaks. Sport and recreation activities could require multiple spaces with each space designed for a specific purpose. Other overlooked spaces can cause frustrations as well. If an equipment repair area isn't planned for, future staff is forced to create a makeshift area. The same is true for equipment staging and issuing areas and mudrooms. How these areas are planned for and where they are located is imperative to prevent costly mistakes in the future. Never underestimate the need for storage.

Laundry Rooms

Laundry areas should be near locker rooms for each of use. Because of heat and humidity, it's essential to isolate this room into a dedicated space and locate it near the main equipment room if possible. Mold, mildew, bacteria, staph problems, and the MRSA virus are just a few of the invisible offenders that can negatively impact the reputation of a sport facility. Spaces that promote air flow and cleanliness can help eliminate these serious threats. As such, plans should be made to ventilate the moisture and humidity that occur in these rooms out of the building.

© Dmitry Kalinovsky/Shutterstock.com

Laundry rooms can create health hazards if not properly maintained and operated.

Toilets

The location and total number of locker room toilets must be carefully considered. One primary consideration is the wet toilet. If the facility includes aquatic elements, then it is likely that wet patrons will use some toilets. For example, wet area toilets should be provided either in a wet area of the locker room or in a restroom directly connected to the aquatic facility. If wet toilet use is anticipated within the locker room, then it is important to also provide dry toilets in another area of the locker room.

Mixing of traffic between wet and dry toilets should be avoided for several reasons. First, no dry person would enjoy sitting on a wet toilet. Second, street shoes in a wet toilet area can lead to slips and falls, and wet bare feet on wet floors soiled by dirt from street shoes is both unpleasant and unsanitary (Petersen & Gonzales, 2013).

The number of fixtures (both water closets and urinals) should be designed to meet the peak demands within a locker room facility. A commonly accepted standard of one water closet per 60 lockers may be adequate for many applications; however, this ratio should be modified as needed to specific needs of facility users (Lavoie, 2005). All toilets should provide privacy for the user; this is typically done with partitions. Selection of partition materials should take into account that most locker rooms have a more corrosive environment than a typical restroom. A growing trend in locker room construction is the creation of individual full-walled toilet rooms for added privacy, each with their own ventilation system (Shaver, 2005).

Finally, the Americans with Disabilities Act of 1990 (ADA) require when six or more toilet compartments and urinals are provided in a multi-user restroom, the restroom must have a minimum of one ambulatory accessible compartment. Men's toilets that have only one urinal are no longer mandated to have an accessible urinal. When multiple single-user toilets are located at one location, only 50% are required to be accessible. The new regulations also contain other technical changes, including changes regarding water closet location and grab bars, clearance, doors, toilet paper dispensers (U.S. Department of Justice, n.d.).

Transgender Facilities

A relatively new, but significant ancillary space to consider, are transgender facilities. The right to restrooms that match one's gender identity have also been recognized in the workplace and are actively being asserted in public accommodations. In Iowa, for example, discrimination in public accommodations on the basis of sexual orientation and gender identity has been prohibited by law since 2007 through the Iowa Civil Rights Act (Fraioli, 2015).

The need for transgender facilities that comply with Title IX are important in educational settings because it fosters campus facilities that are safe and

Signage to designate restrooms for gender accommodation.

inclusive for all to be in compliance with Title IX. These facilities could still be used by other users and could have baby changing stations, be used as family bathrooms, or be used as lactation rooms. Ensuring that general purpose restrooms, residence hall bathrooms, and locker rooms in recreational centers and athletic buildings are addressing the needs of transgender students would work towards achieved compliance. This can be accomplished by creating gender neutral, non-gender, or all gender facilities.

Staff Offices

End users such as facility administrators and staff should deconstruct their existing facility. The term *deconstruction* refers to the process of dismantling or removing useable materials from the structure "…in a manner which maximizes the recovery of building materials for reuse and recycling and minimizes the amount of waste transported for disposal in landfills and transformation facilities" (Dinuba Municipal Code, 2015, para. 8). The design of commercial office space serves to function appropriately, extend human capacity, and enhance productivity. Office space also serves as an aesthetic image of the company's mission (Simonson & Schmitt, 1997). Offices, regardless of type, must be functional; otherwise the spaces will not operate as required. The age of the workforce will have an impact on the habits of those workers. It will also impact the quality of the workplace expectations as well. Interaction and autonomy are the two key factors that must be considered together when understanding an organization's work processes. Space plans have a powerful effect on work processes. Performance is enhanced when space layouts support levels of interaction and autonomy (McGowan & Kruse, 2004). Understanding who will most likely work within organizations should also play a part in how the spaces are designed and furnished. Thus, it is important to understand how people work so spaces can be designed to meet those operational needs. It is also important to take into account ergonomics. It is always best to avoid situations that could result in time off for on-the-job injuries and costly claims (Petersen & Gonzales, 2013).

Deconstruction disassembly and removal of selected or all portions of a facility or structure for recovery and potential reuse.

Special consideration should be given to noise control. Offices where confidential information is discussed should be designed to minimize noise transfer. This can be achieved through many different methods. Walls can be insulated, double pane windows with shades can be installed, ceilings can be insulated, and walls can extend to the underside of the roof structure. Not all of these are necessary in the same wall; each method is a way to achieve low sound transmission. Controlling sound transmission is not just for new construction. Existing walls and ceilings can be modified to easily achieve this goal.

The facility administrator and committee should consider office space from the standpoint of overall space and layout. What works, what doesn't? Are there rooms you would like to realign? Are there places you'd like a double door or an exit? What's the one space you don't have now but would most value in a new facility? How much support space is needed, and how can it be maximized? No two facilities are alike. However, time and equipment investments may be saved when designs that maximize the full amount of cubic space in each room while improving access and traffic flow are considered.

Traffic Flow Issues

The traffic flow within many facilities is complicated because it involves the simultaneous movement of people and equipment. Proper traffic flow minimizes congestion and confusion. Think of designs that encourage multiple lanes of traffic, parking areas, and off-ramps. Planning for a large equipment room for example, will provide the necessary space for gear to get organized and ready to move. This will keep high-traffic areas like adjacent hallways or the gym more open. Estimate the number of people including spectators, players, coaches, support staff, and volunteers moving through the facility during high-traffic times. Anticipate the traffic flow and ensure that directions are simple and obvious. Ensure that the width of hallways and doors are adequate. Wherever possible, design for equipment to move through back doors and secondary hallways. Doors, entrances, and exits should accommodate large equipment. Consider where double doors are necessary and insist on doors free from a center post (mullion) or with an easily removable center post.

Safety Design Considerations

According to Frosdick (2009), safety begins with the design, maintenance, and physical integrity of the facilities so that they do not injure spectators or participants. Safety focuses on the estimation and maintenance capacities of the facilities in which people can safely participate in activities such as the inclusion of buffer zones between activity areas. Further, safety may apply to the design of the parking lot surrounding the facility particularly as it addresses the American Disabilities Act (ADA) of 1990 as well as appropriate design for lighting. Finally, safety design denotes the readiness to deal with emergencies, including those that may require a full or partial evacuation of the facility in a short period of time.

Stolovitch (1995) suggested that facility design for safety should not be considered as an add-on, as this can result in increased cost and vulnerability to potential security-related lawsuits. The process addressed in the early stages of building design can identify safety concerns. However, many sport facilities have not been designed with safety in mind (Gillentine, Miller, & Crow, 2010; Khiun Then & Loosemore, 2005; Miller, 2014; Miller, Veltri, & Gillentine, 2008). Whereas a poorly designed and maintained sport facility provides the conditions that precipitate accidents, one that is well designed can have inbuilt safeguards/barriers that may make it difficult for incidents to occur or that may help stop the chain of events before they result in accidents. In almost all development situations, the design of a sport facility is associated with a host of other factors, such as the culture of the organization, tasks and processes in place, and tools and technology.

Facility design problems generally involve a lack of communication between the architect(s) and facility planning committee. Because of limited opportunities to fund such research, it is prudent to use past research to develop design guidelines. van der Smissen (1990) stated that, "the design, layout, and construction of areas and facilities can provide either safe or hazardous conditions, enhancing or detracting from the activity in which one is engaged" (p. 235). The design of a sport or recreation facility should be thought of as an intricate network of connected elements, including buffer zones, parking lots, and emergency evacuation routes. Mistakes in the design of these interrelated components can create additional pressures onto the others, which may lead to accidents, some of which may be fatal.

Construction Processes

While most sport facility construction work is new, there has been some notable renovation of existing facilities as well (Muret, 2003). According to John McCutheon II, Director of Business Development for Hunt Construction, "it's getting cheaper each year to replace an older facility than it is to get the present one up to standard" (Muret, 2003, para. 18). Of the approximately 124 arena facilities built across the country between 1994 and 2008, each was primarily constructed by different general contractors. Contractors typically do not share cost data with other contractors, as this type of information is a closely guarded trade secret that can give one contractor an edge over another in a competitive bid situation. With this thought in mind, it is likely that only a small minority of contractors who have constructed an arena facility over the last 20 years have constructed multiple facilities and would thus have more than one dataset of historical cost information.

Coordination may be considered the process that makes certain that the interplay of various areas runs smoothly. Chief among the achievable items that may result from proper coordination is the attainment of objectives without wasting time, effort, or money. New construction and renovation projects follow the same basic coordination principles as planning facilitates coordination by integrating the various plans through mutual discussion

Construction Process a process of distinguishing activities and resources needed to make a facility design become a tangible reality.

or the exchange of ideas. This is the framework against which the facility owners/representatives, architects, and builders will work through in various phases of construction. Specifically, these phases are: pre-planning, programming, schematic design, design development, construction documents, bidding, and facility construction. These seven phases will be addressed in the following sections.

Phase I—Pre-Planning Phase

Facility Pre-Planning Phase phase that may include site analysis, programming, construction cost analysis, and value engineering and occurs after some form of funding is available and before design begins.

In this phase, the planning committee is formed and goals for the facility are defined. The most successful committees consist of representatives from a broad range of backgrounds and disciplines. Among the first things the planning committee must do is to decide what sort of *project delivery system* will be used. How will the various parties be related? Will the owner engage a design professional to prepare plans and specifications and then contract separately with a construction contractor? Or will a single entity be responsible for the entire project? Other possible options include several separate specialty contractors, each related by contract with the facility owner, the use of a construction manager as an advisor to the facility manager and planning committee, and the phasing of the project such that individual portions of the field work are started prior to the completion of all design work.

Feasibility Study

Feasibility Study an analysis and evaluation of a proposed project to decide if it is likely to be financially profitable.

A *feasibility study* should be conducted during this phase of construction. The feasibility study should provide extensive investigation and analysis into the design option for the proposed facility. When conducted in the early stages of design, the feasibility study can identify possible logistical challenges or material use that may permit the facility owner to make an educated choice to continue with the proposed project. The feasibility study should consider all the alternatives within the scope of an identified need. It should analyze the social and financial impacts of the proposal and identify the risks involved by studying the:

1. Marketplace
2. Usage and management issues
3. Facility components
4. Location options
5. Financial viability
6. Existing site conditions, utilities, space and programming requirements
7. Environmental issues
8. Associated risks, budgetary and scheduling constraints and logistical considerations.

A feasibility study involves evaluation, analysis, and research for a business to be successful.

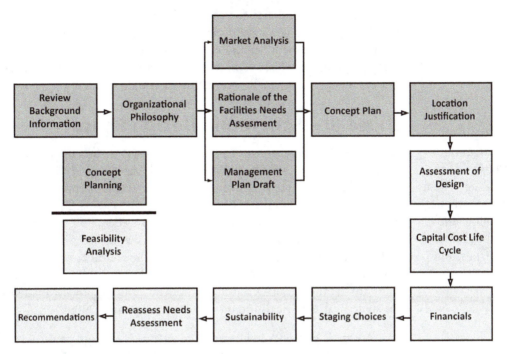

Figure 6.2 Feasibility study steps.

Through the commission of a feasibility study, the likelihood of developing an ineffective facility is significantly decreased while the potential for competency is increased. Figure 6.2 delineates the two-fold nature of the feasibility analysis including the integration of concept planning within the analysis.

Phase II—Programming Phase

Programming phase refers to the process of defining the activities and requirements of the spaces to be designed. The programming phase should start as soon as possible after the project has gotten underway. The purpose of programming is to expand upon and enhance the choice suggested at the end of the feasibility study in phase I. The programming phase includes an assessment of the site and space requirements for the proposed facility, a comprehensive evaluation of the client's programmatic necessities, a project budget and schedule, and an operational plan.

The selected architect will need to know how much space will be needed, how each space within the department will be used, and how the spaces will relate to each other. The architect will use the results of the planning efforts to develop schematic diagrams showing the relationships among the various project components, followed by detailed design of the structural, electrical, and other systems (Egeland, 2009). The architect prepares not only the detailed construction drawings but also written contract conditions containing legal requirements, technical specifications stipulating the materials and the manner in which they shall be installed, and a set of other documents related to the process of selecting the contractor and finalizing the contract.

The rule-of-thumb charts for square footage consideration were designed specifically to help you determine these needs. This is also the best time to compile the equipment list and budgets. Although the final budget will ultimately determine the scope of the project, anyone who's been through this process will agree—"You'll never get what you don't ask for."

Phase III—Schematic Design Phase

Facility Schematic Design Phase description of building systems (structural, mechanical, hvac, plumbing, and electrical), interior and exterior finishes, and the building site.

The *schematic design phase* produces drawings and other documents including a conceptual site plan, preliminary building plans, sections, and elevations including simple diagrammatic documents that define room sizes and relationships as well as single line diagrams of all systems. The selected architect will need to know how much space will be needed, how each space within the department will be used, and how the spaces will relate to each other to address overall relationships and functions. The architect will use the results of the planning efforts to develop schematic diagrams showing the relationships among the various project components, followed by detailed design of the structural, electrical, and other systems (Egeland, 2009).

The schematic phase is often referred to as the 20% design phase as the drawings reveal the project as being 20% into the endeavor (Anderson, Huhn, Rivera, & Susong, 2006). By employing feedback from the facility planning committee and the budgetary information, the architect can start to diagram the facility. It is in this phase that the formalization of the requirements, development of a site survey, completions of the local building restrictions, and preliminary meetings with the local planning commissions will take place. The architect will provide the preliminary site plans, exterior elevations, floor plans, and building sections (Anderson et al., 2006).

It is essential that the facility planning committee review the architectural drawings in stages to make any adjustments to the design. Without such input and agreement to the final schematic, costly and complicated changes may result. To avoid such a situation from occurring a design contract may be developed. The design contract indicates the particular details of the anticipated work from the architect. To ensure that the schematic phase proceeds on schedule, it is recommended that the design contract provide distinct targets that delineate the times that the architect will finish each phase as well as facility planning committee feedback.

After review and revisions, all parties must agree and accept the report before proceeding with the next step in the process. This could also include community or governmental approval to proceed. Approval at this juncture is an indication that the leadership is prepared to proceed and incur additional cost by proceeding. As of this point in project, approximately 20% of the design work has been completed.

Phase IV—Design Development Phase

During the *design development phase*, the more technical issues of constructability and the integration of building systems are addressed. In this step, the size, site location, elevation, look, materials, room sizes and locations, and building systems are finalized. Any changes by the owner will increase design costs, project costs (+/–) as well as the completion schedule.

During the design development phase, the architect will create blueprints by integrating the comments from the facility planning committee. The design development phase will reveal the precise room sizes, ceiling heights and locations of all doors and windows. The electrical, plumbing, and mechanical systems will be finalized during this phase as well. During this phase, the development of the approved schematic design documents will demonstrate elevations, typical construction details, equipment layouts, and diagrammatic layouts of building systems. The design development phase will describe the size and character of the project regarding architectural, structural, mechanical, and electrical systems.

Additionally, draft specifications that indicate installation, inspection, testing, and warrantee requirements will be involved in this phase (Anderson et al., 2006). Clearly written specifications should present a work breakdown structure. The division of work will permit an unmistakable exchange of ideas between the facility planning committee, architect, contractors, subcontractors, and suppliers.

At the completion of this phase state and local permitting submissions are made. The blueprints developed in this stage must be reviewed very carefully by the facility planning committee as project bidding and construction costs will be firmly based on this plan. Any major changes that affect project scope should be avoided at this point unless the revisions are absolutely necessary.

Facility Design Development Phase phase where location of equipment, furniture, electrical and telecommunication services and other user specific requirements are incorporated into the project design.

Phase V—Construction Document Phase

Construction documents are defined as the written and graphic documents prepared and assembled by the architect and engineer design team for communicating the project design for administering the construction contract. The construction documents are comprised of two parts—the Procurement Documents, and the Contract Documents. The sub-parts of these are as follows:

- Procurement documents
- Contracting requirements
- Specifications
- Contract drawings
- Addenda

Prior to visiting with the contractors, the architect will present construction documents that plainly describe the facility and the specifications of the

Facility Construction Document covers the legal, procedural, and construction information, that summarizes the important connections, rights, responsibilities, and relationships that bring a facility into reality.

© Philip Lange/Shutterstock.com

Stadium construction in Doha, Qatar for the 2022 World Cup.

facility. Additionally, the construction phases and timelines for completion will be designated. The approved construction documents provide comprehensive construction drawings and specifications of the proposed facility. The objective of the construction drawings in this phase is to generate schematics and specifications that are comprehensive enough for a contractor to accurately approximate the cost of construction (Anderson et al., 2006). Since these drawings are often referred to as the 100% drawings (Anderson et al., 2006), they are used in the competitive bid process among qualified contractors.

In this phase, bidders or proposers are instructed about the established procedures for preparing and submitting their bids or proposals. These documents are not published and released without the approval of the institution. Approval at this juncture is an indication that the leadership is prepared to proceed to construction pending a successful bidding process that meets the institution's budget. In this portion of work approximately 45% (80% total) of the design work is completed.

Phase VI—Bidding Phase

Based on the chosen delivery method, project bids will be sought among general contractors or through the construction manager to sub-contractors. Regardless of the delivery approach that will be used, the contractors' selection criteria and procedures should be clear, sound, and strictly adhered to, especially in publicly bid work. The contractors and sub-contractors will be chosen predicated on the proposed financial amount of the bids and post bid reviews. In this phase, the attention to detail and communication should facilitate an efficient evolution from design to the construction phase.

Bidding establishing a price an individual is willing to pay for a project.

Competitive *bidding* entails the distribution of complete sets of contract documents to more than one contractor who then bid against each other. Often, the lowest bidder is awarded the contract. The preliminary responsibilities in a competitive bidding process include deciding if the pool of bidders should be open or selective, qualifying contractors, as well as preparing and issuing the bid package. An institution may request multiple types of bids. These include the following:

- Stipulated sum—typical for design/bid/build projects
- Cost-plus—can be used for design/build/bid or design/build
- Unit price—typically used when quantities are unknown. This is typically the norm for civil engineering projects, but can also be for excavation, painting, concrete, etc.

To decide if the bidding process will be open or selective, the architect and the owner must decide whether they will receive better results for a project by choosing from a large or a small pool of bidders. Generally, the more bidders, the more competitive the bidding. Well-designed projects attract bidders because they are confident that the project will go smoothly. Conversely, there are bidders that will pursue poorly designed projects as it presents multiple opportunities to increase their profit through change orders that will likely be required. This type of bidder is taking a gamble that may or may not pay off. Unless the project is negotiated, or if the bidding is to be by invitation only, an "advertisement to bid" is published locally and regionally. In any case, bidders must be qualified and capable of completing the type of work specified.

When the pool is limited, an "invitation to bid" is distributed to contractors based on reputation, recommendation, prior work, financial wherewithal, or previous relationship with the owner or the architect. It is important to note that the invitation to bid as well as the public advertisement supplies a succinct summary of the project. While the legal system often mandates that public works be advertised in available publications such as newspapers, private facilities may elect to publicize their project in trade publications.

Prospective contractors who place bids may be recognized on the basis of their capacity to accept and successfully complete a project. Contractors who may not be in good standing in the profession or may be in a positive association with the owner will need to establish their qualifications prior to the issuance of the bidding documents. To make certain that all of the bidders are committed to their bid and are willing to fulfill the obligations, a form of security such as cash, certified check, or a bid bond (generally equal to 10% of the bid amount) may be required. The bid security may represent a lump sum or percentage of the submitted bid. If a bidder is chosen but declines to perform the work for the amount specified, the bidder may forfeit all or part of the security.

If any of the bidders desire to make any substitutions to the bidding document, the architect must receive a written request a minimum of 10 days prior to the submission date. Before the specific time and date identified in the advertisement or invitation to bid, all bids must be received in writing (verbal bids are usually unacceptable), enclosed in sealed, opaque envelopes. All bids received after the specified time and date will be sent back in the unopened, sealed envelope. When bids are opened in public, they are often read aloud.

When the bid is public, the owner is usually required by law to accept the lowest responsible bidder. However, should the bid be for a private facility, the owner is often not obligated to accept the lowest bid. Regardless of being private or public, the awarding organization should not accept the lowest bidder until the contractor has provided all of the necessary information (Anderson et al., 2006). This information includes documentation identifying that the contractor is properly licensed and meets or exceeds bonding and insurance requirements as well as the qualification and experience minimums.

All bidders should be informed of the decision after a selection has been made. Those parties that were not successful are sometimes provided a list of the final bid figures and the bid deposits are always returned when the contract documents have been returned. It is important to note that when the selected party is told of the decision, it is made in a way that prevents any legally binding agreement prior to the date the contract documents are officially signed. Very often the bids of the next two or three lowest parties are held for a time as a contingency measure.

Phase VII—Construction Phases

Pre-Construction

After the bidding process has been completed, the most common method of managing the construction process is for the selected prime contractor to furnish names of proposed suppliers of materials and equipment, details of the amount of work to be undertaken by the contractor's forces, and a list of intended subcontractors for the architect's approval within seven days of the contract award. A multi-prime delivery method may also be used. The multi-prime method allows a number of subcontractors to enter directly into contracts with the facility owner rather than a prime contractor. The facility owner then hires a construction management company to manage the multiple prime contractors.

Construction

In this phase, the construction documents should provide information regarding the budget, schedule, and scope for the final approval by the owner. This is the final opportunity to confirm that the sport facility is being built according to previously agreed specifications. To ensure that the construction process moves along efficiently, communication and decision-making procedures must be established between the contractor, architect, and owner/head of the facility planning committee. Moreover, communication and decision-making processes must be clearly delineated between the contractor, subcontractors, suppliers, and workers. Effective communication between all of the parties may prevent misunderstandings regarding design, payment or schedule changes, as well as the quality of work expectations or potential disruptions and delays.

© Scruggelgreen/Shutterstock.com

Construction phase of the US Bank Stadium in Minneapolis, MN.

The following items are documents that are often used in the construction phase:

1. *Requests for Information* (RFI)—usually used when the primary decision-maker is not available. The RFI form documents any questions and responses so that all relevant parties are kept up to speed.

2. *Architect Supplemental Instruction* (ASI)—occurs when the architect clarifies items that are unclear to the contractor or provides minor changes that do not warrant a change order or contract sum.

3. *Notice of Delay*—a formal notice that documents a disruption which is perceived as a cause for a delay. Generally, serves to document which party is responsible.

4. *Change Order Requests* (COR)—used when a contractor submits a contract change to the facility planning committee representative, owner, construction manager, or general contractor.

5. Claims—often occur when the owner or facility planning committee representative rejects the change order request and the contractor cannot obtain the perceived compensation.

6. Quality Control Inspection—makes certain that the facility adheres to the expected level of quality concerning contract plans, specifications, and local building codes.

Post-Construction

Contrary to some popular perceptions, the completion of a facility does not occur in one specific time. Rather the facility is completed in segments. For example, the facility offices may be completed before the locker rooms; the basketball court may be completed prior to the swimming pool. As such, the completion of a facility is a continuing process that must have regular and interactive input and communication from all of the involved parties. The process, usually referred to the closeout process, consists of three aspects: substantial completion, punch-list stage, and final completion.

Substantial Completion

While some contracts may provide a definition of *substantial completion*, the American Institute of Architects (AIA) refers to it as work that "…is substantially complete in accordance with the design-build documents and to acknowledge the date when it occurs" (Certificate of Substantial Completion for a Design-Build Project, 2014, para. 1). When substantial completion has been attained, the contractor, the facility representative or owner as well as the architect compile a punch-list of items to be addressed prior to moving on the final completion stage. A punch-list provides a list of items that need immediate attention. Generally, the punch-list identifies contract specifications that are not satisfactory. The contractor must correct the issues identified on the punch-list before being paid. Documents that may be provided during the substantial completion stage are:

Request of Information a formal procedure for accumulating information from prospective suppliers of a good or service.

Architect Supplemental Instruction proper notifications used by architects to circulate supplementary instructions or to instruct that minor modification occur in the project.

Notice of Delay the ability of a spectator to see a predetermined point of focus (such as the nearest touchline or outside lane of a running track) over the top of the head of the spectators sitting immediately in front.

Change Order Requests written instructions by a project owner that orders the contractor to alter contract amount, requirements, or time.

Substantial Completion the phase of completion where the facility is ready to be occupied and used for its intended purpose.

1. As-built drawings—depict all on-site changes, generally in red ink, that were made to the original construction documents.

2. Operation and maintenance manuals—a systematized collection of project technical documents, manufacturer's data, and project site records that is given to the owner at the completion of the project.

3. Labor warranty—states that all of the labor, including subcontractors and suppliers, was performed in a quality manner in accordance with the facility plans and specifications.

4. Special instructions and training—the contractor is often obligated to provide mechanical, electrical, fire alarm, security systems training to the facility staff.

© Dmitry Kalinovsky/Shutterstock.com

Inspection processes both throughout and at the end of the construction phase are important for quality assurance.

Final Completion

The final completion stage begins when the contractor asks for a final inspection by the facility architect and owner/facility planning committee representative. Basically, the final completion may be defined by the date that the owner determines the facility to be complete in all respects, including punch-list work, and ready for final payment. The final completion certificate should identify the name and address of the owner, contractor, and architect. The final completion certificate verifies the date of owner's acceptance, contract number as well as the name of the facility/project, date the certificate was issued, and total cost of construction. Contract warranties begin on the date of final completion unless it was otherwise stipulated in the certificate of substantial completion.

In many cases, the owner may require the contractor to show proof that all invoices have been reconciled or paid. Because many subcontractors and suppliers may not have steady incomes, it is incumbent of the contractor to distribute the payments. The subcontractors and suppliers file a conditional final release to the contractor.

Conclusion

The planning process, including building life cycle considerations, is significant and arduous. The multiple steps in the life cycle analysis or cradle-to-grave approach can seem to be daunting and too much to take in, especially when sport, athletic, and recreational practitioners are likely to see very few major projects in their careers. It is not expected for practitioners to know all these issues by heart and be able to apply these at any given time. The intent of this chapter is to enlighten practitioners. No one wants to be in the dark and reliant on others on every aspect of the LCCA process. This information will allow the practitioner to ask their planners, facilities maintenance and management staff, and budget officers salient questions about current operations, key current and future plans, and to be a major contributing partner to the process.

MINI CASE STUDY

The Miller, Petersen, and Judge (MPJU) Center is the foremost sports and entertainment indoor, multipurpose facility in the region. It has a total seating capacity of 14,500 for baseball, with 14,000 for concerts, and 16,000 for rodeo events. The facility is designed with 45 luxury suites and 1,800 club seats, with parking for 6,200. The MPJU Center is the home of the Troy Jaguars, a AAA minor league baseball team as well as the Lower Alabama Rodeo and Exposition (LARE). The City of Troy originally constructed the $96 million, 19,000 seat capacity facility with the hopes of being awarded a National Basketball Association expansion team. When it was evident Troy would not receive a team, the Jaguars became the anchor tenant. However, with only 26 executive suites and a design better suited to basketball (specifically, poor sight lines and too many seats), the MPJU Center needed to be renovated to fit the needs of the anchor tenant, the Jaguars.

Using the information from the chapter, answer the following:

1. Identify the six design goals listed in the chapter and how they would apply to the renovation of the MPJU Center.

2. Explain how and why lifecycle planning will be significant in planning the MPJU Center.

3. Explain how the basic lifecycle cost analysis would apply to the MPJU Center.

4. List and explain the different life cycle assessment stages for the MPJU Center renovation.

5. Since the facility will be multipurpose, what identify and explain the questions that must be addressed for the renovation to be successful.

6. What spectator seating issues must be taken into consideration for the MPJU Center given the diversity of the activities that will be taking place in it?

7. List and explain concourse design issues that must be addressed in the renovation plan of the MPJU Center.

8. List and explain ancillary space design considerations for the MPJU Center.

9. List and explain facility safety issues that must be addressed during the facility design.

10. Explain what goes on during each of the construction processes such as the pre-planning, programming, schematic design, design development, construction document, bidding, and construction phases.

CHAPTER DISCUSSION QUESTIONS

1. Using the six goals of design principles, explain how you would develop a facility design concept.

2. Discuss the role that you would have an architect play in designing a sport or recreation facility.

3. Explain why life cycle cost analysis is important for the design of a sport or recreation facility.

4. Discuss the differences and importance of cradle-to-cradle and cradle-to-grave concerning the life cycle of building products.

5. Examine the need to have the following facility items: ancillary space, locker rooms, storage and equipment, laundry rooms, toilets, and staff offices. Develop a priority list of these areas and defend your choices.

6. What components would you consider in developing a feasibility study for a new facility?

7. Explain how you, as the facility owner, would be involved in each of the seven construction phases (pre-planning, programming, schematic design, design development, construction documents, bidding, and facility construction).

PRACTITIONER SPOTLIGHT

NAME: Robert LeBarron

ACADEMIC EDUCATIONAL PREPARATION: Bachelor of Arts in Sports Administration, St. Thomas (FL) University.

INDUSTRY EDUCATIONAL PREPARATION: Completed Venue Management School at Oglebay (WV). The Venue Management School (VMS) is considered of the best professional education programs available for venue managers. Those new to the industry, or managers looking to expand their overall understanding, will find solid principles and practices for venue management in the VMS program.

Photo courtesy of Robert LeBarron.

Awarded Certified Facilities Executive (CFE) Designation—A CFE certification is a four-step process, offered at the VMS, which indicates that a facility executive is a skilled manager, committed to the industry, and pledged to continued professional growth and development.

CURRENT ORGANIZATION OF EMPLOYMENT: City of Grand Forks, North Dakota—Alerus Center

CURRENT JOB TITLE: Assistant Director of Alerus Center, Grand Forks, North Dakota

I have been the Assistant Director of the Alerus Center, in Grand Forks, ND since April 2012. Although most public facilities of this type face an uphill battle in getting funding approval, the Alerus Center also overcame a second public vote of confidence, a historic 210 year flood, a redesign, and a roof collapse before becoming the jewel of the Grand Forks crown in February of 2001.

CAREER PATH: I started with an internship in the Miami Arena with the Miami Heat in Leisure Management International. My first entry level position was as Director of Operations for West Palm Beach Blaze Hockey. The West Palm Beach Blaze was a minor professional hockey team based in West Palm Beach, Florida that played in the Sunshine Hockey League from 1992 to 1995. The team played in the West Palm Beach Auditorium, a 5,000-seat multi-purpose arena in West Palm Beach, Florida. Following this position, I was the Box Office Manager for the West Palm Beach Auditorium from 1995 to 1998. From 1998 to 1999, I was the Box Office Manager at the Colorado Springs World Arena, an 8,000 seat multi-purpose arena and entertainment venue. From 1999 to 2001, I served as the Assistant General Manager, Whittemore Center Arena, a multi-purpose arena located at the University of New Hampshire's Durham campus. The arena is home to the UNH Wildcats Hockey. I remained at the Whittemore Center Arena as the General Manager from 2001 to 2004.

From 2004 to 2007, I was the General Manager of the Mullins Center and Ice Rink, a multi-purpose arena, located on the campus of the University of Massachusetts in Amherst, Massachusetts. In 2007, I moved to San Jose State University to become the Assistant Director of the Event Center. The Event Center is a complex comprised of a multi-functional arena and Sport Club fitness center. The center was constructed in 1989 for the purpose of supporting and providing entertainment as well recreational opportunities for the student body and university community. I stayed at San Jose State University until 2009 when I left to become the Executive Director of the Sanford Center, a 4,700-seat multi-purpose arena and convention center in Bemidji, Minnesota. The Sanford Center broke ground in April of 2009 and officially opened doors in October of 2010. From the Sanford Center position, I moved in 2012 to my present position as the Assistant Director of the Alerus Center in Grand Forks, North Dakota.

WHAT IS THE MOST REWARDING ASPECT OF GOING THROUGH CONSTRUCTION PROCESSES FOR YOUR FACILITY?

While at the Sanford Center, I was the Executive Director during the final 10 months of construction and initial year of operations. The most rewarding aspect of the construction process was contributing to the development of a facility that would be used and enjoyed by the community for years. Seeing a building rise up out of the ground and eventually become the center of civic pride in the community brings me a great deal of pride to this day. It was especially rewarding to see ideas and concepts go from paper to construction and then to completion better than I could have ever expected.

Photo courtesy of Robert LeBarron.

The Sanford Center in Bemidji, MN.

WHAT IS THE MOST CHALLENGING ASPECT OF GOING THROUGH CONSTRUCTION PROCESSES FOR YOUR FACILITY?

I consider the most challenging aspect was communicating arena/facility management concepts to the architect and general contractor. While these entities were outstanding at their roles, it became difficult at times explaining why the current design (while functional) was not conducive to operational efficiency. Also it was challenging understanding some of the more difficult technical aspects of construction. For me this was electrical service. Not being an electrical engineer, understanding the complexity and providing an expert opinion was difficult.

WHAT IS A UNIQUE ASPECT OR TASK OF YOUR JOB THAT MANY WOULD BE SURPRISED HEAR ABOUT?

As a General Manager of a facility under construction (or renovation), you often spend more time "talking" about your building than you do actively participating in its construction process. From media interviews to multiple tours to presentations for numerous civic and business organizations, there are days where you spend more time wearing your "public relations hat" than you do wearing your construction helmet.

WHAT DO YOU BELIEVE ARE THE MOST IMPORTANT SKILL(S) TO DEVELOP:

The ability to be organized while multi-tasking projects cannot be overstated. If you are not organized, you cannot adhere to time management which is important to complete construction process. Additionally, I strongly recommend that a young professional develop a general knowledge base of building operations and all of the associated trades (HVAC, electrical, plumbing, information technology, carpentry, etc.)

WHAT PARTING WORDS OF WISDOM DO YOU HAVE FOR STUDENTS AND YOUNG PROFESSIONALS IN THE FIELD?

It is important for young professionals to not appear to that they know everything. A young professional should learn as much about all aspects of facility management from as many people, especially those with experiences, as you can. See the "big picture" and understand how all the pieces fit together to make a successful facility.

Reprinted by permission of Robert LeBarron.

REFERENCES

ADA Accessibility Guidelines. (2002). Dressing, fitting, and locker rooms. Retrieved from https://www.access-board.gov/guidelines-and-standards/buildings-and-sites/about-the-ada-standards/background/adaag#4.35

Anderson, J., Huhn, M., Rivera, D. M., & Susong, M. (2006). Phases of the construction project. Retrieved from: http://apps.americanbar.org/abastore/products/books/abstracts/5190396chp1_abs.pdf

Broadhag, K. (2009a). Lighting can be part of your environmentally friendly gym design. *Club Industry*. Retrieved from http://clubindustry.com/stepbystepdesign/lighting-can-be-part-your-environmentally-friendly-gym-design

Broadhag, K. (2009b). Seeing green in your fitness facility's HVAC system. *Club Industry*. Retrieved from http://clubindustry.com/stepbystepdesign/seeing-green-your-fitness-facilitys-hvac-system

Bynum, M. (January 2005). Changing areas. *Athletic Business*. Retrieved from http://www.athletic-business.com/locker-room/changing-areas.html

Carbone, N. (2012). Top ten worst stadiums in the U.S. *Time Magazine*. Retrieved from http://keepingscore.blogs.time.com/2012/05/10/top-10-worst-stadiums-in-the-u-s/slide/edward-jones-dome-st-louis/

Civil Engineering. (2016). Vertical circulation. Retrieved from http://www.civilengineeringx.com/building-design-and-construction-handbook/vertical-circulation/

Churchill, W. (2003). *Never give in!: The best of Winston Churchill's speeches.* New York, NY: Hyperion.

Consumer Product and Safety Commission. (2015). Maintenance inspections. In *Public Playground Safety Handbook.* Bethesda, MD: U.S. Consumer Product Safety Commission.

Dahnert, R., & Pack, A. (2007). Behind the scenes. *American School & University, 79*(12), 20–22.

deMause, N. (2016). Rams leave St. Louis, Raiders and Chargers in limbo: Winners and losers of the NFL's return to LA. *Vice Sports.* Retrieved from https://sports.vice.com/en_us/article/rams-leave-st-louis-raiders-and-chargers-in-limbo-winners-and-losers-of-the-nfls-return-to-la

Dictionary of Sustainable Management. (2016). *Cradle-to-cradle.* Retrieved from http://www.sustainabilitydictionary.com/cradle-to-cradle/

Didcoe, R., & Saxby B. (2007). *Feasibility study guide: Sport and recreation facilities.* Perth, Western Australia: Western Australian Government. Retrieved from http://www.dsr.wa.gov.au/docs/default-source/file-support-and-advice/file-facilitiy-management/feasibility-study-guide.pdf?sfvrsn=0

Dinuba Municipal Code. (2015). *Construction and demolition debris recycling and reuse ordinance.* Retrieved from http://www.codepublishing.com/CA/Dinuba/html/Dinuba14/Dinuba1464.html

Egeland, B. (2009). Phases of a construction project life cycle—part 2. Retrieved from http://pmtips.net/Blog/phases-construction-project-life-cycle-part-2

Facility Specification Guide. (2016). *Athletic Business.* Retrieved from http://www.athleticbusiness.com/images/pdf/316-SpecGuide_web_high.pdf

Football Licensing Authority. (2008). *Guide to safety at sports grounds* (5th ed.) London, UK: HMSO. Retrieved from www.safetyatsportsgrounds.org.uk/sites/default/files/publications/green-guide.pdf

Fraioli, J. (2015). Transgender in Iowa: Know your rights. Retrieved from http://www.aclu-ia.org/iowa/wp-content/uploads/2015/03/3-26-Iowa-trans-rights-booklet-pdf-with-links.pdf

Fickes, M. (December 1999). Locker room talk. *College Planning & Management, 2*(12), 26–28.

FIFA Stadium Safety and Security Regulations. (n.d.). Field of play. Retrieved from http://www.fifa.com/mm/document/tournament/competition/51/53/98/safetyregulations_e.pdf

Frosdick, S. (2009). Policing, safety, and security in public assembly facilities. *International Journal of Police Science & Management, 12*(1), 81–89.

Gillentine, A., Miller, J. & Crow, B. (November, 2010). Developing a "Best Practice" sport model for tailgating events. *Journal of Event and Venue Management, 2*(2), 54–68.

GSA. (2003). *1.8 Life cycle costing.* Retrieved from http://www.gsa.gov/portal/content/101197.

Hermann, B. G., Kroeze, C., & Jawjit, W. (2007). Assessing environmental performance by combining life cycle assessment, multi-criteria analysis and environmental performance indicators. *Journal of Cleaner Production, 15*(18), 1787–1796.

Horstemeyer, M. F., & Wang, P. (2003). Cradle-to-grave simulation-based design incorporating multiscale microstructure-property modeling: Reinvigorating design with science. *Journal of Computer-Aided Materials design, 10*(1), 13–34.

International Organization for Standardization (ISO) 14040. (2006). *Environmental management-Life cycle assessment-Principles and framework.* Retrieved from https://www.iso.org/obp/ui/#iso:std:iso:14040:ed-2:v1:en

Ive, G. (2006). Re-examining the costs and value ratios of owning and occupying buildings. *Building Research & Information, 34*(3), 230–245.

Khiun Then, S., & Loosemore, M. (2006). Terrorism prevention, preparedness, and response in built facilities. *Facilities, 24*(5/6), 157–176.

Lamberth, C. R. (2005). Trends in stadium design: A whole new game. *Implications, 4*(6), 1–7. Retrieved from www.informedesign.umn.edu

Lavoie, H. (2005). Ancillary areas. In T. Sawyer (Ed.), *Facility Design and Management for Health, Fitness, Physical Activity, Recreation and Sports Facility Development* (11th ed). Champaign, IL: Sagamore Publishing.

Manitoba Culture, Heritage Recreation and Citizenship. (1995/6). *Recreation facilities life cycle management: A planning tool for tomorrow.* Retrieved from http://lin.ca/sites/default/files/attachments/FACENG.HTM#I5

McDonough, W., & Braungart, M. (2010). *Cradle to cradle: Remaking the way we make things.* London, UK: MacMillan Publishers.

McGowan, M. & Kruse, K. (2004). *Interior graphic standards.* Hoboken, NJ: John Wiley & Sons.

Miller, J. J. (2011). Impact of a university recreation center on student retention and social belonging. *Recreational Sports Journal, 35*(2), 117–129.

Miller, J. (2014). When fans rush the court: How do basketball venue managers handle it? *Journal of Facility Planning, Design, and Management, 2*(1), 11–24.

Miller, J., Veltri, F. & Gillentine, A. (2008). Spectator perception of security at the Super Bowl after 9/11: Implications for facility managers. *Sport Management and Related Topics Journal, 4*(2), 16–25.

Muret, D. (2003). Colleges, minors drive bulk of $1.5 B arena tab. *Street & Smith's Sports Business Journal.* Retrieved from http://www.sportsbusinessdaily.com/Journal/Issues/2003/11/20031124/Facilities/CollegeMinors-Drive-Bulk-Of-$15B-Arena-Tab.aspx

National Collegiate Athletic Association. (2013). NCAA best lighting practices. Retrieved from http://www.ncaa.com/news/ncaa/article/2013-11-21/ncaa-best-lighting-practices

Office of Management and Budget. (2015). *Circular A-94 appendix C.* Retrieved from https://www.whitehouse.gov/omb/circulars_a094/a94_appx-c

Petersen, J., & Gonzales, R. (2013). Ancillary areas. In T. H. Sawyer (Ed.), *Facility design and management for health, fitness, physical activity, recreation and sports* (13th ed.). (pp. 71–94). Champaign, IL: Sagamore.

Popke, M. (2006). Safe, easy-to-maintain and cost-effective flooring for locker and shower areas. *Athletic Business*. Retrieved from http://www.athleticbusiness.com/locker-room/safe-easy-to-maintain-and-cost-effective-flooring-for-locker-and-shower-areas.html

Simonson, A., & Schmitt, B. H. (1997). *Marketing aesthetics: The strategic management of brands, identity, and image.* New York, NY: Simon & Schuster.

Stolovitch, D. A. (1995). Drawing security into building design. *Security Management, 39*(12), 69–72.

Tharrett, S. J., McInnis, K. J., & Peterson, J. A. (Eds.). (2007). Risk management and emergency policies. In *ACSM's health/fitness standards and guidelines* (3rd ed.), (pp. 17–23). Champaign, IL: Human Kinetics.

Shaver, J. (2005). Unique fitness settings. *Club Industry*. Retrieved from http://clubindustry.com/mag/fitness_unique_fitness_settings

Snodgrass, K. (2013). *Introduction: Life cycle cost analysis for buildings in easier than you thought.* Retrieved from http://www.fs.fed.us/t-d/pubs/htmlpubs/htm08732839/toc.htm.

U. S. Department of Justice. (n.d.) *Accessible stadiums.* Retrieved from http://www.ada.gov/stadium.pdf

van der Smissen, B. (1990). *Legal liability and risk management for public and private entities: Sport and physical education, leisure services, recreation and parks, camping and adventure activities.* Cincinnati, OH: Anderson Publishing Company.

7

Facility Maintenance

John J. Miller and *J. Patrick Marsh*

OBJECTIVES

After studying this chapter, the student should be able to:

- Understand the importance of interior and exterior facility maintenance.
- Understand the significance of capital improvement planning.
- Comprehend the different types of indoor flooring
- Analyze the advantages and disadvantages of synthetic fields.

KEY TERMS

Ball Bounce

Capital Expenditures

Capital Improvement Plan

Facility Management

Fenestration

Outsourcing

Routine Maintenance

Shock Absorption

Sliding Effect

Synthetic Flooring

Vertical Deformation

Work Order

KEY ACRONYMS

ASTM	American Society for Testing Materials	**HVAC**	Heating, Ventilation and Air Conditioning
CIP	Capital Improvement Planning	**IAAF**	International Association of Athletic Federations
DIN	Deutsches Institut fur Normug eV	**ISO**	International Organization for Standardization
FIFA	Federation Internationale de Football Association (International Soccer Federation)	**VOCs**	Volatile Organic Compounds

Maintenance is an integral component of the complex facility management process.

Introduction

As competitive pressures increase on organizations to be more efficient and effective, a once marginal management activity, maintenance, has become vitally important for facilities (Fraser, 2011). Dekker (1996) and Yamashina (2000) state that in an organization's operational budget, maintenance costs are surpassed only by energy costs. According to Muthu, Devadasan, Ahmed, Suresh, and Baladhandayutham (2000), maintenance activities comprise between 15 and 70% of the total production cost. Facility maintenance will impact not only the daily operations of a facility but also the long-term viability for a sport facility to be functional.

Facility Management profession that joins people, place, process, and technology together to meet the needs of its patrons.

Facility management is an exceedingly multifaceted profession that requires a person to possess various sets of aptitudes and abilities. Due to the high costs associated with building construction or leasing, commercial and private clients of facilities no longer desire reactive actions to facility problems but presume a proactive approach with the management of maintenance (Myeda, Kamaruzzaman, & Pitt, 2011). For both sport and non-sport facilities, the most significant growth is expected to occur in the maintenance management market, as facility managers become increasingly concerned with aging buildings and complying with environmental and safety regulations.

This chapter will consider sport facility maintenance from such a proactive approach, including the importance of effective communication. Additionally, it will include a focus on the routine maintenance through both interior and exterior inspection processes. The planning steps for major maintenance issues will be addressed through the capital improvement planning process. Pragmatic issues related to housekeeping and janitorial services and outsourcing are also addressed. The chapter concludes with a consideration of surfacing choices for flooring and turf along with their maintenance implications.

Facility Management Communication

Communication is a vital part of effective management. Through communication, messages are sent and received. To communicate is to inform to show or to spread information. The communication process as follows:

1. Clarifying the idea or problem.
2. Getting participation in developing a solution to the problem.
3. Transmitting ideas or decisions.
4. Motivating others to take action agreed upon.
5. Measuring the effectiveness of communication.

Communication across levels is significantly improved when opportunities to interact and meet with employees and patrons in informal settings are provided. When such opportunities are offered on a regular basis, three aspects will likely occur: a) management will have a better understanding of what is actually happening in the facility, b) employees and facility patrons will be better able to understand the communications, and c) a decrease of "us" versus "them" thinking resulting in the sense of everyone working toward a common goal (Pfeffer, 1995). For example, if the facility management places a closed sign on a popular basketball court, the employees will be confused and the patrons may be furious. However, this can be minimized if management sends out a message in advance of the actual closing date saying that, after listening to complaints from patrons using the court, the court will be closed for renovations for a short time. By indicating that they have listened and gained an appreciation of the patron complaints, management has a better understanding of the situation. Giving enough time for the facility patrons and employees to read and digest the information will provide them a better understanding of the situation. Finally, the patrons and employees will be more inclined to report other issues that may affect the reputation of the facility.

Successful sport and recreation facilities are busy most the time they are open. As a result, equipment and sport surfaces will incur a great deal of wear and tear over time. It is under such circumstances that the facility manager should communicate, in a timely fashion, to the employees and patrons when, where, what, and for how long routine maintenance procedures will be taking place.

Routine Maintenance

All building materials experience some level of degradation with age and exposure to the environment. Through routine maintenance, the serviceable lifespan of a building will be significantly enhanced. The primary reason for implementing routine maintenance is to ensure that the property is safe and efficiently run. Regrettably, numerous facility supervisors employ the "squeaky wheel" procedure in which little maintenance is done until a failure occurs. Routine maintenance can overcome organizational and operational confusion by instituting a plan to be executed systematically instead of haphazardly in response to a failure or crisis.

Today's facility managers are confronted with ever-increasing challenges to diminish facilities maintenance costs, increase the general efficiency, as well as to advance service quality for the facility users. Until recently, maintenance activities have been thought of as a necessary evil by the various management functions in an organization (Cooke, 2003; Zio, 2009). Often, the facility owners are more concerned about how the building or site will look (i.e. the "wow" factor) on opening day than discussing maintenance plans.

For example, the lighting in a ball field may be aesthetically pleasing. However, it is a significant component of the facility that will need to be consistently addressed to ensure proper functioning, especially if different fields have different lighting systems.

A facility has a lifecycle that assumes when using sustainable and preventative maintenance, the facility will last a certain number of years. Certain amenities have a timeframe as to when they are going to need to be repaired or replaced. Operating equipment in pools might need to be replaced every 5 to 10 years; treadmills and weight training equipment may need replacing every three to five years, and a boiler could need replacing every 15 years. Some public facilities may be challenged to acquire the funding needed to make more expensive fixes if they don't have a maintenance management plan in place. As a result, discussions about a maintenance management plan should take place from the very beginning, during the pre-design phase (Vence, 2014).

The basic roles of maintenance are to maintain structures and equipment, provide product quality, establish safety requirements, and promote cost-effectiveness (Al-Najjar & Alsyouf, 2003). To accomplish these tasks, the facility manager must emphasize routine maintenance that is essential for the upkeep of any sport facility. Routine maintenance is considered to be tasks that do not present a threat to life or property, cause serious disruption to the operation of the facilities, and do not require immediate corrective action. *Routine maintenance* may be defined as an everyday process that is organized to prevent the deterioration of the spaces, structures, and infrastructure associated with the facility. This includes the individual replacement of components and systems that do not necessitate professional engineering or obtaining city or town permits. Usually, routine maintenance activities do not require a modification of space classification or use. Routine maintenance can be expedited by inspecting the external and internal areas of the building that are most likely to become deficient. The following section identifies examples of exterior and interior areas that routine maintenance should be regularly addressed.

Routine Maintenance restores the asset's physical condition and/or operation to a specified standard.

Exterior Inspection Areas

Roofs

One of the most important and problematic areas for facilities is roofing. Ignoring a roof will typically cause significantly more leak-related damages than a roof that is thoroughly inspected on a regular basis. The roof, including structural components, materials, and elements should be inspected at least two times per year. Additionally, it is recommended that the roof be inspected prior to and after a severe weather outbreak (i.e. cold, heat, wind, or rain/snow) to determine what maintenance, if any, is needed. Ice, rain, snow, and wind combined with quickly shifting temperatures and humidity

Table 7.1 *Roofing Checklist*

1. Inspect at least twice a year and after any severe storm

2. Develop a roofing file for the facility; review warranty information

3. Clear roof drains of debris (roof warranties don't cover this)

4. Walk the perimeter to analyze sheet metal, copings, and previously repaired sections

5. Check roof-to-wall connections and examine flashings (at curbs and penetrations, etc.) for wrinkles and tearing.

6. Check on corrosion on metal roofs that may be caused by condensation from copper coils in rooftop HVAC units.

7. Keep traffic off of the roof to avoid membrane damage.

8. Plan a moisture survey every five years to detect wet insulation or leaks.

Adapted from Fricklas, Leeman, Marvin, D'Ascenzo, & Sundin (2009)

impose destruction on roofs. When a roof does not function properly, water from rain, sleet, or melting snow may seep through and produce significant damage. Such damage may cause deterioration to insulation, wood, and drywall, making electrical, plumbing, and HVAC systems vulnerable. After all, in most cases, a roof stands as the primary barrier between the interior of a building and the weather outside (see Table 7.1).

Exterior Walls

The cumulative results of hot sun, high wind, torrential rain or hail, as well as significant amounts of snow and ice over a number of years will often damage even the finest and most competent masonry wall and/or siding work. A routine maintenance inspection may identify cracks in the caulking or mortar joints that could eventually give way to water penetration. Water penetration into mortar may weaken the substance and cause the wall to collapse. The following checklist will be useful in inspecting buildings on a regular basis to determine maintenance needs (see Table 7.2).

Exterior Finishes

Natural finishes, including paint, will show signs of deterioration, peeling, and blistering over time. Exterior finishes should be inspected on a regular basis to determine if a new application of penetrating stain or paint is needed. The need for a re-application of paint or stain may be caused by water vapor or condensation issues, which may be increased depending on the area of the country in which the facility is located. Additionally, considerations that may

Table 7.2 *Exterior Wall Checklist*

1. Masonry: particular focus must be paid to loose mortar joints, cracks, stains, and wet spots on the wall.

2. Mortar: mortar joints must be inspected to verify if they are loose or missing as well as to assess the condition (good, average, poor)

3. Brick: analyze for stains, wet spots, bulges, spalling (result of water entering the brick and forcing the surface to peel off), efflorescence (crystalline deposit), and missing brick

4. Stone: review for wet spots, stains, spalling, bulges, and efflorescence.

5. Stucco/Plaster: examine for cracks, staining, loose stucco, soft spots, blisters or bulges, and falling stucco

6. Siding, Shingles, and Sheathing: scrutinize siding, shingles, soffits and wood trim for cracked, loose, or broken boards; rotted and missing members; signs of veins of dirt (termite tunnels)

Adapted from General Services Administration (2015)

Table 7.3 *Exterior Finish Checklist*

1. Painting: inspect all finished surfaces for signs of peeling, cracks, and alligatoring (patterned cracking in the paint film resembling the scales of an alligator)

2. Decorative Elements: ornamental elements also undergo wear and tear. Inspect not only the ornament but also its supports, such as anchors, for expansion due to rust.

Adapted from General Services Administration (2015)

negatively impact the exterior finish of the facility include water from rain, melted hail or snow that may be trapped behind the exterior siding or roof shingles. The following checklist will be useful in inspecting buildings on a regular basis to determine maintenance needs (see Table 7.3).

Facility Fenestration

Fenestration arrangement, proportioning, and design of windows and doors in a building.

Fenestration is referred to as the arrangement, proportioning, and design of windows and doors in a building. Obviously, doors are needed in any facility, but the number and placement of windows in a facility must also be addressed. Selecting, constructing, or modifying a facility without considering the security consequences for employee and client security and safety can result in lost time and money (U.S. Geological Survey, 2005). There should be a plan to inspect locking devices or controls at perimeter and interior doors on a regular basis as every susceptible point should be protected to deter or prevent unsanctioned entry to the facility. A security review of the perimeter should address ventilation openings, windows, skylights, and any opening 96 square inches or larger that is within 18 feet of the ground (U.S. Geological Survey, 2005). The plan should identify effective key control, including access for facility personnel. Additionally, protective, cleaning, and maintenance forces should be addressed in the plan (U.S. Geological Survey, 2005). The proper upkeep of doors and windows and their optimal performance becomes a vital component of facility routine maintenance.

Fenestration studies have shown increased levels of daylight can reduce absenteeism, increase healing, serve as an effective stimulant to the human visual and circadian systems, and generate feelings of happiness, well-being, and satisfaction (Edwards & Torcellini, 2002). However, in situations where more windows are used in a facility, the likelihood of energy loss in the facility is much greater. Additionally, doors present a major source of energy loss as well. Thus, choosing the proper placement, types, and size of the windows and doors is one of the most important energy decisions for initial facility design. The following checklist will be useful in inspecting buildings on a regular basis to determine maintenance needs (see Table 7.4).

Table 7.4 *Facility Fenestration*

1. Doors: Inspect doors, frames, and weather stripping. Check:

   a. Door alignment

   b. All parts for deterioration

   c. All door hardware for proper operation

2. Windows: Inspect windows for material soundness at sill, joint between sill and jamb, corners of bottom rail and muntins (strip of wood or metal separating and holding panes of glass in a window. Check for:

   a. Proper operation of all sash (including upper sash of double hung units)

   b. Proper operation of hardware

   c. Loose, cracked or missing glazing putty

   d. Soundness of weather stripping

   e. Cracks and other damages to lintel

   f. Rot and/or deterioration of wood framing

Adapted from General Services Administration (2015)

Exterior Ceilings and Decks

Many sports facilities will have outside wooden decks and accompanying shade covers and ceilings. Regarding the deck ceiling, moisture problems can suggest defective drainage or leakage from the roof. The deck roof should be routinely inspected to ensure that moisture is not entering the main structure of the building. The wooden supports and decking should also be inspected for wood-destroying insects such as termites or the presence of fungus. Even if the ceiling and/or deck is composed of chemically treated lumber or synthetic decking products, protective inspections must be made at least twice per year, particularly if the structure is older. The following checklist will be useful in inspecting buildings on a regular basis to determine maintenance needs (see Table 7.5).

Table 7.5 *Exterior Ceilings and Decks*

1. Porch: Make sure water isn't entering the main structure of the building. Also look for:
   a. Peeling paint and water stains on the ceiling
   b. Rotted and warped boards in the deck
   c. Damaged and/or loose steps and handrails
   d. Rotted boards and other damages to ceiling
   e. Cracks and other damages on a concrete floor
   f. Spalling, cracks, loose and/or missing mortar joints on brick or stone

2. Wooden Supports: Insects and fungi can cause considerable damage to the wooden supports of exterior ceilings and decks. Check:
   a. Molds and fungus
   b. Wood rot and termite infestation
   c. Seal of deck at foundation
   d. Corrosion of iron fittings on members

3. Infestation: No matter what protective measures have been taken, a periodic inspection should be made at least every six months. Check for:
   a. The need of treatment for ants and other wood destroying insects
   b. Termites
   c. Damage and rot on all wood members

Adapted from General Services Administration (2015)

Exterior Grounds

The grounds outside of the facility should be correctly graded to guide water runoff away from the facility as well as to prevent standing water, which may attract mosquito breeding. In addition to being routinely inspected and maintained, the outside grounds should always be checked after a heavy rain to determine if drainage is properly occurring. Specific outside areas that should be routinely inspected and maintained include driveways and sidewalks, window wells, storm drains, retaining walls, facility foundation, and landscaping.

Preparing for the colder temperatures that come with the winter months can be a challenge for facilities located in the northern part of the United States. However, facilities located in warm weather climates should always be aware that cold fronts may pass through the region. Regardless of region, in cold weather situations (below 32 degrees Fahrenheit), the grounds crew should make certain that all irrigation backflow system have freeze protection and drain irrigation devices. Sand should be spread on the sidewalks, especially

Table 7.6 *Exterior Grounds Checklist*

---

1. Driveways and Sidewalks: Check for:

   a. Safety hazards (heaves and depressions)

   b. Cracks on and deterioration of paved material

   c. Damages to and curb clearances

   d. Oil stains and pools of water

2. Storm Drains: Check for:

   a. Proper drainage and/or

   b. Clogging of drain line

3. Retaining Wall: Check for:

   a. Cracks, spalling, and freezing

   b. Leaning and bulges

   c. Loose, crumbling, and missing mortar joints

4. Foundation: Inspect to ensure that there is no collection of leaves and other debris at the edges of the foundation and for proper drainage. Check for:

   a. Cracks, spalling and freezing

   b. Leaning and bulges

   c. Loose, crumbling, and missing mortar joints

Adapted from General Services Administration (2015)

when precipitation leading to icing occurs, to minimize patrons slipping and injuring themselves. Finally, de-icing products should be applied to the facility entrances and any exterior steps (Zagrzecki, 2014). The following checklist will be useful in inspecting buildings on a regular basis to determine maintenance needs (see Table 7.6).

Interior Inspection Areas

While the exterior areas of any facility must be routinely inspected, the interior of the facility may also be vulnerable to deterioration if not regularly inspected. At the core of routine maintenance are regularly scheduled inspections, precautionary maintenance actions, and repairs that are directly related to the safe operation of athletic facilities. A timely exposure of facility issues coupled with the quick and efficient response by staff members will positively influence the reputation of the facility. Hospitable environments, working equipment, cleanliness, and good communication may not be the most thrilling side of the business. However, they are crucial for successful, well-run, day-to-day operations. To ensure the sport facilities are sufficiently maintained, the administration of the facility should create and carry out scheduled preventive strategic maintenance plans for all its facilities with all staff members. The following items should be part of the routine maintenance procedure of any facility.

Basement Walls

Basement walls, often referred to as foundation or load-bearing walls, may be exposed to numerous stresses and strains that produce a contraction or expansion of the masonry. As a result, significant problems may occur due to cracks, leaks, or condensation within these walls. It would be wise to routinely inspect and maintain load-bearing walls by checking for loose mortar joints, unusual bulges in the mortar, or water penetration.

Gymnasium

A gleaming hardwood gymnasium floor is a pride point for sport and recreation facilities. However, maintaining a clean floor isn't merely for aesthetics, it may be a safety issue as unkempt floors can become very slippery. In many sport facilities, hardwood floors are used for basketball, volleyball, or racquetball courts. Due to constant use, these types of floors and their finishes may wear down quickly resulting in excessive sliding by the participants or tripping if the boards are damaged. Routine maintenance can reveal whether the wood flooring is cracked or damaged or if the floorboards have warped or twisted to the point of exposing participants to harm.

The appropriate maintenance of a gym floor starts at the entrance of the facility. Entry mats are designed to remove grit from shoes that would scrape and abrade the gym floor almost like sandpaper. Frequent dust moppings, preferably after every two hours of use, may also extend a gym floor's life-cycle, particularly if the gym floors receive constant daily use. However, dust mopping should not be simply pushing a mop back and forth over the floor. Treatments exist that assist in picking up dirt and grit from the floor. Treatments that are selected must be applied properly and in the correct amount. Inappropriate application may result in transferring oil to the floor thereby creating a slip hazard.

Wet mopping also is necessary, though care must be taken because the wrong kind of cleaner or too much water can damage the wood. Wet mopping removes the sweat, soils, and spills that dust mopping leaves behind. Depending on the type of flooring and manufacturer's specifications, "a walk-behind auto scrubber" with white buff pads may be used to clean the floor. Finally, sanding should be done very infrequently and only by a hired professional. It's a delicate process and if done wrong, can ruin your floor.

HVAC (Heating, Ventilation, and Air Conditioning)

The HVAC system (heating, ventilation, and air conditioning) is an essential component of any sport and recreational facility as it creates a comfortable environment for the patrons. While many individuals relate HVAC with temperature control, such a belief overshadows air ventilation as a major element of the system. Although the temperature in the facility is an important part of patron comfort, ventilation introduces fresh air into the facility and removes the old, stale air.

One of the chief functions of the HVAC system is to eliminate the carbon dioxide (CO_2) from inside the facility and replace it with oxygen-rich air from the outside. This is a key point as exercisers increase the amount of CO_2 produced in the facility. Additionally, the HVAC system removes unsafe chemicals such as volatile organic compounds and other small particles, including dust suspended in the air of the facility. Finally, the system minimizes the humidity within the facility by extracting the high water content within the air. Often humidity levels rise due to the sweat produced by exercising patron evaporates into the air. Table 7.7 will show items that should be considered on a HVAC checklist

Table 7.7 *HVAC Checklist*

Thermostat setting assessment	Thermostat maintains, increases, or decreased the facility temperature as needed
Electrical connection check	Connections should be snug, and the voltage and current readings are correct
Condensate drain	Condensate drain should be inspected to ensure that it is not clogged or obstructed
General operation assessment	Confirms that the system starts, runs and shuts off correctly
Outdoor unit inspection	Debris and dirt should be removed from the area around the outdoor HVAC unit
Fan assessment	The motor and blades on the fan should be checked to make sure they are not damaged
Air filter replacement	Air filters should be replaced per manufactures requirements to maintain air flow and air quality
Coil cleaning	The coils on the evaporator and the condenser should be inspected and cleaned regularly
Refrigerant check	Too much or too little refrigerant can be a waste
Blower maintenance	The blower assembly should be cleaned during routine maintenance
Heating elements	For safe operation, gas or oil connections should be clean and unblemished, and there should be no leaks

Adapted from Air Specialist (2016)

Sports Equipment

Just as changing the oil and having the tires regularly inspected impacts the longevity of a vehicle, preventive maintenance is vital to getting the most out of sports equipment. Some of the most fundamental management practices, such as daily walk-throughs and regular cleaning of the equipment and facility, will assist in increasing the lifespan of equipment within the fitness facility. However, these mundane actions are also the most commonly disregarded tasks. It is essential that facility management emphasize to all staff members the significance of routine preventative maintenance.

It is recommended that prior to the daily facility opening, a walk-through should be conducted. During the walk-through, items such as lights, fans, radio, and/or televisions should be tested to see if they are in working condition. Additionally, each piece of equipment such as elliptical, treadmills, steppers, and weightlifting apparatus must be evaluated to ensure that each is working properly. Cable weights, as well as other pieces of exercise equipment that use a pulley system, must be checked daily for frayed cables. If a cable exhibits signs of wear and tear, the machine should be closed for use until repairs have been made (see Table 7.8).

It is strongly recommended that any employee who performs equipment maintenance should be trained by a technician from the manufacturer or qualified local vendor. Should employee training not be a viable option, the organization may purchase a service contract to outsource the maintenance from an equipment manufacturer or local vendor. Maintenance technicians, often representing the equipment manufacturer, will inspect for frayed cables and worn-out belts, as well as clean the internal components of the machine

Table 7.8 *Equipment Service Recommendations*

Treadmills	Clean the motor cover and exposed areas of deck and check the operation of the stop button every week or two. Once a month, vacuum inside the motor electronic compartment and underneath any treadmill that's on carpet. Do not use cleaning solution to wipe the belt; this will impair the lubrication system. Every two to three months, check the belt tension and tracking, and inspect the hardware (nuts and bolts), belt and deck for wear every three to six months.
Elliptical Machines	Clean the console and exterior, depending on the manufacturer's suggestions, remove the cover and clean the area around the alternator every two to three months and ensure that the intermediate shaft belt is tight and centered. Inspect the hardware every six months.
Exercise Bikes	Check the seat attachment handlebars, pedals and crank arm every other month. Tighten pedals and handlebars as necessary. Every three months, clean and lubricate the pedal shaft and listen for squeaks, grinds and any other trouble signs.
Stair Climbers	Inspect pedals and tighten as necessary. Check hardware and conduct an audible inspection every three to six months.
Weight Pulley Systems	Every other week, inspect the cable and handgrips and clean guide rods. Even minor visible damage to cables on strength-training machines is cause for immediate repair. Per the manufacturer's specifications, lubricate guide rods with a Teflon spray, not WD-40. Every three months, check that bolts and screws are tight and that pulleys and any other moving parts are operating smoothly.
Free Weights	Check the bolts, screws and adjustment mechanisms on dumbbells, racks and benches every other week. At the same time, make sure weight collars fit snugly and inspect the weight plates for cracks.

Adapted from Keel (2003)

(York, 2012). If the facility is used a great deal or is located in an area of the country in which dust, cotton fibers, or debris in the air is common, investing in a maintenance contract may be recommended.

Regardless of who maintains the equipment, the one indispensable item that a facility must have is an equipment logbook. Every time a piece of equipment has failed or been serviced, it must be recorded in the logbook as thoroughly as possible. A logbook, when properly used, provides the facility manager a way to view the inventory of the specific equipment that is in the facility, schedule emergency services for any down equipment, track the history of repairs, track the history of maintenance, receive help, download daily walk-through sheets, download specific information on the fitness equipment, and schedule regular preventative maintenance. By maintaining a detailed logbook, the equipment technicians and staff will be able to diagnose the problem better and provide the appropriate corrective actions. The following items are key elements to properly maintain sports equipment.

1. Strictly follow the manufacturer's maintenance instructions. Be sure that the instructions are included in the logbook for staff and technicians

2. Clean all equipment and flooring on a daily basis. Eliminating dust, dirt, and sweat will help maintain the condition of the equipment and flooring for longer use. Vacuuming under the motor cover of a treadmill can expand the life of the belt and deck.

3. Be sure to use the correct cleaning solutions when cleaning the equipment. Using ammonia, bleach, or acid-base cleaning fluids may cause some exercise machines to malfunction.

4. If a piece of equipment needs to be replaced, be sure to use only the parts from the manufacturer. Using a different piece puts the liability on the organization if a patron becomes injured while using the equipment.

5. Clean the upholstery daily to increase the lifespan. Users should be advised not wear clothing with buttons or tabs that can tear at the upholstery.

© Sutichak/Shutterstock.com

A typical restroom layout for males.

Restrooms

Facility managers and custodial workers typically view restroom maintenance as a "must do" task. However, not only should restroom maintenance should never be ignored, it must be performed on a regular schedule. According to Piper (2009) given the longevity of many restrooms, operational considerations such as maintenance costs, cleaning costs, and energy and water use are far more significant than the initial costs. To properly maintain a restroom, the service required to match the anticipated use of the facility must be considered. Additionally, the location of custodial closets should be well thought-out as it impacts as the time required to perform cleaning tasks and increases the chances of an accidental spill of chemicals on corridor carpet and tile.

Restroom housekeeping programs should include effective cleaning as well as hygienic cleaning testing to analyze the progress of the program. Some labor-saving equipment can improve cleaning processes while reducing labor time and cost. For example, steam or vapor cleaning sprays steam to the dirty areas through a special wand and an applicator to which the operator can fasten cleaning towels. The operator wipes all surfaces with the

Table 7.9 *Restroom Checklist*

Acceptable	Needs Attention	
		Toilet and toilet seats cleaned, disinfected, wiped dry
		Urinal handles cleaned, disinfected, wiped dry
		Urinal screens cleaned and blocks replaced
		Sinks and fixtures cleaned, disinfected, wiped dry
		Mirrors cleaned
		Door handles, wall switches and other "high contact" areas cleaned, disinfected, wiped dry
		Soap and paper dispensers disinfected and restocked
		Trash cans emptied, new liners put in place
		Floors freed of paper and trash
		Feminine hygiene dispensers cleaned, disinfected, and restocked, new liners put in place
		Air/odor control systems filled and operating correctly
		Countertops, ledges, etc. cleaned, disinfected, wiped dry
		Floor drains and drain covers are open and free of debris
		Light bulbs functioning
		Ceiling wall vents cleaned, disinfected, wiped dry
		Floor has been mopped clean with a proper cleaning or disinfecting solution
		Restroom looks and smells clean

Adapted from Nyco Products Company (n.d.)

superheated vapor, changing the cloth as it becomes soiled (Bigger, 2004). Managers can invest the savings in more thorough methods that result in a still-higher higher level of cleanliness and greater user satisfaction, and additional value to the facility. The following checklist identifies areas that should be reviewed on a daily basis.

Rows of half-lockers.

Locker Rooms

Locker rooms tend to overlooked initially by many patrons. However, if the locker room does not provide a clean and dry place for members to store personal items, a very negative opinion will most likely be formed. To ensure that patrons will have a positive experience, it is essential that a regular schedule for cleaning and maintenance be maintained.

Locker rooms often need attention on a recurring basis. To make sure that an adequate amount of attention is being paid, the locker room check must be part of the staff's daily duties. It is helpful for a checklist be located near the locker room entrance so employees can use it. One item to include on the checklist include picking up any trash or debris in the area. Wet floors must be inspected as well, particularly if the wet floor (flooring found in the showers and bathrooms) is made of ceramic tile. Ceramic tiles are used in most bathroom and shower areas in sports facilities. While ceramic tiles are usually durable, if they are not routinely inspected and maintained they can become very slippery, resulting in an injury to a facility user. Items to be reviewed include adherence and grouting in the joints, missing tiles, or loose joints.

Since many lockers are located near wet areas, the type of locker chosen for the facility will help maintain the locker room. Selecting solid plastic material instead of metal can decrease locker maintenance time and costs as well as stretch the lifecycle of the lockers. In contrast to metal lockers, solid plastic lockers are relatively impervious to moisture. Thus, plastic lockers have a reputation for being very durable especially in humid or wet environments typical of locker room areas.

Finally, routine inspection of the locker rooms may provide security against potential theft and vandalism. If possible, staff members should inspect the locker rooms at least twice each hour at irregular intervals. In order not to draw attention, staff should be encouraged to go pass through the locker rooms when moving from one part of the facility to another. While theft and vandalism may still occur, such events may be minimized by routine maintenance of the locker rooms.

Table 7.10 *Locker Room Checklist*

DATE	1/22	1/23	1/24	1/25	1/26	1/27
TIME	a.m. p.m.	a.m. p.m.	a.m. p.m.	a.m. p.m.	a.m. p.m.	a.m. p.m.
No standing water						
Floor clear of debris						
No suspicious persons						
No inappropriate behavior						
No electronic devices in use						
Shower area clean and safe						
Sauna area clean and safe						
Hot tub clean and safe						
Restrooms clean and safe						
No bags or unattended items						
Towel bins emptied						
Garbage cans emptied						
Supplies restocked						

Adapted from West Bend (WI) Insurance (n.d.)

These exterior and interior examples are everyday repairs that need to be carried out as a result of normal usage that would improve or maintain the comfort and convenience of the facility's environment. Regardless of the newness of the facility, a concerted preventive maintenance effort is key in determining its success. Patrons will be satisfied that their favorite equipment isn't constantly being repaired or that the locker rooms are safe to store valuables.

Capital Improvement Planning

While regular routine maintenance can assist in equipment safely lasting as long as possible, thereby saving large amounts of money in the long run, sports facilities should also develop and implement a capital improvement plan. A *capital improvement plan*, also referred to as CIP, is a short-range plan, generally lasting between four to ten years. The capital improvement plan assists in classifying capital projects and equipment acquisitions,

Capital Improvement Plan assists in classifying capital projects and equipment acquisitions, planning schedules and potential financing options.

generates a planning schedule, and helps to distinguish potential options for financing the plan. The CIP includes a description of proposed capital improvement projects ranked by priority, a year-by-year schedule of expected project funding, and an estimate of project costs and financing sources. The CIP is a working document and should be reviewed and updated annually to reflect changing community needs, priorities, and funding opportunities. The CIP is often spoken of as a rolling document since older projects drop off and new ones are added each year (Robinson, 1991).

According to Bowyer (1993), a capital improvement project may be defined as a major, nonrecurring expenditure that includes one or more of the following:

1. Any acquisition of land for a public purpose;
2. Any construction of a new facility (a public building, or water lines, playfield etc.), or an addition to, or extension of, such a facility;
3. A nonrecurring rehabilitation (something which is infrequent and would not be considered annual or other recurrent maintenance) or major repair of all or a part of a building, its grounds, a facility, or equipment, provided that the cost is $25,000 or more and the improvement will have a useful life of 10 years or more (such as a roofing or HVAC unit replacement);
4. Purchase of major equipment items such as cardio or strength equipment with an individual cost or total cost of $25,000 or more, and which have a useful life of five years or more;
5. Any planning, feasibility, engineering, or design study related to an individual capital improvement project, or to a program that is implemented through individual capital improvement projects.

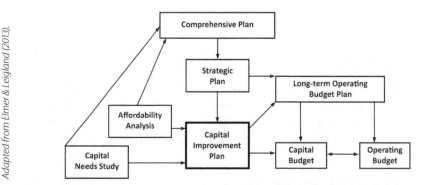

Adapted from Elmer & Leigland (2013).

Figure 7.1 Relationship of capital improvement plan to other documents.

Purposes of Capital Improvement Planning

As mentioned previously, capital improvement planning may be used as a powerful tool in creating a facility comprehensive plan, strategic plan, and other planning documents. The purposes of a CIP include:

1. The repair and replacement of aging infrastructure will take place in a reasonable timeframe.

2. The most economical means of financing capital improvements will be conducted.

3. The public will have a chance to contribute to the budget and financing process.

4. Unforeseen, inadequate planning or pointless capital outlays will be eliminated.

5. Severe increases in tax rates, user fees, and debt levels to pay for unanticipated capital improvements will be minimized.

6. Models of growth and development are aligned with the facility's comprehensive plan (University of Wisconsin-Stevens Point, 2008).

Creating a Capital Improvement Plan

Preparing a capital improvement plan often includes five steps. These steps are 1) project submission; 2) evaluation and selection; 3) financial analysis; 4) plan preparation; and 5) review and adoption. The project submission requires an identification of foreseeable projects in order of priority. Such project requests may include the description and justification of the project; an estimation of the starting project costs; approximation of potential operating and maintenance costs; and recommended funding sources. The second step of evaluation and selection prioritizes and selects the projects predicated on certain criteria such as project demand, as established by an catalog of obtainable land, equipment, and facility conditions; sum of residents served; return on investment, cost savings, or revenue generation; sustainability or energy efficiency improvements; economic, environmental, aesthetic or social impacts; and uniformity with community plans and policies.

The third step is financial analysis. Financial analysis is comprised of an assessment of all pertinent financial data including historical and projected local revenues, expenditures, and debt service. These assessments evaluate the organization's capacity to pay for future planned projects and to choose suitable financing tools. Planned preparation, the fourth step, identifies a directory of suggested undertakings by the funding year, project, and scheduling details, as well as sources of financing. The final step of reviewing and adopting the proposed plan follows a review and revision after which the organization may adopt the CIP and its accompanying budget.

To summarize, capital improvement plans create a relationship between the visions conveyed in the facility comprehensive plans and annual capital expenditure budgets. Capital improvement plans provide a systematic, simultaneous evaluation of potential future projects. While the CIP often functions as a long-range plan, it should be reviewed on a yearly basis and revised as needed. Progressive organizations focus on capital improvement planning as it addresses strategic financial decision-making that may permit the completion of critical projects without financially negative impacts on the facility.

Differences between Maintenance Costs and Capital Expenditures

Captial Expenditures investments that are made to increase the value of the asset.

There are several, yet, subtle differences between maintenance costs and capital expenditures. First, maintenance costs apply to routine actions that keep the building's assets (i.e., security, mechanical and electrical systems) in their original condition. *Capital expenditures* are investments that are made to increase the value of the asset. Routine maintenance restores the asset's physical condition and/or operation to a specified standard, prevents additional wear and tear when a part is no longer useful but cannot be replaced due to lack of finances, serves as a quick but short-term repair, and evaluates ongoing maintenance requirements. Capital expenditure is used when an organization wants to increase an asset's useful function or service capacity, enhance the quality of services, or decrease future operating costs. To summarize, routine maintenance activities can include replacing light bulbs, paint touch-ups in hallways and offices, landscaping, irrigation repairs, pool cleaning, and other frequently performed tasks. Capital expenditures are made when things such as carpet replacement, major lighting or landscape projects, pool deck refurbishment, security system upgrades or replacements, or exterior painting are needed.

Work Order Systems and Tracking

The communication issues between management and maintenance become more difficult as the complexity of maintenance tasks increases. Before the 1950s, maintenance was generally a reactive issue as equipment was repaired after it failed (Penrose, n.d.). In the 1960s, maintenance slowly became more proactive as equipment was analyzed prior to failure. The documentation process for request and completion of facility maintenance and repair work is vital for the effective and safe operation of a sport venue. This documentation process typically revolves around a document called the work order.

Work Order communicates information about services or goods that are needed.

What exactly is a work order? A *work order* communicates information about services or goods that are needed. Usually, a work order provides specific directions for the individual who is charged with completing the task. Depending on the type of work, the request will typically include contact information, a description of the task, location, level of urgency, the date of completion and tracking number. Once the repair or maintenance has been completed, the specific section closes out the work order, which is reported to the initiator. It is important to note that most significant component of the communication network (i.e. work order) is the initiator. If a work order is not completed no communication is taking place. The custodial staff is often the first line of defense when it comes to recognizing maintenance issues.

Work orders are often classified into three primary groups—emergency, urgent, and routine requests. Emergency work orders present conditions that immediately impact the performance and health of those in the facility in a negative fashion. Examples of emergency work orders that could affect the activities of the facility patrons are an electrical power outage, HVAC failure, or burst water pipes. Examples of conditions that would negatively affect the health of the facility patrons include broken windows, a gas leak, defective fire alarms, or scalding hot showers.

Urgent work orders occur when conditions exist that appreciably impair, but do not hamper, facility operations. Urgent work orders are usually unscheduled and reactive. They tend to pose a threat of personal injury, equipment damage, or serious disruption of service but are not considered emergencies. Urgent conditions may include shower or toilet drains that become clogged, handrails that become loosened, or minor water damages. If the problem is not corrected, it could become an emergency condition.

Routine work orders occur when conditions do not pose a threat to life, property or a serious disruption to the operation of the facility. They do not require immediate corrective action and can be scheduled and completed within a specific time period. Examples of routine work orders are painting, carpet or tile repairs, lock changes, pest control, moving or repairing furniture, and hanging bulletin boards, pictures or window blinds.

Tracking

No matter the size, location, or budget of a facility, facility maintenance issues relating to effectively tracking maintenance work orders will exist. Facility management and work order tracking likely consume a large part of a facility manager's time and budget. However, costs can be reduced and efficiency in dealing with facility problems can be increased by making sure that the items are tracked.

A traditional work order system involves requesting a task by word of mouth, a phone call, or email. Following the request, the paperwork is then filled out and communicated to the maintenance team. Upon completing the job, the maintenance workers may or may not report back to management with a status update, and the person who requested the job likely won't know it's been completed until they see it for themselves. Such work order tracking systems may negatively impact effective labor usage, service quality, and tenant or management satisfaction during periods of heavy activity.

Work Order Software

Maintaining a schedule of on-demand maintenance tasks may completely overpower a manual or paper-based work order scheduling system. Moreover, using an outdated work order tracking system can rather easily create a negative impact on service quality and labor. Modern systems found on computers or, in some cases, mobile devices may be used to aid work order tracking, assignment, and reporting. Work order software allows a facilities manager to respond quickly to work order requests from patrons, participants, employees, or staff members. Work order management software allows for the combining of all work order traffic notes, and by doing so, the likelihood of paper requests or scribbled notes being lost or buried is removed. As a result of such increased efficiency, greater management effectiveness, cost savings, and resource availability are realized.

Increasing Tracking Efficiency

According to Cross (2015), five steps may assist in increasing tracking efficiency.

1. Develop a visual workflow chart that shows the inputs and outputs required for processing an order. This is an activity-based workflow system that alters the process from being completed by individuals to synchronization of work activities by individuals.
2. Generation of a scheduling system for the different types of work orders. Job sequencing is employed to prioritize the work orders and ascertain where the request will fall in the processing schedule.
3. Implementation of a tracking system that records the time that work orders are received. Staff members input time information, which authenticates accountability for those charged to complete the work order. This step also provides information to estimate the average amount of time necessary to process an order along each point during the workflow process.
4. Creation of a system for recording and alerting the individual(s) who issued the work order of any delays or failures. This step creates a job history for the different types of work orders that is invaluable in evaluating job performances.
5. Creation of a reporting system that can disseminate the specified aspects communicated in the processing of the order. The fifth step provides information for all parties to review and assess the efficiency, or lack thereof, regarding the work order process.

Housekeeping and Custodial Issues

Custodians and housekeepers are key members of any facility staff since people initially perceive the quality of a facility and equipment by the way it looks. Custodians and housekeepers are usually charged with keeping the facility looking neat, clean and up to acceptable standards. Employing excellent custodial and housekeeping staff members are tremendous assets of the facility. However, despite potentially outstanding custodial and housekeeping services being rendered, many facilities are outsourcing these services with increasing frequency.

Outsourcing Custodial and Housekeeping Services

Two primary reasons that custodial and housekeeping services are being outsourced are increased costs and decreased productivity. A previous survey of facility managers indicated that custodial and housekeeping operations were the primary area for being outsourced to save money for the organization (FMLink & Encompass Global Technologies, 2002). According to McCagg (2001), the cost of hiring in-house staff averages 23% more than contract cleaning services. Moreover, when coupled with high benefit costs, higher costs per square foot exist for an in-house cleaning operation versus an outsourced cleaning operation (Maechling & Bredeson, 2005).

Costs can be measured in various ways such as cost per square foot cleaned, labor costs, supply costs, costs of benefits, and overhead costs. Substantial savings may also be realized since the costs of employee benefits can be circumvented due to *outsourcing*. The subject of benefits is often a costly proposition for in-house operations that requires administrators to create strategies that either counterbalance or reduce the effect of benefit costs (Maechling & Bredeson, 2005).

Outsourcing an arrangement in which one company provides services to another company for another company that could have been provided in-house.

Productivity of facility custodians and housekeepers has also been cited as a reason for outsourcing. In some cases, in-house custodian productivity may fall significantly below industry standards. For example, McCall (2002) reported that in-house custodial services at facilities in New York cleaned fewer square feet per staff member than the accepted national average. The study continues that if the below average facilities increased the efficiency of the custodial staff to meet the national average, an estimated saving of about $640,000 per year would be realized (McCall, 2002). An ancillary component regarding in-house custodial and housekeeping services relates to the lack of personnel training due to the restrictive budgets of the facility. Due to the lack of training, custodial staff members are not being provided professional development opportunities to learn about industry trends. As responsibilities and cleaning equipment change, custodial and housekeeping staff members need training to effectively understand those changes (Bigger & Bigger, 2007).

The efficiency of custodial staff can be connected to in-house versus outsource status.

Advantages of In-House Custodial Operations

Although there are several substantial benefits to outsourcing custodial and housekeeping services, benefits to maintaining such services in-house exist. Bigger and Bigger (2007) highlighted a number of these benefits that include ownership, pride, security, flexibility, and institutional knowledge.

© Keith Homan/Shutterstock.com

Lambeau Field serves as the home venue for the Green Bay Packers of the NFL.

The perception of ownership is important for many employees. When employees have a vested interest in the appearance and cleanliness of a facility, they often become more and more engaged to keep the facility at its most excellent appearance. Additionally, often when individuals are employed in a facility for a period of time, the culture of the organization becomes part of their personal work style. The acceptance of the organizational culture and brand identity of the facility may enhance the employee's perception of ownership. For example, the custodial crews at Lambeau Field in Green Bay, Wisconsin may exhibit increased productivity simply because they work for the Green Bay Packers (organizational culture) at Lambeau Field (brand identity) and have a sense of pride in connection with their work for this franchise.

A custodian who mirrors the organizational culture and promotes the brand identity to guests and customers will help to build associations with others that could ultimately translate into future business opportunities. This is especially true when the staff members understand that the state of the facility reflects their work. If employees have been in a building for numerous years, they tend to get to know the building, its quirks, and departmental needs. Such institutional knowledge provides a significant service when an emergency occurs. Pride in one's work is an additional component to ownership as cleaning and maintenance professionals can take satisfaction and increased self-esteem in serving that role. When custodians have sense of ownership in the organization, they may have an increased interest in ensuring that the facility is safe and secure. In some cases, custodians may prevent thefts because they noticed that something was missing and contacted security.

Mechanical Engineers

The effective integration of the maintenance function with engineering in the organization may save significant amounts of time, money, and other resources regarding reliability, availability, maintainability, and performance issues (Moubray, 2003). An engineering technician creates designs, develops, and maintains different types of machinery. Engineering job responsibilities involve people and resource management. An engineer is also responsible for devising cost-effective methods that can be used to modify different machinery. Engineering job responsibilities also include managing different projects that have been developed, creating the plan and designs for the projects, and giving detailed outlines of project specifications (Moubray, 2003). The person should be able to carry out modifications on projects in case projects turn out unsuccessfully the first time around. A list of responsibilities may include, but are not limited to the following:

1. Design and implement cost-effective equipment alterations to improve safety and reliability;

2. Develop a project specification with colleagues;

3. Discuss and solve complex problems with sub-contractors, suppliers and customers;

4. Ensure the item is constructed reliably to performs consistently;

5. Manage projects using engineering principles and techniques;

6. Consider the implications of issues such as cost, safety, and time constraints (Moubray, 2003).

Engineers discussing a project.

Flooring Selection and Maintenance

Selecting a floor would appear to be relatively simple. A person or committee just has to find a floor that looks good and provides the functionality for an activity. However, when selecting a floor for sports activities, the selection process becomes more complex. For example, sport facility planners did not have to worry about hot yoga, walleyball, or inline hockey needs 10–15 years ago. Additionally, while the sport flooring manufacturing business has exploded in recent years, a uniform standard concerning flooring performance, installation, and design presently does not exist. As a result, the facility manager must deal with a number of products manufactured by a number of different companies as well as the lack of uniform flooring standards. However, several organizations do address parts of these flooring standards that the facility manager should be aware. A sample of these organizations includes:

1. Deutsches Institut fur Normug eV (DIN)—German industrial standards are the most widely used for sports surfaces. While the DIN details performance standards and monitor quality, it does not stipulate design codes. DIN standards were often used in North America before the creation of ASTM F2772 in 2009.

2. American Society for Testing Materials (ASTM)—ASTM standards reveal that a product has passed the codes for a variety of items. It should be noted that ASTM standards tend to appear most frequently in the promotion of artificial turf, multi-purpose and sports needs of American facilities, while the DIN and EN norms only addressed European sports arenas.

3. International Association of Athletic Federations (IAAF)—The IAAF is the world governing body for track and field. Their certification process began in 1999 based upon "the goal that all facilities, synthetic surfaces, implements and equipment built for use in international

competitions conform to IAAF specifications and therefore guarantees the validity of the performances and the quality of the product" (IAAF Track and Field Facilities Manual, 2008, p. 13).

4. The International Soccer Federation (FIFA)—The FIFA Quality Program establishes a flooring standard specific to international soccer surfaces. The dual aim of this project better defines the surface requirements for the elite and lower level competition by creating minimum standards worldwide.

5. International Organization for Standardization (ISO)—The purpose of the ISO is to make certain that products and services are safe, reliable, and of good quality. ISO standards are generated by experts worldwide who form technical committees.

If at all possible, the facility manager should try to consult at least one of these organization websites to gain as much information as possible about specific surface standards that apply to sports activities.

Deciding on a Surface

It is uncommon for a surface to be used for only one activity. Usually, secondary activities will establish the final flooring selection. To address flooring needs, the first action should be to include the owner, the facility manager, the architect, the contractor, representatives of the maintenance staff, the athletic director, the coaches, a community representative for a publicly funded space, and even athletes to decide what's most important for the surface. While architects provide an essential service for designing a facility, they are often at a disadvantage since they "have to know a little bit about everything, and it doesn't always allow them to focus on flooring" (Arhweiler, 2003, para. 20). Second, make a list of the uses of the facility. The flooring materials must be matched to accommodate different performance qualities that are needed for various activities. Third, develop a timeline for the installation of the selected flooring. The flooring must be professionally installed to coincide with the facility opening. Some of the most important items that should be considered are:

1. Installation: Is it difficult to install? Who will be doing the installing? How long will it impact the re-opening of the area?

2. Aesthetics: How does the flooring look? Does it depict the facility owner and/or managers want to portray? Traditional? Contemporary? How does the flooring look under different lighting conditions? Specific details could include court sizes and colors (field, border, circles, etc.).

3. Maintenance: For example, the facility will be open seven days per week for basketball, volleyball, aerobics/fitness, weight training, tennis courts, among many other activities suited to the facility. How will the floor be cared for and how often? What equipment and chemicals are necessary to maintain floor? Will the facility staff realistically be able to handle the maintenance schedule? Can the staff conduct minor repairs or is the manufacturer needed?

4. Durability: How long does this surface last? How long do you want it to last? Look for not only new installations but also installations at least three years old to determine longevity and real maintenance requirements. What types of wear and tear does the product show? How can it be fixed? Does the type of usage you plan affect durability?

5. Performance: Can it handle hosting multipurpose events, if needed? What is this type of floor designed to do best? Does this product work for sports you intend to play? For example, a basketball floor needs to return energy to maximize the ball's bounce, allow participants to jump well, and provide for quick pivot turns. Tennis courts, however, need to return energy for bounce as well but not to the level of a basketball court. Additionally, surfaces such as tennis courts must be designed to allow the athlete to move horizontally, a controlled slide, without fear of injury.

6. Cost: What are the initial costs as well as the overall costs that the facility will need for the duration of the flooring? What are the estimated maintenance costs? How much are the products necessary for maintenance? Is the process to obtain the maintenance products uncomplicated? What may be maintenance cost in employee hours?

7. Safety: Does this floor meet the biomechanical needs of its intended uses? Is there proper cushioning for impact? Does it offer the correct slip coefficient? Is it too slippery or not slippery enough? Does it offer an opportunity for all levels of individuals to participate safely? Have there been any recent recalls by the manufacturer?

Properties of Sports Flooring

Sport facility flooring differs from other types of flooring such as residential or commercial flooring. Do to the activities that take place on it, the type of flooring surface needs must be strongly considered. For example, sports floors can be categorized as point-elastic or area-elastic. Point-elastic surfaces, which are mostly synthetic surfaces, yield to the applied pressure while providing cushioning to absorb energy. Examples of point-elastic flooring include vinyl, rubber, or polyurethane floors.

Point-elastic surfacing may be defined as the "reaction to a local force with a deformation which adapts to the shape of the deforming object" (Nigg & Yeadon, 1987, p. 119). Point-elastic floors perform uniformly throughout the entire playing area. As a result, each area on the floor will have almost equal shock absorption, ball rebound, and vertical deformation qualities. The main advantage of having a point-elastic flooring system is that the adjoining areas of the floor continue to be comparatively unaffected by activity. As such, point-elastic floors cooperate with the individual characteristics (e.g., strength, quickness, speed, etc.) of each athlete.

Area-elastic surfaces, primarily wood, don't give with immediate pressure but bend slightly over a wide area and provide energy return. Because hardwood surfaces are not as flexible as other materials, vertical deformation happens over a large area when a force is applied. The vertical deformation disperses energy farther across the surface. Area-elastic flooring allows a larger area of the surface to return energy to the athlete. For example, when a basketball player runs, each footfall creates energy as it lands. However, an innate component of area-elastic floors is that it performs differently over the entire surface.

Differences between Area-Elastic and Point-Elastic Systems

The primary difference between an area-elastic floor and a point elastic floor is that area-elastic or wood floors disperse energy over a wide surface area while a point-elastic (i.e. vinyl or rubber) sports floor reacts in a more localized area. Whereas wood floors generate concerns about dead spots and resilience, synthetic floors elevate concerns regarding loading, where the cushioning "bottoms out," making a heavy impact on users' joints. Joint load refers to the force put on a weight-bearing or load-bearing joint during activity. Synthetic floors that are 9mm or less will bottom out. However, synthetic systems of a minimum of 15mm will increase users' comfort. When the joint load is excessive over a period of time, the participant may experience severe pain and discomfort in the most affected joint such as the knee.

According to the ASTM, the sport facility manager should take four performance level criteria into consideration. These include:

Shock Absorption calculates the floor's ability to decrease the force of impact.

Vertical Deformation assesses the ability of the floor to deform or "give" when an athlete jumps or falls.

Ball Bounce a measure that determines the precision of the vertical ball behavior.

Sliding Effect sometimes referred to as coefficient of friction or slip-and-slide.

1. *Shock Absorption*: calculates the floor's ability to decrease the force of impact. A boost in shock absorption makes the floor safer for participants of all ages by decreasing the likelihood of long-term injuries.

2. *Vertical Deformation:* assesses the ability of the floor to deform or "give" when an athlete jumps or falls. If the "give" of the floor is too much, it may be equated to running in the sand. However, too little give may result in immediate injuries on impact or falls.

3. *Ball Bounce*: determines the precision of the vertical ball behavior. If the ball rebound is higher and more consistent, the playability of the surface will be better.

4. *Sliding Effect*: sometimes referred to as coefficient of friction or slip-and-slide. The sliding effect occurs when there is an optimal level of grip, the participants can slide in all directions, and the participants can move or pivot safely and easily.

Wood Flooring

Wood is prized for its appearance, its ability to return energy—the level of "bounce"—and its durability. Wood surfacing is a known commodity with a long history of performance that can last between 40–60 years, if properly maintained. However, the proper maintenance of wood requires precise, committed action on the part of the facility manager and staff. Wood surfaces expand and contract depending on the changes of humidity and/or temperature. Such changes require proper ventilation systems to be used. If the wood gets wet and is unattended, it will become damaged. Thus it is extremely important to monitor the floor and clean any spills or leaks immediately. Wood floors also require daily, weekly, and annual maintenance. To maintain a wood surface, dirt should be regularly removed from the surface using a broom or dust mop daily. Track off mats should be utilized at entry points from the outdoors. The floors should be scrubbed with an auto-scrubber or rotary brush scrubber and the appropriate cleaning solutions on a weekly basis. It is important that all water and cleaning solutions be completely removed from the wood surface using a vacuum and squeegee following the cleaning.

When a wood floor is initially installed, planners must select the coating for the floor, which is the finish applied to protect the surface. The two primary options for coating a wood floor are an oil-modified polyurethane, or a water-based polyurethane. Both choices have advantages and disadvantages. Oil-modified polyurethane provides a stronger and longer lasting protective coat and is usually less expensive than a water-based polyurethane. Oil-modified polyurethanes are more difficult to apply to a surface and require a longer curing or drying time. Oil-modified polyurethanes also contain higher levels of volatile organic compounds (VOCs) making them less environmentally friendly than their water-based counterparts. Another significant difference between the two finishes is the color. Water-based polyurethanes provide a clear coat while oil-modifies polyurethanes slightly ambers or darkens the surface.

The surface coating of a wood floor requires annual maintenance. There are three primary methods of maintenance for the coating of a wood floor. The primary method of maintenance for the coating of a wood floor is a simple recoating process. This process takes 3–14 days, depending on environmental factors, and involves screening the surface of the floor and applying another coat of finish. Each layer of finish, particularly with an oil-modified polyurethane solution, ambers the floor deeper. To address the ambering of the floor lines and markings, every two or three recoating processes should include repainting. This process is the same as recoating except a new layer of paint is applied between the screening and recoating steps. The repainting process adds one to five days to the recoating process depending on the number of colors of paint being applied. Finally, every 10–15 years, the floor will need to be refinished. The refinishing process involves sanding the floor to the bare wood, resealing the wood, repainting, and recoating the surface. This full refinishing process can take two to five weeks.

Wood floors can be installed three basic ways, although manufacturers have developed dozens of slightly altered systems. Typically, wood floors are installed over concrete bases. On top is the layer of wood strips, usually maple. Maple is the most common choice for basketball courts, accounting for an estimated 95% of the wood used for professional playing surfaces. Bamboo floors are most often found in college training areas and are often selected for its sustainability.

The refinishing of the Student Life Center at Baylor University. The images show the four steps in refinishing a floor: sanding, resealing, repainting, and recoating.

An anchored system in which the top layer of maple is attached to anchored wood "sleepers" exposed during a floor repair project.

Underneath the top layer is the subsystem, which provides the resilience. It is in the subsystem where the differences in floor installation occur. The three primary types of flooring subsystems are anchored (also referred to as fixed), floating, and anchored-floating. An anchored system is characterized by the top layer of maple being anchored to the concrete base with fasteners or an adhesive. Anchored systems restrict the movement of the floor both vertically and horizontally. Floating systems are not mechanically anchored to the concrete base and are typically installed over a system of wood and/or synthetic pads to provide resiliency. Floating systems do not restrict the movement of the floor vertically or horizontally and are typically the least expensive option. Anchored-floating systems are hybrid systems in which the top layer of maple is anchored to a subsystem of wood and/or synthetic padding that is anchored to the concrete base. These hybrid systems are typically the most expensive subflooring option. Anchored-floating systems restrict vertical movement, but not horizontal movement. Horizontal movement of the floor allows the wood to expand and contract naturally to reduce stress and maintain structural integrity. All three installation systems can be installed as a continuous system or a "sleeper" system. A continuous subsystem has a uniform wood and/or synthetic base, such as continuous sheets of plywood, where a "sleeper" subsystem has a series of "sleepers," wooden support beams such as 2x4s, comprising the subsystem. A continuous subsystem is typically a little more expensive than a "sleeper" system, but provides a more consistent and better performing floor.

Synthetic Flooring

While wood often seems the most obvious choice for gymnasium and multipurpose floors, it may not always be the best solution. Synthetics are generally placed in three discrete categories: urethane, rubber, and PVC (polyvinyl chlorate). While wood is most often the overwhelming selection for courts, synthetic flooring is most often found in weight rooms and cardio equipment areas. Using *synthetic flooring* systems in these areas is prevalent due to their sound- and shock-absorbing capacities. These cushioned floors are available in rolls or tiles.

Synthetic Flooring flooring generally made from urethane, rubber and PVC (polyvinyl chlorate).

Sport facility managers must be aware that synthetic sport surfaces may present certain issues, especially if the facility is multipurpose. For example, synthetic surfaces have been shown to be too frictional with not enough slip (Severn, Fleming, & Dixon, 2010). As a result, manufacturers have revised their products to reduce friction. At the other end of the spectrum, even more frictional synthetics can become slippery when dusty. Owners must also consider the chemicals and aromas involved with installing synthetics when making their choices, especially for facilities that remain open 24 hours a day or get constant, heavy use.

Heavily used multipurpose spaces often don't see enough downtime for the maintenance involved with wood floors. Synthetics can be installed without worrying about humidity or acclimatization, heavy equipment or technical expertise, but they have their own set of installation issues. Owners must make sure the substrate base—the concrete—is free of imperfections, since those will come through, and installers must pay special attention to the seals or seams

This synthetic flooring used in a running track of a fitness center shows signs of excess wear.

© Pressmaster/Shutterstock.com

between rolls, which can create weak spots that can trap water. Many manufacturers and consultants recommend a clear, sprayed-on urethane topcoat to further protect synthetic floors from dust and dirt. While this may increase the floor's shine, it does not affect performance.

Synthetic Turf Selection and Maintenance

Artificial turf, which most manufacturers now call synthetic turf, was introduced to sports activities in the 1966 in the Houston Astrodome. While the initial product offered a way for teams to play sports indoors, major problems related to the lack of "give," which correlated to an individual incurring significant knee and ankle injuries. For example, when an athlete makes a move, the cleats on the bottom of the shoes will penetrate and interlock with the playing surface creating traction forces (Severn et al., 2010). In an interview, Dr. Jason Dragoo, professor at Stanford

© knelson20/Shutterstock.com

Rubberized flooring tiles are often installed in fitness center settings for weight training areas to provide shock absorption and sound reduction.

University School of Medicine, mentioned the issue may be that turf provides too good a grip (Grens, Lies, & Tourtellotte, 2012). Dragoo stated, "So if you are in the wrong position, because your leg doesn't give way as it does on grass, it can distribute that force to your knee and cause an injury" (Grens et al., 2012, para. 15). Thus, the ability to generate traction between a player's footwear and a sporting surface is a critical aspect in the performance of the player as well as safety from lower limb injury (Severn et al., 2010).

Synthetic Turf Maintenance

It is a misconception that the caring of synthetic fields not only requires less maintenance than natural turf grass fields, but they are maintenance free. However, synthetic fields need to have: 1) additional infill, 2) irrigation because of unacceptably high temperatures on warm, sunny days, 3) chemical disinfectants, 4) sprays to reduce static cling and odors, 5) drainage repair and maintenance, 6) erasing and repainting temporary lines, and 7) removing organic matter accumulation (Patton, n.d.). Fouty (2005) cited that the normal annual maintenance costs of her artificial turf fields at Michigan State University ranged from $13,720–$39,220, while the typical annual maintenance costs of her natural turf fields had a similar range of $8,133–$48,960.

Advances in Synthetic Turf

Today's synthetic turf generally has shock pads and infill systems that have provided a safer turf for participants to play. The systems create a more resilient surface, reducing the force of impact. Most of the synthetic turf systems presently used have a shock-absorbing pad installed below them. Additionally, shock pads lengthen the life of a field by reducing compaction. These pads are made from a variety of materials, including polypropylene, rubber, and recycled materials that offer a lifespan of up to 50 years, after which they can be recycled.

The most advanced turf systems imitate the natural grass's response to the way it deforms to player's steps as well as ball bounces and provides adequate slip resistance. Grass fibers, which can be made of polypropylene, nylon or a blend of the two, can be assembled in several ways. Some systems knit fibers together. While more expensive, this method is more stable. Others feature fiber "tufts," similar to what carpeting looks like. Some products even feature shock-absorbing infill materials between each fiber to mimic the play of grass. In addition to the turf fibers, several options are available for the under layers. For the padding underneath, shock-absorbing assemblies include closed-cell foam pads, SBR rubber sheets, or cast-in-place elastic materials called an e-layer. A turf system can even incorporate all of these previously mentioned. More basic methods depend simply on the underlying infill to provide shock absorption.

The next consideration is installation methods. When installing the turf mats, the seams can be glued or sewn together. Glue requires less expertise and costs less, while sewn seams are more expensive but can provide a superior finish. Finally, the striping can consist of painted lines, which are less expensive and easier to change, or inlaid lines, where are more permanent and durable, but can create additional seams in the turf. As such, grounds crews can stripe line markings more easily and other markings on field comprised of synthetic turf.

A soccer field installation of artificial turf.

Although synthetic turf requires no mowing, watering or fertilizing, it has several maintenance issues. For example, the sun's ultraviolet rays can reduce the fibers' strength, make them more brittle, and discolor the turf (Arhweiler, 2003). Additionally, the under layers may become compacted over time rendering the surface similar to concrete, as well as seams separating, and fiber loss. Finally, because synthetic turf doesn't utilize the sunlight to create chemical energy, as a living plant will, it had a tendency to get extremely hot, especially in the early years of its use in the 1960s and 1970s. To alleviate the heat retention issue, synthetic turf manufacturers used research from the automotive industry. By integrating the automotive industry research, manufacturers were able to develop synthetic turf that better reflected the sunlight, which significantly decreased the surface temperature of the material. However, thermal gains with artificial turf remain a concern with some synthetic turf installations (McNitt, Petrunak, & Serentis, 2008).

Synthetic Turf Injury Research

Previous research has suggested that the traditional artificial turf fields increased athlete injury, mainly because of increased surface hardness. In 2006, NFL players were surveyed regarding the type of surface they believed caused more fatigue and soreness. Seventy-four percent of the players perceived that artificial turf systems increased fatigue and soreness (National Football League Players Association, 2006). In another study, Meyers and Barnhill (2004) reported higher incidences of one to two day time-loss injuries, two or more days time-loss injuries, head and neural trauma, and ligament injuries were recorded on natural turf grass fields compared to FieldTurf.

Synthetic turf has been alleged to increase the likelihood of infections among players that play primarily on in-fill systems. A study of high school football players reported an antibiotic-resistant staph infection at a rate of 517 for each 100,000 individuals (Epstein, 2007). This rate is significantly higher than what is reported by the U.S. Centers for Disease Control and Prevention, which revealed a rate for the general population of 32 in 100,000. These infections were mainly related to increased skin abrasions connected with synthetic turf.

Due to a great deal of biomechanical research, product development and testing, synthetic turf is now made to be more forgiving to athletes' bodies and more similar to natural turf. Ekstrand, Timpka, and Hagglund (2006) contrasted injury risk in elite soccer played on artificial turf to natural grass. The results indicated that there was no difference between soccer played on synthetic or natural turf. Five years later, Ekstrand, Hagglund, and Fuller (2011) compared incidences and patterns of injury of female and male soccer teams when played on artificial turf and grass. The results revealed that neither men nor women were significantly different in the type of overuse injuries. However, differences did exist as males were less likely to sustain a quadriceps strain but more likely to sustain an ankle sprain on artificial turf. Soligard, Bahr, and Andersen (2012) analyzed the risk of acute injuries among youth male and female soccer athletes playing on third-generation artificial turf compared with grass. The results indicated that playing on artificial turf increased the likelihood of back, spine, shoulder, and collarbone injuries as opposed to playing on natural grass. While these research articles represent positive findings regarding the use of synthetic turf, more extensive and longitudinal studies are needed.

In-fill systems must now be routinely treated with special disinfectants to reduce the likelihood of infections, adding another cost to the maintenance of these fields. Proper maintenance of a synthetic sports field can increase its longevity and appearance while maximizing its performance and quality of play. Suggestions to provide effective routine maintenance of synthetic sports fields include:

1. Conduct daily inspections—particular attention should be paid to the areas that are most heavily used for wear and seam separation

2. Remove all waste items, airborne contaminants such as leaves, and organic material (such as animal waste) from the surface.

3. Do not permit food, soda, gum, sunflower seeds, tobacco use (chewing or smoking). Do not allow vehicles to be parked on the field.

4. Regularly brush the surface to maintain infill levels, remove debris, and improve the look of the playing field. Using a static brush to maintain the level of the infill and a mechanical sweeper to remove debris, the direction of the brushing should be alternated per manufacturer's instructions between moving length-wise, width-wise and then diagonally across the field.

5. Maintain a maintenance and activity log. Often required by the warranty, every maintenance operation, regardless of how minor, must be recorded in the log. The following information should be included:

   a. Types of activities during the week

   b. Approximate number of hours the field was used

   c. Average number of participants

   d. Type and extensiveness of the maintenance provided, (Synthetic Turf Council, 2013).

As an indication of how far turf has come, FIFA, the International Soccer Federation now states it approves of the use of artificial turf in harsh climates and in stadiums where it is hard to grow and maintain natural grass. The following websites can provide information for a specific sports surface and maintenance:

1. The U. S. Tennis Court and Track Builders Association (www.ustctba.com) provides information regarding tennis as well as track and field.

2. The U. S. Consumer Product Safety Commission (www.cpsc.gov) publishes surface standards and other safety guidelines.

3. The Maple Flooring Manufacturers Association (www.maplefloor.org) offers frequently asked questions, maintenance guidelines, and other relevant information.

4. International Soccer Federation (FIFA) (www.fifa.com/qualityconcept) provides background information on synthetic turf and their standards and testing through the group's Quality Concept program.

5. Synthetic Turf Council (www.SyntheticTurfCouncil.org) provides guidelines for the maintenance of infilled synthetic turf sports fields.

6. USA Football (http://usafootball.com) offers a guide to football field safety and care.

Maintenance, including regular brushing and monitoring of synthetic turfs, must be regularly conducted to warrant the even distribution of the correct quantity of infill in all in-filled synthetic turf surfaces. A synthetic turf surface should never be perceived as maintenance free and the potential of infill contamination must be well thought out from design stage through to operation (James & McLeod, 2010). As more synthetic turf systems are introduced into the sports surface market, questions about the playing surface quality to enable consumers to make informed decisions must be made. Issues such as the surface hardness of these systems affected by infill media depth and type (ratio of sand to crumb rubber), as well as the thickness and type of underlying shock absorbing pad for the safety of participants must be addressed.

Conclusion

When important systems in a sport facility go down, it can be costly and inconvenient. Such critical systems are the lifeline of any facility, that's why a proper routine maintenance program is not an option; it is a necessity. Traditionally, maintenance personnel were only required to concentrate on the rudimentary upkeep of the facility. However, today's personnel must be knowledgeable in a variety of environmentally friendly methods and supplies. Among the items that maintenance personnel must be aware include, but are not limited to, the most current energy issues; toxic materials management; storm water drainage methods; as well as best practices of the heating, ventilation, and air conditioning systems.

Facility maintenance is a crucial process for all sport and recreation facilities. It is vital that facility and event managers understand the importance of a instituting a proactive approach to maintenance in their organizational systems. The use of inspection and checklists, as identified in this chapter is imperative. However, facility management and maintenance is not only about the nuts and bolts. Effective facility management creates a hospitality environment based on positive personal interactions with staff and trainers. An effective maintenance plan is an excellent way of ensuring that a facility is being taken care of. Not only will implementing such a plan keep a building clean, but it will also keep a facility running as efficiently and safely as possible. Ultimately, a facility can have all the bells and whistles, but if members do not feel safe because equipment is consistently faulty, they're not going to join.

CHAPTER DISCUSSION QUESTIONS

1. Why is it important that a facility manager communicate maintenance issues with employees and patrons?

2. What are some ways that facility management can implement routine maintenance procedures in specific exterior areas?

3. In what ways can facility management implement routine maintenance procedures in specific interior areas such as restrooms, locker rooms, etc.?

4. How can capital improvement plans affect the maintenance of a facility?

5. What ways can work order and tracking systems can assist communications between employees and management?

6. Why should facility manager outsource custodial and housekeeping services? Why should facility managers keep maintenance in-house?

7. Why should facilities use either synthetic or wood surfaces? List and discuss five pros and five cons for each type of surface.

MINI CASE STUDY

Miller, Petersen, and Judge University (MPJU) facility maintenance department was organized to manage operations of a multipurpose sport and recreation facility which included a two basketball courts, three racquetball courts, a cardio and weight lifting room, and a six lane, 25-yard swimming pool. Additionally, the facility included both men's and women's locker rooms, each of which had six individual showers and four toilet areas as well as five offices. The director of facility maintenance and the assistant director collected the data on the maintenance management problems, the current approaches to address the problems, information and communication technology (ICT) implementation, and the maintenance management system. A patron registered a complaint regarding a defect in one of the pieces of equipment used in the cardio and weight lifting room. However, the defect findings from the inspection were not similar to the original customer complaint. This was due to unspecific information related to the explanation of the equipment defect. The time range for inspection increased due to the unspecific information contained in the customer complaint. The customer was less technical in knowledge on the equipment defect. Thus, the maintenance manager faced time constraints to execute the necessary maintenance. The additional time for identifying the defect in the inspection impacted the costs for building and equipment maintenance. The facility maintenance budget consisted of both corrective and preventive maintenance. Yet, the staff also found it difficult to estimate the budget expenses for many departments due to many mishandled or and unhandled complaint reports. Finally, most of the maintenance staff was part of the in-house operations at MPJU.

Using the information in this chapter, answer the following items:

1. Identify and explain the steps the director of facility maintenance and assistant director could take to increase communication between staff members and patrons. Second, explain how work order systems and tracking can be used to increase communication between management and maintenance personnel.

2. Identify and explain how routine and preventative maintenance may assist in keeping budget allocations from being overspent.

3. Explain the importance of keeping an equipment logbook for situations described in the above scenario.

4. Explain how proper maintenance of the equipment described above may relate to capital improvement projects.

5. Explain the steps that should be followed for a capital improvement project due to the defects that may appear in the facility equipment.

6. Explain the advantages and disadvantages of in-house custodial maintenance staff as opposed to outsourcing such personnel.

PRACTITIONER SPOTLIGHT

NAME: Lance Rosenberger

ORGANIZATION: Medallion Athletic Products, Inc.

CURRENT JOB TITLE: Vice President, Operations 2006–Present

EDUCATIONAL PREPARATION:

- BS in Industrial Technology, Iowa State University 1996
- Certified Field Builder, American Sports Builders Association

Photo courtesy of Lance Rosenberger.

Lance Rosenberger (orange shirt) updates a client on the progress of an installation.

CAREER PATH: After I finished my degree, I started working for a steel manufacturing company. In 2005, I started working for Medallion. At the time, we were working primarily through subcontractors to build sports fields. We realized that it would be more efficient to have our own crews rather than work through subcontractors and began working towards that model. In 2008, we were able to self-perform our first project and now we have several crews making us a turnkey provider for all of the work in turf and track installations.

WHAT IS THE PROCESS FOR HELPING A CLIENT CHOOSE A SURFACE?

The first thing we do is talk to the client about their intended uses for the facility, their budget for the project, and their timeframe for the project. We then try to point them towards products that will work best for their intended use. Slight variations in the turf work better for different uses. For example, we have surfaces that are designed more for soccer, some that are designed more for football, and some that are designed mainly for field hockey. On the track surface side of the decision, it is really a matter of budget and competition level. A high school on a low budget will usually go with a latex track; a little

The teal turf installed by Medallion at Coastal Carolina University in Conway, SC.

Photo courtesy of Medallion.

better performance track that is a little more expensive would be a urethane track; and if the client has a large budget and wants the best surface we can install a MONDO track, which is what they use in the Olympics. We show the clients samples of the different products and take them to see some of our previous installations. We also put new clients in contact with previous clients to discuss what they liked and what they would do differently. From there we will give a price estimate and either begin designing the project or use the client's architect's plans for the project. Once plans are complete we will give a firm price quote.

WHAT ARE SOME OF THE UNIQUE OR INTERESTING PROJECTS THAT YOU HAVE DONE?

The field installation at Coastal Carolina University was an interesting project. We installed the only teal colored field in the United States. We had a custom teal surface made to match their specific shade of teal as the school color. Not only was the field teal, but all of the surfaces inside of the stadium were teal as well. We also did a baseball complex in Seminole County, Florida. That was a unique project because of its size. There we installed nine, full synthetic, baseball fields.

WHAT IS THE MOST REWARDING ASPECT OF YOUR JOB?

Being able to take a field that is in rough shape and transforming it. We see fields that are not well maintained and don't perform well at all and are able to install a new, high-tech surface. It transforms the entire stadium and can really change the way an entire school feels about their athletic program. It becomes a source of pride. We have had schools make t-shirts because they were so enthusiastic about getting turf. That's pretty cool.

WHAT IS THE MOST CHALLENGING ASPECT OF THIS JOB?

Time constraints are our biggest challenge. We often have clients that don't understand the construction process and have really tight time frames. Most, probably 75%, of the clients want the project done during the summer months, while school is out. It takes about eight weeks to convert an existing football/ soccer facility from a grass surface to a synthetic surface. So we are really busy in the summer.

WHAT IS A UNIQUE ASPECT OR TASK OF YOUR JOB THAT MANY WOULD BE SURPRISED HEAR ABOUT?

When most people see artificial turf, they think that all of the markings are either painted on or installed at the factory. In reality every line, hash mark, logo, etc. are physically cut and installed once the turf is rolled out. All of the markings are made from a colored artificial turf so they will last as long as the field itself.

WHAT ADVICE DO YOU HAVE FOR THOSE SEEKING A SIMILAR CAREER?

Use the American Sports Builders Association as a resource. Their website has a lot of resources for learning about constructing and installing sport surfaces. It also has a listing of builders that are really dedicated to building quality surfaces. Contact a local builder to open communication and network. This industry is a very friendly environment. Most people are very approachable and willing to help individuals seeking to work in this part of the sport industry.

Reprinted by permission of Lance Rosenberger.

REFERENCES

Air Specialist. (2016). What's included on a complete HVAC maintenance checklist. Retrieved from http://www.airspecialist.com/articles/whats-included-on-a-complete-hvac-maintenance-checklist/

Al-Najjar, B., & Alsyouf, I. (2003). Selecting the most efficient maintenance approach using fuzzy multiple criteria decision making. *International Journal of Production Economics, 84*(1), 85–100.

Arhweiler, M. (2003). Tread lightly—A complete guide to selecting the right sports surface. *Recreation Management.* Retrieved from http://recmanagement.com/200305fe00.php

Bigger, A. S. (2004). Restroom cleaning revisited. *Facilitiesnet.* Retrieved from http://www.facilitiesnet.com/plumbingrestrooms/article/Restroom-Cleaning-Revisited-Facility-Management-Plumbing-Restrooms-Feature-1758

Bigger, A. S., & Bigger, L. B. (2007). Contract vs. in-house staff: Finding the right source for custodial and maintenance operations. *The Bulletin.* Retrieved from http://www.acui.org/publications/bulletin/article.aspx?issue=448&id=2298

Bowyer, R. A. (1993). *Capital improvements programs: Linking budgeting and planning.* PAS 442. Chicago, IL: American Planning Association.

Cooke, F. L. (2003). Plant maintenance strategy: Evidence from four British manufacturing firms. *Journal of Quality in Maintenance Engineering, 9*(3), 239–249.

Cross, V. (2015). How to track work orders. *Chron.com.* Retrieved from http://smallbusiness.chron.com/track-work-orders-12254.html

Dekker, R. (1996). Applications of maintenance optimization models: A review and analysis. *Reliability Engineering & System Safety, 51*(3), 229–240.

Edwards, L., & Torcellini, P., (2002). A literature review of the effects of natural light on building occupants. Golden, CO: National Renewable Energy Laboratory.

Elmer, V., & Leigland, A. (2013). *Infrastructure Planning and Finance: A Smart and Sustainable Guide.* London: Routledge.

Ekstrand, J., Hägglund, M., & Fuller, C. W. (2011). Comparison of injuries sustained on artificial turf and grass by male and female elite football players. *Scandinavian Journal of Medicine & Science in Sports, 21*(6), 824–832.

Ekstrand, J., Timpka, T., & Hägglund, M. (2006). Risk of injury in elite football played on artificial turf versus natural grass: A prospective two-cohort study. *British Journal of Sports Medicine, 40*(12), 975–980.

Epstein, V. (2007). Texas football succumbs to virulent staph infection from turf. Retrieved from http://www.bloomberg.com/apps/news?pid=20601109&sid=alxhrJDn.cdc&refer=news

FMLink & Encompass Global Technologies. (2002, January 7). FMLink outsourcing survey. Retrieved from http://www.fmlink.com/Surveys/outsourcing.htm

Fouty, A. (2005). A sport field manager's perspective: Synthetic turf considerations, maintenance costs and concerns. Paper presented at the Synthetic Turf Infill Seminar, Detroit, MI.

Fraser, K. (2011). Maintenance and reliability is strategic to most organizations: So why is there so little empirical research? *Proceedings of the 25th Annual Australian and New Zealand Academy of Management Conference, Wellington, New Zealand.*

Fricklas, R.L. Leeman, M., Marvin, B., D,Ascenzo, W. M., & Sundin, J. (2009). Preventative maintenance checklist: Preserve the integrity of your roofing, lighting, HVAC and plumbing. *Buildings,* Retrieved from http://www.buildings.com/article-details/articleid/6835/title/preventive-maintenance-checklist/viewall/true

Grens, K., Lies, E., & Tourtellotte, B. (2012). Football knee injuries more likely on artificial turf: Study. Retrieved from http://www.reuters.com/article/us-football-idUSBRE84002Q20120501

James, I. T., & Mcleod, A. J. (2010). The effect of maintenance on the performance of sand-filled synthetic turf surfaces. *Sports Technology, 3*(1), 43–51.

Maechling, T., & Bredeson, J. (2005). Discovering value in outsourcing facilities management. *BioPharm International, 18*(5), 66–72.

McCagg, M. (2001). In-house vs. outsourcing: Survey finds in-house cleaning costs more. *Cleaning & Maintenance Management, 38*(6). Retrieved from http://www.cmmonline.com/article.asp?indexid=6631848

McCall, H. C. (2002). A study of custodial staffing levels in school districts: Report published by the State of New York Comptroller's Office. Retrieved from http://www.osc.state.ny.us/localgov/audits/swr/2002mr10.pdf

McNitt, A.S., Petrunak, D.M., & Serensits, T.J. (2008). Temperature amelioration of synthetic turf surfaces through irrigation. *Acta Hortic, 783,* 573–582. DOI: 10.17660/ActaHortic.2008.783.59 http://dx.doi.org/10.17660/ActaHortic.2008.783.59

Meyers, M. C., & Barnhill, B. S. (2004). Incidence, causes, and severity of high school football injuries on fieldturf versus natural grass. *American Journal Sports Medicine, 32*(7), 1626–1638.

Moubray, J. (2003). Twenty-first century maintenance organization: Part 1—The asset management model. *Maintenance Technology*, Applied Technology Publications, Barrington, IL.

Muthu, S., Devadasan, S. R., Ahmed, S., Suresh, P., & Baladhandayutham, R. (2000). Benchmarking for strategic maintenance quality improvement. *Benchmarking: An International Journal, 7*(4), 292–303.

Myeda, N. E, Kamaruzzaman, S. N., & Pitt, M. (2011). Measuring the performance of office buildings maintenance management in Malaysia. *Journal of Facilities Management, 9*(3), 181–199.

Nigg, B. M., & Yeadon, M. R. (1987). Biomechanical aspects of playing surfaces. *Journal of Sports Sciences, 5*(2), 117–145.

Pfeffer, J. (1995). Producing sustainable competitive advantage through the effective management of people. *The Academy of Management Executive, 9*(1), 55–69.

Piper, J. (2009). Minimizing restroom maintenance. *Facilitiesnet.com*. Retrieved from http://www.facilitiesnet.com/plumbingrestrooms/article/Minimizing-Restroom-Maintenance-Facilities-Management-Plumbing-Restrooms-Feature-10626

Robinson, S. (1991). Capital planning and budgeting. *In Local Government Finance* J. E. Petersen and D. R. Strachota (Eds). Chicago, IL: Government Finance Officers Association.

Severn, K. A., Fleming, P. R., & Dixon, N. (2010). Science of synthetic turf surfaces: player surface interactions. *Sports Technology, 3*(1), 13–25.

Soligard, T., Bahr, R., & Andersen, T. E. (2012). Injury risk on artificial turf and grass in youth tournament football. *Scandinavian Journal of Medicine & Science in Sports, 22*(3), 356–361.

Synthetic Turf Council. (2013). *Guidelines for maintenance of infilled synthetic turf sports field.* Retrieved from https://c.ymcdn.com/sites/www.syntheticturfcouncil.org/resource/resmgr/files/stc_guidelines_for_maintenan.pdf

University of Wisconsin—Stevens Point. (2008). Planning implementation tools capital improvement plan. Retrieved from www.uwsp.edu/.../PlanImplementation/Capital_Improvement_Plan.pdf

U.S. Geological Survey. (2005). Physical Security Handbook. Retrieved from http://www.usgs.gov/usgs-manual/handbook/hb/440-2-h/440-2-h.html

Vence, D. (2014). Maintenance-minded. *Recreation Management*. Retrieved from http://recmanagement.com/feature/201410FE05/4

Yamashina, H. (2000). Applications of maintenance optimization models: a review and analysis. *International Journal of Quality & Reliability Management, 17*(2), 132–143.

Zio, E. (2009). Reliability engineering: Old problems and new challenges. *Reliability Engineering and System Safety, 94*(2), 125–141.

Changeover Management and Temporary Venues

8

J. *Patrick Marsh* and *Jeffrey C. Petersen*

OBJECTIVES

After studying this chapter, the student should be able to:

- Understand the various functions of public assembly facilities and how a facility manager must prepare for each function.
- Understand the changeover process and how to efficiently manage changeovers.
- Analyze the construction and use of temporary venues and compare this process to the construction and use of permanent venues.

KEY TERMS

Changeover	Rigging	Zamboni
Man-hour	Temporary Facility	

KEY ACRONYMS

AEG	Anchutz Entertainment Group	**NFHS**	National Federation of High School Associations
AVP	Association of Volleyball Professionals		
CAD	Computer Aided Design	**PAF**	Public Assembly Facility
		UFC	Ultimate Fighting Championship
NCAA	National Collegiate Athletic Association	**WWE**	World Wrestling Entertainment

Introduction

AT&T Stadium in Arlington, TX, as an example of a primary football venue with changeover use capabilities.

The Staples Center in Los Angeles operates as a true multi-purpose venue.

Changeover the process of converting the use of a stadium or arena from the specifications of one sport or event to another different sport or event, also referred to as conversion.

In order to address the high initial investment costs to create facilities for sport or physical activity, two strategies have been developed. These strategies are quite different in their approach but can be equally effective in making a sport facility more financially feasible. The first technique is to create a permanent facility that can be utilized for multiple purposes and events. Such a facility might be designed for a single primary use, yet still maintain the ability to be altered for other uses. AT&T Stadium located in Arlington, Texas and owned by the city would be an example of this facility type. This stadium was designed primarily as a venue for American football and hosts professional football (Dallas Cowboys), collegiate football [Annual Cowboy Classic/Advocare Classic, Texas Farm Bureau Shootout (Baylor and Texas Tech), Southwest Classic (Arkansas and Texas A&M), and the Cotton Bowl Classic], and high school football (various regular season, playoff and state championship games). However the venue has been converted for other uses such as major music concerts (George Strait, U2, Taylor Swift Beyonce and Jay Z), soccer matches (CONCACAF Gold Cup and World Football Challenge matches), boxing matches (Pacquiao/Clottey), and basketball games (including the 2010 NBA All-Star Game & the 2014 NCAA Final Four) along with a variety other events. In contrast, other venues may initially be designed for multiple sports and events as a primary goal such as the Staples Center in Los Angeles owned and operated by Anchutz Entertainment Group (AEG). Staples Center is the home facility for the Lakers (NBA), Clippers (NBA), Kings (NHL) and Sparks (WNBA) along with serving as the standing host of the Grammy Awards. From its inception the Staples Center was designed to be a premier multi-purpose venues currently hosting over 250 events per year as the top concert venue in Los Angeles and hosts numerous other premier sports events like Ultimate Fighting Championship (UFC) events, World Wrestling Entertainment's (WWE) Summer Slam, and the Summer X Games. Regardless of the multi-use facility type, the key to its efficient and effective use is the *changeover* process that converts and prepares a facility to host each different event type. Understanding the changeover processes and the management of such tasks is an important skill set for a facility or event manager.

A second and very different strategy is to avoid the high cost of constructing a permanent structure and instead to invest in a temporary venue or temporary structures that allow non-sport-specific environments to be converted to use for sport and then converted back to their original use. This could range from using an air-supported dome for winter season use of an existing swimming pool or tennis courts, to the construction of a temporary beach volleyball stadium for an Association of Volleyball Professionals (AVP) event, and even to the construction of a hockey rink in a MLB stadium for the NHL Winter Classic. The use of temporary structures can create spaces for sport and/or spectators. These temporary facilities can provide cost-effective solutions and can also create unique experiences for both participants and spectators. For the facility and event manager, it is vital to be able to provide insight and input within decision-making processes between using a temporary venue and constructing a permanent facility.

The changeover process within permanent facilities and the development of temporary venues for sport both have significant and specialized challenges for the facility and event management professional. Therefore, it is important to understand the general concepts and considerations behind each, as well as to delve deeper into the specific applications of these methods to maximize efficiency and revenue generation. When examining the changeover process in a permanent facility or the potential construction of a temporary venue, it is important to understand that the goal is to find the most efficient use of limited resources. The limited resources that a facility and event manager must consider are financial resources, human resources, time, and space. A successful changeover or temporary venue makes the best use of each of these resources to prepare the venue for a successful event.

Changeover Management

Throughout history, public assembly facilities (PAFs) have been used for many different types of events. The Roman Colosseum transformed from an arena for gladiatorial bouts to an aquatic facility hosting mock naval battles. Modern arenas routinely transform from basketball arenas to ice rinks to concert halls. This process of facility transformation is most commonly referred to as changeover, but is also sometimes called conversion within the facility management setting. Regardless of how it is referenced, the changeover of a PAF from one function to another is a very involved process with multiple facets.

- How does the facility need to function for the next event?
- What equipment is needed for the next event?
- Where can the equipment be stored?
- When will the changeover take place and how long will it take?
- Who will provide the labor and how many people will the changeover require?
- Why is the efficient management of the changeover process important?

These are questions that a facility and event manager must answer. The efficient management of the changeover process is vital to the success of a facility. PAFs are built to be used and the value of a facility is a direct product of how often the facility is in use. Facilities ranging from public recreation facilities to large stadiums and arenas routinely host hundreds of different events and/or activities each year. The time it takes to change over a facility from one function to another is the time that the facility is not in use. Having a facility sit dormant is both functionally and financially wasteful. In order to maximize the time that a facility is in use, and the value of the facility, changeovers need to be managed as efficiently as possible.

While there are several essential concepts that must be taken into account when managing facility changeovers, the most important concept to remember is that every facility is different. While many facilities may look very similar during events, the process to get them to that point is often very different. Facilities have different layouts, storage areas, access points, and other structural elements such as seating configurations that can drastically change the way changeovers must be managed. Each facility will also have different staffing in terms of both size and experience. Different facilities also have different equipment. All of these differences make it very difficult to create a standardized method for changeover management. It is vitally important for each facility manager to understand the strengths and the challenges of their facility in order to manage changeovers efficiently. This chapter will explore the key aspects of changeover management and several possible approaches to each aspect. As each aspect is explored, keep in mind that there are multiple ways to approach changeover management and a facility manager must make the best decision for the unique situations presented by each unique facility.

Communication

Perhaps the most essential element to the successful and efficient management of changeovers is communication. Often many people are involved in the changeover process and the facility and event manager is usually the central communication point. The participants, ticket office, marketing department, guest services, media services, and any other involved party are all going to have separate facility related needs that must be accounted for to create an appropriate setup for the event. It is important that the facility and event manager communicate to the changeover crew exactly what is expected in terms of the event setup, including the unique needs of every involved party, the timeframe in which the conversion must be completed, and the resources available for the conversion. It is important to establish open and clear lines of communication with everyone involved and to keep each party informed. The changeover crew cannot create the appropriate seating configuration without knowing what the ticket office has sold for the event. Conversely, the ticket office cannot begin setting up a seat inventory for an event without knowing what the changeover crew is capable of creating.

While this may seem like a very basic concept, the facilitation of effective communication among all of the parties involved in the hosting of an event can be very challenging. Many times the parties involved in hosting an event are not located in the same place and each party is often solely focused on their own specific piece of the event puzzle. The facility and event manager can facilitate communication among the involved parties in several ways. The first is by bringing everyone together in a planning meeting. Facilitating face-to-face communication, and often times introductions, is very effective in opening lasting lines of communication. Whenever possible, the initial large planning meeting for an event needs to take place in the venue where the event will be held. The ability to see the space as a group while discussing the specifics of an event, gives each party a better understanding of the events goals and the challenges associated with meeting those goals. After the initial planning meeting, the facility and event manager should summarize the details discussed in the planning meeting and email them to the entire group. This is the beginning of an email chain that will allow the group to share any additional information or changes with one another. The facility and event manager should continue to check in with each party throughout the time from the initial planning meeting through the day of the event. Finally, the facility and event manager should arrange a walk-through for all involved parties once the event has been set-up to ensure that no final adjustments to the set-up are needed.

Planning

Proper planning is essential to an efficient changeover. The planning process for a changeover begins with an understanding of what the final product will be after the conversion. This is extremely important because it allows the facility manager and the changeover crew to operate efficiently towards the goal. When evaluating what the finished product should look like, there are several factors to consider. The first is the standards for the event that is being hosted. Different events will have different standards and regulations about space and materials. For example, NCAA basketball rule 1-13-4 (2015a) prohibits courtside seating within three feet of the basket stanchion, and NFHS and NCAA wrestling rules 1-2&5 (NFHS, 2015) and 1-8&9 (NCAA, 2015b) require at least five feet of matted clear space around the out-of-bounds circle and an additional 5–10 feet of clear space around the matted area. Meeting these guidelines is essential for athlete safety, and a contest could not be held without conforming to these regulations. It is also important to consider participant and spectator safety, ease of use, and enjoyment when determining how the facility should be set up. Many facilities will use different seating configurations for different events. Having the appropriate configuration and providing the best sightlines can greatly enhance the experience for patrons. All of these factors should be included in preliminary discussions and communication with the event's stakeholders.

Scheduling and Human Resource Management

One of the most important aspects of the planning process is scheduling. The scheduling process for a changeover begins with an understanding of what must take place during the changeover and what the limiting factors are for the changeover. Scheduling for changeovers is often limited by a combination of time and human resources. The appropriate scheduling of both time and human resources is essential to a well-executed changeover. There is usually an inverse relationship between the availability of human resources and the amount of time required to perform a changeover. However, limits on this inverse relationship exist at both ends of the scale. There becomes a point when more people will no longer create a more time efficient process. Conversely, there are tasks associated with many conversions that cannot be completed with only one or two people regardless of the amount of time available. It is important for a facility and event manager to know the limitations on both ends of the scale. For example, the quickest a particular arena can be converted from hockey to basketball may be four hours and require 50 people. The same arena may also be able to convert from hockey to basketball using only four people, but that process would take 24 working hours and be spread out over two days. The four-hour changeover requires 200 *man-hours* of labor, while the two-day changeover only requires 96 man-hours of labor. The appropriate staffing for the conversion is dependent upon the amount of time available. If there is a basketball game later that day or even the next day, then having a larger crew is a necessity; however, if the next basketball game is three days away the smaller crew would be more financially efficient.

Man-hour a unit of measurement for production based upon the amount of work accomplished within a one hour time span by one person.

Managing the human resources for changeovers at a large facility is a very complex task. As was discussed in Chapter 5, human resource management is not only about the number of people working and the amount of time they work. It is also important for a facility and event manager to determine the best way to assemble a changeover crew in terms of full-time, part-time, temporary, and volunteer workers. Changeovers require a high level of knowledge and understanding of the intricacies that are unique to each facility. This level of knowledge and understanding is typically associated with full-time employees. Changeovers are also very sporadic in their scheduling. It is common to have several different events in a row, requiring changeovers for each, followed by several days without any events. This type of schedule is often associated with part-time or temporary employees. Finding the appropriate balance of full-time, part-time, and temporary employees is a function of the needs of the facility and the resources available to compensate the employees. Full-time, skilled employees are more expensive than part-time employees or unskilled, temporary laborers; however, highly skilled employees that are very familiar with the facility are much more efficient in completing changeovers.

The Dean E. Smith Center at the University of North Carolina has a full-time maintenance staff of 11 people that complete all of the changeovers in their facility. The familiarity that the staff has with the facility allows a relatively small number of people to work very efficiently; however, the staff works very long hours and the compensation costs per employee are relatively high. Philips Arena, in Atlanta, takes a different approach to human resource management. Philips employs six full-time changeover specialists and then hires additional temporary laborers based on the need of each changeover. The six full-time employees each oversee a particular section of the arena with which they have become very familiar and they guide the temporary laborers through the changeover. This is financially more efficient than hiring more full-time employees, but the six full-time employees must teach the same tasks to a new group of temporary laborers for each changeover.

Staging

Another essential planning element to an efficient changeover is the appropriate storage and staging of materials and equipment. Having materials and equipment for the next event easily accessible and well organized allows the changeover crew to work through the changeover process efficiently. While this concept seems very straight forward, the efficient and organized storage of materials in many facilities is a challenge due to insufficient storage space. Facility managers must be creative in the storage and staging of materials and equipment for each type of event that the facility hosts. Often this requires moving equipment around in storage in preparation for the next event on the schedule. The ability to efficiently store equipment and materials and move them from storage to staging and to their final installation location is key to a successful changeover. Another important factor to consider when staging materials and equipment for a changeover is the order in which they need to be installed. Materials and equipment being installed first need to be accessible at the beginning of the changeover.

The AT&T Center in San Antonio, Texas utilizes a creative color coding system to stage materials and equipment for changeovers. The floors in the storage and staging areas in the AT&T Center are marked with different colored lines. These lines serve two purposes. First, the lines create boundaries for areas to stage materials and equipment while allowing for easy movement around the staged items. The second purpose is organization. The materials for each task in the changeover process are placed in a different section of the staging area and marked with a different color. This allows separate crews to focus on separate tasks while operating in conjunction with the other crews performing different parts of the changeover.

The AT&T Center in San Antonio, Texas is home to the San Antonio Spurs (NBA), San Antonio Stars (WNBA), San Antonio Rampage (AHL), and the San Antonio Stock Show & Rodeo. Contributed by J. Patrick Marsh.

Equipment

Another key to an efficient changeover is having the appropriate equipment to aid in the process. Every step in the changeover process, from storage to staging to installation, requires equipment to operate in the most efficient manner possible. The equipment can be as simple as having the appropriate screwdriver head attachments for the fasteners being used and as complex as having custom fabricated machinery to assist in certain tasks. A common practice in large facilities to assist in the storage shuffle is the fabrication of custom storage carts. These carts are specially made to fit the unique space limitations of a specific facility and often are created to be stackable with the assistance of a forklift. These carts are an essential part of efficient changeovers because they are used throughout the process for both moving and storing equipment.

As mentioned earlier in the chapter, many facilities are challenged by a lack of storage space. This creates a necessity to become creative with the space available and occasionally to use off-site storage for supplemental space. Both packing an on-site storage room as full as possible and the use of an off-site storage facility have challenges that are often met through the use of specialized equipment. When stacking supplies in a storage room, several types of equipment can be beneficial. These can be as simple as using a ladder or building steps to reach the top levels of storage or as complex as creating custom hoist systems to hang items from the ceiling. Moveable rack storage systems are also common equipment to aid in the efficient storage of supplies. Using off-site storage or procuring materials for a one-time event creates another set of challenges and often requires different equipment. Most large facilities utilize loading docks to unload items being delivered to the facility. These loading docks are sometimes constructed with levers that allow the dock to adjust to the height of the truck making the delivery. When a loading dock is not available, it is often necessary to use a delivery truck with a lift gate to lower the materials and equipment being delivered.

The ability to efficiently move materials and equipment from storage to staging and eventually to the installation site also requires equipment. Storage carts, forklifts, pallet jacks, and small utility vehicles can all be used to move materials efficiently and prevent staff members from having to carry supplies throughout the facility. Once the materials for the next event are in place for installation, there is still a need for equipment to assist in the installation. Everyday hand tools such as screwdrivers, wrenches, hammers, measuring tapes, and levels are commonly used in the installation phase of a changeover. Other common pieces of equipment that are used in facility changeovers include motorized track systems for seating (telescoping bleachers or risers) and power hoists. Power hoists, also referred to as chain hoists, can

Temporary power hoists being used to hang equipment. Contributed by J. Patrick Marsh.

The pallet jack and the forklift are both vital pieces of equipment used in many facility changeovers.

be permanently installed to allow items such as scoreboards or speakers to be moved up and down, or they can be hung temporarily from a *rigging* grid to allow for the use of additional lighting or sound systems.

Rigging a system of cables or chains used to suspend elements from the roof structure of a stadium or arena.

Common Types of Changeovers

Facilities today are capable of hosting a multitude of different events. For each different event that a facility hosts, a corresponding changeover must take place. The sheer number of different changeovers make it impossible to discuss them all, but we will examine a few of the most commonly occurring changeovers.

Practice and Competition

The most common, yet often overlooked, changeover occurs when transitioning a facility from a practice set-up to a competition set-up and vice versa. Happening multiple times each competitive season, the changeover between practice and competition is vital to the success of a facility and the tenants of that facility.

Key Components

Communication with Coaches: It is important that a facility manager knows exactly what each coach wants and needs for a successful practice. This includes the desired space, equipment, surface markings, and any other facility-based requirements the coach may have for an optimal practice. For example, if a team is preparing for an upcoming road game in a hostile environment, the coach may want to have the facility's sound system pipe in crowd noise.

Equipment: An essential component to successfully transitioning between practice and competition set-ups is the efficient storage, set-up, and teardown of equipment. Practice equipment such as additional basketball goals, football blocking sleds, and baseball batting cages or pitching screens must be stored in a place that is easily accessible while not interfering with the competition environment. For example, many basketball teams practice with several additional

McCamish Pavilion at Georgia Tech set-up for a basketball practice. Contributed by J. Patrick Marsh.

goals. Often one of the additional practice goals is also the backup goal for games. It is important to have a place to store the goal during games that is easily accessible but doesn't interfere with the game environment.

Surface Markings: Coaches often want additional surface markings for practice. Creating functional markings that are easily removed is an important aspect of the practice and competition changeover. Markings on an artificial turf surface should be made with a temporary turf paint. These temporary paints are easily removed using a paint removal solution. Markings on a hardwood floor can be made with either a low-adhesive vinyl tape or with a water soluble paint, such as kids' finger paint, and can be easily removed with a wet mop.

Seating Configuration: Many facilities have retractable or portable seating that can be moved to create more space for practice. Seating should only be moved as much as needed to conduct a safe and successful practice or competition. Maintaining sufficient buffer zones between playing surfaces and seating or other stationary objects should be considered in the changeover process.

Hockey and Basketball

Many large arenas host both hockey and basketball. The concurrent seasons and large number of competitions for both hockey and basketball teams mean that these arenas must transition between hockey and basketball numerous times each season. The transition between these two sports is a complex and time-consuming process, often taking in excess of eight hours.

Key Components

Playing Surface: The difference in playing surface is the most obvious challenge in the changeover between hockey and basketball. This challenge is mitigated by the fact that once the ice is made it is rarely removed until the conclusion of the season. Instead of making new ice for each changeover, the ice is covered using a sturdy, insulated cover that is laid over the ice in large 1" thick tiles. A portable hardwood floor is then assembled on top of the insulated ice covering. To transition back to hockey, the hardwood floor and the ice cover are removed and a thin layer of new ice is added to the ice surface using a specialized ice resurfacing machine, commonly called a *Zamboni* or Zamboni machine, after the original inventor of the machine. It is currently the dominant brand in the market.

Zamboni a specialized machine developed to resurface ice in refrigerated rink settings with the name connected to the original inventor; leading manufacturer of these types of devices.

Equipment: A few key pieces of equipment must be stored, assembled, and disassembled efficiently during the changeovers between hockey and basketball. For basketball, the key pieces of equipment are the goals and the scorers and media tables. The scorers and media tables in large arenas often include

LED displays that must be connected to the house system. The key pieces of equipment for hockey are the dasher boards, glass, and netting that surround the ice behind the goal areas. These are heavy, bulky pieces of equipment that must be efficiently stored and transported to and from storage.

Seating Configuration: An NHL hockey rink (200 ft. × 85 ft.) (NHL, 2014) is more than three times as large as an NBA or NCAA basketball court (94 ft. × 50 ft.) (NBA, 2015 & NCAA, 2015a). This means there are drastically different seating configurations for each sport within the same arena. Arenas are typically constructed to the seating specifications of a hockey rink with additional seating provided typically in one of two ways. One method used for the additional space available when converting from hockey to basketball is retractable seating. These seating systems are permanently installed and telescope out either manually or via a motorized roller system and may have tip up chair-back seating or bleacher style seating. In addition to the retractable seating, basketball seating configurations in these arenas often use hundreds of individual chairs that are set out on the floor and on portable risers around the court.

The Staples Center in Los Angeles during a Lakers game. The outline of the hockey rink can be seen in the seating configuration.

The ice resurfacing machine or Zamboni is a vital piece of equipment for creating and maintaining ice surfaces.

Arena to Other Sports

In order to maximize the usage of an arena, facility managers will often book sports other than basketball or hockey such as volleyball, gymnastics, wrestling, and even tennis and arena football. The transition to sports other than those primarily hosted in a facility requires detailed planning to ensure that all of the intricacies and required specifications of the new sport are addressed. It is vitally important that facility managers research the new sport and consult an expert in the sport to ensure that nothing is overlooked. For example, volleyball, gymnastics, and wrestling all have specific requirements for the amount of clear space that must be present between the competition area and any seating, walls, or other obstructions.

Key Components

Playing Surface: Most sports have playing surface specification that may be outlined by the governing body of that sport. While volleyball can be played on a basketball court with the addition of volleyball markings using a low-adhesive vinyl tape, most other sports require the installation of a different surface. Indoor football requires a turf field and gymnastics requires a spring floor and multiple mats. Wrestling requires as many as 10–12 wrestling mats for a large tournament, and tennis requires a portable tennis court similar to a portable basketball court. A facility manager should research the surface needs of each sport being held in the facility and coordinate with an outside source to secure the necessary surface and to ensure the proper installation.

Equipment: Each new sport an arena hosts requires different equipment. Indoor football uses padded hockey dasher boards and two large netting and goal post structures suspended from the rafters. Gymnastics requires several different apparatuses with many requiring anchoring systems to the floor, and volleyball and tennis each require a net system that will typically include a floor sleeve system. In addition to the playing equipment, new sports often require a different timing and scoring system than the traditional arena scoreboard. If the arena uses a traditional scoreboard, often a portable scoreboard will need to be used. If the arena uses a video board display for scoring and timing, new sport specific software will need to be installed.

Seating Configuration: In order to provide the best spectator experience for each sport, a new seating configuration will need to be created. Facility managers should configure the playing surface for each event in the manner that allows the best use of permanent arena seating. Additional temporary seating can be used to create a configuration that allows for the best viewing of the event while maintaining both player and spectator safety.

Football/Soccer and Baseball

Football and baseball teams have shared facilities for over a century where. For example, New York's Polo Grounds played host to the New York Giants baseball team and the New York Giants football team from 1925–1955 (Polo Grounds, 2016). The Oakland Athletics (MLB) and Oakland Raiders (NFL) have shared O.co Coliseum since 1968. Additionally, a number of baseball stadiums have been used for college bowl games such as Yankee Stadium (Pinstripe Bowl), Tropicana Field (St. Petersburg Bowl), and the Rogers Centre (International Bowl). Soccer teams have joined football and baseball in the joint use of some stadiums such as the New York Yankees and FC New York sharing Yankee Stadium. The transition between baseball and either football or soccer is very involved and time consuming, which limits the number of times a stadium manager is willing and able to go back and forth. Additionally, the patrons' viewing experience in multi-purpose stadiums is often sub-par for either or both football/soccer and baseball. This has led to sharp decline in the use and new construction of such facilities.

Key Components

Playing Surface: The necessity for a smooth, dirt surface for a baseball infield stands in stark contrast to the necessity for a sturdy, grass surface needed for both football and soccer. Historically, football teams playing in multi-purpose stadiums would play on the dirt infield until baseball season was finished, then sod would be used to cover the infield for the remainder of the football season. Recently, advances in sod cultivation, specifically the ability to cut sod in longer and wider rolls, has led to sod that is ready for play nearly immediately after installation. This means that stadiums can put down and take up sod more often and play football and soccer on complete grass surfaces. The installation of temporary sod is a very technical process that requires great attention to detail in order to create a smooth surface, free from hazardous seams.

FC New York prepares for a MLS game in Yankee Stadium.

Seating Configuration: The difference in dimensions between baseball and football or soccer makes the configuration of seats a challenge. Many of the multi-purpose stadiums were designed with a circular seating configuration and additional shifting sections that could be moved behind home plate for baseball and behind each sideline for football and soccer. Many baseball stadiums that also host football and soccer will use temporary or portable seating to create seating on the football and soccer sidelines. Proper planning for the installation of temporary seating is essential to the changeover process in order to maintain quality sight lines and preserve the playing surface on which the temporary seating is being installed.

Sport Facility and Other Entertainment

While the primary function of nearly all stadiums and arenas is athletic competition, these facilities often host many other events. Concerts, professional wrestling, rodeo, and extreme sports are just a few of the other types of events that fill out a facility's schedule. While these types of events are common in most large arenas and stadiums, each show has different equipment, a different set-up, and its own unique set of challenges. Proper planning for each unique event is essential to an efficient changeover.

Key Components

Equipment: Each unique event will have different equipment needs. Concerts and professional wrestling have extensive staging, lighting, and audio equipment needs. Often touring shows will provide most of their own equipment, but it is important for a facility manager to work closely with each show's producers to coordinate the acquisition of any additional equipment and to coordinate the load-in and set-up for the show. Set-up for these types of shows often will require extensive assembly and rigging from over-head grids. Many large shows will travel with an equipment crew. However, the facility manager will often need to supplement this staff by providing the traveling crew with additional staff that is thoroughly familiar with the facility.

Surface: Many events held in large stadiums and arenas, such as rodeos, motocross, and monster truck events, require a dirt surface. The installation of a quality dirt surface in these facilities is a complex and detail oriented process. Different events have very different needs for the performance of

Cleanup after a Monster Truck rally at Angel Stadium in Anaheim, CA.

the dirt surface and the surface must be installed accordingly. Rodeos use a 12–14 inch deep mixture of dirt and sand that must be watered, chiseled, and groomed to create a soft surface that is safe for both the animals and the cowboys. Monster truck events, motocross, and BMX events, on the other hand, need a firmer surface to allow for greater traction for the vehicles. In either case, it is important for a facility manager to work closely with event producers to ensure that a quality surface is installed for each event. It is also important that the facility manager protect the primary surface in a facility from the dirt by using an appropriate surface covering. While some arenas may have a base floor surface of concrete that can more easily accommodate the use of dirt-based events, other arenas and stadiums may have permanently installed flooring or turf that often requires multiple layers of surface protection before dirt is brought in.

Seating Configuration: Most facilities have a few different configuration options for outside musical or theatrical shows. The traditional configuration is to build a stage at one end of the facility and place floor seating in rows going out from the stage. In the traditional configuration, the facility will often block off the seats behind the stage due to poor sight lines. The other common seating arrangement is called in the round. This configuration involves building a stage in the center of the facility and placing floor seating 360° around the stage. This configuration often does not require seats to be blocked off due to poor sight lines and allows for more patrons to attend. It is important that the facility manager work closely with each show's production staff and the facility's ticket staff to ensure that each show has an appropriate configuration and floor seating is arranged properly.

Sport Facility and Formal Events

Arenas and stadiums are often the largest facilities in a community and are often used to host large formal events such as graduations, dinners, and receptions. Creating a formal atmosphere in a facility that was designed and constructed for sport can be challenging. A facility manager must pay close attention to every detail in order to successfully transform a sport facility into a formal venue.

Key Components

Furnishings: The key to creating a formal atmosphere in a sport facility is attention to detail in furnishing the event. Formal events require formal furnishings. A facility manager should work closely with event organizers to obtain furnishings that create the appropriate atmosphere. The transformation begins with an appropriate floor covering such a vinyl cover or temporary carpet. Formal tables, chairs, and decorations are an essential element of creating an appropriate environment. A facility manager should work with a rental company and a florist to obtain the appropriate furnishings and decorations.

Seating Configuration: Large formal events often need to maximize the number of people that can be seated comfortably for the event. It is important that a facility manager knows how to make the best use of the space. Formal dinners may use long rows of tables or separate round tables. Each arrangement has different spacing needs to allow for comfortable seating and ease of movement around the tables. Specialized computer aided design (CAD) programs such as Social Tables can assist in creating an efficient layout for nearly any event.

Temporary Venues

While the emergence of multipurpose facilities gives the ability to hold a wide variety of events in a single venue, there are still times when there is not a suitable venue for an event. When there is not a suitable venue for an event, event organizers are faced with a tough decision. Organizers can simply cancel the event, they can build a permanent venue that may only be used a few times, or they can construct a temporary venue. Temporary venues are becoming increasingly popular due to their ability to allow event organizers to reduce construction costs and avoid having vacant or unused facilities. Temporary venues are also becoming increasingly popular for creating unique experiences for fans and participants and driving revenue for the event organizers.

Temporary Facility the creation of a sport venue for a one-time use from a facility or space not originally designed or developed for that sport use.

There are several different types of temporary athletic venues. However, the majority of temporary venues fall into one of three categories. Temporary athletic venues are generally either seating added to an existing competition area, a competition area added to existing seating areas, or a combination of the two. Temporary venues can be as large as creating an entire stadium for the Olympic Games or as small as bringing in a few sets of temporary bleachers for a youth soccer game. Construction sites for temporary venues also vary. Temporary venues can be built in a variety of different spaces including existing athletic venues.

The addition of seating to an existing athletic competition area is a common type of temporary athletic facility. This can be as simple as adding a few sets of rollaway bleachers to create a spectator area for a small event or as complex as adding thousands of bleacher seats and premium seating areas to a golf course to host a major championship. While the scale of these temporary seating structures may be very different, the basic construction concepts are quite similar. Most temporary seating structures are either relatively small, pre-assembled, metal bleachers, or scaffolding systems with seating attached. The construction or installation of any temporary seating structure begins with creating a stable, level surface on which to build. This can be as simple as finding an existing surface to build upon or as complex as creating a base for a scaffolding system on an uneven surface using adjustable legs and laser

Temporary spectator seating at the 18th hole of the 2009 US Open hosted at Bethpage State Park's Black Course in Farmingdale, NY.

The 2009 NCAA Final Four, held at Ford Field in Detroit, MI, was the first Final Four to place the court in the center of the stadium and utilize the entire football seating configuration. Contributed by J. Patrick Marsh.

leveling. Once a stable base has been established, assembly of a scaffolding structure can begin. These structures can be created in a variety of shapes and sizes and are typically finished with metal flooring and either metal bench seating or individual plastic seats.

Adding a playing surface to an existing seating structure creates another common type of temporary athletic venue. The NHL Winter Classic and the NCAA Men's Basketball Final Four are examples of events that are held in temporary venues created inside existing permanent venues. The NHL Winter Classic is an annual outdoor hockey game held on a temporary rink built inside of a large football or baseball stadium. The Final Four is played on a temporary basketball court, built upon a large stage in the center of a domed football stadium. Both of these events create a unique opportunity to have tens of thousands more fans attend the events than if they were played in a typical hockey or basketball arena. Creating these temporary surfaces can be challenging. Creating an NHL quality ice sheet in unpredictable weather conditions takes a great deal of planning and equipment. Creating optimum sight lines for an NCAA basketball court (94' × 50') (NCAA, 2015a) in the middle of a football field (360' × 160') (NFL, 2015) requires building a massive stage that allows for players to safely run out of bounds without falling off and then building a temporary court on that stage. Temporary seating is also built around the stage to allow for higher attendance and to prevent large amounts of empty space around the court.

Temporary athletic venues can also be created by constructing both a temporary playing surface and temporary seating. This is a common practice in creating venues for beach volleyball as temporary seating structures are constructed around a sand court that can be removed following the event. Another example of a venue created using a temporary surface and temporary seating was the Carrier Classic in which a temporary basketball arena was constructed on the flight deck of an aircraft carrier. When creating a temporary venue using both a temporary playing surface and temporary seating the event organizers must address the challenges associated with both components. The Carrier Classic games created a great spectator facility, but the venue had significant problems in creating a safe playing surface. The failure of one aspect of the temporary facility often causes the entire event to fail. This makes attention to detail and having contingency plans essential to the construction of a temporary facility.

Temporary Venue Comparison

Temporary venues are often used to create a unique experience for participants and spectators. These unique experiences are often leveraged to create a demand for tickets and drive revenue for the event organizers. Temporary venues have been constructed to create unique outdoor events for both basketball and hockey with varying degrees of success. Moving sports traditionally played indoors to an outdoor venue creates some unique challenges. The ability of event organizers to address these challenges when constructing a temporary venue is crucial to the success of the event.

Note the multi-level temporary stadium constructed on the beach at this AVP Tour event in Hermosa Beach, CA.

© Photo Works/Shutterstock.com

Carrier Classic

One example of a temporary venue that was constructed to create a unique experience was the Carrier Classic. The Carrier Classic was a series of college basketball games played on the decks of U.S. Navy aircraft carriers. These events were staged on or around Veterans Day and were established in an effort to honor, support, and promote the military services.

The first Carrier Classic game was a great success. The game was played aboard the USS *Carl Vinson* in San Diego, California on November 11, 2011. The construction of a 7,000 seat, outdoor basketball arena on the flight deck of the carrier took nine days. The 150-person crew of civilians and service members began by constructing the temporary seating structures. Four structures, one on each side of the court, were constructed using portable metal framing and individual plastic seats. During the final two days of the construction, a portable, hardwood court was assembled on the flight deck. Crews used a large tarp to cover the floor to prevent moisture from accumulating on the court during the construction process (Whitman, 2011). Recognizing the importance of having a contingency plan, the crew also constructed a 2,500 seat arena in the ship's hanger bay. Fortunately, the weather was beautiful and the game was played on the flight deck as planned as North Carolina defeated Michigan State.

Later iterations of the Carrier Classic were not as successful. The 2012 Carrier Classic was supposed to feature a double header aboard the USS *Yorktown* in Charleston, South Carolina. The first game between the Ohio State and Notre Dame women's teams went off as planned; however, prior to the start of the second game between the Ohio State and Marquette men's teams, conditions changed. As temperatures began to fall during the evening, condensation began to build on the court due to the high humidity, and crews were unable to dry the court sufficiently. Game officials deemed the court unplayable and without a contingency site planned, the game was forced to be canceled.

(Photo was released by the United States Navy with the ID 11111-N-DR-144-999. As a work of the U.S. federal government, the image is in the public domain.)

The inaugural Carrier Classic was played aboard the USS Carl Vinson in San Diego, CA on November 11, 2011.

Similar problems with condensation caused a game aboard the USS *Bataan* in Jacksonville, Florida to be canceled and a game aboard the USS *Midway* in San Diego, California to be postponed by two days (Brennan, 2013).

Stadium Hockey

Another example of a unique sport experience created by the construction of a temporary venue is outdoor NHL hockey. Outdoor hockey in the NHL can trace its roots back to the 1950s when the Detroit Red Wings and Boston Bruins played outdoor exhibitions against non-NHL teams (Pelletier, 2010). The first outdoor game played between two NHL teams occurred in 1991 when the New York Rangers played a pre-season exhibition game against the Los Angeles Kings in 85° F heat at Caesars Palace in Las Vegas (Springer, 1991).

The first regular season iteration of outdoor hockey in the NHL came in 2003 when the Edmonton Oilers hosted the Montreal Canadiens in Commonwealth Stadium for the Heritage Classic. The game was an unprecedented success. Over 750,000 people applied for the chance to buy tickets and a then NHL record crowd of 57,167 braved temperatures below 0° F to watch the game (Allen, 2003). The success of the Heritage Classic led the NHL to create an annual outdoor game called the Winter Classic. Beginning in 2008, the Winter Classic has been played every year on New Year's Day (except when New Year's Day falls on a Sunday; then the game is moved to Monday to avoid conflicting with the NFL). In 2014, the Detroit Red Wings hosted the Toronto Maple Leafs at Michigan Stadium drawing an NHL record crowd of 105,491 (Rosen, 2014). The continued success of the Winter Classic led the NHL to add more outdoor games to its schedule. Dubbed the NHL Stadium Series, additional outdoor games have been played in various locations including warm-weather cites, Los Angeles and Santa Clara, CA.

Outdoor hockey is quite the logistical challenge as making an ice surface and keeping it playable in uncertain conditions is very difficult. The process begins by constructing a subfloor for the rink. The construction of the subfloor provides a sturdy and flat surface upon which the ice rink can be built. Once the subfloor is completed, the rink is constructed using aluminum ice tray panels. These panels have glycol pumped through them, which removes the heat from the panels and allows water to freeze on the surface of the aluminum. The NHL owns their own mobile refrigeration unit, which is used to continuously pump 3,000 gallons of glycol through the aluminum panels. After the aluminum surface is laid, the hockey boards are installed and the ice making process can begin.

The process of making NHL quality ice is very detailed. The process involves adding very thin layers of purified and primed water that freeze to create a very strong and dense surface. The first layer of water is called the bond and is $\frac{1}{32}$ of an inch thick. This layer is painted white with specialty ice paint. Another layer of water is then applied and frozen then the lines and logos are painted. Layers of water are then added by hand until the ice is ½ of an inch thick. Once the ice reaches ½ of an inch thick a Zamboni can be used to add the remaining layers. A Zamboni works by scraping a very thin layer of ice off of the surface, collecting the ice shavings, and then adding a layer of hot water that freezes to make a strong, clear surface. For an outdoor rink this is repeated until the ice reaches a thickness of two inches, twice as thick as an indoor rink. The additional thickness allows for weather related evaporation.

Several weather-related challenges must be addressed when playing hockey outdoors. The most obvious weather-related challenge is precipitation. Rain can create puddles on the ice surface or it can freeze in an uneven manner creating an unplayable surface. Variation in temperatures also creates a variety of challenges. Engineers must continually monitor the temperature of the ice and adjust the amount of glycol flowing through the aluminum panels. Extreme temperatures can also create challenges for the players. An NHL arena is typically kept between 60° and 64° Fahrenheit. Playing in sub-freezing conditions or in 80°F temperatures or higher puts a stress on the players that is atypical from a normal game. The sun also creates challenges. Strong sunshine can not only melt the ice, but it also can create glares on the ice surface that can become dangerous. Finally, wind is a very significant concern. Strong wind can cause the ice to evaporate in unpredictable patterns. This can create an uneven surface that makes it difficult to play hockey at a high level.

Conclusion

The value of an athletic or recreation facility is a function of the amount of time the facility can be used. Facilities are often used for several different types of events and the ability to efficiently changeover the facility from one event to another is crucial to maximizing its usage. Changeover management is a complex process that is unique to each facility; however, the application of several concepts to each unique situation can help facilitate efficient changeovers. Facility and event managers need to effectively communicate with everyone involved in the event, plan with the final product in mind, make efficient use of both time and human resources, and ensure that the staff has access to the appropriate equipment for the changeover.

When there is not an existing facility capable of meeting the needs of an event, the construction of a temporary venue can be a cost-effective alternative to constructing a new permanent facility. Constructing a temporary venue involves creating a temporary seating area, creating a temporary playing surface, or a combination of the two. When constructing a temporary venue, an attention to detail is vitally important to ensure that the seating area and playing surface are safe and that the venue creates a quality experience for spectators and participants.

CHAPTER DISCUSSION QUESTIONS

1. Using a high school gymnasium, a collegiate arena, and/or a professional arena in your state or region as references, create a list of facility and event stakeholders that need to be involved in the planning process for changeovers specific to the facility. Consider each type of event that is held in the facility and the needs specific to each event, and include your plans for both initial and follow-up communication.

2. Using the same facilities and associated events from above as a reference, create a staffing plan for the changeovers in the facility. Weigh the pros and cons of full-time, part-time, temporary, and volunteer staff members to be used within the changeover.

3. Create an idea for an event to be held in a temporary venue that creates a unique experience for participants and spectators. Identify the key elements of the temporary facility that will affect the success of the event. What can be done to ensure that these key elements are successful? Explore and describe other factors will contribute to the success of the event.

MINI CASE STUDY

Rob Smith is the facility manager for John Fields Arena (The Field) on the campus of Southeastern America University. The defending national champion, SEAU Sea Urchins men's basketball team is scheduled to play a nationally televised game at 9:00 pm on Saturday, February 1st. SEAU director of marketing, Brett Hayden, wants to use the big game to draw attention to some of the school's other sport programs. Brett wants to host a "Beauty and the Beast" combined women's gymnastics and wrestling event in The Field prior to the basketball game. Women's gymnastics and wresting normally compete in another facility across campus and the opportunity to compete in The Field is a big deal for each program.

The Field is a 17,000 seat arena with a permanent hardwood floor. Seating surrounding the basketball competition court can be retracted to create 120' × 120' of total floor space. The Field has a full court practice gym, but storage space is limited. Rob must create a plan for the set-up of the "Beauty and the Beast" event and the conversion to basketball.

1. Who should Rob invite to the initial planning meeting for the events?

2. What equipment will Rob need for the events and the transitions between events?

3. What scheduling issues will Rob need to address?

4. How should Rob manage human resources for the changeover?

5. What other issues might Rob encounter?

PRACTITIONER SPOTLIGHT

NAME: Angie Bitting

ORGANIZATION: University of North Carolina

CURRENT JOB TITLE: Director, Dean E. Smith Center
1999–Present

EDUCATIONAL PREPARATION: BA in Radio, Television, and
Motion Pictures, University of
North Carolina, 1986

MEMBERSHIP IN PROFESSIONAL ORGANIZATIONS:

- International Association of Venue Managers (IAVM)
- National Center for Spectator Sport Safety and Security (NCS4)

Photo courtesy of Angie Bitting.

CAREER PATH: I began right after graduation as an intern in the sports information department. After that I had part-time positions in the baseball office and the athletic director's office. I split my days between the two. Then I became the secretary for the director of the Smith Center, then the business manager for the Smith Center, then the assistant director of the Smith Center, and in 1999 I became the director of the Smith Center.

WHAT IS THE MOST REWARDING ASPECT IF YOUR JOB?

Seeing the event go off after all of the hard work and putting all of the pieces together and seeing the people at the event have a good time is very satisfying.

WHAT IS THE MOST CHALLENGING ASPECT OF YOUR JOB?

Coordinating and balancing all of the different aspects of an event. For every event, you deal with so many different entities, and each entity deserves to be treated as the most important part of the event. It is very important that everyone is able to accomplish their unique goals for the event, and balancing everyone in such a way that they are all a priority is challenging.

WHAT IS THE MOST IMPORTANT SKILL FOR FUTURE FACILITY AND EVENT MANAGERS TO DEVELOP?

To be flexible. You can't see things in black and white. There is way too much gray. There's no one right way to do things. You can't be too rigid. You have to be able to adjust and make things work on the fly. Also, listen to the people you work with and know the facility. It's important that you work together as a team to accomplish the same goal.

WHAT ARE SOME OF THE DIFFERENT TYPES OF EVENT THAT YOU HOST AT THE SMITH CENTER?

We have basketball games, commencements (10–12 per year), corporate events, and camps. We used to do a lot of concerts.

WHAT ARE SOME UNIQUE ASPECTS TO CONVERTING THE SMITH CENTER TO HOLD NON-SPORTING EVENTS?

First, we need to protect the floor. The Smith Center has a permanent floor and we have to protect it. We cover it with a vinyl floor cover for commencements, and for concerts we add a layer of plywood on top of the floor cover. For concerts, load-ins are a challenge because we only have one load-in tunnel and forklifts can't drive on the floor. This means we have to load-in one truck at a time and we have to side load the stage, which is very time consuming. Rigging in the Smith Center is very difficult. Any shows that are produced in the round have to be bridled off the superstructure. Concerts are fun, but they are also very challenging. The Smith Center wasn't really built for concerts; it was built for basketball and concerts were an afterthought.

Production rigging in the Smith Center for Late Night with Roy. Contributed by J. Patrick Marsh.

The Dean E. Smith Center at the University of North Carolina. Contributed by J. Patrick Marsh.

WHAT DO YOU DO TO MAKE CHANGE-OVERS MORE EFFICIENT?

It all depends on the event. It's easier to go from a concert to a basketball game than a basketball game to a concert. We don't have much storage so we get creative with the space we do have. We try to take what the next event needs and try to prepare that on the front end. Sometimes that means storing a stage for a concert with the TV truck for a basketball game or storing basketball goals with the production trucks for a concert so they are easily accessible when the changeover begins.

HOW DO YOU STAFF FOR A CHANGEOVER?

We have a 10–12 person maintenance crew that works all of our changeovers as well as day-to-day maintenance of the facility. We have a nine-person housekeeping crew that works all of our events, and they will stay to clean after each event as well. For quick changeovers we will add another housekeeping crew of 15–20 people.

WHAT WAS THE BIGGEST CHANGEOVER YOU HAVE DONE AT THE SMITH CENTER?

World Championship Wrestling (WCW) was a huge production and it was done in the round. It was also my first big event on my own at the Smith Center. Concerts for Reba McEntire and Celine Dion both were huge productions. Each one had 18–19 trucks of equipment.

WHAT IS A UNIQUE ASPECT OF YOUR JOB?

I've gotten to work with some great coaches and great people. I'm able to have a great relationship with our players. To be involved in the Carolina Basketball Family on a day-to-day basis is really special. To be able to work in the building named after Coach Smith is an honor, and I hope to do it justice. I try to run the building in the way he taught his players. Play Hard, Play Smart, and Play Together. We try to apply that to everything we do here. That is how we succeed.

WHAT ARE YOU PARTING WORDS OF WISDOM FOR ASPIRING FACILITY MANAGERS?

It's a job that takes up a lot of your time. It's hard work, but it's also very rewarding. Be willing to do anything and everything you can to make everything work, and give everybody that uses your facility the best experience possible.

Reprinted by permission of Angie Bitting.

MANAGEMENT IN ACTION

World Class Venue Built in a Week with Myrtha Pools

World-class swimming is an immensely popular spectator sport. Swimming in the Olympics, World Championships, and National Championships attracts millions of viewers on television and tens of thousands of in-person spectators. The

Logo courtesy of Myrtha Pools.

growth of swimming as a sport is dependent on spectator access to these large events; however, the infrequency of these major competitions makes building large, permanent spectator facilities for swimming financially impractical. The solution to this challenge is building temporary pools in existing facilities. Myrtha Pools has developed swimming pool construction technology that allows for the temporary construction of a world-class pool that can be disassembled after the competition and installed permanently in another location.

A&T Europe S.p.A. founded in 1961, with its Myrtha Pools brand, has become a world leader in swimming pool technology. Myrtha Pools designs and constructs around 1,500 pools each year and has been responsible for the competition pools at multiple Olympic Games, including the 2016 Rio Games, FINA World Championships, US Olympic Trials, and other major swimming competitions. Some of Myrtha Pools' most notable temporary construction projects have occurred in Omaha, Nebraska at the Century-Link Center. In 2008 and 2012, Myrtha Pools constructed temporary pools for the US Olympic Trials on the floor of the CenturyLink Center creating a 14,500 seat swimming arena. This allowed over 160,000 spectators to attend each event throughout the eight-day US Olympic Trails.

How it Happened

The ability to construct a temporary, world-class pool in a week is the product of innovative design and planning. A typical swimming pool is constructed using concrete and a tile or vinyl lining. The process of pouring concrete requires that the concrete have several weeks to cure in order to create a stable structure. This time factor, combined with the difficulty in moving formed concrete, makes installing a temporary

The CenturyLink Center in Omaha, Nebraska hosted the 2012 US Olympic Swimming Trials in a temporary pool constructed by Myrtha Pools.

concrete pool virtually impossible. Myrtha Pools has been able to create an innovative pool technology using stainless steel and PVC that allows for both a quick and precise installation of a swimming pool.

The installation of the temporary pool in the CenturyLink Center in 2012 began with the house staff from the arena configuring the seats with the first nine rows retracted to create the appropriate space for an Olympic pool and corresponding pool deck. A Myrtha Pools crew of around 40 people then started installation with a stainless steel base frame to form the outline of the pool. Stainless steel pool walls with a factory applied hard PVC coating permanently laminated to the surface, were then attached to the base frame in three feet wide panels and each wall joint was reinforced with steel buttresses. All of the joints in the pool were bolted together to allow for efficient installation and disassembly as well as to prevent corrosion that is common with traditional stainless steel welding.

With the basic structure of the pool in place, the next step was to waterproof the pool. Typically a Myrtha pool would be waterproofed using a special liquid PVC that penetrates and seals the joints between the wall panels; however, for this temporary installation, the pool was waterproofed using a temporary PVC membrane. This allowed the pool to be disassembled following the competition and moved to Boston where it would be permanently installed by a private swim club.

While the pool structure was being constructed, part of the crew was installing the piping, water treatment, and filtration system simultaneously. Once the pool and the filtration system were assembled, a pool deck was then constructed using scaffolding and plywood flooring. The plywood flooring was then waterproofed using a similar membrane to the one used to waterproof the pool. The construction and waterproofing of the deck and pool were designed and installed in such a way that there was no leakage onto any of the permanent arena surfaces. The entire process of constructing the pool, filtration system, and pool deck was completed in seven days. On the eighth day, the Omaha Fire Department filled the pool with water from several adjacent fire hydrants. Once the pool was filled with water, the filtration system was able to chemically balance and heat the pool in two days making the pool ready for competition ten days after the start of construction.

Myrtha Pools specializes in swimming pool design and construction and they pride themselves on their quality and innovation. After over 50 years and thousands of pools, Myrtha has nearly perfected the process of efficient pool installation and has done so with unmatched quality in their final product. Myrtha Pools' partnership with USA Swimming and the CenturyLink Center to create a world-class swimming facility is an example of the great things that can be created when experience and innovation meet a unique challenge. The construction of a temporary pool in a large arena allowed thousands of swim fans to experience the US Olympic Trials. The quality and efficiency with which the pool was constructed and the ability to permanently install the pool after the competition make this a model temporary construction project.

Reprinted by permission of Trevor Tiffany.

REFERENCES

Allen, K. (2003). Backyard memories revived for a night. *USA Today*. Retrieved from http://usatoday30.usatoday.com/sports/hockey/nhl/2003-11-19-outdoor-game_x.htm

Brennan, E. (2013). Aircraft carrier games appear to be kaput. Retrieved from http://espn.go.com/blog/collegebasketballnation/post/_/id/85314/aircraft-carrier-games-appear-to-be-kaput

National Basketball Association. (2015). Official rules of the National Basketball Association 2015–2016. Retrieved from https://turnernbahangtime.files.wordpress.com/2015/11/official-nba-rule-book-2015-16.pdf

National Collegiate Athletic Association. (2015). Men's basketball: 2015–16 and 2016–17 rules. Indianapolis, IN: NCAA.

National Collegiate Athletic Association. (2015). Wrestling: 2015–16 and 2016–17 rules and interpretations. Indianapolis, IN: NCAA.

National Federation of State High School Associations. (2015). 2015–16 NFHS wrestling rules book. Indianapolis, IN: NFHS.

National Football League. (2015). 2015 Official playing rules of the National Football League. Retrieved from http://uaasnfl.blob.core.windows.net/live/1807/2015_nfl_rule_book_final.pdf

National Hockey League. (2014). National Hockey League official rules 2014–2015. Newmarket, Ontario: Raster Graphics.

Pelletier, J. (2010). Red Wings played prison hockey team in 1954. Greatest Hockey Legends. Retrieved from http://www.greatesthockeylegends.com/2010/03/red-wings-played-prison-hockey-team-in.html

Polo Grounds. (2016). Ballparks of baseball: The fields of Major League Baseball. Retrieved from http://www.ballparksofbaseball.com/past/PoloGrounds.htm

Rosen, D. (2014). Big events, venues made up 2014 hockey. Retrieved from https://www.nhl.com/news/big-events-venues-made-up-2014-hockey/c-745693

Springer, S. (1991). Ice in desert? It's no mirage: Hockey: Kings, Rangers play in Caesars Palace parking lot tonight. *Los Angeles Times*. Retrieved from http://articles.latimes.com/1991-09-27/sports/sp-2929_1_parking-lot

Whitman, L. [U.S. Navy]. (2011, November 10). Edited time lapse of USS *Carl Vinson*'s flight deck [Video file]. Retrieved from https://www.youtube.com/watch?v=cGgK-9IbIJ4

9 Sport Facility Safety and Security

John J. Miller

OBJECTIVES

After studying this chapter, the student should be able to:

- Explain the differences between safety and security.
- Understand the liabilities that sport facility managers may face.
- Identify and explain facility security issues such as facility emergencies, terrorism, bomb threats, and fire threats.
- Distinguish between organized and spontaneous terrorism.
- Explain why sport facilities are targets for terrorism, bomb, or fire threats.
- Explain the differences between threat, vulnerability, and criticality assessments.
- Identify different evacuation methods that may be implemented.

KEY TERMS

Active Shooter

Automated External Defibrillator

Bomb Threat

Criticality Assessment

Department of Homeland Security

Emergency Action Plan

Evacuation Routes

Facility Emergency

National Fire Protection Association

Occupational Safety and Health Administration

Organized Terrorism

Safety

SAFETY Act

Security

Spontaneous Terrorism

Sudden Cardiac Arrest

Threat Assessment

Trespasser

Vulnerability Assessment

KEY ACRONYMS

AED	Automated External Defibrillator
DHS	Department of Homeland Security
EAP	Emergency Action Plan
NFPA	National Fire Protection Association
OSHA	Occupational Safety and Health Administration
SAFETY Act	Support Anti-Terrorism by Fostering Effective Technologies Act
SCA	Sudden Cardiac Arrest

Introduction

Safety environmental condition where a person feels comfortable enough to move through it without concern of harm.

Sport facility management and staff are accountable for ensuring that multi-million dollar sport facilities are safe and secure. Sport facility managers have been faced with many *safety* and security issues including crowd management, terrorist threats, medical emergencies, civil riots, weather emergencies, and similar incidents. Adding to these emergency situations is an escalating number of facilities that are designed as "multi-purpose" to host a various events, often simultaneously. While fire marshals, insurance inspectors, building inspectors, police and firefighters may intermittently assess building schematics or perform building inspections, public sport facility managers owe a duty of care to make certain that the areas are reasonably safe and to exercise reasonable care for those who use the building (Dobbs, 2000). As a result, protecting the lives and well-being of the facility employees, clients, patrons, and guests is the number one priority of any facility operation. Thus, it is a considerable responsibility to manage and operate such facilities in the demanding and complex environment of today.

Security the physical and psychological condition of an individual in which the feelings of being safe and free from danger, alarm, or suspicion exist.

Providing for the safety and *security* of participants in a sport facility is one of the most significant challenges that are faced by facility managers. The perception that "it will never happen to me or in my facility" must be guarded against. A facility manager who adopts this type of careless thinking, especially when coupled with poor planning and training, may incur disastrous results when an actual emergency situation occurs.

Safety and Security

A very close relationship exists between the concepts of security and safety. For example, safety and security address with failures that expose others to harm. Additionally, both analyze the circumstances that led to how failures happened. Also, safety and security place additional conditions to decrease the potential or mitigate the consequences of failures. Finally, while security failures can lead to safety concerns such as a bomb threat in a sport facility, safety failures can lead to security concerns such as an accidental electrical failure shutting down the facility's security cameras.

While these two terms are commonly used in many settings outside of facility and event management, it is important to understand that they are closely related but they are not interchangeable. Therefore, it is important to clarify the difference of the two terms. A person's safety has various meanings including freedom from harm, pain, suffering, or loss (O'Shea & Awwad-Rafferty, 2009; Reckelhoff-Dangel & Petersen, 2007; Slovic & Peters, 2006). Additionally, an individual's safety may relate to keeping them from harmful threats or risks (Burns, Mearns & McGeorge, 2006). The safety of a person may convey that the environment is such that the person feels comfortable enough to move through it without concern of harm (Teicholz, 2001). Conversely, an individual's security may be viewed differently from that same person's perception of safety (Slovic & Peters, 2006). Security may be defined as the physical and psychological condition of an individual in which the feelings of being safe and free from danger, alarm, or suspicion exist (O'Shea & Awwad-Rafferty, 2009). Being apprehensive in an environment may suggest that people perceive a lack of security because of the feeling of harm or wrongdoing that may befall them (Teicholz, 2001).

While safety addresses the design issues of a facility, facility security focuses on the measures taken to prevent and deal with danger, such as the prevention and detection of crimes such as theft, damage, or assault; the threat from terrorist attacks, bomb threats and active shooters; fire and medical emergencies. In the event of a serious emergency or disaster, security takes over from safety to clear up the mess, investigate what went wrong and perhaps even enforce accountability (Fosdick, 2009). Firesmith (2003) differentiated safety from security by stating that *safety* is the degree to which *accidental harm* is prevented, detected, and reacted upon, whereas *security* is the degree to which *malicious harm* is prevented, detected, and reacted upon. To put it succinctly, safety is mostly about protecting valuable assets, such as people from harm due to accidents. Security is about protecting those assets from harm from the attacks of others. Developing, implementing, and enforcing policies that provide safety and security in the event of an emergency situation is an essential responsibility of sport facility management and staff.

The Department of Homeland Security (2013, p. 8) identifies following items as responsibilities of a facility manager:

1. Institute access controls (i.e., keys, security system pass codes)

2. Distribute critical items to appropriate managers/employees, including floor plans, keys as well as facility personnel lists and telephone numbers

3. Coordinate with the facility's security department to ensure the physical security of the location

4. Ensure that EAPs, evacuation instructions and any other relevant information address to individuals with special needs and/or disabilities

5. Assemble crisis kits containing: radios, floor plans, staff roster, staff emergency contact numbers, first aid kits, and flashlights

6. Place removable floor plans near entrances and exits for emergency responders

7. Activate the emergency notification system when an emergency situation occurs

An example of spectator screening with bag checks and metal detectors at a FIBA Beach Volleyball Tournament in London.

© Mitch Gunn/Shutterstock.com

Emergency Situation Definition

What is an emergency situation? An emergency situation is any incident, situation, or occurrence that could affect the safety/security of occupants, cause damage to the facility, equipment, and its contents, or disrupt activities of the facility. Emergency situations, ranging from a participant suffering a broken bone to a total evacuation of the facility, can occur without any warning. Regardless of the level of severity, all emergency situations must have a managed response process (Schafer, Carroll, Haynes, & Abrams, 2004). Such a process is referred to as an *emergency action plan (EAP)*.

Emergency Action Plan (EAP) an integrated plan that defines and documents the steps and actions to be taken by the facility staff and public safety agencies.

Emergency Action Plan

Emergency planning often starts with identifying disasters that have recently occurred (Waugh, 2004). Every facility and community is unique and, therefore, each emergency action plan (EAP) must be customized to meet the unique needs of the facility. It is necessary that each facility develop its own EAP taking into consideration the distinctive elements of facility design, facility environment and activities, staff resources, public safety agencies, applicable governmental regulations, operational policies and procedures, political environment and community expectations.

An EAP is an integrated plan that defines and documents the steps and actions to be taken by the facility staff and public safety agencies. An EAP should be designed to consider the extent of an emergency so as to minimize or eliminate the potential harm to occupants of the facility and/or damage to the facility. To do so, an EAP should organize and identify all employee actions during an emergency. Thus, a comprehensive EAP reduces the exposure of harm and results of emergency situations through prevention, early detection, communication, evacuation/relocation (if necessary) and damage control and recovery activities.

Rationale for the Development of an Emergency Action Plan

Well-conceived EAPs, coupled with appropriate employee training will often result in decreased injuries and less structural damage to the facility. Conversely, an ill-prepared plan may lead to disorganized responses, which could lead to confusion, injury, or damage to the property. The development, implementation, and enforcement of an emergency plan will help ensure that the best care will be provided. The following items are some very good reasons why the development and implementation of an emergency plan are important for effective facility management:

1. Good planning, proper staff training and timely execution of an established emergency plan can significantly decrease possible damage and loss caused by an emergency.

2. To meet the professional standards and expectations of providing a safe, non-threatening environment for the facility occupants and to protect the community assets.

3. The development and enforcement of emergency planning process will diminish the legal liability that the facility, staff, and ownership might have when an emergency situation occurs.

4. Potential negative media exposure will be minimized.

5. Increases the likelihood that positive communications will occur among all parties relevant public safety agencies (e.g., fire, police, etc.) linked to the emergency action plan.

Emergency Action Plan as a Federal Requirement

Another significant reason to develop and enforce an EAP is to meet legal public safety requirements (e.g., fire safety, ADA, etc.) outlined by a federal agency such as the *Occupational Safety and Health Administration (OSHA)*. According the Occupational Safety and Health Administration (OSHA) standard 29 CFR 1910.38(a) and standard 29 CFR 1910.38(b) an employer must have a written emergency action plan that is kept in the workplace and is available for all employees to review. Further, OSHA standards 29 CFR 1910.38(c)(2) through 29 CFR 1910.38(c)(6) mandate that an emergency plan should include procedures for: 1) reporting a fire or other emergency, 2) emergency evacuation, including type of evacuation and exit route assignments, 3) employees who remain to operate critical facility operations before they evacuate, 4) accounting for all employees after evacuation, 5) employees performing rescue or medical duties (OSHA, 2013). Additionally, it is recommended that proper coverage of events, maintenance of appropriate emergency equipment and supplies, and utilization of appropriate emergency medical personnel are included as part of the EAP. Thus, not only is it good business, it is federally mandated that a public sports facility possess an emergency action plan.

Occupational Safety and Health Administration (OSHA) an agency of the U.S. Department of Labor that ensure safe and healthful working conditions for men and women by establishing and administering standards through training, outreach, and education assistance.

Components of an Emergency Action Plan (EAP)

An EAP should include input from several different populations such as including your human resources department, facility staff and administration, and local law enforcement and/or emergency responders. An effective EAP includes:

1. A preferred method for reporting fires and other emergencies

2. An evacuation policy and procedure

3. Emergency escape procedures and route assignments (i.e., floor plans, safe areas)

4. Contact information for, and responsibilities of individuals to be contacted under the EAP

5. Information concerning local area hospitals (i.e., name, telephone number, and distance from your location)

6. An emergency notification system to alert various parties of an emergency including local law enforcement and local area hospitals

Combined, the EAP and training exercises will prepare the facility staff to effectively respond and help minimize loss of life or damage to the facility.

Establishing an Emergency Action Plan

Emergencies may be categorized as natural or induced by human agency. Human-induced examples include bomb threats, terrorist attacks, chemical leaks, mechanical/equipment/structure failure, fires, disturbance/riots/other criminal acts; hazardous material release, building evacuation, air conditioning contamination, food poisoning; or suspicious mail/packages. Natural emergencies include events such as hurricanes, tornados, earthquakes, tsunamis, blizzards, ice storms, or flooding (Schafer et al., 2004). While the list of emergencies is long, some of the major areas that an emergency action planning (EAP) committee may consider are facility preparedness, staff training, emergency medical staffing, terrorism (bomb threats and active shooters), fire, and severe weather issues.

An EAP is a vital operating policy for the facility. However, if relevant stakeholder (facility owners, city or federal government officials, fire, police, etc.) support is not garnered, the significance of the EAP becomes greatly minimized to become just another document that gathers dust on a shelf. Their support ensures there is a strong coordinated plan with ownership, the local emergency officials and politicians.

To initiate the EAP process, the support and involvement from upper level facility management is essential. Since upper level facility management personnel are responsible for managing the facilities, they often must communicate with facility ownership (city, county, or private ownership) to create the operating policies and institute the long-range plan to provide overall direction of the facility. The last issue that any upper level facility manager or owner wants to deal with is an emergency situation that has an ambiguous plan.

In addition to including upper level facility management, committee members should be comprised of other facility managers and staff who are well informed regarding the different facility systems, possess the authority and experience to make appropriate emergency decisions, and can implement the plan. The importance of community and stakeholder interactions should not be undervalued when planning for safety and security of a facility. The emergency planning committee should be kept to a manageable size (three to five individuals) to maximize productivity. Preferably, the committee should represent a range of expertise in safety and security management, building design, recreation planning, business/financial management, and facility management. It may not be a requirement for the committee to have knowledge in all of these areas; the specific expertise needed will be determined by the complexity of the proposal. However, it would be beneficial if the committee members had a basic understanding of the various aspects of safety and security planning for a facility. By being involved in the emergency action planning process, the members of the committee will acquire considerable knowledge, understanding, and appreciation of the safety and security needs of the facility.

Broad community participation on a safety and security committee may also identify opportunities to share resources, extend an existing service enter into a partnership or collocate complementary services. Examples of these services may include interactions with the local police, emergency medical technicians, or fire fighters. By creating and developing meaningful relationships with these services, maximum safety and security effectiveness and efficiency may be best attained.

Risk Assessments

At this point in the process, the planning committee should evaluate and assess the probability of the various emergency situations occurring. A risk assessment should identify all threats and hazards to a facility and then place them in a matrix that categorizes risks from high occurrence and high consequences (tornados in the Midwest) to low occurrence and low consequences (single water pipe leak in out building). Other categories are high occurrence and low consequence (Internet probes to facility websites) and low occurrence and high consequence (workplace shooter or terrorist act).

Table 9.1 *Risk Assessment Matrix*

Occurrence	Consequences
1 = Remote	1 = Minimal
2 = Probable	2 = Medium
3 = Highly Probable	3 = Major

Severity		Likelihood	
3	Moderate Risk	Substantial Risk	Critical Risk
2	Tolerable Risk	Moderate Risk	Substantial Risk
1	Minimal Risk	Tolerable Risk	Moderate Risk
	1	2	3

Potential risks are the result of the convergence of three variables: threat, vulnerability, and consequence (Chertoff, 2007). Both threat and vulnerability are influenced by the probabilities of events that are highly uncertain (Chertoff, 2007). As such, sport *facility emergency* planning committees should consider the possible threats, vulnerabilities, criticalities, and consequences of an incident. Each of these components will be briefly discussed in the following sections.

Threat Assessment

The first step in assessing security risks is to conduct a ***threat assessment***. A threat assessment may be used as a decision support tool to assist in creating and prioritizing security-program requirements, planning, and resource allocations (Decker, 2001). When an organization embarks on a risk assessment effort, the team conducting the assessment is searching for potential sources of concern (Frame, 2003). It deals with such issues as how operations might be negatively affected or what weaknesses can be identified. A variety of factors may be used to assess the threat: Is the threat sincere? Can the threat be verified? Is the threat specific and/or impending? How severe is the threat? Such questions characterize the threat conditions of a terrorist incident and provide the appropriate protective measures needed to reduce vulnerabilities.

Vulnerability Assessment

Vulnerability assessment refers to the level to which a target is likely to be attacked and the ability that a target can present to fend off an attack (Decker, 2001). A vulnerability analysis estimates the probability of each type of emergency, potential impact of each emergency and potential resulting problem(s) that will need to be addressed by the emergency plan. The assessment should estimate the potential impact each emergency could have on the operations of the facility.

Thus, a vulnerability assessment assists in the identification of weaknesses that may be exploited and suggest options to eliminate or address those weaknesses (Decker, 2001). For example, a vulnerability assessment might reveal weaknesses in an organization's security systems, training security personnel, a facilities of ingress and egress, or the distance from parking lots to important buildings as being so close that a car bomb detonation would damage or destroy the buildings and the people working in them (Decker, 2001). Additional areas of concern in identifying event vulnerabilities include facility access, food vendor access, areas for concealed threats, security protocol, and access to team locker rooms, as well as lighting and entrance inspections. By properly using a vulnerability analysis, the emergency planning team can determine where the most significant emergency exposures might occur. Once potential vulnerabilities are identified, it is wise for the sport facility manager to prioritize the important aspects of the organization. To do so, a criticality assessment should be conducted.

Facility Emergency an emergency situation is any incident, situation, or occurrence that could affect the safety/security of occupants, cause damage to the facility, equipment and its contents, or disrupt activities of the facility.

Threat Assessment a decision support tool to assist in creating and prioritizing security-program requirements, planning, and resource allocations.

Vulnerability Assessment an evaluation of those areas that are susceptible to a strike through a malevolent attack.

Criticality Assessment

A *criticality assessment* is a practice that recognizes and calculates important assets, infrastructure, and critical functions based on a variety of factors. These factors include the importance of its mission or function of the event, location of the facility in regards to important governmental and financial centers, the number of people that may be at risk, the presence of dignitaries within the people present, or the significance of a structure or system. An example as to why both the number of people and the presence of including dignitaries impacts a criticality assessment would be the 2015 terrorist attacks in Paris where the President of France was in the stadium at the time of suicide bombing outside that location (CNN Library, 2016). Assessing the criticality of a target can help in determining target attractiveness as well as determining which potential areas will receive attention first (Decker, 2001). Thus, criticality assessments are important because they help identify which assets, structures, or functions are relatively more important to protect from an attack. Once a potential target has been identified, the next step for a risk event manager would be to identify and minimize the liabilities of that target through a vulnerability assessment.

Criticality Assessment recognizes and calculates important assets, infrastructure, and critical functions based on a variety of factors.

Assessments should be performed on a regular basis. Information from these assessments provides effective gauges as to how successfully security practices are achieved and maintained within the assessed areas. The outcomes of these assessments should be presented to relevant decision-makers for use as a way to develop additional guidance. An examination of these assessments will allow the relevant decision-makers an appropriate balance of resources to strengthen security.

Emergency Action Plan Procedures

After the potential risks have been assessed, the emergency planning committee should define specific action steps/procedures to be taken in a given emergency. The emergency planning committee should begin with the emergencies that have been assessed as posing the most critical threat to the facility. While every emergency situation is different, the emergency planning committee may find that many of the defined actions and procedures have common ground in many emergency situations. As a result, when an EAP is initially developed various kinds of emergency situations and related issues that apply to the facility should be identified.

© Christopher Boswell/Shutterstock.com

An example of a security camera placement outside a college football stadium facility.

Facility Preparedness

It is the responsibility of the facility director to prepare the facility and facility personnel for potential emergencies. The facility manager needs to identify the location of the emergency power to lighting, closed circuit televisions (CCTV), metal detectors, and public address systems as well as the emergency power to the parking lot lighting. Proper maintenance of all emergency generators and battery-powered areas is essential to emergency preparedness. Additionally, the facility manager should communicate a complete evacuation or shelter in place plan outlining duties and responsibilities to each event staff position.

Staff Training

Miller and Veltri (2001) stated that people and procedures are the two primary security and safety components that need to be addressed in a facility. Yet, previous research has indicated that sport facility and event personnel seldom possess sufficient training (Baker, Connaughton, Zhang, & Spengler, 2007; Goss, Jubenville, & MacBeth, 2003; Miller, Veltri & Gillentine, 2008). Given the "transient" nature of many facility and event staff employees, it is often very difficult to spend a lot of time and resources on training an employee(s) who may only work for a short amount of time. Yet, the most important aspect in securing a facility is the training of personnel.

In fact, many organizations are focusing more and more on the preparedness through appropriate employee training as the principal method for reducing both the frequency and severity of losses over the long term (Cawood, 2002). For this reason, significant training of the event supervisory and lead staff is critical. Training and instruction should be given to other event staff members through pre-event briefings and issuing handheld cards containing information on evacuation procedures. In many instances full-time staff members will provide training and instruction to the part-time or temporary event staff. Specific instructions often will vary for different functions/positions and locations within the facility, as well as for different types of emergencies.

Automated External Defibrillators (AED)

Regular physical activity has been extolled as an important component in living a healthy lifestyle. However, Becker-Eisenberg, Fahrenbruch, and Cobb (1998) warned that health clubs were among the top ten most likely public places with the highest incidence of cardiac arrests.

Sudden Cardiac Arrest condition in which the heart suddenly and unexpectedly stops beating resulting in a stoppage of blood flow to the brain and other vital organs.

Additionally, sporting events in large arenas create challenges regarding the cardiovascular safety of both athletes and spectators. *Sudden cardiac arrest* (SCA) is the leading cause of sudden death in athletes during sport (Maron, Doerer, Haas, Tierney, & Mueller 2009); Harmon, Asif, Klossner, & Drezner, 2011). Viewing sports may increase the risk of an acute cardiac event as well (Katz, Metzger, Marazzi, & Kappenberger, 2006; Wilbert-Lampen, Leistner, & Greven, 2008). Available studies suggest the incidence of SCA is 1–2 per 500,000–600 000 spectators in major European soccer arenas (Borjesson et al., 2011; Leusveld, Kleijn, & Umans, 2008).

While the assistance to the participants may be readily available, barriers exist to provide a sufficiently rapid response in cases of an acute cardiac event in spectators. The number of *automated external defibrillators* needed for a major sporting facility can be calculated to ensure the ability to deliver a shock to a potential victim of SCA anywhere inside the stadium within three to five minutes (Crocco et al., 2004; Motyka, Winslow, Newton, & Brice, 2005). Likewise, the emergency personnel at stadiums should be trained, positioned, and numbered to ensure a rapid response to maximize safety for both athletes and spectators (Crocco et al., 2004). A study by Luiz, Kumpch, and Metzger (2005) revealed that basic life support was provided by employees within two minutes with AED defibrillation and advanced life support within 4 minutes of a sport spectator incurring a SCA. The results revealed that 62% survived without neurological deficits. However, a 2010 study of 190 European major sporting facilities revealed that 36% had no written emergency action plan, 28% possessed no AED and 35% had personnel with no basic CPR training (Borjesson et al., 2010).

Automated External Defibrillators a device that automatically analyzes the heart rhythm and may respond to an electrical shock delivers a shock to restore a normal heart rhythm.

To effectively manage the risks of a SCA or other significant medical emergency occurring, it is recommended that different risk management emergency plans be developed and enacted for athletes and spectators. For example, the facility manager should discuss and collaborate with the team physician to define the different emergency preparations for athletes and spectators. Although team physicians may not be responsible for treating spectator emergencies, they may assist in the development of a risk management emergency action to promote the cardiovascular or other significant injury safety of both athletes and spectators. The facility manager can then implement the emergency action plan by communicating and training the facility support staff.

An example of an AED device with the wrapped electrode pads including instructions.

Emergency Medical Staffing

The appropriate amount and type of emergency medical (EM) staff at events is vital in order to properly respond to situations that might require immediate attention. If EM staff is not in close proximity to the facility, it might be necessary to have them on the premises for these types of events. As such the following items should be followed:

1. Have constant communication with the EM staff in order to assure immediate response.
2. Position the EM staff during events in a predetermined location(s) with the necessary supplies and equipment to best meet the needs of the facility, patrons, and the event.

3. Ensure that in an evacuation some EM staff and supplies are positioned inside as well as outside the facility. In some cases, patrons may be overcome by fumes while trying to evacuate the building. Under such circumstances a trained EM staff member located at facility exit route with appropriate supplies will be able to assist the patrons.

4. Practice the EM response by including all staff and administration

5. During the practice sessions, ensure that the stretcher can bear the weight of a person as well as be able to get to difficult to reach areas, such as steep seating areas.

Fire

At the turn of the 21st century began advances in the design and construction of large and expansive buildings. As a result, governments, industry (insurance) groups, and professional associations began to develop fire and safety codes to protect both life and property. Specifically, the *National Fire Protection Association (NFPA)*, a private enterprise, began writing fire and life safety codes back in 1913.

Table 9.2 *The Ten Most Deadly Property Fires in the United States Since 1900*

Date	Place	Citizens Killed
September 11, 2001	The World Trade Center, New York, NY	2,666
December 30, 1903	Iroquois Theater, Chicago, IL	602
November 28, 1942	Cocoanut Grove night club, Boston MA	492
April 23, 1940	Rhythm Club Natchez, Mississippi	207
January 12, 1908	Rhodes Opera House, Boyertown, PA	170
July 6, 1944	Ringling Brothers Barnum and Bailey Circus, Hartford, CT	168
May 28, 1977	Beverly Hills Supper Club, Southgate, KY	165
February 20, 2003	The Station Nightclub, West Warwick, RI	100
March 25, 1990	Happy Land Social Club, New York, NY	87
December 4, 1980	Stouffer's Inn Hotel Conference Center Venue, Harrison, NY	26

Adapted from Hall (2004)

From 2000 to 2004, public assembly properties, which include sport facilities, averaged 4,900 structure fires annually (Flynn, 2007). These fires caused an average of 1 civilian death, 52 civilian injuries per year and $94.3 million in direct property damage (Flynn, 2007). In 2003, the Station Nightclub fire killed 100 people in the deadliest US fire since the 1990 Happy Land Social Club fire. The potential for a major incident always exists by virtue of the occupancy, but there is also a steady incidence of fires that kill one or two people. The 2003 Station Nightclub fire in West Warwick, RI was a reminder of the enormous potential for loss of life in assembly properties.

© Ververidis Vasilis/Shutterstock.com

Note the fires as part of the aftermath of a clash between POAK fans and riot police during the 2016 semifinal Greek Cup game between PAOK and Olympiacos played at Toumba Stadium.

Some of the considerations to provide safety and security in the facility would be to:

1. Have periodic inspections of the facility by the local fire inspector for fire-prone and hazardous areas.
2. Ensure that the facility has a centralized fire command center or electronic fire box; a familiarization with the fire box in advance so that in case of an emergency; all of the pull stations, various warnings, or emergency announcements are properly initiated.
3. Contact the fire department immediately in the event of a fire even if the fire appears to be under control.

Severe Weather

Weather certainly poses a significant hazard for sports events particularly concerning lightning and tornadoes as potential risks. A sudden change in weather at an open venue or a partial structural collapse might cause occupants to want to escape an area. Additionally, severe weather such as lightning, torrential rain, or tornadoes must be considered as safety and security risks for individuals participating or being spectators at sports events. If the manager of an arena had 10,000 patrons inside at the same time a tornado watch was issued in the community, what emergency operating plan exists to deal with it? What about spectators and participants playing on outside fields? Organized outdoor events, including sporting events at all times of year, should have weather safety plans. People at large sporting events are especially vulnerable because of the difficulties involved in moving large numbers of people. Event coordinators or managers should have a detailed severe weather safety plan in place and practice it.

Lightning over the Ostseestadion or Baltic Sea Stadium home of the FC Hansa Rostock in Rostock, Germany.

On an annual basis, a number of individuals are killed or seriously injured by tornadoes. According to the National Weather Service (2015) from 2005–2014 the average number of fatalities cause by tornadoes was 110 per year in the United States. While tornadoes may be considered the worst fear, lightning is a widespread and serious threat in its own right. Lightning is one of the most common and dangerous weather conditions that impacts outdoor events. According to the National Weather Service from 1979–2008, lightning caused an average of 55–60 fatalities and 400 injuries each year. Most casualties result from inappropriate behavior during thunderstorms, particularly when people are caught outdoors during recreation events or organized sports. It is important to remember that lightning can strike up to 10 miles from a storm as well as from blue sky and in the absence of rain. For example, 10% of lightning happens when there is no rainfall and when blue sky is visible, particularly when summer thunderstorms occur (Sales, 2014). Being aware of, and following, proven severe weather safety guidelines can greatly reduce the risk of injury or death.

To guard against potential injury or death, a sport facility or event manager may consider the following items:

1. Establish a chain of authority that recognizes who can remove spectators, teams, game personnel or other individuals from the field or a given activity.

2. Institute a way to monitor local weather forecasts and/or severe weather warnings.

3. Maintain a list of safe areas for people to find shelter from the dangerous weather.

4. Communicate specific criteria for cancellation, suspension, and resumption of activities. For example, the NCAA policy mandates "waiting 30 minutes after both the last sound of thunder and after the last flash of lightning is at least six miles away, and moving away from the venue. If lightning is seen without hearing thunder, lightning may be out of range and therefore less likely to be a significant threat" (Sales, 2014, para. 16).

5. Employ the recommended safety strategies for severe weather such as lightning, a tornado, or torrential rain.

Terrorism

The world was changed forever on September 11, 2001 because of the terrorist attacks on the United States homeland. Since 2001, terrorism has become a global issue. It is important to note that although the concept of terrorism conjures up certain images, such as the 2001 World Trade Centers, for this chapter terrorism will be used as a way to depict any extremely violent occurrences at sports events. Thus, the words terrorism and violence will be used interchangeably throughout this chapter. Additionally, individuals described as terrorists, in this chapter, are those who unlawfully "use of violence against persons or property to intimidate or coerce a…civilian population, or any segment thereof, in furtherance of…political or social objectives" (FBI, 2006, p. 3).

The possibility of a terrorist attack at sport venues came into detailed focus November of 2015 when a male terrorist with an explosive laden vest tried to gain admittance to the Stade de France in Paris, France. Reports also indicated that terrorists planned to detonate three bombs inside the stadium during a friendly international soccer match several weeks after the Paris attacks. Terrorist attacks have also taken place in the United States. During the 1996 Atlanta Olympics, two people died and more than 100 were injured after a pipe bomb was detonated in Centennial Park, a public downtown area that was not part of the Olympic Village. In 2013, two crude but effective bombs exploded at the finish line of the Boston Marathon killing three and injuring more than 260.

As a result, the facility industry, with its facilities designed for large assembly of people, is a prime target for acts of terrorism. Because they are so strongly associated with the American economy and culture, sports events and facilities have been considered significant targets of violent attacks (Appelbaum, Adeland, & Harris, 2005; Atkinson & Young, 2002). Therefore, it is critical that every facility be properly prepared to deal with this type of high risk.

According to Crenshaw (2000): "Terrorism is meant to hurt, not to destroy" (p. 406). Before the terrorist attacks on September 11, 2001, facility managers generally dealt with inebriated fans, medical emergencies, or thefts. While these issues still occur, the terrorist attacks of September 11, 2001, the rioting by fans after the Stanley Cup Finals, the random active shooters that took the lives of a number of innocents at public and private places, and bomb threats at baseball stadiums illustrate an era of increasingly diverse and significant violence in society. Images of these destructive actions have set into motion a chain reaction that is significantly impacting the sports world.

Generally, it can be said that risk tends to degrade an organization's (or an activity's) value if left unattended (Rescher, 1983). In essence, the value of the event would stem from an interconnected range of "experience elements," such as ambience, event competitiveness, and a various other issues such as weather conditions (Miller, Wendt, & Young, 2010). However, security measures may be perceived as being so heavy that they offset reduced ticket prices, attractive concessions, and the general excitement of attending an athletic contest. As a result, public assembly managers must reassess their safety procedures and risk management assessments plans in order to identify new ways to provide a safer environment for fans and participants.

During a panel discussion, Paul Zoubek, Counsel for the New Jersey Domestic Preparedness Task Force, stated that "Sports are a very symbolic target of terrorism because they are so associated with the globalization of the American economy and the American culture" (Fallon, [quoting Zoubek], 2003, p. 367). As a result, sport facility managers began reassessing their safety procedures, security assessments, and operational plans to identify new ways to provide a safe environment for fans and participants (Fallon, 2003).

Organized Terrorism

Organized Terrorism acts of violence that requires a significant amount of planning, organization, and rehearsal.

Department of Homeland Security (DHS) The United States Department of Homeland Security (DHS) is a cabinet department of the U.S. government with responsibilities for public security.

Terrorism is allied to collective civil violence in the form of organized or spontaneous activities (Borum, 2007). Organized terrorist activities often have a discrete set of objectives when selecting potential targets they believe will further their cause such as media exposure, economic harm, and significant number of potential casualties (Suder, 2004). Such *organized terrorism* requires a significant amount of planning, organization, and rehearsal, such as the incidents at the World Trade Center as well as the Oklahoma City bombing (Cohen, 2001). For example, if the facility manager had received a bomb threat indicating when and where an attack would occur, it would be recognized as organized terrorism.

Sports facilities should be particularly concerned with organized violence for two primary reasons. First, authorities have begun considering athletic facilities among the new types of potential targets. The Federal Bureau of Investigation (FBI) recognized this possibility when it provided sport facility managers a warning after it learned that individuals with possible terrorist connections had downloaded data pertaining to several National Football League facilities (Grace, 2002). In fact, then FBI Director Robert Mueller acknowledged that agents had been directed to look at any potential locations that a terrorist might strike, one of which could be a sports facility (Grace, 2002). Additionally, the *Department of Homeland Security (DHS)* identified a dozen possible strikes it viewed most devastating, including a truck bombing of a sports arena (Lipton, 2005).

Second, sport facilities are attractive targets because, "…with tens of thousands of people in attendance, an attack on a stadium could cause massive casualties with maximum media exposure" (Wade, 2000, p. 18). As such, these facilities are problematic to make safe and secure since large numbers of spectators are constantly entering and leaving the premises. Sports facilities may be categorized as "soft targets" prone to a violent attack. Soft targets are targets that are not well protected so terrorists can gain access to them relatively easily (Clonan, 2002).

Lee, Gordon, Moore, and Richardson (2008) conducted a case study to ascertain the possible economic losses as the result of an organized terrorist event on a sports stadium. They created a hypothetical situation in which a National Football League stadium, seating 75,000 people, was the subject of a bioterrorism attack. Several computer-based simulations were used to determine economic impact of the attacks. The major areas of economic impact were casualties, illnesses, contamination, and business interruption. Casualties were assumed to be 7,000 among stadium attendees and an additional 3,600 from people within the community. A value of a statistical life computation was used to measure economic impact of lost lives. The researchers estimated that 20,000 attendees and an additional 11,000 people from the community would suffer severe illnesses that would require a hospitalization of seven days as well as follow-up medical appointments with the quarantine of the stadium and surrounding area for a month. It was estimated that 50% of the buildings would be uninhabitable for six months and the entire decontamination process would last approximately a year. Lastly, the business effects were thoroughly examined as the incident would probably result in higher risk aversion by the public resulting in less demand for various goods.

The Lee study indicated that if a stadium were to be attacked, attendance would drop at least 8% simply due to the cancelling of games for the month of quarantine. Depending on the extremity of reaction by the public, attendance levels are estimated to drop anywhere from 15% to 40%. Business would also be affected in the form of lost jobs in the immediate area. Using the attacks of September 11 as a model, researchers estimated that 3,793 jobs would be lost for the first year. Ultimately, economic impacts could be estimated to range anywhere from $62 billion to $73 billion. While the results of an attack on a sports facility would not carry quite the economic impact, it would still undoubtedly have a sizeable effect on the economy.

Spontaneous Terrorism sporadic acts of violence that does not possess political goals or organized plans.

Spontaneous Terrorism

Spontaneous terrorism is usually sporadic and does not possess political goals or organized plans (Crenshaw, 2000; Merari, 1978). For example, fans throwing beer bottles at the end of a professional football game when an overturned call occurred in the final minutes or fans burning items due to a team loss in a championship may be regarded as a spontaneous terror attack (Goss, Jubenville, & MacBeth, 2003; Withers, 2002). Moreover, such recent incidents as fans attacking other fans at sports events in San Francisco and Los Angeles may be considered spontaneous terrorist incidents (Associated Press, 2011) and add to the challenges of providing a reasonably safe

© Iurii Osadchi/Shutterstock.com

Fan demonstrating post-match of a soccer event in Kharkov, Ukraine in 2011 as an example of fans engaging in the use of flares or pyrotechnic devices within a sport venue.

environment at sports contests. Such added exposure to harm shifts the paradigm for sport event organizers from safety to security by asking the question: how can identifiable risks be managed at sporting events in today's society?

Support Anti-Terrorism by Fostering Effective Technologies (SAFETY) Act

SAFETY Act part of the Homeland Security Act of 2002 which provides incentives for the development and deployment of anti-terrorism technologies by creating a system of risk management and a system of litigation management

A potential answer regarding how risks may be managed may be the use of the Support Anti-Terrorism by Fostering Effective Technologies (SAFETY) Act. As part of the Homeland Security Act of 2002, Public Law 107-296, Congress enacted the *SAFETY Act*. The SAFETY Act provides incentives for the development and deployment of anti-terrorism technologies by creating a system of "risk management" and a system of "litigation management" (Department of Homeland Security, 2015). While not a regulatory program, the SAFETY Act encourages the development and enforcement of effective anti-terrorism technologies by offering particular liability protections. To clarify, a regulatory program is any authority that develops, implement or enforce regulatory requirements or provides relevant services that apply to emergency prevention, response, or recovery. These authorities usually have local, state, or federal jurisdiction. Familiar examples of such authorities include the local fire department and police or other safety agencies relative to facility operations. It is important that an extensive review be conducted by these authorities to identify the applicable regulatory and safety requirements and regulations that pertain to the facility operation. Although more than 600 technologies have been approved under the SAFETY Act, very few sports facilities have applied for and received the protections provided by the SAFETY Act (Department of Homeland Security, 2015).

Security Training Issues

While terrorism has not been common in sport facilities or events, the tragic incidents at the 2013 Boston Marathon should alert sport facility and event manager of the potential of such an occurrence. Specifically, sport facility and event managers must be concerned about the level of training of security being provided. Experts often refer to security at sports contests as "security theater" that reveals security personnel in uniforms often conducting bag searches (Schrotenboer, 2013). Perhaps such show of security prevented a University of Oklahoma student from blowing himself up in the stadium. However, such "theater" does little to protect fans from what occurred in Boston.

Security company officials and experts say security guards might present the most significant problem in the security of US sporting events (Schrotenboer, 2013). When intelligence is unsuccessful in stopping a terrorist plot before a bomber reaches the gate, the guards are often the next and possibly last line of defense. However, two students documented their ability to sneak into the

2013 Super Bowl. The video revealed that no one checked their credentials (or lack thereof) (Schrotenboer, 2013). In fact, a guard was shown to allow them in without asking any questions.

Two potential reasons have been put forth regarding for lack of security guard training at sports events (Schrotenboer, 2013). First, organizations that employ security guards generally offer sporadic employment that does not pay well. As a result, security guards usually don't stay on the job for more than a year or two. Secondly, many states require minimal, if any, training (Schrotenboer, 2013). Seven states do not mandate any security guard licensing at all. Among those that do, several, including Massachusetts, don't require training. Twenty-three states don't even require applicants to complete any training. Finally, some companies place employees classified as "event staff" in security roles at stadiums to avoid training requirements and increase profits (Schrotenboer, 2013). It should be noted that terrorism manifests itself primarily in two most common forms: active shooters and bomb threats.

State Police Officers in Pennsylvania during a training exercise for crowd control at an arena in Harrisburg.

Active Shooter

The apparent emergence of anti-social behavior has added the potential to an increased exposure of harm to others attending sporting events (Miller & Gillentine, 2006). According to an FBI report, 160 active shooter incidents may have happened between 2000 and 2013. The FBI defines an *active shooter* as "an individual actively engaged in killing or attempting to kill people in a confined and populated area" (p. 5). While no active shooter incidents have occurred at or in sport facilities, it would be prudent for a sport facility manager to collaborate with national, regional, and local law enforcement agencies in developing and implementing an "active shooter" plan.

Active Shooter an individual actively engaged in killing or attempting to kill people in a confined and populated area.

Recognizing Potential Indicators of an Active Shooter

An active shooter may be a current or former employee, or an acquaintance of a current or former employee. Employees typically do not just "snap," but display indicators of potentially violent behavior over time. Intuitive managers and coworkers may notice characteristics of potentially violent behavior in an employee. If these behaviors are recognized, they can often be managed and treated. Under such circumstances, the human resources department should be contacted regarding an employee or coworker who exhibits potentially violent behavior.

Preventing an Active Shooter Situation

To prepare against a potential active shooter situation, the Department of Homeland Security (2008, p. 7) recommends that:

1. Conduct effective employee screening and background checks
2. Create a system for reporting signs of potentially violent behavior
3. Have at least two *evacuation routes* from the facility
4. Post evacuation routes in conspicuous locations throughout your facility
5. Include local law enforcement and first responders during training exercises
6. Encourage law enforcement, emergency responders, SWAT teams, K-9 teams, and bomb squads to train for an active shooter scenario at your location

The first rule in an active shooter scenario is to protect one's own life. When dealing with an active shooter situation, the Department of Homeland Security (2008, pp. 3–4) recommends the following procedures:

1. Establish a chain of authority
2. The facility manager must quickly determine the most reasonable way to protect their own life as customers and clients are likely to follow the lead of employees and managers during an active shooter situation.
3. Evacuate—If there is an accessible escape path, attempt to evacuate the premises. It is important to have an escape route and plan in mind and evacuate regardless of whether others agree to follow.
4. Hide out—If evacuation is not possible, find a place to hide where the active shooter is less likely to find you.
5. Take action against the active shooter—As a last resort, and only when your life is in imminent danger, attempt to disrupt and/or incapacitate the active shooter by acting as aggressively as possible against him/her; throwing items and improvising weapons and committing to your actions.

These steps are often summarized in an easily remembered and prioritized general plan of action for those caught in an active shooter scenario as Run, Hide, Fight.

In an active shooter scenario, communication is a key element. Prepared texts, emails, and/or voice mails must be developed as a way to inform the impacted population (see Table 9.3). Additionally, guidelines should indicate how the facility staff responds prior to and after law enforcement arrives. When officers arrive at the scene the following items must be remembered:

Evacuation Routes the means to send individuals to a place of safety and away from a dangerous area.

1. Establish a chain of authority that identifies who can remove individuals from the area(s).

2. The first officers to arrive to the scene will not stop to help injured persons. Expect rescue teams comprised of additional officers and emergency medical personnel to follow the initial officers. These rescue teams will treat and remove any injured persons. They may also call upon able-bodied individuals to assist in removing the wounded from the premises.

3. Remain calm, and follow officers' instructions

4. Put down any items in your hands (i.e., bags, jackets)

5. Immediately raise hands and spread fingers

6. Keep hands visible at all times

7. Avoid making quick movements toward officers, pointing, screaming and/or yelling (Department of Homeland Security, 2008)

Training graphic for the Run, Hide, Fight response to an active shooter.

To best achieve this understanding, the facility staff and management must undergo proper training, including regular practice training exercises for such an event. The Department of Homeland Security (2008) recommends that the facility conduct mock active shooter training exercises while including local law enforcement as an excellent resource in designing training exercises.

Table 9.3 Active Shooter/Armed Intruder/Shelter in Place Communication Examples

Text: (Organization Name) Emergency! A suspect with a weapon is on campus/facility. Go into nearest room and lock door. Follow instructions from authorities.

Email: (Organization Name) EMERGENCY! There is a suspect with a [type] weapon on campus. [Shots have been fired.] If you are on campus, go into the nearest available room and lock the door. If you are not on campus, stay away. THIS IS NOT A TEST! Wait for the all clear notification from officials or local authorities. For additional information and updates go to (Emergency Website) {End of message}.

Voicemail: This is [name and title] with an EMERGENCY alert from (Organization Name). There is a suspect with a [type] weapon on campus. [Shots have been fired.] If you are on campus, go into the nearest available room and lock the door. If you are not on campus, stay away. THIS IS NOT A TEST! Wait for the all clear notification from College officials or local authorities. For additional information and updates go to (list organization emergency website).

Adapted from: United States Department of Education, n.d.

Bomb Threat

On occasions a sport facility may receive a bomb threat. A *bomb threat* may be defined as:

> *...the communication through the use of mail, e-mail, telephone, telegram, or other instrument of commerce; the willful making of any threat; or the malicious conveyance of false information knowing the same to be false which concerns an attempt being made, or to be made; to kill, injure, intimidate any individual; or unlawfully to damage or destroy any building, vehicle, or other real or personal property by means of an explosive. (University of Tennessee—Martin, 2014)*

Bomb threats are delivered in a variety of ways. The majority of threats are called in to the target. Occasionally these calls are through a third party. Sometimes a threat is communicated in writing or by a recording. A facility must take every bomb threat seriously. There are three potential reasons that a bomb threat would occur. First, the caller has concrete knowledge that an explosive device has been planted in the facility. Second, the caller wishes to generate panic resulting in disruption of normal activities. Third, the caller wishes to express a lack of confidence in the leadership or programs supported by the administration. The targets are not randomly selected but rather are generally chosen due to a political, real, or imagined personal gain to the terrorist. Even if it appears to be a hoax, treat it as if it were not. To do so, it is strongly suggested that:

1. The facility possesses a recording device set up on the phone lines that receive calls during events, and that the individual receiving the call should remain calm, try to record every word spoken by the caller and keep the caller on the line as long as possible.
2. If the caller will not provide the whereabouts of the bomb, this information should be asked for.
3. The caller is reminded that many innocent people could be injured or killed if the bomb is actually detonated in the facility.
4. Any background noises that may provide clues to the caller's whereabouts be identified.
5. The caller's voice can provide clues such as the person's gender, excitement level, accent, or speech impediments.

Should the threat arrive as a written note, every effort must be made to ensure that fingerprints, hand- or typewriting, paper type and postal marks are identified.

Similar to an active shooter situation, the audience in attendance must informed. Since such a situation often occurs at sport contests that takes place in an arena, field, or stadium, there are four primary ways to communicate the situation to the audience: public address system, texts, emails, or voice-mails (see Table 9.4).

Table 9.4 *Example of Bomb Threat Announcement*

PA Announcement: Ladies and gentlemen, I need your attention (say three times). A bomb threat has just been received. We ask your cooperation to evacuate this building quickly by following the instructions from authorities.

Text: (Organization Name) ALERT! (Organization Name) has received a bomb threat at [building]. Evacuate if in that building. Follow instructions from authorities.

Email: (Organization Name) EMERGENCY! A bomb threat has been received by (Organization Name). If you are near campus, prepare immediately for possible evacuation. Listen for instructions from officials or local authorities and follow them quickly and carefully. For additional information and updates go to (Emergency Website) {End of message}.

Voicemail: This is [name and title] with an EMERGENCY alert from (Organization Name). We have received a bomb threat that we deem credible. If you are near campus, prepare immediately for possible evacuation. Listen for instructions from officials or local authorities and follow them quickly and carefully. For additional information and updates go to (Identify emergency website)

Adapted from: United States Department of Education, n.d.

Once a bomb threat has been reported, a complete visual search of the entire facility looking for anything that could appear to be a bomb should be done immediately (Hall, 2004). This is done by assembling the emergency response management team and having them and selected members of their staff search in their respective areas. Planning should include the best way to conduct a search with minimal disruption to the event activity. The local law enforcement agency(s), the fire department (with a possible need to respond), and the appropriate facility officials must be immediately notified. The event's show manager/promoter should be contacted with information of the threat and possible evacuation of the patrons if necessary.

Should an exploding device be found, immediately start evacuation of the area in an orderly fashion using prepared announcements to the patrons and the ushering/security staff. The police and fire department must be notified immediately, as they will be needed to dispose of the explosive device. It is strongly suggested to refrain from radio communication if an object is found, since some exploding devices can be set off by radio waves. If a bomb is not found, the acting facility manager must make the decision, with input from the police representative, whether or not an evacuation of the facility must be made.

Evacuation Procedures

An evacuation may be defined as a temporary relocation strategy of occupants from the facility, or areas of the facility due to a threat or actual occurrence of a hazard. The challenges that all major sporting events face in developing an effective mass evacuation plan include the size of the crowds, parking lot design, and limited egress points from the facility. An exit route to allow for evacuation must be designed to be a permanent part of the facility (29 CFR 1910.36(a)(1). The exit route must be designed to be at least seven feet six inches high (29 CFR 1910.36(g)(1) and at least 28 inches wide (29 CFR 1910.36(g)(2). At least two exit routes must be available in a facility to permit prompt evacuation of building occupants during an emergency. The evacuation routes must be designed to be as far away as possible from each other so if one exit is blocked by fire or smoke, individuals can evacuate using the other exit routes (29 CFR 1910.36(b)(2). Further, for large facilities, more than two exit routes must be available to evacuate safely during an emergency (29 CFR 1910.36(b)(2). Other evacuation design aspects may be found at the Occupational Safety and Health Administration website (https://www.osha.gov/SLTC/etools/evacuation/egress_construction.html).

Evacuation or relocation, if not handled properly, can become an emergency situation by itself and, therefore, must be carefully considered before it is implemented. An evacuation plan should be a major part of an emergency response plan, since every major and semi-major emergency holds a possible need to evacuate some or all of the people in a facility. An evacuation plan needs to be "custom designed" for each facility. When developing an emergency plan some of the important items to always remember are:

1. Chain of command. The worst thing that can happen is a power struggle between the acting facility director and other members of the facility staff or local law enforcement officers as to "who is in charge" and "who makes what decisions." Identify positions and responsibilities; document them; then, train and practice.

2. Egress (exit) from the facility. A plan of alternate exits from every point in the facility needs to be determined and understood by the event staff members working each event.

3. Announcements. Prepared or "canned" evacuation announcements should be prepared in case of an evacuation (see Table 9.4). However, the opportunity to "go off script" must be made available. It is important to remember that only those in position of authority in the chain of command are allowed to "go off script."

4. Patrons or employees with disabilities. Employees designated to assist in emergencies should be made aware of employees and patrons with special needs (who may require extra assistance during an evacuation), how to use the buddy system, and any hazardous areas to avoid during an emergency evacuation.

5. Relationship with authorities. The facility's evacuation plan should include information on what to do with the patrons once they are evacuated outside the facility. Discuss with authorities how evacuees will be transported away from the area if required.

6. Flow time is a component of total evacuation time during which there is crowd flow past a point in the means of egress system. Flow time contributes to the total time needed to evacuate an area after an emergency is detected and an alarm is sounded.

Table 9.5   *Evacuation Announcement Examples*

PA Announcement/Text/Email/Voicemail: This is the (Organization Name) Public Safety. Officers are responding to a report of (**problem**) at (**location**). Calmly evacuate the building using all available exits. Move away from the building. (**Repeat message three times**)

PA Announcement/Text/Email/Voicemail: **Problem Resolved**: This is the (Organization Name) Public Safety. The incident at (**location**) has been resolved and it is safe to return to normal activity. (**Repeat message three times**)

Building Evacuation to a specific direction
PA Announcement/Text/Email/Voicemail: This is the (Organization Name) Public Safety. Officers are responding to a report of (**problem**) at (**location**). Calmly evacuate the building. Avoid (**location**). Go to (**direction/landmark**). (**Repeat message three times**)

PA Announcement/Text/Email/Voicemail: **Problem Resolved**: This is the (Organization Name) Public Safety. The incident at (**location**) has been resolved and it is safe to return to normal activity. (**Repeat message three times**)

Adapted from: United States Department of Education, n.d.

Due to public safety problems that could develop, evacuating the building should be viewed as the "last resort" option and carefully considered before implementing. A building evacuation can become an emergency situation itself. For example, should the bomb threat caller realize that it is the policy to evacuate each time a call is made, he/she can repeatedly call and force the business to close for a time. It is crucial that communication and planning aspects be made in advance regarding how to safely address bomb threats. It is essential that each staff member understand how to handle his or her assignment without delay and without any manifestation of fear. By implementing and training appropriate emergency action plans, the facility manager and staff will be best able to respond to an incident, thereby saving their lives as well as the lives of patrons. Therefore, it is critical that every facility be properly prepared to deal with these types of high-risk events.

CHAPTER DISCUSSION QUESTIONS

1. Discuss the differences and relationships between safety and security.

2. Discuss the importance and proper implementation of an emergency action plan.

3. Discuss the relationships between threat, vulnerability, criticality assessments as components of an effective risk assessment.

4. Identify and explain three ways facility managers may prepare their facility for foreseeable and unforeseeable incidents.

5. Discuss the differences between organized and spontaneous terrorism and ways that may prepare the facility to prevent or respond to threats or incidents.

6. Discuss the procedures facility managers may follow when fire, severe weather, active shooter, and/or bomb threats occur.

MINI CASE STUDY

Lobo Arena is an indoor multipurpose sport and entertainment facility associated with a Division I intercollegiate athletic department in the Mountain West Conference. It seats 15,500 spectators at full capacity for basketball contests and 12,750 capacity for concerts. The Lobos are playing to a full seating capacity against archrival Cougars. With three minutes gone at the beginning of the second half, the ticket office receives a phone call that a bomb will be detonated in arena in 10 minutes. The caller did not indicate where the bomb will be detonated and no further instructions were given. While the caller indicated frustration with some of the university practices, no other reason or organizational affiliation was provided. All of the fans were successfully evacuated from the arena. After a thorough search of the arena, no bombs were detected.

Applying the information in the chapter to this scenario, answer the following:

1. Why are sports facilities potential targets for terrorists' tactics such as bomb scares?

2. What type of terrorism is indicated in the scenario? Explain the reasons for your classification.

3. Identify and explain the reasons that bomb threats occur.

4. What items should the person receiving the phone call note while conversing with the terrorist?

5. Identify and explain the procedures security personnel should follow after a bomb scare is received.

6. Identify and explain evacuation procedures that should be followed after a bomb scare is received.

7. Explain how the facility management personnel assess the risk of a bomb scare.

PRACTITIONER SPOTLIGHT

NAME: Scott Anderson

ORGANIZATION: Pinnacle Venue Services

CURRENT JOB TITLE: Vice President—Security & Fan Experience
Year started in this role—2014

EDUCATIONAL PREPARATION:

- **Undergrad degree:** BA in Physical Education from University of Puget Sound
- **Graduate degree:** MS in Sports Administration from University of Northern Colorado
- **Special Certification(s):** Graduate Venue Management School—IAVM

Photo courtesy of Scott Anderson.

CAREER PATH:

- **Internship(s):** Risk/ Safety Intern—Kroenke Sports & Entertainment
- **Entry level job:** Event Incident Manager—Kroenke Sports & Entertainment

Scott Anderson is a 15-year veteran in facility management with extensive experience in security management, crisis management, risk management, parking, guest services operations, and claims/ incident management. During his 13-year career Scott has been critical in the successful operation of many high profile events including the NBA Finals, NBA Global Games, Democratic National Convention, NCAA Tournament, FIFA sanctioned events, outdoor festivals, and large concerts.

Scott spent the last three years working as the Director of Security and Parking for the San Antonio Spurs organization. During that time Scott was responsible for the overall security/parking management of a wide variety of events including the 2013/14 NBA Finals, 2014 Men's NCAA tournament, River City Rockfest, Warped Tour and many other concerts. During his time with the San Antonio Spurs Scott was instrumental in helping the organization transition event staffing services in-house, which resulted in another #1 ranking in fan experience per the NBA. During Scott's tenure in San Antonio the Spurs were ranked #1 in the NBA in overall experience two out of three years. Scott's other duties for the Spurs organization also included being the Chief Safety Officer, risk manager and claims manager for all company related matters.

Prior to working for the Spurs organization Scott worked as an Event Incident Manager for Kroenke Sports & Entertainment and managed all emergency services and event risk management for three different venues including the Pepsi Center, Dicks Sporting Goods Park, and Paramount Theater.

Scott is a graduate of the University of Puget Sound in Tacoma, Washington and also has a Master's Degree in Sports Administration from the University of Northern Colorado. After successfully transitioning into the sports industry after seven years of management in corporate security, Scott graduated from the International Association of Venue Management's school of Venue Management in 2013.

Scott has also spent the last 15 years conducting a wide variety of trainings that include crowd management, crisis management, emergency procedures, customer service, safety, emergency table-top exercises, and is a certified TEAM (Techniques for Effective Alcohol Management) trainer. He has

Photo courtesy of Scott Anderson.

AT&T Center in San Antonio.

experience conducting joint exercises with both federal and local law enforcement agencies in preparation of large scale events.

Scott shared his insights to some key questions related to his current work in the fields of security and fan experience.

WHAT IS THE MOST REWARDING ASPECT OF THIS JOB?

To me, there is no bigger reward than being part of a successful event and seeing the smiles on the faces of the fans as they exit your facility. For your fans to spend their hard-earned money on attending an event at your venue and walk out of the building with a smile on their face is an amazing feeling. Fans don't always realize the amount of time spent on the overall operation of a single event and to see fans have a safe and enjoyable experience makes all the time and effort worth it.

WHAT IS THE MOST CHALLENGING ASPECT OF THIS JOB?

The most challenging aspect of the job is probably the work schedule and being able to find a good work life balance. In this industry there is really little down time and after a successful event you usually jump right into the next one. Knowing how to manage your time between work and your personal life can be very challenging.

WHAT IS A UNIQUE ASPECT OR TASK OF YOUR JOB THAT MANY WOULD BE SURPRISED HEAR ABOUT?

My job specifically has allowed me to travel to many international locations and even I was unaware of that aspect of the job before I stepped into the role. I have been fortunate enough to travel to and operate successful events in China, Spain, Turkey, Brazil, Italy, Mexico, and the United Kingdom.

ADVICE FOR THOSE SEEKING A SIMILAR CAREER?

Most important skill(s) to develop

- Communication skills—If you want to be successful in the sports and entertainment industry you have to develop advanced communication skills. Communication skills are important in all aspects of our industry and being able to communicate effectively will assist you throughout your career.
- Ability to adapt—In our industry, change is inevitable and your willingness and ability to adapt to change will separate you from the pack. Regardless of the event, a curveball will always be thrown your way and being able to adapt and find solutions to the problem is crucial.

PARTING WORDS OF WISDOM FOR STUDENTS AND YOUNG PROFESSIONALS IN THE FIELD?

While finding an entry level position into the field can be challenging, my recommendation is to take accept any position, including a part-time position, to gain experience and show the value of your skills. In the end, your skills and hard work will put you in a position to advance in the field and attain the job of your dreams.

Reprinted by permission of Scott Anderson.

REFERENCES

Appelbaum, S. H., Adeland, E., & Harris, J. (2005). Management of sports facilities: Stress and terrorism since 9/11. *Management Research News, 28*(7), 69–83.

Associated Press. (2011). Los Angeles Dodgers fans attack San Francisco Giants fan. Retrieved from http://www.azcentral.com/sports/diamondbacks/articles/2011/04/01/20110401los-angeles-dodgers-fans-attacks-san-francisco-giants-fan.html#ixzz1WSR6FmQH

Atkinson, M., & Young, K. (2002). Terror games: Media treatment of security issues at the 2002 Winter Olympic Games. *International Journal of Olympic Studies, 11*, 53–78.

Baker, T. A., Connaughton, D. P., Zhang, J. J., & Spengler, J. O. (2007). Perceived risk of terrorism and related risk management practices of NCAA 1A football stadium managers. *Journal of Legal Aspects of Sport, 13*(2), 145–179.

Beck, U. (2002). The terrorist threat: World Risk Society revisited. *Theory, Culture, and Society, 19*(4), 39–55.

Borjesson, M., Dugmore, D., Mellwig, K. P., van Buuren, F., Serratosa, L., Solberg, E. E., & Pelliccia, A. (2010). Time for action regarding cardiovascular emergency care at sports arenas: A lesson from the arena study. *European Heart Journal, 31*(12), 1438–1441.

Borjesson, M., Serratosa, L., Carre, F., Corrado, D., Drezner, J., Dugmore, D. L. ,...Rasmusen, H. (2011). Consensus document regarding cardiovascular safety at sports arenas. *European Heart Journal, 32*(17), 2119–2124.

Borum, R. (2007). Psychology of terrorism. Retrieved from http://oai.dtic.mil/oai/oai?verb=getRecord&metadataPrefix=html&identifier=ADA494527

Burns, C., Mearns, K., & McGeorge, P. (2006). Explicit and implicit trust within safety culture. *Risk Analysis, 26*(5), 1139–1150.

Cawood, J. S. (2002). Security. In R. W. Lack (Ed.) *Safety, health, and asset protection: Management essentials* (pp. 553–566). New York: Lewis Publishers.

Chertoff, M. (2007). National preparedness guidelines—September 2007. *Department of Homeland Security*. Retrieved from http://www.dhs.gov/xlibrary/assets/National_Preparedness_Guidelines.pdf

Clonan, T. (2002, October 26). Any time any place, *Irish Times*, W1.

CNN Library. (2016). 2015 Paris terror attacks fast facts. Retrieved from http://www.cnn.com/2015/12/08/europe/2015-paris-terror-attacks-fast-facts/

Cohen, A. (2001). Secure in defeat. *Athletic Business*, 25(11), 9–10.

Crenshaw, M. (2000). Psychology of terrorism: An agenda for the 21st century. *Political Psychology, 21*(2), 405–420.

Crocco, T. J., Sayre, M. R., Liu, T., Davis, S. M., Cannon, C., & Potluri, J. (2004). Mathematical determination of external defibrillators needed at mass gatherings. *Prehospital Emergency Care, 8*(3), 292–297.

Decker, R. J. (2001, October). *Homeland security: A risk management approach can guide preparedness efforts.* Retrieved from http://www.gao.gov/cgi-bin/getrpt?GAO-03-102

Department of Homeland Security. (2003). *Evacuation planning guide for stadiums.* Retrieved from http://www.dhs.gov/sites/default/files/publications/Evacuation%20Planning%20Guide%20for%20Stadiums.pdf

Department of Homeland Security. (2008). *Active shooter: How to respond.* Retrieved from https://www.dhs.gov/xlibrary/assets/active_shooter_booklet.pdf

Department of Homeland Security. (2015). *Step-by-step applicant training.* Retrieved from https://www.safetyact.gov/pages/homepages/Home.do

Dobbs, D. B. (2000). *The law of torts.* St. Paul, MN: West Group.

Fallon, R. H. (2003). Legal issues in sports security. *Fordham Intellectual Property, Media, and Entertainment Law Journal, 13,* 349–401.

Firesmith, D. G. (2003). *Common concepts underlying safety security and survivability engineering* (No. CMU/SEI-2003-TN-033). Carnegie-Mellon University, Pittsburgh, PA. Software Engineering Institute.

Frame, J. D. (2003). *Managing risk in organizations.* San Francisco, CA: Jossey-Bass.

Goss, B. D., Jubenville, C. B., & MacBeth, J. L. (2003). *Primary principles of post-9/11 stadium security in the United States: Transatlantic implications from British practices.* Retrieved from www.iaam.org/CVMS/Post%20911%20Stadium%20Security.doc

Grace, F. (2002, July 4). *FBI alert on stadiums.* Retrieved from http://www.cbsnews.com/stories/2002/07/03/attack/main514252.shtml

Harmon, K. G., Asif, I. M., Klossner, D., & Drezner, J. A. (2011). Incidence of sudden cardiac death in national collegiate athletic association athletes. *Circulation*, 123(15), 1594–1600.

Hall, J. R. (2004). Assembly property fires. *Fire Protection Engineering.* Retrieved from http://magazine.sfpe.org/fire-protection-design/assembly-property-fires

Katz, E., Metzger, J. T., Marazzi, A., & Kappenberger, L. (2006). Increase of sudden cardiac deaths in Switzerland during the 2002 FIFA World Cup. *International Journal of Cardiology, 107*(1), 132–133.

Lee, B., Gordon, P., Moore, J., & Richardson, H. (2008). Simulating the economic impacts of a hypothetical bio-terrorist attack: A sports stadium case. *Journal of Homeland Security and Emergency Management, 5*(1), 1–20.

Leusveld, E., Kleijn, S., & Umans, V. A. W. M. (2008). Usefulness of emergency medical teams in sport stadiums. *The American Journal of Cardiology, 101*(5), 712–714.

Lipton, E. (2005, March 16). U.S. report lists possibilities for terrorist attacks and likely toll. *New York Times*, A1.

Luiz, T., Kumpch, M., Metzger, M., & Madler, C. (2005). Management of cardiac arrest in a German soccer stadium. Structural, process and outcome quality. *Der Anaesthesist, 54*(9), 914–922.

Maron, B. J., Doerer, J. J., Haas, T. S., Tierney, D. M., & Mueller, F. O. (2009). Sudden deaths in young competitive athletes analysis of 1866 deaths in the United States, 1980–2006. *Circulation, 119*(8), 1085–1092.

Merari, A. (1978). A classification of terrorist groups. *Studies in Conflict & Terrorism, 1*(3–4), 331–346.

Miller, J., & Gillentine, A. (2006). An analysis of risk management policies for tailgating activities at selected NCAA division I football games. *Journal of Legal Aspects of Sport, 16*, 197–215.

Miller, J. J., Wendt, J. T., & Young, P. C. (2010). Fourth Amendment considerations and application of risk management principles for pat-down searches at professional football games. *Journal of Legal Aspects of Sport, 20*(2), 108–134.

Miller, J., & Veltri, F. (2001). Campus recreation centers: An examination of security issues. *Journal of Legal Aspects of Sport, 11*(2), 169–180.

Miller, J., Veltri, F., & Gillentine, A. (2008). Spectator perception of security at the Super Bowl after 9/11: Implications for facility managers. *Sport Management and Related Topics Journal, 4*(2), 16–25.

Motyka, T. M., Winslow, J. E., Newton, K., & Brice, J. H. (2005). Method for determining automatic external defibrillator need at mass gatherings. *Resuscitation, 65*(3), 309–314.

National Weather Service. (2015). *Weather fatalities*. Retrieved from http://www.nws.noaa.gov/om/hazstats.shtml

O'Shea, L. S., & Awwad-Rafferty, R. (2009). *Design and security in the built environment*. New York, NY: Fairchild Books.

Reckelhoff-Dangel, C., & Petersen, D. (2007). *Risk communication in action: The risk communication workbook*. United States Environmental Protection Agency, Office of Research and Development. Retrieved from http://www.epa.gov/ord/NRMRL/pubs/625r05003/625r05003.pdf

Rescher, N. (1983). *Risk: A philosophical introduction to the theory of risk evaluation and management*. Washington, D.C.: University Press of America.

Sales, L. (2014). Lightning safety. Retrieved from http://www.ncaa.org/health-and-safety/lightning-safety

Schafer, W., Carroll, J. M., Haynes, S., & Abrams, S. (2008). Emergency management planning as collaborative community work. *Journal of Homeland Security and Emergency Management, 5*(1), 1–17.

Slovic, P., & Peters, E. (2006). Risk perception and affect. *Psychological Science, 15*(6), 322–325.

Suder, G. (2004). *Terrorism and the international business environment.* Cheltenham, UK: Edward Elgar.

Teicholz, E. (2001). *Facility design and management handbook.* New York, NY: McGraw-Hill.

United States Department of Education. (n.d.). Emergency notification scripts. Retrieved from rems.ed.gov/docs/.../rems_000111_0001.doc

Wilbert-Lampen, U., Leistner, D., Greven, S., Pohl, T., Sper, S., Völker, C., …Steinbeck, G. (2008). Cardiovascular events during World Cup soccer. *New England Journal of Medicine, 358*(5), 475–483.

Customer Service

Lawrence W. Judge, Shannon Powers, and *Kelsey L. Jones*

OBJECTIVES

After studying this chapter, the student should be able to:

- Define and discuss the importance of excellent customer service during sporting events.
- Restate and give examples of the different kinds of customers at sporting events and their importance.
- Explain the importance of basic customer service needs for a sporting event.
- Understand the different areas where customer service is necessary at a sporting event, including tickets, merchandise, and concessions.

KEY TERMS

Customer Churn

Customer Satisfaction

Customer Service Representative

Frontline Employee

Loyalty

Service

Service Quality

KEY ACRONYMS

ADA   Americans with Disabilities Act

CC   Closed Captioning

CSR   Customer Service Representative

NPA   National Parking Association

Introduction

Service work done for others that is an intangible good that cannot be stored or transported and is simultaneously produced and consumed.

Service Quality a assessment of customer service based upon service encounters in respect to the expectations of the customer.

Quality customer service is imperative to the success of a sporting event. *Service* is intangible in the sense that the customer cannot judge the quality of the product before actually obtaining it (Jang, Ko, & Stepchenkova, 2014). The customer is usually guided by previous experience, the reputation of the organization, and/or the person delivering the service (Kwak, Kim, & Hirt, 2011). *Service quality* has been linked to higher event/game satisfaction and increased behavioral intentions (Yoshida & James, 2010), which may lead to customer retention and long-term profitability (Sturn & Thiry, 1991). Building upon a customer-centric approach to quality customer service, Kelly and Turley (2001) identified, in order, the following aspects as being most important to fans attending sporting events: 1) behavior of employees, 2) fair ticket prices, 3) ease of facility access, 4) fair concession prices, 5) fan seat comfort, 6) game experience/ambiance, 7) show time, 8) convenience of travel and location, and 9) access to smoking sections. Businesses that are "market-oriented" strive to put customers first and are more likely to reach their business goals. Market-oriented firms must have excellent service and include amenities for all types of customers. These customers include the patrons, participants, and the media. "During the planning stages [of any endeavor], it is vitally important to consider every area where the event process may break down and suffer a service failure" (Greenwell, Danzey-Bussell, & Shonk, 2014, p. 181).

Services are perishable. It was noted earlier that a service could not be produced and stored for future use. If no customer reports to a service representative during a sporting event, whatever services the venue could have provided during that period have been lost. Similarly, if a corporate luxury seating box is not rented for a basketball game (i.e., the use of the box seating during that game itself), its use as a service has vanished. In contrast, a manufacturer can continue to produce hard goods and product inventory even though there are no sales at any given moment.

Services vary in quality, whereas goods, such as the quality of a hockey stick, are usually of uniform quality (Kwak, Kim, & Hirt, 2011). There are three reasons for this:

- First, individual differences among service providers in terms of personality, experience, and expertise result in different experiences for the customer. For instance, the leadership offered by different general managers may vary.
- Second, the same employee may not provide the same level of service from one time to another. For example, a basketball coach's lessons may vary in quality from day to day. This could be a function of the coach's level of motivation and fatigue (coaching for five straight hours), stress (pressures affecting family life), and other such factors.

- Third, the quality of the experienced service can be affected by the consumer's psyche. Therefore, a service may be judged good or bad depending upon the consumer's frame of mind. If motivation, fatigue, and stress can affect the service provider, the same factors could also affect the customers. For instance, a customer of a baseball game who has just learned that his tickets are for another day may not be appreciative of the pleasant and warm greetings from the window ticket sales representative. On the other hand, heterogeneity may not be as pronounced in the case of the rental of a headset at a hockey game, where it will be the same day in and day out.

The interface between the producer and the consumer is much more important in the exchange of services than of goods (Kwak, Kim, & Hirt, 2011). A service is intangible because it cannot be scrutinized before purchase; it is perishable because it cannot be stored for future use; it is heterogeneous because it is variable from time to time; and its production and consumption occur simultaneously (Hassan & Lusted, 2012).

Stadium ushers, like these at Wrigley Field, form an integral part of the front lines of customer service in sport venues.

© FFooter/Shutterstock.com

Customer Satisfaction

Customer satisfaction is a marketing term measuring how products or services supplied by a company meet or surpass a customer's expectation. Customer satisfaction is important in providing marketers and business owners with a measurement to manage and improve their businesses. Senior marketing managers find evaluating customer satisfaction useful in managing and monitoring business operations. Customer satisfaction is defined as a pleasurable gratification response toward a good, service, benefit, or reward (Oliver, 1997). Palmatier, Dant, Grewal, and Evans (2006) identified six reasons why customer satisfaction is important:

- It's a leading indicator of consumer repurchase intentions and *loyalty*.
- It's a point of differentiation.
- It reduces customer churn.
- It increases customer lifetime value.
- It reduces negative word of mouth.
- It's cheaper to retain customers than acquire new ones.

Reaping long-term service loyalty is often the key factor that builds competitive advantage for service providers (Javalgi & Moberg, 1997). As previously mentioned, the more satisfied customers are with a purchase or experience,

Customer Satisfaction a measure of how products or services meet or surpass a customer's expectation.

Loyalty customer behavior to consistently purchase a product or brand over a period of time.

the more likely they will become repeat customers or even advocates. In a competitive marketplace where businesses compete for customers, customer satisfaction is seen as a key differentiator. Businesses who succeed in these cut-throat environments make customer satisfaction a key element of their business strategy. Picture two discount ticket companies that offer the same price for tickets. *What will make you choose one over the other?* If you had a recommendation for one, would that sway your opinion? Probably. So how does that recommendation originally start? More than likely it's on the back of a good customer experience. Companies who offer positive customer experiences create environments where satisfaction is high and customer advocates are plenty. This is an example of where customer satisfaction goes full circle. Not only can customer satisfaction help you keep a finger on the pulse of existing customers, but it may also act as a point of differentiation for new customers.

Customer Churn an interruption or loss in a customer's relationship or interaction with a company or product.

What is customer churn? *Customer churn* has been defined as when a customer (merchandise buyer, season ticket holder, etc.) ceases his or her relationship with a company (Kwak, Kim, & Hirt, 2011). Companies typically classify a customer as "churned" after a specific amount of time has elapsed since their last interaction. Customer churn is a key component to business growth. A satisfied customer likely increases the lifetime value of the company. A study by Reel (2009) looking at over 20,000 customer surveys in 40 countries found that a "totally satisfied customer" contributes 2.6 times more revenue than a "somewhat satisfied customer." Furthermore, a "totally satisfied customer" contributes 14 times more revenue than a "somewhat dissatisfied customer." Satisfaction plays a significant role in how much revenue a customer generates for your business.

The White House Office of Consumer Affairs (CSM, 2016) found that an unhappy customer tells between 9–15 people about their experience. In fact, 13% of unhappy customers tell over 20 people about their experience. *That's a lot of negative word of mouth.* How much will that affect the success of the company? Customer satisfaction is tightly linked to revenue and repeat purchases. What often gets forgotten is how customer satisfaction negatively impacts the business. Negative word of mouth is hard to turn around, especially when social media is involved, and is difficult to remove from websites and social media platforms. Losing an unsatisfied consumer is one thing, but completely losing 20 customers because of bad word of mouth is another issue. Acquiring new customers costs six to seven times more than to retaining existing customers (Aaker, 2012). In essence, customers are far more expensive to acquire. The sport industry has spent millions of dollars gaining the attention of customers, nurturing them into leads, and closing them into sales.

In this chapter, the reader will learn about the different customer categories, frontline employee training, ticketing considerations, ancillary services, and how to use customer service to reach business goals.

Customer Categories

Customers can be categorized in many ways; however, in the sport venues and sport event sphere they are best understood in within three distinct groups: *Patrons*, *Participants*, and *Media*.

Patrons: The patrons are consumers attending the event. Typically, these are fans of the teams playing, but can also include people who have a general interest in the event, but no actual ties to the teams. There are different considerations for varying types of customers, including customers paying for differing levels of seats. All patrons must feel like guests and have their needs met. However, will patrons sitting in the upper balcony (sometimes referred to as nosebleed) seats receive the same treatment as those sitting in the box seats? What amenities will be provided in order to help patrons feel welcome and appreciated but not cost the franchise money? These are just a few questions that need to be considered when determining a customer service plan.

Participants: The participants are the athletes, coaches, league staff, officials, etc., and the teams performing in the venue. There are many considerations that need to be attended to in order to execute effective customer service. One of the most pressing needs is ensuring the safety and privacy of the participants. Where are they going to park? What plans do you have to keep fans and media away at appropriate times? Ensuring all parties have a comfortable environment for all their needs, especially places to eat, change, and meet is also important. Participants need to know where to park and directions to and from the venue. Considering all of these things and brainstorming the most efficient way for participants to feel welcome and safe will help the business run efficiently.

Media: Members of the media are considered customers as well. This includes reporters, radio hosts, camera crews, etc. This is especially important in light of research showing a positive relationship between satisfaction and behavioral intention (Kil Kim et al., 2013). In this study, researchers found that the happier the media personnel were, the more likely they were to talk favorably about the venue and event. Considerations for media customers include parking and transportation, technology available, communication, amenities (food, bank, lounges, etc.), and venue size/organization.

Venue and event managers must be cognizant of these distinct groups and develop plans and strategies to meet the unique needs of each group in order to optimize the overall level of success.

Frontline Employee Training

Frontline Employee any employee with direct contact with customers.

Employees who are in direct contact with the customers during an event are called *frontline employees.* These are the employees tending to the concerns, needs, and desires of the customers. Most are motivated to work long hours in hopes to be noticed by upper-level management (Lansberg, 2015). For example, entry-level jobs in baseball that pay relatively low wages have not diminished the competitiveness of the application processes for openings, nor the zeal with which aspiring employees seek to break into the industry (Lansberg, 2015). Major League Baseball (MLB) player agent Joshua Kusnick (2014) sums up the current state of the market well: "Teams always have the advantage when hiring, because so many people are willing to work for next to nothing just to get their foot in the door" (¶ 5). Research shows those working for sport teams and organizations often experience high work stress, poor compensation, and insufficient training (Hartline & Ferrell, 1993). This is concerning because well-trained employees are more motivated to act in ways that will promote and maintain a successful customer service environment (Day, 1994). Further, high-quality service has been linked as an important factor in maintaining customer loyalty and profitability in sports (Sturn & Thiry, 1991).

Along with promotions and lower ticket prices, franchise executives emphasize rolling out the red carpet for customer satisfaction. Franchises spend money training the preferred characteristics frontline employees should embody.

"Market-oriented" business models emphasize the importance of customers and make addressing their needs a top priority. Businesses that emphasize the customer better achieve their objectives (Matsuno, Mentzer, & Oszomer, 2002). Part of this process includes employee training to make sure employees understand the level of service that the business requires (Peccei & Rosenthal, 2001). That way, employees understand what is expected of them and are better able to execute their tasks.

Employees expected to adhere to high levels of standards for customer service typically indicate strong support from coworkers and management (Susskind, Kacmar, & Borchgrevink, 2003). Eisenberger, Huntington, Hutchinson, and Sowa (1986) define support as how employees perceive the company or organization to which they are employed correlated with their personal well-being (as cited in Susskind et al., 2003). High standards and a positive, encouraging work environment are directly related to perceptions of customer service orientation (Susskind et al., 2003). Satisfied customers are a product of exceptional standards and superiors that motivate frontline employees.

Frontline employee success has been linked to the support and guidance from superiors, communication between superiors and their employees, and employees feeling empowered. One review of the literature (Hartline & Ferrell, 1996) stated:

The findings from previous research lead to two major conclusions: (1) managers can influence customer-contact employees' responses so as to enhance service quality and (2) the responses of customer-contact employees heavily influence customers' perceptions of service quality and the service encounter. (Hartline & Ferrell, 1996, pp. 52–53)

It would seem that positive relationships and effective dissemination of business models have a positive impact on how customers experience an event. In many cases, frontline employees are not autonomous in decision making (Boshoff & Allen, 2000). They must check with their supervisors before executing decisions, making it difficult to offer customers rapid service in situations that demand immediate decision making above the frontline employees ability.

In one study, researchers found that communication, training, and managerial coaching were the three factors that most influenced frontline employee empowerment (Ellinger, Keller, & Bas, 2010). A number of studies indicate the importance of human interaction in the determination of satisfactory service (Van Dolen et al., 2004). Hartline and Ferrell (1996) have suggested that customer perceptions of service quality are largely derived from the attitude and behavior of customer contact with employees. This means that those frontline staff who are not only competent but also willing to deal with problems will increase their customers' satisfaction (Bitner et al., 1990).

The empowerment of employees to take customer concerns seriously, quickly handle complaints, solve problems, answer further questions, give feedback and compensate for any cost, is important in satisfying customers and reinforcing their positive attitude towards the relationship with the service provider (Gruber, 2011). Personalizing the service encounter/interaction helps in speeding up the recovery and boosting customer satisfaction and ultimately increasing customer commitment. The key performance factors "Solves Problem," "Respectful Treatment," "Friendliness," "Shows Genuine Care," and "Trustworthiness" have a strong influence on customers' perception of service. Importantly, these attributes are the basic ingredients for the ongoing relationship

Ticker sellers and ticket takers are often early points of contact for customer service in sport.

between the customers and the service provider (Aldlaigan & Buttle, 2005; Rice, 2003). Without these attributes, customers may not have a strong commitment to the relationship and they may consider switching venue and teams to follow (Hocutt, 1998; Pressey & Mathews, 2003). The more franchises enhance and strengthen these attributes, the more likely fans will be retained. Other attributes such as "Sufficient Knowledge," "Listens Carefully," "Demonstrates Understanding," and "Apologizes" have less impact on satisfaction and the long-term relationship.

Ellinger, Keller, and Bas (2010) concluded that human resource departments are imperative in helping frontline employees understand the objectives of their companies and ensure they feel comfortable and empowered, knowing they are giving the best service they can to the customers. MLB is an excellent example of an industry's strategic priority to meet the service needs of consumer expectations. Most sports teams rely on their extensive game-day operations department to train part-time and hourly employees. This typically includes all employees working in concessions, parking, ticketing, and ushering capacities. Unlike other entertainment industries, sporting events are not only evaluated on their customer service but also on winning games. Therefore, sport franchises value external polls that rank such criteria as frontline employee courtesy (with spectators), quality of venue, and fan-friendliness of environment. Ultimately, a good attitude and genuine willingness to help others are very important to fans' opinion of the overall game experience.

ADA Implications on Customer Service

In 1990, the United States congress signed the Americans with Disabilities Act (ADA), which addressed the needs of persons with disabilities. This act prevents discrimination in the workforce and requires all public entities to provide accommodations for anyone with a disability. With an estimated 56.7 million Americans with disabilities, representing 18.7% of the US population, (Brault, 2012), as well as a growing older population that may require similar accommodations, identifying, and meeting the needs of this segment of sport consumers while they are attending sporting events has become a priority for senior management at US sport facilities. Similarly, statistics from Europe suggest that 40% of the total European population could benefit from accessible and inclusive environments, demonstrating "the growing economic influence of sport customers with disabilities" (Paramio-Salcines & Kitchin, 2013, p. 339). Many accommodations are required for people with mobility impairments. Two basic categories of needs are relevant to the sport service experience: physical needs and service needs (James & Grady, 2013). A third category cannot be exclusively categorized as either physical or service need in that physical and service aspects tend to blend together. A list of the categories and various needs identified is provided in Table 10.1. Many venues include the accommodations they offer on their websites so patrons can make preparations.

Table 10.1 *Categories of Needs*

Physical Needs	Service Needs	Blended Needs
Seating	Staff Responsiveness	Crowds
Companion Seats	Staff Awareness	Accidents
Parking	Staff Knowledge	Emergency Evacuation
Line of Sight		Accessible Policies
Restrooms		Role of Companion
Elevators/Ramps		6 hardwood courts
Heat-related Protection		
Assistive Listening Systems		
Signage		

Adapted from James & Grady (2013)

Inside the facility itself, it is important that specific locations for people with disabilities to park, sit, or any other services offered, and have proper signage indicating that disability locations are accessible. Not only does this allow people with disabilities to find these locations easily, but also acknowledges these areas to able-bodied patrons so they know not to use them.

Skulski, Bloomer, and Chait (2002) analyzed the ticket and accommodation policies at various sport and entertainment facilities throughout the United States. They found the level and frequency of accommodations for people with mobility impairments was much greater than the provision of auxiliary aids and services for people with other types of disabilities, such as visual or hearing impairments. In addition, accessibility policies, such as ticket sales policies for patrons with disabilities, varied widely and only 48% of the facilities provided staff training in disability awareness (Skulski et al., 2002). Moreover, there are three critical stages of customer service important for people with disabilities (James & Grady, 2015): before the event, during the event, and after the event. However, certain needs are salient at different stages of the service experience. Table 10.2 outlines particular needs during different stages of service delivery. For example, there is a need for ramps and elevators prior to the beginning of and at the end of an ice skating event.

Going Beyond "Reasonable" for an Overlooked Population

Studies have indicated that the sponsoring organization of a sports event must be cognizant of their legal duties to disabled fans, including addressing risk management issues (Miller & Gillentine, 2006). The question that

Table 10.2   *Particular Needs During Different Stages of Service Delivery*

Pre-Event	During Event	Post-Event
Availability of disabled parking space	Staff responsiveness of ushers in seating sections	Ramp or elevator inside facility
Accessible route from parking lot to stadium	Staff awareness of ushers in seating sections	Directional signage
Ramp or elevator inside venue	Restroom	Navigating through crowd
Directional signage	Navigating through crowd at half time	Ramp outside venue
Restroom		Accessible route from stadium to parking lot
Navigating through crowd		
Staff knowledge (parking, staff, ticket takers, ushers, customer service staff)		
Staff responsiveness (ticket takers, ushers, customer service staff)		

Adapted from James & Grady (2015)

© Dziurek/Shutterstock.com

Provision for seating and services for patrons with disabilities is an important customer service element for sport venues and events.

must be addressed: "Are event and venue managers ensuring that patrons with disabilities have an accessible, safe game, and complete day experience?" An understanding of the duties to create and maintain a reasonably safe environment and to adhere to the ADA regulations, particularly as stipulated in Title II and Title III, is essential to best answer such a question. A game day event staff employee recalled, "When I was at the University of North Carolina, patrons in wheelchairs could not see the banners or the "Jerseys in the Rafters," in the Carolina Coliseum from the wheelchair seating areas. They were blocked by the upper deck. We had a patron ask if there was a way to see them.

Luckily, we were able to take her down to the floor level post-game for a view. This was reasonable. Going during the game or before the game was unreasonable because the only access to the area where she could see the rafters was through the team tunnels which are inaccessible to the general public during games." Holistic responses by *customer service representatives*, as demonstrated above, make game-day experiences for patrons with disabilities inclusive (Gillentine, Grady, Miller, & Pettus, 2016).

ADA Electronic Accessibility

Today, the sport industry communicates with customers and fans using multiple media sources, including television, radio, print advertising, as well as the team website. The ADA's requirement of "effective communication" means that when a sport company chooses a specific media source to reach out to fans, such as the team website, the team must ensure that they are communicating in a similar manner with able-bodied customers and customers with disabilities, given the three components discussed above. Television communication includes "in house" broadcasts and messages within the stadium or arena that are communicated on the scoreboard video screens or monitors within the venue and to ribbon board screens around the venue. Legal precedence was set in the *Feldman v. Pro Football Inc.* case regarding the need to include closed caption messaging for the video content used within the sport venue setting including music lyrics, play information, advertisements, referee calls, and safety/emergency information (Lower & Petersen, 2010). As sport consumers have become increasingly tech-savvy, sport companies have adjusted their marketing strategies to meet their customer's online needs for team and event information. This same desire and need is present for customers with disabilities. This generates a specific need to create sport websites accessible to customers with disabilities because a website is viewed by consumers as more time efficient than communicating with team personnel in other ways, particularly in obtaining information

Customer Service Representatives an employee responsible for maintaining positive relations and goodwill between a business organization and its customers via answering questions, solving problems or providing assistance.

Providing closed captioning for in-house video feeds during sport events is one important accommodation for individuals with disabilities in attendance.

that does not require any personal interaction with the team staff, such as parking locations, listening devices, and gates with escorts (Murphy, Forrest, Wotrig, & Brymer, 1996).

A website that is designed in an accessible format has features that can assist users with a wide range of disabilities. Users with cognitive, learning, or developmental disabilities would likely benefit from screen readers with speech synthesis as well as design of web pages with consistent layouts and color schemes as well as navigation buttons with clear meanings (Smith, n.d.). Users with hearing impairments rely upon text and graphics for information so a web page that utilizes audio clips should provide transcripts for the user. Users with motor disabilities may have difficulty using a mouse or holding down multiple keys simultaneously, while others may need special adaptive software. In designing a web page with these needs in mind, the web page should contain links and hot images that are large enough for users to click on. If the website requires the user to submit forms, often requiring the use of a mouse to complete, the web page should be designed so that there is an alternate means for submitting the form. Web users with visual impairments may use screen readers with voice synthesizers or Braille output. For these users, tables and columns on the web page may be problematic because users who are blind cannot see the images or use mouse-driven forms (Smith, n.d.).

Undoubtedly, adjusting access to the Internet to fully meet the needs of customers with disabilities is not an easy task. However, without modifying sport websites to meet the needs of customers with a disability by providing features such as descriptive alternate text on images and graphics, synchronized captioning, and video captioning, customers with disabilities will face new barriers as more sport businesses expand their sales and service presence in cyberspace (Grady & Ohlin, 2004).

Proactive organizations should see Internet accessibility as an arm of their customer service responsibility. Ultimately, as an opportunity to reach out to individuals with disabilities so that they too may experience the full and equal enjoyment of the sport industry's vast offering of goods and services. From a marketing and finance perspective, a sport company's decision to make a website accessible for visual and hearing impaired has the potential to be a financially lucrative means to attract a largely untapped market (Grady & Ohlin, 2004).

Parking

Provided parking is seen as the "front porch" for many sporting venues (Henao & Marshall, 2012). The challenge of managing a parking facility goes well beyond the moving of cars. Daily operations, upkeep, reporting, marketing, and customer service all need to be running like clockwork. Without all of these cylinders working in sync, a parking lot cannot function properly. Many sport organizations have parking certified parking employees that oversee:

1. **Operations**—Procedural manuals and processes that streamline facility's operations for game days, special events, and possibly outsourcing for daily tenants for non-events. This includes payment stations, strategic flow of general cars coming in and out of lots and garages, and overflow lots. Separate locations for limousine service, taxis, disability drop/pick up.

2. **Reporting**—Automated daily, weekly, and monthly reporting provides accurate data on all aspects of facility's operations. Identify challenges and opportunities while controlling expenses and lowering your costs.

3. **Maintenance**—Short and long-term maintenance plans combined with regular facility inspections and auditing for garage/lot upkeep; parking technology and sustainability; safety; and ordinances.

Transport management is taken so seriously, the National Parking Association Program (NPA), the oldest and most prestigious parking certification program, refer their professionals for jobs in sport management. Established in 1993, More than 500 parking professionals worldwide have earned the designation. NPA's certification program enhances professionalism in the industry, raises the awareness of the impact and importance of the parking industry, and sets a standard for excellence. Eligible parking professionals participate in a comprehensive exam covering 13 key aspects of parking operations, from safety and security to customer service operations to disaster planning, to finance and valet parking operations. Certification is earned through a formal testing system administered by an independent credentialing organization on NPA's behalf and is maintained through continuing education and a periodic recertification process.

Parking costs vary at individual venues. In a 2012, analysis of Denver, Colorado sporting venues the average for on-site parking at football games is $30, the Pepsi Center for NBA and NHL games ranges from $10–$30. Coors baseball field is $15–$17 on game day (Henao & Marshall, 2012). Variations in parking prices can be due to the event type and demand, and often various parking sites and vendors can impact the price point and customer impressions and satisfaction, as parking is often the first point of customer contact on a game/event day. Purchasing prepaid parking can be done in advance at ticket offices or online. On game day, parking attendants ensure the ingress and egress from facility parking areas. They generally perform the following duties: vehicle screening, pre-event parking lot sweep procedures, control traffic flow and parking pass/credential control measures, as well as supervising public tailgating in the parking lots

The management and operation of parking for the sport venue such as this at Levi's Stadium in Santa Clara, CA is another key area for customer service.

(Henao & Marshall, 2012). Parking staff work closely with event security management. If a parking permit holder or their guests' actions are deemed inappropriate or obscene by the management of a sporting venue, they may be subject to discipline. Lastly, parking facilities impact customer satisfaction levels. Managerial concerns should be paid to the improvement of safety, cleanliness, and the customers' lack of tolerance for long wait times.

Ticketing

As technology becomes more central to our lives, many sport venues utilize online websites to sell tickets (Olson & Boyer, 2005). The Internet offers a quick, convenient way to obtain tickets, but offers a unique challenge to service quality for sporting events. There is no customer-employee contact, although patrons expect the online service to run without incident. In one study, Olson and Boyer (2005) found that system effectiveness, order service, cost, and ease of interaction were the most predictive of needing improvement when ordering their tickets for a particular event. This indicates that these four factors are important to consumers when purchasing tickets online. If businesses can incorporate Internet technology into their models while taking these four factors into account, it may help them succeed in this increasingly technological environment.

Customers have a variety of sources to purchase tickets to sporting events. Teams outsource their ticketing sales to secondary companies such as Ticketmaster, Cheap Tickets, and Gametime, to offset their own manpower and overhead costs. Alternatively, companies purchase tickets from teams in bulk and act as discounted ticket liquidators, such as ScoreBig. Many of these companies have convenience fees and other costs associated with purchasing game day tickets. Through exclusive ticketing partnerships, sporting venues can offer rewards, bonuses, and incentives for ticket purchases. Loyal fans can be rewarded for every dollar they spend on tickets, including season ticket renewals and bonus points for special ticket packages (Gennaro, 2013).

Although Internet ticketing is a convenient way to purchase tickets, some patrons still prefer to purchase tickets from the venue's box office. At smaller events, such as youth, recreational, or amateur sports, the only way to purchase tickets is at the box office. In these cases, it is important the ticket office is located in a convenient, visible place and includes adequate resources to sell tickets. Ticket resource management includes an accurate accounting of inventory (seats) and sales. Most sporting companies use computer-based business software for large-scale customer service. Resources may include correct change, a working credit card system, and friendly staff.

According to the 2015 Colloquy Customer Loyalty Census, American households hold memberships in an average of 29 loyalty programs but are active (meaning earn or redeem at least one per year) in only 12 of them. Companies lose money on time and effort, and customers get no more value from the businesses to which they are "loyal." However, consumers think they're being rewarded, and this is good business for companies. For customers, the more applications tied to the experience is another layer of satisfaction. Several programs exist for rewarding customer attendance: mobile applications, ticket and card scans, iPad kiosks, and beacons.

> **Mobile applications:** Fans automatically check-in to sporting events via the application on Android and IOS phones. Ticketers set a geofence, time window, and point value for each event.
>
> **Ticket and card scans:** Through partnerships and partner rewards programs sporting venues are able to offer rewards for ticket scans. Award bonuses points for early arrival and bringing other paying customers earn bigger awards.
>
> **iPad kiosks:** Fans swipe an ID or rewards card to check into an event. A custom kiosk is also used for registration purposes.
>
> **Beacons:** Tiny Bluetooth devices that detect a fan's location. Beacons can be placed at the entrance of a venue, in stores, at sponsor locations or on mobile units. When fans walk past a beacon, loyalty points can be awarded or intelligent push notifications can be sent to their accounts. Beacons are incredibly tiny, unnoticeable, and require little maintenance.

Ticketing is a common entry position for customer service jobs in the sport industry. Moreover, inside sales (IS) are where most ticket sales representatives spend their first year. Inside sales positions are often used like tryouts for a sports team front office. Numerous people try out, but only a select few make the team. In this case, teams hire several new sales representatives and give them a set amount of time (usually six months to one year) to learn the business and demonstrate they have what it takes to help the team achieve its goals. At the end of the session, the highest producers usually get promoted into full-time positions on one of the ticket sales teams. If a full-time position is not available, inside sales managers will do their best to place top producers on the full-time staffs of other franchise. The size of an inside sales team can vary greatly. Many NBA and NHL teams hire 6–15 new reps each off-season; however, there is a growing trend in the NBA for lower-demand teams to have 30 or more inside sales reps in efforts to bolster sales.

Ancillary Services

Merchandizing

Sports enterprises make a large amount of profit from branding and selling their merchandise (Rovell, 2010). Therefore, fans are imperative to the economic success of sport business. The sport world can be a competitive place, with different leagues competing for fans. Cities such as New York City, San Francisco, and Chicago are home to sports teams for each major league sport, and some host more than one team in a major league. One can imagine that these franchises must offer competitive services and merchandise in order to

Whether styled as a concession stand (at the USTA Tennis Center during the US Open) or a full service store (the Ballpark Store at the Tokyo Dome home of the Yomiuri Giants) sport merchandizing within venues is a common point of customer service interaction.

attract and maintain their fan (and customer) base. Aside from strong sport markets and a team's success, Theodorakis, Koustelios, Robinson, and Barlas (2009) found that service quality, especially reliability and responsiveness of the employee, is an important factor in customer "repurchase intention" when fans do not have a high connection with the team. This means that when frontline employees are quick to respond and consistently helpful, fans are more likely to make purchases within that franchise (collectibles, t-shirts, hats, etc.).

Besides the sport venue's official team store, retail booths inside and outside facilities attract a wide variety of customers. The strategy is to use frontline employees to sell consumers merchandise they may not have thought to bring to the event. For example, knit headwear and scarves are sold at outdoor football games in the winter. Picture the weather and the consumer's need to be comfortable; many variables dictate what the vendor deliberately sells to the consumer. Anticipation of customer needs based upon weather and other somewhat predictable conditions or events can lead to greater sales and greater customer satisfaction during the event. Having an adequate stock of rain gear and ponchos for purchase during a game with precipitation could make or break a spectator's experience at the event. The employee's responsibility is to keep merchandise on the shelves before and during the events and to sell as much as possible (Muret, 2014). To expedite sales, retail booths will use kiosks and customized iPads to complete transactions as a "line busting" maneuver, to offset the time buyers spend in lines at the register.

Food & Beverage

The environment at sporting events is an important factor in game satisfaction, impacting customers' intentions to return to the venue in the future (Yoshida & James, 2010). One of the keys to a suitable environment that determines the satisfaction of customers is the availability and quality of food and beverages. The concessions available at sporting events have changed over the course of sport history (Greenwell et al., 2014). Mitch Smith, a reporter for the Chicago Tribune, wrote an article in honor of Wrigley Field's 100th anniversary. Considered the home of the original permanent concession stand, some of the original foods sold at the Chicago Cubs home stadium include Smokie Link hot dogs, slices of pie, peanuts, and popcorn. While the menu has varied greatly, it is still almost impossible to go to a sporting event that does not sell stadium hot dogs (Smith, 2014).

Though most stadiums still sell the classics today, sport venues have started offering premium level choices. These are more expensive than traditional sports concessions, but they embrace the local cuisine of the area. For example, at Toronto's BMO Field, one will find Triple Pork Poutine; their take on Canada's beloved poutine dish. Instead of the traditional fries, gravy, and cheese, this dish adds cheese curds, bacon, sausage, and pulled pork. At Wrigley Field, patrons who want some traditional Chicago cuisine can enjoy the ballpark's bison hot dogs and tater tots (Smith, 2014). Concession workers are required to maintain a clean and safe venue, sell food, beverage, and respond to spills and incidents. The different levels of sport require different services, so one must take this into consideration. At the recreation level, there may be less need to offer a wide-range of concessions. However, regardless of the level of play, many spectators will only continue attending sporting events if food is readily available.

Customer service for food and beverage service can be assessed in many ways. It may be assessed by variety in offerings based on the number and types of products and brands offered the patrons. It can also be assessed by measures of cost and the perception of value for the food and drinks that are purchased. The line length or wait time for service is another important consideration for concessions. In major sport venues, there have also been efforts to keep fans connected to the game or event while making concession purchases. This has been achieved through the widespread use of video monitors covering the game or through the creation of open concourses that have a view of the field/court from the point of sale for food and beverages. Club level seating typically provides a wait service for the spectators that will take personal orders and make delivery directly to the customer in their seats. Ease of payment would be another factor that could influence customer service satisfaction with food and beverage services in the sport setting. From cash-only to credit-only options to payment via credit/debit card, or via phone concessionaires should seek payment options that maximize efficiency, transaction security, and customer preference.

Food and beverage service is another core element of customer service within sport.

Conclusion

There is a need for employees in customer service to understand the fact that customer satisfaction extends from when the idea of attending an event comes to mind through the time they leave the venue (Taylor, 2008). When attendance at sports events is viewed as a means of building community and support for the teams, all individuals including those with disabilities must have an equal opportunity to have the same game day experience as non-disabled spectators. Ease of purchasing tickets, parking, and watching the event encourage fans to purchase concessions and merchandise to support their teams. Finally, from a facility manager's point of view, to understand customers' comments on each single service attribute may be more important than adopting an overarching comprehensive service plan. Focusing on concise and holistic needs of the spectator will increase customer satisfaction. This type of "customer focus" for frontline employees is fostered through effective training programs. When spectators feel safe and well accommodated, customer service has been successful and this helps sporting venues reach their business goals.

PRACTITIONER SPOTLIGHT

NAME: Clancy Holligan

ORGANIZATION: Los Angeles Angels of Anaheim Baseball Club

CURRENT JOB TITLE: Ticket Operations Representative
Year started in this role: 1996

Photo courtesy of Clancy Holligan.

EDUCATIONAL PREPARATION:

- **Undergraduate degree:** BS, in Marketing (University of Colorado)
- **Graduate degree:** M Ed in Sports Management (University of Georgia)

CAREER PATH:

- **Internship(s):** University of Colorado Athletic Department & Orange County, CA Sports Association
- **Entry level jobs:** Angels MLB (Baseball Club) team
- Job path both inside and outside sport (as applicable) leading to this current role:
  1. CU Athletic Department
  2. Orange County Sports Assoc.
  3. Angels Baseball Club

WHAT ARE YOUR PRIMARY RESPONSIBILITIES?

Supervising the ticket operations efforts of the Angels MLB baseball team form the major job responsibilities. My office provides services to event sponsors including coordinating and overseeing the mailing of Angels ticket information, the managing of money and tickets, and the preparing of audit statements. I also hire and train personnel in this area.

WHAT STEPS ARE TAKEN IN CUSTOMER SERVICE TRAINING SPECIFICALLY WITHIN THE AREA OF TICKET OPERATIONS FOR THE ANGELS?

Once hired, the new employee in our area undergoes three to four formal training sessions with long-term employees—people who have proven expertise in sports customer service. Typically the manager of the ticket office or the ticket supervisor oversees the initial stage of training. The second step is observation of the particular staff position for two to three games. Lastly, the new hire is asked if they are ready tostart doing it themselves with supervision. We believe this is the best way to learn—by doing it yourself.

HOW IS SERVICE QUALITY ASSESSED FOR THE ANGELS WITHIN YOUR WORK IN TICKET OPERATIONS?

With the Angels, we only assess the issues that come up either pre-game or during the game. Depending on the severity, we address them either immediately, at the end of the shift or the following day. We strive to embody a team oriented culture. If there are negative aspects to the quality of our product we speak about them respectfully during our staff meetings.

My job is to make sure the number of sold tickets equals the amount of money accrued for all sales. This includes game day, online, external company sales, freebies and promotions, groups, box seats, and season ticket sales. I do this for individual games through the season. If numbers do not balance to zero, I have done something wrong and go back through my spreadsheets until I find the errors. Having spent over 20 years with the Angels ticketing department, leadership expects a high standard of excellence.

WHAT IS THE MOST REWARDING ASPECT OF THIS JOB?

The ticketing representative/manager must work well under pressure and be committed to working in a team environment. Making a difference and giving customers a satisfying experience is the desired reward. When the team (Angels) has a good year, you feel like you did your share to help the organization achieve success.

WHAT IS THE MOST CHALLENGING ASPECT OF THIS JOB?

Three primary things create a big challenge: 1) When I am unable to solve a customer's problem. 2) When a situation arises that I've never seen before. 3) When the team has a bad year, the season can seem very long and can drag on and on. Another one of the most frustrating elements of being a ticket agent is the inability to control the weather as that has a tremendous impact upon turnout and sales for an outdoor venue.

Photo courtesy of Clancy Holligan.

Angel Stadium of Anaheim home venue for the Angels MLB franchise.

WHAT IS A UNIQUE ASPECT OR TASK OF YOUR JOB THAT MANY WOULD BE SURPRISED TO HEAR ABOUT?

Even though, I work for a professional baseball team, I spend most of my day in front of a computer like a lot of people.

WHAT ADVICE DO YOU HAVE FOR THOSE SEEKING A SIMILAR CAREER?

This type of position relies on experience and judgment to plan and accomplish goals. A person in this career path often performs a variety of tasks. This position may lead and direct the work of others. A wide degree of creativity and latitude is expected. Typically this position reports to a manager. A few other specifics are listed below.

WHAT DO YOU BELIEVE ARE THE MOST IMPORTANT SKILLS TO DEVELOP?

I have found that computer skills, financial skills, people skills, and the ability to "think on your feet" are the most critical in this type of job.

WHAT PARTING WORDS OF WISDOM DO YOU HAVE FOR STUDENTS AND YOUNG PROFESSIONALS IN THE FIELD?

Upcoming professionals should do internships, network, work hard, keep their eyes and ears open and your mouth shut. It is vital to be humble and available for whatever work is necessary.

Reprinted by permission of Clancy Holligan.

MINI CASE STUDY

The Importance of Good Customer Service: Case Study with the New York Mets

There is nothing more frustrating in life than facing a stubborn, careless, customer service department. If you work in customer service someday, keep in mind the following rules, they might save or even improve your image. We have all experienced this: automatic hotlines never leading to answers; customer service representatives placating us on the telephone; forcing us to pay extra money to complain; emails never answered; phone representatives transferring our calls to people who cannot help, or even worse disconnecting!

The Mets and the Inexistent Customer Service

Early June 1995, I purchased two tickets on the phone for a Mets vs Colorado Rockies home game on August 13th with my friend. We purchased the tickets way earlier and were ready to go to the game. The problem was that Major League Baseball went on strike the day before. I am a die-hard baseball fan and sided with the owners of Major League Baseball teams collectively proposing a salary cap to their players.

My tickets are changed for another home game that week. All good. We watch the TV report the strike will stop every day and keep the hope alive. The day we're supposed to go to our game the strike is nowhere near over. The next day, I call the ticketing office asking for a full refund. I prepare a polite, detailed, and well organized phone call to describe my exact situation to the Met's ticketing department customer service, convinced that I will get a quick and efficient refund. The phone number is busy multiple times over many hours.

Instead, a few days later, I send an email to the ticketing department. A few minutes later, I receive an auto-reply:

> *Dear Customer,*
>
> *Thank you for your email.*
>
> *We will contact you with an answer to your query as soon as possible. In the meantime, your patience is highly appreciated.*
>
> *Go Mets!*
>
> *Mets Ticket Sales Department*

Great! I will receive a quick answer.

A week later, I still have nothing. I continue to get a busy dial tone. I send another email, copying the original message and asking if my refund is still being handled. Same automatic answer.

Another week passes. I check the website and find that there are several "customer service" lines for ticket refunds. I decide to try calling. This time someone answers me! And the answer is clear and precise: please send us an email………………………………

I send a third email asking if I can expect receiving an answer someday.

> *Dear Mr. Diaz,*
>
> *Thanks for your email.*
>
> *As a refund case, please kindly contact or Ticketing Refund Center at email XXXXX.*
>
> *Thank you.*
>
> *Yours sincerely,*
>
> *The Mets Customer Service & Support Center*

Great, I am now redirected to another customer service center, still from the Mets. Could they not have redirected me in the first place? Anyway, I repeat the same procedure and re-send my email, emphasizing this is already the third one.

Not even an auto-reply.

I go back on the Met's leave a message comments page, and remind them it has been over 45 days since my original complaint and that I have received no feedback so far. I mention that I will take the team to small claims court for my refund and call a New York Times sports writer to share my story.

A few hours later, I receive the following email message:

> *Hi Mr. Diaz, I have contacted the Ticketing Department. A refund regarding your tickets has been made today, you will be contacted shortly.*

They called me finally, asked for my address and sent me a check for the price of the two tickets.

1. As a customer, what do you think of this situation?

2. If you have to hire someone for your customer service, how important is empathy?

3. What is the purpose of a customer service line if it cannot help solve problems?

4. What advice would you give to the Mets ticketing department? Why do you think they failed so miserably?

5. Why did threats from third parties help bolster this case?

REFERENCES

Aaker, D. A. (2012). *Building strong brands.* New York: NY: Simon and Schuster.

Aldlaigan, A., & Buttle, F. (2005). Beyond satisfaction: Customer attachment to retail banks. *International Journal of Bank Marketing, 23*(4), 349–359.

Anderson, E. W. & Salisbury, L. C. (2003) The formation of market-level expectations and its covariates. Journal of Consumer Research, 30 (June), 115–124.

Boshoff, C., & Allen, J. (2000). The influence of selected antecedents on frontline staff's perceptions of service recovery performance. *International Journal of Service Industry Management, 11*(1), 63–90.

Carlzon, J. (1987). *Moments of truth.* Cambridge, MA: Ballinger.

2015 Colloquy Census. (2016). U.S. Customer Loyalty Program Memberships. (Data file). Retrieved from https://www.colloquy.com/latest-news/2015-colloquy-loyalty-census/

Cronin, J. J., & Taylor, S. A. (1992). Measuring service quality: A re-examination and extension. *Journal of Marketing, 56*(3), 56–68.

Customer Service Facts. (2016). *CSM: The Magazine for Customer Service Managers and Professionals.* Retrieved from: http://www.customerservicemanager.com/customer-service-facts/

Day, G. S. (1994). The capabilities of market-driven organizations. *The Journal of Marketing,* 37–52.

Ellinger, A. E., Keller, S. B., & Bas, A. B. E. (2010). The empowerment of frontline service staff in 3PL companies. *Journal of Business Logistics, 31*(1), 79–98.

Frassinelli, M. (2009, March 8). Patriots owner makes sure team's fans always come first on 10th anniversary, ball club is still a hit. *Star-Ledger,* 27.

Gennaro, V. (2013). *Diamond dollars: The economics of winning in baseball.* Purchase, NY: Diamond Analytics.

Gillentine, A., Grady, J., Miller, J. J., & Pettus, K. (2016). Accessible tailgating: An examination of ADA requirements and implications associated with tailgating activities. *Journal of Legal Aspects of Sport, 26*(1), 52–65.

Grady, J., & Ohlin, J. B. (2004). The application of Title III of the ADA to sport websites. *Journal of Legal Aspects of Sport, 14,* 145.

Greenwell, T. C., Danzey-Bussell, L. A., & Shonk, D. J. (2014). *Managing sport events.* Champaign, IL: Human Kinetics.

Gruber, T., Abosaq, I., Reppel, A. E., & Szmigin, I. (2011). Analyzing the preferred characteristics of frontline employees dealing with customer complaints: A cross-national Kano study. *The TQM Journal, 23*(2), 128–144.

Guest Services. (n.d.). Welcome to AT&T Stadium. Retrieved from http://attstadium.com/guests/guestInfo.cfm

Hassan, D. & Lusted, J. (2012). *Managing sport: Social and cultural perspectives.* New York, NY: Routledge.

Hartline, M. D., & Ferrell, O. C. (1993). Service quality implementation: The effects of organizational socialization and managerial actions on customer-contact employee behaviors. *Report-marketing Science Institute, 93–122,* 1–59.

Hartline, M. D., & Ferrell, O. C. (1996). The management of customer-contact service employees: an empirical investigation. *The Journal of Marketing, 60*(4) 52–70.

Henao, A., & Marshall, W. E. (2013). Parking at sporting events stadiums in Denver, Colorado. *Transportation Research Record, 2359,* 17–26.

Herr, P. M., Kardes, F. R., & Kim, J. (1991) Effects of word-of-mouth and product attribute Information on persuasion: An accessibility diagnosticity perspective. *Journal of Consumer Research, 17,* 454–462.

Hocutt, M. A. (1998). Relationship dissolution model: Antecedents of relationship commitment and the likelihood of dissolving a relationship. *International Journal of Service Industry Management, 9*(2), 189–200.

Houston, M., Bettencourt, L., & Wenger, S. (1998). The relationship between waiting in a service queue and evaluations of service quality: A field theory perspective. *Psychology and Marketing, 15*(8), 735–753.

Jang, W., Ko, Y. J., & Stepchenkova, S. (2014). The effects of message appeal on consumer attitude toward sporting events. *International Journal of Sport Communication, 7*(3), 337–356.

Javalgi, R. R. G., & Moberg, C. R. (1997). Service loyalty: implications for service providers. *Journal of Service Marketing, 11*(3), 165–179.

Jiménez, M. A., Moreno, F. C., Núñez-Pomar, J. M., & Hervás, J. C. (2015). Brand perception and its relation to perceived performance of a public sports service. *Engaging Consumers through Branded Entertainment and Convergent Media,* 202–220.

Kelly, S. W., & Turley, L. W. (2001). Consumer perceptions of service quality attributes at sporting events. *Journal of Business Research*, *54*(2), 161–166.

Kil Kim, M., Kim, S. K., Lee, D., Judge, L. W., & Huang, H. (2013). Service quality and satisfaction perspectives at the 2011 International Amateur Athletic Federation (IAFF) World Championships. *Journal of Research in Health, Physical Education, Recreation, Sport, & Dance*, *8*(2), 39–44.

Kusnick, J. (2014, February 11) An agent's take: Three ways to work in baseball. *Baseball Prospectus*. Retrieved from http://www.baseballprospectus.com/article.php?articleid=22791

Kwak, D. H., Kim, Y. K., & Hirt, E. R. (2011). Exploring the role of emotions on sport consumers' behavioral and cognitive responses to marketing stimuli. *European Sport Management Quarterly*, *11*(3), 225–250.

Landsberg, M. (2015). *The tao of coaching: Boost your effectiveness at work by inspiring and developing those around you*. London, England: Profile Books.

Lovelock, C., & Wright, R. (2002). *Principles of service marketing and management*. 2nd ed. Upper Saddle River, NJ: Pearson Education.

Lower, L., & Petersen, J. (2010). Stadium accommodations and jumbotrons. *Journal of Physical Education, Recreation & Dance*, *81*(6), 47–48, 52

Matsuno, K., Mentzer, J. T., & Özsomer, A. (2002). The effects of entrepreneurial proclivity and market orientation on business performance. *Journal of Marketing*, *66*(3), 18–32.

McMillen, J. (2011). Health, wellness, and society: Ambulatory solutions for elderly and aging adults at public venues in the United States. *International Journal of Health, Wellness & Society*, *1*(1), 59–67.

Murphy, J., Forrest, E. J., Wotrig, C. E., & Brymer, R. A. (1996). Hotel management and marketing on the Internet: An analysis of sites and features. *Cornell Hotel and Restaurant Administration Quarterly*, *37*(3), 70–82.

Muret, D. (2014, January, 20). Merchandise record in NFL's sights. *Sports Business Daily*, 3.

Neyr, P., & Gopinath, M. (2005) Effects of complaining versus negative word of mouth on subsequent changes in satisfaction: The role of public commitment. *Psychology and Marketing*, *22*(2), 937–953.

Oliver, R. L. (1997). *Satisfaction: A behavioral perspective on the consumer*. New York: McGraw-Hill.

Oliver, R. L. (1999). Whence consumer loyalty? *Journal of Marketing*, *63*(Special issue), 33–44.

Olson, J. R., & Boyer, K. K. (2005). Internet ticketing in a not-for-profit, service organization: building customer loyalty. *International Journal of Operations & Production Management*, *25*(1), 74–92.

Palmatier, R. W., Dant, R. P., Grewal, D., & Evans, K. R. (2006). Factors influencing the effectiveness of relationship marketing: A meta analysis. *Journal of Marketing*, *70*(3), 136–153.

Peccei, R., & Rosenthal, P. (2001). Delivering customer-oriented behaviour through empowerment: An empirical test of HRM assumptions. *Journal of Management Studies, 38*(6), 831–857.

Pressey, A., & Mathews, B. (2003). Jumped, pushed or forgotten? Approaches to dissolution. *Journal of Marketing Management, 19*, 131–155.

Reel, E. (2009). Beyond customer satisfaction: The competitive advantage and financial benefit in building a loyal customer base. *Business Synergistics International*, Retrieved from http://www.infoquestcrm.co.uk/Beyond_Customer_Satisfaction.pdf

Rice, G. (2003). The challenge of creativity and culture: A framework for analysis with application to Arabian Gulf firms. *International Business Review, 12*(4), 461–477.

Richins, M. (1983) Negative word-of-mouth by dissatisfied consumers: A pilot study. *Journal of Marketing, 47*(1) 68–78.

Rovell, D. (2010, June 14). Publication: MLB will beat NFL in licensing revenue in '10. Retrieved from http://www.cnbc.com/id/37692194/Publication_MLB_Will_Beat_NFL_In_Licensing_Revenue_In_10

Skulski, J., Bloomer, R., & Chait, J. (2002). Accommodating patrons with disabilities: A survey of ticket and accommodation policies for performance venues, theaters and sports arenas. National Center on Accessibility. Retrieved from https://scholarworks.iu.edu/dspace/bitstream/handle/2022/3106/Ticket_Policy_Study_Executive_Summary. pdf?sequence=1

Smith, J. C. (n.d.). Web accessibility. Boston University Libraries. Retrieved from http://www.bu.edu.proxy.bsu.edu/library/instruction/access2.html

Smith, M. (2014, April 8). Where concessions first stood: Stadium dining now a walk-up art form everywhere, but field-to-be Wrigley was first to move vendors out of the aisles. *Chicago Tribune*. Retrieved from http://articles.chicagotribune.com/2014-04-08/sports/ct-wrigley-century-food-met-20140408_1_wrigley-field-beer-and-baseball-concession-stand

Stum, D. L., & Thiry, A. (1991). Building customer loyalty. *Training and Development Journal, 45*(4), 34–36.

Susskind, A. M., Kacmar, K. M., & Borchgrevink, C. P. (2003). Customer service providers' attitudes relating to customer service and customer satisfaction in the customer-server exchange. *Journal of Applied Psychology, 88*(1), 179–187. doi:10.1037/0021-9010.88.1.179

Taylor, N. (2008). *Matchday Travel Own Goal?* Transport Planning Society Bursary.

Theodorakis, N. D., Koustelios, A., Robinson, L., & Barlas, A. (2009). Moderating role of team identification on the relationship between service quality and repurchase intentions among spectators of professional sports. *Managing Service Quality: An International Journal, 19*(4), 456–473.

Wright, P. (1974) The harassed decision maker: Time pressures, distractions, and the use of evidence. *Journal of Applied Psychology, 59*, 555–561.

Yoshida, M., & James, J. D. (2010). Customer satisfaction with game and service experiences: Antecedents and consequences. *Journal of Sport Management, 24*, 338–361.

11

Alcohol Management

John J. Miller and *Lynsey A. Madison*

OBJECTIVES

After studying this chapter, the student should be able to:

- Understand how to conduct beverage sales forecasting.
- Comprehend the revenue issues of alcohol management.
- Explain the association of drinking alcohol and attending athletic games.
- Provide some reasons why tailgating is popular at athletic games.
- Explain why and how alcohol risk management strategies must be employed at sports contests.

KEY TERMS

Binge Drinking

Blood Alcohol Content

Business Invitee

Duty of Care

Foreseeability

Heavy Drinking

Licensee

Premises Liability

Public Invitee

Tailgating

Trespasser

KEY ACRONYMS

BAC Blood Alcohol Content

FIFO system First In, First Out

POS Point of Sales

RM Risk Management

TEAM Techniques for Effective Alcohol Management

TIPS Training for Intervention Procedures

©aceshot1/Shutterstock.com

Alcohol sales within stadiums and arenas for professional sport are commonplace.

Introduction

A sporting event is a social happening, of which the contest itself is only a part. Hocking (1982) referred to differences between the game event, related to action on the field, and the stadium event, which includes the contest and everything else occurring within the facility's boundaries. Alcohol has been linked with sporting events for many years (Gillentine, Miller, & Calhoun, 2008; Nelson & Wechlser, 2003). The decision to sell alcoholic beverages in sports venues requires a venue or event manager to understand a multitude of factors from purchasing and receiving, to serving and forecasting, to managing the risks that involves alcoholic consumption by patrons. Many of the issues of alcohol management concern the operational processes for ordering, storing, serving the product while another range of issues relate to the behavior and risk management issues regarding the duty to providing a safe environment while alcohol is present. Understanding the factors that could potentially impact beverage management provides an avenue for a more successful operation of alcohol sales within sport venues.

Forecasting Beverage Sales

What exactly is forecasting and why is it important? Operating managers need to be able to think both short term and long term in operating their facility. How many guests will be served in a day, week, month, or even year? The ability to understand how many guests will be served answers questions from ranging from expected revenue to purchasing to staffing. Sales forecasting is the prediction of the number of guests that will be served during some predetermined period and the amount of revenue that will be generated from those guests. In managing beverage operations, it is important to keep a distinction between sales (revenue) and sales volume (the number of units sold). An operations manager who understands anticipated sales from revenue and guest counts can maximize revenue potential while minimizing unnecessary costs.

Forecasting beverage sales depends largely on the type of beverage sold such as beer, wine, or spirits. For this chapter, the focus will be on beer as the most commonly consumed alcoholic beverage in sport venues and events. Forecasting beverage sales looks to answer several questions from what kind of beer will guests choose to when sales volumes will increase. By tracking the data from the point of sale, the event and facility manager will know how much of each beer is sold and connect it to the event going on. For example, if a venue hosts a variety of events that ranges in scale and scope, the beverage sales will not create a detailed average because larger events will raise the average, which will result with more product on hand. However, if the data is analyzed from events, which are similar in size and scope with the upcoming event, a better forecast estimate is presented.

Forecasting Using Size and Scope Example

As an example, consider Carter's Coliseum that holds a variety of events from sporting events to concerts. When determining which events to book, one factor considered is the revenue each one will generate. Percentage variance and separated sales histories allow for revenue forecasting related to alcohol sales for these events.

Table 11.1 *Alcohol Sales Forecasting based upon Event Size for Carter's Coliseum*

Event Size	Sales Per Event Last Year	% Increase Estimate	Increase Amount	Revenue Forecast Per Event
>10,000	$42,500	5%	$2,125.00	$44,625.00
10,001–25,000	$57,000	5%	$2,850.00	$59,850.00
25,001–50,000	$84,000	5%	$4,200.00	$88,200.00
<50,001	$108,500	5%	$5,425.00	$113,925.00

Sales Forecasting

Sales forecasting requires understanding sales history. There are numerous methods for tracking an operation's sales from manual to automatic. Computerized sales systems, point of sales (POS) system provides accurate and timely reports with specific sales information. Sales history can be recorded based on total revenue or total volume, deciding between volume and revenue will vary from operation to operation. The least complex method of sales history is based on revenue; however, sales history in terms of revenue is not always a viable option. Regardless of the sales history option selected, it is critical to maintaining accurate and detailed records to assist in successfully forecasting future sales.

Types of Sales Averages

Operation's managers should be familiar with two major types of sales averages: fixed average and rolling average. Fixed average looks at a specific or fixed time period and calculates the average from that time frame. Again, that average may be in revenue or volume. Rolling average looks over a changing time period. So for example, using a fixed average may look at the first 10 days of the month. The average sales from those days will always come from the first through the tenth day of the month. However, using a rolling average looks at a 10-day period that moves forward a day, changing which days are being calculated. The rolling average is innately more complex and time-consuming but the tradeoff is the ability to make more accurate predictions based on more current information. Deciding on whether to use fixed or rolling averages is not an either/or decision; both averages may be used in conjunction to make management decisions.

Sales History

Sales history consists of basic information such as revenue or volume, however, more detailed sales history is required to fully develop effective forecasting. When analyzing beverage sales, and subsequently beverage forecasting, knowing the frequency of the alcoholic beverages sold may improve the overall forecasting. Detailed sales information should be updated after each event held in the venue. Sales history should be kept for a minimum of two years. If the venue is just adding beverage sales, it is even more vital that a sales history is built and maintained to provide support for future decisions. Also included in a sales history may be sales variance. Sales variance looks at the changes over time and shows if sales are increasing, decreasing, or plateauing. Calculating sales variance looks at the difference between current sales (over a specified period) and last year's sales. To be more effective, percentage variance can be calculated to assist in forecasting future sales.

Calculating Percentage Variance

In operating concessions, particularly concessions with alcoholic beverages, being able to accurately ascertain future sales supports a profitable operation. The percentage variance is used in predicting future sales. Depending on the objectives for offering beverages in the venue, management may decide whether forecasting is based on sales or volume. The percentage variance can be applied for either calculation; the method is the same.

Table 11.2 *South Hampton Arena sales history for the first-quarter (Variance ÷ Sales Last Year = Percentage Variance)*

Month	Sales this Year	Sales Last Year	Variance	Percentage Variance
January	$35,000	$34,000	$1,000	2.94%
February	$27,500	$25,000	$2,500	10.00%
March	$36,000	$31,000	$5,000	16.12%
First-Quarter Total	$98,500	$90,000	$8,500	9.44%

Forecasting Using Percentage Variance Example

South Hampton Arena knows their first-quarter sales but wants to forecast what their second-quarter sales will be. The percentage variance during that quarter ranged from 2.94% in January to 16.12% in March. The manager at South Hampton Arena decides to use the first-quarter percentage variance of 9.44%, as it is neither too conservative nor aggressive.

Table 11.3 *South Hampton Arena Sales Forecast using Percentage Variance*

Month	Sales Last Year	% Increase Estimate	Increase Amount	Revenue Forecast
April	$42,500	9.44%	$4,012.00	$46,512
May	$28,000	9.44%	$2,643.20	$54,643.20
June	$44,000	9.44%	$4,153.60	$48,153.60
Second-Quarter Total	$114,500	9.44%	$10,808.80	$125,308.80

Sales Mix

Sales mix looks at the products that are available for purchase. Numerous factors go into determining the sales mix. Using the beverage sales' forecast to determine what products should be offered is one resource. Product availability, cost, and shelf life (how long a product may be used before it expires) must also be taken into consideration when determining which beverages to offer. For example, beer has a significantly shorter shelf life than other beverages, often with an expiration date of only a few months. In order for beverage sales to be profitable, it is imperative that both the forecasting and ordering are as accurate as possible.

To optimize the shelf life and the sale of beer, brand, and packaging have to be considered. On average, operations serving beer offer three to ten choices. The primary factor determining the beer options for concessions will depend on geographic location, clientele, and menu. The geographic location provides several different options on which types of beer to provide to customers. For example, customers in Colorado may have different flavor profiles and preferences than customers in Mississippi.

In locations with greater per capita craft brewers, there is an opportunity to create partnership opportunities within the community as well as providing products that the customers are going to enjoy. The clientele at the venue will also impact product selection as the venues and events at venues will have customers with different preferences. As concession menus become more sophisticated and extensive, the beverage options are following suit. However, the beverages have to match the menu on both scale and price point. The last thing a venue operator wants is to have product going to waste on the shelf because the wrong beverages were selected and they are not being sold.

Along with the product mix, is the packaging is important. Beer typically comes in kegs, bottles, or cans. It is important to recognize that there are advantages and disadvantages to each packaging option. Customers typically have a preference for draft (keg) beer. The advantage to the operator is a lower cost per glass, which in turn means a greater profit margin. However, the disadvantage is that kegs require additional equipment and serving technique.

Keg beer also has the shortest shelf life ranging from 30 to 45 days for a keg that has not been opened (or tapped). Once a keg has been tapped, the shelf life drops to 14 to 21 days depending on the CO_2 pressure and equalization. Additionally, kegs are heavy to move and change when they run out. Draft beer is also the most prone to theft and waste by employees, which can reduce the profit margin. Unlike kegs, cans and bottles can be stored in dry storage, which saves on storage costs. However, they require time to be chilled before serving and take additional space in the concession stand. The decision has to be made whether cans/bottles will be served in a cup or left in their container. Offering cans/bottles increases the number of options available but the profit margin is smaller than draft beer.

Managing Beverage Cost Percentage

The profit margin on beverage sales can increase or decrease based on employee inefficiency, waste (products going out of date or employee waste), or theft. The requirements placed on alcoholic beverage sales often place strict policies that food sales do not have. For example, operations serving alcoholic beverages are subject to tax audits (these may or may not be announced), can be shut down for alcohol law violations, have their alcohol license suspended, and detection of small amounts of theft are difficult to track as they occur but become evident over extended periods of time. Beverage cost percentage is found by dividing the cost of beverages sold by the total beverage sales (Cost of beverages sold ÷ Total beverage sales = Beverage cost percentage).

Beverage cost percentage will vary depending on the type of packaging selected for the operation. Industry averages for bottled beer is 23%–25% while draft beer runs around 20%–22%. While tracking beverage cost percentage is a quick and efficient method for monitoring beverage costs, it is important to understand what the operation's optimal cost percentage is instead of solely relying on the industry averages. Finding optimal cost percentages are determined by examining selling prices, sales mix, and purchasing costs. When determining potential draft beer cost percentages, the sales mix of each draft beer serving size needs to be included in the calculation. Determining bottled beer cost percentage is simply the bottle's cost by its selling price. For example, if Miller Light costs an operating $.75 and is sold for $4.00 a bottle, then the potential cost percentage is 18.75 (.75/4). By comparing their actual cost percentage to their optimal cost percentage, managers and operators are better able to identify flaws and overruns.

A key point of identifying beverage cost percentage is to compare costs to revenue. So if an operation has a beverage cost percentage at 25%, then their gross profit would be 75%. Decrease that cost percentage to 20% and gross profit increases to 80%. Beverage cost percentage helps determine both the selling price and the ideal purchasing price from a vendor. It also helps identify waste and theft via assessment of increases in the beverage cost percentage that could indicate a problem.

Purchasing Beverage Products

Deciding which beverages to purchase utilizes a variety of factors: sales mix, desired beverage cost percentage, vendors, and customer preferences. Beverages offered typically range in quality level in order to satisfy the most customers. The more options offered, both in packaging and brand, the more selection customers will have. However, tracking and monitoring become harder and the potential for theft and waste increases.

An operation may opt to have a combination of draft beer and bottled beer. When selecting this option, draft beer is typically the beer sold most frequently and with the lowest selling price. This is where understanding

© Ffooter/Shutterstock.com

Beverage sponsors and advertisers can impact product and brand offerings at many sport venues.

beverage forecasting comes into play, as you will need to know sales volume and frequency to determine which beer to offer in draft form. The bottled beer options are typically your higher priced drinks and may be less popular. If the operation has partnered with a local brewing company, bottled beer is a great option for packaging choices as the shelf life is longer and there may not yet be an established forecast history.

Vendor selection will vary in each market. However, it is important to shop around and/or negotiate the cost of goods being purchased. Depending on the volume of business and the frequency of deliveries, the price for certain goods can be negotiated. Agreeing to a shorter accounts payable period (when payment is expected) is also a good negotiating tool. Verify the reputation of the vendor for quality and service with their other customers. A vendor has the potential to interfere with the success of the operation so it is important that vendor selection is taken with great care and not chosen haphazardly. Within sport venues, sponsorship agreements with various beverage brands by the team or league can also influence the choice of vendors and products.

In established operations with a history of beverage sales, identifying customer preferences may be easier by utilizing the sales' history. However, if sales' histories are not available, the best starting point to identifying the products that customers want the most is to ask for feedback or suggestions. In today's social media rich climate, that is getting easier and easier to do. During games or events, customers can be invited to text or hashtag their preferences. For example, during a timeout at a basketball game attendants can be shown three beverage options on the video board and told to tweet or post on Instagram their preference. The fan can then connect to the venue on the selected social media site and comment #BaldwinArenaBudLight. An operation may also just elect to start with the basics such as Budweiser, Bud Light, and Michelob Ultra and expand from there.

In purchasing beverage products, it is important to have a dedicated buyer. This person is responsible for placing the order with the vendor. This limits wasted product as well as limiting the opportunity for theft. An operation should have a checks-and-balances system in place to control theft and ensure inventory balance (this will be discussed further in receiving and storing beverages). Once the order has been placed, a copy of the purchase order request should be provided to the person receiving to ensure that extra product from the vendor is not being delivered and subsequently billed to the operation.

Bottles, Cans, or Cups: Making the Best Choice of Beer Service Containers

Determining which container to serve beer in will depend on several factors. If an operation elects to use draft beer, then a cup is clearly the only option. Draft beer provides a higher profit margin as it has a lower cost percentage but the decreased shelf life and potential for theft are factors that need to be considered. While bottled and canned beer have a higher cost percentage, the extended shelf life of the product reduces product waste and is more forgiving in forecasting.

If an operation elects to offer bottled and/or canned beer, either in conjunction with draft beer or as the sole product offering, it must consider whether it is going to pour the product into a cup or leave it in the original container. Service speed will be slower if an operation decides to pour the product. However, costs will increase as the cost of the cup now has to be factored into the already higher price of bottled/canned beer. Not only does the cost of the cup increase the price, sales per hour decrease with the slower service time or labor costs increase with extra personnel to maintain the sales per hour rate.

An operation must also decide what to do with the containers regardless of whether they pour them into cups before serving or serve them in their original container. Recycling aluminum cans is fairly common in most cities; however, glass is not always recycled in smaller locales. Understanding what the local recycling options are prior to making a purchasing decision is important. Sustainability and being environmentally conscious can be used as a marketing tool and building good will in the community. Recycling can also be an additional revenue stream where returning cans provides a refund or they can be sold.

Receiving and Storing Beverage Products

When selecting a vendor, one topic that needs to be discussed is a delivery schedule. The schedule should be set so that delivery does not interfere with the venue's operations business. These set times are called acceptance hours. Certain operations will refuse delivery (refusal hours) between peak hours or scheduled event times to avoid congestion and improper handling of the products. However, depending on the vendor, selection of delivery times may not be possible. The further a location is from the vendor's warehouse, the more difficult it may be to establish a delivery time. Keep in mind, most operations are asking for the same time frame and not all vendors will have the manpower, equipment, etc. to meet those demands.

Depending on the size of the operation, staff responsible for receiving the products needs to be scheduled. The person receiving should be someone other than the person who ordered the product. This ensures that the person ordering is not ordering unnecessary product to either take home for personal reasons or to re-sell and keep the profit. When the delivery comes in, the receiving employee should have a copy of the purchase order request with both the quantity and price. This should be checked against the delivery invoice to check for discrepancies. The receiving employee should not sign the delivery invoice if there is a discrepancy between the original order or if all of the product that is billed on the delivery invoice is not delivered then. Once the order is completely checked in and accounted for, the delivery invoice should be sent to the individual or department responsible for accounts payable. Having a third person or department pay for the invoice is the last part of the checks-and-balances system that should be in place to deter fraud and theft by employees.

The location for receiving should be established prior to delivery. This location needs to be of adequate size to accommodate the delivery and should be kept clear of trash and other obstacles that can impede the delivery. In order to reduce theft, by either the receiving employee or the delivery personnel, the area should be monitored and well lit. Ideally, the storage location is close to the receiving area. If that is not possible, proper equipment should be provided such as carts or hand trucks.

When storing products, it is important to have an established method of product rotation. The shorter shelf life for beer requires ensuring a system is in place so that product does not outdate on the shelf. The FIFO system stands for first in, first out. This means that the product that has been on the shelf the longest is used first. The person responsible for putting the product away will put the new deliveries behind the product that is already on the shelf. This ensures that the oldest product is always closest to the front of the shelves.

For beverages, there are two major storage areas: dry storage and refrigerated storage. Regardless of the storage type, these rooms should be well secured based on the expense and the propensity for theft. Access to these locked storage areas should be limited. These storage areas should be clean, dust-free, and have adequate shelving.

Dry storage for beer should be kept in a cool, dark room between 50° to 70° F. Dry storage for beer is used only for pasteurized canned or bottled beer. Canned beer should remain in the case to limit the amount of dust, dirt, and foreign objects that come into contact with the tops of the cans. Before canned or bottled beer is brought to coolers or iced down, they should be rinsed off to eliminate any debris.

Refrigerated storage is used for keg beer. The temperature in the refrigerated storage should be between 36° and 38° F. Because kegs are unpasteurized, they cannot be used after they have been in the danger zone (40°–140° F) for extended lengths of time as bacteria can start to grow. Therefore it is imperative that they are properly stored immediately upon being received.

Outsourcing of Alcohol Sales at Sports Events

Intercollegiate athletic departments at all levels continue to face financial challenges. When confronted by decreasing budgets and increasing costs, athletic programs usually consider additional sources of revenue. One of these potential sources is the sale of alcoholic beverages on game days, especially if those sales include patrons in general admission, as these individuals comprise the majority of game attendees (Huang & Dixon, 2013). Currently, about 20 colleges nationwide serve alcohol to the general public, and more universities are considering the option (Briggs, 2011). Although the impact of these sales remains largely unmeasured, they could comprise a significant source of revenue to help balance precarious athletic budgets.

A primary method of providing alcohol sales at sports contests is through outsourcing. Outsourcing is a term that is generally employed to address a number of relationships. Specifically, outsourcing is the transfer of liability to another party of a service or function that would have been otherwise handled by the in-house staff. The primary reason for outsourcing is that an organization that specializes in the service or function can offer a higher

A portion of the food court at Madison Square Garden in New York.

Heineken Red Star Café located at the Billie Jean King Tennis Center during the 2014 US Open demonstrates the corporate connection with branding and hospitality at major sport venues.

standard as well as being more cost-effective than might be provided internally. Additionally, outsourcing provides flexibility (often clients want the ability to increase, reduce or alter the scope of a service, at relatively short notice) as well as a decrease in the amount of time and resources spent on non-core activities (Jones, 2009).

When outsourcing concessions operations, several benefits may be realized. One of these benefits is the ability to reorganize the resources of the athletic department to supervise and concentrate on other components of the game event management. A second benefit is the potential reduction the liability of the primary organization in case a patron is injured as a result of alcohol consumption by another patron. However, outsourcing should never be considered a simple delegation of management or strategic responsibility. While operational risk is passed to the outsourced party, strategic risk is not. Thus,

© Leonard Zhukovsky/Shutterstock.com

Moet and Chandon champagne as the official champagne of the US Open.

outsourcing a service or function does not diminish the liability of the primary organization to its patrons.

In many states, the organization promoting or conducting an athletic event such as a duty to use reasonable care for the safety and protection of their business patrons and to employ such care that prudently reasonable individual would use in the same position under similar circumstances (*Pierce v. Murnick,* 1965). The Restatement (Second) of Torts (The American Law Institute, 1965, §342) acknowledged the general duty owed by landowners to their business invitees is to offer reasonable protection from foreseeable criminal assaults. Furthermore, the courts have established that a business invitee is owed the duty to use reasonable care in keeping up the property in a reasonably safe condition as well as the duty to warn of dangers of which the owner has or should have known (*Wolford v. Ostenbridge,* 2003).

In summary, thousands of fans attend intercollegiate football games in the fall on a weekly basis. In addition to viewing the action on the field, attending these games provides an opportunity for these fans to take part in drinking alcohol, sometimes to excess. Although most fans participating in tailgating activities do not act in an unruly fashion, there are potential legal implications for sports event directors. Because they may be liable for the injurious actions of patrons and to guard against legal consequences, sports event directors must be cognizant of their duties for patron safety as they apply to any sports venue. An understanding of the duties required by the law as land possessors to create and maintain a reasonably safe environment and to protect their patrons from the criminal acts of third-parties is crucial. Specifically, sports event directors would be better able to foresee potentially harmful situations and take appropriate measures to manage these risks. This information may aid sport event managers in understanding the importance of the development and implementation of a risk management plan.

Managing Alcohol Consumption Risks

Historically alcohol-related problems have also been shown to be connected with these sporting events (Crawford et al., 2001; Lenk, Toomey, & Erickson, 2009; Vingilis, Liban, Blefgen, Colbourne, & Reynolds, 1992). Thus, one of the major challenges of operating events and venues is that of managing attendee/patron alcohol use (Harris, Edwards, & Homel, 2014). Alcohol consumption has also been identified as a trigger to uninhibited and aroused behavior (Hoaken & Stewart, 2003; Mark, Bryant, & Lehman, 1983). A lowering of inhibitions due to excessive alcohol consumption undoubtedly led to some of the unusual behavior.

Compounding the issue of decreased inhibitions has been the shift of crowd demographics as more women, children, and families are attending sporting events (Madensen & Eck, 2008). Aggressive behavior is more likely if members of the crowd are inebriated (Moore, Flajšlik, Rosin, & Marshall, 2008). As a result, the crowd size increase, the number of intoxicated individuals increase, thereby increasing the levels of crowd violence to the point that attendees are unnecessarily exposed to harm (Moore et al., 2008). According to James Mosher, an expert on alcohol liability, "it's almost a truism that if there's violence at an event, there's usually alcohol involved. If you don't serve it responsibly, you're scaring away some of your best customers" (as cited in Dvorchak, 2005, p. 9).

The amount of alcohol consumed by spectators prior to and during the event is of significant concern regarding alcohol management at sporting events. While the majority of individuals who drink alcohol at sporting events are of drinking age (21), a segment of concern for the sport event manager is the college student who attends intercollegiate athletic contests. In many cases, these young people are too young to legally attend a public tailgate party. As a result, they may drink at private parties in their homes or dorms as a precursor to going out during or after the game. Borsari, Boyle, Hustad, Barnett, Tevyaw, and Kahler (2007) refer these events as "drinking before drinking."

Tailgating at Sporting Events

Tailgating has evolved from a simple gathering of people prior to an event to an international phenomenon in recent years as event administrators of a variety of indoor and outdoor events have embraced and adapted this ritual to fit their specific needs and desires (Anderson, 1997; Cahn, 2003; Duncan, 2004; James, Breezeel, & Ross, 2001; Pedersen & LaBrie, 2007; Read, Merrill, & Bytschkow, 2010; Shivers, 2010). The first occurrence of tailgating at an athletic event anecdotally occurred on November 6, 1869, at the initial intercollegiate football game between Princeton and Rutgers. By many accounts, fans traveled by horse and carriage to attend the contest. Upon their arrival, they were both hungry and thirsty and unpacked the baskets of food and drink they brought with them to the game (Cartwright, 2005). However, Yale University also lays claim to having the first "tailgate" at an intercollegiate athletic contest during the 1904 season. Because there were no opportunities for fans to purchase food and beverages at the contests, fans began to bring their own for the rest of the season (Tailgating America, n.d).

Tailgating a social event held on and around the open tailgate of a vehicle that often involves consuming alcoholic beverages and grilling food.

© Ruth Peterkin/Shutterstock.com

Tailgating fans near outside Doak Campbell Stadium at Florida State University.

Despite the uncertainty regarding the origin of the practice or the term tailgating, what is certain is that tailgating has expanded and evolved over time. Today, fans socializing before sporting and entertainment events has transformed to such an extent that it has been asserted that "...tailgating has become one of the most influential phenomena in today's sport industry" (Miller & Gillentine, 2006, p.1). Through a variety of promotions, event organizers encourage fans to participate in tailgating activities both before and after events. Increasingly, event organizers view tailgating as a highly attractive promotion that can be staged with little or no additional cost to the organization (Hart, 1984). Most often, tailgating is perceived as a safe and enjoyable way for fans to receive an added value of attending a live event (Dent, Pepper, Fields, & Mastorakos, 2004).

Motives to Drink at Sporting Events

Initial research investigating the tailgating phenomena focused primarily on the motives for participation and consumption patterns (Gillentine, 2003; James et al., 2001; Kahle, Kambara, & Rose, 1996; Trail, Anderson, & Fink, 2000). Research findings suggest that a desire for social interaction, togetherness, excitement, and escape serve as fan motives for participating in tailgating events (Gillentine, 2003; James, et al., 2001). James, et al. (2001) suggested that people began tailgating for one reason (i.e., social interaction), and continued tailgating for varied reasons. Identified reasons were spending time with friends (social interaction), (2) consuming food and beverages, (3) the overall atmosphere of tailgating events, and (4) having fun. Gillentine (2003) reported that more than half of the respondents tailgated with more than 10 other fans, further emphasizing the social aspect of tailgating.

Alcohol consumption was also found to be a central aspect in tailgating (Miller & Gillentine, 2006). Additionally, many individuals began their tailgating activities four-to-five hours before the game and continued to tailgate well after the contest (Miller & Gillentine, 2006). Moreover, more than 10% of tailgaters actually missed the event preferring instead to continue tailgating (Gillentine, 2003).

Notwithstanding the perceived carefree nature of tailgating, incidents involving fan behavior during pre and post-event tailgating activities have resulted in injuries and litigation. While most of the reported incidents have involved relatively minor offenses, there have been reports of serious damages to personal and/or public property, drunk and disorderly conduct, unlawful assembly, and even fatalities related to tailgating (Gillentine & Miller, 2006; Mason & Calloway, 2004). For example, in 2004 a North Carolina State University student and his brother were charged with the shooting deaths of two men at a tailgating party. One of the defendants was convicted of first- and second-degree murder and was sentenced to life in prison without parole ("Lawsuits over fatal tailgate," 2008). The other defendant received a 12-year sentence after pleading to lesser felonies. The families of the deceased filed a lawsuit against the company that managed the parking lot where the shootings occurred. A settlement between the families and the company was reached in 2008 ("Lawsuits over fatal tailgate," 2008).

Spectator Drinking at Sporting Events

Many spectators consume excessive levels of alcohol at events, and most of the problems at the events are associated with such overindulgence. Many people are surprised to learn what counts as a drink. In the United States, a "standard" drink is any drink that contains about 0.6 fluid ounces or 14 grams of "pure" alcohol (National Institute on Alcohol Abuse and Alcoholism, n.d.). The percent of "pure" alcohol, expressed as alcohol by volume (alc/vol), varies by beverage. The type of drinks pictured in Table 11.4 are typically available at sports events. However, as the amount of fluid in the container decreases, the percent of alcohol in each increases.

Fans engaged in pre-event drinking as a common occurrence in sport.

Table 11.4   *Alcohol Type, Size, and Percent*

© RealVector/Shutterstock.com	© Valentyn Volkov/Shutterstock. com	© Somchai Som/Shutterstock. com	© gredei/Shutterstock.com
12 oz. beer about 5% alcohol	8–9 oz. malt liqour about 7% alcohol	5 oz. table wine about 12% alcohol	1.5 fl, oz, shot of 80 proof 40% alcohol

Source: National Institute on Alcohol Abuse and Alcoholism, n.d.

Erickson, Toomey, Lenk, Kilian, and Fabian (2011) conducted a study to determine the levels of spectators who were leaving professional sporting events. The results indicated that 40% of the participants had a positive *blood alcoholic content (BAC)*, ranging from 0.005 to 0.217. Individuals who had tailgated prior to the event were 14 times more likely to have a BAC greater than 0.08 (the legal limit in all states). The study also revealed that individuals under the age of 35 were eight times more likely to show a BAC of .08. Finally, spectators attending Monday night football games were found to have three times greater likelihood of having a positive BAC as compared to spectators who attended all of the other NFL games. The last finding supports former

Blood Alcohol Content the amount of alcohol contained in a person's blood.

New York Jets president Steve Gutman assertion that alcohol is entwined into the foundation of the Monday Night Football (Levy, 1989).

Research has also reported that drinking to the point of intoxication or "drinking to get drunk" is the accepted norm for people of all ages and many adult drinkers do not see drinking to intoxication as a problem (De Bonnaire, Kalafatelis, & McMillan, 2004). Negative consequences that are often reported by tailgaters at sporting events include injury, altercations, drinking and driving, and sexual abuse or exploitation (Glassman, Dodd, Sheu, Rienzo, & Wagenaar, 2010). Vingilis et al. (1992) revealed that a higher proportion of alcohol-related traffic crashes occurred following games at a professional sports stadium compared with pregame periods and compared with the same time period on non-game days.

The availability of alcohol allows fans to become intoxicated before they even enter the facility. To that end, several other studies have indicated that "veterans" of tailgating parties often begin drinking as early as breakfast to "get ready" for the big game in university/college property designated for tailgating (Gillentine, 2003, Gillentine & Miller, 2006, Jackson, Polite, & Barber, 2003). Additionally, spectators who attend professional sporting events are more likely to find alcohol being sold within the confines of the stadium. In a survey of 96 food and beverage managers of professional sports stadiums throughout the United States, 89% sold beer, wine, or other alcoholic beverages. Thus, it is apparent that the availability of purchasing alcohol either prior to a game or during is relatively simple.

Student Drinking at Sporting Events

Alcohol is the preferred drug of adolescents in the United States (Ellickson, Collins, Hambarsoomians, & McCaffery, 2004). The foreseeability of alcohol-consumption-related problems linked to university students attending intercollegiate sporting events is high since alcohol consumption has been found to be prevalent prior to, during, and after these events at some universities (Nelson, Lenk, Xuan, & Wechsler, 2010). Occurrences in which disorderly conduct, assaults, and even riots, particularly after an intercollegiate sporting event, has been associated with alcohol use (Anas, 2008; Klein, 2005; Stripling, 2008). Prior studies have found that university students are more likely to drink on game days compared to non-game days (Glassman, Werch, Jobli, & Bian, 2007; Neal & Fromme, 2007; Neal, Sugarman, Hustad, Caska, & Carey, 2005). Additionally, studies have indicated

Tailgating outside Mountaineer Field prior to a University of West Virginia football game in Morgantown, WV.

that more than 40% of college students who drank were "heavy episodic" or "binge" drinkers (Dawson, Grant, Stinson, & Chou, 2004; O'Malley & Johnston, 2002).

According to the National Institute on Alcohol Abuse and Alcoholism (2004), *binge drinking* is "a pattern of drinking that brings blood alcohol concentration (BAC) levels to 0.08 g/dL. This typically occurs after 4 drinks for women and 5 drinks for men—in about 2 hours" (p. 3). Binge drinking is the most common pattern of alcohol use in the United States (Centers for Disease Control and Prevention, 2015). While most people who binge drink are not alcohol dependent (Esser, Hedden, Kanny, Brewer, Gfroerer, & Naimi, 2014), binge drinkers are 14 times more likely to report alcohol-impaired driving than non-binge drinkers (Naimi, Brewer, Mokdad, Clark, Serdula, & Marks, 2003).

> **Binge Drinking** a pattern of drinking that brings blood alcohol concentration (BAC) levels to 0.08.

The Centers for Disease Control (2015) defines *heavy drinking* as males who consume 15 drinks or more per week or females who consume eight drinks or more per week. According to Nelson and Wechsler (2003) college students who consider themselves to be sports fans have a higher probability to engage in "heavy drinking" than other students. Nelson and Wechsler (2003) also reported that universities with a significant percentage of students who were sports fans had increased levels of "heavy drinking" among fans as well as students who were not sports fans. Thus, Nelson and Wechsler (2003) proposed a drinking culture pervaded such "sports oriented" schools.

> **Heavy Drinking** consumption of five or more drinks on the same occasion on each of five or more days in the past thirty days.

Sport event managers who want to effectively manage risks must recognize the value of foreseeability, their legal status regarding premises liability, duty to invitees, and duty to manage the act of third parties. These four areas will be briefly discussed as they pertain to managing tailgating risks in the following sections. The content of the liabilities and duties to be discussed briefly are not meant to be all-encompassing or be taken as legal counsel but rather to give a "snapshot" of the essential legal responsibilities of an organization or individual sponsoring tailgating activities.

Foreseeability

Foreseeability is considered the degree to which the university knew, or should have known, that an invitee may be exposed to the probability of injury. If a harmful situation that occurred on a premise was foreseeable and an individual was harmed, the lack of safety may be the reason or proximate cause of the damage rather than the particular mechanism of the injury (*Turpin v. Granieri*, 1999). For example, Swenson (2012) discusses the Dodgers/Giants rivalry, which has a history of being violent. In 2003 one fan was shot and killed; in 2009 a fan was stabbed. In 2010 on the Dodgers and Giants opening day 132 fan arrests were made, followed by only 72 arrests in 2011 (Swenson, 2012). This history, exposes a foreseeability of potential harm and an argument could be made extra precautions should have been put in place

> **Foreseeability** the degree to which someone knew, or should have known, that another person may be exposed to the probability of injury.

for all future match ups between these teams. The concept of foreseeability in tailgating activities at intercollegiate athletic events was addressed in *Bearman v. University of Notre Dame* (1983). In *Bearman* an intoxicated person who had been at a tailgate party injured the plaintiff. The court stated that it was reasonable for the university to have foreseen that some people become inebriated at tailgate activities and thereby may pose a broad danger to the safety of others. Additionally, Fitzpatrick (2015) discussed the rise in criminal occurrences in and nearby professional sport stadiums. These justify a plausible duty for the stadium owner to take sensible action to avoid foreseeable criminal behavior being aware of such instances.

Premises Liability

Premises Liability holds landowners liable for injuries occurring on their property, including land and facilities.

Trespasser anyone who enters the property without consent from the landowner.

Licensee an individual has the owner's implied consent to be on the premises.

Public Invitee an individual who gains access to the area as a member of the general public with no business relationship with the owner.

Business Invitee an individual is invited to enter the area due to some business relationship, not necessarily monetary in nature.

Premises liability is what holds landowners liable for injuries occurring on their property, including land and facilities. Swenson (2012) explained that stadium owners are not required to guarantee fan safety, but they are duty-bound to take all sensible steps to make their premises as safe as nature realistically permits. The level of duty owed by the organization varies on the status of the individual. The first category, a *trespasser*, is anyone who enters the property without consent from the landowner. This individual is not owed a duty of care. However a duty does exist that the landowner cannot cause intentional injury (Miller & Gillentine, 2006). The second type of entrant is a *licensee*. This individual has the owner's implied consent to be on the premises. It is important to note, even though permission is given to be on the premises there is no guarantee the property is safe. However, should the owner know of a risk or concealed condition there is a duty owed.

The last type of entrant is an invitee, which can actually be broken down into a public invitee or business invitee. A *public invitee* "gains access to the area as a member of the general public" and a *business invitee* "is invited to enter the area due to some business relationship, not necessarily monetary in nature" (Miller & Gillentine, 2006, p. 3). In the event money is exchanged, the highest level of duty is owed to this business invitee. This is an important area to consider in cases of recent hot topic issues of tailgating and pre/post game fan violence cases in the parking lot. For example, in the case of *Stow v. L. A. Dodgers* (2011), Stow successfully demonstrated the slow response and the lack of security in the parking lot where he was injured. It further revealed that the Dodgers did not provide reasonable protection to the business invitee, which extends beyond the inside of the stadium. The court believed that the Dodgers organization should have foreseen this incident due to the alcohol driven culture and rival atmosphere and could have increased security measures. In other words, the Dodgers were responsible for providing alcohol and contributing to the culture of intoxication and therefore owed Stow $13.9 million (Knoll & Kim, 2014).

Duty to Control Third Party Acts

The duty to exercise reasonable care does not exist until the landowner knows or has reason to know from previous experience that there is a possibility that the conduct of third parties may endanger the safety of the visitor (Dobbs, 2000). When a possessor of land opens it for use to the general public, the landholder becomes subject to liability of the public if harm, occurring to a member of that public, is caused accidentally, intentionally or negligently by the act of a third person and the landholder fails to exercise reasonable care (The American Law Institute, 1965, § 344). Reasonable care of a landholder is recognized as discovering acts are being done or likely to be done or give an adequate warning so that the visitor may avoid the harm (Dobbs, 2000).

The consumption of alcohol at athletic events is often blamed for injuries that produce litigation. Inebriated attendees may injure themselves or innocent third parties (*Bearman v. Notre Dame*, 1983). If past experience is such that reasonably careless or criminal conduct on the part of third persons may be anticipated, the landholder may be under a duty to take precautions against it, and provide a reasonably sufficient number of personnel to afford a reasonable protection (Dobbs, 2000). A *duty of care* requires a party to act within a standard of reasonable care while performing any acts that could foreseeably harm others (Dobbs, 2000). Since patrons entering an institution's property for the purpose of watching a football game or any other sporting event are considered business invitees, the institution has a duty to take reasonable safety measures to warn or protect the invitees from foreseeable harmful or criminal acts of a third party (Mallen, 2001).

> **Duty of Care** requires a party to act within a standard of reasonable care while performing any acts that could foreseeably harm others.

Using *Verni v. Lanzaro* to illustrate the potential of alcohol overindulgence, Southall and Sharp (2006) closely examine the alcohol culture that exists within the NFL vis-a-vis marketing, promoting, and advertising. It was this "culture of intoxication" at Giants Stadium that led to a horrific automobile crash in 1999 that left two-year-old Antonia Verni a quadriplegic at the hands of intoxicated New York Giants fan Daniel Lanzaro (Southall & Sharp, 2006). During the criminal trial, Lanzaro was found guilty of vehicular assault and sentenced to five years in prison (Southall & Sharp, 2006). Seeking recovery for her injuries and those of her daughter, Fazila Verni filed a civil suit in 2000 against numerous defendants, including the NFL, the New York Giants, and Aramark (Southall & Sharp, 2006). While the NFL and the New York Giants settled the case prior to trial, in 2006 a jury held New York Giants concessionaires Harry M. Stevens of New Jersey (HMS) and Aramark liable for compensatory and punitive damages in the amount of $110 million, thereby assigning liability for the behavior of drunk (third party) patrons to stadium alcohol vendors (Southall & Sharp, 2006).

The court's decision in *Bearman v. University of Notre Dame* (1983) also illustrates a university's duty for protecting patrons at athletic contests from third parties who had been tailgating. The Bearman's filed suit against Notre Dame for damages resulting from that incident. The Third District Indiana Court of Appeals ruled that:

> Notre Dame was aware that alcoholic beverages are consumed on the premises before and during football games. They also were aware that tailgate parties are held in the parking areas around the stadium. Thus, even though there was no showing that the University had reason to know of the particular danger posed by the drunk who injured Bearman, it had reason to know that some people will become intoxicated and pose a general threat to the safety of other patrons. Therefore, Notre Dame is under a duty to take reasonable precautions to protect those who attend its football games from injury caused by acts of third parties. (p. 1198)

The court agreed that as a broad rule an operator of a place of public entertainment owes a duty to keep the property protected for its invitees, the university had a duty to take reasonable precautions to protect those persons attending the game. As a result, the court found that Notre Dame had a duty to take reasonable safety measures to shield the patrons from injuries caused by the acts of third parties. Although *Bearman v. University of Notre Dame* (1983) is not a precedent setting case; it identifies potential problems that unsupervised tailgating may cause if an institution becomes lax in providing a reasonably safe environment.

Implementation of Alcohol Risk Management Strategies

Ineffective alcohol risk management at sporting events are often accompanied by high-risk behaviors and can lead to a variety of problems. Poorly managed alcohol consumption can exacerbate problems to the point where the event is neither safe nor successful for patrons as well as staff and organizers, and the way that alcohol is consumed at large events can send powerful messages about the acceptability (or otherwise) of alcohol-related behaviors. To minimize the likelihood potentially injurious behaviors and actions will take place, appropriate risk management strategies should be considered. Burke (1999) defined risk as a possible future problem that inhibits the achievement of the primary objectives an organization has outlined. The amount of risk is produced by its impact (e.g., low, medium, or high) and the likelihood of occurrence (e.g. never, sometime, or often). The threat matrix below in Table 11.5 summarizes some of the issues.

Table 11.5 *Threat Matrix*

		Likely	Possible	Unlikely
		Risk of Occurence		
Seriousness of Injury or Damages	Minor	E	F	D
	Medium	B	A	I
	Significant	C	H	G

A—Fisticuffs are reported between tailgaters supporting opposing teams
B—Patron has leg broken due to actions of an inebriated tailgater
C—Grill is tipped over causing coals to spill under a car
D—A tent is blown over scraping a vehicle
E—A tailgater scrapes elbows on pavement playing "tag" football
F—A patron receives cuts on leg from falling on broken glass
G—Tailgater(s) shoot and kill other tailgaters
H—Patron becomes inebriated at tailgating party; kills/paralyzes another while driving home
I—Tailgater becomes over-intoxicated, passes out and becomes comatose

As stated earlier, alcohol consumption is often a focal point at sporting events, with alcohol being strongly promoted within sports stadiums. Southall and Sharp (2006) discussed strategies employed by NFL teams that increased the risk of sales to intoxicated consumers. These authors contended that stadium owners specifically target vulnerable consumers who appear committed to enhancing the game day experience through alcohol consumption (or over-consumption) (Southall & Sharp). Although some professional sports stadiums have taken steps aimed at reducing alcohol-related problems, such as implementing responsible stadium policies (e.g., limiting the number of alcoholic beverages per sale) and participating in an alcohol service training programs for stadiums such as TEAM (Techniques for Effective Alcohol Management) or TIPS (Training for Intervention ProcedureS), many stadiums have a high likelihood of serving alcohol to obviously intoxicated patrons (Toomey, Erickson, Lenk, K. M., & Kilian, 2008). While training programs such as TEAM or TIPS may provide servers and sellers with tools and techniques to recognize and reduce sales to patrons already intoxicated, they cannot completely prevent such sales.

Lenk, Toomey, and Erickson (2009) surveyed local law enforcement and alcoholic beverage control agencies that have professional football, basketball, hockey, and/or baseball stadiums within their jurisdiction. They found that the majority of enforcement agencies commonly received complaints about fights occurring either inside or outside stadiums, property damage at or near the stadiums, and/or intoxicated patrons at the stadiums, but only about half of the agencies conducted alcohol enforcement actions at the stadiums. In another study, Lenk, Toomey, Erickson, Kilian, Nelson, and Fabian (2010) revealed that food/beverage service managers (47%) and stadium managers (42%) were most commonly involved in setting and implementing risk management strategies. Nearly 70% communicated their alcohol policies to the employees at the time they were hired, with periodic follow-up at staff meetings and/or trainings. Stadiums housing football teams appear to have more alcohol control policies than those housing other sports—baseball, basketball, and hockey stadiums. The majority of managers revealed that their stadium had a range of alcohol control policies and practices. For example, all or nearly all reported their stadium allows no more than two alcoholic beverages per sale and their alcohol servers are required to check age identification of patrons who appear younger than age 30. Conversely, only about half prohibit servers younger than 21 years of age from selling alcohol both in seating areas and at concession booths, and approximately one-third designate sections of their stadiums as alcohol-free (Lenk et al., 2010).

Drinking behavior varies considerably by student and college characteristics, by drinking venue and by policies used to control alcohol availability and consumption (Wechsler, Davenport, Dowdall, Moeykens, & Castillo, 1994; Wechsler, Dowdall, Davenport, & Castillo, 1995; Wechsler, Lee, Kuo, Seibring, Nelson & Lee, 2002). Yet, alcohol risk management policies that include supervising the drinking area should be strongly considered. Previous research has indicated that monitoring areas in which alcohol drinking occurred was the only variable that decreased excessive alcohol drinking (Knight, Harris, Sherritt, Kelley, Van Hook, & Wechsler, 2003). Therefore, the implementation of direct monitoring of tailgating and student seating areas of college and university venues would be encouraged.

Miller and Gillentine (2006) investigated the tailgating risk management strategies of 98 NCAA Division I university/college athletic departments. The findings indicated that only 68 of the institutions possessed risk management strategies for tailgating activities, which indicated four primary areas of concern including tailgate parking, alcohol consumption, disposable items (i.e. charcoal grill, glass container, and trash), and stadium re-entry. Surprisingly, only 38% possessed policies regarding tailgate parking hours of operation, 28 institutions indicated that tailgate areas were not monitored, and 75% did not have policies relating to recreational vehicles and tents. Each of these tailgate parking issues could be the proximate cause of a harmful incident. Furthermore, 32 (47%) institutions possessed policies regarding stadium re-entry; lack of such policy allows individuals to leave the stadium and re-enter in an intoxicated state without appropriate checking.

Recommendations

Implementing an alcohol risk management policy should not be designed to create an atmosphere in which the tailgaters cannot enjoy themselves. Rather the policy should provide an environment in which the game attendee is no exposed to unnecessary harm. As improbable as the occurrence of severe injuries is to tailgaters, it does not excuse an organization from recognizing their duty of providing a safe environment. Previous investigations have indicated that drinking alcohol can increase an individual's violent tendencies, especially when placed in an emotionally charged atmosphere (Harford, Wechsler, & Muthen, 2003; Leonard, Quigley, & Collins, 2002). Since drinking alcoholic beverages is a recognized element of tailgating (Gillentine & Miller, 2006; Lebowitz, 2005; Wieberg, 2005) and tailgating may be considered part of the emotionally charged atmosphere often found attending intercollegiate football games, it would be reasonable for the landowner (i.e. university/college/professional team) to anticipate that intoxicated actions of some of tailgaters may endanger others (*Bearman v. Notre Dame*, 1983; *Stow v. L.A. Dodgers*, 2011).

If an organization knows that heavy drinking accompanies tailgating, and heavy drinking by patrons creates an unsafe atmosphere for others, the university, as a landowner, should provide appropriate measures of protection for the patron. A sport facility management should employ a comprehensive risk management plan containing extensive crowd management as well as alcohol management policies. To provide a reasonably safe environment, a written risk management plan for all foreseeable areas in which a person may be exposed to unnecessary harm should be developed. A well-constructed risk management plan should systematically identify the risk, examine the impact as well as the likelihood of the risk occurring, develop strategies to address the risk, and actively administer those strategies. Therefore, an effective alcohol management plan, similar to a crowd management plan, must consider the facility's patrons and their safety. Providing an attractive and safe environment will motivate fans to return to the venue, thus, ensuring a steady stream of revenue. The following considerations will assist facility managers to develop and implement alcohol policies at a facility:

1. Every person attempting to purchase alcohol should have his or her identification checked.
2. Allow no more than two alcoholic drinks should be sold during an individual transaction.
3. Mandate that the size of each serving should be no larger than 12 ounces.
4. Alcohol sales must end at a specific point during the event.

5. Trained crowd management should be stationed at the facility entrances to prohibit intoxicated individuals from entering the facility as well as to prevent patrons from entering the facility with alcoholic beverages.

6. Provide a designated driver program that will build rapport with event patrons while reducing the chances that intoxicated patrons will drive home.

7. Deliberate offering alcohol-free seating sections.

8. Review similar policies of stadiums

9. Proper monitoring and enforcement require visible and active security providers, clearly and easily identified by their clothing.

10. Hold a debriefing session involving police officers, event organizers, and relevant stakeholders.

11. Communicate restrictions on bringing alcohol into the venue, legal requirements to exclude or remove intoxicated patrons, restrictions, or limitations on bringing food and non-alcoholic drink into the venue, and the venue's intolerance of unruly or aggressive behavior.

Conclusion

The management of beverages as it relates to sports venues requires understanding a multitude of factors from purchasing and receiving to serving and forecasting. Understanding the factors impacting beverage management provides an avenue to increase the potential for a successful concessions operation in sports venues. The ability to properly forecast beverage sales, implement and maximize sales mix, manage beverage costs, and negotiate purchasing will result in alcohol sales increasing concession revenue. However, failure to manage these factors can reduce the overall profitability of alcohol sales.

Athletic events are often correctly marketed as an exciting and fan-friendly event appropriate for patrons of all ages. Yet, alcohol is readily available at intercollegiate and professional sporting events. Due to the high level of alcohol sales and consumption at intercollegiate and professional sporting events, there is significant risk for alcohol to contribute to avoidable injuries and deaths associated with these events (Nelson et al., 2010). The lack of alcohol risk management policies at tailgating activities (Miller & Gillentine, 2006) as well as for student populations (Nelson et al., 2010) may generate an atmosphere that allows intercollegiate and professional sports events to be a drinking occasion (Erickson et al., 2011; Gillentine, 2003). The findings of previous research indicate that attending intercollegiate and professional athletic events is linked to permissive drinking environments (Erickson et al.; Gillentine; Miller & Gillentine; Nelson et al.). As such, event administrators need to develop alcohol risk management policies that can increase a safe and enjoyable environment for event attendees.

CHAPTER DISCUSSION QUESTIONS

1. Why is forecasting beverage sales important to consider for a sports event manager? List and explain three items.

2. List and explain the two major types of averages a sport event manager may encounter. Describe the formulas that are used for each type of average.

3. Calculate the percentage variance from the table below

Month	Sales this Year	Sales Last Year	Variance	Percentage Variance
January	$32,000	$30,500		
February	$28,500	$25,000		
March	$36,000	$33,000		
First-Quarter Total				

4. The sport event manager of the Trojan Arena has calculated the first-quarter sales but wants to forecast what their second-quarter sales. While the percentage variance fluctuated during the three months of the first quarter, the manager decides to use the first quarter percentage variance of 8.86%. Using this information with the table below, determine the revenue forecast for each month as well as the entire second quarter.

Month	Sales Last Year	% Increase Estimate	Increase Amount	Revenue Forecast
April	$41,500			
May	$32,000			
June	$39,500			
Second-Quarter Total				

5. Discuss the issues that a sport event manager may face when receiving and storing beverage products.

6. Why is tailgating become so important at sport events? Identify and discuss three reasons.

7. What are some of the major issues of patrons consuming alcoholic beverages prior to, during, and after games?

8. Describe the significant concerns regarding students drinking alcohol at sporting events.

9. Identify the three categories of premises liability and discuss why each of these categories is a concern for a sport event manager.

10. Why should a sport event manager implement alcohol risk management strategies or policies? Describe how you, as the event manager, implement such policies.

MINI CASE STUDY

McBee Stadium is home to the Keljack University (KU) Hippogriffs, a Division I football power. The main athletic rivals of KU, the Jolaur University (JU) Sharks, will be competing for this year's Sea Belt League title with the game hosted at KU. Keljack University provides 800 tailgating spaces on its premises for home games. Patrons may start entering the tailgating areas for a 6:00 p.m. Saturday game start, beginning on Friday mornings at 9:00 a.m., and the tailgating area must be cleared by 6:00 p.m. on Sunday after the game. While security patrols are visible in the tailgate area three hours before and two hours after the Saturday game, their presence is minimal, if not non-existent, on the Friday before the game and Sunday after the game.

It should also be noted that the athletic department at Keljack University has decided to sell draft beer at McBee Stadium for home football games beginning two years ago. It should be noted that McBee Stadium has a capacity of 100,000 spectators, and the game against the Jolaur University Sharks is a complete sell-out. Using the information regarding the tailgate areas at KU as well as their adoption of selling draft beer at home games, answer the following items:

1. What liabilities does Keljack University have to provide a safe environment for their patrons who pay KU to tailgate on the university's premises?

2. Using at least one of the court cases identified in the chapter, explain KU's duty to control third party acts. Further, explain how foreseeability is a significant component in controlling third party acts at home football games.

3. What are some considerations the KU athletic department must address in managing alcohol consumption risks, particularly against an arch-rival such as Jolaur University Sharks?

4. What are some issues that the KU athletic department must address concerning student drinking alcohol at sporting events? Explain at least three issues.

5. Identify and explain at least two methods that KU may institute as part of an alcohol risk management strategy.

6. For the last home game against JU, Keljack University attracted a total of 98,000 spectators. Draft beer sales were $286,000. It is anticipated that an increase of 8% sales will occur for the upcoming game this year. What does the increased amount of an 8% sales increase equal for this game? What will be revenue forecast for the upcoming game against the JU Sharks?

7. Identify and explain at least one advantage and one disadvantage to offer draft beer instead of bottled beer to consumer.

8. Identify and explain at least two concerns an event manager would have about receiving and storing alcohol products.

9. Identify and explain at least two benefits for outsourcing concessions operations?

PRACTITIONER SPOTLIGHT

NAME: Chris Adams

ORGANIZATION: Savor

CURRENT JOB TITLE: Executive Director of Food and Beverage, 2016–Present

EDUCATIONAL PREPARATION:

- BA, Strategic Management and Business Law, University of North Texas, 1996
- TABC, TIPS and TEAM certified

Photo courtesy of Chris Adams.

CAREER PATH: I started working in food and beverage in high school, waiting tables and working in restaurants. I had an internship with a law firm right out of college and I eventually became their director of administration. In 2000, I moved back into food and beverage as a sales and catering manager for Aramark. I was promoted to Director of Market Operations at Aramark in 2002. In 2005, I went to work for Levy Restaurants overseeing all of their premium services for NASCAR and other large events. I was recruited by Sodexo in 2012 to open the food and beverage operations at a new Formula 1 racetrack in Austin, TX and to be a regional manager for them. In 2016, my former boss from Levy approached me about the opportunity here at Savor overseeing all of their Texas and Oklahoma facilities.

WHAT IS THE MOST REWARDING ASPECT OF THIS JOB?

Being a part of something that brings enjoyment to so many people is a part of my role that I find rewarding. I like to take our managers and chefs, who have been working non-stop for several days to prepare for an event, and walk them out into the stands and show them what they are a part of.

WHAT IS THE MOST CHALLENGING ASPECT OF THIS JOB?

Trying to satisfy everybody at an event is a challenge. The trends in food and beverage service change and it can be difficult to know what patrons are looking for. What do patrons mean when they say that they want healthier options? To some that means an all-beef hotdog and a light beer and to others that means vegan and gluten-free options. Trying to meet all of these different needs is the biggest challenge.

WHAT TRAINING SYSTEMS DO YOUR SERVERS UNDERTAKE FROM A LIABILITY AND RISK-MANAGEMENT PERSPECTIVE?

We have all of our servers go through two training courses. Here in Texas, the first one is the Texas Alcoholic Beverage Commission (TABC) seller training course. This can be done on-line or in-person. If any of our temporary employees have experience in food and beverage service, we will allow them to take the on-line course. If not, we recommend them to take the in-person course. In addition to the TABC training, we require servers take either the TIPS (Training for Intervention ProcedureS) or TEAM (Techniques for Effective Alcohol Management) training course. Both of these are nationwide training courses.

WHAT ARE WAYS THAT GOVERNMENTAL REGULATIONS IMPACT YOUR WORK IN ALCOHOL MANAGEMENT PRACTICES IN THE SPORT EVENT SETTING?

The different types of licenses effect what types of alcoholic beverages you are allowed to serve. This applies to any business serving alcohol. In an event facility where you are not operating every day, there are additional components that you have to do to activate your license. You have to notify the governing bodies that you will be using the license and provide the times you will be using the license. You have to make sure that you are only serving alcohol during the licensed times and in the licensed space. If there are different licenses within the same facility, patrons cannot take alcohol from one licensee's area to another. In addition to the licenses, we are responsible for tracking purchases, sales, and inventory and paying the proper taxes on the sales.

HOW DO THE REVENUE STREAMS ASSOCIATED WITH ALCOHOL SALES COMPARE WITH THE REVENUES ASSOCIATED WITH FOOD SERVICE AT THE VENUES YOU HAVE BEEN ASSOCIATED WITH?

The type of event has a significant impact on the types and amounts of products being sold. During a concert, typically about 60% of your overall sales are alcohol. If the event is a family oriented event, there will be more food and soft drinks being sold. For athletic events, the percentage of sales attributed to alcohol varies depending on the time of the event. How long have patrons been tailgating? Is the event during a typical meal time? We have to look at all of these factors and make decisions on how to stock our stands.

WHERE DO YOU SEE THE DIVISION OF RESPONSIBILITY FOR ALCOHOL SERVING PRACTICES AND POLICIES AND ENFORCEMENT WITHIN THE SPORT SETTING?

There isn't any delineation there. It is all about the safety of the patrons. A server at a stadium has about 30 seconds of interaction with a patron and the patron may not exhibit any signs of intoxication. It is important that the servers, the concession managers, the ushers, stadium security, and event management are all cognizant of what is going on and communicate with one another to provide a safe and enjoyable environment for everyone.

WHAT CHANGES IN ALCOHOL MANAGEMENT PRACTICES AND POLICIES HAVE YOU EXPERIENCED IN THIS WORK SETTING, AND WHAT FUTURE CHANGES MIGHT YOU EXPECT?

I remember back in the 1980s it was "just sell them what they want." In the late 1990s and early 2000s, litigation brought an emphasis on responsible alcohol sales to prevent injuries as a result of impairment. We now have limits on the number of drinks one can purchase during a transaction to limit the ability to mass consume alcohol. We are also moving away from allowing people to bring their own alcohol

© Jeff Schultes/Shutterstock.com

Circuit of the Americas, the F1 venue located outside Austin, TX.

into a venue. This was a piggyback on some of the security measures after 9-11, because you don't know what people are bringing in. Going forward, I think you are going to see more training and awareness on the effects of drugs and their interaction with alcohol. The legalization of marijuana in certain states is going to make this an issue that will need to be addressed.

WHAT IS A UNIQUE ASPECT OR TASK OF YOUR JOB THAT MANY WOULD BE SURPRISED HEAR ABOUT?

We review a lot of analytics. It's not just serving hotdogs and beer. You have to consider how you plot locations. Where do you put trashcans and recycle bins? Where do you put a drink cart? You have to know what items sell the best and the locations that some items sell better than others based upon locations. You have to consider sponsorship agreements with beverage brands and how they affect what you stock. It is all part of a big picture that must be analyzed to create the best experience for the patrons.

ADVICE FOR THOSE SEEKING A SIMILAR CAREER?

- Most important skill(s) to develop

There are a lot of skills that you need to take on. It is important that you have a wide range of experience. You don't have to be a chef to grill a hamburger. You don't have to be an HR manager to train a staff. You need to be able to do a little bit of everything. It is important to have an inquiring mind and try to learn as much as you can about all of the different pieces and how they fit together.

PARTING WORDS OF WISDOM FOR STUDENTS AND YOUNG PROFESSIONALS IN THE FIELD?

Make sure that you have fun and enjoy what you do. In athletics, you spend a lot of time at work and it is important that you take some time to stop and realize what you are a part of and enjoy what you are doing. Make sure that to gain a perspective of why you are there and be passionate about what you are doing.

REFERENCES

Apsler, R., & Harding, W. M. (1991). *Responsible alcohol service programs evaluation.* National Highway Traffic Safety Administration. Washington, D.C.

Anas, B. (2008). CU study links football, crime: Research shows spike in arrests on game day. *The Daily Camera.* Retrieved from http://dailycamera.com/ news/2008/jan/23/ cv-study-football-and-crime-are-linked/

Anderson, J. (November, 1997). Team spirits (serving wine at tailgate parties). *Fortune, 136,* 355.

Bearman v. University of Notre Dame, 453 N.E.2d 1196 (Ind. Ct. App. 1983).

Briggs, D. (November, 2011). A revenue stream worth tapping?: Colleges wrestle with the complicated question of alcohol and athletics. *Columbia Daily Tribune,* B1.

Borsari, B., Boyle, K. E., Hustad, J. T., Barnett, N. P., Tevyaw, T. O. L., & Kahler, C. W. (2007). Drinking before drinking: Pregaming and drinking games in mandated students. *Addictive Behaviors, 32*(11), 2694–2705.

Burke, R. (1999). *Project management planning and control.* West Sussex: Wiley Publishing.

Cahn, J. (2003). *Tailgating America 2002.* Retrieved from http://www.tailgating.com/

Cartwright, G. (2005). *Tailgating evolves into American sporting institution.* Retrieved from http://www.baylor.edu/Lariat/news.php?action=story&story=37569

Crawford, M., Donnelly, J., Gordon, J., MacCallum, R., MacDonald, I, McNeill, M., ...& West, G. (2001). An analysis of consultations with the crowd doctors at Glasgow Celtic football club, season 1999-2000. *British Journal of Sports Medicine, 35,* 245–250.

Dawson, D. A., Grant, B. F., Stinson, F. S., Chou, P. S. (2004). Another look at heavy episodic drinking and alcohol use disorders among college and noncollege youth. *Journal of Studies on Alcohol, 65*(4), 477–488.

De Bonaire, C., Kalafatelis, E., & McMillan, P. (2004). *The way we drink: The current attitudes and behaviours of New Zealanders (aged 12 plus) towards drinking alcohol.* BRC Marketing & Social Research/Alcohol Advisory Council of New Zealand: Wellington (NZ).

Dent, G., Pepper, J., Fields, C., & Mastorakos, S. (2004). Unprecedented survey reveals 9 in 10 college students "tailgate" safely. *NCAA press release.* Retrieved from www.ncaa.org/wps/wcm/connect/.../tailgating_press_release.doc?MOD

Dobbs, D. B. (2000). *The law of torts.* St. Paul, MN: West Group.

Duncan, J. D. (2004). *Sport in American culture: From Ali to X-games.* Santa Barbara, CA: ABC:CLIO.

Dvorchak, R. (2005). $135 million jury award forces new look at high cost of sports and drinking. *The Pittsburgh Post-Gazette.* Retrieved from http://www.post-gazette.com/sports/other-sports/2005/04/03/135-million-jury-award-forces-new-look-at-high-cost-of-sports-and-drinking/stories/200504030243

Ellickson, P. L., Collins, R. L., Hambarsoomians, K., & McCaffrey, D. F. (2005). Does alcohol advertising promote adolescent drinking? Results from a longitudinal assessment. *Addiction, 100*(2), 235–246.

Erickson, D. J., Toomey, T. L., Lenk, K. M., Kilian, G. R., & Fabian, L. E. (2011). Can we assess blood alcohol levels of attendees leaving professional sporting events? *Alcoholism: Clinical and Experimental Research, 35*(4), 689–694.

Esser, M. B., Hedden, S. L., Kanny, D., Brewer, R. D., Gfroerer, J. C., & Naimi, T. S. (2014). Prevalence of alcohol dependence among US adult drinkers, 2009–2011. *Preventing Chronic Disease,* 11, E206.

Fitzpatrick, B. (2015). Broken bats and broken bones: Holding stadium owners accountable for alcohol-fueled fan-on-fan violence. *Jeffrey S. Moorad Sports Law Journal, 22*(2), 663.

Gillentine, A. (2003). *Factors associated with participation in pre-game activities.* Paper presentation at Southern District AHPERD. Savannah, GA.

Gillentine, A., Miller, J. & Calhoun, A. (2008). Negligent marketing: What all sport marketers should know. *Journal of Contemporary Athletics, 3*(2), 161–171.

Glassman, T., Werch, C. E., Jobli, E., Bian, H. (2007). Alcohol-related fan behavior on college football game day. *Journal of American College Health, 56*(3), 255–260.

Glassman, T. J., Dodd, V. J., Sheu, J. J., Rienzo, B. A., & Wagenaar, A. C. (2010). Extreme ritualistic alcohol consumption among college students on game day. *Journal of American College Health, 58*(5), 413–423.

Harford, T. C., Wechsler, H., & Muthen, B .O. (2003). Alcohol-related aggression and drinking at off-campus parties and bars: a national study of current drinkers in college. *Journal of Studies on Alcohol, 64*(5), 704–711.

Harris, R., Edwards, D., & Homel, P. (2014). Managing alcohol and drugs in event and venue settings: The Australian case. *Event Management, 18*(4), 457–470.

Hart, D. (1984, June 22). Tailgate promotions help university draw record setting crowds. *East Carolina University Marketing News*, p. 18.

Hoaken, P. N., & Stewart, S. H. (2003). Drugs of abuse and the elicitation of human aggressive behavior. *Addictive Behaviors, 28*(9), 1533–1554.

Hocking, J. E. (1982). Sports and spectators: Intra-audience effects. *Journal of Communication, 32*(1), 100–108.

Huang, K. & Dixon, M.A. (2103). Examining the financial impact of alcohol sales on football game days: A case study of a major football program. *Journal of Sport Management, 27*, 207–216.

Jackson, N., Polite, F., & Barber, A. (2003). *Crossing the legal line: Issues involving tailgating.* Paper presentation at the Society for the Study of Legal Aspects of Sport and Physical Activity. Atlanta, GA.

James, J., Breezeel, G., & Ross, S. (2001). A two-stage study of the reasons to begin and continue tailgating. *Sport Marketing Quarterly, 10*(4), 221–222.

Jones, P. (2009). *Outsourcing: Key legal issues and contractual protections.* Retrieved from http://www.farrer.co.uk/Global/Briefings/Outsourcing%20-%20key%20legal%20issues%20and%20contractual%20protections.pdf

Kahle, L. R., Kambara, K. M., & Rose, G. M. (1996) A functional model of fan attendance motivations for college football. *Sport Marketing Quarterly 5*(4), 51–60.

Klein, G. (2005, June 2). USC bans beer at games. *Los Angeles Times*, p. D1.

Knight, J. R., Harris, S. K., Sherritt, L., Kelley, K., Van Hook, S., & Wechsler, H. (2003). Heavy drinking and alcohol policy enforcement in a statewide public college system. *Journal of Studies on Alcohol, 64*(5), 696–703.

Knoll, C., & Kim, V. (2014). *Dodgers, not McCourt, found liable in Bryan Stow beating case.* Los Angeles Times. Retrieved from http://www.latimes.com/local/crime/la-me-0710-bryan-stow-trial-20140710-story.html

Lawsuits over fatal tailgate shootings settled. (2008, May 21). *WRAL.com.* Retrieved from http://www.wral.com/lawsuits-over-fatal-tailgate-shootings-settled/2922433/

Lebowitz, M. S. (2005). *Yale bans parties before the game.* Retrieved from http://www.thecrimson.com/article.aspx?ref=509514.

Lenk, K. M., Toomey, T. L., & Erickson, D. J. (2009). Alcohol-related problems and enforcement at professional sports stadiums. *Drugs: Education, Prevention and Policy, 16*(5), 451–462.

Lenk, K. M., Toomey, T. L., Erickson, D. J., Kilian, G. R., Nelson, F. D., & Fabian, L. (2010). Alcohol control policies and practices at professional sports stadiums. *Public Health Report, 125,* 665–673.

Leonard, K. E., Quigley, B. M, & Collins, R. L. (2002). Physical aggression in the lives of young adults: Prevalence, location, and severity among college and community samples. *Journal of Interpersonal Violence, 17,* 533–550.

Levy, L. (1989). A study of sports crowd behavior: The case of the great pumpkin incident. *Journal of Sport & Social Issues, 13*(2), 69–91.

Mallen, S. A. (2001). Touchdown! A victory for injured fans at sporting events? *Missouri Law Review, 66*(2), 487–505.

Madensen, T. D., & Eck, J. E. (2008). *Spectator violence in stadiums.* United States Department of Justice: Washington, D. C.

Mark, M. M., Bryant, F. B., & Lehman, D. R. (1983). Perceived injustice and sports violence. In J. H. Goldstein, *Sports Violence.* New York: Springer-Verlag.

Mason, S., & Calloway, V. (2004, September 6). Brothers in custody following fatal shootings outside NCSU game. *WRAL.com.* Retrieved from http://www.wral.com/news/3707350/detail.com.

Miller, J., & Gillentine, A. (2006). An investigation of tailgating policies at Division 1A schools. *Journal of Legal Aspects of Sport, 16*(2), 197–215.

Moore, S. C., Flajšlik, M., Rosin, P. L., & Marshall, D. (2008). A particle model of crowd behaviour: Exploring the relationship between alcohol, crowd dynamics and violence. *Aggression and Violent Behaviour, 13,* 413–422.

Naimi, T. S., Brewer, R. D., Mokdad, A., Denny, C., Serdula, M. K., & Marks, J. S. (2003). Binge drinking among US adults. *Journal of the American Medical Association, 289*(1), 70–75.

National Institute on Alcohol Abuse and Alcoholism. (2004). NIAAA council approves definition of binge drinking. *NIAA Newsletter, 3,* 1–4.

National Institute on Alcohol Abuse and Alcoholism. (n.d.) *Rethinking drinking: What's a standard drink?* Retrieved from http://rethinkingdrinking.niaaa.nih.gov/How-much-is-too-much/What-counts-as-a-drink/Whats-A-Standard-Drink.aspx

Neal, D. J., & Fromme, K. (2007). Hook 'em horns and heavy drinking: alcohol use and collegiate sports. *Addictive Behaviors, 32*(11), 2681–2693.

Neal, D. J., Sugarman, D. E., Hustad, J. T., Caska, C. M., & Carey, K. B. (2005). It's all fun and games…or is it? Collegiate sporting events and celebratory drinking. *Journal of Studies on Alcohol, 66*(2), 291–294.

Nelson, T. F., Lenk, K. M., Xuan, Z., & Wechsler, H. (2010). Student drinking at US college sports events. *Substance Use & Misuse, 45*(12), 1861–1873.

Nelson, T. F., & Wechsler, H. (2003). School spirits: Alcohol and collegiate sports fans. *Addictive Behavior, 28*, 1–11.

O'Malley, P. M., & Johnston, L. D. (2002). Epidemiology of alcohol and other drug use among American college students. *Journal of Studies on Alcohol (Suppl), 14*, 23–39.

Pedersen, E. R., & LaBrie, J. W. (2007). Partying before the party: Examining "prepartying" behavior among college students. *Journal of American College Health, 56*, 237–245.

Pierce v. Murnick, 145 S.E.2d 11 (N.C. 1965).

Read, J. P., Merrill, J. E., & Bytschkow, K. (2010). Before the party starts: Risk factors and reasons for "pregaming" in college students. *Journal of American College Health, 58*(5), 461–472.

Shivers, V. (2010). *Free 'ultimate parrothead parking lot tailgate party' for Jimmy Buffett's Columbia, SC concert.* Retrieved from http://www.examiner.com/x-18204-Jimmy-Buffett-Examiner~y2010m2d19-Free-Ultimate-Parrot-Head-Parking-Lot-Tailgate-Party-for-Jimmy-Buffetts-Columbia-SC-concert.

Southall, R. M., & Sharp, L. A. (2006). The National Football League and its "culture of intoxication": A negligent marketing analysis of *Verni v. Lanzaro. Journal of Legal Aspects of Sport, 16*(1). 121–150.

Stow v. L.A. Dodgers, LLC, No. BC462127 (Cal. Super. Ct., L.A. Cnty. May 24, 2011)

Stripling, J. (2008). Learning to binge. *The Gainesville Sun.* Retrieved from http://www.gainesville.com/article/20080228/NEWS/802280317/0/search

Swenson, S. J. (2012). Unsportsmanlike conduct: The duty placed on stadium owners to protect against fan violence. *Marquette Sports Law Review, 23*, 135–153.

Tailgating America. (n.d.) Retrieved from http://tailgating.com/Trivia.htm.

The American Law Institute ("ALI"). (1965). *Restatement of law (second), torts.* St. Paul, MN: American Law Institute Publishers.

Toomey, T. L., Erickson, D. J., Lenk, K. M., & Kilian, G. R. (2008). Likelihood of illegal alcohol sales at professional sport stadiums. *Alcoholism, 32*(11), 1859–1864.

Trail, G. T., Anderson, D. F., & Fink, J. (2000). A theoretical model of sport spectator consumption behavior. International *Journal of Sport Management, 3*, 154–180.

Turpin v. Granieri, 133 Idaho 244, 985 P.2d 669 (1999).

Verni v. Lanzaro, Docket No. BER-L-10488-00 (Superior Ct. N.J. Law Div. Bergen County, Oct. 16, 2003).

Vingilis, E., Liban, C. B., Blefgen, H., Colbourne, D., & Reynolds, D. (1992). Introducing beer sales at a Canadian ball park: The effect on motor vehicle accidents. *Accident Analysis & Prevention, 24*(5), 521–526.

Wechsler, H., Davenport, A., Dowdall, G., Moeykens, B., & Castillo, S. (1994). Health and behavioral consequences of binge drinking in college. A national survey of students at 140 campuses. *Journal of American Medical Association, 272*(21), 1672–1677.

Wechsler, H., Dowdall, G. W., Davenport, A., & Castillo, S. (1995). Correlates of college student binge drinking. *American Journal of Public Health, 85*(7), 921–926.

Wechsler, H., Lee, J. E., Kuo, M., Seibring, M., Nelson, T. F., & Lee, H. (2002). Trends in college binge drinking during a period of increased prevention efforts. Findings from 4 Harvard School of Public Health College alcohol study surveys: 1993–2001. *Journal of American College Health, 50*(5), 203–217.

Wieberg, S. (2005, November 21). *Colleges are reaching their limit on alcohol.* Retrieved on from http://www.usatoday.com/news/nation/2005-11-16-colleges-alcohol_x.htm

Wolford v. Ostenbridge, 861 So. 2d 455 (Ct. App. Fla. 2003).

Media Support

Lawrence W. Judge and *J. Patrick Marsh*

OBJECTIVES

After studying this chapter, the student should be able to:

- Explain the importance of media support in major sport events.
- Understand and list examples of the media needs that are required in a sport facility.
- Understand the changing needs and role of sport media in a technological society.
- Describe some of the facility and space needs associated with sport media within and around sport venues.

KEY TERMS

External Media	Internal Media	Press Row
In-House Media	Press Box	

KEY ACRONYMS

DAS	Distributed Antenna Systems	**OBS**	Olympic Broadcasting Service
ISDN	Integrated Services for Digital Network	**PBWA**	Professional Basketball Writers Association
IT	Information Technology	**UGC**	User-Generated Content
LED	Light Emitting Diode		

Introduction

From mega-sporting events to high school and even youth sporting events, athletics are now subject to (and the subject of) accelerating media representations such as television coverage and media advertisements. Since the Los Angeles Olympic Games in 1984, the International Olympic Committee (IOC) has realized the media value of the largest multi-sport event in the world and how important the media is in managing representations of host cities, games organizers, sponsors, sporting federations and the IOC itself (Miah & Garcia, 2012). The IOC (and its soccer counterpart, FIFA) now exerts tight control of its lucrative media rights, tying local organizing committees contractually within the Host City Contact to return significant profits to the sanctioning body. Host cities for mega-sporting events strive to profit from the event by not only spending money to make the event great but in turn by making a profit from the number of individuals who attend their event and spend money in their city. However, as new user-generated content (UGC) has proliferated over the last two decades, a multi-dimensional and contested media space has emerged around the not only the Olympic Games but also all other high profile sport events. UGC via Facebook, YouTube, or blogging sites is continuing to show explosive growth. Between 2009 and 2016, the monthly active users of Facebook have skyrocketed from 197 million to 1.654 billion (Facebook, 2016). An increase in UGC and media use may have an impact on the attendance of mega-sporting events, due to the ease of access to stay updated remotely.

The rise in media coverage of athletics is not limited to mega-events. In 1979, 24-hour sports programming was born with the launch of ESPN. In the years since, ESPN has flourished and expanded, and new sports networks have emerged. There are now more than 50 sports television networks in the United States alone. This has led to an exponential increase in the number of live sporting events being broadcast. The rise of the 24-news cycle and the ease of communication through social media have even further advanced the demand for sports media content. The sports media is no longer solely focused on the most elite events. Media coverage of small college, high school, and even some youth sporting events is becoming more commonplace. Thus, it is important for facility managers at all levels of athletics to understand the role of media and media support and its importance to the success of sporting events and sport, overall.

Providing access and working space for the media and press is an important provision in sport facility and event management.

Sport Media

According to Stoldt, Dittmore, and Branvold (2012), media is the most popular form of public relations in sport. Public relations uses media to coordinate communication from teams to the press as well as to provide the public with sports news and information. In addition, public relations promotes interest in sport and increases a team's visibility through the use of media outlets. The goal of the media relations, overall, is to develop a relationship between the media and the sport organization itself (Mullin, Hardy, & Sutton, 2007). Event managers rely on the media and publicity for the success of an event. For example, the 2012 London Olympic Games reached the highest number of people in Olympic Games history with 3.6 billion viewers, while also providing more media coverage of the Games than ever before. The definition and role of sport media is constantly changing with new technology. In this chapter we will discuss the channels the media uses to reach sporting fans, both traditional and emerging, and how facility and event managers can best support each channel. Without the media, audiences would not have remote access to sport events thus it is imperative for media members and facility and event managers and organizers to work in unison to provide the best coverage possible.

External, Internal, and In-House Media

There are three primary classifications of media coverage of an event based upon the affiliation of the outlet covering the event: external media, internal media, and in-house media. While there are three primary classifications, it is best to think of these classifications as existing on a spectrum of media coverage. *External media* are media outlets that cover an event and have no affiliation to the organization hosting the event. External media outlets generally pay a media rights fee to the host organization and most of the control over what is shown during the broadcast lies with the broadcast company. ESPN broadcasting Monday Night Football and TBS broadcasting the Final Four are examples of external media. When sport organizations and governing bodies like the IOC, FIFA or, the NFL have their own media team providing coverage, it is referred to as internal media. An *internal media* team allows the company to cover the event the way they want to, with a very direct say in what is published via print, television, radio, etc. The IOC's internal media is run by Olympic Broadcasting Service (OBS). OBS works as the "host broadcaster" for the IOC wherever the current Olympic Games are being held. Because the OBS is part of the International Olympic Committee, they are able to provide viewers with the best possible broadcasting experience due to their direct relationship with the IOC. Having an internal broadcasting team helps the IOC to keep the coverage of the games consistent and recognizable from year to year. Other examples of internal media outlets include the NFL network, NBA TV, and the MLB Network. From a facility and event management perspective, internal and external media support are very similar. The venue has the same responsibilities in providing support to internal and external media outlets, and the technical aspects

External Media
broadcast media outlets covering an event and have no organizational affiliation to the event host (team or governing body).

Internal Media
broadcast media coverage of an event by the sport organization or governing body with their media personnel.

In-House Media event media coverage that is only for the patrons attending the event such as video board feeds, public address announcements, in-house mobile apps content or game programs.

of the broadcast remain relatively consistent regardless of the broadcaster. *In-house* media is media coverage that is only for the patrons at the event. In-house media includes video board feeds, public address announcing, game programs, and in-house mobile apps. In-house media is typically supported differently from other types of media because it is generally broadcast by the venue. In-house media uses the venue's equipment and personnel requiring more detailed support from the facility manager. The lines between the different types of media, however, are becoming increasingly blurred. It is becoming more and more common for in-house media feeds to be broadcast externally through on-line platforms such as university websites and lower tier carriers like ESPN3. Organizations are also partnering with external media outlets to form hybrid internal-external media networks. The Big Ten Network is a partnership between the Big Ten Conference and Fox and the Longhorn Network is a partnership between the University of Texas at Austin and ESPN. These partnerships give the sport organizations an increased voice in the broadcasting of their events while avoiding the logistical challenges of operating its own internal media network.

Credentialing

The primary media support functions of a facility and event manager are to provide access to both the space and technology necessary for members of the media to cover the event properly and ensure that media coverage does not interfere with the event's participants and spectators. Both of these functions are accomplished in large part through a credentialing process. Credentialing is the process by which a facility and event manager identifies all of the people involved in the hosting of an event, including media members, and the access and technology or equipment needs of each person. The facility and event manager then issues an appropriate credential to each person, which gives them access to the spaces and equipment necessary to perform their job functions. In the case of media credentialing, media members will generally be given access to a game viewing area such as a *press box*, media row, or field level access, a media work space, a press conference room, and/or sometimes locker rooms at specified times. These spaces will be equipped with all of the power and technological features necessary for the media members working in each area. Along with allowing access to the appropriate spaces, credentials also prevent access to restricted areas. By setting clear boundaries for media access, a facility and event manager can effectively accommodate the needs of the media while maintaining a clear and safe environment for participants and spectators.

Press Box an enclosed working space for broadcast and print media members provided in stadiums at a high vantage point separate from general spectators.

Television Needs

Individuals are able to indirectly engage in sporting events by looking to mass media support. The television has been the most popular source of media for sports. Television coverage of large sporting events is vital in order to make financial and economic gains (Barget & Gouget, 2012). For example, an estimated over 114 million viewers tuned into the 2015 Super Bowl XLIX via the CBS network. In addition, the 2012 London Olympics had more than 219 million viewers. These examples of mega-sporting events and the number of viewers tuned in to them indicate the magnitude of television coverage. Sport facility management must ensure that they are providing the most clear and visually appealing broadcast for audiences that are looking to view a sporting event from the comfort of their own home. Sport organizations are continually changing their rules, schedules, and packaging in order to meet the needs of television broadcasting (Coakley, 2005; Jhally, 1989). In the World Cup, for example, FIFA identifies three required stadium zones related specifically to the media including a media tribune, a media center and a broadcast area (FIFA, 2012). Through the use of television, an incredible array of sporting events are broadcast to the homes of almost all Americans.

Supporting the needs of a television production is a complex and detailed process. Television productions have a variety of space and technological needs from the venue in order to broadcast an event. While the size and scope of television broadcasts of sporting events can vary greatly, the basic facility based components remain the same. Television productions need facility support for their video, audio, talent, and transmission. Support for each of these components includes both space and the ability to connect equipment.

The facility based needs for a television production begin with a space to park and power the television production truck(s) and the satellite uplink truck(s). Television productions of sporting events are produced using mobile production units. These units contain all of the audio, video, and production equipment for the broadcast. These trucks must be parked in close proximity to the venue and have access to a power source. All of the audio and video equipment for the television production will be connected to the mobile production unit and engineers, producers, and the director will produce the broadcast from inside of the truck. In addition to the production truck, a satellite

Reserved areas or platforms for television camera are an important feature in a media-friendly sport venue. Contributed by J. Patrick Marsh.

Specialized cameras and equipment may provide unique viewing for the fans watching on television, but may also impede the sightlines of spectators in the venue.

Space for broadcast production trucks and satellite uplinks can be an important space consideration for sport facilities.

uplink truck will also need to be parked near the production truck and a power source. The satellite uplink truck will also need an unobstructed path to the satellite. Obstructions such as trees or buildings can prevent the signal from reaching the satellite and disrupt transmission of the broadcast.

Facilities hosting a televised sporting event will also need to provide support for the audio and video equipment that the television production uses. Television productions use multiple cameras and multiple microphones to capture the sights and sounds of the event. This equipment must have a space to operate and a connection to the production unit. In most facilities that were designed to host televised events, camera platforms are incorporated into the design and provide space for the camera without interfering with participants or spectators. Often these camera platforms are also fitted with structured cabling. Structured cabling is a system of audio and video connection boxes throughout the facility that are pre-wired to a large connection box by the production truck parking location. When existing camera platforms are not present, an area for the cameras will need to be created, and connection cables will need to be run from the camera location to the production truck. When creating an area for a television camera, it is important that the facility and event manager work closely with the television production crew to create a space that fits the location and functionality needs of the television production without creating a disturbance to participants or spectators. This means that the camera and its cabling need to be in locations which do not create a safety hazard nor restrict the view of participants or spectators. In addition to cameras, television production crews will also position microphones throughout the facility to capture ambient noise. As with cameras, the facility and event manager must work closely with the production crew to ensure that the placement of microphones meet the needs of the production without hindering participants or spectators.

A typical connection box on a camera platform.
Contributed by J. Patrick Marsh.

A typical connection box for television production truck located just outside the venue. Contributed by J. Patrick Marsh.

The final component in meeting the needs for television coverage is support of the on-air talent. The on-air talent requires a combination of both audio and video support from the facilities staff, and the media relations or sports information staff should provide information to the broadcasters regarding the teams, stats and facilities. As was the case with audio and video support, talent support requires space. Television broadcasts need a space for the on-air talent that allows broadcasters to call the game and also allows for them to appear on screen when necessary. This means that the space needs to either be large enough to accommodate video cameras or be in a location in which other cameras for the production have a clear line of sight. In stadium settings, a portion of the press box may be separated and designated as a television booth or area for the broadcasters. In arena settings, these television areas are typically near the playing area in a *press row*. The space for the on-air talent also needs to include space and connections for their audio equipment, a statistics monitor, monitors of the game video feed, lighting for the broadcasters, and a workspace for the broadcasters' notes. A unique space need for on-air television talent is the necessity for their broadcast space to be located on the same side of the playing area as the main video cameras. If the broadcasters are calling the game from a point of view that is different from the main cameras, their call will not coincide with the video that viewers are seeing.

Field-side or court-side areas for in game broadcast or for pre-, post-, or halftime shows can create another space need for broadcast media.

Set-ups for on-air talent require an intricate system of cameras, microphones, lighting, video displays, and support technicians. Contributed by J. Patrick Marsh.

Radio Needs

Radio has the ability to reach out to audiences in ways other media cannot. From high school sports to professional sports, radio broadcasters paint the picture of the event for individuals who are miles away without the accessibility to a television in real time (Smith, 1995). Audiences are able to listen to sport broadcasts from the comfort of their home, in their car, while exercising, and places where other forms of media are not easily accessible. Through the use of radio, audiences can listen directly and immediately to many types of sporting events. Conveniently, there are sport-centered radio stations that allow for a connection between broadcasters and audiences, thus enhancing the experience of indulging in radio use for sport entertainment (Keith,

Press Row working space for broadcast and print media members provided in an arena or gym at a location close to the playing area and separated from general spectators.

2002). Radio has only expanded the range and types of audiences who have the ability to listen to many types of sporting events.

Radio is one of the oldest forms of mass media used to broadcast sports to the public. The first sporting match ever broadcasted live was a boxing match. In April of 1921, a sports editor for the *Pittsburgh Post*, Florent Gibson, gave a play-by-play to the surrounding areas of the Johnny Ray-Johnny Dundee fight via KDKA. KDKA became the nation's first radio station in 1920, when it made its first broadcast out of Pittsburgh. In August, just a few short months after the Ray-Dundee fight, KDKA broadcast the first live baseball game: Philadelphia Phillies versus the Pittsburgh Pirates (Bohn, 2011).

Radio broadcasts are relatively simple for a facility to accommodate. All that is needed for a radio broadcast is a space for the broadcasters and a mode of transmission. The space for radio broadcasters is typically located in the press box or at a courtside table and consists of a workspace large enough to accommodate the broadcast team's equipment and notes. Unlike television broadcasters, radio broadcasters do not need to be located on a specific side of the field or court. In addition to a workspace, radio broadcasters need a mode of transmission for the broadcast. Radio broadcasts of athletic events are not transmitted over the airways directly from the competition venue. They are instead sent back to a radio station by connecting a remote broadcasting unit to a phone line and transmitted over the airways by the radio station. This means that the host facility must provide phone lines for each broadcast team. Originally, these broadcasts were sent using an analog phone line; however, most current remote broadcasting equipment is designed to be transmitted through digital audio lines called Integrated Services for Digital Network (ISDN) lines. When hosting an event with radio broadcasts, it is important for the facility and event manager to communicate with the radio broadcasters in advance to ensure that the appropriate lines are installed in the appropriate locations and that enough separate lines are provided for the number of broadcast crews present for the event.

© *Everett Historical/Shutterstock.com*

Graham McNamee, one of the most famous radio personalities of the 1920's, broadcasting game two of the 1924 World Series at Griffith Stadium in Washington, D.C.

Print Media Needs

Programs, brochures, and newspaper access are important to event managers of sport facilities. From advertising prior to an event, to the occurrence of the event, to after the event, print media is vital for audiences to stay engaged in what is happening in the sports world. Brochures and advertisements allow audiences to have access to the details of an event; programs that are available to individuals in attendance at an event can contain information on the athletes as well as other important information such as the team's record, upcoming events, and even local attractions. For those individuals who are unable to attend an event and do not have access to viewing it live, newspapers allow for a recap. Also, a large increase in Internet reports has recently become vital in the way that audiences seek engagement in sport. Print media in the form of advertisements and news reports provides audiences with detailed information to promote and support an athletic event or team.

From a facility and event management perspective, supporting the needs of print media can be broken down into supporting writers and supporting photographers. Media support for writers includes access to game viewing (typically within the press box for stadiums or the press row for arenas), access to game statistics, access to participant interviews, and a workspace. These viewing areas typically include a table or counter space, at least one power outlet per person, and Internet access. During the game, media members should be provided with game statistics either in the form of printed box scores at regular intervals or through live stats monitors in the media viewing area.

After the conclusion of the game, media members will need access to participants for interviews. Interviews can be conducted in a

A press conference area during the 2012 Snowboard World Cup.

Media seating in a press box with the power and hard-wire Internet connections available for each media member. Contributed by J. Patrick Marsh.

designated interview area or in the team locker rooms. Media access to athletes is often set by league policy. It is important that the facility and event manager know these policies and facilitate the appropriate access. In the event that there is not a policy in place for media access, the facility and event staff must communicate with the participants and the media to determine the appropriate access for interviews. This includes the number of participants the media will be permitted to interview, where the interviews will take place, and the timing of the access. Typically participants will be granted a "cooling off" period before the media is allowed access and there will be a time limit on the participants' availability. Historically, media access to locker rooms has been a point of contention in the sports world due to differing opinions on the appropriateness of access by members of the opposite sex; however, courts have ruled that reporters should have equal access to locker rooms regardless of gender. If the media is granted access to the locker rooms, all working media must be granted the same access.

Writers also need access to a workspace following the competition to write their stories. Writers typically have a deadline to submit their stories and

Photographer work area during a Copa America soccer match. Also note the microphone positioned to capture ambient noise from the match. Contributed by J. Patrick Marsh.

must work from the competition venue immediately following the event in order to make their deadline. The workspace for writers can be in a separate media workroom, the media viewing area, the interview room, or any space where there is access to power and Internet.

Media support for photographers is primarily about determining where photographers can position themselves and their cameras. This requires interaction between the facility and event manager and the photographers to provide the best access while maintaining a safe playing area, free from obstructions. Often photographers will be limited to certain areas around the playing area for taking traditional photographs. In addition to traditional point and shoot photography, photographers will often place remote cameras in different locations throughout the facility to capture unique images. It is extremely important that the facility and event manager work closely with photographers using remote cameras to ensure that these cameras are both mounted in an area that does not interfere with the competition or spectators and that the cameras mounted in a safe and secure fashion. In addition to access to camera positions, photographers also need a workspace following the game to edit and upload their photos. Prior to digital photography, facilities needed to have a dark room for photographers; however, now, photographers are able to use the same workspace as writers.

Professional Organizations

Many writers and reporters who specialize in sports media have the opportunity to join and participate within professional organizations associated with their sport or event. Professional organizations provide a bridge between the professional sporting world and journalist, acting as a union to ensure the rights and respect of their members. The Professional Basketball Writers Association (PBWA) is just one example of these professional organizations, with approximately 175 members. The PBWA describes itself as a "nonprofit membership organization comprised of people who regularly cover the NBA for newspapers, magazines and websites" (Schmitt-Boyer, 2013). PBWA was founded in 1972 to give sports reporters and broadcasters better working conditions, with more consistent access to locker rooms or practices. During the early 1970s the NBA had no system that detailed the rights and access to be given to journalists, making it tough to report consistently. Since the PBWA's founding in 1972, "press seating and pre- and post-game access to locker rooms improved considerably" (Schmitt-Boyer, 2013). It has its own awards as well, honoring coaches, players, and public relations departments of NBA teams that show exceptional professionalism and cooperation with the media. An elected membership committee grants PBWA membership; members are vetted to make sure they meet PBWA criteria. PBWA criteria include being a regular contributor to newspapers or magazines that cover professional basketball frequently—usually on a daily basis—as well as generating content that is original and honest.

As the landscape of coverage changes in professional sports, professional organizations like the PBWA ensure that journalists and media are given the fair and necessary tools to provide accurate and detailed coverage to fans. These organizations include general associations across multiple sports like the National Sports Media Association (NMSA), and other sport specific groups like the Pro Football Writers of America (PFWA), the Baseball Writers Association of America (BBWAA), and the Professional Hockey Writers Association (PHWA) to name a few.

Digital and Social Media

Over recent years, both the IOC and FIFA have had to deal with the threat posed by digital and social media acceleration that has transformed the landscape for media and communication around their event assets. Having previously been preoccupied with the management, control, and protection of all media, these sanctioning bodies are now faced with an audience of confident digital media users keen to produce their own content and share it instantly across their social networks. Media users are able to do this without ever having to interact with established media platforms, or adhere to the strict licensing and brand protection guidelines governing the Olympic Games and FIFA World Cup.

The concepts of both speed and acceleration are important. New media tools and technologies allow for the participation, distillation and instant mediatization of experiences at, and distant from, mega-sporting events. Speed and acceleration in the distribution of information allow for information to be transported as soon as possible so that individuals are not missing any action. The high speed and acceleration allow for audiences to have an experience as if they are present at the event. As Redhead (2007, p. 238) suggests, using mobile devices (whether smartphones or tablets) enables participants to take pictures or videos and "instantly send those photos to either friends who are absent from the stadium or, increasingly, to new media companies that request fans' pictures of events at games as part of their UGC news gathering." Redhead associates the emergence of new media and its accessible tools with the notion of accelerated modernity evident in mediatized sporting events. This speed creates challenges of control and management for event owners and corporate sponsors alike in providing selective reformulations of events that suit their dominant narrative. For example, the IOC was, until recently, vociferous in their protection of official Games venues to the point where only rights holders could distribute photographs taken in these spaces. However, once the IOC eventually realized the power of social media in 2008, it quickly reviewed its approach to image distribution recognizing the fallacy of trying to lock down a community of (young) audiences it really needed to reach and bring into the (so-called) Olympic Family.

Media is the most widely used form of public relations in the sports industry. Through television, radio, and social media, audiences are able to remotely engage in sporting events from the comfort of their own home. Access to information via media outlets is fast, easy, and user friendly. Sport fans are able to stay up to date with information on their favorite teams and athletes as well as the occurrences of mega-sporting events.

Smartphones and Apps

Smartphones and apps have made it even easier for people to access sporting events, no matter where they are. ESPN is one of the channels providing cable customers with the ability to stream coverage live on their phone. As long as a customer has a subscription to a service provider, they are able to watch the game on their smartphone or tablet live, for no extra charge, by signing in with their account information. While regular television still has significantly more views, the ESPN Watch app has been downloaded 25 million times, and will only continue to grow. Comedy Central, Cartoon Network, CBS, ABC, and HBO are just a few of the channels joining the mobile movement. These carriers have the same requirement as ESPN Watch: asking the customer to use cable login information to access episodes. These apps, which require a subscription to cable, are referred to as TV Everywhere apps. Viewing of the TV Everywhere apps increased 264% from 2013 to 2014, with the main rise in viewership being the sports broadcasts (Wood, 2014). TV Everywhere apps are fairly new, with most being introduced only three or four years ago. With video views on mobile devices up 57% from 2013 to 2014, their growing popularity is undeniable (Wood, 2014). In the 2014 Winter Olympic Games, digital video views rose by 334% from the 2010 Games in Vancouver ("Sochi," 2014). Broadcasting companies purchased more digital hours of Olympic coverage in 2014 than they did traditional television hours.

Recognizing this growing trend, CBS announced that it will stream all commercials live for the 2016 Super Bowl. While Super Bowl advertisements have been streamed live before, CBS's announcement will mark a significant change in the number. During the 2015 Super Bowl only 18 out of the 70 plus advertisers chose to live stream the commercials (Steinberg, 2015). Providing the commercials on TV as well as on a mobile app will allow the advertisements to reach more customers, as well as a slightly different demographic. These added benefits offered by live streaming has caused CBS to raise the price of airtime for the 2016 Super Bowl commercials by around half a million dollars.

Super Bowl ads are some of the most coveted air spots of the year when it comes to sports media. Streaming these ads live online, as well as on television, shows the growing popularity of watching things digitally. It highlights, as well, the shift sport media is making to accommodate this growing popularity in smartphone and app usage.

Twitter

Live-tweeting, the process of tweeting about an event while watching it live, has become a cultural phenomenon: the 28.4 million tweets during the 2015 Super Bowl, using the hashtag #SB49, makes that apparent (Spangler, 2015). Whether it's the Super Bowl or the AMA'\s, the Twittersphere loves live-tweeting to express their opinion. Social media makes everyone a journalist, and live tweeting is a prime example. Almost all channels have embraced this live-tweeting trend. While watching a sporting event, or even a TV show re-run, channels have started including hashtags in the corner of the screen to encourage viewers to tweet about the program. This gets the word out to millions of potential viewers, piquing their interest and encouraging them to tune in via television or online streaming. While this is a win-win as far as publicity goes, this practice of live-tweeting offers unsolicited advice from amateur, at home viewers; especially when it comes to sporting events. Live tweeting is not intended to offer just a dry, play-by-play of a game. The idea of live tweeting is to attach a personal opinion or sentiment onto the current play. If during a Super Bowl viewers disagree with a referees call, it wouldn't take more than 30 seconds to send out a tweet trashing the referees, and using an effective hashtag to get the opinion "trending" on Twitter. Play-off and regular season games in almost any sporting event division tend to "trend" on Twitter. For an event to "trend" on Twitter, it must solicit a certain number of hashtags or mentions, demonstrating to the Twitter world how many people are tuned in. NBA, NFL, MLB, NHL, and many worldwide soccer games can always be counted on to earn thousands of tweets from fans.

To someone not watching the actual game, live-tweets, and the opinions attached to them, can be taken as fact. Live-tweeting and sporting events are intertwined in today's world. The 2014 FIFA World Cup set the record for most tweeted about sporting event. The Germany-Brazil semifinal match generated 35.6 million tweets (Sweeney, 2014).

Despite the threats social media may pose to IOC, FIFA, and other governing sport bodies there is no denying that it is here to stay and growing quickly. Many television networks are taking advantage of the rapid growth by encouraging social media users to post their thoughts and opinions of an event using hashtags provided for that specific event. This allows social media users to not only post their thoughts on the event, but also to connect with others who may have the same ideas, thus creating social connections among individuals via the Internet.

Fantasy Sport Leagues

The practice of live-tweeting sporting events shows something important about the younger generation of sport fans: they enjoy being engaged. For the younger generation, it's no longer enough to sit and passively watch the games. Whether it's video games, live-tweeting or fantasy leagues, Millennials cannot get enough of interactive fandom.

Fantasy leagues especially have enjoyed popularity. Fantasy football allows a fan to join a "league" that is either private or public. After joining a league, the fan is in charge of drafting players, one or two per position to have a full team. In essence, they create their "dream team." How well-or poorly-an athlete does in actual NFL games is reflected in the fantasy league. If a player scores several touchdowns or rushes an impressive amount of yards, the fan will gain points. The fan is in complete control of his or her fantasy league: if a player is injured or performing poorly, they can choose to bench or trade a player for free agents. Managing a team correctly, as well as picking the right players, can rack up points, leading to victory in fantasy leagues. Similar fantasy leagues are also in place for other sports such as hockey, baseball, soccer, and basketball.

As early as 1989, one million Americans were already playing fantasy football. Fantasy leagues have been whole-heartedly embraced by professional sporting organizations. Both the NBA and NFL have tabs prominently displayed on their main webpage that lead fans to the fantasy section of the website. Here, enthusiasts can sign up or manage their team.

In 2013, the Fantasy Sports Trade Association calculated that Americans spent around $15 billion dollars on their fantasy teams. In comparison, the NFL's revenue in that same year was $10 billion. That $15 million dollars comes from the over 33 million people who participate in fantasy football leagues each year. Of those 33 million, over six million are women (Steinberg, 2014). The amount of individuals who participate in fantasy sports and the money they spend per year reflects the magnitude of the effect that media has on our society today. Media users are always looking for ways to connect and communicate with others through the Internet, and fantasy leagues make this idea more accessible.

The modern fan is always tuned in to sports media. Fantasy leagues make it even more important for fans to tune into media. During the fantasy season, participants become obsessed with game outcomes and stats. They need to know what is happening with a player or his injuries 24/7. This causes people to tune into more traditional forms of media (e.g., TV, apps, websites) more often than usual. This also results in participants cheering for individuals rather than teams, indicating a change in the competitive team sport environment that has been popular in past years.

Whether it's the Watch ESPN app (streaming games on-the-go) or reading tweets, enthusiasts today have access to an unprecedented amount of facts and coverage. Fantasy leagues offer fans a way to put their knowledge of the game and players to use. Fantasy is the next step in offering the public as much sports related media as possible. It can be estimated that this form of sport engagement will continue to become more of a trend among social media and media users.

Internet and Cellular Service Support

Managing Internet and cellular service access has become one of the most important aspects of media support for facility and event managers. In addition to meeting the needs of media members working events, the desire of spectators for mobile access to the Internet has placed a premium on facility Internet and cellular service. Management of Internet and cellular service within a facility is a highly technical and complex process that will require the assistance of information technology (IT) professionals; however, it is important for facility and event managers to have a solid understanding the necessary access points in order to communicate these needs to the providers. The first type of Internet access necessary for a sport facility is wired Ethernet access. Wired Ethernet access is needed in most of the media areas within the facility including the TV production truck area, press seating areas, radio seating areas, media work spaces, and broadcast booths for on-air talent. Sport facilities also need to have Wi-Fi networks available for everyone in the facility. In facilities that host events with large crowds and large media coverage, high capacity wireless networks are becoming a necessity. In providing Wi-Fi access during sporting events, it is prudent for a facility to use different networks for different groups of users. There should be separate networks for house use, media use, and spectator use. Separating these networks provides the facility staff and the media with Wi-Fi access that is unaffected by the volume of use by spectators. In addition to Internet access, there is becoming an increasing demand for high capacity cellular service in large venues. When tens of thousands of people gather in a small area, the capacity of traditional cellular towers to handle the capacity of calls, texts, and cellular Internet access is insufficient. The use of distributed antenna systems (DAS) can greatly enhance the cellular service capacity in large facilities by providing an overlapping system of access points that boost cellular signals while mitigating interference.

LED Placement and Use

Media and aspects of media support ultimately strive to make a sport experience satisfying to sports fans. While many individuals obtain information from participation in social media, attending a sporting event live and in-person creates an entirely different experience. Creating an easily accessible and comfortable experience for audiences is an important element of the live in-venue sport experience, and efficient, reliable lighting, video boards and sound systems add greatly to this overall experience. Lighting in sport facilities has evolved over the years. The use of light-emitting diode (LED) lighting has steadily increased within

© FFooter/Shutterstock.com

At the time of its installation in 2009 the video board in Kaufman Stadium (Kansas City, MO) was the largest outdoor video board.

The video board at NRG Stadium in Houston, TX shows how video, scoreboard, and advertising content can be integrated. Contributed by J. Patrick Marsh.

sport facilities. LED displays are often being used in video boards, fascia displays, and scoreboards allowing audiences to more easily view video, advertising, scores and statistics on a visibly appealing monitor.

LED displays can be used in a variety of different locations throughout a facility and can provide a variety of different uses. LED displays can be used to create large video board displays, fascia displays along the front of seating tiers, and court or field side displays. In many large facilities, LED displays are installed throughout the facility and are connected using an integrated operating system. These integrated operating systems allow all of the LED displays throughout the facility to be operated in conjunction with one another to create a unified visual experience for the event and its spectators. Integrated operating systems for LED displays allow for the integration of timing, scoring, and statistical content with video content, event graphic content, and advertising content. The seamless integration of advertising content with other event related content is an extremely valuable revenue-producing tool for facilities and events. Thoughtful placement and operation of integrated LED displays create advertising content that is visible not only to the spectators in the facility, but also to television audiences and in photographs of the event. Marketing and advertising professional are able to quantify the number of advertising impressions through the LED displays and negotiate advertising rates based upon the results.

LED lighting can be seen not only on video boards, scoreboards, and other graphic displays, but in illuminating playing surfaces for athletes and aiding in the spotlight introductions of athletes. LED lighting is economically efficient and energy saving. Compared to commonly used halogen lights and metal halide lights, which consume 900 watts of power, LED lights only consume 150 watts of power while providing the same light intensity. This decrease in energy use produces an increase in energy savings (Steinbach, 2013). One prime example of this is the Dee Event Center, part of Weber State University's campus in Utah. LED lighting uses 70% less energy. Since switching to LED high bay lighting, the Dee Event Center has created an annual savings of $40,000 ("LED lighting," 2014). In addition to energy efficiency, LED fixtures are also more functional than traditional halogen lighting. LED lights reach full brightness between one and two seconds after being turned on compared to several minutes with halogen lights. This is helpful for the preparation of sport events as well as in the event of a power outage, thus LED lighting is becoming the standard in the sport industry for both primary and emergency backup use.

Audio Needs and Acoustics

In a large sport facility, it is vital that audio and acoustics are controlled in order to ensure that the audience has a comfortable and enjoyable experience. Audio and acoustics are used in facilities to relay information to the individuals in the audience, via a sound system. For instance, broadcasters who are announcing the game need to be heard at a comfortable noise level. Video displays and music entertainment contribute to the overall experience for audiences, as well. Having good audio and acoustics contributes to the audience satisfaction. If individuals cannot hear the information that is being given, they may become frustrated. On the other hand, if the sound system volume is too loud, individuals may be uncomfortable and tempted to leave the event. Control of audio and acoustics to ensure that the sound is at a reasonable and effective level is important during a sport event.

Designing an audio system for sports stadiums is a much bigger job than just picking the best brand of speakers. The first thing to be considered for an audio system is whether the complex is indoors or outdoors. While running audio through an indoor arena is difficult, it does not require as much maneuvering as outdoor stadiums. Indoor and outdoor stadiums indicate different audio needs between the two types of facilities.

Designers tend to approach sound for outdoor stadiums in one of two ways: multiple speakers coming from a single spot in the arena, or smaller sound systems scattered across the arena. Outdoor stadiums are a vastly different environment than indoor stadiums. Thus, implementing audio and acoustics in an outdoor stadium will be different from those of an indoor stadium. The main goal of these two environments, overall, is to ensure that the audience has a comfortable, enjoyable, and productive experience. Being able to hear clearly and at a comfortable noise level is vital for both outdoor and indoor facilities during events.

For outdoor stadiums, a distributed sound system, using scattered speakers, is agreed by experts to be the preferred audio method. However, many stadiums may not have the money or structure for setting up the distributed speakers. Setting up audio in just one area of the stadium is more cost effective, and it makes maintenance much easier.

Whether a stadium is open on one end, or fully enclosed, plays a huge factor in designing an audio system as well. With an open-ended stadium there is a greater chance of sound leaving the stadium in windy conditions. Both distributed and single-source sound systems face the effects of weather. Temperature, wind, and precipitation all play a role in the amount and quality of sound that encompasses the entire stadium.

In most large stadiums and arenas, these audio systems work in-sync with large LED-video screens that provide entertainment and replays to the audience during a sporting event. If an arena is using these screens to broadcast videos to the crowd, the distributed sound system offers a superior experience to the viewer. If a stadium chooses to use single-source audio, the video being shown may appear out of sync with the audio coming from the narrator. When the speakers are located in only one part of the stadium, it takes longer for the sound to reach some members of the audience based on location. This produces a lapse between the movement of the narrators' lips and their actual words for some viewers, creating an unpleasant experience for fans (Steinbach, 2013).

Entertainment vs. Coverage

With the world's increasing technology, the media is able to provide fans with unprecedented amounts of access to their favorite sports, teams, and events. However, with all these new coverage opportunities come new problems. ESPN, for example, offers 24-hour sports coverage on their TV channel(s) as well as online, via their mobile app, and even in their magazine. All this coverage has caused critics to question if the coverage is too much, transforming journalistic reporting into entertainment. ESPN even describes themselves as "the worldwide leader in sports entertainment." Convenience and ease of access to these events via a mobile device is beneficial and ideal to sports fans. However, too much emphasis upon information and entertainment may be an overload to fans if it lacks needed context, insight, and analysis that would be part of journalistic coverage. Social media and media overall allows for individuals to be connected at all hours of the day. As technology continues to advance, and new types of sports coverage emerge, this balance between entertainment and coverage will be a question for fans and critics alike to answer.

Sport fans are allowed access to major sporting events, athletes, and breaking news in the sport world via Smartphones and apps. With coverage provided at all times, the desire for viewing a sporting event live can be diminished. Fans may be satisfied with participating in sporting events remotely, without experiencing live sport action. Viewing sport news, scores, and highlights online is a completely different experience than being present at a live event. The value of attending a live sporting event should not be diminished with the increased use of media. Indeed, extra effort is required by sport marketers and facility managers to provide unique content and experiences for those attending events live.

Conclusion

Overall, without the media, sport events would not be as widely known and popular as they are today. The sport industry provides a great deal of entertainment for the global population for spectators at the event, and the media allows even more individuals access to sporting events from a distance. Individuals are also able to communicate and connect with other media users via social media outlets.

Media has developed over the years just like the sports it covers. The media concentrates on everything from lighting and acoustics to apps and television coverage to give viewers the best sport experience possible. Media, ultimately, allows sport enthusiasts to be knowledgeable on the latest news of their favorite athletes and teams. With coverage and updates available to consumers non-stop, it is up to the press to continue to find ways to grow with the fans and keep sports an essential part of the public's day. It is also up to those operating sport facilities and events to take the necessary steps to assist the media with their coverage by providing policies, procedures, and facility spaces that assist with the sport media work within sport.

PRACTITIONER SPOTLIGHT

Photo courtesy of Dawn Ellerbe Crawford.

NAME: Dawn Ellerbe Crawford

ORGANIZATION: California State University Northridge

CURRENT JOB TITLE: Associate Athletics Director for Marketing, Branding and Fan Development

DESCRIBE YOUR ROLE AT CSUN: I started at CSUN in August of 2013. In my position, I oversee the Athletic Department's marketing, promotions, and community engagement efforts. This includes marketing efforts for the CSUN Athletics Department and 19 Varsity Sports with a focus on men's and women's basketball, volleyball, soccer, baseball, and softball for regular season and post season play.

I oversee special events for the department and lead our community engagement efforts. I supervised the event management team responsible for game day operations at all athletic facilities and game day support for all televised home events. I manage our spirit teams (dance, cheer, and pep band) and act as the liaison between Athletics and our campus departments.

EDUCATIONAL PREPARATION:

- **Undergrad degree:** University for South Carolina, BA Journalism
- **Graduate degree:** University of Wyoming, MA Communications
- **Special Certification:**

  NCAA Leadership Institute Graduate: Class of 2011

  National Association for Collegiate Women's Athletic Administrators (NACWAA) Institute for Administrative Advancement: Graduate 2008

INTERNSHIP(S): University of South Carolina Media Relations, Summer 1996
University of South Carolina Facilities Management, Summer 1997

ENTRY LEVEL POSITIONS: Marketing Assistant Colonial Life Arena, Columbia, SC
Executive Suites Coordinator for William Brice Stadium, University of South Carolina, Columbia, SC 2006–2008

CAREER PATH: Assistant Track and Field Coach
University of Wyoming, Laramie WY 1997–2000

Director of Marketing, Varsity Sports
University of South Carolina, Columbia, SC 6/2005–7/2008

Director of Marketing, Events and Public Relations
University of South Carolina, Columbia, SC 7/2008–8/2009

Assistant Athletic Director, Marketing
Cal State University East Bay, Hayward CA 8/2009–2013

Associate Athletics Director for Marketing, Branding and Fan Development
Cal State University Northridge, Northridge, CA 2013–present

DESCRIBE THE IMPORTANCE OF MEDIA SUPPORT IN COLLEGE ATHLETICS.

Both media and sports information departments are critical for the growth of an Athletic department. Shaping the message within your internal media department will ultimately help shape the external message that is shared via news and media outlets.

The Athletics department media relations directors work as the publicity arm of the department, helping share its news and special interest stories with the community. Media outlets amplify those stories to help reach fans, alumni, recruits and more. SIDs make it easier for the media to accurately and positively cover your department because they feed stories directly to reporters that are already stretched thin. A strong relationship with the media generates more coverage more often, resulting in more attention for the department and fan affinity.

WHAT ARE SOME OF THE GAME DAY RESPONSIBILITIES WHEN WORKING WITH MEDIA IN COLLEGIATE SPORT?

Game day responsibilities in working with the media include:

- Preparing press box, or press table for game day media. The media should have stats, player information, team rosters, printers, appropriate technology, and Internet connection. Insure that press boxes are stocked with updated player information.
- Preparing arena or stadium for television games. This should include parking of TV trucks, liaison for the TV crew access to arena or stadium.
- Confirming media attendance and securing credentials for media.
- Facilitate various requests by media members for information, statistics, etc.
- During the actual games, responsible for distributing statistics to the media in attendance. And after the game, tasks include drafting press releases and recaps.
- Overseeing post-game press conference, timeout and in game interviews. Scheduling time for media to speak with coaches and student athletes and making sure the athletes are prepared to answer questions.

HOW DO YOU HANDLE MEDIA WHEN SOMETHING GOES WRONG?

As Philip Lesly says in *Lesly's Handbook of Public Relations and Communications*, a good crisis plan should: 1) Establish among everyone in the organization that it will put first the interest of the people concerned, 2) Make it clear that the organization will be as open as possible about what happened as the facts and conditions permit, 3) Give priority to resolving the emergency and protecting people affected, and 4) Emphasize that the organization will be fair to all, including critics or opponents who may have instigated the problem.

The Matadome serves as the home arena for CSUN basketball and volleyball

Crisis communications is no longer reserved for big business and corporations. It's important for college athletics departments to have a plan in place to anticipate problems that may arise. The best way to face the situation is to face it straight on. The longer you allow the media to question the situation the faster they will form and distribute their own answers.

The first action should be to assemble a team. While the incident in question may be of concern to the athletics department often times it will affect the University as a whole.

The team should consist of the University President or representative, the Athletics Director, the Director for University Communications, the Athletics Communication Director, and the head coach or department head directly involved in the crisis.

The second action will be to designate a spokesperson, and agree on a consistent message the university will use to address the crisis. The message should include the allowable facts, be timely, straight forward and honest with the goal to re-establish trust and credibility with university stake holders.

Social media plays a central part in any communications plan. If used correctly, social media could be the most effective and timely strategy for controlling a crisis situation within college athletics. The message via social media must be consistent with the media message and all parties involved must work together to share the same message.

WHAT IS THE MOST REWARDING ASPECT OF THIS JOB?

The most rewarding part of my job is being able to serve and support the student athlete. I appreciate opening the newspaper or watching the news and seeing one of our students on the sport page or during the newscast. As we grow our relationships with the media, our fan affinity continues to grow which leads to increased attendance at our home sporting events. Knowing my work has led to a sold out arena full of cheering fans in support of the student athletes is quite rewarding.

WHAT IS THE MOST CHALLENGING ASPECT OF THIS JOB?

It's a misconception that all athletics departments have large budgets. One of the challenges I have is continuing to create positive environments for our student athletes and fans with limited resources.

Much of our success relies on the performance of the teams, the interest of the media to cover our events, and the fans choice to visit our facilities. Living in the Los Angeles area provides a unique challenge as there are a number of professional sports teams and cultural events for our news media to cover.

WHAT DO YOU BELIEVE ARE THE MOST IMPORTANT SKILL(S) TO DEVELOP?

The most important skill would be relationship building, effective written and verbal communications skills, basic graphic design skills, a strong work ethic, and a resourceful positive attitude.

WHAT PARTING WORDS OF WISDOM DO YOU HAVE FOR STUDENTS AND YOUNG PROFESSIONALS IN THE FIELD WHEN WORKING WITH MEDIA?

Regardless of which side of the media you chose for your career, there will be WORK.

I would advise any young professional entering the world of College Athletics to be ready for challenges and have an open mind to different opportunities within the department. While we tend to focus on the next opportunity we rarely take time to master our current position, it's important to continue to learn and improve where you are. I would strive to make myself indispensable, while opportunities will present themselves to move on/up in the industry, you always want to leave your current institution better than you found it.

Reprinted by permission of Dawn Ellerbe Crawford.

MINI CASE STUDY

It is Senior Night and a Division II basketball team has their last home game of the season. The coach asks that the players refrain from posting anything about the event on social media and ask that parents and significant others do the same. At the start of the event, barely any fans are in the stands. As the announcer begins starting line-ups, fans are startled by the volume of the announcer's voice that is extremely loud. They were unable to see player information on the scoreboard because there were lights out that had not been replaced. To make up for the lack of visual representation of the players and the game, the announcer attempted to comment second-by-second, but the sound was not fixed. A majority of the fans began leaving the game, including parents, before the end of the game and Senior Night activities.

1. Why do you think few fans showed up for the event?

2. Of the fans that were present, why did they leave the event early?

3. How could the fan experience have been improved?

4. Discuss the positives and negatives of media support in such a setting.

CHAPTER DISCUSSION QUESTIONS

1. Define media support. What is the difference between internal and external media?

2. Explain the importance of media support in major sporting events, such as the Olympics/Paralympic Games.

3. List the forms of media that are required in a sport facility and the use of each one.

4. How has new technology such as Twitter, mobile apps. and fantasy games helped media's traditional coverage of sports? How has it harmed traditional coverage?

5. Describe a mega sporting event that used lighting and acoustics effectively. Describe an event where lighting and acoustics were used ineffectively.

6. Discuss the critics who believe 'coverage' has become entertainment in today's sports media. Do you agree or disagree, and why?

REFERENCES

Barget, E., & Gouguet, J. J. (2012). The impact on tourism of mega-sporting events: The stakes of foreign spectators. *Tourism Review International, 16*(1), 75–81.

Bohn, M. K. (2011). Sports on the radio, 1921: The first wireless revolution. Retrieved from http://www.bohnbooks.com/2011/04/17/sports-on-the-radio-1921-the-first-wireless-revolution/

Coakley, J. J. (2005). *Sport in society: Issues and controversies* (7th ed.). Boston: McGraw-Hill.

Costello, S. (2015, February 24). 47 Great Apps for Watching TV on the iPhone. *About Tech*. Retrieved from http://ipod.about.com/od/bestiphoneapps/tp/Great-Apps-For-Watching-Tv-On-The-Iphone.htm

Covell, D., Hess, P., Siciliano, J., & Walker, S. (2007). *Managing sports organizations*. (2nd ed.) (pp. 82–114). Burlington, MA: Butterworth-Heinemann Publications.

Facebook. (2016). Number of monthly active Facebook users worldwide as of 2nd quarter 2016 (in millions). In Statista - The Statistics Portal. Retrieved from http://www.statista.com/statistics/264810/number-of-monthly-active-facebook-users-worldwide/

FIFA. (2012). *FIFA stadium safety and security regulations*. Zurich: FIFA.

Goff, B. (2013, August 20). The $70 billion Fantasy Football Market. *Forbes*. Retrieved from http://www.forbes.com/sites/briangoff/2013/08/20/the-70-billion-fantasy-footballmarket/#5a4ba34641b76000e60441b7

International Olympic Committee. (2014). IOC Marketing: Media Guide Sochi. Retrieved from http://www.olympic.org/Documents/IOC_Marketing/Sochi_2014/IOC_MEDIA_UIDE_2014.pdf

Jhally, S. (1989). Cultural studies and the sports/media complex. In L. A. Wenner (Ed.), *Media, sports, & society* (pp. 70–93). Newbury Park, CA: Sage.

Keith, M. (2002). *The Radio Station*, (6th ed.). Burlington, MA: Elsevier/Focal Press

LED Lighting Moving Up the Ranks for Sports Facilities. (2014). *GE Lighting*. Retrieved from http://www.gelighting.com/LightingWeb/na/images/VERT004-LED-Lighting-Growth-in-Sports-Arenas-White-Paper_tcm201-96394.pdf

Mullin, B. J., Hardy, S., & Sutton, W. A. (2007). *Sport marketing* (3rd ed.). Champaign, IL: Human Kinetics Publishers.

Pomerantz, D. (2014, January 27). ESPN tries to have it both ways. *Forbes*. Retrieved from http://www.forbes.com/sites/dorothypomerantz/2014/01/27/espn-tries-to-have-itboth-ways/

Redhead, S. (2007). Those absent from the stadium are always right: Accelerated culture, sport media and theory at the speed of light. *Journal of Sport and Social Issues*, *31*, 226–341.

Schmitt-Boyer, M. (2013). Our beginning. *Professional Basketball Writers Association*. Retrieved from: http://probasketballwriters.org/pbwa-beginning/

Smith, C. (1995). *The Storytellers: From Mel Allen to Bob Costas: Sixty years of baseball tales from the broadcast booth*. New York: Macmillan.

Sochi 2014 Global Broadcast and Audience Report. (2014). *Kantar*. Retrieved from http://www.olympic.org/Documents/IOC_Marketing/Sochi_2014/sochi-2014-globalcoverage-audience-summary-vaug14.pdf

Spangler, T. (2015, February 2). Super Bowl on social: Twitter, Facebook, tally records for NFL championship game. *Variety*, Retrieved from http://variety.com/2015/digital/news/super-bowl-on-social-twitter-tallies-28-4-milliontweets-during-tv-telecast-1201421151/

Steinbach, P. (2013). Designing sound systems to meet stadium audio challenges. *Athletic Business*. Retrieved from http://www.athleticbusiness.com/designing-sound-systems-to-meet-stadium-audio-challenges.html

Steinberg, B. (2015, July 28). CBS will live-stream Super Bowl ads in big move for media industry. *Variety*. Retrieved from http://variety.com/2015/tv/news/super-bowl-ads-livestream-cbs-tv-commercials-1201549892/

Steinberg, L. (2014, August 29). The fantasy football explosion. *Forbes*. Retrieved from http://www.forbes.com/sites/leighsteinberg/2014/08/29/the-fantasy-football-explosion/#69a3875e5458d10e5d95458d

Stoldt, G. C., Dittmore, S., & Branvold, S. (2012). *Sport Public Relations* (2nd ed.). Human Kinetics.

Sweeney, M. (2014, July 14) World Cup final breaks Facebook and Twitter records. *The Guardian*. Retrieved from https://www.theguardian.com/media/2014/jul/14/world-cup-final-breaks-facebook-and-twitter-records

Wood, M. (2014, June 4). TV apps are soaring in popularity, report says. *Bits*. Retrieved from http://bits.blogs.nytimes.com/2014/06/04/report-tv-apps-are-soaring-in-popularity/?_r=0

13

Booking and Scheduling Events

John J. Miller

OBJECTIVES

After studying this chapter, the student should be able to:

- Understand the relationship between booking and scheduling an event.
- Understand ways to organize scheduling an event.
- Comprehend the importance of contract negotiations.
- Analyze the different elements of a contract.
- Differentiate between the use of insurance and indemnification.
- Examine issues regarding holding dates.
- Appreciate the different types of riders.

KEY TERMS

Acceptance	Gantt Chart	Liquidated Damages
Booking Agent	Indemnification	Offer
Consideration	Insurance	Punitive Damages
Contract	Intention	Scheduling
Contract Clause		

KEY ACRONYMS

COI	Certificate of Insurance		**NRD**	Non-Refundable Deposit
HR	Hospitality Rider		**PR**	Production Rider
MR	Merchandise Rider		**ROS**	Run of Show

Introduction

Sport and fitness venues often have spaces that may be used in a multitude of different ways. For example, sports arenas, stadiums, and multipurpose fitness facilities may be suitable to host a wide variety of different sports events as well as concerts, religious gatherings and political conventions. However, large sport venues such as stadiums and arenas may be much more limited in available dates for other events due to the hosting their primary tenants' contests. Sports arenas often depend on concerts and family shows to enhance their revenue generation. Yet, there are only so many tours, and some venues miss out on shows depending on the planned routingof the tours and their market and venue size. As a result, when facility tenants can fill only so many dates at the facility, the gap becomes greater between events. These dark days, in which the facility is not at all used, are the curse of a sport facility's survival.

All of the numerous types of sport facilities and venues can be profitable by providing the right services. To do so stadium managers should try to schedule innovative and unique events such as a way to utilize the venue on a dark day. Sport facilities offer owners, operators, managers, and other connected stakeholders the opportunity to generate revenue through a number of creative planning forms. The way to fill the dark days and develop revenue production is consistently and properly book and schedule special events that are not typically associated with the venue. For example, MetLife Stadium (home of the New York Jets and New York Giants) hosted nine concerts in 2014 (Muret, 2014). Altogether the stadium booked more than 20 non-NFL events drawing a minimum of 35,000 attendees. Among these events held at the stadium was a Jehovah's Witnesses international convention that drew 50,000 participants over six nights and an AMA Monster Energy Supercross that attracted over 62,217 fans (Muret, 2014). Additionally, these bookings extended out to MetLife Stadium's parking lot where joint events such as Color Me Rad, in which competitors run a 5K course while people throw washable paint at them drew 15,000 to 20,000 people (Muret, 2014).

MetLife Stadium in East Rutherford, NJ, hosts numerous events outside of the NFL contests of the New York Jets and New York Giants.

© Richard Cavalleri/Shutterstock.com

Sports teams are often housed in sport stadiums and arenas as the primary tenants. A primary tenant may be recognized as being entitled under an agreement to the use and occupy a premises to the exclusion of others. For example, the men's and women's basketball teams at Troy University are considered the primary tenants of the Trojan Arena. As primary or anchor tenants, the teams may have input into the use of the arena while in season, including play-offs. Additionally, these teams will often have precedence in using the facility during the off-season for camps and training.

In more recently built venues, the significance of the primary tenant is significantly related to the design of the facility. In many cases, the design becomes an extension of the team brand. However, primary tenants are not the only ones who can generate revenue for a sports facility. Indoor facilities that designed to host sporting and events are often constructed to accommodate one or multiple primary tenants. In fact, facility construction sometimes includes adjacent practice facilities for the primary tenants to increase event bookings.

The design of the new Yankee Stadium is an extension of the New York Yankee team brand.

Booking

For nearly 40 years, booking managers have become more and more aggressive in booking events at their facilities. Gone are the days when booking managers (who were usually the facility managers) waited to have events or acts contact them to be booked at their facility. Nowadays, the booking manager is more likely to take the risk of becoming the presenter of the event or act. By doing so, the booking manager, as the event presenter, must have a deeper understanding and more control of the event that may benefit both the organization and the community.

Scheduling and booking can be as simple as planning practice and game schedules for a single community recreation center or gym.

Competition for events in most markets is deep, as is the struggle to find and attract new populations. To be successful, a booking manager must create a positive reputation throughout the industry. To develop deep-rooted and trusting relationships in the industry, a booking manager must be honest and honorable when dealing with event promoters. A successful booking manager must be flexible during the period of contract negotiation with events. In order to thrive, a booking manager must hire and retain skilled staff to market and promote events. Finally, a successful booking manager must be ready, willing, and able to take some risks by assuming the role of co-promoter if necessary.

For the purposes of this chapter, the term *booking manager* will be used to identify the person responsible for booking events or acts for the facility. Booking takes into consideration the programming of a facility's master calendar in combination with mission statement. The booking manager must always be reminded of three significant questions. First, how does the

Booking and scheduling can be as complex as a global act like U2 in their massive 360 degree concert tour of 2009.

Tailgate parties are a way for sport event managers to build fan camaraderie, use all areas near the facility and increase revenue production.

event or act fit into the mission statement? A booking manager needs to identify the facility's goals and objectives, as stipulated in the mission statement, to ensure that they comply with the booking efforts. Second, does the event have the capability of being financially successful for the facility? A third question asks about the safety and legality of the event in question. If it is not already, how can it become safe and legal? By understanding the gaps of unique aspects that different entertainment and sport activities may offer to a community, the chance of increasing revenues may be attained.

One of the most significant booking responsibilities is management of the venue schedule. Booking can only occur if the facility is available, but entails more than just checking availability. A facility needs to assess an event's quality, the terms of the contract, a promoter's reputation, and other variables. The goal of the booking manager is to produce a well-rounded schedule. While the manager's job is to maximize bookings, it is more difficult with a stadium than an arena. The reason that fewer non-sport events can play in stadiums is due to stadiums being significantly larger than other venues and most other events cannot attract stadium-sized crowds. Thus, stadium managers have become increasingly effective in creating events for their venues that take advantage of all available spaces (e.g., tailgate parties).

Regulation of Booking Agents and Agencies

Booking Agent person responsible for booking events or acts for the facility.

*Booking agent*s concentrate on finding live appearances or bookings for performers. In basic terms, the booking agent loosely schedules events based on the restrictions presented by management and expectations as to where the act can and should play. In the traditional model, the agent goes back and firms up each market, often completing deals with the venues in each city. Because booking agents find and negotiate employment for artists, a role similar to employment agencies, some states regulate them through labor laws. For example, California law falls under the Talent Agencies Act while the New York laws are governed by the Consumer Protection Law (Roos, 2008). Almost 50% of all states in the United States mandate that a person possess a special license to be a booking agent (Roos, 2008). Given the extent of the entertainment industry in each state, it is not surprising that the strictest regulations are in California and New York (Roos, 2008).

In both California and New York, anyone who wants to find, secure, or try to secure dates for artists must apply to the commissioner of labor to obtain a license. One exception is anyone working in New York City must apply to the city commissioner of consumer affairs (Waddell, Barnet, & Berry, 2007). Both states require many steps, including completing an application form that reveals the names of all of the owners of the agency and examples of each contract form to be used by the agency, as well as an exclusive agency agreement and performance agreements-relating to the artist. The office of labor, or consumer affairs, will also launch an investigation of the agency owner's character. Besides application and license fees, both states require each applicant to post a $10,000 surety bond to use in case the agency refuses, or is unable to pay money to the artists they represent.

Scheduling

A significant part of the booking process is to schedule the types of events and timing of their use of the facilities. A booking manager creates a schedule or calendar of events for the facility. Although often used interchangeably, booking is dissimilar from scheduling. *Scheduling* refers to identifying and securing the specific dates and times for the event. Scheduling is the creation of a strategy of desired events and what is normally scheduled during the year. Every public assembly venue should possess a written mission statement that is regularly reviewed by its governing board. A written mission statement should have two important purposes. First, the mission statement must unambiguously identify the purpose of the venue. Second, it should provide a foundation for the governing body to make policy decisions regarding issues of scheduling and booking priorities.

Scheduling ability to find an appropriate time for a booked event.

Once the calendar is created, the manager needs to develop a plan for fulfilling all activities needed to produce the event. The scheduling calendar used to manage the venue's availability in regards to dates and area size may be considered the most essential element a booking manager possesses. Booking puts the scheduling strategy into motion. However, scheduling is not easy as the needs of the many will be heard. Scheduling issues may arise when more than one party wants to use the same area of the facility. An example of a scheduling issue could occur if a college team as the primary tenant of the facility qualifies and is chosen to host a play-off game on the same date that a concert is booked. In such cases, the concert will need to be re-scheduled as the primary tenant holds precedence over any other activity. Effective scheduling is also important when the facility a number of various activities being conducted. Imagine trying to run a basketball tournament, conduct yoga classes, supervise the weight and fitness room, and manage a volleyball league in the same week, sometimes at the same time, without good scheduling. Finally, good scheduling practices can remove potential discriminatory practices. Should all games for a basketball league be played in a relatively convenient time in the evening, while a volleyball league is relegated to another, more difficult time simply because basketball is considered a major sport? Does the schedule require the women's hockey team to practice from 10:00 p.m. to midnight while the men's hockey team always practices from 4:00 p.m. to 6:00 p.m. because of gender? Good scheduling can go a long way in preventing potential discriminatory practices.

On a larger scale, scheduling and revenue producing opportunities may be gained by hosting concerts for national and international touring musical performers. Scheduling acts that draw crowds beyond the capacity of an indoor arena are often options for further facility use. Visits by major religious figures, such as the Pope, have graced outdoor sports venues. Ultimately, the venue schedule should provide the best possible mix of events that meet the needs of the community, users, and the venue. A diversified event program, properly scheduled and effectively presented, requires a clear understanding of expectations of the events, the event's consumers, and the venue's governing body, coupled with an understanding of the venue's physical and/or personnel limitations. Accurate scheduling procedures enable management to prevent double bookings, which may result in losing an event. To ensure that the scheduling calendar is correct, it must be meticulously supervised with absolute integrity and accuracy so that profits and patron relationships can be increased.

Gantt Charts

Gantt Chart a graphic representation which depicts the amount of work done or production completed in certain periods of time in relation to the amount planned for those periods.

An accepted way to schedule is through the use of Gantt charts. A ***Gantt chart*** is a type of bar chart that illustrates a project schedule. A Gantt chart allows the organization to define dependencies between resources in the project.

The process of developing the Gantt chart requires group members to focus clearly on the tasks that must be completed to reach their objectives and goals. Ideally, a Gantt chart should be regularly updated to manage the process and eliminate foreseeable problems (DeMeyer, Loch, & Pich, 2002). Gantt charts were used to coordinate activities so orders would flow smoothly. Charts showed managers the progress of an order as it moved between work centers and the time planned for each (Wilson, 2003). These were described as "layout charts" (see Figure 13.1).

Gantt charts have seen a revival in their popularity (Wilson, 2003). They provide a quick and easily understood means for describing project activities and this attraction has stimulated their use in microcomputer based project management packages. Gantt charts are not solution techniques but they facilitate communications between the analyst and user, and provide a powerful method for implementing interactive approaches to scheduling (Perry & Rumpf, 1996).

© John T Takai/Shutterstock.com

Figure 13.1 Gantt chart example.

Diverse Scheduling Options

At many successful facilities, the revenue sources for sports facilities are often diversified. As a result, facilities must attempt to create a diverse scheduling calendar to the types of event mixture that will be conducted. To attain a diversified schedule, a comprehensive awareness and appreciation of the community must exist. For adequate event diversification, variables such as facility ownership/governance, community social and economic climate, community demographics, and availability of attractions with ancillary support capabilities should be considered.

A diversification of quality events will drive people to the facilities. The more people who attend an event equates to increased ticket revenue. Moreover, ancillary revenues such as merchandise, food and beverage, and parking will also increase. For example, a facility will have a more difficult time attracting crowds by offering the same event 15 times over a two-week period. In contrast, by varying the types of events, different types of spectators will be attracted for different reasons. For example, a Disney family event will attract a specific type of individual when compared to a World Wrestling Entertainment event. Additionally, the Disney event may result in more food sales while the WWE event may generate more alcohol sales. Finally, but importantly, facilities will realize that greater sponsorship opportunities will be possible due to the facility offering various events, thereby attracting diverse populations of event attendees. As can be viewed in Table 13.1, the top 50 ticket sales tours represented divergent talents from classic and present country and rock stars, the circus, wrestling, and the Harlem Globetrotters to Captain America, Iron Man, and the rest of the Marvel Universe heroes.

© Anton_Ivanov/Shutterstock.com

The Marvel Superheroes entertain audiences in movies and on live show tours.

Table 13.1 *2015 Year End Worldwide Ticket Sales Top 50 Tours*

Rank	Total Tickets	Act
1	2,364,390	One Direction
2	2,273,328	Taylor Swift
3	1,578,003	Ed Sheeran
4	1,365,006	Foo Fighters
5	1,363,190	Kenny Chesney

6	1,286,416	U2
7	1,231,375	Luke Bryan
8	1,178,958	Ringling Bros. and Barnum & Bailey Circus
9	1,118,036	World Wrestling Entertainment
10	1,031,496	Violetta
11	938,668	Fleetwood Mac
12	875,232	Zac Brown Band
13	871,493	Maroon 5
14	832,406	Cirque du Soleil—Varekai
15	823,016	Def Leppard
16	790,555	Ariana Grande
17	784,757	5 Seconds of Summer
18	760,308	Dave Matthews Band
19	737,516	Imagine Dragons
20	700,305	Garth Brooks
21	696,787	Shania Twain
22	669,055	Winter Jam/Skillet
23	650,228	Florida Georgia Line
24	644,280	Madonna
25	628,733	The Rolling Stones
26	624,495	Billy Joel
27	618,193	Jason Aldean
28	617,634	Kevin Hart
29	614,517	Chris Brown
30	595,077	Cirque du Soleil—Quidam
31	568,553	Cirque du Soleil—Amaluna
32	563,459	Katy Perry
33	562,102	Neil Diamond

34	561,038	J. Cole
35	556,980	The Harlem Globetrotters
36	551,693	Take That
37	515,875	Andre' Rieu
38	507,281	Cirque du Soleil—Kurios
39	504,731	Eric Church
40	498,941	Cirque du Soleil—Totem
41	485,177	Brad Paisley
42	477,003	Marvel Universe Live
43	453,320	Paul McCartney
44	450,174	Juan Gabriel
45	442,337	Rush
46	440,743	The Illusionists
47	438,236	Helene Fischer
48	433,363	Train
49	433,219	Van Warped Tour
50	429,672	Nicki Minaj

©Pollstar. Reprinted by permission.

Negotiating the Basic Terms of a Contract

Every facility manager must be able to negotiate a contract that outlines the terms and conditions for the use of the facility. Similar to selecting appropriate events, negotiation is a complicated skill. Essentially, negotiation calls for an individual who can collaborate with producers, booking agents, and promoters to get the show for an affordable price. Typical kinds of contracts that a facility manager may need to negotiate include

The Harlem Globetrotters continue to be a top booked act globally entertaining through basketball in venues both large and small.

licensing agreements, ticketing-service providers, food and beverage services, and artist/talent.

The basic terms of a contract are negotiated between the agent (who represents the act), and the booking agent (who represents the event promoter) (Waddell et al., 2007). The agent and booking agent begin negotiations through a series of telephone calls or emails, which they debate, the fundamental deal points such as venues, date, and fee structure of the proposed event. When the discussion leads to an overall agreement, the booking agent and agent authenticate the deal in writing.

During the negotiating process, the contract terms must ensure that stipulations of the contract are plainly delineated and approved to by all parties. The primary focus for conducting an event is the deal the booking agent strikes with the act (Barnett, 1987). A contract is an agreement between at least two parties to conduct an event and/or activity. Contracts should include, but are not limited to:

1. Identifying the details of the parties to the contract, including any sub-contracting arrangements
2. Duration of the contract
3. Clauses that further explain the goods and/or services that will be received or provided, including key deliverables
4. Payment details and dates, including possible provision for interest applied to late payments
5. Any required insurance and indemnity provisions
6. Guarantee provisions
7. Special conditions or requests often in the form of a rider

The negotiation of the key issues of the contract advances toward the written agreement when the booking agent submits an offer form, which covers the basic deal points, including the fee structure (Caves, 2000). While the offer form possesses important information, it is the not the actual contractual agreement. Rather, the offer form indicates that the booking agent is willing to receive the legal written contract from the agent of the act (Barnett, 1987). After receiving the offer form, the agent presents it to the act's manager for final approval of the offer. In order to ensure that all necessary information is contained in the offer form, the agency for which the agent works may create a standard offer form. Some agencies have an online offer form to standardize and expedite the offer process.

© Randy Miramontez/Shutterstock.com

Cirque du Soleil has created a number of traveling shows that have proven popular bookings in arenas.

Details of a Contract

There is no particular format that a contract must adhere to. Usually, a contract will include either expressed or implied terms that will provide the foundation of the agreement. When the act is satisfied with the booking agent's offer, the contract, which is often a written legal document that describes the terms and conditions of the deal, is then signed by both parties. The three fundamental elements of a legally binding contractual agreement: the offer, consideration, and acceptance—must be revealed.

Offer

A contract is a promise or a set of promises for the breach of which the law gives a remedy, or the performance of which the law in some way recognizes as a duty (RESTATEMENT (SECOND) OF CONTRACTS § 1 (1981). An *offer* will lapse when: a) the time for acceptance expires; b) the offer is withdrawn before it is accepted; or c) after a reasonable time in the circumstances (generally the greater the value of the contract, the longer the life of the offer).

Offer a promise made in exchange for performance by another party.

To be considered a legally binding agreement, the offer must be presented without fraud, coercion, or deception. Any misrepresentation of the act by the agent may cause the offer to be considered fraudulent and the agreement may be nullified in court. For example, when the lead singer for the act has left the band and the agent fails to reveal the change to the booking agent, the booking agent may rightfully claim that there was deceit in the offer and seek to have the agreement invalidated.

Consideration

In order for a contract to be binding it must be supported by valuable *consideration*. In other words, one entity promises to do something in return for a promise from the other party to provide a benefit of value (the consideration). This element of the contract process is what each party provides to the other party as the agreed price for the other's promises. Often, the consideration is in the form of a payment of money but it does not always have to be. In fact, the form of payment may be anything of value including the promise not to do something, or to refrain from exercising some right. These contract conditions are essential to the agreement. If the contract provisions are not met, the contract may be terminated.

Consideration in contract law the item provided is exchanged for another consideration.

Intention

A contract mandates that the parties intend to enter into a legally binding agreement. The parties entering into the contract must intend to create legal relations and comprehend that the agreement can be enforced by law. To enter into the contract, the booking agent must have the legal capacity to

Intention create legal relations so as to denote whether a court should presume that parties to an agreement wish it to be enforceable at law.

evaluate and accept the offer. When the offeree is a minor, he or she typically has limited capacity to enter into the legal contractual agreement. However, minors may be allowed to undergone the legal process to be judged to have the capacity to sign the agreement themselves. Individuals under the influence of alcohol or drugs may have limited capacity to evaluate and accept an offer, but the person who willingly drank alcohol or consumed "recreational" drugs generally does not have a strong defense.

Although the agent prepares and presents the performance agreement, the act is bound to the terms of the agreement and the agent merely represents the act. Therefore, the offeror (the party presenting the offer to enter into the agreement) is typically the act or the company formed by the act (McKendrick, 2014). The offeree (the party who receives the offer) is typically the booking agent. The booking agent may accept the offer as it is presented in the original agreement or negotiate to modify it (Waddell et al., 2007). Although the booking agent may legally decline to accept the offer contained in the performance agreement, he or she generally would not have sent the offer form if the deal were not attractive. When the booking agent does not negotiate further or accept the offer, the agent may hesitate to work with the booking agent in the future.

Acceptance

Acceptance expressly stated or implied approval to the terms of an offer.

Acceptance, another necessary element of the legally binding contract, is demonstrated by the signature of both parties and the date when signed by each party (Judicial Education Center, 2015). By accepting the offer, the talent agent indicates that he or she understands the terms and conditions contained in the agreement, including those presented in the additional terms and the riders. Furthermore, by accepting the offer, the talent agent agrees to fulfill each promise described in the agreement.

An offer can only be accepted by a person invited to accept it (Judicial Education Center, 2015). Similar to the way it is determined whether an offer was made, an objective standard is used to determine if there has been an acceptance. A number of offers and counter offers may be made before the agreement is finalized. An indication as to which party makes the final offer is insignificant. Rather it is the acceptance of the offer that brings the negotiations to an end by establishing the terms and conditions of the contract. The person signing the contract (offeree) may be held personally liable for promises made in the contract (Waddell et al., 2007). In addition to the signatures of each party and the date when signed, the acceptance of terms may include:

1. The typed or printed name of the person signing on behalf of each party
2. The legal entity—act or company—for which each party is signing
3. The title of the offeror and offeree
4. The legal capacity of the individual signing the agreement when representing the organization (Waddell et al., 2007).

The contract must list all of the event requirements as well as guidelines, policies, and procedures for using the facility. In most cases, a booking will not be completed if the client amends or changes the terms of the contract unless the booking manager gives prior approval. Should the clients cancel the event, they often are required to pay compensation to the facility, which the clients acknowledge a genuine pre-estimation of the financial loss incurred by the facility.

Contract Clauses

In many cases, additional clauses may be included as part of the *contract*. A major *contract clause* is force majeure. *Force majeure*, otherwise known as an "act of God" permits an act to cancel, without legal responsibility, when conditions stated in the contract are met (Mercante, 2005). For example, if severe lightning is occurring in the immediate area while a performance or athletic activity is being conducted, the event may be cancelled. Inclement weather is addressed in the contract as part of the force majeure clause. In some cases, the performers may indicate that they, not the booking agent, will determine when the performance may be delayed or cancelled (Waddell et al., 2007).

©prudkov/Shutterstock.com

Severe rain and lightning may cause the act to cancel.

Default by booking agent occurs when the act includes a clause that gives them the right to cancel a performance if the agent does not live up to the conditions listed in the contract. The act may also include a clause that identifies them as *independent contractors*. In other words, the act is not an employee or employer of the venue. This clause also establishes that the contract does not create a partnership with the venue.

Verbal Contracts

Contracts can be presented verbally (spoken), written or a combination of both. Although the act and booking agent may form a verbal, unwritten performance agreement, enforcing it is difficult. When one party disagrees with the other's recollection of the stated promises, it is unlikely that valid evidence exists to help resolve the disagreement. Because performance agreements, even simple ones, contain many mutual promises, the written agreement is always better than the verbal agreement.

Many entertainment projects that involve substantial capital investments frequently proceed on the basis of unsigned "deal memos" and draft agreements with uncertain legal enforceability (Barnett, 2015). In some cases,

Contract a written or spoken agreement that is may be enforced by law.

Contract Clause specific provision or section within a written contract that distinctly delineate the duties, rights and privileges that each party has under the contract terms.

the courts may empathize with individuals who have relied on promises that would seem to be legally enforceable but are not binding contracts (Wilkinson-Ryan & Hoffman, 2015). Verbal agreements are based on the good faith of all parties but can be challenging to substantiate. According to Barnett (2015), a less formal contract (i.e. a verbal contract) reduces the enforceability of the terms. The lack of enforceability creates an opportunity for one of the parties to withdraw or adjust contract terms. Alternatively, the more formal contract (i.e. written contract) increases the enforceability of the agreement (Barnett, 2015). Thus, it is strongly recommended (where possible) for business agreements to be in writing, to avoid problems when attempting to establish the existence of a contract.

Breach of Contract

When a failure to fulfill the promises identified in the performance agreement occurs, that party is in breach of contract. When breach of contract occurs, the injured party may seek a remedy, usually through monetary recompense for the damages. There are three different types of damage recompense. Compensatory damages is the amount of money that the injured party would have earned had the contractual promises been achieved. When the defendant is determined to be in breach of contract, compensatory damages that equal the amount of money the court believes the plaintiff would have earned is awarded. Conversely, when the plaintiff is determined to be in breach of contract, the defendant may be awarded the amount equal to the estimated profit that the court believes would have been earned from the performance.

Damages

Punitive Damages occurs when damages exceed simple compensation and awarded to punish the defendant.

Punitive damages are awarded in addition to compensatory damages. Punitive damages serve the dual purposes of punishing past wrongdoing and deterring future wrongful behavior (*Rodriguez v. Suzuki Motor Corporation*, 1996). Punitive damages may be awarded if fraud was present in the offer or if the contract falsely stated that the venue had been secured (Waddell et al., 2007). Under the common law approach, the amount of punitive damages is initially determined by the jury and may be later upheld by the court. The main reason to assess punitive damages on the offending party is to deter similar conduct (Russell, 2015).

Liquidated Damages monetary compensation for a loss or injury to a person, person's rights, or person' property generally stipulated in the contract.

Liquidated Damages

As opposed to punitive damages, a *liquidated damages* clause is not to punish the person that breaches the contract. Liquidated damages is the specified amount of money that must be paid by the party in breach of contract. The parties agree to a specified amount of money that must be paid if one of them does not follow the terms of the contract. The rationale to include this type of clause is to make certain that the failure of one party to adhere to the contract does not unlawfully or fraudulently damage the other party. Additionally, the agreed sum must be a realistic evaluation that any possible damage may be caused due to the breach of contract. Thus, the person who breaches the contract understands ahead of time how much they would owe the other party. As such, liquidated damages clauses may function as insurance for both parties.

Insurance and Indemnification

Insurance

It is strongly recommended that the allotment of legal liability and the corresponding responsibility to pay for losses should be governed by the contract. Performance and venue rental contracts usually require the booking agents to assume legal responsibility for any injuries that may occur. As such, the booking agent must be able to possess a valid certificate of insurance (COI). While a COI certifies that an insurance policy has been purchased, it is not a substitute for the actual policy.

While *insurance* will not automatically decrease the risk of damages, it can assist the organization from possible catastrophes. To provide the best protection possible, the venue manager and supporting venue should consider several different types of insurance. One type of insurance is *general liability insurance*, which provides the organization with financial protection in case an audience member, venue staff, or local crew among others is injured. The venues generally necessitate the promoter to have a general liability policy of at least $1 million, depending on the size of the venue, recognition of the act, and/or the number of attendees (Waddell et al., 2007).

Insurance practice by which an organization provides a guarantee of compensation for specified loss, damage, illness, or death in return for payment of a premium.

Event cancellation insurance is a policy that reimburses the promoter for the net cost caused by the event being cancelled, postponed, or rescheduled (Waddell et al., 2007). The event cancellation policy depicts the potential events or conditions such as catastrophic weather conditions and delays in transportation. Generally, causes of cancellation that are not identified in the policy such as acts of terrorism or war may be included in the policy for an additional cost (Waddell et al., 2007).

A third type of insurance that is becoming increasingly important is *pyrotechnic insurance* as many entertainment acts and sports teams use such shows of display during the event. When the general liability policy fails to include potential injuries to the audience, fans, or the participants due

© melis/Shutterstock.com

Pyrotechnic displays are dangerous but commonplace at concerts.

to pyrotechnics, the booking agent must insist that it is addressed in the contract. In addition to pyrotechnic insurance, most cities require a permit for the use of pyrotechnics. It is important for the booking agent to discuss every detail of the use of pyrotechnics with the talent agent and obtain the appropriate permits. Most states require the pyrotechnic operator of the display must be certified by the state. Additionally, the operator is responsible for making certain that the display conforms to the state standards.

The 2003 Station Nightclub fire in West Warwick, RI was a reminder of the enormous potential for loss of life in assembly properties. The Station fire, one of the deadliest nightclub blazes in US history, was started by pyrotechnics during a concert for the band Great White resulting in 100 people being killed and 230 injured. Owners of the nightclub stated that they had no knowledge the band planned to use fireworks. However, Great White lead singer Jack Russell said, "Our tour manager set that up with the club" (CNN.com, 2003). Ultimately, Great White did not have the required city permit for a pyrotechnics display. The danger of fire is a significant concern in public assembly facilities and since the early 1900s there have been a number of significant fire related incidents that are summarized in Table 13.2.

Table 13.2 *Ten Worst Fire Related Fatalities in the U.S. since 1900*

Date	Place	Citizens Killed
September 11, 2001	The World Trade Center, New York, NY	2,666
December 30, 1903	Iroquois Theater, Chicago, IL	602
November 28, 1942	Cocoanut Grove night club, Boston, MA	492
April 23, 1940	Rhythm Club Natchez, Mississippi	207
January 12, 1908	Rhodes Opera House, Boyertown, PA	170
July 6, 1944	Ringling Brothers Barnum and Bailey Circus, Hartford, CT	168
May 28, 1977	Beverly Hills Supper Club, Southgate, KY	165
February 20, 2003	The Station Nightclub, West Warwick, RI	100
March 25, 1990	Happy Land Social Club, New York, NY	87
December 4, 1980	Stouffer's Inn Hotel Conference Center Venue, Harrison, NY	26

Adapted from Hall (2004)

Indemnification

As with any transaction, the party with the most power is likely to dictate the terms. The typical allocation of liability can be modified by the use of hold harmless/*indemnification* clauses in contracts. These kinds of clauses can assign liability between the acts and the organization for injuries to third parties. These clauses mandate that one party to the contract (indemnitor) pay for the legal defense costs and pay damages (settlement or adverse jury costs) on behalf of the other party to the contract (indemnitee) under certain specified circumstances (Sadler, 2010).

The hold harmless/indemnification clause may be written to provide three different outcomes (Sadler, 2010). In the first outcome, the limited form involves each party to be responsible for the legal defense, settlement, and adverse jury verdict costs only to the extent of their respective negligence. Secondly, the intermediate form mandates that one party be responsible for 100% of the total liability in the event that they are either totally or partially negligent. The third outcome compels one party to be responsible even if the other party is 100% negligent (Sadler, 2010).

Similar to other types of contractual negotiations, the party in power will usually try to influence the intermediate form or broad form provision over the party that is not in power. However, the most reasonable consequence will occur when the limited form is employed. The reason is that this will force both parties to be responsible to the extent of their own negligence and to pay the legal defense. However, the limited form provision does provide for a contractual remedy, which is likely to be more efficient than the common law remedy under tort. The contractual remedy makes it easier, less expensive, and more certain for the indemnitee to enforce its rights under the legal system when only the indemnitor is at fault (Sadler, 2010).

Indemnification compensation for loss or damage to provide security for financial reimbursement in case of an identified loss sustained by the person.

Holding Dates

The facility management industry is one of personal and professional associations in which formal rules do not exist between booking managers and promoters of acts or events. Unless the event is very famous and has a proven track of strong ticket sales, without a trustful relationship between booking manager and promoter, booking and scheduling an event becomes exceptionally challenging. Without this relationship a booking manager may require a non-refundable deposit for a tentative hold date, or dates.

A hold refers to a time slot requested as long as there is not already a signed rental agreement with another client for that time slot. A promoter may hold dates of a facility in several different ways. *First option* occurs when a space hold is offered by the facility. The promoter of the event possesses the first right of refusal and is subject to the terms of the agreement until a previously specified release date. Should this occur, the time holder must either proceed to contract or release the booking. The *second option* happens when the space hold is accepted by the facility as a secondary option to a first space holder. For example, an event holds the first option for specific dates. A second option occurs when a potential client asks to hold an event on the same dates that the first option. If the client holding the first option withdraws, the second option is offered the opportunity to hold the event. A second option hold becomes first option in the event of release of the first option hold.

A *prospect hold* occurs when a hold reserves a space exclusive of an assurance of an agreement. Prospect holds can be on first option or second option basis and can be disputed depending to the conditions of the policy. A *tentative hold* arises when a facility space is provisionally held for a certain date until the activity is definitely booked. A tentative hold may be released or contested if the agreement as well as the deposit are not tendered by the due date. Finally, a *definite hold* confirms a space hold when the agreement has been received and the rental deposit has been collected. A definite hold cannot be challenged.

Hold Date Challenges

A facility may reserve final judgment to accept, change, refuse, or terminate bookings as stipulated in the agreement. Challenges generally pertain to first option/prospect holds and to tentative holds when the agreement has not been accepted by the due date. Non-confirmed holds tend to be non-binding and open to challenge by other potential users. Should another potential event challenge a hold, the first party may be compelled to either release the hold or re-confirm within a specified amount of time. If a challenge is not met, the dates and facilities will be relinquished to the challenging party/and or facility.

A challenge is commenced when a second option group (challenger) is ready to contract dates and space for which there is already a first option hold in place. The second option group may contest the first option hold by dispatching a deposit, at the facility's discretion, of up to 100% of the estimated rent for the requested booking and signing a conditional license agreement with the facility. The facility will then notify the first option group of the challenge, and give the first option group an opportunity to: a) meet the challenge by posting a deposit equivalent to that posted by the challenging group, b) execute a license agreement or other acceptable binder with the facility, or c) release the space/dates. Should the first option group meet all of these stipulations, the facility will usually return the requested deposit to the second option group.

Deposits

Usually, all holds require a deposit. Groups with several holds must maintain a full deposit on file at all times. A deposit establishes a commitment to occupy a space on the specified dates. Generally, an executed license agreement is required. Additionally, the facility may command a contingency deposit for certain kinds of events or acts. The contingency deposit is determined by the facility manager predicated in the possible risk the facility may assume on the event or act being booked. An example of a standard rental deposit schedule is as follows:

Percentage Payable	Payment Due Date
50%	Upon signing the license agreement
50%	One to two months before the move-in day

Non-Refundable Deposit

A non-refundable deposit is basically the vendor's way of saying, "These are the damages I will suffer if you terminate the contract. I am permitted to them without having to do anything else." The non-refundable deposit (NRD) demonstrates the objective to actually purchase the contracted service. In exchange for the deposit, the parties agree not to accept other commitments. These deposits guarantee that the booking agent nor the entertainment talent will not cancel or withdraw from the performance without just cause (Moffett, 2006). When the deposit has been accepted, it becomes the consideration upon which the talent is obligated to deliver the service. Such deposits are non-refundable as they represent a promise to perform. Should the entertainer fail to make good on that promise, the non-refundable deposit returns to the facility. When the event price is significant, the non-refundable deposit may be comprised of several payments on a pro-rated schedule as the event draws near (Moffett, 2006).

Riders

A rider is an attachment to the basic agreement that describes additional requirements the booking agent must provide to assist the act, including their technical, hospitality, security, and merchandising needs. Because many of the rider requests proposed for inclusion by a major touring act are related to and under the supervision of the production manager, these provisions may be included in one comprehensive document known as the *production rider (PR)*. Each condition presented in the riders, no matter how insignificant it may seem to the booking agent, is a legal part of the agreement. When the booking agent ignores an obligation contained in the rider, the act may consider the buyer in breach of the contract, demand full payment, and refuse to perform. However, the act is unlikely to enter into a legal fray with the booking agent unless the cause of the breach is a major omission, including failure to obtain liability insurance, required licenses and permits, and failure to provide adequate state set, sound systems, and lighting.

The act's team creates the riders that are unique to the act and the tour (Waddell et al, 2007). The act typically has a rider for one-off or fly dates. One-off dates relate to shows that are not part of a structured tour. For such concerts, the booking agent provides all technical support except the acts backline gear and their instruments. The size of the anticipated venue is the major consideration when creating the language for the riders. Riders for stadium tours are much more extensive than are those of arena tours, and those for theater and club performances are less complicated than arena show riders (Waddell et al., 2007).

As the production elements of concerts have grown in size and sophistication, the riders have increased in length. The technical rider and performance agreement for the Beatles 1964 tour was six pages long. A major stadium tour today may have riders that are more than 100 pages long. The rider for a major tour typically contains the key contacts for the act. This allows the booking agent's staff and venue's employees to communicate with the appropriate representatives for the act. The contacts may include the booking agency, manager or management firm, tour manager, production manager, tour merchandising company, the company responsible for creating tour advertising, and the tour press coordinator.

Hospitality Rider

The task of keeping the event entertainment happy backstage is often the responsibility of the booking agent. Such responsibilities are predicated in a *hospitality rider (HR)*. A hospitality rider is a contractual document negotiated between the entertainment talent and the booking agent (Waddell et al., 2007). It identifies all of the relevant information and requests made by an artist for the venue. Most are pretty standard requests: type of beer, towels, water, dietary restrictions, technical specifications, and so on.

Although there is a common misconception that hospitality riders are simply lists of ridiculous requests for backstage comforts, the overwhelming majority of requests in the hospitality rider of a major act are reasonable and necessary. Nourishing food, including fresh vegetables and fruit, may seem like a nuisance to the booking agent but it is a valid request for the act and their crew who often spend more than twelve hours in the venue. The hospitality rider often includes the following items:

1. The type of ground transportation needed to carry the act from the airport to the hotel, hotel to venue, venue to the hotel, and hotel to the airport.
2. Description of the kind of hotel accommodations desired when the tour does not use a travel agency.
3. The number of dressing rooms needed and the accommodations in the dressing rooms such as the number of towels, room temperature, lighting for make-up, number of restrooms.
4. Food and beverage requirements including breakfast, lunch, dinner, and after-show refreshments.
5. Food and beverage requests for the act's entourage.

But many artists do include clauses that border on the over-specific and ridiculous, the most infamous story being Van Halen demanding all brown M&Ms to be removed from the dressing room. However, although it was promoted as an example of rock star overindulgence, lead Van Halen singer David Lee Roth claimed it was a way for the band to see if the venue management was paying attention to the details in the rider. Roth stated, "So in the middle of this huge contract rider… it was like a Chinese phonebook…I had them place a clause, in the middle of nowhere. If I saw brown M&Ms on a catering table, then I knew the pro-

Rock and Roll Hall of Fame band Van Halen has stipulated that a certain color M&M could not be included in their hospitality rider.

©s_bukley/Shutterstock.com

moter did not read the full rider" (Callahan, 2014, para. 9). If brown M&M's appeared a breach of contract could ensue, the show could be canceled, and the promoter would have to pay in full (Callahan, 2014).

The Technical Rider

The technical rider provides information regarding the physical area, the local personnel, the electrical power, and the equipment that the act requires when they arrive at the venue. When the act is touring without sound and lights, their technical rider provides a detailed description of the sound and lighting systems, which the local booking agent must provide. The technical rider may include the following:

1. The location of the house console and monitor console in the venue. With large productions, it is more and more common for the title artist to be completely in-ear and carrying his own monitor desk.

2. Specify whether the artist is traveling with a monitor engineer or one should be provided.

3. The dimensions of the stage risers including height, length, and width.

4. The stage plot, the diagram of instrument, amplifier, microphone, and direct input box locations on the stage. The stage plot is a picture of everything on stage and should be extremely detailed, down to electricity drops.

5. The input list describing the microphone and direct input signal feeding each channel of the sound console.

6. The lighting plot indicating the types of lighting instruments, their locations, and color of each piece of lighting equipment.

7. The rigging plot diagramming all rigging points and the maximum weight that each rigging point can hold.

8. The electrical power requirements including amperage, phase, and grounding for the sound and lighting systems.

9. List of offices needed for the production staff and tour management and staff and the number of telephone lines, high speed Internet connections, electrical power outlets, and photocopiers.

10. Request for a local physician to be available in case a member of the tour needs attention.

Security Rider

The security rider explains the needs and conditions to protect the act, their crew, and their equipment. When the act has a tour security director, the rider identifies him or her and requests that the local booking agent provide a copy of the security rider to the venue security director. The security rider may include the following items:

1. A condition that warrants and guarantees proper security for the act, the act's personnel, any guests of the act, and the act's equipment, including their instruments.

2. A request for the name and phone numbers of the venue's security officer, key venue administrators, local police, and appropriate state and federal law enforcement officials.

3. A stipulation that all contact information be in the possession of the tour security director no later than 15 days prior to the act's arrival.

4. A request for copies of the security plan, including a method statement (general description of how the local security staff will protect the act); risk assessment (an estimate of the dangers the act may encounter); the emergency evacuation plan (identifying the exit locations and means of transportation when an emergency such as a bomb threat or natural disaster occurs).

5. A request to schedule a security meeting including the tour security director, venue security director, and local security representative providing the event security, police and fire department representatives before noon of the day of the performance.

6. A request to hold a security briefing minutes prior to the doors opening for the paid ticket holders.

7. A copy of each incident report, description of any injury or arrest must be provided to the tour's security coordinator.

8. A request to hold a security de-briefing after the concert to discuss any incident that may have occurred.

9. Description of the stage barrier, the portable structure placed between the audience and the stage, and the number and type of security personnel to be positioned near the stage barrier.

10. Condition that only authorized venue employees and local stage crew be allowed in the venue during stage check.

11. A request that no beverages may be sold in glass or metal containers when the show is in an arena, stadium or outdoor festival concert.

Merchandise Rider

Merchandise sold at the venue is a major source of income for the act. The right to sell merchandise that includes the act's name or image is under the control of the act. The act typically hires a tour merchandising company to manage and market their tour merchandise. The merchandising company and the act's team create a rider that defines the terms and conditions that the local venue must follow in exchange for a percentage of the merchandise sales. However, when the booking agent is an independent concert promoter who rents the venue, he or she usually does not receive a percentage of the merchandise sales. The merchandise rider may include the following items:

1. A most favored nation's clause—this clause requires the booking agent to negotiate the lowest merchandising rate (the percentage of merchandise income that the act pays the venue).

2. Language indicating that the act's merchandising company has sole and exclusive rights to sell non-food and non-beverage items including audio and video recordings, photographs, T-shirts, or program books that embody the likeness, name, or image of the act.

3. A clause that specifies the booking agent's obligation to prevent the sale or distribution of merchandise, especially counterfeit merchandise, by anyone other than the act's representative inside or outside of the venue.

4. A statement that will provide the space, stands, and tables to sell the act's merchandise before, during, and after the show.

A poorly written rider may cause post-contract signing cost add-ons that could very likely ruin the budget. However, there are a number of benefits of a well-written rider. One of the most important benefits of a well-written rider is that it assists the client in deciding, before signing the contract, whether the accrued cost of the production is a feasible business decision. A second benefit of a well-written rider is that it provides the production company with the information needed to accurately assess a price to the client. The initial communication will ascertain the attitudes of all parties when the band arrives at the venue on show day. In short, a well-written, accurate technical rider will ensure that game day is smooth, seamless, and devoid of unpleasant surprises.

Timing Schedule/Run of Show

Creating an outstanding event is not as easy as it sounds. There are many variables and logistics, and organization is crucial. The first thing an event manager should do when planning an event is to create a Run of Show (ROS) document. Simply put, this document details when each part of your event happens and who is responsible for making it happen.

The parties will often agree to a "run of show" deal in which the fee is intended to cover the services for the entire length of production. There can be conflicting understandings to what run of show means. For example, a production company may anticipate that a run of show deal refers to the lack of overages and that no matter how long the shoot lasts, the flat fee covers all production services. Conversely, the talent may consider a run of show agreement to relate to the fees that cover the scheduled period as of the start of the event.

Any event with some type of activity on a stage needs a Run of Show document that instructs the behind-the-scenes players what to do. Whether it relates to stage managers, lighting technicians, audio technicians, technical directors, or the announcer, the Run of Show serves as the architectural blueprint and road map for a successfully executed program. When crafting the ROS, the event manager should consider what the large items and sections of the event are and write them down in detail. These items may include staffing, event rental items, or attendee gifts among others. Additionally, the date, time, staff assignment and venue in which the event will take place should be written down. When the run of show is completed it is important to communicate it with all staff members. Failing to plan is planning to fail, but the run of show document will help mitigate these risks.

Conclusion

Correct booking and scheduling will generally be directly related to the generation of sales, which only reinforces its importance. Many entertainment and sports venues greatly rely on appropriate booking and scheduling to conduct their operations. To do so, these venues need to consider a number of items including diversification of the events, entering into contracts, and ways to protect themselves as well as their clients. The greatest responsibility of any public facility is to book events that present a full and diverse schedule consistent with the mission, public purpose, and economic expectations. Event activity, the result of successful booking, is important to the communities served by public assembly venues. They are important because they improve the quality of life, generate positive economic impact, and increase local, regional, and national visibility. Ultimately, the key to a venue's success is the ability to effectively identify and book events as expected by venue ownership and desired by the marketplace.

CHAPTER DISCUSSION QUESTIONS

1. Discuss the need for state regulations to oversee booking agents and agencies. Who or what are these regulations designed to protect? What examples can you provide?

2. How is booking and scheduling of acts intertwined? Can you have one without the other?

3. What are the advantages of booking and scheduling diverse events? What are some examples of diverse events that are booked and scheduled in a sports facility?

4. What are the elements of a contract? What happens if one of the elements is missing?

5. Why are written contracts/agreements recommended over verbal contracts/agreements?

6. Discuss the differences between punitive and liquidated damages as they apply to booking and scheduling events.

7. Explain the differences and similarities between insurance and indemnification.

8. Discuss the different types of riders and why they are important to understand when booking and scheduling an event.

MINI CASE STUDY

Part 1

The Miami American Airlines Arena seats up to 20,000 visitors and lists the Miami Heat of the National Basketball Association as its anchor or primary tenant. Additionally, this arena can be set up in five different primary configurations for events other than professional basketball such concerts and special events such as ice shows or the the circus. Moreover, the American Airlines Arena has also hosted boxing, religious, corporate, and Monster Truck events. Given that the Miami Heat, as the primary tenant, hosts professional basketball games beginning in early September with preseason games and ending in late April at the earliest depending upon the level of participation in the NBA playoffs, please explain the following:

1. How does the knowledge of facility use by the Heat impact the booking managers' responsibilities and goals?

2. How does the knowledge of facility use by the Heat impact the booking managers' scheduling responsibilities?

3. How would the booking manager use a Gannt chart in the scheduling of events for the American Airlines Arena?

4. Given that the American Airlines Arena is located in Miami, what types of events should a booking manager consider to ensure a diverse schedule of events are offered throughout any given year?

5. When the booking manager finds a date to schedule a concert, explain the contract elements a booking manager must understand.

6. Why should insurance be considered when holding an event? Identify and explain the different types of insurance that may be used for a rock and roll concert at the American Airlines Arena.

Part 2

Assume that you are working in the capacity of the booking manager for the American Airlines Arena and you have booked a national caliber band for a one-night concert. This band's manager has expressed disappointed with the original sound system during rehearsals claiming that vocals were not intelligible and that the music sounded loud but not lifelike. There were concerns during rehearsals that the vocals and music lacked power and presence. As a result, this band scheduled for the concert is threatening to cancel their performance. Using this information respond to the following items:

1. How would a rider be useful in this situation?

2. What type of rider would be used regarding the sound system? What are the elements of this type of rider?

PRACTITIONER SPOTLIGHT

NAME: Frank Roach

ORGANIZATION: University of South Carolina and Clear Channel Entertainment

CURRENT JOB TITLE: Senior Instructor, University of South Carolina

MOST RECENT PRACTITIONER JOB TITLE: Vice President, Venue Relations and Programming; Clear Channel Entertainment (now, Live Nation Entertainment)

EDUCATIONAL PREPARATION: Bachelor of Science in Government, College of William and Mary, Williamsburg, VA Master in Public Administration, Golden Gate University, San Francisco, CA

Photo courtesy of Frank Roach.

CAREER PATH: My first position was as the Administrative Assistant for the Department of Commerce in Hampton, VA. I was involved in convention and tourism promotion, as well as promotion of sports, concerts, and other events at the Hampton Coliseum and in other city locations. However, for my first "real" job in the facility management industry I served as the Assistant Director of the Hampton Coliseum a multipurpose arena in Hampton, Virginia from 1975–1979. During my four-year stay, I was able to double the number of booking at the Hampton Coliseum. For the next 15 years (1979–1994), I was the Vice President, Routing & Tours for the Ringling Bros. and Barnum & Bailey Combined Shows, Inc. (now Feld Entertainment). While at Ringling Bros. and Barnum & Bailey, I booked and negotiated arena contracts for two units of the circus and four units of Walt Disney's World on Ice. All told, I have booked more than 25,000 performances in more than twenty countries around the world. From 1994–1996, I served as the Vice President of Family Entertainment for MCA Concerts. In this position I established and directed the family touring unit, which produced and operated "Mighty Morphin Power Rangers Live." In 1996 until 1999 I was the President and CEO of TourVen, Inc, which was based in Burbank, California. TourVen served as management and marketing consultant to touring attractions, venues and other sports and entertainment. While I was at TourVen we provided tour scheduling, marketing, and consulting services for the highly successful "Barney's Big Surprise" tour and to various other sports, entertainment, and venue operations. From 1999 to 2003, I was the Vice President, Venue Relations and Programming, Clear Channel Entertainment. After I left Clear Channel Entertainment, I decided to go into academia. I was a Senior Instructor in the Department of Sport and Entertainment Management at the University of South Carolina from 2003 to 2015. In 12 years as a Senior Lecturer in the Department of Sport & Entertainment Management at the University of South Carolina I developed and taught courses in Event Management, Live Entertainment, and Venue Management. In addition to being a Senior Instructor, I served as the interim chair of the department for one year.

WHAT IS THE MOST REWARDING ASPECT OF BOOKING AND SCHEDULING EVENTS?

The relief you feel in getting all of the pieces to fit together in the right order to maximize revenue. It takes a great deal of time communicating with all of the parties to make sure the show is done correctly.

The Hampton Coliseum in Hampton, VA, a multi-purpose arena managed by Roach early in his career.

Photo courtesy of Frank Roach.

WHAT IS THE MOST CHALLENGING ASPECT OF BOOKING AND SCHEDULING EVENTS?

Getting all of the pieces to fit together in the right order; it's somewhat akin to putting together a big jigsaw puzzle without having access to how the final product should appear.

WHAT IS A UNIQUE ASPECT OR TASK OF YOUR JOB THAT MANY WOULD BE SURPRISED HEAR ABOUT?

In booking a tour, you work from most important markets to least important rather than from start to finish chronologically. This means that you may have shows booked in Orlando, Nashville, Chicago, and Raleigh, NC. However, as you move through the process, New York City becomes available but is only open on the dates for the Raleigh show. Since New York is the biggest market, and therefore has the most revenue to gain, you add in New York and reschedule the Raleigh show, for example. Hopefully, the reschedule dates for Raleigh show does not conflict with the others. If it does, then the Raleigh show may be cancelled since it is the smallest market. If you get the New York show, Chicago would be next, then Orlando, Nashville, then Raleigh. Geography aside, you always book and schedule from the market that is the most lucrative to the least lucrative. At least, if you want to make the most money you do it that way.

WHAT DO YOU BELIEVE ARE THE MOST IMPORTANT SKILLS TO DEVELOP?

The most important skills to develop, in my opinion is being able to analyze data, negotiate, people skills, and intuition (although I am not sure that last one is a skill but it's really necessary). In essence, you will need to understand the basic facts to allow you to make money (which is the bottom line in this business). However, you need to be able to communicate and listen to the other parties involved. You cannot rely so much on the facts that you forget you are dealing with people who have the same goal as you do, to put on a good show. Intuition comes from experience and being able to understand the booking and scheduling process as well as the other people involved in the process. Paying attention to these details helps.

WHAT PARTING WORDS OF WISDOM DO YOU HAVE FOR STUDENTS AND YOUNG PROFESSIONALS IN THE FIELD?

In the more than 30 years in the industry, I have found that there are three items that each student or young professional interested in this type of position. First, develop an appreciation for math (finances) and logic; this is all about problem solving. Second, devote time to understanding every aspect of the industry; to book successfully you must understand production, marketing, finance, and operational logistics as well as understanding the needs and desires of the venues you are playing. There are no short cuts. Third, you will be gone from home a great deal. If you have one, be sure your significant other is okay with you being gone. If you are single, do not own a pet. Finally, be sure to register for TSA Precheck because you are going to spend a lot of time going through airports.

Reprinted by permission of Frank Roach.

REFERENCES

Barnett, R. E. (1987). Squaring undisclosed agency law with contract theory. *California Law Review, 75*(6), 1969–2003.

Barnett, J. M. (2015). Hollywood deals: Soft contracts for a hard market. *Duke Law Journal, 64,* 605–669.

Callahan, S. (2014). Rock stars' wackiest backstage demands. *New York Post*. Retrieved from http://nypost.com/2014/10/11/rock-stars-wackiest-backstage-demands/

Caves, R. E. (2000). *Creative industries: Contracts between art and commerce.* Cambridge, MA: Harvard University Press.

CNN.com (2003). At least 96 killed in nightclub inferno. Retrieved from http://www.cnn.com/2003/US/Northeast/02/21/deadly.nightclub.fire/

De Meyer, A., Loch, C. H., & Pich, M. T. (2002). Managing project uncertainty: from variation to chaos. *MIT Sloan Management Review, 43*(2), 60.

Hall, J. R. (2004). Assembly property fires. *Fire Protection Engineering.* Retrieved from http://magazine.sfpe.org/fire-protection-design/assembly-property-fires.

Judicial Education Center. (2015). Elements of a contract. Retrieved from http://jec.unm.edu/education/online-training/contract-law-tutorial/contract-fundamentals-part-2

McKendrick, E. (2014). *Contract law: text, cases, and materials.* United Kingdom: Oxford University Press.

Mercante, J. E. (2005). Hurricanes and act of God: When the best defense is a good offense. *University of San Francisco Maritime Law Journal, 18,* 1–38

Moffett, B. (2006). *Booking the contract.* Retrieved from http://www.proformancedj.com/download/articles/contract.pdf

Muret, D. (2014). Variety pays off as venues fill event dates. *Street & Smith's SportsBusiness Journal.* Retrieved from http://m.sportsbusinessdaily.com/Journal/Issues/2014/07/21/In-Depth/Events.aspx

Perry, M., Foley, P., & Rumpf, P. (1996). Events management: An emerging challenge in Australian higher education. *Festival Management and Event Tourism, 4*(3–1), 85–93.

Pollstar. (2015). 2015 year end worldwide ticket sales: Top 100 tours. Retrieved from http://www.pollstarpro.com/files/charts2015/2015YearEndWorldwideTicketSalesTop100Tours.pdf

Roos, D. (2008). *How booking agents work.* Retrieved from http://entertainment.howstuffworks.com/booking-agent.htm

Russell, L. (2015). Statutory caps on punitive damages: Are they infringing on your rights? *Missouri Law Review, 80,* 853–869.

RESTATEMENT (SECOND) OF CONTRACTS § 71 cmt. a (1981).

Rodriguez v. Suzuki Motor Corp., 936 S.W.2d 104, 110 (Mo. 1996).

Waddell, R. D., Barnet, R., & Berry, J. (2007). *This Business of Concert Promotion and Touring.* New York, NY: Crown Publishing Company.

Wilkinson-Ryan, T., & Hoffman, D. A. (2015). The common sense of contract formation. *Stanford Law Review, 67,* 1269–1301.

Wilson, J. M. (2003). Gantt charts: A centenary appreciation. *European Journal of Operational Research, 149*(2), 430–437.

14

The Bidding Processes

Lawrence W. Judge

OBJECTIVES

After studying this chapter, the student should be able to:

- Define and discuss the three techniques that are used during the bidding process.
- Restate and give examples of the basic steps in the bidding process.
- Explain the importance of the eight essential factors for successful bids in relation to mega-events.

KEY TERMS

Bid Fee

Candidature Process

Host

Host Fee

Legacies

Olympic Agenda 2020

Relationship Marketing

KEY ACRONYMS

CFP   College Football Playoff

IOC   International Olympic Committee

NGB   National Governing Body

NGO   Non-Governmental Organization

RFB   Request for Bid

RFI   Request for Information

RFP   Request for Proposal

Introduction

The business world of sport requires supplies, information, and, of course, money. Companies often exchange these things via bids. The bidding process in sport can encompass several different applications. The use of a bidding process for sport facility design and construction has been covered within Chapter 6 of this text. Other applications of bidding for the purchase of major supplies, equipment or services have been mentioned in the chapters covering planning and budgeting (Chapter 4) as well as in the area of facility maintenance (Chapter 7). However, the primary focus of bidding for the purposes of this chapter will be on the process of obtaining the rights to host a sport event by a city or nation through the creation of a proposal or candidacy that is reviewed or approved by a sport governing body or rights holder.

In the United States, bidding goes on for nearly every NCAA (National Collegiate Athletic Association), NJCAA (National Junior College Athletic Association) and NAIA (National Association of Intercollegiate Athletics) national event. NGB (National Governing Bodies) like USA Track and Field or USA Swimming and NGOs (Non-Governmental Associations) like AAU Volleyball or the National Senior Games of many sports put their championship event sites out for bid. Many high school associations have also started to adopt bidding processes for events and venues (Seifried, Turner, Kristy, Mahony, & Pastore, 2007). Many other nations follow similar bid processes for major sport events, and most international events also follow a bid process for the determination of host locations for events. While mega-events like the Olympic Games or the World Cup may be the first global events that come to mind, there are many other international events that attract great interest in the bidding process. This would include more global multi-sport events like the Commonwealth Games, the Pan American Games or the X Games, other single sport international federation championships such as the Rugby or Cricket World Cup or the IAAF Track and Field World Championships, or tour stops such as ATP and WTA events in tennis or PGA and LPGA events in golf and many others.

There are three types of bidding techniques: RFIs (request for information), RFPs (request for proposal), and RFBs (request for bid). Each has its own unique purpose for a company or organization; for example, the RFI is often used to explore whether a company's service offering will meet the needs of the organization, while an RFB gets to more detailed aspects of the project including but not limited to timelines and financials. A well-organized bidding process can allow people to exchange goods, information, and money while minimizing many legal issues associated with contracting the event. Much of the bidding that occurs in the professional sports world revolves around the locations for mega-events, which are discussed further in Chapter 15. Many different locations bid for the chance to host these types of events. Cornelissen and Swart's article (2006) discusses how beneficial hosting one of these events (in the article's case, South Africa hosting the World Cup in 2010) is to countries socially, economically, and politically. Pomfret, Wilson, and Lobmayr (2009) explain the actual bidding process for mega-events, starting with individuals who stand to benefit from a successful bid. These individuals then form a lobby group and make contributions to the government for support of their bid proposal. However, the public is paying for the bidding process and the subsequent hosting of the event. Much of the general public does not realize that if the cost of these mega-events runs over a host city's budget, the taxpayers must pay for the deficit. Many lobbyists and political figures state that the benefits of hosting a mega-event are grand. In reality, this is not typically the case, as we will discuss later on in the chapter. Once a city determines it would

© lazyllama/Shutterstock.com

A bid to host the Olympic Games presents a complex process for a potential host city.

like to bid, they must often win a bid process at the national level. Only then do they bid at the international level—usually directly to the event holders such as the International Olympic Committee (IOC).

The Basic Steps in the Bidding Process

Whether you are the sport organization requesting the bids or the organizing committee or venue pitching to be selected, the basic steps are typically the same. Keep in mind that the product purchasing processes for bidding may be similar to the bidding process for a major sporting event. However, it does not mirror these processes completely. Completing the bidding process by following correct stipulations could be the difference between securing a bid and losing a bid along with its economic benefits.

Specifications

While discussing the specifications for the bidding process, the IOC will serve as the example bidding committee. The first step in the bidding process encompasses determining the specifications for an event. For the IOC, event specifications could include size and safety of a city, amount of public transportation available, or a country's climate during the time of the Olympics. The IOC must develop specifications for the bidding process. For example, if they need a building constructed, a schematic or blueprint must be developed first. All of the specific details for the entire project must be outlined in the proposal.

Request for Bids

After the specifications of the event have been developed, the IOC must request that bids be made. This can involve sending out invitations to bid on projects and posting the opportunity online or in some other publicly accessible forum. In some cases, the sports organizations will only request bids from a pre-selected list of *host cities* or countries in an attempt to save time and ensure quality. In other situations, the bid opportunity may be open to anyone who qualifies to bid on it. For certain events that are co-funded by government agencies, the law may require that the bids be posted publicly for a period of time.

Bidding

After the information about the project has been distributed to countries and cities, the bidding process begins. The bidding process can differ, depending on the rules set by the IOC, or other sporting organization. In some cases, sealed bids will be submitted, and the sporting organization will evaluate them. Sealed bids will contain a bidder's plans and costs for the event in a written proposal or with diagrams; this way the bidder does not present information as a spoken proposal. In other cases (more closely related to product bidding), a more informal bidding process will be involved in which the simply give a total amount required for completion of the work. Whether a bid is sealed, informal, or oral, the bidder must follow stipulations set in place by the IOC, or any other governing sport body.

A review of required bid documents made in 2013 determined that 83% of bids required a standardized questionnaire and 67% of bids included a comprehensive candidate file or bid book (Walmsley, 2013). The questionnaire system used by many sport organizations/rights holders fosters an easier and more standardized method for comparing the submitted bids. The candidate file or bid book requirement is typically viewed as more detailed and comprehensive than the survey methods. Some federations/rights holders require the submission of both within the bid process.

Reviewing the Bids

The IOC, and any other sports organization accepting bids, will typically set a deadline for when the last bids will be accepted. Once that deadline is reached, the committee will begin reviewing the bids. The length of time that it takes to review the bids could vary, depending on the number of bids received. The review process often involves evaluating the various bids against criteria pre-determined by the committee, such as resources, budgets, and timelines.

The review process can also include direct contact and interaction between the bidders and the rights holders through site inspection visits, formal presentations or both. An analysis of the use of face-to-face contact in the bid review process has been reported by Walmsley (2013) at the rate of 80% for bid presentations and 63% for site inspection visits.

Awarding the Contract or Bid

After the bids have been thoroughly reviewed, the sport organization or governing body will award the contract/event to one bidder. When bidding for smaller less competitive events, the bidder with the most financially appealing bid package will often be awarded the bid. For example, when it comes to bid packages for mega-events such as the Olympics, World Cup, bids that provide the greatest benefits for the event and surrounding community are often given careful consideration. The IOC will have pre-determined criteria that aid in their selection of a host city. Because these sporting events operate on such a large scale, a bid will be awarded to the city who proposes the most effective and feasible plan. In a bid for the Olympics, host cities are more likely to be awarded based on their benefits and legacy plan, rather than cost. Those involved in the actual vote or decision-making process within the sport organization or rights holder group varies. In some cases all members/nations of a sport federation or governing body will be included in the bid selection process, while in other cases the by-laws of the organization by having appointed an executive board or special council to award the bid. Walmsley (2013) reports that approximately one-third (35%) of bids are currently determined by a full membership vote while almost two-thirds (65%) are determined by an executive board or committee.

Stages of Bidding: RFIs, RFPs and RFBs

RFIs

RFI stands for "request for information." The purpose of this is to gather information on the capabilities and services of the companies around them. The IOC could use RFIs to obtain information on the current facilities, climate, or financial situation offered by the prospective host country. This is typically a step in the planning process for requestors in order to learn about the options—after which they compare their options. Contracts are not usually awarded to anyone after an RFI.

RFPs

RFP stands for "request for proposal." This is when the IOC or governing sport body announces that they have a desire to begin the search for a host city or country. This usually occurs through a bidding process. Countries may respond to the RFP with proposals for the project.

The requestor includes the following in its RFP: purpose and scope of project, specifics, timeline, contract type, data requirements, terms and conditions, goods/services needed, how the proposals will be evaluated, special requirements, and the format of the proposals (found from businessdictionary.com). In this bidding process, contracts and proposals are negotiated, and the contract is awarded to bidders based on the over-all package, not necessarily just on price.

RFBs

RFB stands for *request for bid*. A RFB is a way of bidding for an item that is usually commonplace, with lots of competition (the article uses copy paper as an example). Usually, the main factor in deciding where to place a RFB is price, because the other factors are the same across all boards (Darden, 2009). These are related to, as stated above, the request for proposal (RFP) and the request for information (RFI). Each works in a similar way, just desiring different things. An RFB is giving out a bid for a specific item, usually for less than asking price. The company/group/individual selling the item will usually negotiate with the bidder until a price is reached that both are satisfied with. RFBs for sporting events tend to differ in their price focus. While RFBs for product bids tend to use price as a deciding factor, the IOC will focus on price, community support and other tangible and intangible factors before completing this final step.

Bid Team/Committee

A bid team is the group of people who work together to plan and submit bids. This includes both the internal players—people on the team directly affected by the bid, and external players—people who are not affiliated with the group placing the bid but recruited to help. They are responsible for making sure that the bid is well prepared, there is a strategy at hand, and the bid is followed up with and taken care of in a timely fashion. It is important that the bid team stays together throughout the bid process because they need to work as a team in case of an issue or a counter proposal once the bid is made (Christiansen & Copp, 2014; Laryea, 2013). Each prospective host city/country will prepare a bid team. External bid players will often consist of former Olympic Athletes who can also serve as ambassadors for the bid team to the prospective host community.

Bid Preparation

When preparing the bid, it is important to have a clear, obvious statement of the permissions, limitations, and goals. Christiansen and Copp (2014) have a list of tips for preparing a bid, including reading directions carefully, speaking only to people those that the governing body permits contact with during the bidding period, proofreading the bid, having financing secured, obtaining local support, and being realistic, unbiased, and consistent. Often, in larger organizations, both the company seeking the bid—as well as the company providing a response—are required to work through their respective procurement organizations, who are charged with managing the entire process in a manner that solicits the appropriate information and protects company and individual interests.

Bid and Host Fees

The sport organizations or governing bodies are typically seen as the "rights holder" for the various events and championships that they put out for bid.

These rights holders typically will require some level of payment related to the event within a bidding fee a hosting fee or both. A *bidding fee* is an upfront charge to the city/region or organizing committee that is required at the time of submission of the bid materials and paid to the rights holder. For example, the International Ski Federation (FIS) introduced a bidding fee in 1997 in an effort to generate revenue to grow the sport and to focus candidates upon all aspects of the comprehensive bidding process. According to FIS Secretary General, Sarah Lewis:

> *The whole process completely changed in so far as candidates have to pay a significant, non-refundable registration fee and provide a fixed number of training days. The funds from the registration fees are used for the program for developing ski nations, which is a very extensive program of camps, seminars, coaching courses and educational sessions. That has been instrumental in increasing the number of nations active and increasing their (participation) level. (Walmsley, 2013, p. 41)*

An advantage to this bid fee system is that the bid fee creates a more efficient process as candidate sites must much more carefully consider the commitment to the bid process.

A *hosting fee* is a payment to the rights holder upon securing the event bid. Hosting fees may be somewhat less common than bidding fees because some rights holders prefer revenue sharing with minimum guarantees to would not cap earning for an event that becomes highly commercially successful. In 2013 it was reported that 68% of events charged bidding fees ranging from a low of $1,088 to a high of $650,000, and that 54% of event charges hosting fees ranging from a low of $5,441 to a high of $1,124,000 (Walmsley, 2013).

Bid Fee a payment required to the event rights holder from the city/organizing committee due at the time the bid is submitted.

Host Fee a payment required to the event rights holder based upon being awarded the bid for the event.

Factors for Successful Bids on Mega-Events

Because of the significant investments made during the bid process by candidate cities and organizing committees, much effort has been made to determine what exactly leads to success in this bid process. At least eight common factors related to bid success have been identified including accountability, political support, relationship marketing, ability, infrastructure, bid team composition, communication and exposure, and existing facilities (Westerbeek et al., 2000).

Accountability

Sport commissions are often developed in various cities and regions that seek to bring mega-events to their areas. These organizations often develop bids as part of their work/mission. Accountability refers to the ability of the bid team/organizers to deliver on what their event outline is. This means they must be able to market and promote the city and the event in a way that is attractive to the event holders (e.g., IOC), stakeholders (i.e., financial backers of the event), and the public in order to host a successful event that leaves a lasting legacy for the sporting organization.

Political Support

This factor refers to the idea that the bid committee needs to have the support of political entities in the city as well as the surrounding area. Governmental bodies need to support the hosting of this event in order to help financially, as well as to allow organizers access to public facilities to be used for the event. They also may be integral in helping staff the event.

Another caveat to this factor refers to the national and global implications of the politics in the host country. The bid committee must be aware of policies that will affect the event being hosted, as well as the attendees. For example, there was much political and social uproar surrounding the 2014 Sochi Winter Olympics and Russia's unpopular policies regarding homosexuality.

Relationship Marketing

Relationship Marketing marketing activities designed to develop and manage long-term relationships and build trust with customers.

This was the least important factor out of the eight. However it was still deemed important. *Relationship marketing* refers to the individuals that make up the bid committee and the influence on the people around them in order to help make their bid a successful one.

Ability

This was deemed the most important factor because it refers to the ability to organize and plan the sporting event. It is important that the members of the bid committee have expertise in event planning; however, it was important that individuals with specific experience with a large sport event be included. It is important to have the "sport" expertise so the committee can make the appropriate decisions in order to make a sporting event successful since this may be a unique event unlike many others.

Infrastructure

This factor refers mostly to the new buildings that would be constructed for the event. There must be an adequate location that is accessible for all persons wishing to attend. Secondary to this is the attractiveness of the proposed buildings and the population of the area in which the facilities are to be built. If there is a large population, then it is more likely that many people will be attending the event. When constructing buildings for the Olympics, host cities will often spend more money on developing the region than on the arenas necessary to host the competition. New facilities like hotels (including high end rooms), restaurants and other dining options, ground and air transportation upgrades and corporate entertainment options are often developed as part of the bid package for a mega-event.

For example, Sochi spent $7 billion on venues for the 2014 Olympic Games, while $44 billion was spent on developing the region in order to make it a prime tourist destination both during and after the games (Kresova & Prutz, 2014). This sort of development included hotels, transportation and other tourist infrastructures. While the actual Olympic venues are important for the Games, it is this type of city and regional development that creates memorable games, adding to the overall hosting atmosphere of the city. Of the 400

Olympic Park represents only a portion of the development of buildings and infrastructure for the Sochi Olympic Games in 2014.

structures built for the Olympic Games, only 11 of them were actually used to host competitions. Sochi greatly expanded their hotel offerings for the games, with over 40,000 rooms available for tourists.

The transportation infrastructure of Sochi changed drastically in preparation for the Games. Sochi constructed a "new airport, road junctions, roads, and rail links" (Kresova & Prutz, 2014, p. 156). In addition to adding hundreds of kilometers in roads, Sochi upgraded its energy system. The largest energy project involved both the heat and power station of the newly remodeled train station, which cost $856 million. While audiences might consider Olympic Games infrastructure to consist only of competition venues, a host city undergoes many more infrastructure projects: "the Olympics is not only the most modern sport facilities and stadiums, but it is also the most complex engineering infrastructure, without which the competition conduction would be impossible" (Kresova & Pruts, 2014, p. 156). Competitive, transport, energy, telecommunications, and tourist infrastructures must all be budgeted for and carried out in order for a successful Olympic Games to take place.

When Beijing hosted the Olympics in 2008, a large part of their infrastructure planning included the environmental and pollution aspects. A part of their environmental infrastructure plan included ridding the city of smoke polluted air and replacing it with clean air for both tourists and Olympic athletes. A large portion of this environmental initiative involved running a pipeline from Northern Shaanxi to Beijing in order to transport the more natural gas to the Olympic host city. This dedication to Beijing's environmental infrastructure was a huge part of China's proposal for the 2008 games. In the proposal, Beijing promised that the "city's natural gas annual supply capability shall reach 5 billion cubic meters" (2008 Beijing, 2008, p. 21). The city promised to achieve this by using geothermal, solar, wind and biomass energy sources (2008 Beijing, 2008). While clean air was a massive part of Beijing's environmental infrastructure plan, the city also concentrated on water pollution, drinking water supply, waste, and eco-friendly agriculture (2008 Beijing, 2008). Environmental infrastructure is important to any landscape where buildings are being constructed and landscapes are being changed, but it proved to be paramount to China's bid in 2008.

For bidding processes such as NCAA championship events, where new structures are not commonly erected, the meaning and budget of infrastructures is not as expensive and construction-heavy. While new structures are occasionally constructed in an effort to attract NCAA championship events, in most of these cases, infrastructure is more about maintaining and upgrading the current facilities.

Bid Team Composition

A variety of talent, age, gender, and skills were important for a successful bid. It was also important for former athletes or "high profile board members" to be on the committee in order to show the event holders that they had experts on their team. This variety was important because it made the bid committee versatile and full of all the skills necessary in order to be successful.

Communication and Exposure

This factor refers to the communication and IT systems available to individuals during the event. This is necessary in order for the media to successfully cover the event. This is important to event holders and stakeholders in order to enhance the image/reputation of the event. Communication and exposure are also important to enhance public opinion. Positive exposure allows the host city and event holders to reap the full benefits of hosting the event (e.g., economic impact through increased tourism from viewers who want to visit because they watched the event on the television).

Existing Facilities

This was important for many reasons. One is that the ability of existing facilities that can accommodate the new sporting events, as well as housing for visitors, indicates that the city has hosted a similar event in the past. Facilities can be an extrinsic indicator that the city has a legacy of hosting. Thus event holders are more likely to choose that particular city. Further, if there are

© Nando Machado/Shutterstock.com

These banners in London from 2010 were part of the unsuccessful bid campaign for the 2018 FIFA World Cup.

© Thomas Barrat/Shutterstock.com

This 2009 display was part of an effort to impress the Olympic Evaluation Committee's visit to Chicago as a candidate for the 2016 Summer Olympics.

existing facilities, it shows that the city is willing and able to host an event of this magnitude. Lastly, many cities begin constructing facilities prior to winning a bid. This shows the event holders, stakeholders, and community that the facilities will have a lasting positive impact on the community due to the possibility that the city will lose the bid so the facility will have to be used.

General Bidding Information

Bidding for a major sport event can offer many benefits to the hosting region. However, it can be very risky as well. The largest risk would be losing the bid entirely after many resources were used in the initial process; host nations spend millions of dollars on bidding alone. London spent $13–25 million on the bidding process while pursuing the 2012 Games (Poast, 2007). The city or region engaging in the bidding process incurs a large amount of debt: monetary and other resources, as well as time. Bidding is an investment that only provides a monetary return if the bid is won. If the bid is lost, then the public is left paying for this with little return. Masterman (2008) proposed that cities wishing to bid for an event need to plan for lasting "physical legacies." He acknowledges the high cost, therefore risk, of bidding for an event and proposes that cities preparing to win a bid should also plan how this preparation can leave a legacy in the case they lose the bid. This can help protect the investment of the city as well as protect the future bidding of hosting the Olympic Games. Regardless, it is known there is a large amount of prestige and legacy in hosting mega-events.

With advances in today's media presence, cities and regions can be showcased and promoted through hosting these events. This creates "event-driven tourism" that encourages long-term contributions to the economy.

The research is equivocal in whether these events provide social and economic benefits in the long term. It is the goal of many sporting events, especially the Olympics, to bring international cooperation, push host communities to the forefront of the world stage, and promote positive ideals. Therefore many developing regions want to host these events in order to reap the financial and social benefits. However, many successful bids are based on legacy or the city's previous success with hosting sport events. This is not likely for the developing regions in question. Further complicating the process for these developing countries is the cost of bidding, as the time and resource investment required for a successful bid is expensive and there is often resistance within the country because many citizens may believe that the money is better spent on the welfare of its own population.

NCAA Bidding

The NCAA holds a bidding process for a wide variety of it championship events, but most notable is the selection process for the host city of the Final Four for men's basketball. Because the Final Four is a smaller scale than

The NCAA utilizes a bid process for many of its championship events including all rounds of the Men's Basketball Tournament.

the Olympics, the bidding process and requirements are slightly different. For the IOC bidding process, the host city is often forced to erect new arenas, stadiums and lodging to house competitors; thus, their bids include not only a cities current amenities but future ones to be constructed if the bid is secured. For the Final Four, the NCAA examines city's already existing facilities. When Indianapolis hosted the Final Four in 2015, the NCAA bid committee examined the Indianapolis Colts' Lucas Oil Stadium, as well as the cities current hotels and public transportation system before making their decision. As in the Olympic bidding process, the community's spirit and desire to host the event is factored into the decision. The NCAA committee has several requirements when selecting a host city for the Final Four tournament: arenas and stadiums must hold a minimum of 60,000 spectators, while the city must be able to provide 10,000 hotel rooms within a reasonable distance of the tournament arenas. For the Final Four as well as any NCAA event bid, every bid must be associated with a member or host school that is connected to the bid.

As in the IOC bidding process, the first step for a prospective host city/school is to formally announce their intent to bid. Host cities have one month between the time the NCAA announces the beginning of the bidding process until the deadline for a formal bid intent is due. One month later, the prospective host cities second submissions are due to the NCAA. These submissions include "draft budget, hotel rates and confirmation of adherence to the NCAA's bid specifications" (Men's Final, 2013). The next step occurs when NCAA staff members meet with a representative from the prospective host city's bid team a month after the budgets are submitted. The finalists are announced a month after the representative meetings. Once the finalists are announced, they have six months before final bids are due to the NCAA. Final presentations are made before the winning host city is announced after a five-month decision period by the Final Four committee (Men's Final, 2013). The Final Four has certainly grown in its popularity over the years since the NCAA held its first championship tournament for men's basketball in 1939. Table 14.1 details the Final Four city and venue location over the history of this event. It is of interest to note that the first use of a major stadium venue over a basketball arena occurred in 1971 with the Astrodome hosting the Final Four. The last time that a traditional basketball arena hosted the Final Four was in 1996 when Kentucky bested Syracuse in front of a crowd of 19,229 in the Continental Airlines Arena in New Jersey (Guglielmo, 2016).

While the Final Four may be the most recognizable and largest in size, scope and media attention of the NCAA championships, the NCAA sponsors 89 championships on an annual basis with nearly all going through a bid

Table 14.1 *NCAA Men's Basketball Final Four Sites*

Year	City	State	Arena/Stadium Name	Championship Team
2021	Indianapolis	Indiana	Lucas Oil Stadium	TBD
2020	Atlanta	Georgia	Mercedes-Benz Stadium	TBD
2019	Minneapolis	Minnesota	U.S. Bank Stadium	TBD
2018	San Antonio	Texas	Alamodome	TBD
2017	Glendale	Arizona	University of Phoenix Stadium	TBD
2016	Houston	Texas	Reliant Stadium	Villanova
2015	Indianapolis	Indiana	Lucas Oil Stadium	Duke
2014	North Texas	Texas	AT&T Stadium	UConn
2013	Atlanta	Georgia	Georgia Dome	Louisville
2012	New Orleans	Louisiana	Mercedes-Benz Superdome	Kentucky
2011	Houston	Texas	Reliant Stadium	UConn
2010	Indianapolis	Indiana	Lucas Oil Stadium	Duke
2009	Detroit	Michigan	Ford Field	North Carolina
2008	San Antonio	Texas	Alamodome	Kansas
2007	Atlanta	Georgia	Georgia Dome	Florida
2006	Indianapolis	Indiana	RCA Dome	Florida
2005	St. Louis	Missouri	The Dome at America's Center	North Carolina
2004	San Antonio	Texas	Alamodome	UConn
2003	New Orleans	Louisiana	Mercedes-Benz Superdome	Syracuse
2002	Atlanta	Georgia	Georgia Dome	Maryland
2001	Minneapolis	Minnesota	Hubert H. Humphrey Metrodome	Duke
2000	Indianapolis	Indiana	RCA Dome	Michigan State
1999	St. Petersburg	Florida	Tropicana Field	UConn
1998	San Antonio	Texas	Alamodome	Kentucky

1997	Indianapolis	Indiana	RCA Dome	Arizona
1996	East Rutherford	New Jersey	Continental Airlines Arena	Kentucky
1995	Seattle	Washington	Kingdome	UCLA
1994	Charlotte	North Carolina	Charlotte Coliseum	Arkansas
1993	New Orleans	Louisiana	Mercedes-Benz Superdome	North Carolina
1992	Minneapolis	Minnesota	Hubert H. Humphrey Metrodome	Duke
1991	Indianapolis	Indiana	RCA Dome	Duke
1990	Denver	Colorado	McNichols Sports Arena	UNLV
1989	Seattle	Washington	Kingdome	Michigan
1988	Kansas City	Missouri	Kemper Arena	Kansas
1987	New Orleans	Louisiana	Mercedes-Benz Superdome	Indiana
1986	Dallas	Texas	Reunion Arena	Louisville
1985	Lexington	Kentucky	Rupp Arena	Villanova
1984	Seattle	Washington	Kingdome	Georgetown
1983	Albuquerque	New Mexico	The Pit	N.C. State
1982	New Orleans	Louisiana	Mercedes-Benz Superdome	North Carolina
1981	Philadelphia	Pennsylvania	Spectrum	Indiana
1980	Indianapolis	Indiana	Market Square Arena	Louisville
1979	Salt Lake City	Utah	Jon M. Huntsman Center	Michigan State
1978	Saint Louis	Missouri	St. Louis Arena	Kentucky
1977	Atlanta	Georgia	Omni Coliseum	Marquette
1976	Philadelphia	Pennsylvania	Spectrum	Indiana
1975	San Diego	California	San Diego Sports Arena	UCLA
1974	Greensboro	North Carolina	Greensboro Coliseum	N.C. State

1973	Saint Louis	Missouri	St. Louis Arena	UCLA
1972	Los Angeles	California	LA Sports Arena	UCLA
1971	Houston	Texas	Astrodome	UCLA
1970	College Park	Maryland	Cole Field House	UCLA
1969	Louisville	Kentucky	Freedom Hall	UCLA
1968	Los Angles	California	LA Sports Arena	UCLA
1967	Louisville	Kentucky	Freedom Hall	UCLA
1966	College Park	Maryland	Cole Field House	Texas Western
1965	Portland	Oregon	Memorial Coliseum	UCLA
1964	Kansas City	Missouri	Municipal Auditorium	UCLA
1963	Louisville	Kentucky	Freedom Hall	Loyola (IL)
1962	Louisville	Kentucky	Freedom Hall	Cincinnati
1961	Kansas City	Missouri	Municipal Auditorium	Cincinnati
1960	San Francisco	California	Cow Palace	Ohio State
1959	Louisville	Kentucky	Freedom Hall	California
1958	Louisville	Kentucky	Freedom Hall	Kentucky
1957	Kansas City	Missouri	Municipal Auditorium	North Carolina
1956	Kansas City	Missouri	Municipal Auditorium	San Francisco
1955	Evanston	Illinois	Wels-Ryan Arena	San Francisco
1954	Kansas City	Missouri	Municipal Auditorium	LaSalle
1953	Kansas City	Missouri	Municipal Auditorium	Indiana
1952	Seattle	Washington	Hec Edmundson Pavilion	Kansas
1951	Minneapolis	Minnesota	Williams Arena	Kentucky
1950	New York	New York	Madison Square Garden	CCNY
1949	Seattle	Washington	Hec Edmundson Pavilion	Kentucky
1948	New York	New York	Madison Square Garden	Kentucky
1947	New York	New York	Madison Square Garden	Holy Cross

1946	New York	New York	Madison Square Garden	Oklahoma State
1945	New York	New York	Madison Square Garden	Oklahoma State
1944	New York	New York	Madison Square Garden	Utah
1943	New York	New York	Madison Square Garden	Wyoming
1942	Kansas City	Missouri	Municipal Auditorium	Stanford
1941	Kansas City	Missouri	Municipal Auditorium	Wisconsin
1940	Kansas City	Missouri	Municipal Auditorium	Indiana
1939	Evanston	Illinois	Patten Gymnasium	Oregon

Adapted from www.fanbay.net/ncaa/final4.htm

process. A six-month long bid process has been adopted by the NCAA that begins with a release of bid specifications in mid-June, followed by intents to bid submission required in early August with final bids due in mid-September. Finalists are notified at the end of October, and the winning bid sites are announced in mid-December. In 2013, the NCAA implemented this new process and awarded 523 sites (294 final sites plus 229 prelim sites) for events from 2014–2018 ("NCAA Championships," 2013). This new process drew a total of 1,984 bid applications resulting in just over 26% of bid applicants securing their desired bid. Within each of these selection processes, each sport had a committee, per each of the three divisions, and each committee was charged to select the host site that would provide the best experience for the student-athletes, coaches, and spectators.

Collegiate football operates in a much different fashion. While the NCAA works through a bid process for the Division III, Division II and the Division I FCS levels, the FBS level of Division I has a unique structure. The post post-season play at the FCS level occurs through a bowl game system plus the College Football Playoff (CFP), currently including four-teams. The roughly 40 bowl games offer bids to teams from specific conferences that are contractually tied to the individual bowl games. Additionally, there is a group of "New Year's Six" bowl games that have a rotational structure for two of these bows serve as the hosts of the national semifinal games. The "New Year's Six" bowls include the Rose Bowl in Pasadena, CA; the Sugar Bowl in New Orleans, LA; the Orange Bowl in Miami, FL; the Cotton Bowl in Arlington, TX; the Peach Bowl in Atlanta, GA; and the Fiesta Bowl in Glendale, AZ. Beginning in 2015, the College Football Championship Game has been played at a neutral site that has been determined through a bid process operated by the CFP management committee. Two requirements for the bid are that the stadium must have a minimum capacity of 65,000 and it cannot be in the same city as a semifinal game for that year. Since its inception the College Football Championship Game has included the following hosts: 2015 AT&T Stadium in Arlington, TX; 2016 University of Phoenix Stadium in Glendale, AZ; 2017 Raymond James Stadium in Tampa, FL; 2018 the new Mercedes-Benz Stadium in Atlanta, GA; 2019 Levi's Stadium in Santa Clara, CA; and 2020 the Mercedes-Benz Superdome in New Orleans, LA (Scarborough, 2015).

IOC Bidding

While bidding to host a sporting event of this magnitude can be broken down into seemingly simple steps, the reality of the bidding process is very time consuming and labor intensive, especially for the Olympic Games.

Before a host city can enter bidding at the international level, it must be approved at the national level first. A host country may have several cities that wish to make an Olympic bid. If this is the case, the country's NOC (National Olympic Committee) must vote on and select one city to represent the nation in the international bidding arena. Up until the bid for the 1956 games, multiple bids from the same country were allowed for different cities. Nations including Italy, Germany, Switzerland, and the United States all have made bid efforts with multiple cities for the same games. None were greater than the 1936 Winter Olympics that saw seven bids from US cities including the winning bid from Lake Placid, NY. However, after the Summer Olympic bidding for the 1956 games concluded with six bids submitted by cities within the United States, the IOC restructured the bid process to allow only one bid per nation.

The IOC elects an Olympic host city seven years before the actual games. However, the IOC begins the process of selecting candidates a full ten years before the games.

The IOC begins inviting cities that have expressed an interest in hosting to start putting together a bid ten years prior to an event. This is called the "Invitation Phase" and is not considered a commitment to bid. The IOC holds a workshop for the cities considering candidacy that outlines benefits of hosting the games as well as what is necessary to bid. After the Invitation Phase, potential bidders can become committed candidate cities. In the three years between the initial bidding request and the host city election, the IOC hosts multiple workshops for the bidders. During this time, they also review proposals submitted by candidate cities that come in three stages:

Stage 1: Vision, Game Concept, and Strategy

Stage 2: Governance, Legal, and Venue Funding

Stage 3: Games Delivery, Experience, and Venue Legacy

After all bidders have submitted these three proposals over a time frame of three years, the IOC selects its host city for the Olympic Games to be held

Candidature Process
a two-year process undertaken by cities undertaking a bid for the Olympic Games.

Olympic Agenda 2020
a strategic plan for the Olympic movement designed to enhance the dialogue between the IOC and the candidate cities and to foster bid proposals that will deliver excellent Games, meeting the needs of the city and region to ensure a positive, long-term, sustainable legacy without compromising the field of play for the athletes.

seven years later. These three stages are called the "*Candidature Process*," and are part of a formal bidding process. This new bidding process, part of Olympic Agenda 2020, was just approved by the IOC in 2014, and aims for "greater dialogue between the IOC and the Candidate Cities (All About, 2015). The *Olympic Agenda 2020* outlines the IOC's goals for future candidate processes and places increased importance on "sustainability" for host cities. The IOC describes the Olympic Agenda 2020 as an attempt "to reinforce alignment between a city's long-term development plans and the Games, enabling cities to pursue the promotion of sustainable Games solutions and feasible long-term impacts which meet their needs (All About, 2015)."

Criteria of a Host City

When voting on a host city, one of the most important factors the IOC looks at is the economic stability of the country and government. As mentioned earlier, taxpayers and the federal government end up paying for a large portion of the Olympic Games, as a host city's government and sponsors can rarely cover the cost on their own. Due to the taxpayers' role in paying for the Olympics, the IOC prefers to select countries with a larger population. This makes the economic factor of a host city arguably the most important. For the 2000 Olympic Games bid, former President Ronald Reagan outspokenly endorsed Berlin, Germany as the host. Reagan cited that it would be a politically smart move, and would encourage unity in the host city and country. Despite the IOC's agreement that it would be a symbolic choice from a political standpoint, Berlin was eliminated in the second round of voting due to its unstable economy (Poast, 2007).

Research shows that over the years, choosing a city that is agreeable to the United States may have been a factor during voting. American broadcasting corporations like NBC, ABC, Fox etc., make up 80% of the IOC's broadcasting profits during the games. In addition, many of the Olympics' sponsors, who purchase logo use rights to the game, are American corporations. With this in mind, it is widely speculated that the IOC chooses a host city whose time zone will align better with American viewers. The political standing of a potential host city in conjunction with America's political views is also a consideration of the IOC. If they pick a host city with a government that does not align with US preference, they risk a boycott of the Olympics, which would result in a loss of broadcast and sponsor income.

Those who are more critical of the IOC's choices have expressed the opinion that the preference of the IOC president plays a big role, as well as bribes from candidate cities to other members of the IOC. Former IOC President, Juan Antonio Samaranch, came under heavy fire when the 1992 Summer Games were awarded to Barcelona—his hometown. Many in the media believed that this blatant and inappropriate use of power warranted his resignation. President Samaranch did not resign, and the incident cast an unflattering light on the way a host city is chosen by the IOC (Mason, Thiboult, & Misener, 2006). One of the most talked about bribe scandals in the IOC came during the choice of Nagano, Japan and Salt Lake City, United States, to host the 1988 and 2002 games. During a preliminary visit to the candidate cities IOC members received bribes. These events caused the IOC to add an amendment to their charter, forbidding the IOC committee from visiting prospective cities during the candidature process (Poast, 2007).

Table 14.2 provides a summary of the both the candidates and the ultimate host city for the Summer Olympics from the beginning of the modern Games. While the early iterations of the Olympics often had limited numbers of cities and nations pursuing the bid to host the Games, the growth of the Games popularity and prestige can be seen in the number of bids as well as the changes in cities vying for the opportunity to host.

Table 14.2 *Summer Olympic Games Host Cities and Bid Candidate Cities*

Year	Olympiad	Bid Winner/ Host City	Bid Cities (in order of ballot results) *cancelled or withdrawn bids not listed*
2020	XXXII	Tokyo, Japan	Istanbul, Turkey; Madrid, Spain; Baku, Azerbaijan; Doha, Qatar
2016	XXXI	Rio de Janeiro, Brazil	Madrid, Spain; Tokyo, Japan; Chicago, USA; Baku, Azerbaijan; Doha, Qatar; Prague, Czech Republic
2012	XXX	London, UK	Paris, France; Madrid, Spain; New York, USA; Moscow, Russia; Leipzig, Germany; Rio de Janeiro, Brazil; Istanbul, Turkey; Havana, Cuba
2008	XXIX	Beijing, China	Toronto, Canada; Paris, France; Istanbul, Turkey; Osaka, Japan; Bangkok, Thailand; Cairo, Egypt; Havana, Cuba; Kuala Lumpur, Malaysia; Seville, Spain
2004	XXVIII	Athens, Greece	Rome, Italy; Cape Town, South Africa; Stockholm, Sweden; Buenos Aires, Argentina; Istanbul, Turkey; Lille, France; Rio de Janeiro, Brazil; St. Petersburg, Russia; San Juan, Puerto Rico; Seville, Spain
2000	XXVII	Sydney, Australia	Beijing, China; Manchester, United Kingdom; Berlin, Germany; Istanbul, Turkey
1996	XXVI	Atlanta, USA	Athens, Greece; Toronto, Canada; Melbourne, Australia; Manchester, United Kingdom; Belgrade, Yugoslavia
1992	XXV	Barcelona, Spain	Paris, France; Belgrade, Yugoslavia; Brisbane, Australia; Birmingham, United Kingdom; Amsterdam, Netherlands
1988	XXIV	Seoul, South Korea	Nagoya, Japan

1984	XXIII	Los Angeles, USA	*No other bids*
1980	XXII	Moscow, USSR	Los Angeles, USA
1976	XXI	Montreal, Canada	Moscow, USSR; Los Angeles, USA
1972	XX	Munich, Germany	Detroit, USA; Madrid, Spain; Montreal, Canada
1968	XIX	Mexico City, Mexico	Detroit, USA; Lyon, France; Buenos Aires, Argentine
1964	XVIII	Tokyo, Japan	Detroit, USA; Vienna, Austria; Brussels, Belgium
1960	XVII	Rome, Italy	Lausanne, Switzerland; Brussels, Belgium; Budapest, Hungary; Detroit, USA; Mexico City, Mexico; Tokyo, Japan
1956	XVI	Melbourne, Australia	Buenos Aires, Argentina; Mexico City, Mexico; Chicago, USA; Detroit, USA; Minneapolis, USA; Philadelphia, USA; San Francisco, USA; Montreal, Canada
1952	XV	Helsinki, Finland	Los Angeles, USA; Minneapolis, USA; Amsterdam, Netherlands; Detroit, USA; Chicago, USA; Philadelphia, USA; Athens, Greece; Lausanne, Switzerland; Stockholm, Sweden
1948	XIV	London, UK	London selected without election after end of WWII
1944	XIII		*Cancelled due to WWII*
1940	XII	Tokyo, Japan*	Relocated to Helsinki, Finland; *Cancelled due to WWII*
1936	XI	Berlin, Germany	Barcelona, Spain; Alexandria, Egypt; Budapest, Hungary; Buenos Aires, Argentina; Cologne, Germany; Dublin, Ireland; Frankfurt, Germany; Helsinki, Finland; Lausanne, Switzerland; Nuremberg, Germany; Rio de Janeiro, Brazil; Rome, Italy
1932	X	Los Angeles, USA	*No other bids*
1928	IX	Amsterdam, Netherlands	Los Angeles, USA
1924	VIII	Paris, France	Amsterdam, Netherlands; Barcelona, Spain; Los Angeles, USA; Prague, Czechoslovakia; Rome, Italy
1920	VII	Berlin, Germany	*Games Cancelled due to WWI*

1916	VI	Berlin, Germany	Alexandria, Egypt; Amsterdam, Netherlands; Brussels, Belgium; Budapest, Hungary; Cleveland, US; *Cancelled due to WWI*
1912	V	Stockholm, Sweden	*No other bids*
1908	IV	London, UK	Rome, Italy; Milan, Italy; Berlin, Germany
1904	III	St. Louis, USA	Chicago, USA
1900	II	Paris, France	*No other bids*
1896	I	Athens, Greece	*No other bids*

Adapted from gamebids.com

In a recent analysis of determinants of successful bidding for hosting the Winter Olympics, researchers found ten to be the most influential (Feddersen & Maennig, 2012). These included altitude of the bidding city, low average precipitation of the bidding city, snow levels of the bidding city, existing sport facilities, population of the bidding city, small distance of Olympic village from the sport facilities and airport, hotel availability for the staff, volunteers, media personnel, etc., and the absence of inflation and corruption. Although the Winter Games have a shorter history and more lengthy set of geographic and climatic constraints than the Summer Olympics, there is still a tremendous interest in hosting them. Table 14.3 displays the host and candidate cities for the Winter Olympic Games beginning in 1924 with the inaugural event. While the Olympics have suffered cancellation due to global conflicts during World War I and II, there have been two occasions where the city awarded the bid did not host for financial reasons. First, in 1908 the city of Rome was awarded the Games, but financial constraints due to a volcanic eruption in nearby Mount Vesuvius caused the Olympics to be hosted by London, England. More recently in 1976, the City of Denver, Colorado was awarded the Winter Olympic Games. However, the citizens of the state voiced both environmental and economic concerns regarding the bid and in 1972 both the state and the city of Denver voted against taxpayer support of the Olympic Games prompting the Organizing Committee to withdraw their bid (Moore, 2015). The IOC ultimately awarded the 1976 Winter Olympics to Innsbruck, Austria, as this city had previously hosted in 1964 and had much of the infrastructure already in place.

Table 14.3 *Winter Olympic Games Host Cities and Bid Candidate Cities*

Year	Olympiad	Host City	Bid Cities (in order of ballot results)
2022	XXXIII	Beijing, China	Almaty, Kazakhstan
2018	XXXII	PyeongChang, South Korea	Munich, Germany; Annecy, France
2014	XXXI	Sochi, Russia	PyeongChang, South Korea; Salzburg, Austria; Almaty, Kazakhstan; Borjomi, Georgia; Jaca, Spain; Sofia, Bulgaria
2010	XXX	Vancouver, Canada	PyeongChang, South Korea; Salzburg, Austria; Andorra la Vella, Andorra; Berne, Switzerland; Harbin, China; Jaca, Spain; Sarajevo, Bosnia-Herzegonvina
2006	XXIX	Turin, Italy	Sion, Switzerland; Helsinki, Finland; Klagenfurt, Austria; Poprad-Tatry, Slovakia; Zakopane, Poland
2002	XXVIII	Salt Lake City, USA	Ostersund Sweden; Sion, Switzerland; Quebec City, Canada; Graz, Austria; Jaca, Spain; Poprad-Tatry, Slovakia; Sochi, Russia; Tarvisio, Italy
1998	XXVII	Nagano, Japan	Salt Lake City, USA; Ostersund, Sweden; Jaca, Spain; Aosta, Italy
1994	XXVI	Lillehammer, Norway	Ostersund, Sweden; Anchorage, USA; Sofia, Bulgaria
1992	XXV	Albertville, France	Sofia, Bulgaria; Falun, Sweden; Lillehammer, Norway; Cortina d'Ampezzo, Italy; Anchorage, USA; Berchtesgaden, West Germany
1988	XXIV	Calgary, Canada	Falun, Sweden; Cortina d'Ampezzo; Italy
1984	XXIII	Sarajevo, Yugoslavia	Sapporo, Japan; Gothenburg, Sweden
1980	XXII	Lake Placid, USA	N/A
1976	XXI	Denver, USA	Sion, Switzerland; Tampere, Finland; Vancouver-Garibaldi, Canada
1972	XX	Sapporo, Japan	Banff, Canada; Lahti, Finland; Salt Lake City, USA
1968	XIX	Grenoble, France	Calgary, Canada; Lahti, Finland; Sapporo, Japan; Oslo, Norway; Lake Placid, USA

1964	XVIII	Innsbruck, Austria	Calgary, Canada; Lahti, Finland
1960	XVII	Squaw Valley, USA	Innsbruck, Austria; St. Moritz, Switzerland; Garmish-Partenkirchen, Germany; Karachi, Pakistan
1956	XVI	Cortina d'Ampezzo, Italy	Colorado Springs, USA; Lake Placid, USA; Montreal, Canada
1952	XV	Oslo, Norway	Cortina d'Ampezzo, Italy; Lake Placid, USA
1948	XIV	Saint Moritz, Switzerland	Lake Placid, USA
1944	XIII	Cortina d'Ampezzo, Italy	Montreal, Canada; Oslo, Norway; *Cancelled due to WWII*
1940	XII	Sapporo, Japan	*No other bids, Cancelled due to WWII*
1936	XI	Garmisch-Partenkirchen, Germany	Montreal, Canada; St. Moritz, Switzerland
1932	X	Lake Placid, USA	Montreal, Canada; Oslo, Norway; Yosemite Valley. USA; Lake Tahoe, USA; Bear Mountain, USA; Duluth, USA; Minneapolis, USA; Denver, USA
1928	IX	St. Moritz, Switzerland	Davos, Switzerland; Engelberg, Switzerland
1924	VIII	Chamonix, France	*No other bids*

Adapted from gamebids.com

Benefits of Bidding and Hosting

Bidding for and hosting these mega events promises social and economic benefits for the host country; making the cost incurred by starting a bid seem like a good investment to the hopeful host cities. Research from the 2012 London Games showed that the country enjoyed a £9.9 billion boost just 12 months after the Games. A study done by the University of Oxford projects that the Games will have fostered £16.5 billion for the economy by the year 2017. The London Games came at a time when there was a worldwide recession. The Games helped to create jobs, especially in the construction field. During the 2012 games, London saw 1.2% decrease in the unemployment rate (London 2012, 2015).

Binyaman Applebaum (2014), an economist reporter for the *New York Times* believes that the benefit of hosting the World Cup or Olympic Games does not lie in monetary return value. Applebaum points out that there is little evidence to show that hosting these mega-sporting events have the desired economic outcome. He argues that many host cities fail to look at the amount of money the city would have generated without the sporting event; he uses the 2012 London Games as an example. During the games, London theatres stopped performances of musicals and plays, and the British Museum was down 200,000 visitors. Economists forget to factor in this loss of revenue that would be generated by tourists if the Games were not being hosted. According to Applebaum, many of the host countries don't expect profit from hosting such events. He describes hosting the Olympic Games or World Cup as "a debutante's ball for emerging countries." In this way, countries are symbolizing their rising economic power when making a bid; they are signaling to other nations that they are a worthy investment of capital. This idea is explored further in an article for *Third World Quarterly*, concluding "Once a country is able to break into the international arena of hosting mega-events, this creates the ripple effect of attracting more and often bigger mega- events. Once on the mega-event circuit, there is an aspiration to hold more" (Swort & Bob, 2004). This approach seems to work, as countries that host the Olympics generally experience a growth in trade.

Many developing countries make a bid to host the Olympics or World Cup in the hopes that it will create a fully developed economy and country. When Cape Town, South Africa made a bid for the Games in 2004, their bidding presentation focused mainly on the event being an immense developmental opportunity for the country. However, while host development is a goal for the Olympics, Cape Town ultimately lost the bid by ignoring the two main priorities of the IOC: "sport and commerce" (Swart & Bob, 2004). Critics are still divided on the actual benefits that hosting these mega-sporting events provide. Whether the benefits are an instant monetary boost to the economy or a slow growth in trade, the prestige and excitement surrounding a host city cannot be denied.

Legacies

Legacies comprise material and non-material changes (positive or negative) that occur in a host city, region, or nation in relation to the sporting event and remain after the event concludes.

These economic and social benefits for the host company of the Olympics are referred to as *legacies*. In recent years the IOC has made a push for host countries' proposals to include these legacies in their bids. In 2002, the IOC added another mission statement to their Charter: "mission number 14 placed an emphasis the need for hosts to strive for positive legacies that benefit the quality of life in the city, region, and country" (Sant & Mason, 2015). Vancouver was the first city to sign the newly amended Charter contract when hosting the 2010 Winter Games. While the Charter does give a general definition of legacies, the IOC leaves it up to each candidate city to specify the legacies that would be unique to their city and country. The legacies are what the bid committee and investors focus on in order to receive favorable public opinion. A united and supportive public is essential for a successful Olympic bid. In the time leading up to the bidding and voting process, bid committees will use media to highlight and publicize these expected legacies.

Politics and Bidding

As discussed earlier, holding these mega-sporting events reflects positively on the host country if the event goes well. In the same way, the Olympics or World Cup reflects positively on the current political regime of the host country. The political parties who can successfully bid and pull off a mega-event obtain positive favor from not only national citizens but also other global governments. Many politicians see this immense media opportunity: "mega-events are used as global advertisements for the host state, producing and spreading a certain image for market purposes" (Persson & Petersson, 2014).

Similarly, if the event goes wrong, the current government takes the blame for the failed scheme. Former British Prime Minister Tony Blair is one example where a political figure profited from the mega-event. When London hosted the Olympics in 2012, Blair was given immense credit for London receiving the bid and held popular public favor (Jennings, 2013).

Research has shown that those bidding for the Olympics often underestimate the cost and overestimate the benefits. These bidders continue to underestimate costs even though research has shown that "With great regularity, the final cost of the Games exceeds the original projections of planners, while the forecast benefits either fail to materialize or are not measured after the event is over" (Jennings, 2013). The total cost of the London games was budgeted at around £1.3 billion. The final cost was upwards of £9.3 billion: a massive overrun of the budget. This optimism is often accredited to "strategic misinterpretation" that is used by political parties or stakeholders. They advertise these lower costs, higher benefits games as a way to convince citizens that the bid is a worthy investment (Jennings, 2013).

Modern Olympics and Business

In an article for Political Studies Review, Jonathon Grix (2013) argues that "sport is taking more of a back seat to politics." According to Grix, the Olympics has become a corporate entity that is more concerned about revenue for corporate sponsors and IOC profit than it is about the "legacies" of the games. In his article, Grix quotes John Sugden and Alan Tomlinson's theory that: "The most compelling and fundamental change is the way the Olympics have moved steadily and inexorably away from being an amateur, peoples', sporting festival towards a state-choreographed, commercially driven, internationally controlled, media mega-event" (p. 21). Whether or not the business aspect of the Games is overshadowing the sport is arguable, but the fact that business allure plays a huge role is not. While hosting the games does create excitement and high morale for a city, the business and economic aspects of the games are what really prompt countries to engage in bidding.

The Olympic Games have changed with the times to become the mega-event the world knows and loves. Although the games still captivate the public with their show of sheer talent and physicality, the political and business finesse of these modern games is equally as impressive.

Urban Development of Host Cities and the Consequences

Once a bid is secured, the host city begins to build arena structures, hotels, transportation routes, and other structures that they have deemed necessary to host the Games or World Cup. All this new development within host cities has made critics question whether this new development is actually beneficial for the host citizens once the event is over. All this sudden development of land within a city is done with the intention to "evoke a certain image of the place and a status for those experiencing it, rather than those living in the city" (Andranovich, Burbank, & Heying, 2001). This development of urban areas for mega-events creates a 'tourist bubble, an area that is "romanticized, nostalgic, sense of history and culture" (Andranovich et al., 2001). This "tourist bubble" portrays a sometimes unrealistic version of the host city to the media, ignoring impoverished or imperfect urban areas. The major criticism is that these improvements are made with the temporary visitors in mind, instead of permanent residents. These criticisms may have bearing on the IOC's new Olympic Agenda 2020 discussed above, which aims to create more sustainable games for host cities.

Bidding Scandals

While the bid process has become a common method for the determination of host venues and cities for various sporting events around the world, this process is not without potential problems. With the immense competition and at times political pressure and prestige associated with bid success, corruption in the form of bribes and other unethical inducements made toward decision makers in the bid award continues to be a concern. While bid processes are generally designed to create an equitable opportunity for potential hosts to make their case for hosting an event, bid scandals are especially problematic for the sporting events that tout fair competition and the "level playing field" as foundational values.

While the bid processes for sport organizations both large and small are susceptible to bribery and corruption, the scandals at the most prominent levels of sport, the Olympic Games and the World Cup, have garnered tremendous attention in recent years. The bribery scandal involving the Salt Lake City bid for the 2002 Winter Olympics created a major issue for the IOC. What began as a television report in November 1998 linking college scholarship funding for the daughter of an IOC member to American University in Washington by the Salt Lake Organizing Committee, quickly escalated to include numerous IOC officials and ultimately expanded to investigations of other

Olympic bids in addition to the Salt Lake City Games. This scandal led to internal investigation by the IOC via the Pound Commission along with several external bodies including: the Mitchell Commission (USOC), the Board of Ethics Commission for SLOC, and the US Federal Bureau of Investigation (FBI) (Mallon, 2000). A total of ten IOC members lost their positions by either expulsion or resignation due to the bribery investigations. Two major reform outcomes were noted in the response to this scandal. The first was the establishment of an independent, eight-member, Ethics Commission that developed a code of ethics along with enforcement processes. The second was the formation of the 82-member IOC 2000 Commission that provided 50 reform recommendations for the Olympic Movement that were adopted in 1999 (Mallon, 2000). The elements from the commission's report related specifically to bid and candidature status are summarized in Table 14.4.

Table 14.4 *A Summary of IOC 2000 Commission Reform Recommendations Related to Bid and Candidature Procedures*

45	The IOC will disclose the allocation of funds to each NOC and IF and each entity of the Olympic Movement will submit to the IOC an accounting of its expenditure of funds provided by the IOC.
47	Each bid city must disclose the source of funding for bid expenditures, which will be audited at the conclusion of the bid process.
48	The IOC will encourage NOCs and Ifs to disclose their sources and uses of funds.
50	New Candidature Procedure: A new bid acceptance phase will be instituted, with multiple recommendations as follows:
50.1	Strict minimum technical requirements will be applied to the selection of a bid city.
50.2	A new bid acceptance process in which representatives of the IOC, IFS, NOCs, athletes and external experts will examine the proposed bids and recommend to the IOC Executive Board which cities should be accepted as candidate cities.
50.3	The IOC will enter into a contractual agreement with the NOC and the Bid Committee.
50.4	The IOC will issue candidate city manuals and prepare candidature files.
50.5	An Evaluation Commission will be formed to visit each of the candidate cities.
50.6	Selection of final candidate cities, if necessary. The Executive Board may reduce the number of candidates by selecting a limited number of cities.
50.7	It is not considered necessary for IOC Members to visit the candidate cities nor for the representatives or candidate cities, or third parties acting on their behalf ("agents"), to visit IOC Members.

Adapted from Mallon (2000)

The bid for the 2002 Winter Games held in Salt Lake City resulted in a major scandal of corruption of the process in bribes made to many IOC selection committee members.

Despite these reform efforts made at the turn of the century, the 2020 Olympic bid awarded to Tokyo came under scrutiny in 2016 for payments of almost $2 million for consulting fees to a Singapore-based company, Black Tidings, that has links to persons involved in other IOC and IAAF investigations (Lawton, 2016).

The World Cup experienced a major scandal related to bids and bribes that began with United States FBI and Internal Revenue Criminal Investigation Division investigations resulted in indictments of 14 individuals and the arrest of seven FIFA officials in Zurich, Switzerland in May 2015 (Gibson & Gayle, 2015). These initial investigations and arrests were linked to over $100 million in bribes and kickbacks spanning three decades including the 2010 World Cup bid from South Africa, and they triggered new or additional criminal investigations of FIFA officials' corruption in other nations including Columbia, Costa Rica, Germany, and Switzerland (Fortino, 2015). This FIFA corruption scandal led to the replacement of Sepp Blatter as FIFA President and a temporary suspension of the 2026 World Cup bidding process.

It is imperative that sport organizations operating as rights holders for any given event establish and clearly communicate bid processes to candidates and ethical standards for those involved in bid assessments and selection. It is equally important for those involved within the development of bids and candidatures to understand the moral and legal consequences that can be associated with improper actions taken in the efforts to secure a bid. While the two examples of bribery and corruption are only briefly mentioned above, they do draw attention to the perceived high stakes involved within the bidding process for elite sporting events.

Conclusion

Bidding on these mega-sporting events is seen as a major investment for host cities and countries. While the exact benefits of hosting Olympic and FIFA games are still widely disputed, the publicity, heritage and excitement surrounding these type of mega-events cannot be ignored. Despite the uncertainty of these benefits, the bidding to host these mega-events creates frenzy during each bid season, sometimes causing the IOC and FIFA to be put in compromising situations due to bribery. Westerbeek's Eight Essentials for making bids reveals a skeletal outline for the planning and resources that go into the bidding process. When applying for a bid, it is essential to make sure a proposal covers all necessary criteria. Likewise, it is important for the IOC and FIFA to outline their demands and expectations for potential bidders. Both parties need to create proposals /guidelines that take into consideration budget, timelines, and federal/state laws.

CHAPTER DISCUSSION QUESTIONS

1. Explain the differences between RFBs, RFIs and RFPs.

2. Which of Westerbeek's Eight Essential Factors for a Successful Bid is the most important, and why?

3. Define the IOC's steps for becoming an Olympic Host City.

4. What are Olympic "Legacies," and what role do they play in a cities bid for the Olympics?

PRACTITIONER SPOTLIGHT

NAME: Dana Schoenwetter

ORGANIZATION: United States Olympic Committee

CURRENT JOB TITLE:

Photo courtesy of Dana Schoenwetter.

- Associate Director, Operations—Chula Vista Olympic Training Center
- **Year started in this role:** 2010

EDUCATIONAL PREPARATION:

- **Undergrad degree:** BA in Spanish, Psychology Minor

CAREER PATH:

- **Internship(s):** Team Manager for Soccer 2 years in college
- **Entry level job:** US Soccer Administrative Assistant for National Teams Dept.
- Job path both inside and outside sport (as applicable) leading to this current role
  - US Soccer 1996–2000
    - Promoted within US Soccer to National Teams Coordinator then Team Administrator for the Women's National Team
  - Boston Breakers (Women United Soccer League) 2000–2003
    - Director of Soccer
    - League folded in 2003
  - Consultant to USOC then US Soccer—Team Manager for the Paralympic Soccer team (2003–2013)
  - Consultant—Champions World (summer of 2003)—professional soccer game and venue management
  - National Sports Center for the Disabled—2005–2007
    - National Programs Manager
  - Rush Soccer 2007–2010—General Manager

An aerial overview of the United States Olympic Training Center in Chula Vista, CA.

HOW IS THE BIDDING PROCESS RELATED TO YOUR POSITION AT THE OLYMPIC TRAINING CENTER?

As the associate director of operations, I am very involved in event management. The Chula Vista Olympic Training Center (CVOTC) hosts many events including training camps, clinics, competitions and Olympic qualifying events. We have a competitive advantage over many facilities because of the great weather in the metro San Diego area. Our venue also has outstanding onsite housing and dining facilities.

At the CVOTC we have to put together bid packages to host events like development camps, clinics, and high-level competitions. We have hosted international events like the Thorpe Cup which was a track and field competition in the heptathlon and decathlon between the United States and Germany. We have also hosted the International Association of Athletics Federations (IAAF) Level V Coaches Education Academy multiple times. The CVOTC regularly hosts track and field meets, BMX competitions, and multiple archery contests.

WHAT IS THE KEY TO A SUCCESSFUL BIDDING PROCESS?

The key to a successful bid package is understanding the nature of the competitive bidding process. A "competitive bidding process" means a non-discriminatory bidding process that provides for the participation of a sufficient number of undertakings and where the ability to host an event is granted on either the basis of the initial bid submitted by the bidder. The process should be open to and provide adequate incentives to both existing and future generators. A competitive bidding process on the basis of clear, transparent and non-discriminatory criteria, effectively targeting the defined objective, will be considered as leading to reasonable rates of return under normal circumstances. A competitive bidding process should offer a transparent route to market for existing and potential new market entrants. Take pride in your facility/venue. The competition venue "Field of play" is the ultimate focal point of hosting events whether large or small—all functions and traffic flows converge there.

HAS THE CVOTC EVER BEEN UNSUCCESSFUL IN THE BIDDING PROCESS?

Of course we have. My advice is "don't discount a losing bid" because much can be learned from it. Behind the scenes, every winning— and losing—bid represents weeks, months and sometimes years of planning, preparation, and collaboration. You learn each time you undertake the bidding process.

WHAT IS THE MOST REWARDING ASPECT OF THIS JOB?

Working with the great group of athletes we have here and hopefully having a positive impact on their life and successes.

WHAT IS THE MOST CHALLENGING ASPECT OF THIS JOB?

It is making this place a world-class training center with a limited staff and a limited budget.

WHAT IS A UNIQUE ASPECT OR TASK OF YOUR JOB THAT MANY WOULD BE SURPRISED HEAR ABOUT?

Many people are not aware that the USOC is the only Olympic Committee that receives no government funding.

WHAT PARTING WORDS OF WISDOM DO YOU HAVE FOR STUDENTS AND YOUNG PROFESSIONALS IN THE FIELD?

Expect to have to work hard for most of your career. Nothing should be below you/you are not too good for any task.

Reprinted by permissions of Dana Schoenwetter.

MINI CASE STUDY

A medium-sized city in the southwestern United States is hoping to win a bid for the next available summer Olympics. This city has placed an unsuccessful bid in the past and some of its citizens were upset over the "waste of money and resources." This caused inflation in the local economy and there were rumors of corruption in the city government. Although this was 20 years ago and the political personalities involved are no longer in place, the citizens are wary of supporting a new bid. Further complicating matters is the lack of available facilities and space to build.

1. What steps can a bid committee from this this city take to plan a successful bid?

2. What type of individuals (roles, background, experience, etc.) should be included on a bid committee from this city?

3. What steps might the bid committee take to help convince its citizens that this will be beneficial to them in the long run?

REFERENCES

2008 Beijing Olympic Games Action Plan. (2008, July 1). *Chinese Law and Government*, 41(4), 20–29.

All About the Candidature Process. (2016). *Olympic.org*. Retrieved from http://www.olympic.org/all-about-the-candidature-process

Andranovich, G., Burbank, M., & Heying, C. (2001) Olympic Cities: Lessons learned from mega-event politics. *Journal of Urban Affairs*, 23(2), 113–133.

Applebaum, B. (2014, August 5). Does hosting the Olympics actually pay off? *The New York Times*. Retrieved from http://www.nytimes.com/2014/08/10/magazine/does-hosting-the-olympics-actually-pay-off.html?_r=1

Bidding Process. (2014). *FIFA*. Retrieved from http://www.fifa.com/governance/competition-organisation/bidding-process.html

Business Dictionary. (2016). *Web Finance*. Retrieved from http://www.businessdictionary.com

Christiansen, E., & Copp, K. (2014). The process of applying for a license in a new gaming jurisdiction: Do's and D\don'ts. *UNLV Gaming Research & Review Journal, 18*(2), 113–124.

Cornelissen, S., & Swart, K. (2006). The 2010 Football World Cup as a political construct: the challenge of making good on an African promise. *Sociological Review, 54,* 108–123. doi:10.1111/j.1467-954X.2006.00656.x

Darden, E. C. (2009). Bidding for trouble. *American School Board Journal, 196*(7), 36–37.

Feddersen, A., & Maennig, W. (2012). Determinants of successful bidding for mega events: The case of the Olympic Winter Games. In Maennig, W., & Zimbalist, A. S. (Eds.), *International Handbook on the Economics of Mega Sporting Events.* Northampton, MA: Edward Elgar Publishing.

Fortino, M. (2015, May 28). Columbia joins investigation into FIFA corruption. *Columbia Reports.* Retrieved from http://colombiareports.com/colombia-joins-investigation-into-fifa-corruption/

From Candidate to Host City. (2015). *Olympic.org.* Retrieved from http://www.olympic.org/host-city-election

Gibson, O., & Gayle, D. (2015, May 27). FIFA officials arrested on corruption charges as World Cup inquiry launched. *The Guardian.* Retrieved from https://www.theguardian.com/football/2015/may/27/several-top-fifa-officials-arrested

Grix, J. (2013). Sport politics and the Olympics. *Political Studies Review. 11,* 15–25. doi: 10.1111/1478-9302.12001

Guglielmo, G. (2016). The dome effect isn't real: The NRG effect is complicated. *FiveThirtyEight.* Retrieved from http://fivethirtyeight.com/features/the-dome-effect-isnt-real-the-nrg-effect-is-complicated/

Jennings, W. (2013). Governing the games: High politics, risk and mega-events. *Political Studies Review, 11,* 2–14.

Kresova, N., & Prutz, N. (2014, July 1). The most expensive Olympic Games in history: Sochi 2014. *European Journal of Economic Studies. 9*(3), 155–161.

Laryea, S. (2013). Nature of tender review meetings. *Journal of Construction Engineering & Management, 139*(8), 927–940. doi:10.1061/(ASCE)CO.1943-7862.000066

Lawton, M. (2016, May 13). Tokyo's 2020 Olympics bid team defend two payments to company at center of athletics corruption scandal. *The Daily Mail.* Retrieved from http://www.dailymail.co.uk/sport/sportsnews/article-3589588/Tokyo-s-2020-Olympics-bid-team-defend-two-payments-company-centre-athletics-corruption-scandal.html

Legacies and Impacts. (2015). *International Olympics Committee: The Olympic Studies Centre.* Retrieved from https://stillmed.olympic.org/media/Document%20Library/OlympicOrg/Olympic%20Studies%20Center/List%20of%20Resources/Resources%20available/Library/Olympic%20Games%20legacies%20and%20impacts%20bibliography%202015.pdf#_ga=1.152999612.423837759.1449172814

London News. (2013, August 8). *Olympic.org.* Retrieved from http://www.olympic.org/news/london-2012-to-provide-long-lasting-economic-benefits/207219

Mallon, B. (2000). The Olympic bribery scandal. *Journal of Olympic History*. Retrieved from http://library.la84.org/SportsLibrary/JOH/JOHv8n2/johv8n2f.pdf

Mason, A., Misener, L., & Thibault, L. (2006) An agency theory perspective on corruption in sport: The case of the International Olympic Committee. *Journal of Sport Management, 20*, 52–73.

Masterman, G. (2008, January). Losing bids, winning legacies: An examination of the need to plan for Olympic Legacies Prior to the Bidding. In *Proceedings: International Symposium for Olympic Research* (p. 171). International Centre for Olympic Studies.

Men's Final Four bid process underway. (2013, September 19). NCAA.com. Retrieved from http://www.ncaa.com/news/basketball-men/article/2013-09-19/mens-final-four-bid-process-under-way

Merriam-Webster. (2015). *Merriam Webster Inc.* Retrieved from http://www.merriam-webster.com/dictionary

Moore, J. (2015, April 7). When Denver rejected the Olympics in favour of the environment and economics. *The Guardian*. Retrieved from https://www.theguardian.com/sport/blog/2015/apr/07/when-denver-rejected-the-olympics-in-favour-of-the-environment-and-economics

NCAA championships site selections (2013). NCAA.com. Retrieved from http://www.ncaa.com/news/ncaa/article/2013-12-06/ncaa-championships-site-selections

Persson, E., & Petersson, B. (2014). Political mythmaking and the 2014 Winter Olympics in Sochi: Olympism and the Russian great power myth. *East European Politics, 30*(2), 192–209.

Poast, P. (2007). Winning the bid: Analyzing the International Olympic Committee's host city selection. *International Interactions, 33*, 75–95. doi: 10.1080/03050620601157470

Pomfret, R., Wilson, J., & Lobmayr, B. (2009). Bidding for sport mega-events. *The University of Adelaide, School of Economics Working Paper Series, 0089*(30), 1–28.

Raviv, Y. (2008). The role of the bidding process in price determination: Jump bidding in sequential English auctions. *Economic Inquiry, 46*(3), 325–341. doi:10.1111/j.1465-7295.2007.00088.x

Sant, S., & Mason, D. (2015). Framing event legacy in a prospective host city: Managing Vancouver's Olympic bid. *Journal of Sport Management, 29*, 42–56.

Scarborough, A. (2015). Atlanta, Santa Clara, New Orleans land CFP title games for 2018–20. *ESPN.com*. Retrieved from http://www.espn.com/college-football/story/_/id/14052099/atlanta-santa-clara-new-orleans-land-cfp-title-games-2018-20

Seifried, C.S., Turner, B., Kristy, K., Mahony, D., & Pastore, D. (2007). The diverse landscape of championship and playoff site selection procedures across high school athletics. *International Council for Health, Physical Education, Recreation, Sport, and Dance, Journal of Research, 2*(1), 37–42.

Swart, K., & Bob, U. (2004). The seductive discourse of development: The Cape Town 2004 Olympic bid. *Third World Quarterly, 25*(7), 1311–1324. doi:10.1080/014365904200281294

Walmsley, D. (2013). *The bid book: Matching sports events and hosts*. London, England: SportBusiness Group.

Ward, H., & John, P. (2008). A spatial model of competitive bidding for government grants: Why efficiency gains are limited. *Journal of Theoretical Politics, 20*(1), 47–66.

Westerbeek, H., Smith, A., Turner, P., Emery, P., Green, C., & van Leuwenn, L. (2000). *Managing Sports Facilities and Major Events.* Windsor Locks, CT: Yankee Clipper Books.

Xi-Liu, Z. (2014). Cost control method and software in bidding process based on gray system forecast. *Journal of Control Science & Engineering*, 1–6. doi:10.1155/2014/296241

15 Mega-Events and Sport Festivals

Lawrence W. Judge and *Jeffrey C. Petersen*

OBJECTIVES

After studying this chapter, the student should be able to:

- Define and discuss mega-events and their importance.
- Explain the positive and negative impacts a mega-event has on the hosting site.
- Give examples of how mega-events have evolved in the last 100 years.
- Describe how national and state level sport festivals relate to mega-events like the Olympic Games.

KEY TERMS

Gentrification	Infrastructure	Major Event
Giga-Event	Mega-Event	Sports Festival

KEY ACRONYMS

EMT Emergency Medical Technician	**TOP Program** The Olympic Partner Program
FIFA Federation Internationale de Football Association	**UEFA** Union of European Football Associations
IOC International Olympic Committee	

Introduction

Sport festivals also referred to as multi-sport events, have formed the foundation for the development of mega-events. The Olympic Games are the oldest and most notable of sport festivals from the ancient world, but they were far from the only athletic games held in the ancient world. There have been records of at least 126 sites that held athletic festivals in the Greco-Roman world with Sparta, Athens, and Ephesus hosting multiple annual, biennial, or quadrennial events in their history (Harris, 1979). These historical contests from antiquity created a model type for the formation of multi-sport events in the modern era, and this modern era began with the revival of contests held at the national and regional levels. This included games in England like the Cotswold "Olympicks" held from 1612 to 1852 and the Much Wenlock Games held from 1850 to 1895, the Drehberg Olympics in Germany from 1776 to 1799, and the Zappas Olympics or Greek National Games held in 1859, 1870, 1875, and 1888 (Bell, 2003). These and other similar multi-sport festivals cultivated the formation of the modern Olympic Games as the first modern international multi-sport event.

Sports Festival a multi-sport event held over a period of multiple days utilizing multiple venues.

The largest and oldest of the modern international **sports festival**s would be the Olympic Games. The modern Olympic Games were founded in 1894 under the leadership of French historian Pierre de Coubertin, who was dedicated to the promotion of physical education and sport. These first games were held in 1896 in Athens, Greece, with fewer than 250 athletes from 14 countries competing in a total of 42 events (Wallechinsky, 1992). The Olympic Games have continued to evolve and develop over the years as the number of events, countries represented, and participants continue to grow. The Winter Olympic Games were added in 1924 in an effort to promote additional events and expand the geographical and seasonal reach of the Games. That same year, the Games became a truly international competition, with 3,000 athletes from over 44 countries competing in the summer Games in Paris (Wallechinsky, 1992). While very few major changes were made to the overall structure of the Games as a whole, new sporting events, participating countries, and competitors were added with each successive Games. By the time the Olympic Games returned to Athens in the summer of 2004, more than 11,000 athletes were competing from 201 countries. The event had grown over 44 times the number of athletes and over seven times the number of participating countries by the time it had made its way back to Athens, just a little over a hundred years later. Since the 2004 Athens Games, the Olympics have continued to expand with the 2016 summer Olympics held in Rio de Janeiro, Brazil, boasting 11,303 athletes from 205 different countries, participating in 306 medal events ("Rio 2016," 2016).

The Olympic Games became the first of the mega-events in sport, and their tremendous popularity and success has spawned the creation of numerous other international, national, and even state level sport festivals. However, the question of defining what exactly determines a mega-event and determining when the Olympic Games transitioned from their rather modest beginnings to the stature of mega-event must be determined. Although the

Olympics are the pinnacle of the sport festival in terms of size and scope, not every sport festival would qualify as a mega-event. Additionally, other events with a singular sport focus or even a single event focus have the potential to be classified as mega-events. Therefore, this chapter will attempt to create a working definition of mega-events in sport and apply this definition to a number of sport events with global impact. The chapter will also explore the benefits and problems associated with mega-events, and apply this examination to smaller scale sport festivals and sport events.

Defining Mega-Events

While the rise of global sporting events has a history of more than a century, the development and use of the term *mega-event* is a fairly recent development. It began within the academic discipline of tourism in 1987 where a gathering of scholars met at a conference under the theme of "The Role and Impact of Mega-Events and Attractions on Regional and National Tourism Development" (Müller, 2015b, p. 628). The proceedings of this conference resulted in a working definition based heavily on the work of Ritchie and Yangzhou (1987), and it defined a mega-event as "major one-time or recurring events of limited duration, which serve to enhance the awareness, appeal and profitability of a tourism destination in the short and/or long terms" (p. 20). This initial working definition remained primarily connected to the attraction of tourists as the primary component of the mega-event. Horne (2007) on the other hand, defined mega-events simply as an event that would "have significant consequences for the host city, region or nation… and attract considerable media coverage" (p. 80). These two definitions show scholarly disagreement on the international/national angle of a mega-event and whether the event could be annual. As you can see, these definitions did not use number of spectators or participants to define a mega-event, but rather economic impact, media coverage, tourism, and popularity.

This early definition began to expand outside of the realm of tourism through the work of Roche (1994) who viewed mega-events as "short-term events with long-term consequences for the cities that stage them" (p. 1). These long-term consequences or costs could include the creation of *infrastructure* and event facilities along with the accompanying long-term debts. The long-term consequences could also serve to project or create a new or renewed positive image and identity for the host city via television and other national and international media coverage.

Roche further expanded his mega-event definition in 2000 to include aspects of government and non-government organization in the events as:

> *Large scale cultural (including commercial and sporting) events which have a dramatic character, mass popular appeal and international significance. They are typically organized by variable combinations of national governmental and international non-governmental*

Mega-Event an extremely large event of global significance in size and scope related to attendance, media coverage, total budget, and total infrastructure development (rating 7–10 on the Müller scale) such as the World Cup or Winter Olympic Games.

Infrastructure the basic physical structures for organizational and societal enterprise such as buildings, roads, power and water supplies.

organizations and thus can be said to be important elements in 'official' versions of public culture (Roche 2000, p. 1).

This expanded definition shows the importance of the international sport governing bodies like the International Olympic Committee (IOC) or the Federation Internationale de Football Association (FIFA) and their work with the national or local governments in the creation of such an event.

A direct connection to competitive sport aspect of the mega-event was made by Mills and Rosentraub (2013), and they combined the transformative aspects of the event with costs and media coverage to define the mega-events as follows:

Significant national or global competitions that produce extensive levels of participation and media coverage and that often require large public investments into both event infrastructure, for example stadiums to hold the events, and general infrastructure, such as roadways, housing, or mass transit systems (p. 239).

This definition would encompass the largest and most complex types of international sporting events like the Olympic Games and World Cup along with national-level events of significant impact.

Most recently, the mega-event has been expanded into a more comprehensive four-part definition. Müller (2015b) describes mega-events as "ambulatory occasions of a fixed duration that 1) attract a large number of visitors, 2) have large mediated reach, 3) come with large costs and 4) have large impacts on the built environment and the population" (p. 629). As an ambulatory occasion, the mega-event may be recurring on an annual, biennial, or quadrennial timeline, but it would have a different location for each iteration. This four-part definition can form an effective means for determining sporting event status if consensus for the measures in each of the four categories can be determined.

Mega-Event Characteristics and Measures

In order to fully apply the proposed mega-event definition, each of the four components must be explained and quantified. The first mega-event requirement is that the event must attract a large number of visitors. However, defining exactly what constitutes a visitor and determining the actual number of visitors present numerous challenges. The lack of direct data or primary surveys has caused ticket sales to be used as a proxy measure for visitors (Richie & Yangzhou, 1987). The utilization of ticket sales for estimations of total event attendance can provide a comparable set of data for nearly all sport-related events. Establishing the number of visitors required to reach the status of mega-event is another point that is debated. While early research by Marris (1987) called for a minimum threshold of one million visitors for mega-events, the most recent model calls for at least one half million visitors to qualify for a minimal level of mega-event qualification with the greatest level of recognition in the visitors scale for events drawing three million or more total visitors (Müller, 2015b).

The second mega-event characteristic calls for the event to have large mediated reach. While the direct consumption of a mega-event via personal attendance is important, the consumption of mega-events through the media reaches a far greater number of people. While various rating systems may seek to estimate the number of media viewers via television and other digital platforms, these estimates are prone to exaggeration and manipulation (Horne, 2007). Therefore, Müller (2015b) proposed the use of the dollar value of the media broadcasting rights as a more directly comparable measure of the level of media coverage and consumption associated with an event. The scaled values for mediated reach range from a low of $100 million for minimal consideration up to a maximal allocation of $2 billion or more in expenditure for broadcast rights associated with an event. Table 15.1 illustrates the tremendous growth of the media rights value of the Summer Olympic Games from 1960 to 2012. This includes an average increase in broadcast right fees of 206% from the prior Games. In comparing the nominal costs, the total broadcast rights first exceeded $1 billion with the 2000 Sydney Games and topped $2 billion in the 2012 London Games. The fees paid to secure broadcasting rights do demonstrate the market value of mega-events to a growing global audience, and the rate of growth in nominal cost with each Olympic cycle would far exceed the rise of costs associated with inflation at a global level.

While the first two mega-event characteristics are output-focused with potential revenue generation through tourism/event attendance and media following, the third and fourth components of the mega-event designation deal with input factors or costs. Total event costs are the basis used for the third defining factor of mega-events. Total costs would incorporate both infrastructure and operational elements of the event budget. The infrastructure would include new construction and upgrades to facilities, transportation, and utilities related to the event. Operational costs would be related to organizing the event itself including costs such as salaries for personnel along with associated costs for food service, information and communication technologies, and security to name a few. Mega-events are bound with a high level of complexity that is combined with a time pressure or deadline for completion. These two factors frequently create cost overruns from the original budget projections. For example, the Summer and Winter Olympic Games from 1968–2012 have averaged a total cost of 179% above the event budget (Flyvbjerg & Stewart, 2012). The level of total costs associated with mega-events would typically range from the hundreds of millions to the multiple billions of dollars. In fact, Müller (2015b) proposed a scale of spending for mega-events that ranged from the lowest end of $1 billion dollars to the highest end exceeding the $10 billion dollar level.

Table 15.1 *Summary of Summer Olympic Broadcast Rights*

Year	Host City	Total Broadcast Rights in millions (nominal USD)	Percent Increase from Prior Games	Countries and/ or Territories Covered
1960	Rome	$1.2	—	21
1964	Tokyo	$1.6	133%	40
1968	Mexico City	$9.9	619%	N/A
1972	Munich	$17.8	180%	98
1976	Montreal	$34.9	205%	124
1980	Moscow	$88.0	252%	111
1984	Los Angeles	$286.9	326%	156
1988	Seoul	$402.6	140%	160
1992	Barcelona	$636.1	158%	193
1996	Atlanta	$898.3	141%	214
2000	Sydney	$1331.6	148%	220
2004	Athens	$1494.0	112%	220
2008	Beijing	$1739.0	116%	220
2012	London	$2569.0	148%	220

Adapted from IOC (2014)

The fourth and final component of the mega-event definition is associated specifically with the significant impacts on the built environment and on the population of the host city or the host nation. This characteristic can also be viewed as a form of urban transformation. While the development of built environment is a portion of the total costs discussed in the third characteristic, for many events classified as mega-events a high percentage of total costs are related to capital expenditures. For example, the 1964 Tokyo Olympic Games dedicated 97% of its spending on infrastructure and the 1984 Los Angeles Games used 50% of the total budget for facility and infrastructure (Liao & Pitts, 2006). More recently, Müller (2015b) reported that 90% of the 2010 FIFA World Cup budget and 66% of the 2012 London Olympics total budget was spent on capital projects for facilities and infrastructure. Müller's quantified scale for urban development investment levels for mega-events mirrors the total cost scale, and it begins at the low end of $1 billion dollars and must exceed $10billion to reach the upper end of the scale. A summary of the event classification matrix for mega-events proposed by Müller is provided in Table 15.2. This matrix provides a score of zero to three for each of the four mega-event characteristics. The resulting total score from the matrix is then interpreted from the largest of events as a new classification of giga-event that would rate at the highest scale level in at least three of the four categories, to the mega-event scoring 7–10 points, and down to the major event that would score from 1–6 total points on the matrix.

Table 15.2 *Event Classification Matrix*

Size	Visitor Attractiveness *Ticket Sold*	Mediated Reach *Broadcast Rights Fees*	Cost *Total Cost*	Transformation *Capital Investment*
XXL *3 points*	> 3 million	> $3 billion USD	> $10 billion USD	> $10 billion USD
XL *2 points*	> 1 million	> $1 billion USD	> $5 billion USD	> $5 billion USD
L *1 point*	> 0.5 million	> $0.1 billion USD	> $1 billion USD	> $1 billion USD
giga-event 11–12 total points, mega-event 7–10 total points, major event 1–6 total points				

Adapted from Müller (2015b)

This model does create a comprehensive approach to the definition of mega-events, and its initial application to a selected group of events appears acceptable. However, the application of such a model will likely need to remain flexible in the attachment of cut-off values within each of the four quantified scales. These values may require adjustment from the initial proposal, and they most certainly would need to be adjusted over time as the rates of growth for *major event*s through giga-events appear to greatly outpace the rates of inflation globally.

The application of Müller's four-part model was made to several events from the time span of 2010–2013 including the 2010 Asian Games, 2010 Commonwealth Games, 2010 Expo (World Fair), 2010 World Cup, 2010 Winter Olympics, 2011 Pan American Games, 2012 European Football Championship (UEFA), 2012 Summer Olympics, 2013 Universiade, and the 2013 NFL Super Bowl. Table 15.3 summarizes the data of the four mega-event factors with visitor attraction measured via ticket sales, with mediated reach measured through broadcast rights fees, with total cost measured through event budget, and with population and built environment impact measured through spending on facilities and infrastructure. These 10 events provided a wide range of values in each of the four categories, and the final analysis

Major Event an important event of global or regional importance related to attendance, media coverage, total budget, and total infrastructure development (rating 1–6 on the Müller scale) such as the Super Bowl.

Giga-Event a new classification for an event at the very largest scale of size and scope related to attendance, media coverage, total budget, and total infrastructure development (rating 11–12 on the Müller scale) such as the Summer Olympic Games.

resulted in the London Olympics qualifying as a *giga-event*, rating at the highest levels of all variables except for built environment impact falling $0.7 billion short of the top rating. Six events were categorized as mega-event, and interestingly Expo 2010 as a trade fair scored 9 points despite having no media broadcast rights. Interestingly, the Super Bowl qualifies only as a major event as only the broadcast rights category earned points on the scale values. This scale application demonstrates the need to assess events on multiple variables in order to better assess an events impact and importance. However, the value and importance of major events and even of events that do not reach major status on this scale should not be completely discounted as such events can still have a significant impact on a given local community. While the specific qualifications of a mega-event will likely be debated for years to come, critics and supporters can agree that mega-events impact host cities economically, provide wide popularity (nationally or internationally), garner considerable media coverage, and cause the host city/nation to incur large costs.

Table 15.3 *Application of the Event Classification Model with Scale Point Values*

Event	Location and Year	Tickets Sold in million	Broadcast Rights USD million	Total Costs USD billion	Capital Investment USD billion	Scale Point Totals	Event Class
Summer Olympics	London 2012	8.2 (3)	2569 (3)	14 (3)	9.3 (2)	11	Giga
UEFA	Ukraine/Poland 2012	1.4 (2)	1076 (2)	48 (3)	47.1 (3)	10	Mega
World Cup	South Africa 2010	3.1 (3)	2408 (3)	5.5 (2)	5.0 (2)	10	Mega
Expo	2010 Shanghai	73.0 (3)	— (0)	55 (3)	53.2 (3)	9	Mega
Asian Games	2010 Guangzhou	2.0 (2)	75 (0)	18 (3)	16.9 (3)	8	Mega
Winter Olympics	2010 Vancouver	1.5 (2)	1280 (2)	7.5 (2)	4.3 (1)	7	Mega
Commonwealth Games	2010 Delhi	1 (2)	52 (0)	6.1 (2)	5.3 (2)	6	Mega
Universiade	2013 Kazan	0.7 (1)	32 (0)	7.2 (0)	6.9 (2)	5	Major
Pan American Games	2011 Guadalajara	0.6 (1)	45 (0)	1.3 (0)	1.2 (0)	1	Major
Super Bowl	2013 New Orleans	0.07 (0)	166 (1)	0.8 (0)	0.04 (0)	1	Major

Adapted from Müller (2015b)

With an event like the Olympics, the huge cost of hosting the event to the standards now required by the International Olympic Committee (IOC), as well as providing adequate security, almost necessitates an infusion of taxpayer or governmental money from the host nation. Because public funds, as well as sponsorship and marketing funds, typically go into hosting these events it is important to have a bidding process in which locations are bid on according to the desirability of their organizational plan. For this reason, it is important that any location hoping to host the event have an organized plan of action that supports the interests of its community and those bidding.

Closing Ceremonies at the Sochi Games in 2014 at the Fisht Olympic Stadium.

Positive Impacts of Mega-Events

Examples of impacts to the local economy range from generating capital due to increased tourism, providing improvements to infrastructure within that community, and portraying the host city in the most positive light with glamorous media coverage. Mega-events also increase employment, both on a short-term and permanent basis in many job sectors. Infrastructure and employment impacts are a result of the building of sports arenas and lodging for tourists and competitors. These facilities, if designed accordingly, can go on to be used by the community for other purposes following the game, thus creating permanent employment opportunities.

Not only do mega-events have a physical impact on their host communities, they have a socio-cultural impact as well. They can impact the mental and physical wellbeing of the citizens and the community itself. Through the exciting and inclusive nature of mega-events, communities come together to promote, participate in and enjoy the event together as a whole. This can lead to an increase in mental health by being a part of something as special as a mega-event. This is evidenced by the increase in sport participation in Barcelona after the 1992 Olympic Games (Malfas et al., 2004).

A mega-event also involves political decision-making and involves the strategies of a country's government. Political involvement is mostly on a direct basis, but their policies can also be indirect, primarily depending on the structure and attitude of the government. The government will usually advocate for the economic benefit a mega-event would have for the country; a mega-event is conceived as an economic initiative.

Mega-events can provide a positive financial impact on the host communities if organized properly. This usually comes in terms of attracting visitors to the area who tend to spend money at local hotels, restaurants, and businesses. Crompton and Lee (2000) recommend that event planners utilize economic impact reports in the place of financial reports when displaying the impact of an event. The difference between the two is that financial reports include only the numbers spent and earned at the actual event. Although economic reports are a little more guesswork, they estimate the amount that visitors spend in the whole area, not just at the event itself and how those funds cycle and recycle through the local economy. This is beneficial because it can show the residents of the area the impact the event has on their lives. One researcher proposed that economists tend to over-estimate the economic impact mega-events have on local economy (Matheson, 2008), however many entities use economic impact to convince cities to host these events. Mega-events need the support of the governmental structure of the area as well as the residents, so any report that shows that the event will create jobs and an influx of cash into the local economy will help garner positive support for the event. It is also important to take into consideration the sustainability of the facilities built for mega-events. The sustainability of these facilities will have a direct effect on the local economy. The 2004 Olympic Games were held in Athens, Greece. According to an article written by Nick Malkoutzis (2012), the hosting cost of the event equated to 11 billion dollars, making it the most expensive Olympic event to ever be held up to that point in time. Because Athens had made no plan for sustainability, the numerous facilities built for the event became vacant buildings that were of little or no use to the local community after the games had ended. Since the Athens organizing committee had spent an enormous amount of money but failed to sustain what they had built in a way that would continue to create profit, it resulted in a detrimental decline in Greece's economy and almost sent the country into an economic collapse. On the flip side, economies can be impacted in a very positive way if the money for events is spent in a sustainable manner. According to the IOC, London was essentially able to pull itself out of an economic recession by hosting the 2012 Olympic Games ("London 2012 to Provide," 2013). The facilities built for the event not only created jobs for the event itself, but also remained sustainable in the local community and resulted in employment gains after the games had ended. This idea of sustainable facilities is now essential for a city/country to win the bid for hosting the Olympics. The IOC makes the economy of the host country one of their priorities; they want the Olympics to bring a positive impact to a city's economy, like London in 2012 rather than a detrimental one such as Athens in 2004.

Negative Impacts of Mega-Events

While there are a number of both real and perceived benefits associated with hosting a mega-event, there are also many potential problems connected to the planning and operations of a mega-event. Müller (2015a) identified problematic factors as a "mega-event syndrome" connected to the planning process including overpromising benefits, underestimating costs, event priorities taking over urban planning priorities, allocating public resources for private interests, and suspending the regular rule of law.

Table 15.4 *Summary of the Mega-Event Syndrome*

Symptom	Definition	Outcome
Overpromising benefits	Overestimating the event's positive effects	• Misallocation of funds • Trust loss with citizens
Underestimating costs	Actual budget exceeds original plan	• Budget Shortfalls • Cost overruns (profiteering) • Poor construction quality
Event takeover	Event priorities usurp the normal planning priorities	• Oversized infrastructure • Unfinished infrastructure • Event needs replace community needs
Public risk taking	Public funds risked for private gain	• Public funding provided for limited to no public benefit • Profiteering
Exception of rules	Regular rule of law suspended	• Resident displacement • Limited public input • Reduced public oversight
Elite capture	Resource distribution not equitable	• Gentrification • Fragmented urban design layout
Event fix	Mega-event viewed as the quick fix for major planning obstacles	• Event overrides city or national funding priorities • Regular planning process bypassed • Event as an unsuccessful lever for urban development

Adapted from Müller (2015a)

Mega-events begin with a bid process, but the bid-books developed in these processes typically put forth a best-case or ideal scenario. The economic impacts in these plans are often overstated or inflated. The total costs for mega-events tend to exceed initial estimates for several reasons. First mega-events have a fixed deadline for completion and this drives up prices related to rush construction orders. As the event deadline approaches, profiteering occurs where premiums are paid to contractors to meet looming deadlines. The relatively long implementation period make the construction and other costs subject to inflation. While most communities have urban planning processes in place, the mega-event needs crowd out the existing priorities and funding. For example, mass transit systems built specifically to serve an

Olympic Park area where competitive venues may be clustered are seldom needed in the same capacity post-event. Changes or exception to the normal rule of law has been associated with the hosting of mega-events. Sport governing bodies may require tax exemptions on certain event revenues, such as the 2014 World Cup in Brazil, where it was estimated that $250 million in tax revenue to the country was lost due to special exceptions required (de Paula, 2014). Laws may be amended via targeted legislation or to obtain private property for redevelopment for mega-event venues and infrastructure that can displace residents (Davis, 2011). While mega-events promoters boast broad benefits to the general population, the wealthy tend to capitalize to the greatest degree. The Stratford area of East London (location of the Olympic Park) experienced accelerated *gentrification* after the redevelopment of the area. Original residents were displaced as the area became attractive for wealthy residents and the price structure of the area was altered (Watt, 2013).

Gentrification a renewal and or renovation of deteriorated urban neighborhoods via an influx of more affluent residents, resulting in increased property values that displace lower-income residences and small businesses.

Evolution of Mega-Events

Tracing the evolution of mega-events from their earliest manifestations to the imposing examples of the modern Olympic Games can reveal some fascinating similarities; however, many aspects of these mega-events have changed. The earliest Games in the modern series shared the stage with global trade festivals (for example, the World Fairs in Paris, 1900 and St. Louis, 1904). A number of the publications produced by these festivals are held by the British Library, as are materials from a wide range of other early festivals. Studied in conjunction with the official Olympic Games reports, many of which contain exhaustive details about the planning carried out by the host city, much can be learned about the beliefs and ambitions these events hold in common. One of the biggest changes in mega-events is due to developments in media technology. Before television and other types of technology like social media were developed, mega-events focused primarily on the game itself instead of on outside sponsors and advertisers. Until the 1970s, Olympic athletes were not permitted to take money from any advertisers or even to be a professional athlete. However, this early adherence to the ideal of amateurism made the Olympics less appealing to some who had the abilities to go pro. In order for the games to truly bring together the best athletes in the world, the IOC and its international sport federations amended rules and policies over time in order to allow professional athletes to participate and for athletes to openly accept sponsorships. With the allowance of professional athletes into the Olympics came the increased promise of corporate sponsorships for these world-renowned athletes and for the event itself.

Because of this, mega-events have several sponsors that are prominently featured before and during the events. Because of the many diverse and popular forms of media (television, computers, phones, etc.), mega-events have consequently gained a larger and more diverse population of viewers. Sponsorship has led to mega-events being advertised on everything from television commercials to fast food meal bags.

Sponsorships have become an integral part of the modern-day Olympics; both the individual sponsorships awarded to athletes and the commercial sponsorships (The Olympic Partner Program or TOP). Coca-Cola first became an official Olympic sponsor in 1928 and has since become the Olympics "longest standing sponsor" ("IOC Marketing Report," 2014). Another longtime sponsor is McDonalds. The fast food provider has spent 38 years as the official restaurant of the Olympic Games. This title allows them to use Olympic memorabilia in marketing campaigns and secure building spots for McDonald's restaurants within the Athletes Village and Main Media Centre. Atos, an information technology corporation based out of France, has been the IOC's official IT partner and sponsor for the last seven years, becoming a part of the exclusive TOP program in 2002 during the Salt Lake City Games. General Electric also has a standing partnership with the IOC that began in 2005; GE provides infrastructure necessities for all Olympic venues. These sponsorships between the IOC and successful corporations provide mutually beneficial relationships that enhance the overall viewership and success of the Olympic Games (IOC Marketing Report, 2014).

Due to a larger population of viewers and a great deal of advertising (helped in part by the partnerships mentioned above), mega-events have grown greatly in size. Once focused on the sport itself, mega-events now contain an array of focuses including not only sports, but the specific athletes and sponsorships as well. Furthermore, because of the unique nature of mega-events and the modern ease of travel, mega-events have become just as much about the location and tourism as it is about the sport itself. Mega-events have also grown in the diversity of participation. The Olympics started off as a competition between able-bodied men in sports focused primarily on strength. Through time, however, the Olympic Games have evolved to include not only able bodied men, but also able bodied women and athletes with disabilities. Additionally, the events are no longer centered solely upon strength, but also include endurance, skill in accuracy, and even creative performance.

Another important event to consider in the evolution of mega-events would be the World Cup. The FIFA World Cup, known more commonly just as "World Cup," is the largest international football (soccer) competition and is comprised entirely of senior men's national teams. The tournament began in 1930 and has been held every four years except 1942 and 1946 due to World War II. Since its start in 1930 with 12 nations participating along with the host nation Uruguay, the tournament has expanded to host 32 teams, giving more countries a chance to participate both in the World Cup and through the qualifying process. The long-standing success of the World Cup coupled with the growth of women's sport led to the creation of the Women's World Cup. This was first held in China in 1991 with 12 nations participating. This mega-event was expanded to 16 teams in 1999 and further increased to 24 teams in 2015. Both the World Cup and Women's World Cup are held every four years and have been strategically timed to fall outside of the cycle of the Summer Olympic Games. The competition for men is hosted in the midpoint between Summer Games while the women hold their event in the year immediately prior to the Summer Olympics.

The worldwide exposure of the World Cup has increased dramatically, primarily due to advances in media coverage and technology, and the immense global interest in the sport has thus qualified it as yet another mega-event.

International and National Sport Festivals

The success of the Olympic Games spawned a tremendous growth for other sport festivals on an international level. Table 15.5 details the growth of international sport festivals on an annual basis for the ten decades following the inaugural modern Olympic Games in 1896. A number of these sport festivals have direct affiliations with the Olympic movement such as the Pan American Games, the African Games, or the Asian Games. However, the majority of international sport festivals are organized independently from the Olympic movement. These international sport festivals have been organized by a number of different factors including: geographic area (i.e. Central American and Caribbean Game or Mediterranean Games), language (i.e. Francophone Games or Pan Arab Games), age (i.e. World Masters Games or the Youth Olympic Games), occupation (i.e. Universiade/World University Games or Military World Games), and disability (i.e. Paralympics or Special Olympics World Games) (Bell, 2003).

Table 15.5 *Growth of International Sport Festivals and Games 1896–2000*

Year	1901	1911	1921	1931	1941	1951	1961	1971	1981	1991
Event #s	1	3	4	6	0	10	10	11	15	40
	1902	1912	1922	1932	1942	1952	1962	1972	1982	1992
	0	1	4	7	0	4	8	9	22	28
1903	1913	1923	1933	1943	1953	1963	1973	1983	1993	
1	3	3	4	0	8	9	14	21	48	
1904	1914	1924	1934	1944	1954	1964	1974	1984	1994	
1	1	7	6	0	5	5	13	19	41	
1905	1915	1925	1935	1945	1955	1965	1975	1985	1995	
1	1	3	9	0	7	9	19	28	54	
1896	1906	1916	1926	1936	1946	1956	1966	1976	1986	1996
1	1	1	4	3	2	6	10	12	25	50
1897	1907	1917	1927	1937	1947	1957	1967	1977	1987	1997
0	0	2	3	6	2	7	10	15	35	68
1898	1908	1918	1928	1938	1948	1958	1968	1978	1988	1998
0	1	0	10	6	3	5	7	16	25	62
1899	1909	1919	1929	1939	1949	1959	1969	1979	1989	1999
0	2	2	2	4	6	9	11	17	38	68
1900	1910	1920	1930	1940	1950	1960	1970	1980	1990	2000
0	1	1	8	1	5	6	13	11	38	57

Adapted from Bell (2003)

While few sport festivals are able to rise to the level of a mega-event, the multiple sport offerings of the sport festival create similar challenges regarding the need for a wide variety of venues to host multiple and varied sport competitions. Sport festivals typically have larger total numbers of athletes participating in the varied events. While it is unlikely that many, if any, of these other international sport festivals will develop into mega-events these events do provide positive economic and participation benefits. This trend of growth for multi-sport festivals on an international level appears to show potential to continue.

Many of these international festivals employ drama and spectacle to underline and promote the values of local, national, or international organizing committees or groups. The level of media attention for these non-mega-events is far less focused on the fame of individual athletes or on the elite level of competition. Most of these sport festival participants are not celebrities or world-renowned athletes. These festivals give hard-working and more common athletes the opportunity to demonstrate what they have trained for and the skills they possess. These festivals typically place a greater emphasis on the experience of the participants over the experience of the spectators.

One example of a participant focused sport festival would be the World Police and Fire Games. This is a biennial, international event where police officers, firefighters, and customs and correction officers participate during a 10-day slate of athletic competitions. This festival began in 1985 in San Jose, California with almost 5,000 competitors ("CPAF History," n.d.). It has since been held in multiple nations including Canada, Ireland, Spain, and Australia, with the 2015 edition hosted in Fairfax, Virginia, USA. This event has grown to more than 12,000 competitors drawing from over 70 different countries. It is one of the top three largest amateur sporting events in the world and continues to grow and expand with over 60 sport and contest offerings and over 1,600 medal events in various age and gender categories ("About the Games," 2015).

Another example of a sports festival is the Arnold Sports Festival, held at the Ohio Expo Center in Columbus, Ohio. This event is held annually in Columbus, and like the Olympics features a wide variety of sporting events. The Arnold Sports Festival centers around the "Arnold Classic," a body builder competition named after Arnold Schwarzenegger but features about 50 other sports that span all age groups. This event has grown exponentially since its beginnings in 1989 and now attracts more than 175,000 spectators and over 18,000 competitors annually. The event and its unique format have been expanded to multiple sites and continents hosting an event called the Arnold Classic including Africa, Asia, Australia, Europe, and South America (Associated Press, 2016).

In addition to international sport festivals, a number of multi-sport events have been developed that are exclusively for the citizens or residents of a single nation. The oldest of these national festivals would be the Chinese National Games started in 1910 and reorganized as the National Games of China in

© Rena Schild/Shutterstock.com

A competitor in the Ultimate Firefighter competition obstacle course during the 2015 World Police and Fire Games in Fairfax, VA.

© A.RICARDO/Shutterstock.com

The "Arnold Classic" a bodybuilding contest remains a foundational element of the annual Arnold Sport Festival in Columbus, OH.

1959. In Korea, the National Sports Festival can be traced back to the 1920s, and after Korea's liberation post World War II the event has been hosted annually since 1950 in South Korea. The size and scope of this national event is impressive. For example, the 2014 festival on Jeju Island utilized 74 different venues to host 44 official and three exhibition sports drawing nearly 19,000 athletes and just over 6,000 officials ("95th National," 2014). In the United States, a national sport festival was initiated in 1978 under the auspices of the U.S. Olympic Committee. This festival was designated to operate in the three non-Summer Olympic years in order to provide American athletes with an experience similar to the Spartaki-ade festival held in the Soviet Union. The U.S. Olympic Festival operated as the largest amateur event in the country from 1978 until it was discontinued after the 1995 festival in Denver, Colorado (Hersh, 1995). The public interest and support of the national sport festival in the United States also helped to spawn the development of amateur sport festivals at the state level.

State Games

In the United States, the development of Olympic-style sports festivals at the state level (for both recreational and competitive opportunities) was begun in the late 1970s. The state of New York was the first to develop a state games program with the launching of the Empire State Games in 1978. This first state-based event became the model for other states and drew more than 100,000 participants at its peak (Andreatta & Johnson, 2014). The growth of state games fostered the development of a professional organization, the National Congress of State Games (NCSG), in 1988. The NCSG is connected to the United States Olympic Committee (USOC) through the community-based partner program of multi-sport organizations. This USOC partnership helps to meet the goal of promoting and supporting physical fitness and public participation in athletic activities through the state games as a developmental program. This partnership requires at a minimum that such events include two or more sports included within the Olympic, Pan American or Paralympic Games. The National Congress of State Games formed a new event open to medalist from all state games competitions in 1999 called the State Games of America. This event has been held every two years on an odd-year basis and has grown to include over 50 events.

Table 15.6 *State Games Members*

Region	State	Event Name	Year Founded
1	Connecticut	Nutmeg State Games	1989
1	Massachusetts	Bay State Games	1982
1	New Jersey	Garden State Games	1983
1	New York	Empire State Games	1978
1	Pennsylvania	Keystone State Games	1983
1	Virginia	Virginia Commonwealth Games at Liberty University	1989
2	Alabama	Alabama Sports Festival	1982
2	Florida	Sunshine State Games	1980
2	Georgia	Georgia Games	1989
2	Kentucky	Bluegrass State Games	1985
2	Louisiana	Louisiana State Games	2014
2	Mississippi	State Games of Mississippi	1991
2	North Carolina	Powerade State Game of North Carolina	1983
3	Iowa	Iowa Games	1987
3	Kansas	Sunflower State Games	1990
3	Michigan	Meijer State Games of Michigan	2010
3	Minnesota	Star of the North State Games	1988
3	Missouri	Show-Me State Games	1985
3	Nebraska	Cornhusker State Games	1985
3	Oklahoma	The State Games of Oklahoma	1983
3	Texas	Games of Texas	1986
3	Wisconsin	Badger State Games	1985

4	Arizona	Grand Canyon State Games	1993
4	California	California State Games	1988
4	Colorado	Rocky Mountain State Games	2001
4	Montana	Big Sky State Games	1986
4	New Mexico	New Mexico State Games	1989
4	Oregon	State Games of Oregon	1986
4	Utah	Utah Summer Games	1986
4	Washington	Washington Games	1996
emerging	New Hampshire	Granite State Games	2016
emerging	Wyoming	Wyoming State Games	2016

Adapted from stategames.org

Facility Considerations

Certainly facilities need to prepare for mega-events and sport festivals accordingly. These facilities include, but are not limited to the arenas in which competitions will be held, locations for athletic practice, boarding facilities for competitors, and facilities for tourism such as hotels, restaurants, and shops. Due to the large number of spectators in attendance, it is important to make sure that the facility is inspected and there is enough room for all attendees. Much consideration should be given to the fact that there may be a large number of disabled attendees; so it is important to include handicap accessibility in all facilities, if possible. The facility should also be inspected for any potential damage, fire hazards, or other hazards that could place participants and/or spectators in danger. Also, making sure that current security measures are arranged and implemented is very important (Coaffee et al., 2011).

Competitive Venues

As mentioned in previous chapters, the IOC has taken an avid interest in sustainability for the host country when it comes to facilities constructed for the Olympic Games. The IOC specifies to its host cities "build for legacy, adapt for Game time (with temporary solutions)" ("Host City Contract", 2015). Due to this, Beijing focused heavily on this idea of sustainability when constructing stadiums for its Olympics. China placed emphasis on their plan to utilize as many current stadiums as possible with alterations, instead of constructing new. In their plan, Beijing stated that while approximately 19 new stadiums would be constructed, six of them would be temporary, and the other 13 would contain plans to show sustainability for not only future tourism, but for citizen recreational purposes as well. In the modern games, competitive venues must not only be constructed with the needs of athletes and spectators in mind, but with the post-Olympic needs as well. There is an increasing push to design competitive venues that are functional, without being luxurious. With recent Olympics reaching astounding costs for host countries (Sochi's 2014 Winter games cost Russia $51 billion), the focus has turned to constructing facilities that meet requirements and practical needs, without unnecessary and costly amenities ("Development of Olympic Venues," n.d.). The IOC expects a detailed plan of venue sustainability. They provide this checklist to host cities, and ask that all elements be included in the legacy plan:

- the expected benefits at Games-time;
- the post-Games use of key Olympic venues and infrastructure;
- how the Olympic Games fit into the city/region's long-term planning strategy;
- financial planning; and
- pre-Games and post-Games ownership and responsibility for operations of the venues and infrastructure built for the Games (as determined by the OCOG in collaboration with the delivery partners) ("Host City Contract," 2015).

The IOC also demands that competitive venues comply with "international health, safety, and environmental best practices," as well as providing adequate accessibility for those with "mobility, vision, hearing or intellectual impairments," allowing them to enjoy the Olympic and Paralympic games "independently, equitably and with dignity"("Host City Contract," 2015).

Athlete Housing and Dining Facilities

Worldwide, multi-day events such as the World Cup and the Olympics need to have special accommodations in place for athletes when they are not participating, such as temporary housing, practice facilities, and dining. This may require the construction of new facilities if the ones available will not suffice. The IOC has a compliance list for athlete housing as well, with standard space requirements, as well as amenity requirements. For example, athlete bedrooms must be at least nine square meters, while main dining halls in Olympic village are required to cover at least 6,000 square feet ("Host City Contract," 2015). There are even specifications for how often housekeeping cleans, and what services they will provide.

London created a $1.5 billion, 2.7 million square foot Olympic village for hosting the 2012 Olympic Games. The village included sleeping accommodations for 16,000 athletes and Olympic personnel. The sleeping arrangements were compared to college-style dorm rooms-serviceable and comfortable, but by no means luxurious. The kitchen and cafeteria facilities are always a major concern for Olympic facilities, and London's cafeteria was constructed to seat 5,000 people. The cafeteria was constructed to fit the needs of the athletes based on these consumption predictions:

- 60,000—Number of meals expected to be served during the games
- 25,000—Loaves of bread expected to be consumed by athletes
- 90 tons—Amount of seafood expected to be consumed
- 360 tons—Amount of fruit expected to be served (Jamieson, 2012).

The IOC requires at least one dining hall in Olympic Village to be open 24 hours, and to provide hot meals at all times. Menus even have to be pre-submitted to the IOC for approval ("Host City Contract," 2015).

For athletes, the Olympic Villages' sleeping and dining accommodations are some of the most important aspects that aid them in a successful Olympic performance. When planning venues, it is important for directors to consider numbers like these in order to create facilities that can effectively meet the needs of such a large crowd. As part of the Olympics new sustainability agenda, London planned to turn these athlete accommodations into family style apartments after the games.

Already existing facilities must also be taken into consideration as well. As was previously stated, mega-events can have a large impact on tourism to the location. It is important to take into account that tourists will create a high demand in shops, hotels, restaurants, and other local attractions. For this reason, already existing facilities may need to expand or hire additional employees to meet the consumer demands that come with the mega-event being held. This can lead to high costs in infrastructure development for the city but also bring forth a large influx in employment.

To better understand the facility challenges for a mega-event, consider the 2014 Winter Games in Sochi, Russia. The Winter Olympics pose a significant facility challenge in that the nature of the event requires both large indoor venues coupled with more remote mountain-based venues. As such, Sochi was organized into two clusters, a coastal cluster in Sochi for the ice-based competitions, and a mountain cluster in the Krasnaya Polyana Mountains for the ski and sliding based competitions. Six primary venues were developed in the coastal cluster while five venues were established in the mountain cluster as detailed in Table 15.7. With a plethora of new venues and additional infrastructure costs, the Sochi Games were the most expensive at $51 billion compared to the $40 billion spent on the next most costly Beijing Summer Games of 2008 (Yaffa, 2014).

Table 15.7 *Summary of the Competitive Venues of the 2014 Sochi Games*

Cluster	Venue	Event(s)	Capacity	Cost in million (USD)	New or Renovated
Costal	Bolshoy Ice Dome	Hockey	12,000	336	N (2012)
Costal	Fisht Olympic Stadium	Opening & Closing Ceremony	40,000	631	N (2013)
Costal	Shayba Arena	Hockey	7,000	116	N (2013)
Costal	Ice Cube Curling Center	Curling	3,000	24	N (2012)
Costal	Alder Arena Skating Center	Speed Skating	8,000	246	N (2012)
Costal	Iceberg Skating Palace	Figure Skating, Short Track Speed Skating	12,000	270	N (2012)
Mountain	Laura Biathlon & Ski Complex	Biathlon, Cross Country Skiing	7,500	2478	N (2013)
Mountain	Rosa Khutor Extreme Park	Snowboarding, Freestyle Skiing	6,250/4,000	113	N (2012)
Mountain	Rosa Khutor Alpine Resort	Alpine Skiing	7,500	396	N (2011)
Mountain	RusSki Gorki Jumping Center	Ski Jumping	7,500	298	N (2013)
Mountain	Sanki Sliding Center	Bobsled, Luge, Skeleton	5,000	249	N (2013)

Adapted from "Interactive Venues" (2014) and Müller (2014)

Other Infrastructure Development

In order to have a successful mega-event, the proper buildings and other support structures are necessary to provide for transportation and access to water, energy, and eliminating waste. For example, the people of Rio de

An aerial view of the sliding center "Sanki" for the 2014 Winter Games in Sochi.

The RusSki Gorki Jumping Center used in the 2014 Sochi Winter Games.

Janeiro spent billions of dollars on sporting, tourist, transportation, and security infrastructures for recent mega-events that they have hosted in the past several years, such as the World Cup and Olympic Games (Gaffney, 2010). Gaffney notes that mega-events, in a way, become their own little societies due to these infrastructures because different rules apply at these events. Olympic Villages and venues require power, water, sewage, and adequate building accommodations, much like any other type of society. Certain specifications, especially in the matter of security, also need to be in place to keep everyone safe and happy. Infrastructures that need to be constructed for mega-events include buildings, policies, and organizational strategies.

While Olympic venues are created with athletes in mind, it is also necessary to consider the needs of the spectators. Concession and beverage vendors are available to spectators 24/7, just like the athletes. Spectator refreshment menus are submitted to the IOC as well, in order to comply with regional and religious preferences of all attending. The IOC requires its competitive venues to be designed with updated international health and safety standards to create an infrastructure that is safe and enjoyable for spectators.

Mega-events often include some aspect of political overtone where the host country and event holders can showcase new and attractive policies to a global audience. This is especially evident in bidding on which country/city will host the Olympic Games. For example, in order to win the bid for the 2014 Winter Olympics, the Sochi Bidding Committee promised four core elements within their bid:

1. "Accessibility for disabled individuals,
2. Development of a robust volunteer movement,
3. Implementation of green building standards, and
4. National adoption of Olympic Values (respect, excellence, and friendships)"

   (Alekseyeva, 2014, p. 162).

As one can see, two of these initiatives were based on current topics that are gaining research attention as well as political attention worldwide, for accessible and green infrastructure development. Unfortunately, there have been many complaints that these ideals were not upheld and were even violated in the process of building for the 2014 Sochi Winter Games. For this reason mega-events, such as the Olympic Games, can greatly impact the relations between countries.

Special Considerations for Mega-Events

Since mega-events often offer a world-stage for premiere athletes and performers in general, there are special considerations for these events such as large-scale security needs, volunteer organization, and athlete/performer needs. It is important to keep all participants safe from unruly spectators and other potentially dangerous individuals, because one cannot predict what people will do. If individuals are not trained on the proper emergency protocols, it would be incredibly easy for something to go wrong and for someone to get hurt. Individuals planning mega-events have been on high alert ever since 9/11, which changed the way our nation viewed security (Giulianotti & Klauser, 2010). For example, Brazil spent more than five times the amount on security in 2014 than South Africa did in 2010 in order to ensure the safety of the participants (Sim, 2014). Further, globalization and industrialization create opportunities for all nations to host international events. Local security in nations who do not typically host mega-events need to implement new policies and design new security systems in order to ensure the safety of everyone involved. An added benefit of hosting is that the enhanced security system is maintained once the mega-event is over and remains useful in keeping the citizens safe.

The tragic event that unfolded at the Munich Olympics in 1972 demonstrates the importance of the exceptional security needs associated with a mega-event in sport. Often referred to as the Munich Massacre, 11 people lost their lives after athlete housing facilities were infiltrated by eight heavily armed members of the Black September faction of the Palestinian Liberation Organization. The group's initial plan was to take hostages in an attempt to have negotiations met to free imprisoned Palestinians in both Germany and Israel, but when negotiations were not met, lives were lost. Initially, the Palestinians were able to breach security by simply scaling the six-foot fence around the athletes' compound (Berger, 2015). Since the massacre at the Munich Olympics, many mega-events have upped security as a top priority in the infrastructure design for the event. In 1972, Munich had a meager $2 million security budget, and as both the Games and the security risks have grown and developed that security budget had skyrocketed to over $1 billion by the 2004 Games in Athens (Maslin, 2005). The Munich Massacre shifted the priority of the Olympics to the security of venues and infrastructures, just as much as the games and events themselves. Security for the modern Olympics means plenty of surveillance and intelligence as well as police and military personnel (Bernhard & Martin, 2011).

The 9/11 terrorist attacks on the United States have been another cause of heightened security in the modern Games. Voulgarakis, the head of 2004 Olympic security in Athens, described how planning security post 9/11 was a daunting prospect for anyone because "no state had adapted mega-event plans to consider a scenario like 9/11" (Bernhard & Martin, 2011). As mentioned in previous chapters, Olympic host cities are often selected based on political and economic success at the time. Hosting provides a country with the chance to display the "affirmation of elite status that is part and parcel of hosting the games" (Bernhard &Martin, 2011). This government-placed "symbolic importance" of the Games, combined with the sheer international size of the event, justifies the increased security concerns and spending that have surrounded the modern Games. It is important to have both local and multi-national security systems in place in order to ensure the safety of all persons involved in the mega-event.

Table 15.8 *Security Expenditures for Olympic Summer Games 1984–2004*

Games	Expenditures (USD)	Cost per athlete (USD)
Los Angeles (1984)	$79.4 million	$11,627
Seoul (1988)	$111.7 million	$13,312
Barcelona (1992)	$66.2 million	$7,072
Atlanta (1996)	$108.2 million	$10,486
Sydney (2000)	$179.6 million	$16,062
Athens (2004)	$1.5 billion	$142,897
Beijing (2008)	$6.5 billion	$594,041
London (2012)	$1.6 billion	$148,588
Rio (2016)	$2.2 billion	$196,815

Adapted from Black (2012); Coaffee, Fussey, & Moore (2011) and Azulai (2016)

One final consideration for mega-events is the need for an effective volunteer organization. This topic is more fully discussed in Chapter 5 on Human Resource Management and in Chapter 10 on Customer Service, but it is important to utilize community volunteers in order to staff mega-events. A mega-event would have no chance of success without the contribution of skills, time, and commitment by the numerous volunteers who respond to the organizing committee's calls (Strigas & Jackson, 2003). For example, approximately 29,000 volunteers participated in the 1984 Los Angeles Olympic Games, and this level more than doubled at the Athens 2004 Olympic Games with a combined total of 60,000 volunteers serving at the Olympics and Paralympics (Giannoulakis, Wang, & Gray, 2007). For the Sydney Olympic Games of 2000, a total of 40,000 volunteers worked during the event, and the 2016 Olympics and Paralympics in Rio required 70,000 volunteers

(Associated Press, 2014). As each mega-event grows larger, the number of local volunteers increases with the demands for completing a successful event. This is a cost-effective strategy, especially if organizers take the steps to assure that the volunteers are well trained.

Conclusion

Perhaps the most important reason to legitimize the decision to host a mega-event is not strictly the impact on a country's economy, but how it changes the legacy of the place where it is held. As stated before, a mega-event is deemed a mega-event because of its size and scope in relation to visitors attracted, media coverage, total budget/costs and its impact on the built environment and citizens. While sports boosters routinely claim large benefits from hosting mega-events, the overwhelming majority of independent academic studies of these events have shown that their economic impact appears to be limited. The gross impact of these huge games and tournaments is undoubtedly large, attracting tens or hundreds of thousands of live spectators as well as television audiences that can reach the billions. The net impact of mega-events on real economic variables such as taxable sales, employment, personal income, and per capita personal income in host cities is negligible. However, examples in this chapter, including the rise out of an economic recession in London and a fall into an economic crash in Athens, Greece, show that mega-events can certainly have a direct economic impact on a location given the right conditions.

MINI CASE STUDY

A medium sized city in the United States debating on whether or not to host a mega-event. The city has recently hosted a small-scale festival that brought in tourists from around their state. The city leaders felt this stimulated their economy and provided just what they needed to make some much needed updates to their downtown area. They are considering placing a bid to host a national event. However, in order to host this event, they will need to make even more updates to their downtown, including implementing a new citywide security system, constructing a new arena venue, and upgrading the existing arena downtown. The city has contracted you as an expert on mega-events to help them make this imperative decision.

1. What are some of the projected costs and benefits of hosting this event?

2. What developments will they need to consider?

3. Discuss the potential economic impact this event may have on the city.

CHAPTER DISCUSSION QUESTIONS

1. Why is a mega-event considered a mega-event?

2. What are the major potential impacts on a local economy associated with hosting a mega-event?

3. Research a recent global sport event and evaluate its classification based upon Müller's (2015b) scale.

4. List examples of events/venues that the hosting site needs to consider and implement in order to host a mega-event.

5. Give an example of how facilities can accommodate for disabled attendees.

6. Why is security an important aspect of infrastructure design? Provide examples of how to make a mega-event more secure.

PRACTITIONER SPOTLIGHT

Photo courtesy of Frank Caraway.

NAME: Frank Caraway

ORGANIZATION: University Athletic Association, University of Florida

CURRENT JOB TITLE:

- Assistant Manager—Gale Lemerand Athletic Center
- **Year started in this role:** 2005

EDUCATIONAL PREPARATION:

- **Undergrad degree:** University of Florida BS, ESS
- **Graduate degree:** University of Florida MESS

CAREER PATH:

- **Internship:** Track and Field Programs, University of Florida
- **Entry level job:** Student Manager, University of Florida Women's Track and Field team

WHAT IS THE MOST REWARDING ASPECT OF THIS JOB?

My work is most rewarding when the athletes, coaches, and guests are happy. The most rewarding aspect of the job is when the event is running home competitions and you know that you have been successful in planning for it. Also, you have the opportunity to work and learn from a diverse group of successful professionals.

WHAT IS THE MOST CHALLENGING ASPECT OF THIS JOB?

The most challenging aspect of this job is not to become overwhelmed with the scope of the event and ensuring that you have enough volunteers to make the event go off smoothly. There are so many moving parts to putting on a large event. You must also be able to come to terms with the fact that no matter how well you plan, there will be something that comes up and you must be able to adapt.

WHAT IS A UNIQUE ASPECT OR TASK OF YOUR JOB THAT MANY WOULD BE SURPRISED TO HEAR ABOUT?

The aspect that many would be surprised to hear about is the number of hours that go into making an event happen. Planning starts a year in advance. There are multiple meetings and phone calls to vendors. It is not only the time spent on the day of the event, but the set-up before and the clean-up after that people are not aware of. I do not want my coaches to have to get involved in this event. Their job is to coach!

The Lemerand Athletic Center on the campus of the University of Florida in Gainesville.

HOW DOES PLANNING AND SET UP FOR MEGA-EVENTS OR TOURNAMENTS DIFFERENTIATE FROM SINGLE GAME COLLEGIATE EVENTS?

Event planning is not rocket science, but it requires an acute organization and constant attention to detail. The setting of objectives is important for the entire event. There are a lot of similar aspects. However, planning and set-up for a mega-event is different just due to numbers. You have to start your planning months in advance to make sure you are ready for the event. A lot of the single game set-up is the same as for the mega-event, but you have to multiply things due to numbers. Major events have a much larger budget and many moving parts.

WHAT TYPES OF MAJOR EVENTS HAVE YOU BEEN A PART OF?

Some of the largest and most complex events I have worked with include the Florida Relays (4,200 competitors, 220 University/Club teams, 330 High School teams), the Mountain Dew Cross-Country Invitational (30 Colleges with men's and women's teams, plus 100 High Schools with boys' and girls' teams), and the Gator Gallup (1,200 participants) as a community-based road race.

WHICH WAS YOUR FAVORITE, AND WHY?

The Florida Relays are at the top of my list because of the number and diverse scope of participants. You have high school athletes competing in the same venue as Olympic Gold Medalists.

IS THERE ANY COMPONENT YOU BELIEVE CAN REALLY SEPARATE A WELL-PLANNED MEGA-EVENT FROM AN UNSUCCESSFUL ONE?

Communicating clearly, planning for the unexpected and reigning in your budget will all help your event go without a hitch. I believe that the number and quality of the volunteers you have working your event can really separate a well-planned mega-event from an unsuccessful one. While it is important that you have enough volunteers, if you have a lot of volunteers that do not want to do any actual work, you are going to be fighting an uphill battle. Working with a team of people will make life easier. I was lucky to work under great leaders and mentors in Coach (Tom) Jones and Coach (Larry) Judge. They helped me learn to be clear in setting goals on what you are aiming to achieve from a project or event. The size of this event team will vary depending on the scale of the event. Don't make the event team too big, as management by large committee rarely works for this kind of activity. Make sure everyone knows and understands their role and responsibilities. Use small teams with a team leader reporting back if necessary, as this will reduce the number sitting round the table as part of the core team.

WHAT DO YOU BELIEVE ARE THE MOST IMPORTANT SKILLS TO DEVELOP?

A strong work ethic is vital. It is important that you communicate and work well with others. An ability to adapt and not become set in your ways is also important.

WHAT PARTING WORDS OF WISDOM DO YOU HAVE FOR STUDENTS AND YOUNG PROFESSIONALS IN THE FIELD?

It can be a very rewarding field but be aware of the time commitment and make sure you do not burn out. Also, as I've only worked at the University of Florida, I only know the way we do things here. But this is a dream job and a great place to work! I would recommend working at several places so you can get a different feel.

Reprinted by permission of Frank Caraway.

REFERENCES

About the Games. (2015). *World Police and Fire Games*. Retrieved from http://fairfax2015.com/

Alekseyeva, A. (2014). Sochi 2014 and the rhetoric of a new Russia: Image construction through mega-events. *East European Politics, 30*(2), 158–174. doi:10.1080/21599165.2013.877710

Andreatta, D., & Johnson, J. (2014, April 17). Empire State Games officially kaput. *Democrat and Chronicle*. Retrieved from http://www.democratandchronicle.com/story/news/2014/04/17/empire-state-games-disolve/7820979/

Associated Press. (2016, March 4). The series of sports festivals co-founded by American actor Arnold Schwarzenegger is adding two new versions of the Arnold Classic for a total of six this year, each on a different continent. *U.S. News and World Report*. Retrieved from http://www.usnews.com/news/entertainment/articles/2016-03-04/schwarzenegger-sports-fests-now-in-africa-asia-for-6-total

Associated Press. (2014, October 25). Unpaid volunteers worth millions to Olympic Games. *USA Today*. Retrieved from http://www.usatoday.com/story/sports/olympics/2014/10/25/unpaid-volunteers-worth-millions-to-olympic-games/17898595/

Azulai, Y. (2016, July 31). Israeli security co ready for Rio Olympics. *Globes*. Retrieved from http://www.globes.co.il/en/article-israeli-security-co-ready-for-rio-olympics-1001142963

Bell, D. (2003). *Encyclopedia of international games*. Jefferson, NC: McFarland & Company.

Berger, D. (2015). Tragedy in Munich. Retrieved from http://www.nps.gov/dabe/tragedy-in-munich.htm

Bernhard, D., & Martin, A. K. (2011). Rethinking security at the Olympics. In C. J. Bennett and K. D. Haggerty (Eds.). *Security games: Surveillance and Control at Mega-Events.* (pp. 20–35). New York, NY: Routledge.

Black, M. (2012, July 30). Winner's curse? The economics of hosting the Olympic Games. *CBC News.* Retrieved from http://www.cbc.ca/news/canada/ winner-s-curse-the-economics-of-hosting-the-olympic-games-1.1186962

Coaffee, J., Fussey, P., & Moore, C. (2011). Laminated Security for London 2012: Enhancing Security Infrastructures to Defend Mega Sporting Events. *Urban Studies, 48*(15), 3311–3327. doi:10.1177/0042098011422398

CPAF History. (n.d.) California Police Athletic Federation. Retrieved from http://www.cpaf.org/5/ index.htm?winscn=Main|history.htm&win=Main

Crompton, J. L., & Lee, S. (2000). The economic impact of 30 sports tournaments, festivals, and spectator events in seven U.S. cities. *Journal of Park & Recreation Administration, 18*(2), 107–126.

Davis, L. K. (2011). International events and mass evictions: A longer view. *International Journal of Urban and Regional Research, 35*(3), 582–599.

de Paula, M. (2014). *The 2014 World Cup in Brazil: Its legacy and challenges.* Sao Paulo, Brazil: Heinrich-Boll-Stiftung.

Development of Olympic Venues and Related Facilities. (n.d). *Beijing International.* Retrieved from http://www.ebeijing.gov.cn/Government/Mayor_office/Mayor_bulletin/t929892.htm

FIFA (n.d.). Bidding Process. Retrieved from http://www.fifa.com/governance/competition-organisation/bidding-process.html

Flyvbjerg, B. & Stewart, A. (2012). *Olympic proportions: Cost and cost overruns at the Olympics 1960–2012.* Oxford: Said Business School. Retrieved from http://eureka.sbs.ox.ac.uk/4943/1/ SSRN-id2382612_(2).pdf

Gaffney, C. (2010). Mega-events and socio-spatial dynamics in Rio de Janeiro, 1919–2016. *Journal of Latin American Geography, 9*(1), 1–29.

Giannoulakis, C., Wang, C. H., & Gray, D. (2007). Measuring volunteer motivation in mega-sporting events. *Event Management, 11*(4), 191–200.

Giulianotti, R., & Klauser, F. (2010). Security governance and sport mega-events: Toward an interdisciplinary research agenda. *Journal of Sport & Social Issues, 34*(1), 49–61.

Harris, H. A. (1979). *Greek athletes and athletics.* Bloomington, IN: Indiana University Press.

Hersh, P. (1995, July 27) Olympic Festival's success may cause it's demise. *Chicago Tribune.* Retrieved from http://articles.chicagotribune.com/1995-07-27/ sports/9507270075_1_olympic-festival-individual-sports-federations-olympic-teams

Horne, J. (2007). The four "knowns" of sports mega-events. *Leisure Studies, 26*, 81–96.

Host City Contract: Operational Requirements. (2015). *International Olympic Committee*. Retrieved from http://www.olympic.org/Documents/Host_city_elections/Host_City_Contract_Operational_Requirements_September_2015.pdf

Interactive: Venues of the Sochi 2014 Olympics (2014, January 11). *Toronto Metro*. Retrieved from http://www.metronews.ca/sports/2014/01/11/interactive-the-venues-of-the-sochi-2014-olympics.html

International Olympic Committee. (2014). *Olympic marketing fact file*. Retrieved from https://stillmed.olympic.org/Documents/IOC_Marketing/OLYMPIC_MARKETING_FACT_%20FILE_2014.pdf

International Olympic Committee (2013). Factsheet: London 2012 facts and figures. Retrieved from https://stillmed.olympic.org/media/Document%20Library/OlympicOrg/IOC/Olympic_Games/Olympic_Legacy/London_2012/Legacy/EN_London_2012_Facts_and_Figures.pdf

International Olympic Committee Marketing Report: Sochi 2014. (2014). *Olympic.org*. Retrieved from http://www.olympic.org/Documents/IOC_Marketing/Sochi_2014/LR_MktReport2014_all_Spreads.pdf

Jamieson, A. (2012, July 2). Inside London's Olympic Village: World's top athletes to share college dorm-style rooms. *NBCNews*. Retrieved from http://worldnews.nbcnews.com/_news/2012/07/02/12509629-inside-londons-olympic-village-worlds-top-athletes-to-share-college-dorm-style-rooms?lite

Liao, H. & Pitts, A. (2006). *A brief historical review of Olympic urbanization*. The International Journal of the History of Sport, 23, 1232–1252.

London Olympics 2012: Planning a Sustainable Olympic Games. (n.d). *Partnership for SDG's*. Retrieved from https://sustainabledevelopment.un.org/partnership/?p=2207

London 2012 to provide long-lasting economic benefits. (2013, August 8). Retrieved from http://www.olympic.org/news/london-2012-to-provide-long-lasting-economic-benefits/207219

Malfas, M., Theodoraki, E., & Houlihan, B. (2004, September). Impacts of the Olympic Games as mega-events. In *Proceedings of the Institution of Civil Engineers, Civil Engineering* (No. 157, pp. 209–220). Thomas Telford for ICE.

Malkoutzis, N. (2012, August 2). How the 2004 Olympics triggered Greece's decline. *Bloomberg*. Retrieved from http://www.bloomberg.com/bw/articles/2012-08-02/how-the-2004-olympics-triggered-greeces-decline

Marris, T. (1987). The role and impact of mega-events and attractions on regional and national tourism development resolutions. *Tourism Review, 42*, 3–12.

Maslin, J. (2005, December 15). A massacre in Munich, and what came after. *The New York Times*. Retrieved from http://www.nytimes.com/2005/12/15/books/a-massacre-in-munich-and-what-came-after.html?_r=0

Matheson, V. (2008). Mega-events: The effect of the world's biggest sporting events on local, regional, and national economies. In D. Howard & B. Humphrey (Eds.). *The business of sports* (Vol. 1, pp. 81–99). Westport, CT: Praeger.

Mills, B. M., & Rosentraub, M. S. (2013). Hosting mega-events: A guide to the evaluation of development effects in integrated metropolitan regions. *Tourism Management, 34,* 238–246.

Müller, M. (2014). After Sochi 2014: Costs and impacts of Russia's Olympic Games. *Eurasian Geography and Economics, 55*(6), 628–655.

Müller, M. (2015a). The mega-event syndrome: Why so much goes wrong in mega-event planning and what to do about it. *Journal of the American Planning Association, 81*(1), 6–17.

Müller, M. (2015b). What makes an event a mega-event? Definitions and sizes. *Leisure Studies, 34*(6), 627–642.

Rio 2016. (2016, August 22). This was Rio 2016: The Olympic Games in numbers. Retrieved from https://www.rio2016.com/en/news/rio-2016-the-olympic-games-in-numbers

Ritchie, J. R. B., & Yangzhou, J. (1987). The role and impact of mega-events and attractions on national and regional tourism: A conceptual and methodological overview. In AIEST (Ed.), *Proceedings of the 37th Annual Congress of the International Association of Scientific Experts in Tourism (AIEST) in Calgary* (pp. 17–58). St. Gallen: AIEST.

Roche, M. (1994). Mega-events and urban policy. *Annals of Tourism Research, 21,* 1–19.

Roche, M. (2000). *Mega-events and modernity.* London: Routledge.

Strigas, A. D., & Jackson Jr., E. N. (2003). Motivating volunteers to serve and succeed: Design and results of a pilot study that explores demographics and motivational factors in sport volunteerism. *International Sports Journal, 7*(1), 111–123.

Sim, D. (2014, June 10). Brazil World Cup 2014: Security costs five times as much as South Africa. *International Business Times.* Retrieved from http://www.ibtimes.co.uk/brazil-world-cup-2014-security-costs-five-times-much-south-africa-1452064

Wallechinsky, D. (1992). *The complete book of the Olympics.* Boston: Little, Brown & Co.

Watt, P. (2013). "It's not for us": Regeneration, the 2012 Olympics and the gentrification of East London. *City, 17*(1), 99–118.

Yaffa, J. (2014). The waste and corruption behind Sochi's enormous price tag. *BloombergBusiness,* Retrieved from: http://www.bloomberg.com/news/articles/2014-01-02/the-2014-winter-olympics-in-sochi-cost-51-billion

95th National Sport Festival comes to Jeju (2014, October 16). *The Jeju Weekly.* Retrieved from http://www.jejuweekly.com/news/articleView.html?idxno=4406

16

Tour and League Events

Lawrence W. Judge and *Jeffrey C. Petersen*

OBJECTIVES

After studying this chapter, the student should be able to:

- Describe how league and tour events are both similar and different from mega-events.
- Understand the difference between leagues and tour events and be able to give examples of each.
- Explain how and where league events originated.
- Identify how tour events impact a community or region.
- Explain and provide examples of the crossover between league and tour based sport organizations.

KEY TERMS

Ecological Footprint

Season

Sport League

Sport Tour

KEY ACRONYMS

AAU	Amateur Athletic Union	**NABBP**	National Association of Base Ball Players
APFA	American Professional Football Association	**NASCAR**	National Association for Stock Car Auto Racing
ATP	Association of Tennis Professionals	**NBA**	National Basketball Association
F1	Formula 1	**NFL**	National Football League
FIFA	International Federation of Association Football	**PGA**	Professional Golf Association
MiLB	Minor League Baseball	**WNBA**	Women's Professional Basketball Association
MLB	Major League Baseball	**WTA**	Women's Tennis Association
MLS	Major League Soccer		

Mazda Stadium in Hiroshima, Japan is a key venue in the Nippon Professional Baseball League.

Introduction

Global sporting events like the Olympics and the FIFA World Cup have proven to be immensely popular as spectator events. For example, fairly recent Olympic Games have sold a tremendous amount of total tickets including 8.3 million for the 1996 Atlanta Games, 6.8 million for the 2008 Beijing Games and just over 9 million for the 2012 London Games ("Olympics Ticket Sales," 2016). Similarly the 2010 World Cup in South Africa tallied 2.2 million tickets sold while the 2014 Rio World Cup tallied 2.58 million tickets (Rapp, 2014). However, a number of other sport events and organizations that operate primarily on a national or regional level attract large numbers of participants and followers, and these events usually are broadly classified as either league or tour events. In the 2014–2015 year, 10 sport leagues had a

Table 16.1 *Top Ten Sport Leagues by Total Attendance per Season 2014–2015*

League	Nation/ Region	Sport	Total Season Attendance
Major League Baseball (MLB)	USA & Canada	Baseball	73,739,622
Nippon Professional Baseball (NPB)	Japan	Baseball	22,859,351
National Basketball Association (NBA)	USA & Canada	Basketball	21,905,470
National Hockey League (NHL)	USA & Canada	Ice Hockey	21,528,192
National Football League (NFL)	USA	Gridiron Football	17,606,643
English Premier League (EPL)	UK	Association Football	13,943,910
Bundesliga	Germany	Association Football	13,311,136
La Liga	Spain	Association Football	10,171,062
Serie A	Italy	Association Football	8,866,274
Ligue 1	France	Association Football	8,024,973

Adapted from Gaines (2015)

total attendance above 10 million. This was topped by Major League Baseball that totaled almost 74 million fans in the 2015 season (see Table 16.1). Given this tremendous level of spectator attendance, it could be argued that the total continued impact of sport leagues and tours far surpasses the total impact of the global mega-events of the Olympics and World Cup.

Sport leagues and tours create a lengthy season of games and tournaments that generates a broad impact across many cities and venues over a sustained period of time, and in most cases this format of play is repeated on an annual basis year after year. While the attendance at a given single game or tournament is important, the contribution to the cumulative total for the season is even more vitally so. The structure of each league or tour also influences the importance of each individual game or contest as well as the total length of the season. Each game or tournament should be designed to add value to the overall product and generate interest in the sport as a whole. Table 16.2 identifies the top sport leagues throughout the world based upon average attendance per game. Interestingly, there is a tremendous amount of variation in the order and even inclusion of leagues when considering the two variables of average game attendance and total season attendance for league-based sports.

Sport Leagues an organization of team sports dependent upon the use of a home venue. Within leagues, a group of teams competes either at their home venue or the home venue of another league member throughout a set season of competition.

Table 16.2   *Top Ten Sport Leagues by 2015 Average Game Attendance Levels*

League	Nation/ Region	Sport	Average Game Attendance
National Football League (NFL)	USA	Gridiron Football	68,776
Bundesliga	Germany	Association Football	43,500
English Premier League (EPL)	UK	Association Football	36,695
Australian Football League (AFL)	Australia	Australian Football	32,346
Major League Baseball (MLB)	USA & Canada	Baseball	30,346
Indian Premier League (IPL)	India	Cricket	27,833
La Liga	Spain	Association Football	26,766
Nippon Professional Baseball (NPB)	Japan	Baseball	26,458
Canadian Football League (CFL)	Canada	Gridiron Football	25,286
Serie A	Italy	Association Football	23,332

Adapted from Gaines (2015)

Tour based events also boast significant levels of event attendance. As the most popular form of auto racing, Formula 1 (F1), drew a total race day attendance of 1,096,328 for its 13 events in 2015 averaging 84,333 per race with this total expanding to 2,974,923 when attendance for the total race weekend was taken into account (Collatine, 2016). The Professional Golf Association (PGA) set a single round attendance record in 2016 with 201,003 fans in Scottsdale, Arizona filling the third round session of the Waste Management Phoenix Open (Wacker, 2016). Perhaps the largest of the tour events from a spectator perspective is the Tour de France. This event is a tour of 21 day-long stages that occur over 23 days in 21 different locations or courses. Because the courses vary each year and occur on open roads, only estimates of the total spectators lining the roads for the Tour de France can be made with the 2016 race drawing approximately 15 million fans for an average of just over 714,000 per stage (Matuszewski, 2016).

Spectator attendance and ticket sales remain a foundational element of revenue for sport. According to a report by PricewaterhouseCoopers (2010), the largest revenue sector for sport globally was gate revenue that accounted for $43.2 billion or 37.8% of all sport revenues in 2009. A more recent study, specific to North American sport, showed gate receipts as the top revenue sector totaling $18.3 billion or 28.6% of all sport revenues in 2015 (Broughton, 2016). While media rights, sponsorship, and merchandising also provide significant revenue streams for sport organizations, the gate revenues remain at the top demonstrating the importance of the host venue in generating funds. The tremendous earning connected directly to the venue through spectator attendance highlights the importance of facilities to both league and tour events.

Sport leagues and sport tours both seek to engage fans in their local and regional areas to attend their event or follow via the media. Additionally sport leagues and sport tours will also seek to attract sport tourist or fans outside the local area to travel in order to attend an event. However, there are also a number of distinct differences in the organizational structure and operation of league and tour events in sport.

Sport League Organization

Team sports are most commonly organized into leagues. These leagues establish a schedule of contests or games that will occur over the course of a competitive season. These contests become recurring events at the home venues associated with each team. This organization allows for a schedule where events usually consist of a group of individual athletes or teams coming together in one location to play a sport. Generally, league events revolve around a group of teams and their respective season. Most, if not all, league events take place in the home venues of the member teams orchestrating about half of a season's games being played at the home venue of each league member. Some examples of US professional leagues include NFL, NBA, MLB, MLS, WNBA and others. However, much of intercollegiate sport and interscholastic sport at an amateur level in the United States follows league principles with conferences and leagues setting master schedules and organizing post-season tournament play. A common thread among all sports leagues is a structure that allows teams or individuals to compete against each other in a nonrandom order on a set schedule, usually called a *season*. The results of these individual competitions or games in the season determine an overall champion or establish qualification for a post-season championship tournament.

According to Noll (2003), there are five major areas that each sport league must address including:

1. Format—methods of scheduling or regular season and post-season championship contests;

2. Hierarchy—relationships amongst leagues of higher and lower caliber;

3. Multiplicity—number of leagues at the same hierarchical level;

4. Membership—conditions for team entrance or exit from a league; and

5. Governance—methods for creating and enforcing league rules.

Season an organized system of games or matches played within a sport league structure, or an organized group of tournaments, races, or events within a sport tour structure.

The five areas can be illustrated in the sport of baseball and within the current structure of Major League Baseball. Currently, MLB follows a format of 162 total games for each of its 30 teams within the regular season. These games are structured for each team as follows: 19 games × 4 opponents within same division (76 games total), 6 or 7 games × 10 opponents interdivision within same league (66 games total), 20 interleague games with opponents from the opposite league (American or National). The MLB post-season to determine the overall champion was last updated in 2012. This structure includes a single game wildcard playoff that is followed by a pair of divisional series (best 3 of 5 games) with the top rated team from the three divisions playing the wild card winner and the other two division winners facing one another within both the National League and the American League. The winners of each divisional series play in a league championship series (best 4 of 7 games) to determine the winners of the National League and American League Pennant. The post-season concludes with the World Series (best 4 of 7 games) between the American League and National League Champions. This type of organization demonstrates an application of the concept of format to the organization of MLB.

Hadlock Field in Portland, Oregon, is the home venue of the Portland Sea Dogs, one of 253 minor league teams officially connected to MLB.

© Eric Broder Van Dyke/Shutterstock.com

Table 16.3 *A Summary of Minor League Baseball (MiLB) Hierarchy*

League Level	League Members	Total Teams
AAA or Triple-A	3 (International League, Pacific Coast League, Mexican League	46 (with 16 in the Mexican League)
AA or Double A	3 (Eastern League, Southern League, Texas League)	30
A+ or Class A Advanced	3 (California League, Carolina League, Florida State League)	30
A or Class A	2 (Midwest League, South Atlantic League)	30
A Short Season	2 (New York-Penn League, Northwest League)	22
Rookie Advanced	2 (Pioneer League, Appalachian League)	18
Rookie	3 (Arizona League, Gulf Coast League, Dominican Summer League, Venezuelan Summer League)	77

Adapted from Cronin (2013) and milb.com

MLB provides a hierarchy of various levels of league play at the professional level. While the major leagues represent the highest level of play, MLB also directly oversees 253 minor league teams with affiliations to MLB franchises through Minor League Baseball (MiLB). These lower level leagues are divided into seven levels of play that are summarized in Table 16.3. These leagues are differentiated by length of season, age/experience of players, or location.

Major League Baseball can also demonstrate the principle of multiplicity. MLB is organized into two separate leagues, the American League and the National League each with 15 teams. Each of these leagues is also divided into three geographic divisions (East, West, and Central). Baseball also demonstrates multiplicity at the minor league level where multiple leagues exist at each level of minor league play, and they are organized primarily based upon geographic region.

Membership for teams within MLB is strictly controlled, and therefore minor league affiliations with the MLB franchises is also regulated by MLB policies and rules. MLB also is regulated under the leadership of the Commissioner as elected by the franchise owners. The league characteristic of governance is evident in that under the authority of the Office of the Commissioner of Baseball official playing rules for the game are published each year.

These five common characteristics of leagues are evident in sport leagues around the world. Each league has its own unique variations and range widely in their size, scope, and composition. Leagues span from young children participating in sports leagues at their local YMCA to leagues of professional athletes around the nation and the world. The size of these league events certainly varies by the age and skill level of the athletes participating. Young athletes who are just starting out generally only have an audience consisting of friends and family, while professional athletes have thousands or even hundreds of thousands of fans attending their competitions.

Development of American League-Based Sports

Baseball was the original league sport in the United States, and set an example for league organization that was emulated in other sports within the country and around the world. The first written rules for baseball were seen in 1845, and were established by the Knickerbocker Base Ball Club of New York City. A little over ten years later in 1857, a conference of amateur teams was called in order to decide rules; 25 teams were represented at the conference. This conference ended in the formation of the National Association of Base Ball Players (NABBP), America's first structured baseball league (Lahman, 1995). Until the late 1850s, baseball's primary participants came from those who lived in the New York area. The years after the Civil War saw baseball's popularity spread across the country (Spread of Baseball, 2016). During this time, players were still amateurs without direct pay for their play, until the Cincinnati Red Stockings decided to become a professional team in 1869. There were only 14 rules in the original league document, and the games played by the Knickerbocker Club were considered intramural within the league.

In 1875, the NABBP was disbanded in favor of the formation of the National League. The National League differed from the NABBP in its ownership; the National League was owned and run by businessmen under the leadership of William Hulbert, whereas the NABBP teams were owned and operated by players. The National League added more structure to the game of baseball in the form of scheduling, fixed ticket prices, and athlete contracts (Lahman, 1995).

Throughout the late 1800s and early 1900s baseball saw the rise and fall of many different leagues as the sport tried to find its footing in the combination of business and sport. Union Association, Player League, and Federal League all tried and failed to create a lasting league. The American League was formed as a professional major league in 1901 under the leadership of Ban Johnson with teams in eight cities including Baltimore, Boston, Chicago, Cleveland, Detroit, Milwaukee, Philadelphia, and Washington D.C. (Poremba, 2000). Today, Major League Baseball is comprised of two leagues: the National and American Leagues. Each league consists of 15 teams, combining for a total of 30 teams in the Major League.

Currently, the MLB competes in a season that lasts from April to October, ending with the World Series, which is the MLB's championship series between the American League and National League champion teams. These post-season championship games are played in a rotational basis at the "home" venues of the participating teams, showing one of the reasons MLB is such a true league sport. Table 16.4 shows attendance at MLB games during the regular season in 1935, 1975, and 2015, spanning eighty years and three generations.

Table 16.4 *A Comparison of MLB Game and Season Attendance*

Team	2015 (30 Teams)		1975 (24 teams)		1935 (16 teams)	
	Average Game Attendance	Total Season Attendance	Average Game Attendance	Total Season Attendance	Average Game Attendance	Total Season Attendance
Arizona Diamondbacks	25,681	2,080,145	—	—	—	—
Atlanta Braves	24,709	2,001,392	6,683	534,672	(Boston) 3,103	(Boston) 232,754
Baltimore Orioles	29,246	2,281,202	13,015	1,002,157	(St. Louis) 1,065	(St. Louis) 80,922
Boston Red Sox	35,564	2,880,694	21,587	1,748,587	7,070	558,568
Chicago Cubs	36,039	2,919,122	12,776	1,034,819	8,995	692,604
Chicago White Sox	21,677	1,755,810	9,269	750,802	6,108	470,281
Cincinnati Reds	29,870	2,419,506	28,588	2,315,603	5,898	448,247
Cleveland Indians	17,361	1,388,905	12,213	977,039	5,164	397,615
Colorado Rockies	30,948	2,506,789	—	—	—	—
Detroit Tigers	33,655	2,726,048	13,235	1,058,836	13,100	1,034,929
Houston Astros	26,587	2,153,585	10,593	858,002	—	—

Kansas City Royals	33,439	2,708,549	14,220	1,151,836	—	—
Los Angeles Angels	37,195	3,012,765	13,064	1,058,163	—	—
Los Angeles Dodgers	46,479	3,764,815	31,350	2,539,349	(Brooklyn) 6,111	(Brooklyn) 470,517
Miami Marlins	21,633	1,752,235	—	—	—	—
Milwaukee Brewers	31,390	2,542,558	14,980	1,213,357	—	—
Minnesota Twins	27,408	2,220,054	8,990	737,156	—	—
New York Mets	31,725	2,569,753	21,365	1,730,566	—	—
New York Yankees	39,430	3,193,795	16,513	1,288,048	8,885	657,508
Oakland Athletics	21,829	1,768,175	13,278	1,075,518	(Philadelphia) 3,239	(Philadelphia) 233,173
Philadelphia Phillies	22,606	1,831,080	23,571	1,909,233	2,601	205,470
Pittsburg Pirates	30,847	2,498,596	15,875	1,270,018	4,583	352,885
San Diego Padres	30,367	2,459,752	15,824	1,281,747	—	—
Seattle Mariners	27,081	2,193,581	—	—	—	—
San Francisco Giants	41,678	3,375,882	6,456	522,919	(New York) 9,478	(New York) 748,748
St. Louis Cardinals	43,468	3,520,889	20,674	1,695,270	6,573	506,084
Tampa Bay Rays	15,322	1,287,054	—	—	—	—
Texas Rangers	30,764	2,491,875	14,099	1,127,924	3,312	255,011

Toronto Blue Jays	34,505	2,794,891	—	—	—	—
Washington Nationals	32,344	2,619,843	(Montreal) 11,213	(Montreal) 908,292	—	—
MLB Total	910,847	73,719,340	369,431	29,789,913	95,285	7,345,316
MLB Average per team	30,362	2,457,311	15,393	1,241,246	5,955	459,082

Data adapted from baseball-refernce.com

The data presented regarding the individual franchises in MLB demonstrates the growth of the league in team members from 16 to 24 to 30 since 1935. Additionally, the total attendance for MLB has increased just over ten-fold since 1935 and currently leads all sport leagues attendance globally.

Baseball, though still tremendously popular in the United States, pales in comparison to modern day American Football and the National Football League (NFL) in average spectators per game. The National Football League (NFL) was formed in 1920 initially as the American Professional Football Association (APFA). Many early NFL teams started in small markets in the Midwestern part of the United States. For example, Muncie, Indiana was once home to a National Football League team. The Muncie Flyers were one of the 11 charter members of the NFL (then called the American Professional Football Association) competing in 1920 and 1921 before disbanding (Crepeau, 2014; Sawyer & Judge, 2012). Eventually, most of these small town franchises moved or were replaced with the big city teams known around the nation in present day. However, several traditional smaller-market teams have remained, like the Green Bay Packers and the Buffalo Bills of the NFL.

By the start of the first season, the NFL brought together a total of 15 teams under the influence of key leaders like George Halas, Joe Carr and Jim Thorpe who was elected as the first president of the APFA (Crepeau, 2014). The league began to organize its operations with a number of steps aligning with Noll's (2003) five areas of league operation. Early meetings of the leagues' leadership sought to formalize and regulate the schedule of games, control the bidding process for players, regulate salary levels, and prevent the raiding of rosters by other teams (Crepeau, 2014). At the conclusion of the first season, this new league was far from successful from a financial perspective, and the team membership fee for the coming year was cut in half from $100 to $50. Despite these challenges, the league grew to 21 teams starting the second season in 1921; however, only 13 teams remained viable by the end of that season. From these rather meager beginnings, the most influential and powerful sport league has developed.

Special Considerations for Leagues

There are several special considerations related to league based sports that will influence the management of facilities for these events. First, the venue itself is highly valued, as it is viewed as the home of the team. This connection with the facility extends from the athletes and team staff to the spectators. There is often a high level of pride associated with this home venue. Because the facility hosts numerous home contests through each season, league-based sports will often have larger numbers of total employees as well as a greater number of full-time employees than tour based sport venues. This can be advantageous from a staff training and operational perspective as the employees have numerous opportunities to host games or matches during a season, and this can lead to more opportunities to make adjustments and improvements based on feedback from recent past performances. As many league-based sports have repeat customers or even season ticket holders, there is a good opportunity to develop relationships between these members of the fan base and the venue employees. While the repetition of hosting home contests can be draining, league sports also have a nearly equal number of contests played away from the home venue. The time periods during the season with away games creates an opportunity for employees to recuperate from the high workloads associated with home games.

With a large number of home contests played each season, fluctuations in attendance and lower interest during the regular season can become problematic for some teams. Mills and Fort (2014) explain that attendance, even at professional sporting events, can be rather unpredictable. They state that "No form of outcome uncertainty (game, playoff, or across seasons) matters for attendance in hockey or baseball regardless of which game uncertainty variable is used". So, it is important for facilities to be prepared for tremendous possible fluctuations in crowd size within home events.

Another issue that occurs with league events is the lack of spectators during the regular season for games against non-marquee opponents within the league. A great example of this can be seen in recent years within the NFL. The regular season of the NFL gets far lower levels of spectatorship in comparison to the playoffs and conference championship games. It is not until the NFL moves into the playoffs that the attendance and spectatorship increase significantly. During the 2015 regular season, Fox drew 20.75 million viewers per broadcast (Deitsch, 2016). In comparison, the 2015 Super Bowl alone drew in 114.4 million viewers (Pollota, 2015). The NFL appears to face a problem of lack of spectatorship in venues and in the media within the regular season. This can cause financial issues if large sums of money are being spent in the operation of numerous games in which fewer tickets are sold and television viewings are lower. In response to such factors, facility managers need to have contingency planning for event staffing related to the changing demands based upon the level of attendance.

Tour Events

While the league structure is the most common model of organization and operation for team sports, the tour event is more prevalent for individual sports. Some prominent examples of professional sport organizations that operate as tour events include the Professional Golf Association (PGA) tour, NASCAR and Formula 1 (F1) racing, as well as the professional tennis tours such as the Association of Tennis Professionals (ATP) World Tour and the Women's Tennis Association (WTA) Tour.

Sport Tour a group of tournaments established around a single sport or single ownership/leadership that travels from city to city around a nation, region, or even the world and brings high caliber athletes and events to various fan bases.

A *sport tour* would be defined as a group of tournaments established around a single sport or single ownership/leadership that travels from place to place. These tournaments may move from city to city around a nation, region, or even the world, and the goal of this traveling event is to bring high caliber athletes and events to various fan bases. The variation of location can help to expand the level of exposure of the sport, as well as energize communities to engage and participate in this limited opportunity to attend. While the Olympic Games and FIFA's World Cup do technically qualify as tour events, their sheer size elevates them to the status of mega-events. Tour events are not limited only to high-caliber professional sports and athletes. A number of tour events focus more on participation than spectators. In the United States, a number of youth club sports operate in a tour manner. The Amateur Athletic Union (AAU) operates basketball and volleyball through numerous large tournaments typically held on weekends at a regional or national level. These tournaments are held in large sportsplex facilities to maximize the number of contests played within a short timeframe. Traveling teams in youth soccer follow a similar model and play in large tournaments on a regular basis for their competition traveling to different cities for exposure to various new teams, as well as for exposure to college coaches for potential recruitment for athletic scholarships.

Just as television and multi-media coverage is better than any other time in history, so is the ability to travel. This ability to travel has increased the reach of many tour events to individuals outside of the local market allowing travel to a new city or nation to take part in a sports event. An increasing number of sports fans want to experience sporting events live and in person. Every season, sports fans are traveling by land, sea, and air to spectate sports on a first-hand basis. This sport-based travel is connected to those who desire to watch a contest live in a new place as well as those that seek to participate in a sporting event as an athlete. This increased ability of individuals to travel in order to view these events in person has allowed many tour events to expand and thrive.

INDYCar Series

Some tour events in sport are better known than others, and they can be a prime source of income for locations if they are well known. For example, the Indianapolis 500 is only one race in a series of INDYCar races that occur around the United States (15) and Canada (1). Although there are 16 races in this series, the Indianapolis 500 is by far the best known, and it creates the largest single event on an annual basis for the city of Indianapolis. The first Indianapolis 500 was held on Memorial Day of 1911. The Indy 500 track, officially known as the Indianapolis Motor Speedway, was the first track to be built specifically for automobile races, and was constructed as a 2.5 mile oval. In 2011, an estimated 300,000 spectators attended the Indianapolis 500 (Leerhsen, 2011).

The INDYCar series tours the United States and Canada from the spring to early fall, following a grueling schedule as illustrated in Table 16.5. The INDYCar series includes drivers from all over the world. These drivers compete on "super-speedways, short ovals, road courses and temporary street circuits" (What is INDYCar, 2016). There is a point system in place throughout the tour season, and the driver with the most points at the end of the tour is declared champion, receiving around $1 million in additional prize money at the conclusion of the tour season. The INDYCar governing body was founded in 1994, after a split of the former governing body.

NASCARs Brickyard 400 as a "secondary" event held at the IMS that began in 1994 as the first race other than the Indy 500 to be held since 1916.

Indianapolis MotoGP event demonstrates additional uses for the IMS venue originally developed for one main event the Indy 500.

Table 16.5 *The 2016 INDYCar Schedule and Venues*

Date	Race	State	Venue Name	Venue Type
March 13	Firestone Grand Prix of St. Petersburg	Florida	N/A	Temporary Circuit Streets
April 2	Desert Diamond West Valley Phoenix Grand Prix	Arizona	Phoenix International Raceway	Tri-Oval Track
April 17	Toyota Grand Prix of Long Beach	California	N/A	Temporary Circuit Streets
April 24	Honda Indy Grand Prix of Alabama	Alabama	Barber Motorsports Park	Permanent Circuit

May 14	Angie's List Grand Prix of Indianapolis	Indiana	Indianapolis Motor Speedway	IMS Grand Prix Course Permanent Circuit
May 29	100th Running of the Indianapolis 500	Indiana	Indianapolis Motor Speedway	Rectangular-Oval
June 4	Chevrolet Dual in Detroit Race 1	Michigan	Raceway at Belle Isle Park	Temporary Circuit Streets
June 5	Chevrolet Dual in Detroit Race 2	Michigan	Raceway at Belle Isle Park	Temporary Circuit Streets
June 11	Firestone 600	Texas	Texas Motor Speedway	Oval
June 26	Kohler Grand Prix	Wisconsin	Road America	Permanent Circuit
July 10	Iowa Corn 300	Iowa	Iowa Speedway	Oval
July 17	Honda Indy Toronto	Ontario	Exhibition Place	Temporary Circuit Streets
July 31	Honda Indy 200 at Mid-Ohio	Ohio	Mid-Ohio Sports Car Course	Permanent Circuit
August 21	ABC Supply 500	Pennsyl-vania	Pocono Raceway	Tri-Oval
September 4	Grand Prix at the Glen	New York	Watkins Glen International	Permanent Circuit
September 18	GoPro Grand Prix of Sonoma	California	Sonoma Raceway	Permanent Circuit

Adapted from Indycar.com

In order to further illustrate key components of tour sport organization two examples of sport tours will be considered including INDYCar and the Women's Tennis Association (WTA).

A review of these 16 races reveals 14 different race locations/venues with the Indianapolis Motor Speedway hosting two events in May including one Grand Prix circuit race and the Indy 500 on the oval track, and Detroit hosting two races in two days at Belle Isle. Five of these races occur on temporary street circuits (St. Petersburg, Long Beach, Detroit, and Toronto), and five other road circuit courses occur on permanent tracks in Alabama, Wisconsin, Ohio, New York and California. The balance of these tour event races occurs at permanent oval racing tracks like the Phoenix International Speedway,

Indianapolis Motor Speedway, Texas Motor Speedway, Iowa Speedway, and Pocono Raceway. The spectator attendance at the INDYcar races is an important revenue stream, but published official data is scarce with only the Grand Prix of Alabama reporting official attendance for 2016 at 83,765 (DiZinno, 2016). No other races reported official attendance, but the 100th running of the Indianapolis 500 in 2016 was sold out with an estimated 350,000 spectators in attendance for the race (Carter, 2016).

A tour sport like INDYcar is dependent upon appropriate venues to host each race that can provide a course that is safe for the drivers and a course that provides the necessary seating and amenities for the spectators. The use of temporary venues with street circuits was used for 31% of the races in 2016. This type of venue has the advantage in that there is no permanent construction of facilities that might sit idle for much of the rest of the year. A track with a singular primary event, like the Indianapolis Motor Speedway (IMS) with the Indy 500, must seek other opportunities to host other events throughout the balance of the year. While the IMS does host two INDYcar events each year, the facility has also served as the host venue for NASCAR's Brickyard 400 since 1994, and a MotoGP race from 2008–2015. The IMS has attracted other unique racing events recently like the Red Bull Air Race for 2016 that drew nearly 40,000 spectators (McCutcheon, 2016).

WTA Tour

The Women's Tennis Association is another example of a tour event. The 2016 WTA tour schedule included a total of 61 tournament events with several different categories including Grand Slam (4), WTA Finals (1), Summer Olympics (1), Premier Mandatory (4), Premier 5 (5), Premier (12), International (33), and the WTA Elite Trophy (1). The WTA Tour holds matches and tournaments all over the world, from Brisbane to Istanbul, as well as within the United States ("WTA 2016 Calendar," 2016). Unlike the INDYCar tour, which runs from March-September, the WTA begins in January and finishes in October. WTA ranks their participants in two different categories: singles and doubles. Scores are calculated based on performances during WTA tournaments. For singles players, 16 tournaments are taken into consideration, and for doubles 11 tournaments are used. The WTA attaches stipulations to the way that points are accumulated for their ranking systems. For example, some of the points accumulated over the 52-week period must come from the four Grand Slam events (Wimbledon, the French Open, the US Open, and the Australian Open) and other mandatory premier tournaments. In order to be listed on WTA Rankings, athletes must receive points from three tournaments (at least), or 10 single/double points from all tournaments ("All About Rankings," 2016). Professional tennis is a unique tour sport that has distinct organizations that operate for the men's and the women's competitions. However, a number of tournaments are combined with both men and women participating at the same tournaments. This occurs at each of the four Grand Slam events annually, and these events draw the greatest levels of spectators within the tour as displayed in Table 16.6

Table 16.6 Grand Slam Tennis Tournament Attendance (ATP & WTA combined)

Tournament	Location	Year	Total Attendance
Australian Open	Melbourne, Australia	2015	703,899
French Open	Paris, France	2015	463,328
Wimbledon	London, England	2015	484,391
U.S. Open	Flushing Meadows, New York	2015	691,280

Adapted from Carter (2016)

The French Open held at Rolland Garros.

As mentioned above, the WTA tour lasts ten months out of the year, as compared to INDYCar's seven. This lengthy season takes a physical toll on athletes, and the international location of the tournaments is daunting from a travel and expense perspective as well. The length of the season combined with the physical tolls brought on by frequenting different time zones has caused players to speak out against the WTA and the ATP. Andy Roddick, a former professional tennis player, was quoted as saying, "I think too much is asked of us, playing 11 months of the year. At a certain point you would hope [the ATP and WTA] would start respecting [the players] opinions a little more" (Wertheim, 2008). While no changes have been made to the WTA or ATP tour schedule, one can expect that Roddick's comments will not be the last complaint regarding a grueling tour schedule. Regardless of the difficulty of the schedule, the fact that there are so many different places that hold these tournaments makes the WTA tour another prime example of a tour event.

Impacts of Tour Events

Similarly to mega-events and sport festivals, tour events can affect a community in more than one way. Collins (2012) discusses this at length in his article discussing the locations of the 2007 Tour de France. He says that there are both economical (usually positive) and environmental (unfortunately usually negative) changes that occur when a huge number of tourists come to an area; communities should keep this in mind when deciding whether or not to host a tour event. An example of the negative environmental impacts of tour events can best be seen when examining the Tour de France. The Tour de France takes place for nearly all of July, and the course covers approximately

2,200 miles. According to a study by Cardiff University, an ecological footprint of 57,990 global hectares was created by the 2.85 million spectators attending the prologue and stage one of the 2007 Tour de France (MacMichael, 2012). This concept of *ecological footprint* serves as a measurement of the impact of the event in terms of the area of productive land and water required to produce the goods consumed and to assimilate the wastes produced. This large ecological footprint for the Tour de France is not necessarily due wholly to the competition itself but rather, the popularity of the event and the tourism that it attracts.

The Tour de France draws the largest number of spectators of any sport event over its 21 stages.

Like mega-events, this tour event attracts thousands of spectators, and with many spectators comes a greater demand for hotels, restaurants, shops, and entertainment attractions. For this same reason, Tour de France has a highly positive impact on the country's economy. For this reason, like mega-events, committees planning tour events should keep in mind the ecological footprint and devise ways to combat the negativities associated with the event. With such large effects on economy, environment, and fandom it would seem that tour events almost mirror mega-events, but it is important to keep in mind that tour events are, in fact, different from mega events because of their timing and locations.

Ecological Footprint the total impact of a sport event on the environment measured in hectares of productive land required to produce all goods consumed and handle the wastes produced.

Some tour events have smaller impacts, and it is easier to distinguish these tour events from mega-events as they are smaller and are usually geared towards the athletes themselves and less towards the spectators who may come to watch them. These events, called ultra-endurance events, are not funded by the communities, but positively influence these communities because of the athletes willingness to fund themselves throughout the event. According to Discovery News (DNews, 2013) some of the most notable ultra-endurance events are Race Across America (3,000 cycling race), Marathon de Sables (150 mile stage race run in the Sahara Desert of Morocco), Iditarod Trail Invitational (a 350 and 1,000 mile fat bike, foot and ski race along the Iditarod Sled Dog course) and the Ironman World Championship (triathlon in Hawaii with 2.4 mile swim, 112 mile bike and marathon run). These events, though lesser known than Tour de France, are races that take place over a great span of land and directly affect the places in which the athlete travels. These ultra-endurance events help to distinguish between tour and mega-events because they are smaller in nature while still benefitting the local economy along the route. Athletes participating in these races must usually provide for all of their needs including lodging, medical staff, and support teams. As the locations do not provide such accommodations, money is being added into the community by the athletes and spectators rather than spent. For example, a change in the 2015 course for the Iditarod Trail Invitational in Alaska in 2015

© James Carnegie/Shutterstock.com

Ultra-Endurance events like the Marathon de Sables in the Sahara Desert still create significant economic and environmental impacts.

had significant impacts on several small rural villages that lost their checkpoint status due to low snow levels. Three different checkpoints reported lost revenues that were very significant to their limited business including Yentna Station Roadhouse with $3,000 to $5,000 in estimated losses, Skwentna Roadhouse with $15,000 to $20,000 in estimated losses, and Winterlake Lodge with $25,000 to $40,000 in estimated losses (Skvorc, 2015). Although these losses in revenue pale in comparison to mega-events, they remain quite significant for the small and isolated rural communities. Though these ultra-endurance tour events and stage races are lesser known, they are important in understanding the scope of tour events.

Special Considerations for Tour Events

Several special considerations need to be taken into account when hosting a tour event. First, the mobile and traveling nature of tour events in many cases relies upon venues that may only be used for a single primary event each year. This can be positive from the perspective that tour events do not usually require a great deal of construction or reconstruction on an annual basis once the initial facilities have been established. However, this limited level of facility use only for the tour event can create pressure for facility managers to develop other potential uses and events for the facility in order to increase revenue generation and decrease the time periods that the facility sits idle.

The facility and event staff associated with a tour event is typically smaller in size due to the singular nature of the tour event at any particular location. This often creates a heavier reliance on part-time and temporary staffing for tour events compared to many league based venues. While some tour management staff may work on a full-time basis while traveling from event site to event site, much of the venue staff are associated with the local venue, and this can create challenges in that key managers may have a limited time of working together within the tour event.

Another special consideration to take into account with tour events are sponsorships. Ferreira (2008) describes some of the sponsorship aspects of the tour and the vital importance of giving sponsors the proper advertising, hospitality and product use as stated in their contract; failing to do so could end in a hefty lawsuit. Title sponsorship of tour events has become a common element for many tour events. Many of the corporations making major investments in title sponsorship packages expect to see a return on this investment through increases in their business in sales or even their overall company valuation in the stock market. A recent study of title sponsors in NASCAR and the LPGA found significant stock price increases on both the announcement date and the event date for corporations engaged in title sponsorship contracts (Kudo, Ko, Walker, & Connaughton, 2015).

Volunteerism in Tour and League Events

Volunteers may be a smart way to provide effective services for attendees as well as offset the high cost of running a sport facility or operating a major event. It is important that volunteers are trained in all aspects of customer service (see Chapter 10 on customer service) and it may be beneficial to provide incentives to help foster their service in future events. The costs associated with offering incentives may actually be recovered through lower costs in training volunteers if one can attract a consistent set of returning or repeat volunteers. Love, Hardin, Koo, and Morse (2011) found that individuals volunteered at a sport event because they perceived it to enhance themselves, they wanted to be altruistic, they saw this as an opportunity to escape, they thought it would enhance their career, they had an interest in the sport, and/or for the prestige of the event. Volunteerism may easily be found among fans that show an active engagement with the sporting events (e.g. those who attend many of the events). Therefore the recruitment of potential volunteers can often begin with current or past spectators or participants in an event.

Customer Satisfaction in Tour and League Events

Spectators form a group of primary customers and are an imperative part of tour and league events as they provide the financial means to sustain these types of events over time. Therefore, understanding the reasons individuals attend events and what leads to customer satisfaction during the event are both important factors for facility and event managers to consider. Lambrecht, Kaefer, and Ramenofsky (2009) assessed factors contributing to customer attendance and satisfaction at a golf tournament and found course accessibility, restrooms, and helpfulness of the staff to be important to customers' satisfaction.

Other researchers found there were four different benefit subcategories within sport spectators including personal, sociocultural, economic, and environmental (Driver & Bruns, 1999; Lyu & Lee, 2013). Each of these subcategories is associated with different behaviors encountered or experienced while at the event, which all contribute to spectator satisfaction and intention to attend another event. Jun and Seung (2015) found that customer satisfaction may even be linked to attributions of game outcomes in sports and could be explained by attribution theory. Although these results may be specific to the population and event in these particular studies, it speaks to the need for facility managers to consider these four areas when hosting an event. For these reasons, facility managers must also take into account that customer satisfaction may rely heavily on the money invested into making the facilities appealing and comfortable. In order to maximize the profitability of such events and foster event success, there needs to be a focus on the features and amenities within the venues for the benefit of the spectators.

Cross Over of League and Tour Events

While it is helpful to understand the very different way that league and tour events are structured and organized, there continues to be a growing number of sports that have begun to combine elements of leagues and tours within their operations. This has created a number of events associated with a traditional league that has adopted aspects of tour structure. To better understand this concept, it will be helpful to consider sport organizations that operate almost exclusively as a league. Major League Baseball, National Association Basketball, and the National Hockey League would be such sports as all regular season games and post-season games occur in the home venue of one of the two teams competing. The All-Star Games composed of top players selected from all member teams is also hosted in a home venue of one of the franchises. However, not all leagues fully utilize a league format for every aspect of their operation.

The National Football League operates in a slightly different manner, but the majority of its regular season contests are still held in the home venues of its members like a traditional league. However, the NFL has adopted several features that align with sport tours. The first tour element of the NFL would be the hosting of the Super Bowl or league championship game in a neutral site that is bid upon by prospective cities to host the prestigious event. Although the host venue is often an NFL venue, it has also been hosted in college stadiums such as Rive Stadium (Super Bowl I), Stanford Stadium (Super Bowl XIX) and the Rose Bowl (Super Bowls XI, XIV, XVII, XXI, XXVII) (Fischer, 2015).

Another manifestation of a tour element in the NFL has been the creation of regular season games being hosted internationally in neutral venues during the regular season. This began in 2005 when the Arizona Cardinals played the San Francisco 49er in Azteca Stadium in Mexico City and was spread to a long term contract for NFL games to be played in London at Wembley Stadium through 2020 (Siefert, 2016). These international initiatives were led by the entire league to foster the international growth of the sport. These new international moves by the NFL show one example of how a league sport is crossing into tour event territory by using the location of an event as a major selling point. Now spectators are given the incentive to buy tickets not only for the game itself but also for the idea of visiting a new country. While seeing a foreign country is an incentive for current fans, the ultimate goal of playing these games overseas

© Nando Machado/Shutterstock.com

NFL marketing on Regent Street in London promoting its game held in Wembley Stadium.

is to engage new fans across the globe thus increasing the number of spectators.

Collegiate football is another sport that primarily competes within a league structure at the highest level or Football Bowl Subdivision (FBS) of the NCAA. The regular season is conducted primarily in the home venues of the universities, but the post-season conference championship games and the bowl games are played at neutral sites, and these post-season games operate as tour events where the host city seeks to attract spectator tourist spending and media attention through the hosting of these games. These conference championship games and bowl games are associated heavily with the leagues or conferences in negotiating the participating teams and locations.

Participants at the start of the Rock "n" Roll Marathon in Los Angeles.

Collegiate basketball at the highest level operates most of its regular season within a league structure with games played in the home venues of teams during the conference or league schedule. However, the early season includes many tournaments and special games held in neutral site venues that operate more like a tour event. Additionally, the post-season tournament to determine the national championship is operated directly by the NCAA. This event popularly known as March Madness encompasses a tour-event atmosphere with different sites used for eight Opening Rounds plus the First Four, four Regional Finals, and a Final Four. Each site within the tournament acts as a stop of the tour and brings new teams to various cities and arenas to attract both new spectators to the event from the local area as well as traveling fans directly supporting their teams.

The crossover of events types has also expanded to traditional stand-alone events like marathon races transforming into branded tour events. The Rock 'n' Roll San Diego Marathon was established in 1998 as a unique running event that incorporated live bands along multiple points of the 26.2-mile course. The creation of the Rock 'n' Roll Marathon fused a mass participation race with over 20,000 entrants with a highly competitive elite race and with a fun festival atmosphere. The popularity and success of the event led to its spread to 31 events in other cities and countries for both the marathon and half marathon distances and is now under the leadership of Calera Capital, a for profit business enterprise (Reavis, 2016).

In essence, this race organization group has packaged the organization and operation of these distance running events into a global tour of the Rock 'n' Roll brand of races. This format of touring endurance race events with professional for-profit management groups now include Run Disney marathon and half marathon races, Ironman triathlon races, and Tough Mudder obstacle course racing series. These types of popular tour events began with a single event that expanded to multiple cities nationally and internationally, with each race acting as a tour stop with an emphasis upon local participants to compete rather than for the professional athlete to perform for spectators.

Conclusion

Sport leagues and sport tours are the primary organizational structures for team and individual sports. Each of these organizational structures has implications for the venues and the management practices in place. Sport leagues and tours have grown in their size and scope, and for this reason, communities must plan carefully when deciding to host a sport league or a tour event. Financial resources must be spent to meet the demands of the spectators, but careful planning can yield monetary benefits for a community.

As stated before, as league and tour events grow in size, so do their economic and ecological impact on the locations in which they are held. Because these events are becoming more impactful, it is also important for those hosting these events to have a plan of action to raise the economic benefits and lower the ecological footprint. Facility and event managers should take the necessary action to provide the proper facilities and adequate security needed to ensure a successful event and to maximize the benefits to the local community.

While sport leagues and sport tours have distinct characteristics, there has been a growing trend to incorporate crossover elements to many sport leagues where many pre-season and post-season events have incorporated elements of tour sport characteristics. Many of these creative applications of crossover have expanded the markets and popularity of sport and have provided innovations for sport events and facilities.

MINI CASE STUDY

Assume that you are in the role of General Manager for a multi-purpose arena with a seating capacity of 6,300. The arena includes an ice sheet for hockey and other ice events and a hardwood court for basketball and volleyball and other sports. This arena currently serves as the home venue for a team in the National Basketball Association Developmental League (NBA D-League) as a primary tenant. As the General Manager of the arena, you have been charged with increasing the usage of the facility, and two primary options have been developed. The first option is to enter a contract with a new minor league hockey franchise that would include a season of 15 home games. The second option would include contracting with several tour or tournament events including three components: hosting the conference championship tournament for a mid-major NCAA Division I conference in men's basketball, hosting the conference championship hockey tournament of an NCAA Division I men's hockey league/conference, and to host an exhibition basketball game with the Harlem Globetrotters. A comparison of these two options yields projections of a similar amount of total event sessions/games and initial projections of similar spectator numbers. Given this scenario, you need to determine whether to go with the league option or the tournament/tour option. In your analysis consider the following issues:

1. Determine a list of advantages and disadvantages for the league option with minor league hockey.

2. Determine a list of advantages and disadvantages for the tournament/tour option.

3. Project the possible impacts in event staffing for each option, and consider the marketability of the events within each option.

4. How would the location of the city with this venue (geographic region and size of the market) impact your decision as the General Manager?

CHAPTER DISCUSSION QUESTIONS

1. Briefly describe how league and tour events compare and contrast to Mega-events.

2. Apply Noll's (2003) five elements of league structure (format, hierarchy, multiplicity, membership, and governance) to one of the following examples: professional hockey in the United States and Canada, collegiate football in the United States, collegiate basketball in the United States, or professional basketball in the United States and Canada.

3. Name one example of a league event and one of a tour event. How do these events differ?

4. Describe and give examples of crossover within league events, tour events and stand-alone events in sport

PRACTITIONER SPOTLIGHT

NAME: Keisha Dunlap

ORGANIZATION: Conference USA

CURRENT JOB TITLE: Senior Associate Commissioner

- **Year started in this role:** August 2016, 12 total years at C-USA

Photo courtesy of Keisha Dunlap.

EDUCATIONAL PREPARATION:

- **Undergrad degree:** Eastern Illinois University, BA in Economics
- **Graduate degree:** Eastern Illinois University, Master of Science in Physical Education w/ option in Sports Administration

CAREER PATH:

- **Internship(s):** Graduate Assistant with EIU track team, Internship with Loyola College: Compliance Department
- **Entry level job:** University of Arkansas (2 years): Compliance office in Women's Athletic Department and NCAA Champs Life Skills

- **Job path both inside and outside sport leading to this current role:** I took a position at Conference USA during their headquarters transition to Dallas, Texas. My first position was Assistant Director for Championships and then I moved to Director of Sport Services, Assistant Commissioner for Sport Services, Associate Commissioner and finally to my current position as Senior Associate Commissioner.

WHAT IS THE MOST REWARDING ASPECT OF THIS JOB?

I think our goal here in servicing our membership and being a resource to each member is the best part of my job.

WHAT IS THE MOST CHALLENGING ASPECT OF THIS JOB?

It's challenging to service each of our membership institutions while being fair to all. If you are looking at it from each individual institution, the priorities are different. At the conference office, we are trying to achieve the best possible solution for everyone not just the individual school.

HOW DOES THE CONFERENCE/LEAGUE DEVELOP AND IMPLEMENT MASTER SCHEDULES (WHO HAS INPUT/HOW APPROVED) AND WHAT IS THE TIMING IN THIS PROCESS (HOW FAR IN ADVANCE DEVELOPED)?

Ideally in all of our team sports we would like to be at least two years out. But with the great deal of recent change in C-USA with realignment, we have been forced to change our scheduling format more than we would normally do so. We have scheduling guidelines for each sport developed by our members, usually this includes coaches and/or administrators from each member school. We work with an outside company to build the actual schedule. We send the company our scheduling guidelines, and they create a number of scheduling options for us to choose from. We will get fifty or so options and begin a lot of back and forth to tweak details in order to find the right fit. The C-USA staff makes the final decision as long as it satisfies the format and guidelines. We do give schools an opportunity to look it over as a draft before it is implemented in the event that we missed a conflict.

HOW DOES THE LEAGUE DETERMINE SINGLE VERSUS MULTI-SITE CHAMPIONSHIP TOURNAMENT PLAY? HOW ARE REVENUES FROM THESE TOURNAMENTS/ CHAMPIONSHIPS ALLOCATED?

Some sports are on rotation. For example, with outdoor track and field and cross-country, we will build out a rotation for as many years out as we have teams interested in hosting as long as they meet the minimum requirements to host. Other sports we bid no more than two years out. For example, in men's and women's soccer, volleyball, and softball we don't take all conference teams to the tournament. We want to be sure those who bid have a competitive chance of making the tournament in order to increase attendance. Other sports are conducted at neutral sites. For swimming and diving, none of our conference members currently has facilities that would allow us to host a championship meet, so a neutral site is the most logical solution. In golf, coaches prefer a neutral site to allow an even playing field during competition by eliminating a home course advantage. In this case, the site location decision is driven by coaches' recommendations.

Revenue distribution depends on the situation and championship. Typically, football and basketball are revenue generating events, and we have specific distribution models in place for those sports. Other sports have a small guarantee with the remaining funds going to the host site. For some of our smaller championships, the funding for building rental and other operational items will come from conference budgets and shared expenses among the competing members.

Tip-off of the Conference USA Men's Basketball Tournament at Legacy Arena in Birmingham, Alabama.

Photo courtesy of Keisha Dunlap.

HOW IS THE CONFERENCE STAFF INVOLVED IN THE OPERATION OF REGULAR SEASON CONTESTS AS WELL AS SEASON ENDING CHAMPIONSHIP TOURNAMENTS?

For regular season we rely on game management staff at each of the sites. We do conduct a game management call for each team sport at the beginning of the season. We ask for a member of that game management staff, a member of the coaching staff and the sport administrator to participate in a conference call so all of our member schools are hearing the same things from us on game administration expectations.

For conference tournaments, our conference staff will be onsite and serve as game administrators during the entirety of the championship. We do utilize volunteers and the host institution to provide support in a number of areas.

HOW IS THE CONFERENCE/LEAGUE INVOLVED IN THE SELECTION OF GAME/ CONTEST OFFICIALS?

For officials, we have coordinators for each of our sports. They are independent contractors that are responsible for assigning officials for games/matches.

HOW IS THE CONFERENCE/LEAGUE INVOLVED MEDIA COVERAGE AND MEDIA CONTRACTS FOR CONFERENCE/LEAGUE GAMES AND END OF SEASON CHAMPIONSHIPS?

As of 2016, Conference USA has our own online streaming service for all conference competitions (CUSA.tv). We have a communications staff assigned to each of our sports and they work with the media posts at each of our sites. During championships, we send at least one person to help cover media requests for photography, interviews, filming, etc. We also send someone from our multimedia department to cover social media or an on camera person to collect video for replay and highlights.

WHAT IS A UNIQUE ASPECT OR TASK OF YOUR JOB THAT MANY WOULD BE SURPRISED HEAR ABOUT?

Every day is very different. I can have a to do list that sits on my desk every day and maybe only get one or two things done on that list in the course of the week. So many things pop up on any given day and it's my job to handle each of those situations. The expectation is that I have the answer to the questions that come in and that often takes time. One email or phone call can change the path of your entire day and you have to be ready and willing to go with that.

WHAT DO YOU BELIEVE ARE THE MOST IMPORTANT SKILL(S) TO DEVELOP?

You have to be flexible and able to multi-task. Discipline and organization are very important as this job requires you to put in a lot of hours and there is a lot of travel. You have to be knowledgeable in your role and up to speed on national issues and how they affect the Conference in order to fulfill the needs and questions of the membership institutions.

WHAT PARTING WORDS OF WISDOM DO YOU HAVE FOR STUDENTS AND YOUNG PROFESSIONALS IN THE FIELD?

Always treat people with respect and do it with a smile on your face. Your attitude and demeanor are so important. Learn to not take things personally and realize this is an often highly emotional field where you have to be able to fix problems without escalating situations. Be kind. This is a small world and a negative encounter can follow you throughout your career.

Reprinted by permission of Keisha Dunlap.

REFERENCES

All About Rankings. (2016). *WTA*. Retrieved from http://www.wtatennis.com/all-aboutrankings

A Brief History of Baseball. (1995). *Sean Lahman*. Retrieved from http://www.seanlahman.com/baseball-archive/brief-history-of-baseball/

Broughton, D. (2016). Slowdown seen for media. *Street & Smith's SportsBusiness Journal, 19*(26), 1, 33.

Carter, A. (2016, January 20). Grand Slam 2016: Tennis' four majors by the numbers. *Forbes*. Retrieved from http://www.forbes.com/sites/alikocarter/2016/01/20/grand-slam-2016-tennis-four-majors-by-the-numbers/#43b2e11820de

Carter, A. (2016, May 26). 8 things the 100th Indy 500's projected attendance will be as big as. *Indy Star*. Retrieved from http://www.indystar.com/story/sports/2016/05/25/things-100th-indy-500s-projected-attendance-big/84942590/

Collatine, K. (2016, February 15). What race attendance figures tell us about the state of F1. F1Fanatic, Retrieved from http://www.f1fanatic.co.uk/2016/02/15/what-race-attendance-figures-tell-us-about-the-state-of-f1/

Collins, A., Munday, M., & Roberts, A. (2012). Environmental consequences of tourism consumption at major events: An analysis of the UK stages of the 2007 Tour de France. *Journal of Travel Research, 51*(5), 577–590. doi:10.1177/0047287511434113

Coopers, P. W. (2010). Changing the game: Outlook for the global sports market to 2013. *PricewaterhouseCoopers*. Retrieved from http://www.academia.edu/247749/The_Outlook_For_The_Global_Sports_Market_to_2013

Crepeau, R. C. (2014). NFL football: *A history of America's new national pastime*. Champaign, IL: University of Illinois Press.

Cronin, J. (2013). Truth in the minor league class structure: The case for reclassification of the minors. *Baseball Research Journal, 42*(1). Retrieved from http://sabr.org/research/truth-minor-league-class-structure-case-reclassification-minors

Deitsch, R. (2016). Why there is no ceiling in near future for NFL ratings, more media circus. *Sports Illustrated*. Retrieved from: http://www.si.com/more-sports/2016/01/10/media-circus-nfl-playoff-ratings-espn-nbc-cbs

DiZinno, T. (2016, April 25). Barber reveals weekend attendance figure of 83,765, *NBC Sports*. Retrieved from http://motorsports.nbcsports.com/2016/04/25/barber-reveals-weekend-attendance-figure-of-83765/

DNews. (2013). The world's 8 most grueling endurance events. Retrieved from http://news.discovery.com/adventure/extreme-sports/8-most-grueling-events-130429.htm

Driver, D., & Bruns, D. H. (1999). Concepts and uses of the benefits approach to leisure. In E. I., Jackson & T. I., Burton (Eds). *Leisure studies: Prospects for the twenty-first century* (pp. 349–369). State College, PA: Venture.

Ferreira, M., Hall, T. K., & Bennett, G. (2008). Exploring brand positioning in a sponsorship context: A correspondence analysis of the Dew Action Sports Tour. *Journal of Sport Management, 22*(6), 734–761.

Fischer, D. (2015). *The Super Bowl: The first fifty years of America's greatest game.* New York, NY: Sports Publishing.

Gaines, C. (2015, May 22). The NFL and Major League Baseball are the most attended sports leagues in the world. *Business Insider.* Retrieved from http://www.businessinsider.com/attendance-sports-leagues-world-2015-5

Kudo, M., Ko. Y. J., Walker, M., & Connaughton, D. P. (2015). The influence of title sponsorships in sports events on stock price returns. *International Journal of Sports Marketing & Sponsorship, 16*(2), 118–137.

Leerhsen, C. (2011).100 Years of the INDY 500. *Sports Illustrated, 114*(22). Retrieved from: http://web.b.ebscohost.com/ehost/detail/detail?vid=11&sid=f42bf86f-c94b-487a-8a14-abf5fcedcf67%40sessionmgr110&hid=102&bdata=JnNpdGU9ZWhvc3QtbGl2ZSZzY29wZT1zaXRl#AN=61012875&db=aph

MacMichael, S. (2012, November 27). Competing British Tour de France bids jockey for position ahead of ASO decision. *Road.cc.* Retrieved from http://road.cc/content/news/71195-competing-british-tour-de-france-bids-jockey-position-ahead-aso-decision

Matuszewski, E. (2016, July 1). The Tour de France: Cycling's most famous race by the numbers. *Forbes.* Retrieved from http://www.forbes.com/sites/erikmatuszewski/2016/07/01/the-tour-de-france-cyclings-most-famous-race-by-the-numbers/#d0325454f90e

McCutcheon, M. (2016, September 28). 40K people expect for this weekend's Red Bull Air Race at IMS. *WTHR.com.* Retrieved from http://www.wthr.com/article/40k-people-expected-for-this-weekends-red-bull-air-race-at-ims

Mills, B., & Fort, R. (2014). League-level attendance and outcome uncertainty in U.S. pro sports leagues. *Economic Inquiry, 52*(1), 205–218. doi:10.1111/ecin.12037

Noll, R. (2003). The organization of sports leagues. *Oxford Review of Economic Policy, 19*(4), 530–551.

Olympics Ticket Sales. (2016). Tulsa 2024. Retrieved from http://www.tulsa2024.com/Olympics_ticket_sales

Owen, P. D., & King, N. (2015). Competitive balance measures in sports leagues: The effects of variation in season length. *Economic Inquiry, 53*(1), 731–744. doi:10.1111/ecin.12102

Pollotta, F. (2015). Super Bowl XLIX posts the largest audience in T.V. history. *CNN Money.* Retrieved from: http://money.cnn.com/2015/02/02/media/super-bowl-ratings/

Poremba, D. L. (2000). *The American League the early years.* Chicago, IL: Arcadia Publishing.

Rapp, T. (2014, April 1). United States buys more World Cup tickets than any non-Brazilian nation. *BleacherReport.* Retrieved from http://bleacherreport.com/articles/2013461-united-states-buys-more-world-cup-tickets-than-any-non-brazilian-nation

Reavis, T. (2016, June 3). Rock 'n' Roll Marathon history. Retrieved from https://tonireavis.com/2016/06/03/rock-n-roll-marathon-history/

Seifert, K. (2016, May 5). How American football is becoming a worldwide sport. *ESPN.com*, Retrieved from http://www.espn.com/nfl/story/_/id/15273529/how-american-football-becoming-worldwide-sport-europe-china-beyond

Skvorc, C. (2015, March 7). Dollars lost, spirit of Iditarod maintained at original checkpoints. *Mat-Su Valley Frontiersman.* Retrieved from http://www.frontiersman.com/business/dollars-lost-spirit-of-iditarod-maintained-at-original-checkpoints/article_d24c8ff8-c552-11e4-acc4-37b5bbbdab52.html

Spread of Baseball. (2016). *Baseball Memory Lab: MLB.* Retrieved from http://mlb.mlb.com/memorylab/spread_of_baseball/index.jsp

Wacker, B. (2016, February 6). New attendance record set at TPC Scottsdale. PGATour.com. Retrieved from http://www.pgatour.com/news/2016/02/06/attenance-record-round-3-saturday-waste-management-phonenix-open-tpc-scottsdale.html

Wertheim, L. (2008). World of hurt. *Sports Illustrated 109*(02) 70–70. Retrieved from http://web.a.ebscohost.com/ehost/detail/detail?vid=3&sid=46863f68-4b2f-42a5-af1d88005f7f7a7f%40sessionmgr4003&hid=4106&bdata=JnNpdGU9ZWhvc3QtbGl2ZSZz29wZT1zaXRl#AN=35353980&db=aph

What is INDYCar? (2016). *Indycar.com.* Retrieved from http://www.indycar.com/FanInfo/INDYCAR-101/What-Is-INDYCAR

WTA 2016 Calendar. (2016). *Women's Tennis Association.* Retrieved from http://www.wtatennis.com/SEWTATour-Archive/Archive/AboutTheTour/TourCalendar_2016.pdf

17

Facility and Event Impact and Legacy

Jeffrey C. Petersen and *Seth Dorsey*

OBJECTIVES

After studying this chapter, the student should be able to:

- Define and differentiate economic impact and legacy.
- Identify the facility costs and public and private financing trends for professional sport in the United States.
- Identify the primary variables of economic impact analyses in sport and describe how they can be potentially misused.
- Apply the concept of legacy to the specific sport venues and events.

KEY TERMS

Benefit Driver	Direct Impacts	Induced Impacts
Cost Driver	Double-Counting	Legacy
Cost Measurement Omission	Economic Impact Analysis	Multiplier
	Indirect Impacts	Narrow Perspective Bias

KEY ACRONYMS

BEA	Bureau of Economic Analysis	**REMI**	Regional Economic Modeling Incorporated
CBA	Collective Bargaining Agreement	**RIMS II**	Regional Input-Output Modeling System II
DS	Direct Spending		
EIA	Economic Impact Analysis	**SUI**	Stadium Utilization Index
NASC	National Association of Sports Commissions	**TEI**	Total Economic Impact
		TVS	Total Visitor Spending
OGI	Olympic Games Impact		

Introduction

In 2007, the sport facility and stadium world entered a new era with the opening of the first billion dollar sport facility. The opening of the new Wembley Stadium in London with a capacity of 90,000 and a cost of $1.25 billion launched this era. Many other venues quickly followed including Cowboy Stadium (now AT&T Stadium) in Arlington, Texas at $1.3 billion in 2009, Yankee Stadium in New York City at $1.5 billion in 2009, and Met-Life Stadium in East Rutherford, New Jersey at $1.6 billion in 2010. The "bottom line" question behind the building of any of these new facilities might be "is it worth it?"

This question should be broadly considered examining both economic and non-economic elements as well as short term and long term time frames. This same question could and should be applied to any sport event or sport facility from the local to the global scale. In an effort to answer such a question, a variety of methods and approaches have been developed including the consideration of economic impact and legacy as part of the justification for staging sport events and/or constructing sport facilities.

The escalating costs associated with sport facility construction and with the hosting of major events that require facility investments is of great concern not only to those involved in the management and operation of sport but also for the residents and citizens that often will support the funding of these facilities via taxes and other governmental subsidies. The considerable facility costs can be seen in global events like the World Cup as well as in the professional leagues at a national or regional level. For example, the facility costs for the four World Cups held from 2002–2014 each exceeded $1.7 billion including existing, renovated and new facilities (see Table 17.1). This level of expenditure for a single month-long event must be balanced with an assessment of the impact of the event itself and the long-term legacy of these facilities and their future use.

Cape Town Stadium also known as Green Point Stadium was a new $600M venue used in the 2010 World Cup in South Africa.

Table 17.1 *World Cup Stadium Construction Costs*

Year & Location	Total Venues	New or Major Renovation Venues	Total Construction Cost in millions (USD)	Average Cost Per Seat (USD)
2002 Korea/Japan	20	19	$4,627	$5,070
2006 Germany	12	0	$1,986	$3,442
2010 South Africa	10	5	$1,794	$5,299
2014 Brazil	12	10	$3,605	$5,514

Adapted from Preuss, Solberg and Alm (2014)

Facility Costs and Financing Trends in the U.S. Professional Leagues

Since 1990 there has been a tremendous level of investment in stadiums and arenas for professional sport across the "Big 4" leagues within the United States. From 1990 to the present those costs have totaled just over $36.8 billion dollars. This investment in facilities for professional sport has also incurred a tremendous amount of public funding totaling just over half (53.3%) for all facilities constructed or undergoing major renovation during that time period. While an understanding of this total investment is valuable, it is equally important to examine the similarities and differences amongst each of the four leagues as well as the details of the individual franchises' venues to more fully grasp the nature of these investments and the differences that occur.

The National Football League has the largest venues of the professional leagues in America, and it is composed of 32 teams. Since 1990, each of these 32 teams has experienced new facility construction or renovation totaling over $13.8 billion as detailed in Table 17.2. These 31 building projects have garnered the highest level of public funding compared to the other three professional leagues with an average of 70.8% of the cost covered by public funds. This public funding has varied greatly depending on the stadium and the host community. The MetLife Stadium, where the Jets and Giants play, received no public funding. However, nine teams were fully funded by taxpayer dollars: Indianapolis, Cincinnati, Buffalo, Tampa Bay, San Diego, Jacksonville, St. Louis, and Atlanta for the Georgia Dome. Only six of the 31 projects were stadium renovations with just over 80% of the projects involving construction of a completely new venue. The NFL construction included five projects with a total cost of over $1 billion each, and the addition of a new venue in the Los Angeles area is projected to have a total development cost of $2.6 billion (Ponsford, 2016).

Table 17.2 *NFL Stadium New Construction and Major Renovation Since 1990*

Team	Stadium	Opened	Capacity	Nominal Cost (in millions)	Public Cost	Public Percent
Atlanta	Mercedes-Benz Stadium	2017	71,000	$ 1,400	$ 200	14%
Minnesota	U.S. Bank Stadium	2016	65,000	$ 1,061	$ 498	47%
San Francisco	Levi's Stadium	2014	68,500	$ 1,200	$ 850	71%
New Orleans	Mercedes-Benz Superdome (reno)	2011	73,000	$ 505	$ 490	97%
Giants/Jets	MetLife Stadium	2010	82,500	$ 1,600	—	0%
Kansas City	Arrowhead Stadium (reno)	2010	76,416	$ 375	$ 250	67%
Dallas	AT&T Stadium	2009	85,000	$ 1,150	$ 325	28%
Indianapolis	Lucas Oil Stadium	2008	67,000	$ 720	$ 720	100%
Arizona	Univ. of Phoenix Stadium	2006	63,400	$ 71	$ 267	72%
Philadelphia	Lincoln Financial Field	2003	69,596	$ 285	$ 228	80%
Green Bay	Lambeau Field (reno)	2003	80,735	$ 295	$ 251	85%
Chicago	Soldier Field	2003	61,500	$ 600	$ 450	75%
New England	Gillette Stadium	2002	68,756	$ 325	$ 33	10%
Houston	NRG Stadium	2002	71,500	$ 300	$ 225	75%
Detroit	Ford Field	2002	65,000	$ 300	$ 219	73%
Seattle	CenturyLink Field	2002	67,000	$ 300	$ 201	67%
Pittsburgh	Heinz Field	2001	68,400	$ 230	$ 150	65%
Denver	Sports Authority Field	2001	76,125	$ 365	$ 274	75%
Cincinnati	Paul Brown Stadium	2000	65,515	$ 400	$ 400	100%
Cleveland	FirstEnergy Stadium	1999	67,431	$ 283	$ 255	90%
Tennessee	Nissan Stadium	1999	69,149	$ 290	$ 220	76%

Buffalo	Ralph Wilson Stadium (reno)	1999	73,079	$ 63	$ 63	100%
Baltimore	M&T Bank Stadium	1998	71,008	$ 220	$ 176	80%
Tampa Bay	Raymond James Stadium	1998	65,890	$ 169	$ 169	100%
San Diego	Qualcomm Stadium (reno)	1997	70,561	$ 78	$ 78	100%
Washington	FedEx Field	1997	73,000	$ 250	$ 70	28%
Oakland	O.co Coliseum (reno)	1996	53,252	$ 200	$ 200	100%
Carolina	Bank of America Stadium	1996	73,778	$ 248	$ 52	21%
Jacksonville	Everbank Field	1995	67,246	$ 121	$ 121	100%
St. Louis	Edward Jones Dome	1995	66,000	$ 280	$ 280	100%
Atlanta	Georgia Dome	1992	71,250	$ 214	$ 214	100%
32 of 32 teams with construction/renovation					Average Public Funding	70.8%

Adapted and expanded from data from Baade and Matheson (2011)

For the National Hockey League (NHL) 23 of the 30 franchises are located in the United States, and each of these teams has significantly renovated or constructed a new arena since 1990 for a total cost of $5.66 billion. Table 17.3 details these facility investment projects with all but one of these projects being construction of a new arena. While four franchise facilities in the U.S. were fully funded by public funds (Phoenix, Minnesota, Nashville, and Anaheim), there were also four team's facilities fully funded with private funds (Columbus, Philadelphia, Boston, and Chicago). The mean percentage value for public funding of NHL facilities located in the U.S. over this time period was 45.4%. Additionally, a total of four of the seven Canadian teams in the NHL played in new venues constructed since 1990. The NHL also shares eight of these 23 American venues as home court for teams with the National Basketball Association.

© Mark Herreid/Shutterstock.com

U.S. Bank Stadium opened in 2016 in Minneapolis, Minnesota as a fully enclosed stadium with a total cost of just over $1 billion.

Table 17.3 *NHL Arena New Construction and Major Renovation in the U.S. Since 1990*

Team	Arena	Opened	Capacity	Nominal Cost (in millions)	Public Cost	Public Percent
Detroit	Little Caesars Arena	2017	20,000	$ 627	$ 285	45%
NY Islanders	Barclays Center*	2012	15,795	$ 637	$ 150	24%
Pittsburgh	Consol Energy Center	2010	18,387	$ 321	$ 130	40%
New Jersey	Prudential Center	2007	17,625	$ 375	$ 210	56%
Phoenix	Gila River Arena	2003	17,125	$ 180	$ 180	100%
Dallas	American Airlines Center*	2001	18,532	$ 420	$ 210	50%
Columbus	Nationwide Arena	2000	18,144	$ 175	—	0%
Minnesota	Xcel Energy Center	2000	17,954	$ 130	$ 130	100%
Denver	Pepsi Center*	1999	18,007	$ 160	$ 35	22%
Los Angeles	Staples Center*	1999	18,230	$ 375	$ 59	16%
Carolina	PNC Arena	1999	18,680	$ 158	$ 98	62%
Florida	BB&T Center	1998	19,250	$ 212	$ 185	87%
Washington	Verizon Center*	1997	18,506	$ 260	$ 60	23%
Nashville	Bridgestone Arena	1997	17,113	$ 144	$ 144	100%
Philadelphia	Wells Fargo Center*	1996	19,537	$ 206	—	0%
Buffalo	First Niagara	1996	19,070	$ 128	$ 55	43%
Tampa Bay	Amalie Arena	1996	19,204	$ 160	$ 120	75%
Boston	TD Garden*	1995	17,565	$ 160	—	0%
Chicago	United Center*	1994	19,717	$ 175	—	0%
St. Louis	Scottrade Center	1994	19,150	$ 170	$ 35	20%
Anaheim	Honda Center	1993	17,174	$ 123	$ 123	100%
San Jose	SAP Center	1993	17,562	$ 163	$ 133	82%
NY Rangers	Madison Square Garden (reno)*	1991	18,006	$ 200	—	0%
23 out of 23 NHL teams based in the U.S.				Average Public Funding		45.4%

*shared venue with NBA franchise   Adapted and expanded from data from Baade and Matheson (2011)

The National Basketball Association currently includes 30 teams with 29 franchises located within the United States. Since 1990, a total of $6.45 billion has been invested in NBA arenas in the United States, and this impacted 27 of those 29 teams. Table 17.4 displays the construction cost details that averaged 58.4% in public financing. This public support ranged from four projects with no public funding (TD Garden in Boston, Wells Fargo Center in Philadelphia, Madison Square Garden in New York, and EnergySolutions Arena in Salt Lake City) to a total of 12 teams that were 100% publicly funded for their project. It is also of interest to note that the city of Memphis constructed two new arenas during this relatively short timeframe (the Pyramid and the FedEx Forum). The vast majority (83.3%) of these construction projects for the NBA were for new venues with only five venues undergoing major renovations during this time.

Nationwide Arena in Columbus, Ohio opened in 2000 and was the last NHL arena in the U.S. that was completely funded from private sources at a cost of $175 million.

© aceshot1/Shutterstock.com

Table 17.4 NBA Arena New Construction and Major Renovation in the United States Since 1990

Team	Stadium	Opened	Capacity	Nominal Cost (in millions)	Public Cost	Public Percent
Sacramento	Golden 1 Center	2016	17,500	$ 477	$ 255	53%
Brooklyn Nets	Barclays Center*	2012	17,732	$ 637	$ 150	24%
Orlando	Amway Center	2010	18,846	$ 480	$ 430	90%
Oklahoma City	Chesapeake Energy Arena (reno)	2010	18,203	$ 121	$ 121	100%
Charlotte	Time Warner Cable Arena	2005	19,077	$ 265	$ 265	100%
Memphis	FedEx Forum	2004	18,119	$ 250	$ 250	100%
Phoenix	Talking Stick Resort Arena (reno)	2004	18,055	$ 67	$ 10	15%
Houston	Toyota Center	2003	18,055	$ 235	$ 192	82%
San Antonio	AT&T Center	2002	18,581	$ 186	$ 158	85%

Oklahoma City	Chesapeake Energy Arena	2002	18,203	$ 89	$ 89	100%
Dallas	American Airlines Center*	2001	19,200	$ 420	$ 210	50%
Indianapolis	Bankers Life Fieldhouse	1999	18,165	$ 183	$ 183	100%
Atlanta	Philips Arena	1999	18,118	$ 214	$ 63	29%
Denver	Pepsi Center*	1999	19,155	$ 160	$ 35	22%
Lakers/Clippers	Staples Center*	1999	18,997	$ 375	$ 59	16%
New Orleans	Smoothie King Center	1999	16,867	$ 114	$ 114	100%
Miami	American Airlines Arena	1998	19,600	$ 213	$ 213	100%
Washington	Verizon Center	1997	20,356	$ 260	$ 60	23%
Golden State	Oracle Arena (reno)	1997	19,596	$ 121	$ 121	100%
Philadelphia	Wells Fargo Center*	1996	20,328	$ 206	—	0%
Boston	TD Garden*	1995	18,624	$ 160	—	0%
Portland	Moda Center	1995	19,980	$ 262	$ 35	13%
Seattle	Key Arena (reno)	1995	17,072	$ 75	$ 75	100%
Cleveland	Quicken Loans Arena	1994	20,562	$ 152	$ 152	100%
Chicago	United Center*	1994	20,917	$ 175	—	0%
Phoenix	America West Arena	1992	18,422	$ 90	$ 90	100%
New York	Madison Square Garden (reno)*	1991	19,812	$ 200	—	0%
Salt Lake City	EnergySolutions Arena	1991	19,911	$ 93	—	0%
Memphis	Memphis Pyramid	1991	20,142	$ 65	$ 65	100%
Minneapolis	Target Center	1990	19,356	$ 104	$ 52	50%

30 projects impacting 27 of 29 teams located in the U.S.

Average Public Funding **58.4%**

*shared venue with NHL franchise

Adapted and expanded from data from Baade and Matheson (2011)

Major League Baseball (MLB) currently includes 30 franchises with 29 of those teams within the United States. Since 1990, 100% of the MLB teams in the U.S. have constructed a new stadium or completed major facility renovations, with the city of Atlanta constructing two new stadiums for the Braves during this time span. Table 17.5 displays the construction cost details that averaged 60.9% in public financing ranging from a low of 4% for construction of AT&T Park in San Francisco to five teams that garnered 100% public funding (Chicago White Sox, Oakland Athletics, Tampa Bay Rays, Pittsburgh Pirates, and Washington Nationals). The ongoing renovations of Wrigley Field in Chicago represent the only MLB construction project that did not garner any level of public funding. A total of 5 of the 29 projects were stadium renovations with the vast majority (83%) as new constructions.

© littleny/Shutterstock.com

The Barclays Center in Brooklyn, New York is one of the newer NBA facilities that opened in 2012 that serves as the home venue for the Brooklyn Nets as well as the NHL's New York Islanders.

Table 17.5 *MLB Stadium New Construction and Major Renovation in the United States Since 1990*

Team	Stadium	Opened	Capacity	Cost (000s) (Nominal)	Public Cost	Public Percent
Chicago (Cubs)	Wrigley Field (reno)	2019	42,495	$ 575	—	0%
Atlanta	SunTrust Park	2017	41,500	$ 622	$ 397	64%
Miami	Marlins Field	2012	36,742	$ 525	$ 370	70%
Boston	Fenway Park (reno)	2012	37,673	$ 285	$ 40	14%
Minnesota	Target Field	2010	39,021	$ 544	$ 392	72%
NY Mets	Citi Field	2009	41,922	$ 600	$ 164	27%
NY Yankees	Yankees Stadium	2009	49,642	$ 1,300	$ 220	17%
Kansas City	Kaufmann Stadium (reno)	2009	37,903	$ 250	$ 175	70%
Washington	Nationals Park	2008	41,341	$ 611	$ 611	100%
Cardinals	Busch Stadium	2006	43,975	$ 365	$ 45	12%
San Diego	PETCO Park	2004	41,164	$ 457	$ 304	66%

Philadelphia	Citizens Bank Park	2004	43,651	$ 346	$ 174	50%
Cincinnati	Great American Ball Park	2003	42,319	$ 325	$ 280	86%
Pittsburgh	PNC Park	2001	38,362	$ 262	$ 262	100%
Milwaukee	Miller Park	2001	41,900	$ 400	$ 310	78%
Detroit	Comerica Park	2000	41,574	$ 300	$ 115	38%
Houston	Minute Maid Park	2000	41,574	$ 265	$ 180	68%
San Francisco	AT&T Park	2000	41,915	$ 357	$ 15	4%
Seattle	Safeco Park	1999	47,574	$ 518	$ 392	76%
Arizona	Chase Field	1998	48,519	$ 349	$ 238	68%
LA (Angels)	Angel Stadium (reno)	1998	43,250	$ 118	$ 30	25%
Tampa Bay	Tropicana Field	1997	31,042	$ 208	$ 208	100%
Atlanta	Turner Field	1997	49,586	$ 235	$ 165	70%
Oakland	O.co Coliseum (reno)*	1996	35,067	$ 200	$ 200	100%
Denver	Coors Field	1995	50,398	$ 215	$ 168	78%
Cleveland	Progressive Field	1994	38,000	$ 175	$ 91	52%
Texas	Globe Life Park	1994	48,114	$ 191	$ 135	71%
Baltimore	Camden Yards	1992	45,917	$ 110	$ 100	91%
Chicago (Sox)	U.S. Cellular Field	1991	40,615	$ 167	$ 167	100%
29 of 29 MLB teams located in the U.S.				Average Public Funding		**60.9%**

*facility shared with NFL franchise   Adapted and expanded from data from Baade and Matheson (2011)

Economic Impact Analysis

Given the significant level of financial resources invested and the high degree of public funding that is often connected with constructing sport venues and hosting major events, it is not surprising that methods have been developed to assess the impact of these events and facilities in both the short term and the long term doing so in both economic terms and more intangible terms. As such, economic impact analysis (EIA) and legacy have become the two primary forms of analysis to examine the outcomes of a sport event or sport venue.

For every facility that is built, there are financial resources that are invested in order to transform the facility from an idea or concept on paper to a tangible product in which sport can be played. Once the facility has been constructed, it continues to affect resources in many ways including operational costs, maintenance costs and various revenues gained or lost from the events being held within the venue. Before a public entity like a city, county, or state or a private entity like a business or investor group decides if they would like to build or renovate a facility within their borders, they typically conduct research and make projections in order to determine whether the project is realistic and beneficial financially. One type of study that falls within such research is called an economic impact analysis.

Marlins Park, one of MLB newer venues, opened in 2012 with a cost of $622 million.

In the broadest sense, an *economic impact analysis* seeks to study and quantify the effects of a change or disruption in an economic system caused by climatological, environmental, physical, or other changes. This analysis simulates these changes via mathematical modeling (such as input-output models and economic simulation models) that can focus upon linkages among various industries, economic sectors, and external factors. Specifically within the context of sport, the economic impact is defined as "the net economic change in a host community that results from spending attributed to a sport event or facility" (Crompton, 1995, p. 15). The underlying purpose for many of these studies is to measure and quantify the economic benefits that would be gained from the sport event or sport venue.

An economic impact analysis measures the effect of a sport event or sport facility within a particular community in three primary ways. The first measures how much the sport event or facility is generating new revenue or spending within the host community through sales. This would be spending in conjunction with a facility or event where the funds come from individuals or sources outside the community itself. The second area of impact would be in individual income and would be measured in the degree that individual income levels within the community change due to the sport event or facility. The employment measure, as the third component, identifies the production of new jobs in the community that are created in relation to the event or facility.

Each of these impacts is viewed to have a continuous impact as the flow of funds associated with each of the three areas is viewed to cycle through several rounds of exchange in the host community. Most broadly interpreted, this cycling of exchange creates a total economic impact through three levels: direct impacts, indirect impacts, and induced impacts (Plumstead, 2012). *Direct impacts* are the actual revenues generated by the sport event including the local spending by the non-local participants and spectators. *Indirect impacts* are classified as additional input purchases made by local businesses,

Economic Impact Analysis a mathematic modeling to estimate the multiple impacts of a new facility or event in a local area in the area of spending, income, and employment through direct, indirect and induced effects.

Direct Impacts the initial round of spending associated with a facility or event within a local economy.

Indirect Impacts additional spending by businesses within the local area that is directly linked to the initial spending or direct impact of an event.

Induced Impacts a tertiary spending increase in a local area associated with an increased personal income level tied to a sport event or facility.

Multiplier a quantity used to estimate the indirect and induced impacts for spending, income and employment within a given region for economic impact calculations.

not necessarily directly involved in the event, as a result of the direct impact. For example, a visiting participant purchases meals in local restaurants that in turn prompts the local restaurant owners to make additional purchases from suppliers and hire more workers. The third level, *induced impacts*, are additions to local spending by the local residents who received more income due to the event itself. Because of this cycling effect, *multipliers* are used to estimate the full impact of each dollar initially spent or generated for an event or facility.

Depending on the needs of those involved with the facility or event, an EIA can be conducted before the event or construction begins (ex ante), or it can be completed after the event or construction has been completed (ex post). In efforts to build public interest or support for a facility or event, an ex ante EIA may be beneficial. Because ex ante analyses are based upon a greater number of assumptions that must be made before an event is held or a venue is constructed, an ex post EIA will often create a more accurate assessment of the outcomes. However, even the ex post EIA is still built upon assumptions, but the ex post has a greater amount of established data to begin the analysis than the ex ante. There may also be occasions where it would be beneficial or even necessary to conduct both an ex ante EIA and an ex post EIA for the same event or facility. This can be especially impactful if an organizing committee can demonstrate that the actual event or facility exceeded the initial estimates provided during the planning and/or funding phase.

The skill sets and technical abilities to conduct a comprehensive EIA is likely beyond the typical practitioner in facility and event management. Such assessments are commonly conducted by academicians in economics or sport management or by consulting firms skilled and experienced in conducting and presenting results from an EIA. However, an understanding of some of the basic terms and variables of economic impact analysis are important to the knowledge base of a sport facility or event manager.

Initially, when sport economists and sport management researchers began to raise questions over the proper and improper application of economic impact, the use of economic impact analysis as a sole indicator of event success or value came under greater scrutiny in the political realm when used in garnering support for sport events and facilities (Crompton, 1995; Crompton & McKay, 1994). Some of the early studies of EIA in sport dating back to the 1970s (Noll, 1974; Rosentraub & Nunn, 1978) and the 1980s (Baade & Dye, 1988; Burns, Hatch, & Mules, 1986; Ritchie, 1984) provided a mix of both positive and negative outcomes associated with event and facility funding for sport. However, by the 1990s a growing body of research began to document findings of economic impact surrounding sport teams and stadiums that in general were not meeting the claims of facility/event proponents (Baade, 1994; Chapin, 1999; Colclough, Deellenbach, & Sherony, 1994; Noll & Zimbalist, 1997). Much of these early studies focused upon major professional sport leagues within the United States and North America. The first assessment of sport facility EIA in Europe was conducted regarding the World Cup stadium construction in Germany and found no significant effects in employment or income related to this facility development (Feddersen, Grotzinger, & Maennig, 2009).

While there has been a greater level of study and documentation of EIA for mega-events, there has also been notable examination of the economic impact of smaller scale events and facilities. For example, an EIA study of the 2005 Pan American Junior Athletic Championships revealed that this event generated $5.6 million in economic impact during this 4-day track and field competition in Windsor, Ontario (Taks, Kesenne, Chalip, Green, & Martyn, 2011). Similarly, a study of collegiate club sport found that a four-day club hockey national championship tournament created almost $2 million in economic impact for the city of Fort Collins, Colorado (Veltri, Miller, & Harris, 2009). At the lower tier professional level, a study of minor league baseball from 1985 to 2006 showed that AAA and Advanced A league teams and AA and rookie league stadiums were all associated with significant economic impact in the local income levels (Agha, 2013). The assessment of economic impact has been applied to very small scale local and regional contests, as well. Crompton and Lee (2000) examined 14 local sport events like recreational soccer, softball, basketball, and swim events across multiple cities in the U.S. finding direct sales impacts ranging from just over $21,000 to $1.15 million. A study of small-scale local swim meets in the United Kingdom noted more than 80,000 GBP in spending over a span of eight days of events (Wilson, 2006). These examples illustrate the value of smaller scale sport events to local and regional economies and demonstrate the ability to apply EIA methods to events across a broad spectrum of sizes.

Economic Impact Analysis Variables

Each industry that wants to conduct an economic impact analysis would have different variables to place into the analysis. Agha and Taks (2015) mention multiple variables that are directly related to the realm of sport with respect to both the benefit drivers and cost drivers. Examples of *benefit drivers* in the realm of sport are: new local spending, increased local spending, job creation, tax revenues, and intangible benefits.

New local spending and increased local spending sound as if they are the same thing, but there are slight differences between the two. New local spending is a focus on spending that comes in from people who do not live in the immediate area. Examples of these people could be visitors, outside companies, or workers who move into the area. Increased local spending is an increase in the money spent by people who live in the immediate area due to the new facility being built.

Agha and Taks also describe several *cost drivers* such as crowding out of visitors, locals, and other business activity, leakages, and opportunity costs. Crowding out is when local people or businesses move out of the area or avoid the area on game days due to the new facility. Leakages, on the other hand, focus on the money that is typically spent locally but is now spent

Benefit Drivers factors adding to the economic impact of an event or facility such as increased or new spending, job creation and tax revenues.

Cost Drivers factors reducing the economic impact of an event or facility such as crowding out, leakages and opportunity costs.

non-locally due to the new facility. Finally, opportunity costs focus upon money spent on the facility that would otherwise be spent on something else in that local community if the facility was not being built.

While there are a number of differing methodologies used in the calculation of economic impact, it is helpful to examine at least one basic model to illustrate some basic applicable principles. The National Association of Sports Commissions (2000) provided a three-step model to help standardize economic impact calculation. The first step, summarized in Formula 1, seeks to estimate total visitor spending (TVS), and this is determined as the net product of the number of out of town visitors (OTV), the average spending per day for these visitors (ASD), and the number of days for the event (ND).

Formula 1: $TVS = OTV \times ASD \times ND$

The second step is to create an estimate of the direct spending (DS) associated with the event as represented in Formula 2. This value is determined by adding the total administrative operations (TAO) spending due to hosting the event with the total visitor spending (TVS) from formula 1.

Formula 2: $DS = TAO + TVS$

The final step is summarized in Formula 3 which calculates the total economic impact (TEI) as the product of the direct spending (DS) and the regional multiplier (RM). An NASC whitepaper suggested a range of spending multipliers ranging from 1.3 to 1.85 depending upon the population of the community hosting the event (Rishe, 2007).

Formula 3: $TEI = DS \times RM$

The combination of these three formulas represents a very basic conception of the spending portion of an economic impact analysis. The income and employment elements would also need to be considered for a complete EIA.

Misapplication in Economic Impact Analysis

Economic impact analyses at their root are complex mathematical formulas and models that will go beyond the scope of this chapter. Accordingly, the data that is provided when creating the analysis is vital to the creation of a useful and accurate analysis. When collecting the data, there are several different areas in which they could be misapplied to the analysis creating a skewed if not completely misleading analysis (Chang, Kim, & Petrovickova, 2015). John Crompton has noted several different factors that have been mistaken or misrepresented when it comes to economic impact analysis.

First, according to Crompton (1995) is a misrepresentation of the employment multiplier. When a new facility is built, jobs are typically created due to the increased demand that comes from the vast amount of construction that is required. This factor also needs to include the employment that is fostered once the facility is opened and is being run.

Second, is the use of "fudged" multipliers. Crompton mentions that each event or facility needs to be evaluated properly and independently. Using a standard multiplier from another region or industry sector or over-estimating the multiplier value creates a misrepresentation of the total economic impact.

Third is an omission of opportunity costs. In order to achieve a proper economic analysis you must look at the alternatives on which money could be spent. An example of this would be using tax dollars to pay for part or all of a new facility. An opportunity cost arises within such a scenario. These tax dollars could be spent on education or rebuilding roads, but instead they will be going toward the sport facility.

Another common problem encountered with EIA is only accounting for benefits, not costs. There is obviously a huge focus on the benefits and revenues that will come from a new facility, but the costs must be considered as well. If only the benefits are entered into the analysis and not the costs, then a true analysis that considers all aspects of the new facility will not be obtained.

Bias in Economic Impact Analysis

When a facility is going to be built, there is often an economic impact analysis that is conducted to help determine if the proposed facility is a good investment for the city. There can be numerous different motives surrounding the efforts to build a new facility, which can lead to different biases in the economic impact analysis. These biases can be positive or negative in nature, meaning the economic impact analysis can be affected by the person or group who collects the data or by those who conduct the analysis. Evers, Hiligsmann, and Adarkwah (2014) noted several different areas of bias that have a tendency to be placed into economic impact analysis. Below are some of these biases that cause omission of relevant costs and outcomes or overestimation of costs and outcomes.

The first bias is referred to as a *narrow perspective bias*, which means that there is a use of a restricted perspective which will lead to omissions of important costs and outcomes, as these costs and outcomes are regarded as irrelevant from a narrower perspective. In this case, the person who is collecting the data is not looking at all possible outcomes in order to achieve the proper information. The potential spending and benefits as well as costs should be viewed from a wide or societal perspective in relation to the event or facility.

The second bias is a *cost measurement omission* bias. This bias involves leaving out measurement items that might count against the desired benefit outcomes of the event or facility. Essentially, this cost measurement omission bias leaves out important cost considerations in order to have a more favorable valuation.

The final bias of note is the *double-counting* bias. This is when a parameter that is added in the analysis is counted more than once. In this case, the data is doubled in order to achieve the valuation that is desired. This can most

Narrow Perspective Bias an error in assessing economic impact where the broader impacts of cost and benefits associated with a facility or event are not considered.

Cost Measurement Omission an error in assessing economic impact where only benefits are considered and opportunity costs are not accounted for.

Double-Counting an error in creating accurate estimates of total out of town visitors for an event that results in an overstatement of total economic impact.

commonly occur when determining the attendance or number of partici-pants where surveys or headcounts can inaccurately inflate the total impact. These are just a few of the biases that alter the accuracy and efficacy of an EIA, but ideally an EIA will be completed in a manner that limits biases as much as possible.

Crompton and Howard (2013) have questioned the use of EIA for sport projects in general as they only represent the economic benefits and fail to consider the cost components. These costs include explicit opportunity costs such as the costs for the facilities and/or events themselves, the land and infrastructure costs along with the ongoing operations and maintenance costs. For example, annual maintenance expenses for new professional ven-ues average $3–4 million for MLB, $2–3 million for the NFL, and $2 million for NBA and NHL arenas (Long, 2013). There are also implicit opportunity costs associated with sport projects such as foregone property taxes (Cromp-ton & Howard, 2013). A recent analysis of professional teams in the "Big 4" leagues found that 110 of the 120 franchises do not pay property taxes (Long, 2013). This represents tax revenues not being collected by the home commu-nity. Conducting an analysis that lacks cost considerations creates a definite bias in the EIA process.

Multipliers

When money is initially spent on any event, facility, or purchase, there is an economic impact. That economic impact has further implications than just the initial purchase. The money continues to flow throughout the economy and essentially has a ripple effect. This continued flow of funds in the local community is called the multiplier effect. This multiplier effect has several dif-ferent layers, but for the purpose of this chapter, we will focus on the primary area of the multiplier effect which is the simple spending multiplier. The simple spending multiplier shows us how much the economic output increases with an increase in spending. A basic example of this is found in how an increase in ticket sales for a high school football team can impact a community.

East Town High School generally has great support for their football pro-gram with superb levels of ticket sales. By hosting a key game with an out of town rival, East Town's athletic department earned an additional $10,000 of income compared to prior years. East Town spent some of those earn-ings for additional game workers, but is now looking to improve its grass for the stadium field. The school decides to spend $5,000 of these additional earnings on new topdressing and seeding for their field using Greenturf Solutions which is owned by a local resident Russell Green. That means Russell earns an additional $5,000. Some of those funds will be used for labor that can impact personal income and jobs that can in turn gener-ate more local spending. But other portions create new income for the owner. Russell spends $1,000 of that $5,000 in earnings at Jane's sporting goods store (a local business) to purchase sporting goods for his kids. The $1,000 that is spent creates a new profit source for Jane. She uses some of the money to cover additional business expenses and then some as additional income. As you can see, the initial $10,000 round of spending actually led to two more rounds of spending, with smaller amounts each time cycling through the community. In this simplified example, $10,000 of revenue from East Town High School led to an increase in economic output of $10,000 + $5,000 + $1,000 = $16,000.

Thus, the initial increase in revenue for East Town High School had a ripple effect that netted far more than the initial $10,000. In order to attain a proper economic analysis, all of the different rounds of spending that are likely to occur after the initial spending must be taken into account. This simple example demonstrates the impact of such an event on spending, income and jobs. The example can also be interpreted within aspects of direct, indirect and induced impacts of the event.

Because the exact data regarding multiple rounds of spending are very difficult to precisely determine, multipliers are utilized within the EIA formulas. These multipliers are determined by geographic region and by the size of the community involved. Table 17.6 summarizes recommended multipliers from the National Association of Sports Commissions (NASC) for use in the determination of EIA for event bidding. However, multiplier determination is typically more complex than this table suggests.

Table 17.6 *NASC Recommended Multipliers based upon Population*

Community Population	Spending Multiplier	Income Multiplier
Under 500,000	1.30	0.38
500,000 to 1.5 million	1.41	0.48
1.5 to 3.0 million	1.53	0.58
3.0 to 5.0 million	1.69	0.61
Over 5 million	1.85	0.64

Adapted from Rishe (2007)

In the United States, multipliers were initially developed and standardized in the 1970s through the Bureau of Economic Analysis (BEA). These multipliers were refined and adjusted as the Regional Input-Output Modeling System (RIMS II) by the Department of Commerce in the 1980s and again in the 1990s. There are unique multipliers developed for the spending, income and employment areas of the EIA for each of 172 distinct Metropolitan Statistical Areas (MSAs) within the nation and for 490 distinct industry segments. With such a level of complexity, there are several software systems that have been created to conduct EIA including the already mentioned RIMS II along with the more advanced IMPLAN and REMI.

IMPLAN, short for Impact Analysis for Planning, is a software system designed to conduct economic impact assessments that foster the development of local-level input-output models to estimate the economic impact of all industry types including new professional sports teams, or recreation and tourism events. IMPLAN was originally developed for the U.S. Department of Agriculture Forestry Service as an economic model, and it has expanded in its specific areas of application to nearly all industry sectors. REMI, or Regional Economic Modeling Incorporated, has created a modeling system that integrates the strengths of four major modeling approaches: input-output, general equilibrium, econometric, and economic geography. Each of these modeling systems has common applications across all types of EIA projects.

Facility Financing

There are a multitude of different ways to finance the construction or major renovation of a facility or venue. This includes options such as public funding, private funding, and other various financing methods. According to Shisler and Kim (2013), prior to the 1960s the majority of sports facilities were privately owned. Since the 1960's facility financing has shifted more toward public funding. In this current era, the combinations of funding range from fully public to fully private and with varied combinations of public and private financing techniques. Table 17.7 summarizes commonly used methods for direct public funding, indirect public funding and private funding used for facility construction in sport. Each of these options has their own unique set of positives and negatives that should be fully investigated for each specific community. A successful example of public funding is the 2001 move of the Vancouver Grizzlies to Memphis. The arena was publicly funded by the city of Memphis and cost $250 million to build. The Grizzlies had been in operation for ten years and had an economic impact analysis conducted regarding the outcomes of the move. It was found that the Grizzlies generated an economic impact of $233 million per year in the Memphis area. The Grizzlies also created 1,374 full-time jobs due to their move to Memphis (Shisler & Kim, 2013).

The FedEx Forum was a $250M new venue constructed as part of the relocation of the Vancouver Grizzlies of the NBA to Memphis, TN.

In contrast, the Montreal Expo's move to Washington D.C. to become the Washington Nationals in 2005 does not have a comparably successful outcome. The Nationals had a publicly funded facility that cost around $611 million. The new ballpark was envisioned to revitalize an area within Washington D.C. but has yet to fully accomplish that goal. Attendance was at 79% in 2012 at just under 33,000 attendants per game in a venue that holds 41,222 (Shisler & Kim, 2013). The balance of initial investments with final outcomes must be fully assessed to understand the relative value or lack of value for such public spending.

Opposite of public funding, sport organizations can seek to generate needed funds for an event or facility through private sources. The Minnesota Vikings constructed a new football facility that opened in 2016 partially via funding from three private banks: Goldman Sachs, U.S. Bank, and Bank of America. This strategy was taken by the Vikings after the 49ers chose to take this route with their nearly $1 billion investment in Levi's Stadium and its huge success in regard to funding through bank loan syndication. The remaining part of the Vikings new stadium came via public and state funding from the state of Minnesota and the city of Minneapolis. In return for funding, these private investors typically expect an interest or predetermined amount to be repaid to the bank within a pre-established timeframe (Kaplan, 2013).

Private grants are also an option for sport organizations to utilize for assistance in building their facilities. These grants can be found at many major

Table 17.7 *Summary of Public and Private Facility Funding Sources*

Direct Public Funding Sources	Indirect Public Funding Sources	Private Funding Sources
• General Obligation Bonds	• Land Donations	• Lease Fees—User Fees
• Certificates of Participation	• Infrastructure Improvements	• Naming Rights—Corporate Sponsorship
• Revenue Bonds	• Tax Abatements	• Naming Rights—Donor Recognition
• Tax Increment Financing (TIF) and Property Taxes		• Private Grants (sport leagues or federations)
• Sales Tax		• In Kind Services & Goods
• Tourism and Food & Beverage Taxes		• Private or Professional Fundraising
• Sin Taxes		• Vendor Financing
• Sale of Government Assets		
• State Appropriations		
• Ticket or Parking Tax/ Surcharge		
• Lottery Revenues		
• Player Income Tax		

Adapted from Brown, Rascher, Nagel & McEvoy (2010) and Seymour (2013)

athletic associations such as U.S. Soccer, U.S. Tennis Association, or via corporate sources such as the Nike Endowments, etc. (Seymour, 2013). This option is likely more feasible for smaller-scale and community development-based projects, not professional sport facilities, but it is still indeed an option.

Private funding through grassroots fundraising efforts is another option for smaller venues to increase available dollars. This can be done via selling various products: commemorative brick pavers, parking spaces, seats, and even candy bars. This often brings in less than 10–20% of a projected budget, but it can provide some assistance toward your goal. The main attraction in this private funding route is the public awareness and involvement that comes from your grassroots efforts (Seymour, 2013). These efforts may not make the bank for you initially but can help with getting people into the venue once it has been built.

Aside from public and private funding, there are also several other miscellaneous areas of funding that can be achieved. Sponsorship is a major area in which financing can be increased via naming rights for a venue. When the venue is being built the naming rights to the track, scoreboard, press box, and even the facility itself can be sold for a given period of time. This helps with the initial funding and even covering facility maintenance costs throughout the facilities tenure. Donor In-Kind Goods and Services is more of a local appeal on getting a facility built. In this type of fundraising, the fundraising group identifies various businesses that could potentially perform in-kind services that would be of benefit for the project (Seymour, 2013).

Let's take, for example, a local high school building a new baseball field. The fundraising group could reach out to fence manufacturers, landscaping companies, sprinkler system and irrigation contractors, sporting goods stores, and other local vendors who might be willing to donate supplies or labor that would provide assistance in building the new facility. Such donations are not direct monetary contributions, but they have value in reducing the total funding that will be needed for the project.

As you can see, there are many options to attain funding to build a new facility or renovate an existing one. There are both the private and public sectors that each provide different forms of support, and then other various fundraising options that may assist with the financing needs.

Legacy

Legacy a long-term measure of event outcomes that remain after the event including those planned or unplanned, positive or negative, and those tangible or intangible.

Political leaders, policy planners and event organizers tout the benefits of major special events, but the short-term economic impact evaluations don't always demonstrate the desired outcomes: therefore, the need has arisen for longer term and broader evaluations of event outcomes that are referred to as event *legacy* (Thomson, Schlenker, & Schulenkorf, 2013). The development and increasing use of the concept of legacy can be tied to sport mega-events and more specifically the Olympics and the World Cup.

The first major legacy conference/symposium was hosted by the International Olympic Committee (IOC) in November 2002 and resulted in the publication of a retrospective work highlighting the legacies associated with the Olympics from 1984 to 2000 (Moragas, Kennett, & Puig, 2003). However, the earliest application of the term legacy in relation to the context of events and sport can be traced back to the early 1990s. Getz (1991) first identified legacy as "The physical, financial, psychological, or social benefits that are permanently bestowed on a community or region by virtue of hosting an event. The term can also be used to describe negative impacts such as debt, displacement of people, pollution, and so on" (p. 340). While the aforementioned Olympic Symposium generated a flurry of nine different legacy definitions and applications (Thomson, Schlenker, & Schulenkorf, 2013), the work of Gratton and Preuss (2008) has provided the most concise application of the term legacy as the "planned and unplanned, positive and negative, intangible and tangible structures created through a sport event that remain after the event" (p. 1924). This legacy definition will serve as the working definition of the term throughout this chapter.

The use of legacy has been increasing both in the development of sport event bids and in the ongoing assessment of major sport event outcomes. A focus on initial planning for the legacies for sport events has served to reinforce the concept that mega-events can be positive forces for urban development (Holt & Ruta, 2015). Indeed legacy planning has been viewed as a method that can help to maximize the positive impact of mega-events in sport (Jago, Dwyer, Lipman, van Lill, & Vorster, 2012). However, the broad concept of legacy has created challenges in developing specific and consistent measures for assessing the outcomes of the event. Questions of what should be measured, what methods are best or appropriate for measurement, and when and for how long these measurements should occur all must be answered in order to fully assess legacy.

This expansive definition of legacy would encompass economic impact as a component but could include so much more. For example, UK Sport along with a number of British agencies for sport, tourism and economic development created an assessment process called the eventIMPACTS toolkit that measures legacy across five broad categories including: attendance, economic, environmental, social, and media. This model expanded in Table 17.8 provides one possible application of impact that would include broad aspects regarding an event or facility in sport.

The IOC has sought to provide more direct linkage to post-event reporting and legacy. They now release a summary factsheet for each of the Games and a review of the 2012 London Games and the 2014 Sochi Games reveals a number of common broad legacy categories including: Sports Legacy, Urban Legacy, Economic Legacy, Environmental Legacy, and Social Legacy. A summary of some of the key legacy outcomes from the 2012 and 2014 Games within each category is presented in Table 17.9.

Table 17.8 *Legacy Evaluation Categories from eventIMPACTS Toolkit Model*

Legacy Category	Sub Categories	Private Funding Sources		
Attendance	Attendance numbers	Demographic Profiles	Advanced Measures	
Economic	Basic Measures	Intermediate Measures	Advanced Measures	
Environmental	Basic Measures	Intermediate Measures	Advanced Measures	
Social	Satisfaction	Identity and Image	Participation	Volunteering and Skills
Media	Coverage Volume	Engagement and Tone	Value	

Adapted from www.eventimpacts.com

While a reporting of legacy outcomes is important in order to generate accountability at the end of the event process and legacy period, legacy outcomes and measures do not occur without detailed planning. Legacy planning has been most highly developed to date within the Olympic Games movement, and this has included the sanctioning of the Olympic Games Impact (OGI) study. The IOC issued a draft of 126 impact indicators in December 2006, of which 73 were mandatory and 47 were optional. This study's name was revised to the OGI study and the revised indicators were included in the OGI Technical Manual of 2007 (Vanwynsberghe, 2015).

These impact indicators are measured over a 12-year time period that spans from nine years prior to the Games to three years after the conclusion. This three-year post-event portion of the impacts falls into a legacy period with the factors assessed being broadly categorized into economic, socio-cultural, and environmental areas.

While much of the planning and reporting of legacy for sport events emphasizes the tangible and more easily measured aspects of legacy, there are also intangible event outcomes. The intangible benefits most commonly touted within the conception of event legacy are rises in civic and national pride and national exposure via the event hosting, but these intangible benefits are difficult to assess directly. Civic pride brings intangible psychological value to the countries hosting the event (Matheson, 2006). There has been direct research to support such an increase in pride with major events such as the World Cup (Alegi, 2010) and the Youth Olympic Games (Leng, Kuo, Baysa-Pee, & Tay, 2014). This enhancement of national identity and pride is also

Table 17.9 *Selected Legacy Outcomes from Recent Olympics*

Legacy Category	2012 London Games	2014 Sochi Games
Sports Legacy	• Six primary venues available for elite and community sporting events post Games • 12,000 schools in England participated in the 2012 School Games in interschool regional and national sport festivals	• Fisht Olympic Stadium will be used for the 2018 FIFA World Cup • Boshoy Ice Dome converted to multi-purpose sports center and home of a Kontinental Hockey League (KHL) team
Urban Legacy	• Olympic Village converted into 2,800+ flats • 6.5 billion GBP invested in transport infrastructure	• 367km of roads and bridges and 200km of railways with 54 bridges and 22 tunnels built • 60 new educational, cultural and health facilities constructed
Economic Legacy	• 1.2% reduction in London's unemployment rate • Oxford Economics study estimates 16.5 billion GBP in Games impact from 2005–2017	• 70,000 people employed in Olympic construction projects • Sochi business activity increases 178.8% form 2005–2010
Environmental Legacy	• Development of 45 hectares of habitat with a 10-year ecological management plan • 98% of demolition waste recycled	• 16.2 billion RUB in sustainable development projects during Olympic construction • 97% of construction waste recycled
Social Legacy	• "Get Set" education program taught Olympic values and global citizenship to 6.5 million students in 25,000 schools • 70,000 Games Maker volunteers served during the Olympics	• 5 million Russian schoolchildren received lessons on Olympic values and the Sochi Games • 25,000 volunteers served during the Olympic and Paralympic Games

Adapted from IOC Factsheets (2012 & 2014)

referred to at times as the "feel good effect" that can be noted amongst the population of the city or nation (Jaska, 2011).

An example of legacy planning specifically in the area of environmental impact can be seen in the preparations made for the 2012 Olympic Games in London. A key to London's successful bid to host the Olympics was the focus on sustainability in their proposal and the ways that this aspect of the bid would specifically align with the environmental legacy of the Games. London listed their sustainability goals for the 2012 Olympics as follows:

1. Climate change: minimizing greenhouse gas emissions and ensuring legacy facilities are able to cope with the impacts of climate change.

2. Waste: minimizing waste at every stage of the project, ensuring no waste is sent to landfill during Games-time, and encouraging the development of new waste processing infrastructure in East London.

3. Biodiversity: minimizing the impact of the Games on wildlife and their habitats in and around Games venues, leaving a legacy of enhanced habitats where we can, e.g. the Olympic Park.

4. Inclusion: Promoting access for all and celebrating the diversity of London and the UK, creating new employment, training and business opportunities.

5. Healthy living: Inspiring people across the country to take up sport and develop active, healthy, and sustainable lifestyles (London Olympics 2012, n.d.).

These goals, established in the planning process, connected with longer term legacy outcomes expected through the hosting of the Games. This dedication to sustainability and legacy helped to bolster the bid, making them a more favorable host choice. The impact of sustainability and environmental initiatives have also been shown to influence the perceptions of visitors and residents at the World Cup events (Govender, Munien, Pretorius, & Foggin, 2012) and at the Olympics (Liyan, Zhang, Xingdong, & Connaughton, 2011).

Facility Legacy Examples

While it has been established that event legacy extends to factors well beyond sport facilities, the sport venues remain an area of heavy emphasis within legacy planning, assessment and reporting. This may be in part due to the high visibility of the venues as a tangible and long-lasting connection to an event that has concluded. In order to maximize the legacy benefits for a facility, there must be considerable and specific planning for transition from a major global event use to local or regional use. Such a transition can also incur considerable additional costs. To illustrate this process a few recent examples will be considered.

The planning and execution of a legacy can include significant additional costs to the event or facility. For example, the Water Cube hosted the swimming and diving competitions for the 2008 Olympic Games in Beijing. After the games, one-half of the Water Cube (approximately 6,000 square meters) was renovated at a cost of $51M into the largest indoor water park in Asia (Farrar, 2010). This post-Olympic facility conversion opened two years after the Games with the facility boasting a wave pool, hot tub spa area, a lazy river, and 13 water slides. As a competition swimming pool has very limited use outside of hosting major meets, the conversion to a recreation destination for children, youth, and families has a much wider appeal to the general public in Beijing. A comprehensive legacy plan must account for such post-Olympic renovation costs within the planning and budget for the Games.

The Olympic Games have suffered from several examples of negative legacies as well. For example, the 2004 Games in Athens spent more than double its original hosting budget and within four years after the Games, at least 21 of the event's venues were considered abandoned (Black, 2012). These legacy struggles related to Olympic facilities in Athens highlight the potential problems in fully realizing the legacy plans and bringing them to fruition after the Games conclude (Kissoudi, 2008). A review of Olympic Games from the 1970s and 1980s shows tremendous variation in their success from a financial legacy perspective. While the 1984 Games in Los Angeles were considered a model for revenue generation via the Games, the 1976 Games of Montreal generated a cost over 13 times the original budget of $1.6 billion, and the debt from those Games in 1976 took 30 years to retire (Todd, 2016; Wilson, 2015).

The water park renovation of the Water Cube represents a legacy plan component of the 2008 Olympic Games.

The facility use component of legacy for mega-events has become increasingly important especially in light of the fact that a new measure for the productivity of stadium use post-event has been developed known as the Stadium Utilization Index (SUI) (Pruess, Solberg, & Alm, 2014). This index demonstrates the aggregated annual demand upon the facility, and it is calculated by multiplying the number of events by the average attendance and dividing that product by the stadium capacity. The value of this index increases by a greater number of events being held as well as having a high rate of attendance. Such an index allows for comparison of venues of various size and levels of use with one measure. An application of this index to the 2002 World Cup in Japan/Korea with 19 venues ranging from 0.15 to 46.45 resulted in an average SUI of 8.38. Used again for the 2006 World Cup in Germany with 9 venues ranging from 2.56 to 34.64 resulted in an average SUI of 16.67 (Preuss et al., 2014). The use of this index may have helped Germany in their legacy planning to get better use of their facilities after the conclusion of the World Cup. Such results create a standard of comparison for various single stadiums or for entire events related to effective facility utilization. The continued use of the SUI can allow facility legacy evaluation to move beyond anecdotal accounts of facility use to a more clear and quantifiable measure.

In addition to post-event facility use, the legacy concept has also been extended to include grassroots sports development as a desired event impact. For example, the 2010 World Cup in South Africa included the construction of a number of Football for Hope Centers in addition to the existing 20 artificial football pitches distributed across 16 African countries (Horne, 2014). Also as part of a legacy plan, a total of 800 legacy bags of football equipment were distributed to clubs and schools across the country (Paula & Bartelt, 2014). These types of legacy initiatives to enhance sport participation and interest at the grassroots level of the local population has become a more prominent part of legacy planning, and it may also contribute to the more intangible outcomes of the event in the influence of the attitudes of the local residents.

Conclusion

The construction and operation of sport facilities along with the hosting of sport events can be a costly endeavor. Therefore, both EIA planning and the broader legacy planning are valuable in helping to determine the short-term economic impact of a large facility or event and the long-term impact through legacy. Both of these methods of analysis should be fully utilized when looking to build a new facility or host a mega-event, and the results of these processes should be communicated with the appropriate stakeholders.

CHAPTER DISCUSSION QUESTIONS

Describe the level of spending and the public and private financing found within professional sport venues in the United States.

1. Identify and describe the three ways events or facilities impact the economy.

2. Find an example of a recent sport event in your region and provide examples of direct, indirect, and induced impacts associated with this example.

3. Explain the use of multipliers in the EIA process and describe how such multipliers are determined.

4. Identify some of the primary software systems used to assess EIA.

5. Define event legacy and explain how legacy differs from economic impact.

6. Obtain a copy of the IOC Factsheet from the most recent Olympic Games, and classify the legacy components from this document in the following categories: planned or unplanned, positive or negative, and tangible or intangible. Add additional legacy outcomes that are not mentioned directly in the IOC report for those Games.

MINI CASE STUDY

Assume that you are employed as the city manager for the city of Abilene, Texas, and you are considering the possibility of bringing independent league professional baseball to your city. You have been approached by a group of investors associated with the Pecos League of Independent Baseball who propose that the city support the construction of a new $4.5M multi-use baseball stadium. The stadium would serve as the home venue for this new franchise team and could also serve as a home venue for a local high school or university in the city. Additionally, the site could be used for concerts and other sporting events. This stadium would include artificial turf and seating for 4,000. The investor group proposes that the city fund 80% of the venue construction, and the investor group would supply the other 20%. The Pecos League plans to operates on a 70 game condensed schedule (35 home games), and the investor group and new team management would share 25% of all ticket and vending proceeds with the city for all events held at the new venue.

1. Describe how the generally isolated location of Abilene might impact the use of economic impact calculations regarding out of town visitors and how the smaller city population might impact multipliers in the economic impact analyses.

2. How does the balance of public and private funding for this proposed new venue for the independent baseball team compare with the public and private funding levels seen in MLB (see Table 17.5)?

3. Apply the IOC legacy categories (Sports Legacy, Urban Legacy, Economic Legacy, Environmental Legacy, and Social Legacy) to this potential project and identify possible positive legacy elements that could be associated with this new franchise and facility.

4. What specific events and event categories would you suggest for maximizing the use of this venue other than the 35 home games for the proposed Pecos League franchise?

5. What public funding sources (direct and/or indirect) and private funding sources would you project as the most probable and beneficial for this venue construction project and why (see Table 17.7)?

6. After considering the above mentioned factors, would you as the city manager support the construction of this newly proposed venue? Why or why not?

7. What other factors would be important for you to take into consideration connected to the concepts of economic impact and legacy for this example?

PRACTITIONER SPOTLIGHT

NAME: Scott Wysong

ORGANIZATION: University of Dallas and Wysong Brand Solutions, LLC

CURRENT JOB TITLE: Associate Professor in the Satish & Yasmin Gupta College of Business 2001–Present

EDUCATIONAL PREPARATION:

- BA in Economics, Vanderbilt University
- MBA, University of Texas at Arlington
- PhD in Marketing, University of Texas at Arlington
- International Association of Venue Managers, Research Committee

CAREER PATH: Several key steps in my career related to conducting economic impact analyses include first doing

Photo courtesy of Scott Wysong.

economic impact analyses as a project for sport management students at the University of Dallas working with the American Airlines Center in downtown Dallas. This initial experience led to more opportunities to provide economic impact analysis work on an ongoing basis with the Shreveport-Bossier Sports Commission. Then I took steps to organize and operate my own consulting company, Wysong Brand Solutions, LLC.

Photo courtesy of Scott Wysong.

The Louisiana High School Wrestling Championships sponsored by the Louisiana High School Athletic Association has been assessed via an economic impact analysis to determine its impact on the local economy of the hosting community.

WHAT TYPE OF SPORT AND ENTERTAINMENT ORGANIZATIONS HAVE YOU WORKED WITH?

I have been able to work with a number of sport organizations to date such as:

the American Airlines Center, the Frisco RoughRiders, the Shreveport-Bossier Sports Commission, the Independence Bowl, the Louisiana High School Athletic Association, and CenturyLink Center (Bossier City, LA).

WHAT ARE SOME OF THE KEY STEPS IN COLLECTING DATA AND CONDUCTING AN ECONOMIC IMPACT ANALYSIS?

I hire temporary workers and train them in how to approach people and collect data, then we go to an event and conduct the survey with attendees. The first question we ask is their zip code. Even if they don't want to answer any more questions, we know where they are from. We want to separate visitors into two categories, "Day Trippers" and "Overnighters." We ask questions to determine how much money they have spent and/or plan to spend on their trip. This includes food, lodging, shopping, entertainment, etc. If needed, we will send a follow-up email after the event for more detailed information. From this we are able to generate a report for the client.

HOW DO YOU REPORT YOUR ANALYSIS TO THE CLIENT?

I start with the methodology of the study and the number of responses. Then I report the direct economic impact, the indirect economic impact, and the total economic impact. The direct economic impact is a simple formula of the number of attendees multiplied by the number of days they were in town for the event multiplied by the amount of money they spent per day. The direct economic impact is then multiplied by a multiplier that represents the recirculation of the money spent by visitors in the local economy. The multiplier that is used is always a debated topic. Clients want to use as large of a multiplier as possible to show the greatest economic impact. I use a multiplier of 1.75 that comes from the Dallas Convention & Visitors Bureau. I think that is a good, conservative number for the Southern United States. The total economic impact is the sum of the direct and indirect economic impact. On top of that I also report media impact. There is software that can be used to determine how many times a location is mentioned during a broadcast or online. For example, how many times is Shreveport mentioned during the broadcast of the Independence Bowl? From this, a dollar amount can be assigned to the value of the media exposure during the event.

HOW DOES AN ACADEMICIAN CREATE OPPORTUNITIES TO DO CONSULTING WORK IN THE AREA OF ECONOMIC IMPACT ANALYSES?

A lot of my opportunities come from networking and word of mouth. I am very upfront with clients. I send them a written proposal that outlines what I will do in the analysis, the exact cost, and the date that the final report will be submitted. I take pride in my reputation and do what I tell the clients that I am going to do, and I think they appreciate that.

WHAT IS THE MOST REWARDING ASPECT OF CREATING ECONOMIC IMPACT ANALYSES?

I like to see our work put to use. Some of my analyses were used to help pass a hotel/motel tax increase in Shreveport. A piece of this increase will go to the Shreveport-Bossier Sport Commission to help them recruit amateur sporting events to the area. Another piece of this funding will also go to the Independence Bowl to help them negotiate better tie-ins with conferences.

WHAT IS THE MOST CHALLENGING ASPECT OF THIS JOB?

Collecting the data is formidable. Walking up to a complete stranger and asking them to take a survey can be uncomfortable. Sometimes people can be rude and you can't take it personally. Sometimes the temporary workers will walk off and I will have to stay late to get the numbers needed for the proper analysis.

WHAT IS A UNIQUE ASPECT OR TASK OF YOUR JOB THAT MANY WOULD BE SURPRISED TO HEAR ABOUT?

That every survey/event analysis conducted is different. They all have unique aspects. For a Mardi Gras parade in Shreveport, for example, there were estimations of the number of people in attendance that varied by 100,000 people. Conducting a study of a Taylor Swift concert posed many issues in working with the security staff and security measures in place. During a high school football event, there were four games in a row and it was difficult to determine where the impact of one game ended and another began. Ultimately, there isn't a cookie cutter approach to conducting these analyses and that makes it fun and keeps it interesting.

WHAT ADVICE WOULD YOU OFFER TO THOSE SEEKING A SIMILAR CAREER:

I think students need to intern and volunteer as much as possible. If students are interested in doing economic impact analyses, they should contact their local convention and visitor bureau. These bureaus would like to do an economic impact analysis for every event they have, but that isn't feasible. Volunteer to do a study and gain some experience. If you mess it up, try again.

Reprinted by permission of Scott Wysong.

REFERENCES

Agha, N. (2013). The economic impact of stadiums and teams: The case of minor league baseball. *Journal of Sports Economics, 14*(3), 227–252.

Agha, N., & Taks, M. (2015). A theoretical comparison of the economic impact of large and small events. *International Journal of Sport Finance, 10*(3), 199–216.

Alegi, P. (2010). *African soccerscapes: How a continent changed the world's game.* Athens, OH: Ohio University Press.

Baade, R. (1994). *Stadiums, professional sports, and economic development: Assessing the reality.* Chicago, IL: Heartland Institute.

Baade, R. A., & Dye, R. F. (1988). Sports stadiums and area development: A critical review. *Economic Development Quarterly, 2*(3), 265–275.

Baade, R. A., & Matheson, V. A. (2011). Financing Professional Sport Facilities. College of the Holy Cross, Department of Economics Faculty Research Series, Paper No. 11–02. Retrieved from http://college.holycross.edu/RePEc/hcx/Matheson-Baade_FinancingSports.pdf

Black, M. (2012, July 30). Winner's curse? The economics of hosting the Olympic Games. *CBC News.* Retrieved from http://www.cbc.ca/news/canada/winner-s-curse-the-economics-of-hosting-the-olympic-games-1.1186962

Brown, M. T., Rascher, D. A., Nagel, M. S., McEvoy, C. D. (2010). *Financial management in the sport industry.* New York, NY: Routledge.

Burns, J. P. A., Hatch, J. H. & Mules, T. J. (1986). *The Adelaide Grand Prix: The impact of a special event.* Adelaide: The Centre for South Australian Economic Studies.

Chang, S., Kim, H. K., & Petrovickova, K. (2015). Uses and abuses of economic impact studies in tourism. *Event Management, 19*(3), 421–428.

Chapin, T. (1999). *Urban revitalization tools: Assessing the impacts of sports stadia at the microarea level* (Unpublished doctoral dissertation). University of Washington, Seattle, WA.

Colclough W. G., Daellenbach L. A., Sherony, K. R. (1994). Estimating the economic impact of a minor league baseball stadium. *Managerial and Decision Economics, 15*, 497–502.

Crompton, J. L. (1995). Economic impact analysis of sports facilities and events: Eleven sources of misapplication. *Journal of Sport Management, 9*(1), 14–35.

Crompton, J. L., & Howard, D. R. (2013). Costs: The rest of the economic impact story. *Journal of Sport Management, 27*(5), 379–392.

Crompton, J. L., & Lee, S. (2000). The economic impact of 30 sports tournaments, festivals and spectator events in seven U.S. cities. *Journal of Park and Recreation Administration, 18*(2), 107–126.

Crompton, J., & McKay, S. (1994) Measuring the economic impact of festivals and events: Some myths, applications and ethical dilemmas. *Festival Management and Event Tourism, 2*(1), 33–43.

Evers, S. M., Hiligsmann, M., & Adarkwah, C. C. (2015). Risk of bias in trial-based economic evaluations: Identification of sources and bias-reducing strategies. *Psychology & Health, 30*(1), 52–71.

Farrar, L. (2010). Beijing's Water Cube now has slides, rides, a wave pool and spa. *CNN Travel,* Retrieved from http://travel.cnn.com/explorations/play/beijings-watercube-water-park-now-open-040746/

Feddersen, A., Grotzinger, A. L., & Maennig, W. (2009). Investment in stadia and regional economic development—Evidence from FIFA World Cup 2006. *International Journal of Sport Finance, 4,* 221–239.

Getz, D. (1991). *Festivals, special events, and tourism.* New York: Van Nostrand Reinhold.

Govender, S., Munien, S., Pretorius, L., & Foggin, T. (2012). Visitors' perceptions of environmental impacts of the 2010 FIFA World Cup: Comparisons between Cape Town and Durban. *African Journal for Health, Physical, Education, Recreation & Dance, 18*(1 Supp.), 104–111.

Gratton, C., & Preuss, H. (2008). Maximizing Olympic impacts by building up legacies. *The International Journal of the History of Sport, 25*(14), 1922–1938.

Holt, R., & Ruta, D. (2015). *Routledge handbook of sport and legacy: Meeting the challenge of major sports events.* London, UK: Routledge.

Horne, J. (2014). Managing World Cup legacy. In S. Frawley & D. Adair (Eds.), *Managing the Football World Cup* (pp. 7–24). Basingstoke, UK: Palgrave MacMillan.

International Olympic Committee. (2015). Factsheet: Sochi 2014 facts and figures. Retrieved from https://stillmed.olympic.org/media/Document%20Library/OlympicOrg/Games/Winter-Games/Games-Sochi-2014-Winter-Olympic-Games/Facts-and-Figures/Factsheet-Facts-and-Figures-Sochi-2014.pdf

International Olympic Committee. (2012). Factsheet: London 2012 facts and figures. Retrieved from https://stillmed.olympic.org/media/Document%20Library/OlympicOrg/IOC/Olympic_Games/Olympic_Legacy/London_2012/Legacy/EN_London_2012_Facts_and_Figures.pdf

Jago, L., Dwyer, L., Lipman, G., van Lill, D., & Vorster, S. (2012). Optimising the potential of mega-events: An overview. *International Journal of Event and Festival Management, 1*(3), 220–237.

Jaska, K. L. (2011). Sports and the collective identity: The effects of athletics on national unity. *SAIS Review, 31,* 39–41.

Kaplan, D. (2013). Vikings pick three banks for stadium financing. *Street & Smith's Sportsbusiness Journal, 16*(23), 6.

Kissoudi, P. (2008). The Athens Olympics: Optimistic legacies post-Olympic assets and the struggle for their realization. *International Journal of the History of Sport, 25*(14), 1972–1990.

Leng, H. K., Kuo, T., Baysa-Pee, G., & Tay, J. (2014). Make me proud! Singapore Youth Olympic Games and its effect on national pride of young Singaporeans. *International Review for the Sociology of Sport, 49*(6), 745–760.

Liyan, J., Zhang, J. J., Xingdong, M., & Connaughton, D. P. (2011). Residents' perceptions of environmental impacts of the 2008 Beijing Green Olympic Games. *European Sport Management Quarterly, 11*(3), 275–300.

London Olympics 2012: Planning a sustainable Olympic Games. (n.d.). *Partnership for SDG's.* Retrieved from https://sustainabledevelopment.un.org/partnership/?p=2207

Long, J. G. (2013). *Public/private partnership for major league sport facilities.* New York, NY: Routledge.

Matheson. V. A. (2006). Mega-events: The effect of the world's biggest sporting events on local, regional, and national economies. College of the Holy Cross, Department of Economics Faculty Research Series, Paper No. 16–10. Retrieved from http://college.holycross.edu/RePEc/hcx/Matheson_MegaEvents.pdf

Moragas, S. M., Kennett, C., & Puig, B. N. (2003). *The legacy of the Olympic Games, 1984–2000.* Lausanne: International Olympic Committee.

National Association of Sports Commissions. (2000). *Economic impact study.* Cincinnati, OH: National Association of Sports Commissions.

Noll, R. (Ed.) (1974). *Government and the sports business.* Washington, DC: Brookings Institute.

Noll, R. G., & Zimbalist, A. (1997). *Sports, jobs and taxes: The economic impact of sports teams and stadiums.* Washington, DC: Brookings Institute.

Paula, M. D., & Bartelt, D. (2014). *World Cup for whom and for what? A look upon the legacy of the World Cups in Brazil, South Africa and Germany.* Rio de Janeiro, Brazil: Heinrich Böll. Retrieved from https://www.boell.de/sites/default/files/worldcup_forwhom_forwhat.pdf

Plumstead, J. (2012). Economic impact analysis: 2012 Americas school of mines. *PricewaterhouseCoopers,* Retrieved from https://www.pwc.com/gx/en/mining/school-of-mines/2012/pwc-realizing-the-value-of-your-project-economic-impact-analysis.pdf

Ponsford, M. (2016, January 19). Los Angeles to build world's most expensive stadium complex. *CNN,* Retrieved from http://www.cnn.com/2016/01/19/architecture/new-nfl-stadium-los-angeles/

Preuss, H. (2007). The conceptualisation and measurement of mega sport event legacies. *Journal of Sport & Tourism, 12*(3–4), 207–228.

Preuss, H., Solberg, H. A., & Alm, J. (2014). The challenge of utilizing World Cup venues. In S. Frawley & D. Adair (Eds.), *Managing the Football World Cup* (pp. 82–103). Basingstoke, UK: Palgrave MacMillan.

Rishe, P. (2007). Calculating and reporting economic impact results: A guide for NASC Members. *NASC Whitepaper,* Retrieved from https://www.sportscommissions.org/Portals/sportscommissions/documents/webinars/economic_impact_tool_and_whitepaper.pdf

Rosentraub, M. S., & Nunn, S. R. (1978). Suburban city investment in professional sports: Estimating the fiscal returns of the Dallas Cowboys and Texas Rangers to investor communities. *American Behavioral Scientist, 21,* 393–414.

Seymour, W. J. (2013). Non-traditional funding alternatives for public athletic facility projects. *Sportsturf, 29*(1), 28–31.

Shisler, M., & Kim, J. C. (2013). A closer look at public financing of sport stadiums and arenas. *Chronicle of Kinesiology & Physical Education in Higher Education, 24*(1), 18–23.

Taks, M., Kesenne, S., Chalip, L., Green, B. C., & Martyn, S. (2011). Economic impact analysis versus cost benefit analysis: The case of a medium-sized sport event. *International Journal of Sport Finance, 6*(3), 187–203.

Thomson, A., Schlenker, K., & Schulenkorf, N. (2013). Conceptualizing sport event legacy. *Event Management, 17,* 111–122.

Todd, J. (2016, July 6). The 40-year hangover: How the 1976 Olympics nearly broke Montreal. *The Guardian.* Retrieved from https://www.theguardian.com/cities/2016/jul/06/40-year-hangover-1976-olympic-games-broke-montreal-canada

Vanwynsberghe, R. (2015). The Olympic Games Impact (OGI) study for the 2010 Winter Olympic Games: Strategies for evaluating sport mega-events' contribution to sustainability. *International Journal of Sport Policy and Politics, 7*(1), 1–18.

Veltri, F. R., Miller, J. J., & Harris, A. (2009). Club sport national tournament: Economic impact of a small event on a mid-size community. *Recreational Sports Journal, 33*(2), 119–128.

Wilson, R. (2006). The economic impact of local sport events: significant, limited or otherwise? A case study of four swimming events. *Managing Leisure, 11*(1), 57–70.

Wilson, W. (2015). Sports infrastructure, legacy and the paradox of the 1984 Olympic Games. *International Journal of the History of Sport, 32*(1), 144–156.

18 Sport and Recreation Facilities as Leverageable Assets

Marshall J. Magnusen

OBJECTIVES

After studying this chapter, the student should be able to:

- Understand the importance of recruiting to the short- and long-term success of non-profit and for-profit sport and recreation organizations.
- Understand the importance of turnover and retention management strategies to the short- and long-term success of non-profit and for-profit sport and recreation organizations.
- Explain how facilities can impact the recruiting efforts of non-profit and for-profit sport and recreation organizations.
- Explain how facilities can impact turnover and the retention management efforts of non-profit and for-profit sport and recreation organizations.
- Clarify how academic, recreational, and sport facilities can function as strategic assets that can be leveraged by non-profit and for-profit organizations to attract and keep highly desirable stakeholders ranging from students to student-athletes and from sports fans to sport teams.
- Discuss how cities and states use sport facilities as part of their strategic efforts to either lure a professional sport franchise or retain an existing sport franchise.

KEY TERMS

Customer Lifetime Value	Organizational Culture	Retention Management
Human Capital Theory	Recruitment	Theory
Human Resource Management	Resource Leveraging	Turnover

KEY ACRONYMS

CFP	College Football Playoff		**HCT**	Human Capital Theory
CLV	Customer Lifetime Value		**HRM**	Human Resource Management
FBS	Football Bowl Subdivision		**MLS**	Major League Soccer

NACUBO	National Association of College and University Business Officers
NBA	National Basketball Association
NCAA	National Collegiate Athletic Association

NHL	National Hockey League
NFL	National Football League
STEM	Science, Technology, Engineering, and Math

Introduction

Human Resource Management the process of recruiting, hiring, training, and managing individuals within an organization so that they become more valuable organizational assets.

Business organizations often spend hundreds of thousands of dollars recruiting employees and even more in their efforts to retain them. Research conducted by Bersin and Deloitte, which is a company that provides research-based strategies designed to help team managers and business executives enhance organizational performance via improved *human resource management* (HRM) strategies, determined most businesses spend between $3,000 and $4,000 per hire. They also estimated that US corporations spend over $72 billion annually on recruiting and staff retention (Bersin, 2013). Computer chipmaker, Intel, for example, announced they would be making a $300 million investment in the development, recruiting, and training of female and other groups of under-represented computer scientists at the 2015 Consumer Electronics Show in Las Vegas (Lev-Ram, 2015).

Colleges and universities, no differently than companies such as Intel, invest a tremendous amount of time, energy, and fiscal resources into their efforts to recruit and retain talented students, student-athletes, and organizational personnel (Magnusen, Kim, Perrewé, & Ferris, 2014; Treadway, Adams, Hanes, Perrewé, Magnusen, & Ferris, 2014). In a financial report produced by the *Chronicle of Higher Education*, nearly 50 percent of all National Collegiate Athletic Association (NCAA) Division I athletic departments doubled or tripled their recruiting budgets from 1997 to 2007 (Sander, 2008). According to the most current data available from the U.S. Department of Education's Office of Postsecondary Education, Division I football bowl subdivision (FBS) schools spent on average around $800,000 on recruiting expenses for men's teams for the 2014–2015 reporting year. Only a handful of schools, including Louisiana-Monroe, Ball State, and Troy, spent under $250,000 on recruiting for men's sports.

Table 18.1 includes recruiting and financial information about the Top 25 teams represented in the final regular season College Football Playoff (CFP) selection committee ranking for the 2015–2016 season. Information about collegiate recruiting expenses for the 2014–2015 fiscal year was gathered from the Department of Education website (http://ope.ed.gov/athletics/), which includes data for nearly every Football Bowl Series (FBS) school. Although the website does not provide sport specific recruiting spending information, women's recruiting expenses are separated from men's recruiting expenses. Football-only recruiting expenses are not separated from basketball-only recruiting expenses. Even so, it is highly likely that the majority of the men's sport recruiting expenses for most FBS schools stem from football, given both its popularity and large roster size. For the CFP Top 25, the average amount spent on recruiting for men's sports during 2014–2015 was $1,050,948.

Table 18.1 *Recruiting, Performance, and Financial Information for the 2015–2016 NCAA Division I Football CFP Top 25*

2015–2016 NCAA Division Football CFP Top 25

Final CFP Rank	School	Conference Affiliation	Regular Season Record	ESPN Recruiting Class Rank	Recruiting Expenses for Men's Sports
1	Alabama	SEC	14–1	2	$1,683,337
2	Clemson	ACC	14–1	8	$1,317,961
3	Stanford	Pac-12	12–2	13	$1,001,323
4	Ohio State	Big 10	12–1	5	$1,214,871
5	Oklahoma	Big 12	11–2	21	$1,800,535
6	Michigan State	Big 10	12–2	22	$1,087,467
7	TCU	Big 12	11–2	23	$570,428
8	Houston	American	13–1	30	$412,534
9	Iowa	Big 10	12–2	49	$1,041,747
10	Ole Miss	SEC	10–3	4	$767,335
11	Notre Dame	Independent	10–3	16	$1,751,090
12	Michigan	Big 10	10–3	6	$1,554,421
13	Baylor	Big 12	10–3	17	$835,578
14	Florida State	ACC	10–3	1	$936,791
15	North Carolina	ACC	11–3	34	$1,008,744
16	LSU	SEC	9–3	3	$1,277,315
17	Utah	Pac-12	10–3	38	$712,330
18	Navy	American	11–2	Not Top 75	Not Reported

19	Oregon	Pac-12	9–4	32	$1,110,417
20	Oklahoma State	Big 12	10–3	46	$835,284
21	Wisconsin	Big 10	10–3	41	$602,921
22	Tennessee	SEC	9–4	14	$1,550,029
23	Northwestern	Big 10	10–3	52	$603,421
24	Western Kentucky	Conference USA	12–2	Not Top 75	$306,394
25	Florida	SEC	10–4	12	$1,240,487

Data adapted from http://espn.go.com and http://ope.ed.gov/athletics/

What should be evident from the provided examples is that organizations across a variety of industry sectors, from the tech sector to intercollegiate athletics, invest heavily in recruiting and retention activities. At first glance, such spending might appear excessive, Indeed, in some cases, spending millions of dollars on recruiting-related expenditures may raise eyebrows. For example, prior to the start of the 2015 football season, lawmakers in South Carolina approved Clemson University's request for a second aircraft for the school's athletic department. The estimated cost of the jet ranged from $3.4 million to $5.9 million, and it would be purchased using the combination of athletic revenues and the school's booster club. In addition to the purchase price, estimated annual maintenance and staffing costs for the jet are expected to exceed $500,000 (Smith, 2015). Still, there are several very important reasons for colleges and universities, athletic departments, and sport and recreation organizations, in general, to allocate considerable resources to their recruiting and retention efforts.

First, people (stakeholders) are the foundation that will either make or break an organization (Schneider, 1987). Take into account how sport and recreation professionals in leadership roles may often times end up in the difficult position of having to determine how they can create a competitive advantage for their organizations while lacking the financial resources to hire expensive consultants and purchase the latest and greatest equipment and technology. Though such a task may sound daunting, a way exists for individuals ranging from high school and college athletic directors to private sector recreation and sport professionals in leadership positions to create sustainable competitive advantages for their organizations in the midst of challenging economic times. The way, quite simply, rests with an organization's human capital. Few organizational practices will contribute to the lasting success of an organization and its capacity to remain competitive with (if not gain a competitive advantage over) rivals than the recruitment, selection, and development of exceptional talent (Barney, 1991; Becker & Huselid, 1998; Crook, Todd, Combs, Woehr, & Ketchen, 2011).

Second, stakeholder disengagement and turnover can be incredibly costly to organizations. Direct replacement costs of an employee can range from 30–400% of the individual's annual salary depending on the industry and whether the individual being replaced is an entry-level or a high-level employee. Replacing six entry-level employees earning an average salary of $40,000 could cost an organization close to $100,000 because 40% of $40,000 is $16,000 per employee (Borysenko, 2015). Further, stakeholder disengagement does not end with employees. Students, student-athletes, and even sport and recreation consumers are key organizational assets that need to be recruited and retained.

With respect to the latter categorization of stakeholders, sport consumers, a particular area of importance is the concept of *customer lifetime value* (CLV). The lifetime value of customers to an organization represents the value of their expected benefits minus their anticipated burdens (costs). Consider how losing season ticket holders can be problematic for professional sport teams. A 50% retention rate requires a sport team to replace its season ticket holder fan base every two years. That is just not realistic. Accordingly, many professional sport teams have a formula for calculating the value of individual season ticket holders to a franchise. This helps the sport franchises better understand how much they should spend to keep a season ticket holder so that they can create a more stable product and grow their sport brands.

Customer Lifetime Value the expected benefits of customers minus their expected costs.

Discussed in the ensuing sections of this chapter are the importance of effective organizational recruitment and retention practices and how facilities can be used by 1) colleges and universities to attract and retain students, 2) college athletic departments to attract and retain student-athletes, 3) sport and recreation organizations to appeal to and keep organizational personnel, and 4) college athletic departments and professional sport teams to attract and retain sport consumers. Explored as well is how cities and states use facilities to attract and retain professional sport franchises.

People Make the Place: Why Recruiting Investment Matters

Does it make sense for a hospital to underinvest in medical technology, equipment, and facilities? Does it make sense for a construction company to invest in outdated machinery? No, absolutely not. Inadequate technology, equipment, and facilities can decrease productivity, damage a reputation, and cost a company time, money, and future business. Thus, it makes little sense for non-profit and for-profit organizations in the sport and recreation sectors to insufficiently invest in recruiting practices that can help them better identify, attract, and retain individuals who, quite honestly, are their biggest assets. Consider the importance of recruiting and personnel decisions in the example of LeBron James's journey from Cleveland to South Beach.

LeBron James is one of the world's most famous and popular athletes. He has won three National Basketball Association (NBA) championships, an

NBA scoring title, and four most valuable player awards. He was selected by the Cleveland Cavaliers as the first overall pick in the 2003 NBA Draft. This selection by the Cavaliers was supposed to propel them to the upper echelons of the NBA and yet, from 2003–2010, the Cavaliers only made it to the NBA Finals once. In 2007, they lost to the San Antonio Spurs in the finals. James became a free agent, eventually signing with the Miami Heat where he would play in four consecutive NBA Finals from 2010–2014, winning NBA championships in 2012 and 2013.

According to Forbes contributor, Vick Vaishnavi, the lesson from this journey is quite recognizable and simple. Do not be like the 2003–2010 Cleveland Cavaliers organization. Vaishnavi examines the importance of "A-Players" to the success of organizations in a series of articles published by Forbes.com, which is the online counterpart of Forbes magazine—a leading business publication on finance, investing, technology, leadership, and entrepreneurship. He states that "...a company staffed with talented and dedicated employees provides itself the best possible chance at succeeding in a daunting marketplace" (Vaishnavi, 2013, para. 1). Vaishnavi uses the Cavaliers-Heat situation that transpired with LeBron James to illustrate his point.

LeBron James, a superstar, was frustrated with the lack of talent surrounding him. This lack of talent contributed in large part to his decision to join the very talented Heat. Unlike his former team, the Heat had "A-Players" and James was able to surpass his previous success with the Cavaliers in only a couple years. What is the take-home message? Again, it pertains to recruiting. "A-Players" are of paramount importance to organizational success for several keys reasons: 1) they tend to put forth maximum talent and effort; 2) they recognize and can recruit other "A-Players" to a team; and 3) they want to work with other "A-Players" because they want to see their see their talent and effort reciprocated in their teammates (Vaishnavi, 2013).

When properly executed, recruiting and personnel selection methods can be very successful in targeting desired individuals, thus saving organizations time, money, and labor (Bowen & Ostroff, 2004; Magnusen et al., 2014; Magnusen & Todd, 2015; Terpstra & Rozell, 1993). The information provided in this section underscores the importance of recruiting. Regardless of whether it is a student-athlete, star player, graduate assistant, facilities manager, or league commissioner, effective HRM practices within a multitude of for-profit and non-profit organizations can lead to more efficient and productive workplaces (Schmidt & Hunter, 1998; Todd, Magnusen, Andrew, & Lachowetz, 2014).

Turnover is Costly: Why Retention Investment Matters

Does turnover matter? Unquestionably. Derrick Hall, President of the MLB's Arizona Diamondbacks, commented that employee turnover can cripple an organization. Hall noted, "We're in an industry where early entry jobs are extremely difficult, the turnover is devastating" (Belzer, 2015 para. 6). So from this perspective, employees rather than customers must be the top priority of an organization.

Turnover in the specific context of the business workplace is when an employee either voluntarily (e.g., the individual decides to leave for another job opportunity) or involuntarily (e.g., an individual is fired) leaves an organization and the organization must then replace the lost employee. The underlying concept of retention also can be applied to more than just employees. Retaining desired individuals (e.g., talented students, exceptional student-athletes, loyal customers) is absolutely important to colleges and universities, athletic departments, and professional sport teams.

Retention management encompasses "the entire human resource management policies for retaining the current or expected high-performing employees within organizations for long periods of time, enabling them to exercise or develop their capabilities" (Yamamoto, 2011, p. 3550). Similar to definitions of turnover, *retention management* is often defined by the context of the business workplace in mind. Even so, the basic idea of retention management is applicable to individuals, such as students or customers, who are not categorized as full-time employees. A key reason that retention management strategies are important to organizations is that turnover is expensive. In the case of organizational personnel, a general rule of thumb is that "…depending upon the complexity of the job and the level of management, the cost of turnover can equal anywhere from one month's to several years' salary for a departing employee. The more complex the job and the higher level of the job, the greater the cost" (Lawler, 2015, para. 1).

Another reason turnover is important to organizations is that it affects organizational performance. After examining 48 months of turnover data from a major US retail chain, a pair of scholars from the Harvard Business School reported associations between employee turnover and decreased performance, as measured by customer service and profit margin. In sum, turnover meant the company's employees were less likely to deliver optimal service and sell a higher volume of products (Ton & Huckman, 2008).

Just as skilled and experienced employees are difficult for a retail chain to replace, so too are talented student-athletes and competent coaches difficult for athletic departments to replace. For example, the University of Virginia's football program has won 15 games and lost 33 games from 2012–2015. During that time, seven quarterbacks transferred from the school, including three consecutive incumbent starters (Kurz, 2015). The inability of the football staff at the University of Virginia to stop the migration of quarterbacks has undoubtedly contributed to the football team's on-field woes.

Several topics have been reviewed in this chapter so far, including recruiting, retention management, and turnover. The importance of each of these areas to non-profit and for-profit organizations has been discussed but not explicitly connected to facilities. This salient connection should not go unnoticed. Facilities can function as immensely important *leverageable* assets when it

Turnover stakeholders leaving an organization.

Retention Management policies and behaviors designed to retain stakeholders an organization deems desirable.

Resource Leveraging presenting critical features of an entity (e.g., sport organization, city) to recruits and current stakeholders in ways that increase recruits' and stakeholders' levels of interest, attraction, and commitment to accepting offers from the focal entity.

Lucas Oil Stadium, current home of the NFL's Indianapolis Colts, has a capacity of nearly 65,000.

comes to recruiting key stakeholders (e.g., employees, student-athletes, consumers) and keeping those stakeholders satisfied, committed, and stationary. Further, professional sport franchises, though outside the customary focus of most HRM theory and scholarship, can be the target of cities' and states' strategic efforts to attract and/or retain them using the promise of new sport facilities. Evaluate the classic case of the Baltimore Colts and the circumstances surrounding the National Football League (NFL) team's move from Baltimore to Indianapolis.

The Indianapolis Colts were not always in Indiana. From 1953 to 1983, the Colts were based in Baltimore, Maryland. What led in large part to the controversial change in venue? Facilities. Robert Irsay, the then-owner of the Baltimore Colts, was unsatisfied with Memorial Stadium. He wanted a new stadium but faced resistance from politicians in Maryland's legislature as well as opposition from the state's governor and comptroller. By 1977, minimal progress had been made by the city of Baltimore or the state of Maryland to break ground on a new stadium. Irsay, frustrated with the situation, received permission from the NFL owners to move his franchise to a new city. Indianapolis saw an opening. While the decision-makers in Baltimore floundered and made threats (including seizing ownership of the Colts via eminent domain), Mayor Hudnut of the city of Indianapolis offered Irsay's team a $4,000,000 training complex, a $12,500,000 loan, and usage of the then-new $77.5 million, 57,980 seat Hoosier Dome. The offer was accepted, and the NFL was forever changed. On March 28, 1984, the Baltimore Colts became the Indianapolis Colts (Euchner, 1993; Morgan, 1997).

Having provided a foundation that brings awareness to the significance of recruiting and retention efforts to various types of organizations, what follows in this chapter is an explanation of how facilities can be linked to organizational recruitment and retention efforts. In the ensuing section, theory is used to illustrate just how facilities may help organizations in both recruiting and keeping desirable individuals. From there, the usage of facilities to recruit and retain preferred individuals is explored using college and university students, NCAA Division I student-athletes, sport and recreational organization employees, sport consumers, and sport franchises.

Connecting Recruiting and Retention Efforts to Facilities

A key goal of research is to systematically gather, organize, and synthesize information to answer questions. Theory serves as a starting point for research. It provides a framework for explaining a particular phenomenon and also may serve as the basis for research and practical application. In sum, research represents a systematic attempt to provide answers to questions and *theory* provides the set of beliefs or assumptions that help guide the systematic answering of questions. After selecting a theory, a researcher develops a research plan that corresponds to the selected theory, gathers data, analyzes the data, and then interprets the results and forms a conclusion about whether or not the theory was confirmed.

Theory beliefs or assumptions that guide the systematic answering of research questions.

Theory can be used to explain the connection between facilities and the recruiting and retention management efforts of athletic departments, professional sport teams, and institutions of higher education. Moreover, a wide assortment of theories can be used to explain any particular phenomenon. In this section, two different theoretical perspectives are brought to bear in articulating the expected relationships between facilities and both recruiting and retention respectively. The reputation/information framework (Berkson, Ferris, & Harris, 2002) is used to explain how facilities can be used by organizational leaders to attract desirable individuals. Next, human capital theory (HCT) is offered as a possible explanation for how facilities can influence the retention and turnover of key stakeholders.

How Facilities Can Impact Recruiting

The reputation/information framework (Berkson et al., 2002) is one way to understand how facilities can function as leverageable assets during the recruiting process. This framework is grounded in an organization-based *recruitment* perspective, and it explains the importance of effective recruitment programs in maximizing job candidates' job offer acceptance in a highly competitive marketplace. Central to the framework is information because it was argued by the researchers as being at the center of a recruit's level of attraction to an organization. Job attributes (e.g., compensation, hours) and organizational reputation, for example, are often times key sources of information for individuals as they evaluate potential employers. Persuasive communication by recruiters was offered as a specific mode of information transmission that helps business firms leverage job attributes and reputation information as a strategy to attract and then sign top talent in a competitive labor market. Rational persuasion, in this context, occurs when a recruiter uses logical arguments, facts, and data to try to convince sought-after individuals that they should join the recruiter's organization.

Recruitment the process of identifying, attracting, and selecting suitable candidates for specific positions within an organization.

Facilities, no differently than academic reputation or salary, represent a key piece of information—leverageable asset—that can be used by organizational personnel to attract students, student-athletes, front office staff and coaches, consumers, and even sport franchises. Tommy Frazier, Jr., for example, is one of the greatest players in the history of college football. Frazier played for the University of Nebraska. From 1992–1995, he won two national championships, four Big Eight conference championships, and had a 33–3 record as a starter. He is also a member of the College Football Hall of Fame (elected in 2013). What helped convince Frazier, who at the time was the third rated football recruit in the country, to sign with a football program that had repeatedly been blown out in recent bowl games? Facilities apparently played a huge role in his decision because, when Tommy Frazier visited the school on a recruiting trip in the fall of 1992, he was amazed by the vastness of the 30,000 square-foot weight room and the sprawl of a 3 million dollar indoor practice field that put the Cornhuskers a decade ahead of most programs (King, 2005).

When discussing recruiting, Wanous (1980) observed that the "traditional philosophy of recruitment can be best summarized as the practice of selling the organization to outsiders" (p. 35). The research piece by Berkson et al. (2002) conceptualizes the traditional philosophy of recruitment by characterizing the recruitment interview processes as a vehicle for key individuals involved in the recruitment process (e.g., athletic directors, college coaches, school admissions personnel) to actively promote important and attractive features of the organizational context to desired individuals. How well a chosen resource (e.g., facilities) or collection of resources (e.g., academic reputation, facilities, location, cost, availability of desired major) is managed by an individual involved in the recruiting process will determine whether performance translates into subsequent recruitment effectiveness for an organization (Magnusen, Mondello, Kim, & Ferris, 2011; Magnusen et al. 2014).

How Facilities Can Impact Retention

Human Capital Theory belief that organizational productivity rests with the individuals who comprise an organization.

The next theory, *human capital theory* (HCT), is a perspective that can be used to explain how facilities can impact retention. This theory proposes that the knowledge, skills, and abilities of an organization's workforce are the driving force of firm productivity (Becker, 1964). Organizational productivity rests with the individuals who comprise an organization. According to an HCT viewpoint, losing valuable personnel means a decrease in human capital and a decrease in human capital is likely to lead to a decrease in organizational efficiency and effectiveness (Huselid, 1995). The same can be said for students, student-athletes, and sport consumers.

Though sport consumers are not employees, they are valuable stakeholders. Sports do not exist absent satisfied consumers. Just as losing key personnel can hurt the productivity of an organization so too can losing sport consumers damage the viability of collegiate and professional sport organizations. So, for academic, sport, and recreation organizations, the retention of valued stakeholders (from students to consumers) is highly likely to be linked to organizational performance and success.

What can be done to retain valued stakeholders? Training and development, compensation, perks, and facilities are several ways in which organizations can invest in their human capital and, by extension, hopefully enhance organizational performance. Think through how the decision to stay or leave an organization requires stakeholders to engage in some form of costs and benefits analysis. An ambitious athletic director at a mid-major NCAA Division I school such as Boise State may be offered a job at a larger NCAA Division I institution such as the University of Florida (UF). This individual is unlikely to leave the current place of employment if the potential benefits do not outweigh the current costs (monetary, psychological, or otherwise). Athletic success can be achieved at both schools. However, the facilities at UF and the resources to upgrade and expand the UF facilities far exceed what Boise State has presently and what it can offer in the future. Notably, Florida's 2014–2015 athletic budget was $103.3 million, with $23 million allocated to a renovation of the office of student life and academic advisement center (Jones, 2014). Boise State's athletic department budget is not even half of UF's athletic department budget. Such noticeable differences in athletic department budgets and the capability to build and/or significantly renovate athletic facilities could hold significant sway over the athletic director's decision to leave Boise State for UF even though the position in Gainesville would not come without numerous burdens (e.g., the immense stress that often stems from sky-high expectations to compete for conference championships and national championships on an annual basis).

Failure to retain students on a consistent basis is problematic. Steady failure to retain employees is a major concern. Failure to keep customers on a regular basis is also problematic. Reductions in the quality and quantity of an organization's human capital can have negative organizational consequences. Overall, what matters according to HCT is that regularly losing key stakeholders is expected to drain an organization's human capital. Therefore, it is of the utmost importance that organizations invest in their stakeholders, and facilities are one way in which such investments can be made by schools, athletic departments, and professional sport teams.

Facilities and the Recruitment and Retention of College and University Students

A major trend amongst institutions of higher education is to build and then market impressive recreation centers to lure and retain students (Pyle, 2011). These investments are more than marketing ploys. According to Matthew Hamill, senior vice president of the National Association of College and University Business Officers (NACUBO), facilities and perks are "responses to consumers demand. And the reality is that students are increasingly demanding these kinds of services and opportunities" (Podolsky, 2014, para. 2).

Winters in Ohio can be frigid. In the city of Cincinnati, from December to February the average high temperature does not exceed 45°F and the average low temperature is under 32°F (U.S. Climate Data, 2016). Fortunately, for students at the University of Cincinnati, the Richard Lindner building has over 200,000 square feet of recreation facility. The facility has three pools, a climbing wall, a suspended track, over 21,000 pounds of weights, a juice bar, and a convenience store.

In comparison, both the University of Texas and the Ohio State University have over 500,000 square feet of indoor recreation space. That is more than double what the University of Cincinnati offers students. As two of the best recreation centers in the entire country, the amenities at both of these state flagship institutions include pools, climbing walls, large gyms, indoor tracks, volleyball courts, basketball courts, dance studios, and racquetball courts (Lange, 2015).

Facilities to attract and retain students also extend beyond the realm of indoor recreation centers. Michigan Technological Institution owns and operates a 112-acre ski hill (Podolsky, 2014). Similarly, Dartmouth College, an Ivy League school located in Hanover, New Hampshire, owns and operates Dartmouth Skiway. The mid-sized ski area was first opened for the 1956–1957 season. The ski area is comprised of the lower slopes of two mountains, 2,110 foot Holts Ledge and 2,282 foot Winslow Ledge.

Colleges and universities also use facilities to engage in targeted recruiting efforts, such as building a new law school, business school, or facilities devoted to Science, Technology, Engineering, and Mathematics (STEM) so as to better attract the finest and brightest students in each of the aforementioned areas of study. Institutions of higher education, similar to their athletic department counterparts, are in a competition to build facilities that will attract highly talented and intellectually gifted individuals. Business schools across the United States, for example, are seemingly sparing no expense in their efforts to attract highly competent and motivated students to their programs. Consider the following comparisons between the costs associated with a new football stadium and several new business schools.

Baylor University completed a brand new football stadium on the Brazos River in 2014. McLane Stadium, named for Drayton McLane, Jr., an alumni of Baylor and one of the richest Americans (ranked #324 in 2015 on the Forbes 400 list of Richest Americans) seats a capacity crowd of 45,000, has six founder's suites, 39 regular suites, 79 Loge boxes, and 1,200 outdoor club seats (Olson, 2013). The stadium cost more than $250 million to construct. That price may seem staggering until you compare it to several business schools.

The new School of Management building at Yale University.

Stanford's business school spent roughly $350 million on its new campus. Columbia Business School raised a staggering $600 million to complete its new campus in West Harlem (Build It, 2014). In fact, it is not uncommon for new or heavily renovated business schools to cost over $100 million. The Wharton School of Business at the University of Pennsylvania and the Ross School of Business at the University of Michigan cost $140 and $145 million respectively. Yale's School of Management had award-winning architect, Lord Norman Foster, build a $180 million structure for the school so that it might better keep pace with Ivy League rival Harvard (Staley, 2010).

Finally, community colleges are looking to attract and retain students no differently than traditional four-year institutions. To do so, community colleges are investing in facilities, with particular reference to housing. In 2000, 222 community colleges offered housing. In 2012, that number had nearly doubled to 391 institutions providing housing (Gilbert, 2012). Presently, there are just over 1,100 community colleges and over 25% of those offer housing. These efforts are designed to improve community colleges' recruiting and retention efforts by helping the two-year institutions have a similar feel to four-year institutions (Sheehy, 2015).

Facilities and the Recruitment and Retention of NCAA Division I Student-athletes

Facilities are often times noted to be an important factor for Division I recruits (Jessop, 2012; Pauline, Pauline, & Stevens, 2007; Shelton, 2014; Wise & Casadonte, 2014). Tom Gabbard, the Senior Associate Athletics Director at Virginia Tech, once remarked, "The folks you see building new facilities around the country know what a great recruiting tool they can be" (Broughton, 2009, p.24a). For many college and university athletic departments, sport facilities (e.g., stadiums, locker rooms, nutrition centers, practice facilities) are viewed as indispensable recruiting tools (Magnusen et al., 2014). Take into consideration the following facts and observations about facilities and recruiting:

- Over $15 billion was spent on sport facilities in the United States from mid-1990 to 2005 (King, 2005).
- A survey from AECOM and Ohio University shows that "more than eight in ten participating ADs plan to make significant investments in facilities over the next five years to target potential recruits and spectators. Of those, one in five plans on spending more than $50 million on renovations and new construction projects" (AECOM, 2014, para. 3).
- "If you don't have facilities, it's hard to attract top talent…so if we can add a new facility it will accentuate everything we have," said UCLA head coach Jim Mora. (New Football Facility, 2013, para. 8).
- Gerry DiNardo, an analyst for the Big Ten Network, labeled the athletic facilities at the University of Minnesota as the worst in the conference. His comments were not altogether unreasonable. Dean Johnson, chairman of the Board of Regents, described the facilities as "third-rate," which is why he, along with school president Eric Kaler championed a complete overhaul of the Golden Gopher's facilities. In 2015, they received final approval for a $166 million Athletes Village that will include a football performance center, football indoor practice facility, basketball development center, and a center for academic and athletic excellence (Lerner, 2015).

- Former University of Texas head football coach Charlie Strong once said "You don't always want to make it about facilities. But that's what it's really coming to" (Howe, 2014, para. 10).

Being a Division I student-athlete is an enormous investment of time and effort on the part of the student-athletes. Much of their college experience will be spent at the athletic facilities. Indeed, a criticism of NCAA Division I sports is that the student-athletes do not have sufficient time to be students. Surveys conducted by the NCAA have shown that athletes in sports such as baseball, basketball, and football self-report spending at least 40 hours a week on sport participation and training while in-season (O'Shaughnessy, 2011). The matter of whether or not college athletes have time to be students is a discussion best left for a different book, but the hours invested in sport do underscore the allure of top notch facilities to student-athletes. When so much of student-athletes' time is spent on sport participation, they are going to want to spend it in the best possible facilities.

There are a multitude of notable sport facilities and stadiums at the NCAA Division I level. A top 10 list of NCAA Division I football teams with the largest stadium capacities is provided in Table 18.2.

Table 18.2 *Top 10 Largest College Football Stadiums in NCAA Division I Athletics*

Largest College Football Stadiums (2015–2016 Season)

Rank	School	Conference	Stadium Name	Stadium Capacity
1	University of Michigan	Big Ten	Michigan Stadium	109,901
2	Penn State	Big Ten	Beaver Stadium	107,282
3	Texas A&M	SEC	Kyle Field	102,733
4	Ohio State	Big 10	Ohio Stadium	102,329
5	Louisiana State University	SEC	Tiger Stadium	102,321
6	University of Tennessee	SEC	Neyland Stadium	102,037
7	University of Alabama	SEC	Bryant-Denny Stadium	101,821
8	University of Texas	Big 12	Darrell K Royal—Texas Memorial Stadium	100,119
9	University of Southern California	Pac-12	Los Angeles Memorial Coliseum	93,607
10	University of Georgia	SEC	Sanford Stadium	92,746

Adapted from www.worldstadiums.com

The Bleacher Report website produces a power ranking of what they believe to be the top 25 facilities and stadiums in college football. In 2015, the Top 10 college football stadiums included (from tenth to first): Husky Stadium (University of Washington), McLane Stadium (Baylor), Memorial Stadium (Clemson), Ohio Stadium (Ohio State University), Sanford Stadium (University of Georgia), Michigan Stadium (University of Michigan), Notre Dame Stadium, Autzen Stadium (University of Oregon), Tiger Stadium (LSU), and the Rose Bowl (UCLA) (Pedersen, 2015). Though it is debatable as to which schools have the most appealing and striking facilities and stadiums, there are several schools that tend to garner considerable attention from the media, recruits, coaches, and institutions across the United States. Of particular note are the University of Oregon and the University of Alabama.

The University of Oregon has risen to a place of prominence in NCAA Division I athletics thanks in large part to contributions from billionaire benefactor Phil Knight, the founder of Nike. "We are the University of Nike," Jeff Hawkins, the senior associate athletic director of football administration and operations, once remarked (Bishop, 2013). In comparison to Oregon, the University of Alabama is home to one of the most storied football programs in the entire country. Bear Bryant, Alabama's legendary football coach won six national championships and 13 conference championships over his 25-year career at the school that began in 1958. Presently, under current head coach Nick Saban, the Crimson Tide represent one of the most successful football programs in Division I athletics over the past decade. Since arriving in Tuscaloosa in 2007, Coach Saban has won four national championships and four conference championships.

Building cutting-edge facilities can most certainly help boost recruiting, improve student-athlete satisfaction and success, and contribute to a school having a national sports presence. The University of Oregon is home to numerous truly impressive facilities. Most notably, the Hatfield Dowlin Complex is considered to be the Taj Mahal of college football facilities. The 145,000 square foot complex (with 60,000 addition square feet of parking) was reportedly built for just under $70 million (Bishop, 2013). Here are just a few examples of what the facility includes:

- Over 250 televisions, 170 seat theater room, arcade games, and locker rooms covered in Nike football leather.
- An actual duck, rugs woven by hand in Nepal, and a weight room with Brazilian hardwood floors.
- A 40-yard electronic track inside the weight room that measures the force of each step and the efficiency of each athlete's run.
- Underwater treadmills, a fully stocked protein and juice bar, and a multi-level locker room complete with flat-screen televisions and gaming consoles.

Additional impressive facilities are the University of Oregon include the John E. Jaqua Academic Center and Matthew Knight Arena. The former facility is a 40,000 square foot state-of-the-art academic learning center. The new

The John E. Jaqua Academic Center on the campus of the University of Oregon.

Interior shot of the Matthew Knight Arena on the University of Oregon Campus.

Bryant-Denny Stadium at the University of Alabama.

center replaced the Mac Court Annex, which was only an 8,000 square foot facility. The first floor of the academic center includes a café and a heritage space that recognizes past, present, and future student-athletes. The facility also includes 114-seat auditorium, 35 tutor rooms, 25 faculty and advising offices, conference room, computer lab with 54 computer stations, and 40 study carrels.

The latter facility, the Matthew Knight Arena, is a 420,000 square foot facility. It includes two regulation-size basketball court as well as one regulation-size volleyball practice court. The arena also has a nutrition bar, athletic training and rehabilitation facility, and a weight training facility.

The Alabama Crimson Tide also have notable facilities, with specific reference to the football facilities. The Tide play their football games at Bryant-Denny Stadium. This stadium has a seating capacity over 100,000, thus making it one of the largest stadiums in the world. In addition to Bryant-Denny Stadium, the football facilities inside the Mal M. More Athletic Facility are impressive as well.

The Mal M. More Athletic Facility is a state-of-the-art facility of just under 40,000 square feet. Inside the facility is an atrium that houses crystal football replicas of the football programs most recent national titles. There is a 212 seat theater room, billiards room, and an arcade that does not require quarters. The training facilities have a TRAZER video training system as well as an anti-gravity treadmill, which is a device developed by NASA engineers. The hydrotherapy room has a pool that is 30 feet long, eight feet wide, and adorned with four waterfalls. Additionally, the practice facilities include cooling tents, temperature-controlled benches, and a shoe-drying room (Manfred, 2013; Muma, 2013).

Facilities and the Recruitment and Retention of Sport and Recreation Professionals

Schools and athletic departments invest millions of dollars into facilities to attract and retain the most talented students and student-athletes. So, when it comes to discussions about recruiting and retention in academia and athletics, the conversation often times gets directed toward those two groups. However, recruitment and retention efforts are not isolated to students and student-athletes. Not to be passed over is another category of valuable organizational assets: employees. Consider how much of the turnaround of Major League Soccer (MLS) stems from its decision to hire and retain a single person, Don Garber.

Over a decade ago, Garber, a former senior vice president/managing director of NFL International, was named the commissioner to a struggling soccer league. Despite criticisms at the time (e.g. he had no soccer background), this personnel decision has paid off greatly for MLS. The league has seen an astonishing turnaround as it has gone from near extinction to a remarkable success. Even though the MLS is still losing money, it is poised for tremendous growth. Almost all of the MLS teams now compete in stadiums specifically built for them, including several of which were built without public funds. Lew Wolff and John Fisher, owners of the San Jose Earthquakes, paid $100 million to build their team's new, 18,000 capacity stadium (Painter, 2015). Average attendance for the MLS is at its highest levels (over 21,000, which is more than top leagues in Brazil and France), it has 20 teams worth around $3.14 billion combined, and the league just signed an eight-year contract with ESPN, Fox, and Univision worth $720 million that runs from 2015–2022 (Baxter, 2015; Tannenwald, 2015).

Robert Kraft, the owner of the MLS's New England Revolution and the NFL's New England Patriots, nominated Garber for the position after getting to know him in the NFL. When speaking about Garber, Kraft remarked, "He's had 15 tremendous years. We know how critical commissioners are in these different sports leagues. I think back to when we were paying to get games on TV, and now we have a lucrative contract. We're a league of 20 teams going to 22 in 2017 [with Atlanta and Los Angeles FC] and then to 24" (Wahl, 2014, para. 10). From contraction to expansion, Garber took his league out of the darkness (Parker, 2014).

Personnel equal policy in any organization. What does that statement mean exactly? Leaders and their teams both craft the vision and strategic means through which to achieve the vision. Again, this is why it is of the highest importance for organizations to not only invest in the recruiting of highly talented people but invest heavily in retaining their most productive employees. Facilities are one way to do this. In the case of college sports, facilities can attract coaches and athletes. Recruits, especially elite recruits, want impressive facilities. Coaches also want those facilities to better attract and sign such highly talented athletes. By extension, impressive facilities as well as the capacity to build new facilities and/or renovate existing facilities are factors that may help schools attract and keep highly competent athletic directors.

The potential for an athletic director to establish himself or herself as a successful and competent professional is far greater at institutions that have state-of-the-art facilities and continued capacity to build impressive facilities than at institutions whose facilities are lacking and will continue to lack in the foreseeable future. Facilities can be used to attract athletes and coaches with high value in the sport marketplace. More competent and skilled coaches and athletes can lead to greater athletic success. Greater athletic success can often result in increased giving to athletics (Stinson & Howard, 2004; Stinson & Howard, 2008). More money for athletics can lead to even greater facilities. The development of this type of cycle would be very attractive to athletic directors looking to establish themselves as the leaders at the helms of successful athletic departments poised for current and future growth.

Valued personnel to sport and recreation organization can be executive personnel, front office staff, and, in the case of professional sports, the athletes. For example, since mid-2000, numerous teams throughout the NBA have invested in state-of-the-art practice facilities to attract and retain desirable talent. The Nets, Wizards, Clippers, Cavaliers, Jazz, Thunder, and Pelicans are just a few teams that have built or significantly renovated existing practices facilities since 2005. Why the rise in practice facility construction? The answer goes above and beyond providing a centralized facility for team members to practice and train. A training facility is supposed to be a recruiting and retention tool because players spend more time at the training facility than the arena. Though this doesn't always end up being the case (e.g., the Cavaliers built a spectacular facility that did not keep LeBron James from going to the Heat), training facilities are increasingly being viewed by the leadership of NBA teams as a key recruiting and retention tool (Net Income, 2013).

In sport, as in all industries, some organizations are better to work for than others. According to a list compiled by *Forbes*, the following organizations are the top five to work for in sport (Belzer, 2015):

1. Arizona Diamondbacks
2. Cleveland Cavaliers
3. GMR Marketing
4. Ohio State University Department of Athletics
5. Navigate Research

What differentiated highly desirable organizations from less desirable employers? The answer is surprisingly simple. Sport organizations that were labeled as the best were also the ones where workers believed "they were more than just a replaceable cog in a giant machine" (Belzer, 2015, para. 5). Bonuses, perks, continuing education and training, positive recognition, and facilities amenities (e.g., on-site gym, employee cafeteria, on-site childcare facility) are all ways in which sport and recreation organizations can keep employees happy, motivated, and productive (Hull, 2013). Indeed, when it comes to the latter option, sport and recreation professionals may consider looking to the wide world outside of sports for inspiration.

What can the sport and recreation professionals learn from the technology, consulting, healthcare, retail, and consumer good sectors? They can learn quite a bit when it comes to leveraging amenities and facilities to attract and keep top talent. Many of the best places to work in general fall into one of the aforementioned sectors. According to data gathered by Glassdoor, a recruiting and job placement website that boasts over 8 million company and CEO reviews, the top places to work in 2015 were the following businesses (Smith, 2015):

1. Google
2. BAIN & COMPANY
3. Nestlé PURINA
4. f5
5. BCG
6. Chevron
7. H-E-B
8. IN-N-OUT BURGER
9. McKinsey & Company
10. Mayo Clinic

Google is at the top of the 2015 list. The company facilities include a variety of amenities including massage tables, relaxation chambers, wellness centers, bocce courts, a bowling alley, a real fireman's pole, a slide—yes, a slide—and a roller hockey rink (Koetsier, 2013; Simoes, 2013). Even though the company has been on the list for nearly a decade, 2015 was the first time the company took the pole position. Devoting more time to work-life balance and families apparently helped the tech giant claim the top spot. Specifically, the company offered increased maternity as well as paternity leave and reworked on-site daycare facilities so that they better accommodated the needs of Google employees (Dill, 2015).

It is unlikely that colleges and universities, athletic departments, and even some professional sport teams have the capability to consistently devote the same amount of financial resources to facilities for their respective students, student-athletes, and employees that companies such as Google, f5, H-E-B, Proctor and Gamble, and Apple can devote to their employees. Nevertheless, looking to other sectors to gain a better understand of how they attract and retain talented employees is an excellent idea for sport and recreation industry professionals. The learning process can be as simple and straightforward as identifying companies that are highly rated by their employees, determining why they are such wonderful places to work, and then strategizing ways in which to adapt and adopt the best practices of top companies.

Facilities and the Recruitment and Retention of Sport Consumers

Game day at Louisiana State University (LSU) is an experience unlike anything else in college football. LSU ranked third in attendance during the 2014 season, trailing only Ohio State and Alabama, according to statistics from the NCAA. Over 13 games, the Tigers drew just under 1.2 million fans (Sanoski, 2015). Further, more than two-thirds of LSU football fans are reported to tailgate for at least five hours before kick-off. Tiger fans take football and their game day experience seriously. ESPN writer Jim Caple once wrote: "So welcome to LSU, where the football is so good the earth moves, where the tailgate chow is so good the Food Network should own broadcast rights, and where the entire atmosphere is so special that people from the other side of the world would rather spend their days listening to a tiger's roar in Death Valley than go home to the peace and comfort of the Shire" (Caple, n.d.).

Attendance may not be an issue for LSU, Ohio State, or Alabama, but getting sport consumers in seats is becoming progressively challenging for many sport teams at both the collegiate and professional levels. The personal home viewing experience is on the rise, which is a key threat, if not the number one threat, to viewer attendance at actual sporting events. According to Lee Igel, a professor of sport management at New York University, "The drop-off in attendance for live sporting events is getting worse. You've got a lot of competing factors in this, even bad weather. But with the economy still sorting itself out, there's the huge cost of going to live events plus fighting through traffic and parking just to get to the games. And even more important is the experience of watching games in the comfort of your home on a big screen without the hassle at a stadium. That keeps a lot of people away" (Koba, 2013, para. 5–6).

A growing awareness of the importance of optimizing the fan experience at sport events by sport professionals has led to concerted efforts by sport teams to deliver an entertaining and valuable product on the field, rink, or court as well as in the stands. This is being done across sport industries and in a variety of ways. Toyota Motor Sales and International Speedway Corporation is heavily invested in enhancing the experiences of racing fans with "Wi-Fi, larger and more comfortable seating, escalators, twice the number of restrooms and large concourses with all the bells and whistles fans expect of a modern, major sports facility" (Cain, 2014, para. 4).

The University of Iowa invested approximately $50 million into their football stadium, Kinnick Stadium. The home of the Hawkeyes' football team now includes high-tech amenities, such as interactive kiosks, a 2,100 square foot player lounge with computer stations, and a public viewing area with video displays (Beahm, 2014). Alabama State University installed over 30 iPad point of sale (POS) systems at its football stadium. The POS units, which were installed at every concession stand, have an incredibly helpful feature for attendees and the Hornets. The units can operate even if there is a power outage. Because the units can function offline, consumers can still get concessions, and the university can still generate revenue that otherwise may have been lost (Boudevin, 2013). Another example of integrating technology and facilities to enhance the fan experience comes from what is likely to be an unexpected source: the NFL's Jacksonville Jaguars. The last time the Jaguars had a winning record was in 2007 when they went 11–5. They have now struggled for over a decade, failing to win even five games from the 2011–2015 seasons. Though the Jaguars have one of the worst teams in the NFL, they also have one of the best and most unique stadiums in the league.

Exterior view of Everbank Field, home to the NFL's Jacksonville Jaguars. The stadium is located in downtown Jacksonville.

© Rob Wilson/Shutterstock.com

Chad Johnson, the team's senior vice president of sales, wanted to get imaginative. He knew his team was not performing well on the field, and because of that harsh reality, the team had tarps over the empty seats. The team transformed the former tarp areas into premium spaces for "…businesses who want to entertain some of their clients or even their employees. What we've built here you can't get anywhere else" (Rovell, 2014, para. 6). The Jaguars removed nearly 10,000 seats from the north end zone. In place of seats, the section now boasts a two-level party deck that includes 16 cabanas and two pools. At midfield, fans can make dinner reservation and eat at the 50-yard line. The stadium also has the largest HD LED video screens of any professional or collegiate sport team in North America.

The Dallas Cowboys used to have the largest HD video displays in North America. The total viewing area of their video screens is just over 11,000 square feet (Oliver, 2009). In comparison, the Jaguars have video displays mounted at each end zone that are longer than the field itself. They stand 60 feet high, 362 feet wide, and provide a total of 21,700 square feet of digital canvas for spectators at EverBank Field to enjoy (Tarantola, 2014). Nothing sells out a stadium better than a winning team. However, if you're going to watch the home team lose, you might as well do it surrounded by amazing amenities such as a pool, cabana, and gargantuan LED screens.

The common thread connecting the aforementioned examples is the sport teams' laser-like focus on optimizing sport consumers' game day experiences. In 1998, a poll by ESPN reported that over 50% of sports fan said they would rather attend a game than watch at home. By 2011, only 29% reported they preferred being at the game (Rovell, 2012). With the myriad ways to enjoy sports at home and on the go, building innovative facilities that incentivize attendance through optimizing fan experience has become a top priority for sport teams at the collegiate and professional levels.

The future of sport facilities is maximizing the fan experience. Experiences attract consumers. Experiences sell tickets. Experiences promote positive word-of-mouth. Experiences get fans off their couches and into seats at an actual sporting event. Experiences are what many industry experts view as the essential component of sport organization's marketing and sales formulas. How do you attract and retain sport consumers? Facilities and the experiences provided in and around those facilities. Thus, sport teams need to ensure they are optimizing the fan experience and providing fans the right value proposition in that, when they spend their hard-earned money to physically attend, they believe they are getting a satisfactory value in return.

Facilities and the Recruitment and Retention of Sport Franchises

Much of the management theory and research on recruiting and retention in the workplace is focused on human resources, a categorization which can be applied to students, student-athletes, and employee, but traditionally not professional sport franchises. Professional sport franchises are often owned by a single individual (Mark Cuban) or family (Glazer family or Steinbrenner family), a group of investors (Guggenheim Partners group), or a corporation (Rogers Communication). Franchises are comprised of individuals, but are not themselves individuals. This much is obvious, but worth noting because efforts by cities and states to both attract and retain professional sport franchises are often very similar to the human recruiting and retention efforts of non-profit and for-profit organizations. Cities and states tend to use new sport facilities to attempt to lure and/or retain professional sport franchises in ways similar to how schools use recreational facilities to attract and satisfy students or athletic departments use a new stadium to entice and retain student-athletes and coaches. Accordingly, how cities and states use facilities to attract and keep sport franchises is discussed in this chapter.

The Baltimore Colts example, which already was discussed in this chapter, is a classic case of how facilities can be used as part of a larger package deal to attract the ownership of a professional sport franchise. That sort of municipal-, state-, and league-level political behavior is not uncommon in the realm of professional sports. More recently, Arthur Blank, the majority owner of the NFL's Atlanta Falcons, made it clear to politicians in Georgia and Atlanta that he was considering relocating his team unless he got a new stadium. Investors in Los Angeles (LA) had shown strong interest in moving the Falcons to LA, and were actively courting Blank to make that move a reality. Note, these interactions transpired several years before the St. Louis Rams would officially head back to LA. It is difficult to say whether or not Blank was seriously considering relocating his team. What is clear to say is that he used that information to subtly pressure politicians in Atlanta as well as the Governor of Georgia to take a more proactive lead on public financing of a new stadium to replace the Georgia Dome, a facility that opened in 1992 (Manasso, 2013).

In the end, Arthur Blank got his way. The Falcons remained in Atlanta, awaiting the 2017 completion of the new, $1.4 billion Mercedes-Benz Stadium. When commenting on the new stadium, Mike Gomes, senior vice president of fan experience for the Falcons, commented that the team's goals "…is to build upon the marvel of the physical structure to create a fully immersive experience for our fans—one that is memorable, fun, shareable and personal…an experience unlike any they've had before so they can't wait to come back" (Reimagined Experience, 2016, para. 5). The stadium, which totals two million square feet, should be a game-changer for the city of Atlanta. When finished, it will have an engineered roof that opens in less than 10 minutes, 2,000 digitals displays, ultrafast Wi-Fi, and numerous spots to eat, drink, and socialize while watching the Atlanta Falcons or Atlanta United FC of the MLS.

New Atlanta Stadium construction site. When completed, the stadium will serve as the new home of the NFL's Atlanta Falcons.

The Falcons did not relocate, but that is not the case with several other professional sport teams. In 2016, the St. Louis Rams relocated to Los Angeles, the second-largest media market in the United States, as a result of the NFL owners approving Rams owner Stan Korenke's ambitious and calculated plan to shift his team from the Midwest to the West coast. The Rams were located in LA from 1946 to 1994, but moved to St. Louis because of a dwindling fan base and an inability to secure a new or improved facility in the LA area. St. Louis, as part of the relocation deal, agreed to build a taxpayer-financed stadium, the Trans World Dome (now known as the Edward Jones Dome). Ironically, facilities contributed in part to the Rams departure from St. Louis.

Attempting to keep the Rams from moving to LA, the city of St. Louis developed a plan of action related to their facilities. The plan included a $1.1 billion stadium along the Mississippi River that would replace the obsolete Edward Jones dome. This proposal, which stood in stark contrast to the owner of the Rams self-funding the building of a stadium in Inglewood, California, faced a number of hurdles including public financing concerns (e.g., getting legislative approval) and a request for $200 million from the NFL, which was double what league policy allows for the financing of new stadiums (Logan, 2015). The hurdles to stay in St. Louis ended up being too high and, after receiving the approval of 30 of 32 NFL owners, the Rams returned to LA (Dixon, 2016). What is more, the Rams soon may have company. Both the San Diego Chargers and Oakland Raiders have been floated as possible teams to join the Rams in the City of Angels.

Another interesting example of a team leaving a city for better facilities is the case of the Seattle SuperSonics moving to Oklahoma City for the 2008–2009 season. At the time of the move, the Sonics were the fourth NBA to relocate since 1985. Previous relocations included the Charlotte Hornets to New Orleans, the Kansas City Kings to Sacramento, and the Vancouver Grizzlies to Memphis (Allen, 2008). The NBA approved the sale of the SuperSonics to an Oklahoma City investment group for approximately $350 million at the end of 2006. Come April of 2008, the NBA owners met and near unanimously approved (by a vote of 28–2) relocating the franchise from Seattle to Oklahoma City. Though efforts were made by the city of Seattle to keep the team, such efforts were not met with success. Indeed, on July 8, 2008, mere months after the vote by the NBA owners, Greg Nickels, then mayor of Seattle, held a press conference where he announced the team could leave straight away in exchange for $45 million (Farmer, 2012). The deal was done. History was made.

As was the case with the St. Louis Rams moving to LA and the Baltimore Colts moving to Indianapolis, the City of Seattle wanted the team to stay but an agreement between the city and the executive leadership of the Sonics could not be reached. When speaking on the matter, Sonics chairman Clay Bennett made clear the team had made strong good-faith efforts to keep the team in Seattle but, ultimately, the Sonics "could not engender the leadership of the marketplace to support a new building" (Allen, 2008). In comparison, Oklahoma City approved a $121 million sales-tax package to build a new practice facility for the team as well as renovate the city's existing Ford Center Arena. Further, the "Oklahoma Legislature sweetened the pot for the NBA…approving a payroll-tax rebate for the Sonics worth an estimate $60 million over 15 years. The state House approved the measure 67–32 and sent it to Gov. Brad Henry, who swiftly signed it into law" (Allen).

For fans of the Sonics, there is still hope that the team one day will return to Seattle. Investor Chris Hansen wants to bring an NBA franchise back to Seattle so long as Seattle will help pay for an arena. He also has expressed an interest in bringing a National Hockey League (NHL) team to Seattle. Such plans may be wishful thinking on the part of Hansen. A facilities dispute contributed in part to the Sonics leaving for Oklahoma City and a facilities dispute is hurting the chances of a triumphant return to Seattle for the Sonics. The arena issue with the Sonics, which as of 2016, was still being debated, remains contentious and unlikely to be resolved in the foreseeable future unless Hansen, the Seattle Sports Commission, city officials, Port of Seattle commissioners, and various labor groups who rely on the port of Seattle (the proposed site of the new arena) can come to terms (Browning, 2016).

Conclusion

In closing, it is very important that for-profit and non-profit organizations invest in recruiting so that they can attract key individuals as well as invest in retention management strategies in order to better satisfy and retain the individuals they want to keep. This chapter examines the relationship between facilities and the recruiting and retention practices of non-profit (e.g., colleges and universities) and for-profit (e.g., professional sport teams) organizations. Specifically shown in this chapter is how facilities can be leveraged by various entities to attract desired individuals and, in certain cases, actual sport franchises. Institutions of higher education can use facilities to attract and retain students. Athletic departments can leverage facilities to interest and keep desired student-athletes and coaches as well as other key organizational stakeholders such as athletic directors. The recruiting and retention of sport consumers is another way for athletic departments and professional sport teams to leverage their sport facilities. Lastly, cities and states can use facilities to attract and retain professional sport franchises.

PRACTITIONER SPOTLIGHT

NAME: Glenn More

ORGANIZATION: Baylor University

CURRENT JOB TITLE: Head Softball Coach

EDUCATIONAL PREPARATION: Northwestern State University, Bachelor's Degree in General Studies with a minor in History

Photo courtesy of Glenn Moore.

CAREER PATH: I started out with a desire to coach and teach high school. I finished up my degree at Northwestern State as student assistant in softball, which piqued my interest in coaching softball. From there I went into high school coaching (baseball and football) and teaching (history, marriage, and family), and it wasn't too long until I figured out that the classroom wasn't my cup of tea or something I desired. Then I had a door open at William Carey College. They started a softball program and asked me to interview for the head coach job. I was offered the job and took it in part because they would allow me to be softball coach and serve as a youth minister. While I was the head coach at William Carey, I also was in charge of a travel ball team. That provided me with opportunities to recruit because, quite honestly, I had little to no recruiting budget. LSU started a softball program a couple years after I took the position at William Carey. My travel ball team had the top pitcher in the south on it. So, through the recruiting process from LSU as well as my relationship with the pitcher, I was offered the pitching coach job at LSU. At first, I turned the job down. In fact, I did so on two occasions because I was happy with where I was. I was a single guy with a meal ticket and free lodging—just didn't have a lot of need for a lot of stuff at the time and the glamor of the job wasn't that important. Anyways, I eventually went there (LSU), and within the second year, the head coach was let go. I took over as interim head coach and then became the head coach for the next year. Two years later, Baylor called and asked me to come interview for my current post. LSU had made some promises. So, I thought that the job offer from Baylor might motivate LSU to fulfill some facility issues that we had and I felt we were up against. Some of their promises they were dragging their feet on, which ultimately was the sort of issue that led me to interview for the job at Baylor. I came over to Baylor for an interview and fell in love with the school. I thought they had a great vision—saw a budget and a vision unlike what we were experiencing at the time at LSU. Sixteen years later and this is where I still am.

WHAT ARE THE SKILLS AND ABILITIES THAT BEST ENABLE YOU TO EFFICIENTLY AND EFFECTIVELY DO YOUR JOB?

Honesty and being real with them (the student-athletes). Reputation is important as well. I think our reputation as a staff amongst softball players is that we know we're not perfect and we're not going to hide it from you. We're going to be upfront and honest with you to the best of our ability. We're knowledgeable in what we do and I think we've networked with enough coaches to the point where we're able to find the athletes we need to be successful because coaches trust us with their athletes. So trust. The ability to build trust with athletes and coaches is key.

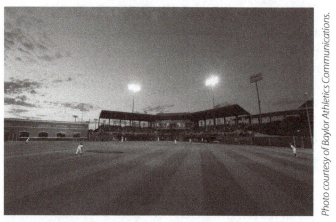

Getterman Stadium with the indoor practice facility along the right field line.

Photo courtesy of Baylor Athletics Communications.

WHAT RECRUIT CHARACTERISTICS ARE IMPORTANT TO YOU?

I get that question quite often to be honest with you. I'd be lying if I didn't say talent was the number one factor. We won't offer on talent alone, but it has to be significant first of all. Once we determine an athlete has the talent and motivation to compete at the NCAA Division I level, we examine the intangibles that qualify a kid to be a Baylor softball athlete. Their work ethic, academic ability, personality, and character—what kind of person they are—are very important factors to us.

HOW DO FACILITIES IMPACT TO YOUR ABILITY TO RECRUIT SOFTBALL PLAYERS TO BAYLOR?

Facilities are a strong reason I left LSU to come to Baylor. They signal to recruits the level of commitment a school has to the sport. When I first came to Baylor, softball wasn't that old and people were just doing the bare minimum. So, in context, when I saw the commitment Baylor made nearly two decades ago, I could tell that their intentions were to do really well at the sport. I was asked many times why I would leave an SEC power like LSU to come to a private school in the Big 12. Well, it was all about their commitment from an athletic standpoint. Facilities were a physical expression of Baylor's commitment to the softball program. Further, my budget was nearly twice what I had at LSU from a travel standpoint. Boosters at Baylor are more supportive of this program than what I saw at LSU and the facilities are what I think are the equalizer when you talk about the unleveled playing field that comes with being at an expensive, private institution compared to the costs of attending a state school.

Kids come here and they really want to compete and train in our facilities. So, in sum, practice facilities and stadiums are very important to recruits. At Baylor, for example, we have indoor and outdoor facilities, which is a big deal when you consider that 99% of NCAA Division I softball programs do not have an indoor facility or do not have an indoor facility as nice as our facility.

HOW DO YOU STAY CURRENT?

Well, we, of course, have conventions. We also bring speakers to our own clinics, and you know we just stay up to date with relevant companies via trade publications and chatting with colleagues. We have two great sponsorships with Under Armour and Wilson. They keep us up to date with equipment and apparel. A big part of our philosophy at Baylor is to be able to provide our athletes with anything they could get at other institution. Thus, it's our job to know what's going on. Equipment and apparel are big deals, and much of what we find out about these items comes through networking with vendors at conventions.

WHAT ARE THREE WAYS IN WHICH ASPIRING SPORT PROFESSIONALS CAN BETTER POSITION THEMSELVES FOR SUCCESS IN COLLEGE SPORTS?

First of all, I would say you have to have the resources in place so building that booster club and taking care of your donors and making them feel a part of our program helps give you the resources you need. Once you can provide the resources then it's a lot easier to recruit those athletes. Next is treating your athletes right. I think this means doing your best to provide them a great environment but also not abusing them or abusing your coaching power. I just don't think kids play as hard for you in those situations. Take care of them academically, give them what they need to be successful in the classroom and make sure your support staff does this as well. We're very blessed here at Baylor, and the kids are well taken care of with academic support. So if they're successful there, then it's going to transfer to the field and they're going to come out every day and play better because they're comfortable in the classroom. So that's my top three.

TECHNOLOGY & INNOVATION SPOTLIGHT

Advent and the Florida State Seminoles: Facilities as Experiences that Move People

"FSU Utilizes New Football Facilities to Attract Top Recruits" read the headline of a *Forbes* article published in September 2014. The upgrades to the football program facilities, which cost roughly $5 million, were part of the "Champions Campaign," a $250 million fundraising effort to enhance existing athletic facilities and increase the number of fully-funded athletic scholarships. Spending millions,

even hundreds of millions of dollars, is not uncommon for an athletic program in the upper echelon of NCAA Division I athletics. Indeed, the Oregon Ducks' new football facility cost nearly $70 million. What is worth mentioning about the FSU facilities is how they integrated tradition and technology to create facilities that would satisfy current student-athletes as well as capture the attention and imagination of potential student-athletes. To do this, FSU partnered with Advent, a Nashville-based company whose college sport clientele includes the University of

© Nagel Photography/Shutterstock.com

"Unconquered" statue in front of Doak Campbell Stadium on the Campus of the Florida State University.

Southern California, Stanford, Maryland, Georgia, BYU, Notre Dame, and Mississippi State among numerous other schools.

Advent as a company has a focus on branding within the facility environment and seeks to develop spaces that are dynamic and engaging for the brand, such as FSU football. Advent uses the facility itself to tell a story that builds upon and connects with the brand via "targeted messaging, stimulating graphics, and innovative problem solving" (Our Story, 2016). FSU wanted its facilities to be more than bricks and mortar; the institution wants its facilities to be a source of pride for current players and tell a story to recruits. The desire by FSU to have their facilities tell a narrative resulted in a business relationship with Advent, a company that specializes in helping brands tell their stories through facilities. According to Jessop (2014), Advent determined that FSU should highlight the three Heisman Trophies awarded to former players. Advent also accentuated the FSU athletic department's relationship with Nike through interactive video board technology. This technology allows recruits and players to mix-and-match FSU's various uniform components to customize potential game-day combinations. Advent also created a setting for FSU to incorporate a full-size ESPN College Gameday broadcast desk within its football facility. This mock broadcast desk even included a backdrop wall of photos depicting the traditional College Gameday sign holders (Jessop, 2014).

Advent combines technology and research about top college football to create their facility designs. For instance, Advent's research shows contemporary recruits (i.e., "Millennials") tend only to remember information about a program that goes three seasons back. That includes great players, national championships, and even Heisman trophy winners (Jessop, 2014). So, in the case of FSU, highlighting its multiple national championships in the 1990s and emphasizing players such as Derrick Brooks, Deion Sanders, Warrick Dunn, and Charlie Ward would not be as relevant and appealing to current recruits as showcasing its 2013 national championship, Jameis Winston, the 2013 Heisman trophy winner, its string of Atlantic Coast Conference (ACC) football championships from 2012–2014, and the fact that from 2013–2015, the Seminoles had almost 30 players drafted to the NFL.

The example of Advent and the Florida State Seminoles brings to light a relatively new way in which businesses and athletic departments can re-envision sport facilities. This demonstrates unique ways that universities might seek to utilize facilities to engage current and potential student-athletes to gain an advantage in recruiting. Athlete engagement is critical, "and for the millennial athlete engagement is about more than a campus tour and nice dinner. It's about helping the athlete see how he can fit into a story bigger than himself and into a story that is unlike one being told anywhere else" (Jessop, 2014, para. 10).

TECHNOLOGY & INNOVATION SPOTLIGHT

XYCAST: No wireless signal? No cellular network? No problem.

In 2011, Stanford University partnered with AT&T to become its first college to offer free Wi-Fi hotspots throughout its athletic facilities, including Stanford Stadium (Yasin, 2011). Texas Christian University also partnered with AT&T to offer Wi-Fi and DAS accessibility. In 2013, 345 Wi-Fi access points were installed in the school's Amon G. Carter Stadium along with 140 DAS antennas (Kapustka, 2013). Sport fans want to be connected—not only to their favorite team, but to their mobile devices. As a result, colleges and professional sport teams invest millions of dollars in stadium infrastructure to enhance connectivity for consumers. This comes with tremendous challenge.

Both Stanford Stadium and Amon G. Carter stadium have capacities around 50,000. The top five stadiums in college football have over double that capacity. Michigan Stadium, known as the "The Big House," has the greatest capacity in all of college sports with a capacity of nearly 110,000. The stadiums at Penn State, Ohio State, Texas A&M, and the University of Tennessee are not far behind with capacities over 100,000. In the NFL, MetLife Stadium, home of the New York Giants and Jets, has the largest capacity at nearly 83,000. The top 10 venues in the NBA (in terms of capacity) have seating capacities that exceed 20,000. Whether it is 20,000 or 100,000, the challenge of connectivity comes when you have a packed stadium or arena and everyone wants to connect simultaneously. The demands for mobile connectivity seemingly exceeds the supply in and around sporting events even after colleges and professional teams invest millions to update their network infrastructure.

XYCAST, a company founded by Bruce Cox, believes it has an answer to the challenge of mobile connectivity and an enhanced game day experience for fans. According to the official company Website (www.xycast.com), XYCAST aims to make mobile devices the equivalent of an "interactive personal jumbotron" for fans. The company offers a distinctive wireless data broadcasting network that does not need Wi-Fi or cell network connectivity. XYCAST is similar to AM/FM radio. If you are in range, you can receive content so long as you have a mobile smartphone, the credit-card sized XYCAST Personal Data Receiver (PDR), and a XYCAST-powered App. Once the App is launched, the XYCAST broadcast will provide venue and event-specific custom content on the fan's mobile device. The sport teams can customize the content to their fans, providing them with broadcast video highlights, pictures, audio files, score updates, stats, instant messages, promotions, and even interactive games.

Presently, XYCAST and its PDRs are not available for most sport teams as the company determines best programming and entertainment features for its network. The broadcast system was beta-tested in 2014 using football fans at Auburn University, Florida State University, the Naval Academy, the University of Michigan, and the University of South Carolina. If the technology continues to be well-received by fans and sport organizations, and the company can determine an adequate monetization strategy, XYCAST may become a staple of the fan experience at venues across the collegiate and professional sport ranks.

INDUSTRY SPOTLIGHT

The Arizona Diamondbacks and Zappos: Lessons in Organizational Culture

Both the Arizona Diamondbacks and Zappos are considered to be great places to work. What do the MLB team and online shoe and retailer have in common? They both have exceptional organizational cultures. Zappos, for example, has an employee retention rate of 95% and over 75% of the company's customers order more than once from the retailer. As a result, Zappos is often heralded as a model of an employee—and customer-centric organizational culture (Moran, 2013).

© 360b/Shutterstock.com

Zappos as a leader in organizational culture.

Organizational Culture the set of communal expectations that help guide individual behaviors by implicitly and explicitly outlining what constitutes suitable behavior for a variety of organization-specific situations.

Organizational culture represents a set of shared assumptions that help guide employee behavior by implicitly and explicitly defining what is appropriate behavior for a variety of work-related situations (Ravasi & Shultz, 2006). Culture affects how people interact with each other as well as how organizational members interact with others, such as clients and the local community. So, in terms of organizational culture, what is a major takeaway from the Arizona Diamondbacks and Zappos? The culture that has been created in both organizations is structured in a way that all employees feel connected and empowered.

© Doug James/Shutterstock.com

Chase Field, home to MLB's Arizona Diamondbacks, is shown with both the top and side windows open.

Zappos has the "Face Game." The way the game works is that "when you log into the computer system, after you enter your password, a face pops up of a fellow employee and you're asked to enter the person's name. Whether you answer correctly or not, you see a bio and profile—another way of getting to know your fellow workers and building culture" (Hollender, 2013, para. 13). The Diamondbacks also have a culture where employees are connected and every voice can be heard.

Derrick Hall, the current President and CEO of the Arizona Diamondbacks, wants every employee from the groundskeeper to the front office staff, to have a chance to influence the direction of the organization. Specifically, Hall explains that employees are involved in "…all aspects of the organizations decision making process" (Belzer, 2015, para. 10).

Culture should not be discounted as it can contribute to employee satisfaction and commitment as well as a company's overall profitability and success. Culture is more than a motto or a series of bullet-points. Culture is also more than amenities and cutting-edge facilities. Even though facilities can be the physical embodiment of an organization's culture, they are not the originators of an organization's culture. Having an on-site gym, cafeteria, and relaxation rooms may be physical representations of a commitment to employee health and well-being, but they will likely ring hollow among employees unless the organizational culture truly embodies and consistently conveys a commitment to employee health and well-being. Facilities can unquestionably contribute to an organization's culture. However, in order for a truly great organizational culture to emerge, it must be integrated into all areas of the organization—not just the facilities—by both its leaders and employees.

CHAPTER DISCUSSION QUESTIONS

1. Why is recruiting important to the short-term and long-term success of non-profit and for-profit sport and recreation organizations?

2. How can turnover positively and negatively impact sport and recreation organizations?

3. Why are retention management strategies important to the short-term and long-term success of non-profit and for-profit sport and recreation organizations?

4. How can facilities impact the efforts of NCAA Division I athletic departments to recruit student-athletes? Of cities and states to attract a professional sport franchise?

5. How can facilities impact the efforts of college and universities to retain students? Of professional sport teams to retain sport consumers?

6. What is a research theory? Discuss how Berkson et al.'s (2002) reputation/information can be used to explain how facilities can function as leverageable assets during the process of recruiting highly-rated high school athletes.

7. How might facilities impact the retention of athletic department employees according to HCT?

8. How do the athletic facilities at your school compare to the Big Ten and SEC powerhouses' facilities that are some of the best in the nation? Identify two schools from the Power Five conferences (i.e., ACC, Big 12, Big Ten, Pac-12, and SEC) and compare the sport facilities at those schools to the athletic facilities at your school.

9. Advent is a company that specializes in helping brands tell their stories through their facilities. Assume the role of a college athletic director or president of a professional sport team. Next, imagine you could hire Advent or a similar company to have your facilities be a source of pride for current players as well as future potential players. What story would you want your facilities to tell and why? What would need to get done in order for the facilities to tell the desired narrative?

10. The Equity in Athletics Data Analysis Cutting Tool (EADACT) is available via the Office of Post-secondary Education of the U.S. Department of Education. Visit the following website: http://ope.ed.gov/athletics/. Look up your school, then look up a rival school. How do they compare? For instance, what are the operating (game-day) expenses at your school compared to the operating expenses at your rival's school?

MINI CASE STUDY

ATHLETIC SUCCESS AS A CATALYST FOR NEW SPORT FACILITIES: THE CASE OF THE WILD BOARS AT MIDWEST UNIVERSITY

Dr. Lee Penning is the athletic director of a mid-major Division I athletics program. She has served in this role for nearly a decade. When she arrived to the school, she made the recruiting and retention of highly talented coaches and student-athletes a top priority. Dr. Penning believes that people make the place, and this belief has proven to be true. The athletics program has gotten steadily better every year under her leadership. A decade after she arrived, the Wild Boars of Midwest University experienced their most successful year competing in NCAA Division I sports. Five teams won conference championships, one team won a national championship, the football team made it to a "New Year's Six" bowl game, and both the men's and women's basketball teams made it to the Elite 8 of the NCAA men's and women's basketball tournament respectively. Although Dr. Penning is very excited about the banner year her athletic department experienced, she is also concerned about the ability of her teams to continue to compete at the highest level of Division I athletics absent significant changes to the athletic facilities at Midwest University.

The athletic facilities at Midwest University are dated. Half of the school's conference foes have built new sport facilities or significantly renovated their existing sport facilities over the past five years. What is more, two schools are scheduled to break ground on new football and basketball facilities next year. The facility projects taking place within the conference, combined with the myriad building activities of athletic departments outside of Midwest University's conference, could make it very difficult for the Wild Boars to maintain, if not exceed, their current level of athletic success.

Without new, state-of-the-art facilities, Dr. Penning worries that she will have difficulty recruiting and retaining highly competent and successful coaches. She is also concerned that her coaches will struggle to land the recruits they need to compete for conference and national championships. With such concerns in mind, Dr. Penning develops a strategic plan of action that she believes will help her athletics department rise to and remain a serious competitor at the top echelon of Division I sports. Facilities play a key part in her strategic plan. Over the next 10 years, she wants a new football stadium and practice field, renovations to the men's and women's basketball arena, a new baseball/softball complex, and a new athletic performance facility complete with a nutrition center. However, before she can execute her strategic plan, she has to present it to and get approval from Midwest University's Board of Regents. This will be no easy task given that, collectively, her plan requires the institution to raise approximately $250 million to pay for the projects. Still, Dr. Penning is determined to transform the success of the current year into a catalyst for future growth and continued athletic department prosperity and success.

1. What types of information should Dr. Penning present to the Board of Directors? How come?

2. What types of information should Dr. Penning avoid mentioning to the Board of Directors? How come?

3. How should Dr. Penning organize and package the information she is presenting so as to better convince the Board of Directors to agree to her strategic plan?

4. How can the theories provided in this chapter be used to help Dr. Penning make her case to the Board of Directors?

REFERENCES

AECOM. (2014). *Concerted effort to attract recruits, remain competitive and deliver distinctive game day experience, despite funding challenges.* [Press release]. Retrieved from http://www.aecom.com/press/concerted-effort-to-attract-recruits-remain-competitive-and-deliver-distinctive-game-day-experience-despite-funding-challenges/

Allen, P. (2008, April 19). NBA approves Sonics' move to Oklahoma City *The Seattle Times.* Retrieved from http://www.seattletimes.com/sports/nba-approves-sonics-move-to-oklahoma-city/

Barney, J. (1991). Firm resources and sustained competitive advantage. *Journal of Management*, 17, 99–120.

Baxter, K. (2015, December 15). MLS goes from near extinction to remarkable success. *LA Times.* Retrieved from http://www.latimes.com/sports/soccer/la-sp-soccer-baxter-20151206-story.html

Beahm, D. (2014, October 24). The most technologically advanced football stadiums. *Sport Techie.* Retrieved from http://www.sporttechie.com/2014/10/24/the-most-technologically-advanced-college-football-stadiums/

Becker, G. (1964). *Human capital*. New York, NY: Columbia University Press.

Becker, B. E., & Huselid, M. A. (1998). High performance work systems and firm performance: A synthesis of research and managerial implications. *Research in Personnel and Human Resources Management, 16*, 53–101.

Belzer, J. (2015, Mar 2). The best organizations to work for in sports. *Forbes*. Retrieved from http://www.forbes.com/sites/jasonbelzer/2015/03/02/the-best-organizations-to-work-for-in-sports/?utm_content=buffer839aa&utm_medium=social&utm_source=twittercom&utm_campaign=buffer

Berkson, H. M., Ferris, G. R., & Harris, M. M. (2002). The recruitment interview process: Persuasion and organization reputation promotion in competitive labor markets. *Human Resource Management Review, 12*, 359–375.

Bersin, J. (2013, May 23). Corporate recruiting explodes: A new breed of service providers. *Forbes*. Retrieved from http://www.forbes.com/sites/joshbersin/2013/05/23/corporate-recruitment-transformed-new-breed-of-service-providers/#36c0676d6f85

Bishop, G. (2013, August 2). Oregon embraces 'University of Nike' image. *New York Times*. Retrieved from http://www.nytimes.com/2013/08/03/sports/ncaafootball/oregon-football-complex-is-glittering-monument-to-ducks-ambitions.html?_r=0

Borysenko, K. (2015, April 22). What was management thinking? The high cost of employee turnover. *Talent Management and HR*. Retrieved from http://www.eremedia.com/tlnt/what-was-leadership-thinking-the-shockingly-high-cost-of-employee-turnover/#

Boudevin, J. (2013, September 17). New ASU stadiums installs ipad POS. *Venues Today*. Retrieved from http://www.venuestoday.com/news/detail/revel-pos-0917

Bowen, D. E., & Ostroff, C. (2004). Understanding HRM-firm performance linkages: The role of the "strength" of the HRM system. *Academy of Management Review, 29*, 203–221

Broughton, D. (2009, November 8). Tech finds home in locker rooms. *SportsBusiness Journal*. Retrieved from http://www.sportsbusinessjournal.com/article/63995

Browning, P. (2016, March 15). Sonics fans turn out for arena proposal, as do opponents. *KUOW.org*. Retrieved from http://kuow.org/post/sonics-fans-turn-out-arena-proposal-do-opponents

Build it and they may come. (2014, January 18). *The Economist*. Retrieved from http://www.economist.com/news/business/21594316-management-schools-are-building-spree-risk-some-build-it-and-they-may-come

Cain, H. (2014, February 6). Toyota becomes first Daytona rising partner. *Nascar.com*. Retrieved from http://www.nascar.com/en_us/news-media/articles/2014/2/6/daytona-rising-toyota-founding-partner-daytona-international-speedway.html

Caple, J. (n.d.). *ESPN*. Retrieved from http://espn.go.com/page2/s/caple/030918.html

Crook, T. R., Combs, J. G., Todd, S. Y., Woeher, D. J., & Ketchen Jr., D. J. (2011). Does human capital matter? A meta-analysis of the relationship between human capital and firm performance. *Journal of Applied Psychology, 96*, 443–456.

Dill, K. (2014, December 10). The best places to work in 2015. *Forbes*. Retrieved from http://www.forbes.com/sites/kathryndill/2014/12/10/the-best-places-to-work-in-2015/

Dixon, S. (2016, January 12). NFL approves Rams to LA, Chargers option to join. *Yahoo! Sports*. Retrieved from http://sports.yahoo.com/news/ap-source-nfl-committee-picks-combined-over-rams-220949398--nfl.html

Euchner, C. C. (1993). *Playing the field: Why sports teams move and cities fight to keep them.* Baltimore, MD: The Johns Hopkins University Press.

Farmer, S. (2012, June 16). *How the Sonics became the Thunder: A timeline. Los Angeles Times.* Retrieved from http://articles.latimes.com/2012/jun/16/sports/la-sp-0617-sonics-thunder-timeline-20120617

Gilbert, M. (2012, December 24). *Diverse.* Retrieved from http://diverseeducation.com/article/50264/

Hollender, J. (2013, March 14). Lessons we can all learn from Zappos CEO Tony Hsieh. *The Guardian*. Retrieved from http://www.theguardian.com/sustainable-business/zappos-ceo-tony-hsieh

Howe, J. (2014, August 18). Patterson, Strong say facilities upgrades on the way. *247Sports*. Retrieved from http://texas.247sports.com/Bolt/Patterson-Strong-say-facilities-upgrades-on-the-way-30386879

Huselid, M. A. (1995). The impact of human resource management practices on turnover, productivity, and corporate financial performance. *Academy of Management Journal, 38*, 635–672.

Jessop, A. (2012, December 14). The surprising factors driving college football recruits' college decision. *Forbes*. Retrieved from http://www.forbes.com/sites/aliciajessop/2012/12/14/the-surprising-factors-driving-college-football-recruits-decision/

Jessop, A. (2014, September 20). FSU utilizes new football facilities to attract top recruits. *Forbes*. Retrieved from http://www.forbes.com/sites/aliciajessop/2014/09/20/fsu-utilizes-new-football-facilities-to-attract-top-recruits/

Jones, D. (2014, June 11). Florida's 2014–15 athletic budget exceeds $103 million. Retrieved from http://www.floridatoday.com/story/sports/college/university-florida/david-jones/2014/06/10/university-florida-athletic-budget-103-million/10289783/

Kaputstka, P. (2013, October 25). Horned Frogs get AT&T Wi-Fi, DAS for TCU stadium. *Mobile Sports Report*. Retrieved from http://www.mobilesportsreport.com/2013/10/horned-frogs-get-att-wi-fi-das-for-tcu-stadium/

King, B. (2005, December 5). Race for recruits. *SportsBusiness Journal*. Retrieved from http://www.sportsbusinessdaily.com/Journal/Issues/2005/12/20051205/SBJ-In-Depth/Race-For-Recruits.aspx

Koba, M. (2013, July 17). Keeping fans in the stands is getting harder to do. *Yahoo! Sports*. Retrieved from http://sports.yahoo.com/news/nba--keeping-fans-in-the-stands-is-getting-harder-to-do-005355696.html

Koetsier, J. (2013, May 8). This Google office has a real fireman's pole, slide, cattle walkway, and more (gallery). *Venture Beat*. Retrieved from http://venturebeat.com/2013/05/08/this-google-office-has-a-real-firemans-pole-slide-cattle-walkway-and-more-gallery/

Kurz, H., Jr. (2015, May 16). Former Virginia starting QB Greyson Lambert to transfer. *Yahoo! Sports.* Retrieved from http://sports.yahoo.com/news/former-virginia-starting-qb-greyson-lambert-transfer-172357166--ncaaf.html

Lange, A. T. (2014, March 24). The college recreation centers in America. *Men's Health.* http://www.menshealth.com/fitness/coolest-college-rec-centers

Lawler, E. E., III. (2015, July 21). Rethinking employee turnover. *Forbes.* Retrieved from http://www.forbes.com/sites/edwardlawler/2015/07/21/rethinking-employee-turnover/

Lerner, M. (2015, October 9). U regents expected to approve $166 million Athletes Villages. *Star Tribune.* Retrieved from http://www.startribune.com/u-regents-expected-to-approve-166-million-athletes-village/331279731/

Lev-Ram, M. (2015, January 12). The powerful woman behind Intel's new $300 million diversity initiative. *Fortune.* Retrieved from http://fortune.com/2015/01/12/intel-diversity/

Logan, T. (2016, March 31). St. Louis pitches new stadium plan to keep the Rams. *LA Times.* Retrieved from http://www.latimes.com/business/realestate/la-sp-sn-st-louis-pitches-stadium-plan-20150109-story.html

Magnusen, M. J., Kim, Y. K., Perrewé, P. L., & Ferris, G. R. (2014). A critical review and synthesis of student-athlete college choice factors: Recruiting effectiveness in NCAA sports. *International Journal of Sports Science & Coaching, 9,* 1287–1288.

Magnusen, M. J., Mondello, M., Kim, Y. K., & Ferris, G. R. (2011). Roles of recruiter political skill, influence strategy, and organizational reputation in recruitment effectiveness in college sports. *Thunderbird International Business Review, 53,* 687–700.

Magnusen, M., & Todd, S. (2015). Coming soon to a sport and entertainment organization near you: Video realistic job previews as a way to increase the quality of applicant pools. *Sport & Entertainment Review, 1,* 91–97.

Manasso, J. (2013, January 29). Report: LA group courted Blank about Falcons. *Fox Sports.* Retrieved from http://www.foxsportssouth.com/01/29/13/Report-LA-group-courted-Blank-about-Falc/landing_falcons.html?blockID=856211&feedID=4368

Manfred, T. (2013, July 22). Alabama's new $9 million football facility is like something out of MTV Cribs. *Business Insider.* Retrieved from http://www.businessinsider.com/alabama-football-facility-pictures-2013–7

Moran, G. (2013, March 6). *Entrepreneur.* Zappo's secrets to building an empowering company culture. Retrieved from http://www.entrepreneur.com/article/226003

Muma, S. (2013, August 1). Alabama's new football facility: A photo tour. *SB Nation.* Retrieved from http://www.sbnation.com/college-football/2013/8/1/4578810/alabama-football-building-pictures

Morgan, J. (1997). *Glory for sale: Fans, dollars, and the new NFL.* Baltimore, MD: Bancroft Press.Net Income. (2013, December 20). Brooklyn Nets are latest NBA team to build a practice facility. SB Nation. Retrieved from http://www.netsdaily.com/2013/12/20/5215118/brooklyn-nets-are-latest-nba-team-to-build-a-practice-facility

New football facility. (2013, October 7). *Daily Bruin*. Retrieved from http://dailybruin. com/2013/10/07/editorial-new-football-facility-necessary-to-attract-top-recruits/

Olson, M. (2013, December 4). Stadium next step toward Baylor's future. *ESPN*. Retrieved from http://espn.go.com/blog/big12/post/_/id/76791/stadium-next-step-toward-baylors-future

Oliver, S. (2009, September 29). Mitsubishi HD display at Cowboys Stadium is the world's largest (by a country mile). *Hot Hardware*. Retrieved from http://hothardware.com/news/ mitsubishi-hd-display-at-cowboys-stadium-is-worlds-largest-by-a-country-mile

O'Shaughnessy, L. (2011, February 18). Do college athletes have time to be students? *CBS Money Watch*. Retrieved from http://www.cbsnews.com/news/ do-college-athletes-have-time-to-be-students/

Our story—Advent. (2016). Retrieved from http://adventresults.com/about/

Painter, K. L. (2015, May 19). When building MLS stadiums, formulas are all over the map. *Star Tribune*. Retrieved from http://www.startribune.com/ april-23-when-building-mls-stadiums-formulas-are-all-over-the-map/301011471/

Pauline, J. S., Pauline, G. A., & Stevens, A. J. (2007). Influential factors in the college selection process of baseball student-athletes. In J. H. Humphrey (Ed.), *Issues in contemporary athletics* (pp. 135–144). New York, NY: Nova Science Publishers, Inc.

Pedersen, B. (2015, June 2). Power ranking top 25 college football stadiums of 2015. *Bleacher Report*. Retrieved from http://bleacherreport.com/ articles/2480668-power-ranking-top-25-college-football-stadiums-of-2015/

Podolsky, D. (2014, September 22). How do schools market themselves to attract students? *US News*. Retrieved from http://www.usnews.com/news/college-of-tomorrow/articles/2014/09/22/ how-do-schools-market-themselves-to-attract-students

Pyle, E. (2011, January 10). Colleges' new rec centers lure students. *The Columbus Dispatch*. Retrieved from http://www.dispatch.com/content/stories/local/2011/01/10/colleges-new-rec-centers-lure-students.html

Ravasi, D., & Schultz, M. (2006). Responding to organizational identity threats: Exploring the role of organizational culture. *Academy of Management Journal, 49,* 433–458.

Reimagined experience. (2016). Retrieved from http://mercedesbenzstadium.com/stadium-info/ reimagined-experience/

Rovell, D. (2014, June 9). Jaguars to have poolside cabanas. *ESPN*. Retrieved from http://espn. go.com/nfl/story/_/id/11055495/jacksonville-jaguars-poolside-cabanas-stadium

Rovell, D. (2012, November 16). Best seats in the house. *ESPN*. Retrieved from http://espn.go.com/espn/otl/story/_/id/8636927/ nfl-taking-note-many-fans-watching-games-tv-beats-going-stadiums

Sander, L. (2008, August 1). Have money, will travel: The quest for top athletes. *Chronicle of Higher Education*. Retrieved from http://chronicle.com/article/Have-Money-Will-Travel-th/28750/

Sanoski, S. (2015, May 14). *Greater Baton Rouge Business Report.* Retrieved from https://www.businessreport.com/article/attendance-lsu-football-games-third-highest-us-last-season

Schmidt, F. L., & Hunter, J. E. (1998). The validity and utility of selection methods in personnel psychology: Practical and theoretical implications of 85 years of research findings. *Psychological Bulletin, 124,* 262–274.

Sheehy, K. (2015, February 9). Dorms help give 2-year colleges a 4-year feel. *U.S. News & World Report.* Retrieved from http://www.usnews.com/education/community-colleges/articles/2015/02/09/dorms-help-give-2-year-colleges-a-4-year-feel

Shelton, C. (2014, November 19). Campus facilities impact recruiting. *The Cougar.* Retrieved from http://thedailycougar.com/2014/11/19/campus-facilities-impact-recruiting/

Simoes, M. (2013, February 7). Why everyone wants to work at big tech companies. *Business Insider.* Retrieved from http://www.businessinsider.com/everyone-wants-to-work-at-tech-companies-2013-1

Smith, J. (2014, December 10). The full list: The best places to work in 2015. *Business Insider.* Retrieved from http://www.businessinsider.com/top-places-to-work-in-2015-2014-12

Smith, T. (2015, April 22). Clemon's getting a CJ2+ business jet for recruiting. *Greenville Online.* Retrieved from http://www.greenvilleonline.com/story/news/politics/2015/04/22/south-carolina-lawmakers-approve-purchase-clemson-university-citation-business-jet/26176477/

Staley, O. (2010, August 24). Harvard business school drives Yale and MIT's edifice complex. *Bloomberg.* Retrieved from http://www.bloomberg.com/news/articles/2010-08-25/harvard-business-school-drives-yale-and-mit-s-edifice-complex

Stinson, J. L., & Howard, D. R. (2003). Scoreboards vs. mortarboards: Major donor behavior and intercollegiate athletics. *Sport Marketing Quarterly, 13,* 129–140.

Stinson, J. L., & Howard, D. R. (2008). Winning does matter: Patterns in private giving to athletic and academic programs at NCAA Division I-AA and I-AAA institutions. *Sport Management Review, 11,* 1–20.

Tannenwald, J. (2015, December 13). MLS, U.S. soccer officially announce new TV deal with ESPN, Fox, Univision. *Philly.com.* Retrieved from http://www.philly.com/philly/blogs/thegoalkeeper/Live-MLS-US-Soccer-officially-announce-new-TV-deal-with-ESPN-Fox-Univision.html

Tarantola, A. (2014, July 26). The world's largest HD LED display takes over Jacksonville. *Gizmodo.* Retrieved from http://gizmodo.com/the-worlds-largest-hd-led-display-takes-over-jacksonvil-1610836380

Terpstra, D. E., & Rozell, E. J. (1993). The relationship of staffing practices to organizational level measures of performance. *Personnel Psychology, 46,* 27–48.

Todd, S. Y., Magnusen, M., Andrew, D. P. S., & Lachowetz, T. (2014). From great expectations to realistic career outlooks: Exploring changes in job seeker perspectives following realistic job previews in sport. *Sport Management Education Journal, 8,* 58–70.

Ton, Z., & Huckman, R. S. (2008). Managing the impact of employee turnover on performance: The role of process conformance. *Organization Science, 19,* 56–68.

Treadway, D. C., Adams, G., Hanes, T. J., Perrewé, P. L., Magnusen, M. J., & Ferris, G. R. (2014). The roles of recruiter political skill and performance resource leveraging in NCAA football recruitment effectiveness. *Journal of Management, 40,* 1607–1626.

U.S. Climate Data. (2016, March 1). Climate Cincinnati—Ohio. Retrieved from http://www.usclimatedata.com/climate/cincinnati/ohio/united-states/usoh0188

Vaishnavi, V. (2013, May 10). The importance of hiring 'A-Player'. *Forbes.* Retrieved from http://www.forbes.com/sites/vickvaishnavi/2013/05/10/the-importance-of-hiring-a-players/#28d02e7158f9

VanderMey, A. (2012, February 24). Inside Google's recruiting machine. *Fortune.* Retrieved from http://fortune.com/2012/02/24/inside-googles-recruiting-machine/

Wahl, G. (2014, December 3). 15 years of the Don: Under Garber, MLS stayed afloat, has taken strides. *Sports Illustrated.* Retrieved from http://www.si.com/soccer/planet-futbol/2014/12/03/don-garber-mls-commissioner-major-league-soccer

Wanous, J. P. (1980). *Organizational entry: Recruitment selection, and socialization of newcomers.* Reading, MA: Addison Wesley.

Wise, S., & Casadonte, L. (2014, March 11). $25 million practice facility to help VCU Rams recruit top basketball talent. *WTVR.* Retrieved from http://wtvr.com/2014/03/11/vcu-basketball-complex/

Yamamoto, H. (2011). The relationship between employee benefit management and employee retention. *The International Journal of Human Resource Management, 22,* 3550–3564.

Yasin, K. (2011, May 19). Stanford teams with AT&T to enhance sports-venue Wi-Fi. *Palo Alto Online.* Retrieved from http://www.paloaltoonline.com/news/2011/05/19/stanford-teams-with-att-to-enhance-sports-venue-wi-fi

3 P Model—the inter-relationships among three primary factors (place, process, and people) for the management of facilities and events in sport.

Acceptance—expressly stated or implied approval to the terms of an offer.

Active Shooter—an individual actively engaged in killing or attempting to kill people in a confined and populated area.

Allocation of Resources—this theory holds that under competition, the owner of resources (capital, human, natural) will seek to use the resources in the most profitable way.

Amphitheater—an oval shaped arena completely surrounded by seating developed by the ancient Romans.

Ancillary Space—spaces that are used to house or contain operating, maintenance, or support equipment and functions.

Architect—a person who designs buildings as well as often supervises the construction.

Architect Supplemental Instruction—proper notifications used by architects to circulate supplementary instructions or to instruct that minor modification occur in the project.

Arena—completely enclosed sport venue providing playing space on a central area, court, or floor with a high ceiling clearance surrounded by spectator seating.

Automated External Defibrillators—a device that automatically analyzes the heart rhythm and may respond to an electrical shock delivers a shock to restore a normal heart rhythm.

Ball Bounce—a measure that determines the precision of the vertical ball behavior.

Benefit Driver—factors adding to the economic impact of an event or facility such as increased or new spending, job creation and tax revenues.

Bid Fee—a payment required to the event rights holder from the city/organizing committee due at the time the bid is submitted.

Bidding—establishing a price an individual is willing to pay for a project.

Binge Drinking—a pattern of drinking that brings blood alcohol concentration (BAC) levels to 0.08.

Blood Alcohol Content—the amount of alcohol contained in a person's blood.

Bomb Threat—the malicious conveyance of false information knowing the same to be false which concerns an attempt being made, or to be made; to kill, injure, intimidate any individual; or unlawfully to damage or destroy any building, vehicle, or other real or personal property by means of an explosive.

Booking Agent—person responsible for booking events or acts for the facility.

Budgeting—a plan of operations based on estimates of income and expenses over a given time period.

Business Invitee—an individual is invited to enter the area due to some business relationship, not necessarily monetary in nature.

Candidature Process—a two-year process undertaken by cities undertaking a bid for the Olympic Games.

Capital Expenditures—investments that are made to increase the value of the asset.

Capital Improvement Plan—assists in classifying capital projects and equipment acquisitions, planning schedules and potential financing options.

Certification—the validation of specific professional training related to a professional practice or professional organization.

Change Order Requests—written instructions by a project owner that orders the contractor to alter contract amount, requirements, or time.

Changeover—the process of converting the use of a stadium or arena from the specifications of one sport or event to another different sport or event, also referred to as conversion.

Circus—a venue for horse and chariot races used within ancient Rome.

Compensation—the salary or pay an employee receives for performing a job.

Comprehensive Master Plan—a long-range and general plan to guide land and building development based upon committee assessment of data.

Concourse—a circulation area providing direct access to and from spectator accommodation, via stairways, ramps, vomitories, or level passageways, and serving as a milling area for spectators for the purposes of refreshment and entertainment. It may also provide direct access to toilet facilities.

Consideration—in contract law the item provided is exchanged for another consideration.

Construction Process—a process of distinguishing activities and resources needed to make a facility design become a tangible reality.

Contract—a written or spoken agreement that is may be enforced by law.

Contract Clause—specific provision or section within a written contract that distinctly delineate the duties, rights and privileges that each party has under the contract terms.

Cost Driver—factors reducing the economic impact of an event or facility such as crowding out, leakages and opportunity costs.

Cost Measurement Omission—an error in assessing economic impact where only benefits are considered and opportunity costs are not accounted for.

Cradle-to-Cradle—process in which all material inputs and outputs are viewed as technical (recycled or reused items with no loss of quality) or biological nutrient (items that can be composted or consumed).

Cradle-to-Grave—refers to a process in which an organization being accountable for the removal of goods it has manufactured without putting the components back into service.

Criticality Assessment—recognizes and calculates important assets, infrastructure, and critical functions based on a variety of factors.

Customer Churn—an interruption or loss in a customer's relationship or interaction with a company or product.

Customer Lifetime Value—the expected benefits of customers minus their expected costs.

Customer Satisfaction—a measure of how products or services meet or surpass a customer's expectation.

Customer Service Representatives—an employee responsible for maintaining positive relations and goodwill between a business organization and its customers via answering questions, solving problems or providing assistance.

Deconstruction—disassembly and removal of selected or all portions of a facility or structure for recovery and potential reuse.

Department of Homeland Security (DHS)—The United States Department of Homeland Security (DHS) is a cabinet department of the U.S. government with responsibilities for public security.

Diffusion of Innovation—a theory describing the communication and spread of an innovation over time in a social system.

Direct Impacts—the initial round of spending associated with a facility or event within a local economy.

Division of Labor—the separation of tasks within a system.

Double-Counting—an error in creating accurate estimates of total out of town visitors for an event that results in an overstatement of total economic impact.

Duty of Care—requires a party to act within a standard of reasonable care while performing any acts that could foreseeably harm others.

Ecological Footprint—the total impact of a sport event on the environment measured in hectares of productive land required to produce all goods consumed and handle the wastes produced.

Economic Impact Analysis—a mathematic modeling to estimate the multiple impacts of a new facility or event in a local area in the area of spending, income, and employment through direct, indirect and induced effects.

Egress—action of going out of or exiting a facility.

Emergency Action Plan (EAP)—an integrated plan that defines and documents the steps and actions to be taken by the facility staff and public safety agencies.

Emotional Intelligence—the ability of individuals to recognize the emotions of others and themselves and to use this recognition to guide their thinking and behavior in the pursuit of one's goals.

Employee Benefits—non-monetary compensation awarded to employees by employers. Benefits can include health benefits, special perks or vacation time.

Employee Development—an employer supporting an employee by providing access to training programs that introduce new skills to the employee and organization.

Evacuation Routes—the means to send individuals to a place of safety and away from a dangerous area.

Expectancy Theory—this theory postulates that an individual will select a specific behavior over other behaviors based upon the expected result of the selected behavior.

External Media—broadcast media outlets covering an event and have no organizational affiliation to the event host (team or governing body).

Facility Construction Document—covers the legal, procedural, and construction information, that summarizes the important connections, rights, responsibilities, and relationships that bring a facility into reality.

Facility Design Development Phase—phase where location of equipment, furniture, electrical and telecommunication services and other user specific requirements are incorporated into the project design.

Facility Emergency—an emergency situation is any incident, situation, or occurrence that could affect the safety/security of occupants, cause damage to the facility, equipment and its contents, or disrupt activities of the facility.

Facility Management—profession that joins people, place, process, and technology together to meet the needs of its patrons.

Facility Pre-Planning Phase—phase that may include site analysis, programming, construction cost analysis, and value engineering and occurs after some form of funding is available and before design begins.

Facility Programming Phase—involves collecting information from the anticipated facility occupants and user groups through focus group and/or individual interviews.

Facility Schematic Design Phase—description of building systems (structural, mechanical, hvac, plumbing, and electrical), interior and exterior finishes, and the building site.

Feasibility Study— an analysis and evaluation of a proposed project to decide if it is likely to be financially profitable.

Fenestration—arrangement, proportioning, and design of windows and doors in a building.

Fieldhouse—a large multipurpose indoor facility that typically incorporates an indoor track plus additional court facilities.

Foreseeability—the degree to which someone knew, or should have known, that another person may be exposed to the probability of injury.

Front Line Employee—any employee with direct contact with customers.

Gantt Chart—a graphic representation which depicts the amount of work done or production completed in certain periods of time in relation to the amount planned for those periods.

Gentrification—a renewal and or renovation of deteriorated urban neighborhoods via an influx of more affluent residents, resulting in increased property values that displace lower-income residences and small businesses.

Giga-Event—a new classification for an event at the very largest scale of size and scope related to attendance, media coverage, total budget, and total infrastructure development (rating 11–12 on the Müller scale) such as the Summer Olympic Games.

Gymnasion—a multi-use public venue for recreation, athletic practice, and physical education in ancient Greece.

Gymnasium—an indoor facility with high ceilings for sport competition, practice and/or physical education.

Hawthorne Effect—the concept of the increased attention of being a subject in a study creating a temporary increase in productivity.

Heavy Drinking—consumption of five or more drinks on the same occasion on each of five or more days in the past thirty days.

Hippodrome—a venue for horse and chariot races developed in ancient Greece.

Host (Host City)—a city or nation providing facilities for an event or function.

Host Fee—a payment required to the event rights holder based upon being awarded the bid for the event.

Human Capital Theory—belief that organizational productivity rests with the individuals who comprise an organization.

Human Resource Management—the process of recruiting, hiring, training, and managing individuals within an organization so that they become more valuable organizational assets.

In-House Media—event media coverage that is only for the patrons attending the event such as video board feeds, public address announcements, in-house mobile apps content or game programs.

Indemnification—compensation for loss or damage to provide security for financial reimbursement in case of an identified loss sustained by the person.

Indirect Impacts—additional spending by businesses within the local area that is directly linked to the initial spending or direct impact of an event.

Indoor Practice Facility—large indoor practice facilities with artificial turf that provide large spaces for practice in inclement weather conditions.

Induced Impacts—a tertiary spending increase in a local area associated with an increased personal income level tied to a sport event or facility.

Infrastructure—the basic physical structures for organizational and societal enterprise such as buildings, roads, power and water supplies.

Ingress—a place or means of access or entrance to a facility.

Insurance—practice by which an organization provides a guarantee of compensation for specified loss, damage, illness, or death in return for payment of a premium.

Integrated Planning—planning process linking the organization's values, vision, mission and priorities and all departments/areas with the event or facility plan.

Intention—create legal relations so as to denote whether a court should presume that parties to an agreement wish it to be enforceable at law.

Internal Media—broadcast media coverage of an event by the sport organization or governing body with their media personnel.

Legacies—comprise material and non-material changes (positive or negative) that occur in a host city, region, or nation in relation to the sporting event and remain after the event concludes.

Legacy—a long-term measure of event outcomes that remain after the event including those planned or unplanned, positive or negative, and those tangible or intangible.

Licensee—an individual has the owner's implied consent to be on the premises.

Life Cycle Assessment—a technique to measure the environmental effects related to all the periods of a product's life from cradle to grave.

Life Cycle Cost—process that considers the total expenditures of project options to choose the design that best guarantees the facility will offer the lowest overall cost of ownership in relationship with quality and function.

Line of Sight—the ability of a spectator to see a predetermined point of focus (such as the nearest touchline or outside lane of a running track) over the top of the head of the spectators sitting immediately in front.

Liquidated Damages—monetary compensation for a loss or injury to a person, person's rights, or person' property generally stipulated in the contract.

Loyalty—customer behavior to consistently purchase a product or brand over a period of time.

Major Event—an important event of global or regional importance related to attendance, media coverage, total budget, and total infrastructure development (rating 1–6 on the Müller scale) such as the Super Bowl.

Man-hour—a unit of measurement for production based upon the amount of work accomplished within a one hour time span by one person.

Management by Objectives—a managerial concept by which managers manage their employees by setting specific, short-term goals for employees, and the organization then works towards those goals.

Maslow's Hierarchy of Needs—a pyramid structure for human motivation beginning with physiological needs and moving up through safety and security, love and belonging, self-esteem, and culminating in self-actualization.

Mega-Event—an extremely large event of global significance in size and scope related to attendance, media coverage, total budget, and total infrastructure development (rating 7–10 on the Müller scale) such as the World Cup or Winter Olympic Games.

Motivator-Hygiene Theory—a two-factor model for factors that create job satisfaction and job dissatisfaction.

Multiplier—a quantity used to estimate the indirect and induced impacts for spending, income and employment within a given region for economic impact calculations.

Narrow Perspective Bias—an error in assessing economic impact where the broader impacts of cost and benefits associated with a facility or event are not considered.

Natatorium—a building containing a swimming pool or an indoor competitive swimming and diving facility.

National Fire Protection Association (NFPA)—an association that generates and maintains private, copyrighted standards and codes for usage and adoption by local government including firefighter equipment that is used while engaging in hazardous material (hazmat) response, rescue response, and firefighting.

Notice of Delay—relates to the point of time for which the project has been extended or work has not been performed because conditions that were unanticipated when the parties entered into the construction contract.

Occupational Safety and Health Administration (OSHA)—an agency of the U.S. Department of Labor that ensure safe and healthful working conditions for men and women by establishing and administering standards through training, outreach, and education assistance.

Offer—a promise made in exchange for performance by another party.

Olympic Agenda 2020—a strategic plan for the Olympic movement designed to enhance the dialogue between the IOC and the candidate cities and to foster bid proposals that will deliver excellent Games, meeting the needs of the city and region to ensure a positive, long-term, sustainable legacy without compromising the field of play for the athletes.

Organizational Culture—the set of communal expectations that help guide individual behaviors by implicitly and explicitly outlining what constitutes suitable behavior for a variety of organization-specific situations.

Organized Terrorism—acts of violence that requires a significant amount of planning, organization, and rehearsal.

Outsourcing—an arrangement in which one company provides services to another company for another company that could have been provided in-house.

Palaistra—a structure with an open courtyard for training and combat sports in ancient Greece built in combination with gymnasion and track or as a stand-alone structure.

Pankration—a combative submission sport combining the skills of wrestling and boxing.

Performance Management—a communication process where employer and employee collaborate to attain the organization's specific goals.

Place Attachment—a concept from environmental psychology describing the emotional connection between a person and a place that is founded on a three component model of person, process and place.

Premises Liability—holds landowners liable for injuries occurring on their property, including land and facilities.

Press Box—an enclosed working space for broadcast and print media members provided in stadiums at a high vantage point separate from general spectators.

Press Row—working space for broadcast and print media members provided in an arena or gym at a location close to the playing area and separated from general spectators.

Public Invitee—an individual who gains access to the area as a member of the general public with no business relationship with the owner.

Punitive Damages—occurs when damages exceed simple compensation and awarded to punish the defendant.

Recreation Center—a multipurpose facility designed for the pursuit of fitness, wellness, and sport based upon the needs of the users.

Recruitment—the process by which an organization enlists new workers and members; the process of identifying, attracting, and selecting suitable candidates for specific positions within an organization.

Relationship Marketing—marketing activities designed to develop and manage long-term relationships and build trust with customers.

Request of Information—a formal procedure for accumulating information from prospective suppliers of a good or service.

Resource Leveraging—presenting critical features of an entity (e.g., sport organization, city) to recruits and current stakeholders in ways that increase recruits' and stakeholders' levels of interest, attraction, and commitment to accepting offers from the focal entity.

Retention Management—policies and behaviors designed to retain stakeholders an organization deems desirable.

Rigging—a system of cables or chains used to suspend elements from the roof structure of a stadium or arena.

Routine Maintenance—restores the asset's physical condition and/or operation to a specified standard.

Safety—environmental condition where a person feels comfortable enough to move through it without concern of harm.

SAFETY Act—part of the Homeland Security Act of 2002 which provides incentives for the development and deployment of anti-terrorism technologies by creating a system of risk management and a system of litigation management.

Say's Law—a product is no sooner created, than it, from that instant, affords a market for other products to the full extent of its own value.

Scheduling—ability to find an appropriate time for a booked event.

Scientific Management—the application of scientific and engineering principles to management.

Season—an organized system of games or matches played within a sport league structure, or an organized group of tournaments, races, or events within a sport tour structure.

Security—the physical and psychological condition of an individual in which the feelings of being safe and free from danger, alarm, or suspicion exist.

Selection—the process of choosing someone (or something) deemed to be the most acceptable candidate.

Service—work done for others that is an intangible good that cannot be stored or transported and is simultaneously produced and consumed.

Service Quality—a assessment of customer service based upon service encounters in respect to the expectations of the customer.

Shock Absorption—calculates the floor's ability to decrease the force of impact.

Sliding Effect—sometimes referred to as coefficient of friction or slip-and-slide.

Spontaneous Terrorism—sporadic acts of violence that does not possess political goals or organized plans.

Sport League—an organization of team sports dependent upon the use of a home venue. Within leagues, a group of teams competes either at their home venue or the home venue of another league member throughout a set season of competition.

Sport Tour—a group of tournaments established around a single sport or single ownership/leadership that travels from city to city around a nation, region, or even the world and brings high caliber athletes and events to various fan bases.

Sports Festival—a multi-sport event held over a period of multiple days utilizing multiple venues.

Sportsplex—a large multiple field and/or multiple court complex used for competitive or recreational sport.

Stadium—a spectator venue associated with a running track (stade) in ancient Greece typically with sloped surroundings on three sides; an outdoor or domed facility that provides a large space typically with turf to host sport and other non-sport events.

Strategic Facility Planning—a connection of an organization's strategic planning to a mid- or long-term facility plan.

Strategy—a method or plan chosen to bring about a desired future state such as goal achievement or problem solution.

Substantial Completion—the phase of completion where the facility is ready to be occupied and used for its intended purpose.

Sudden Cardiac Arrest—condition in which the heart suddenly and unexpectedly stops beating resulting in a stoppage of blood flow to the brain and other vital organs.

Sustainability—the use of materials or methods that do not use resources that cannot be replaced and that do not harm the environment.

Synthetic Flooring—flooring generally made from urethane, rubber and PVC (polyvinyl chlorate).

Tailgating—a social event held on and around the open tailgate of a vehicle that often involves consuming alcoholic beverages and grilling food.

Temporary Facility—the creation of a sport venue for a one-time use from a facility or space not originally designed or developed for that sport use.

Theories X and Y—two competing theories on the motivation of workers. Theory X assumes that workers are intrinsically lazy, and Theory Y assumes that workers are intrinsically motivated.

Theory—beliefs or assumptions that guide the systematic answering of research questions.

Threat Assessment—a decision support tool to assist in creating and prioritizing security-program requirements, planning, and resource allocations.

Trespasser—any individual who enters a property without the express or implied consent of the facility owner; anyone who enters the property without consent from the landowner.

Turnover—stakeholders leaving an organization.

Values—principles or standards related to significance or importance for person or organization.

Vertical Circulation—the movement of people and/or products between floors of multi-level facilities.

Vertical Deformation—assesses the ability of the floor to deform or "give" when an athlete jumps or falls.

Vision or Vision Statement—a statement of an organization's desired achievements or accomplishments in the mid-term or long-term future.

Vomitory—an access route built into the gradient of a stand, which directly links spectator accommodation to concourses, and/or routes for ingress, egress or emergency evacuation.

Vulnerability Assessment—an evaluation of those areas that are susceptible to a strike through a malevolent attack.

Work Order—communicates information about services or goods that are needed.

Zamboni—a specialized machine developed to resurface ice in refrigerated rink settings with the name connected to the original inventor; leading manufacturer of these types of devices.

AAU	Amateur Athletic Union		**CMP**	Comprehensive Management Plan
ACA	Affordable Care Act		**COI**	Certificate of Insurance
ADA	Americans with Disabilities Act		**COR**	Change Order Requests
ADAAG	Americans with Disabilities Act Accessibility Guidelines		**COTA**	Circuit of the Americas
AED	Automated External Defibrillator		**CSR**	Corporate Social Responsibility
AEG	Anchutz Entertainment Group		**CSR**	Customer Service Representative
AFL	American Football League		**DAS**	Distributed Antenna Systems
AIA	American Institute of Architects		**DHS**	Department of Homeland Security
ALSD	Association of Luxury Suite Directors		**DIN**	Deutsches Institut für Normung eV
APFA	American Professional Football Association		**DS**	Direct Spending
ASI	Architect Supplemental Instruction		**EAP**	Emergency Action Plan
ASTM	American Society for Testing Materials		**EAP**	Employee Action Plan
ATP	Association of Tennis Professionals		**EEOC**	Equal Employment Opportunity Commission
AVP	Association of Volleyball Professionals		**EIA**	Economic Impact Analysis
BAC	Blood Alcohol Content		**EMT**	Emergency Medical Technician
BEA	Bureau of Economic Analysis		**F1**	Formula 1
BFOQ	bonafide occupational qualification		**FBS**	Football Bowl Subdivision
CAD	Computer Aided Design		**FC**	fixed costs
CBA	Collective Bargaining Agreement		**FIFA**	Federation Internationale de Football Association (International Soccer Federation)
CC	Closed Captioning		**FIFO system**	First In, First Out
CFP	College Football Playoff			
CIP	Capital Improvement Planning		**FINA**	Fédération Internationale de Natation
CLV	Customer Lifetime Value		**FLSA**	Fair Labor Standards Act

FMLA	Family and Medical Leave Act	**MLS**	Major League Soccer
FUTA	Federal Unemployment Tax Act	**MR**	Merchandise Rider
GHG	Ggreen house gas	**NABBP**	National Association of Base Ball Players
HCT	Human Capital Theory	**NACUBO**	National Association of College and University Business Officers
HID	High Intensity Discharge		
HR	Hospitality Rider	**NASC**	National Association of Sports Commissions
HRM	Human Resource Management		
HVAC	Heating, Ventilation and Air Conditioning	**NASCAR**	National Association for Stock Car Auto Racing
IAAF	International Association of Athletic Federations	**NBA**	National Basketball Association
IAVM	International Association of Venue Managers	**NCAA**	National Collegiate Athletic Association
IFEA	International Festival and Events Association	**NCS4**	National Center for Spectator Sports Safety & Security
IFMA	International Facility Management Association	**NFHS**	National Federation of State High School Associations
IOC	International Olympic Committee	**NFL**	National Football League
IP	integrated planning	**NFPA**	National Fire Protection Association
ISDN	Integrated Services for Digital Network	**NGB**	National Governing Body
ISO	International Organization for Standardization	**NGO**	Non-Governmental Organization
		NHL	National Hockey League
IT	Information Technology	**NPA**	National Parking Association
KSAs	knowledge, skills and abilities	**NPV**	Net Present Value
LCA	Life Cycle Assessment	**NRD**	Non-Refundable Deposit
LCCA	Life Cycle Cost Analysis	**OBS**	Olympic Broadcasting Service
LED	Light Emitting Diode	**OGI**	Olympic Games Impact
LPGA	Ladies' Professional Golf Association	**OSHA**	Occupational Safety and Health Administration
MBO	Management by Objectives		
MiLB	Minor League Baseball	**PAF**	Public Assembly Facility
MLB	Major League Baseball	**PBWA**	Professional Basketball Writers Association

PGA	Professional Golf Association
POS	Point of Sales
PPBES	planning programming budgeting evaluation system
PR	Production Rider
PSL	Personal Seat License
REMI	Regional Economic Modeling Incorporated
RFB	Request for Bid
RFI	Request for Information
RFP	Request for Proposal
RIMS II	Regional Input-Output Modeling System II
RM	Risk Management
ROS	Run of Show
RPS	Request for Professional Services
SAFETY Act	Support Anti-Terrorism by Fostering Effective Technologies Act
SCA	Sudden Cardiac Arrest
SCAN	strategic creative analysis
SFP	strategic facilities plan
SLP	systematic layout planning
SMA	Stadium Managers Association
SMART Goals	strategic, measurable, attainable, realistic and timely goals
STEM	Science, Technology, Engineering, and Math
SUI	Stadium Utilization Index
TEAM	Techniques for Effective Alcohol Management
TEI	Total Economic Impact
TIPS	Training for Intervention ProcedureS
TOP Program	The Olympic Partner Program
TQM	Total Quality Management
TVS	Total Visitor Spending
UEFA	Union of European Football Associations
UFC	Ultimate Fighting Championship
UGC	User-Generated Content
VC	variable costs
VIK	value in kind
VOCs	Volatile Organic Compounds
WNBA	Women's Professional Basketball Association
WTA	Women's Tennis Association
WWE	World Wrestling Entertainment
YMCA	Young Men's Christian Association
ZBB	zero based budget

Index

Q

Quality, Productivity and Competitive Position, 87
quality control inspection, 219
quid pro quo sexual harassment, 156

R

Race Across America, 525
racing venues, 46–49
radio, 395–396
recreation centers, 57–59
recruiting and retention efforts to facilities, 578–579
    college and university students, 581–583
    NCAA Division I Student-athletes, 583–586
    sport and recreation professionals, 587–589
    sport consumers, 590–592
    sport franchises, 592–594
recruiting investment, 575–576
    facilities, 579–580
recruitment, 162, 579
Regional Economic Modeling Incorporated (REMI), 554
Regional Input-Output Modeling System II (RIMS II), 553
relationship marketing, 450
REMI. *See* Regional Economic Modeling Incorporated (REMI)
request for bid (RFB), 448
request for information (RFI), 219, 447, 448
Request for Professional Services (RPS), 186
request for proposal (RFP), 186, 447, 448
resource leveraging, 577
restrooms, routine maintenance, 242–244

retention investment, 576–578
    facilities, 580–581
retention management, 577
retractable roof stadiums, 44–45
revenue generation, mega-event, 481
RFB. *See* request for bid (RFB)
RFI. *See* request for information (RFI)
RFP. *See* request for proposal (RFP)
rider
    hospitality rider (HR), 432–433
    merchandise rider, 435
    one-off or fly dates, 431–432
    production rider (PR), 431
    security rider, 434–435
    technical rider, 433–434
rigging, 279
RIMS II. *See* Regional Input-Output Modeling System II (RIMS II)
risk
    assessments, 303–304
    management, 170
Rive Stadium, 528
Roach, Frank, 438–440
The Rock 'n' Roll San Diego Marathon, 529
Roman Colosseum, 7–8
Rome, sport events and facilities, 7
roofs, routine maintenance, 232–233
ROS. *See* Run of Show (ROS)
Rose Bowl, 528
Rosenberger, Lance, 265–267
round-robin play, 63
routine maintenance, 231–232
    exterior inspection areas, 232–238
    interior inspection areas, 238–245
routine work orders, 249
Royal Swimming School, 54
RPS. *See* Request for Professional Services (RPS)

rubberized flooring tiles, 259
Run Disney marathon, 529
The Rungrado May Day Stadium, 46
Run of Show (ROS), 435–436
The RusSki Gorki Jumping Center, 498

S

safety, 298–299
    design considerations, 210–211
    needs, 91–92
    and security, 303
SAFETY Act. *See* Support Anti-Terrorism by Fostering Effective Technologies (SAFETY) Act
sales mix, alcohol management, 360
Salt Lake City bid, 468–470
saunas, 59
Say, Jean-Baptiste, 84–85
Say's law, 84–85
SCA. *See* sudden cardiac arrest (SCA)
SCAN. *See* strategic creative analysis (SCAN)
scenario planning, 113
scheduling
    booking and, 415–416
    definition, 417
    diverse, 419–421
    Gantt charts, 418
    and human resource management, 276–277
    and revenue producing opportunities, 418
    written mission statement, 417
schematic design phase, 214
Schoenwetter, Dana, 471–473
School of Management building, Yale University, 582
Science, Technology, Engineering, and Mathematics (STEM), 582
scientific management, 85–86

CPSIA information can be obtained
at www.ICGtesting.com
Printed in the USA
LVHW030712250619
622244LV00002B/6/P